$1840G

FASHION MERCHANDISING

AN INTRODUCTION

FOURTH EDITION

Elaine Stone

ASSOCIATE PROFESSOR AND
COORDINATOR OF THE SMALL BUSINESS CENTER
FASHION INSTITUTE OF TECHNOLOGY
NEW YORK, NEW YORK

CONTRIBUTOR
Jean A. Samples

INSTRUCTOR
HOUSTON COMMUNITY COLLEGE
HOUSTON, TEXAS

Gregg Division
McGraw-Hill Book Company
New York • Atlanta • Dallas • St. Louis • San Francisco
Auckland • Bogotá • Guatemala • Hamburg • Johannesburg • Lisbon
London • Madrid • Mexico • Montreal • New Delhi • Panama • Paris
San Juan • São Paulo • Singapore • Sydney • Tokyo • Toronto

Sponsoring Editor: Mary Alice McGarry
Editing Supervisor: Nina Levy Girard
Design Supervisor/Text Designer/Cover Designer: Nancy Axelrod
Production Supervisor: Priscilla Taguer

Photo Editor: Bill Jones
Cover Photographer: Wolfson Photography Inc.

Library of Congress Cataloging in Publication Data

Stone, Elaine.
  Fashion merchandising, an introduction.
  Rev. ed. of Fashion merchandising / by Mary D.
Troxell, Elaine Stone. 3rd ed. c1981
  Includes bibliographies and index.
  1. Fashion merchandising—United States. 2. Clothing
trade—United States. I. Samples, Jean A.
II. Troxell, Mary D. Fashion merchandising. III. Title.
HD9940.U4T74 1985   687'.068'8   84-21769
ISBN 0-07-061742-2

Fashion Merchandising: An Introduction, Fourth Edition

1 2 3 4 5 6 7 8 9 0   DOC DOC   8 9 2 1 0 9 8 7 6 5

ISBN 0-07-061742-2

Fashion Merchandising: An Introduction, Fourth Edition, prepares students to enter the fashion business with knowledge of concepts and practices of the different levels of the fashion business. The subtitle (An Introduction) has been added to stress the survey and overview nature of this edition. The text treats the subject matter largely in terms of men's, women's, and children's apparel and accessories. However, the concepts it develops are equally applicable to the merchandising of other fashion-influenced goods, such as home furnishings and household linens.

At the request of our users, we have changed the focus of the book to reflect the survey nature of an introductory course by (1) removing the chapters that detailed the buying function and the supporting services for that function, (2) adding new chapters on the business of fashion and entrepreneurship, and (3) expanding the material on children's apparel, intimate apparel and cosmetics, domestic fashion markets, trends in fashion retailing, resident buying offices, and auxiliary services into separate chapters.

ORGANIZATION OF THE TEXT

The fourth edition of *Fashion Merchandising: An Introduction* uses classroom-tested organization of the previous editions. It is structured according to the following sequential learning order: Unit 1. The Dynamics of Fashion; Unit 2. The Producers and Marketers of Fashion; Unit 3. The Merchandising of Fashion; Unit 4. Careers in Fashion.

Unit 1: The Dynamics of Fashion

The first five chapters acquaint the student with the fundamentals of fashion and the basic principles that govern all fashion movement and change. This unit also teaches the fundamentals of the business of fashion. This unit provides many new examples and features a number of new illustrations.

Chapter 1, "The Nature of Fashion," introduces fashion terminology, examines the components of fashion, and explains why fashion is always subject to change. Chapter 2 explores the manner in which economic, sociological, and psychological factors influence fashion demand. Chapter 3 discusses the rhythmic changes in silhouette, the cyclical movement of fashion, and how to predict fashion trends with relative accuracy. Chapter 4 explains how fashions start; the roles and responsibilities of designers, manufacturers, and retailers; the major theories relating to fashion adoption and dissemination; and why most people follow rather than lead fashion change. Chapter 5 explores the scope of the fashion business, explains the different types of business organizations, and allows the student to investigate the different forms of business structure.

Unit 2: The Producers and Marketers of Fashion

The next nine chapters of the text trace the history and development, organization and operation, merchandising and marketing activities, and trends of industries engaged in producing and marketing fashion.

Chapter 6 discusses textile fibers and fabrics. Chapter 7 explains the renewed vigor of the fur industry and the widespread appeal of leather apparel and accessories. Chapter 8 explores the women's apparel industry with emphasis on future trends. Chapter 9 covers children's apparel, both boys and girls. Chapter 10, which has been expanded, details the operations of the innovative menswear market. Chapter 11 explores the excitement and opportunities of the fashion accessories market. Chapter 12 emphasizes the intimate apparel industry and also spotlights the cosmetic industry with its glamorous aura. The domestic fashion markets are individually detailed for students in Chapter 13. Chapter 14 explores the major foreign markets and sources of fashion inspiration.

Unit 3: The Merchandising of Fashion

Chapter 15 examines the major types of retail organizations that operate as distributors of fashion goods to the consumer. Chapter 16, "Trends in Fashion Retailing," is a completely new chapter. It explores for the student new, exciting, and innovative ways of distribution. Chapter 17 covers in depth resident buying offices and the changes occurring in that field. The fashion auxiliary services are explained in Chapter 18, with emphasis on advertising and publicity.

Unit 4: Careers in Fashion

This unit offers guidelines and suggestions to those having career goals in fashion, starting with entry-level positions.

Whether a student's interests are in design, manufacturing, small-business ownership or management, or in some phase of a related service-oriented business, Chapter 19 of the text describes each of the possible fields and helps the student identify specific jobs of interest in the fashion industry. It ensures that students understand the skills, training, and experience required for entry into each job and the "how to" of job search. Chapter 20 is devoted to helping students who want to be "their own boss" investigate the possibilities of entrepreneurship in the fashion business.

FASHION FOCUS

A new feature of this edition, the "Fashion Focus," highlights interesting people, places, and products that impact on the subject matter of the chapter in which they appear. These are informal, informational articles that focus upon the fashion aspect of the chosen subject. They are appropriate for class discussions and library research projects.

GLOSSARY

This edition provides a glossary of over 250 frequently used industry terms. A knowledge and understanding of the "language" of fashion gives students a firm footing upon which they can "step-out" into the industry and know they are speaking the right language.

END-OF-CHAPTER ACTIVITIES

Each of the 20 chapters in the text concludes with three kinds of student-oriented activities designed to enrich and reinforce the instructional material. A "Merchandising Vocabulary" section in each chapter explains fashion and merchandising terms introduced for the first time in that chapter. The student will recognize these terms when they appear in subsequent chapters.

"Merchandising Review" asks questions about the key concepts of each chapter. These questions provoke thought, encourage classroom discussion, and develop recall of the material presented in the text.

The section called "Merchandising Digest" consists primarily of an excerpt from the text. It asks the student to explain the significance of the excerpt and to support the explanation with specific illustrations. This activity affords the student an opportunity to apply theory to actual situations and to draw on his or her own background and experiences.

END-OF-UNIT ACTIVITIES

A popular feature that is repeated in this edition is the "Fashion Project," drawn from authentic merchandising situations, which ends each unit. These fashion projects emphasize and reinforce the instructional elements brought out in each unit. The projects enrich instruction and suggest to students that fashion merchandising is a dynamic and exciting field.

INSTRUCTOR'S MANUAL AND KEY

An instructor's manual and key is available to adopters at no cost. It includes a number of options for organizing the fashion merchandising curriculum, contains general suggestions for teaching the course, and provides an annotated bibliography of books and trade journals. It also contains supplementary assignments for each unit. The key to the text includes answers to all end-of-chapter and end-of-unit exercises.

A popular feature is a test bank of five tests containing test material for the units, and a final examination. The tests are composed of 500 objective questions and are ready to duplicate.

ACKNOWLEDGMENTS

The authors are grateful to the many educators and businesspeople who have given them encouragement, information, and helpful suggestions for this new edition.

We would like to acknowledge the assistance of Patricia Breen of the Fashion Institute of Technology who reviewed the previous edition and made many helpful suggestions for the new edition. The library staff at the Fashion Institute of Technology also provided valuable research and fact-checking skills.

The following educators reviewed the manuscript for this new edition and advised the authors of their needs and preferences:

Susan Davis
University of Wisconsin
Menomanie, WI

Jerry Roberts
Hinds Junior College
Raymond, MS

Claire Woods
Bermuda College
Bermuda

Joann McKenna
Webber College
Babson Park, FL

Sylvia Sheppard
Fashion Institute of
Design & Merchandising
Los Angeles, CA

The authors are also indebted to the following industry experts who read and critiqued the specific chapters mentioned for accuracy, up-to-date information, and completeness:

Robert Beaulier (Ch. 5)
Fashion Institute of Technology
NYC

Jess Chernak (Ch. 7)
American Fur Industry, Inc.
NYC

Arthur Levinson (Ch. 7)
Fashion Institute of Technology
NYC

Robert Salem (Ch. 8)
Smart Parts
NYC

Rosa Rosa (Ch. 9)
Fashion Institute of Technology
NYC

Jack Hyde (Ch. 10)
Fashion Institute of Technology
NYC

Ruth Siegel (Ch. 11)
R. N. Koch, Inc.
NYC

Jack Tepper (Ch. 11)
Footwear Industry Consultant
NYC

Sylvia Forrest (Ch. 12)
Fashion Institute of Technology
NYC

Lewis Spaulding (Ch. 12)
Fashion Industry Consultant
NYC

Jack Mizrahi (Chs. 15 & 16)
Strawberry Fields
Jacksonville, FL

Elaine Nathan (Chs. 15 & 16)
B&N Printing Co.
NYC

Marjorie S. Deane (Ch. 17)
Tobé Associates, Inc.
NYC

Mary Collins (Ch. 18)
Mary Collins Public Relations Co.
NYC

Alvin Wormser (Ch. 20)
Fashion Institute of Technology
NYC

The authors of this edition acknowledge the many contributions of Mary Troxell, who first conceived the idea for this text and who worked on the first three editions, beginning in 1970. We are proud to follow where she has led.

Elaine Stone
Jean Samples

CONTENTS

UNIT 2
THE PRODUCERS AND MARKETERS OF FASHION 101

UNIT 3
THE MERCHANDISING OF FASHION 301

UNIT 4
CAREERS IN FASHION 379

UNIT 1. THE DYNAMICS OF FASHION

Fashion is a force—a powerful force of constantly altering patterns of change and growth. Its movement affects the fates of the designers and manufacturers who distribute it and the lives of the consumers who follow its dictates. All of its facets taken together add up to a multibillion dollar industry. Fashion today is big business.

Fashion is also a science. It involves known facts and basic principles, and its actions and reactions can be predicted based on those facts and those principles.

Unit 1 is about the **dynamics** of fashion. The term refers to a basic force and the laws relating to that force that explain its patterns of change and growth. This unit, therefore, discusses the nature of fashion and how it works. It explains the fundamentals of fashion and the relationships between fashion and the factors that affect it. Some of the topics taken up in the five chapters that make up this unit include:

- The nature of fashion—its basic vocabulary, its various components, its intangible elements, and the principles that relate to its adoption.

- The environmental factors—economic, sociological, and psychological—and how they influence fashion interest and demand.

- The movement of fashion—how fashions change and how an understanding of this movement can be used to analyze and predict fashion trends.

- The leaders of fashion—how fashion is disseminated and the role of designers, producers, and retailers.

- The business of fashion—the scope of the industry, its growth and expansion, and the various forms of business ownership.

Understanding the dynamics of fashion is critical to the success of anyone interested in marketing and merchandising fashion, both at at wholesale and at the retail level. Fashion is serious business.

1. THE NATURE OF FASHION

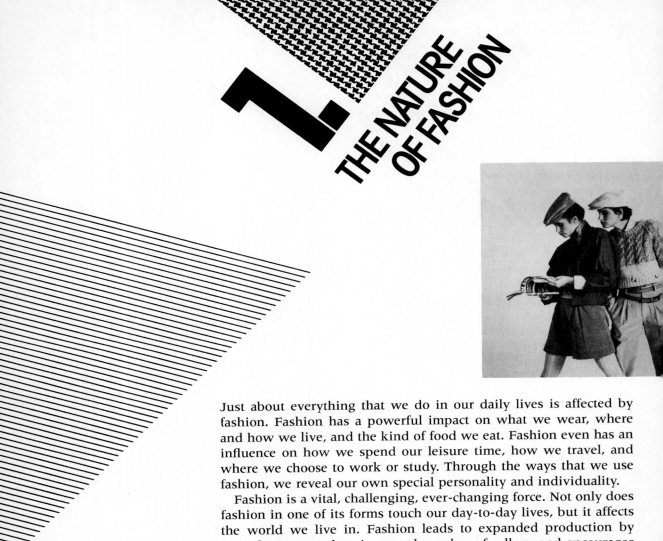

Just about everything that we do in our daily lives is affected by fashion. Fashion has a powerful impact on what we wear, where and how we live, and the kind of food we eat. Fashion even has an influence on how we spend our leisure time, how we travel, and where we choose to work or study. Through the ways that we use fashion, we reveal our own special personality and individuality.

Fashion is a vital, challenging, ever-changing force. Not only does fashion in one of its forms touch our day-to-day lives, but it affects the world we live in. Fashion leads to expanded production by manufacturers and an increased number of sellers, and encourages more consumers to buy. It thus leads to expansion of the world marketplace.

Webster defines fashion as "prevailing custom, usage, or style,"[1] and in this sense its influence is all-encompassing. The term is used here in a somewhat narrower way, but one that takes into account the fact that fashion has far-reaching effects on the world. "Fashion" here will mean the style or styles of clothing and accessories prevailing at a particular time.

Fashion today is big business; thousands of people are employed in either the fashion industries or the fashion business. The **fashion industries** are considered to be those engaged in producing the materials used in the production of apparel and accessories for men, women, and children, including the merchandise categories known as "boys' wear" and "girls' wear." Throughout this book, any reference to "fashion industries" means these, unless others are specifically mentioned. The broader term **fashion business** includes all industries and services connected with fashion: manufacturing, distribution, advertising, publishing, and consulting—any business concerned with goods or services in which fashion is a factor.

Marketing is a total system of business activities designed to plan, price, promote, and place (distribute) want-satisfying products and services to present and potential customers. The total process of marketing is now beginning to be applied to the products and services of the fashion industries; the result is called **fashion marketing**; that is the marketing of fashion-related apparel and accessories to the ultimate consumer. The topic of this book is narrower than fashion marketing; we are concerned with **fashion merchandising**, which refers to the *planning* required to have the right fashion-oriented merchandise at the right time, in the right place, in the right quantities, at the right prices, and with the right sales promotion.

MISCONCEPTIONS ABOUT FASHION

As the power of fashion to influence our lives grows, three misconceptions about it continue to be widely held. The first and most common misconception is that designers and retailers dictate what the fashion will be and then force it upon helpless consumers. It has been said that the industry is composed of "obsolescence ogres." In reality, the consumers themselves decide what the fashion will be by accepting or rejecting the styles that are offered. They are, in truth, "variety vultures."

The second misconception is that fashion acts as an influence on women only. Men today are as influenced by and responsive to fashion as women. Fashion is the force that causes women to raise or lower their skirt lengths, straighten or frizz their hair, and change from sportswear to dressy clothes. Fashion is also the force that influences men to grow or shave off their mustaches and beards, choose wide or narrow ties and lapels, and change from casual jeans into three-piece suits.

The third misconception is that fashion is a mysterious and unpredictable force. Actually, its direction can be determined and its changes predicted with remarkable accuracy by those who study and understand the fundamentals of fashion. Fashion was once considered an art form controlled by designers who dictated its content. But fashion has now evolved into a science that can be measured and evaluated.

THE TERMINOLOGY OF FASHION

Fashion is a complex subject—one that intrigues and fascinates, and has been studied throughout history. In the study of fashion today, certain words and phrases are used over and over again: "high fashion," "mass fashion," "style," "design," "taste," "classic," and "fad." The exact meanings of these terms must be understood so that concepts can be discussed without confusion. One of the major pioneers in the field of fashion merchandising was Dr. Paul H. Nystrom. The definitions used in this section are his and are generally accepted in the academic study of fashion.[2]

Fashion

A style that is accepted and used by the majority of a group at any one time, no matter how small that group, is a **fashion**. Short skirts, pointed-toe shoes, long hair, beards and mustaches, and natural makeup have all been fashions. And no doubt each will again be accepted by the majority in a group of people with similar interests or characteristics—for example, college students or young career-oriented men and women.

Fashions can be categorized according to the group to which they appeal. **High fashion** refers to those styles or designs accepted by a limited group of fashion leaders—the elite among consumers—who are first to accept fashion change. High-fashion styles or designs are generally introduced and sold in small quantities and at relatively high prices to socialites, entertainers, and fashion innovators. **Mass fashion**, or **volume fashion**, refers to those styles or designs that are widely accepted. These fashions are usually produced and sold in large quantities at moderate to low prices and appeal to the greatest majority of fashion-conscious consumers.

Style

A style is a characteristic or distinctive mode of presentation or conceptualization in a particular field. Styles exist in writing, speaking, home decorating, and table manners, to name a few examples. In apparel, **style** is the characteristic or distinctive appearance of a garment—the combination of features that makes it different from other garments. For example, jackets are one style of apparel, pants are another, and skirts are another. Sometimes certain characteristics are so special and individual within a large style classification that they develop into their own style. For instance, all blazer jackets have a distinctive appearance that makes them different from all other types of jackets.

Although styles come and go in terms of acceptance, a specific style always remains a style, whether it is currently in fashion or not. Thus some people adopt a style and wear it regardless of current fashion.

Some styles are named for the period of history in which they originated—Grecian, Roman, Renaissance, and Empire, for example. When such styles return to fashion, their basic elements remain the same. Minor details are altered to reflect the taste or needs of the era in which they reappear. For example, the Empire style of the early nineteenth century featured a waistline cinched high up under the bust. That style can still be bought today, but with modifications for current fashion acceptance.

In the fashion industry, **style** is used by manufacturers and retailers to refer to the number assigned to each individual item produced. The item is then referred to as "style 999" or "style number 999" (or just "number 999"), which identifies it for manufacturing and ordering purposes. In this instance, the word "style" takes the place of the word "design" as defined in the following section.

Design

A **design** is a specific version of a style. The skirt, for example, is a style in women's apparel. The many variations in which the skirt is available are the designs—gored, A-line, box-pleated, and knife-pleated, to name a few. The coat is a style. The variations in body length and width, and in neckline and sleeve treatment, constitute the various designs of the coat. Manufacturers usually produce several designs or variations of a popular style. A cardigan sweater, for example, may be designed with variation of shoulder treatment or may or may not have pockets.

Taste

The Latin proverb *"De gustibus non est disputandum"* means "There can be no disputing taste." According to another well-known proverb, "There is no accounting for taste." "Taste" can be defined as the ability to discern and appreciate that which makes for excellence at a particular time in a particular circumstance.

In fashion, **taste** refers to an individual's opinion of what is and what is not attractive and appropriate for a given occasion. Good taste in fashion, therefore, means sensitivity not only to what is artistic but also to what is appropriate for a specific situation. A style may be beautiful. But if inappropriate to the particular circumstances, it may not be considered in good taste. Even in the liberated atmosphere of the 1970s when so many dress codes disappeared, certain standards of good taste still prevailed. One might have dared to wear a see-

When the Empire style of the early 1800s recurred in the 1950s, it did so with modifications.

through blouse to the office, for example, but it would not have been considered in good taste.

Nystrom described the relationship between taste and fashion this way: "Good taste essentially is making the most artistic use of current fashion . . . bridging the gap between good art and common usage."[3]

Timing, too, plays a part in what is considered good or bad taste. British costume authority James Laver saw the relationship between taste and fashion in terms of its acceptance level. A style, he said, is thought to be:[4]

"indecent"	10 years before its time
"shameless"	5 years before its time
"outré"	1 year before its time
"smart"	in its time
"dowdy"	1 year after its time
"hideous"	10 years after its time
"ridiculous"	20 years after its time

While the time an individual fashion takes to complete this course may vary, the course is always a cyclical one. (See Chapter 3.) A new style is often considered daring and in dubious taste. It is then gradually accepted, then widely accepted, and finally gradually discarded.

Although most fashions in the past strictly followed Laver's cycle, some fashions of the fifties and the sixties have deviated. Due to the troubled world scene and the electronic explosion, the fashion cycles of some fashions have become shorter and have repeated themselves within a shorter space of time. Television reruns have enabled 1980s college students to view a 1950s situation comedy, *Leave It to Beaver*. Life as depicted on this show was less complicated and problematic than today. The college students viewing the show became nostalgic for the time period and adopted its clothing. Thus, they did not view the clothing as being ridiculous 20 years after its time.

A Classic

Some styles or designs continue to be considered in good taste over a long period—exceptions to the usual rapid movement of styles through their fashion life cycles. A **classic** is a style or design that satisfies a basic need and remains in general fashion acceptance for an extended period of time.

Almost every wardrobe has some classics in it, and some wardrobes are mostly classics. A classic is characterized by simplicity of design as well as length of time in fashion. The shirtwaist dress has been a classic for many years. So have the simple pump (shoe) and the cardigan sweater.

A Fad

A fashion that suddenly sweeps into popularity, affecting relatively few of the total population, and then quickly disappears is called a **fad**. Fads are usually exaggerated in design. A typical example of a fad is the weird, wildly dyed "punk" hairdo sported by a small group of young people in the early and mid-1980s.

Fads follow the same cycle as fashions do, but their rise in popularity is much faster, their acceptance much shorter, and their decline to obsolescence much more rapid than that of true fashions. Because they can come and go in a single season, fads have been called "miniature fashions." See the illustration of the "Urban Cowboy" fad at the right.

The chemise, or sack dress, is probably the outstanding example of the fad phenomenon. After an instant rise to popularity in the late 1950s, it quickly passed from the fashion scene. A few years later, the chemise reappeared as the shift. In 1974, the chemise again appeared in the Paris collections, modified to eliminate its former disadvantages. American manufacturers quickly reproduced it in several versions and in a wide price range. That the

chemise, in its various manifestations, has again appeared in the 1980s is strong evidence that it, too, will become a fashion classic.

Another fad also may be on its way to a longer life. For decades, ballet dancers have used leg warmers to protect their valuable legs during and after strenuous exercise and dancing. And there the knowledge and use of leg warmers ended. But in early 1982, leg warmers were suddenly adopted by high school and college students, doubtless made aware of them by the movie (and later TV show), *Fame*. Worn over panty hose or pants, they provided the wearer with warmth as well as a very "in" look. Finally, by early 1983, leg warmers were being worn with short shorts on the streets of Southern California where the temperatures are far from chilly. Thus, it appears that leg warmers are moving from fad into the mainstream and so to a more general acceptance.

The Urban Cowboy fad, marked by western hats, glittery shirts and lizard boots, lasted just 2 years.

COMPONENTS OF FASHION

Fashion design does not just happen, nor does the designer wave a magic wand to create a new design. Fashion design involves the combination of four basic elements or components: silhouette, detail, texture, and color. Only through a change in one or more of these basic components does a new fashion evolve. This is true of any fashion-influenced product, from kitchen appliances to automobiles, from apartment houses to office buildings, and from accessories to apparel.

Silhouette

The **silhouette** of a costume is its overall outline or contour. It is also frequently referred to as "shape" or "form."

It may appear to the casual observer that women have worn countless silhouettes throughout the centuries. Research shows, however, that there are actually only three basic forms—straight, or tubular; bell-shaped, or bouffant; and the bustle, or back-fullness—with many variations.[5]

Since the mid-eighteenth century, these three basic silhouettes have consistently come into fashion in the same sequence, each recurring approximately once every 100 years and lasting for about 35 years. For example, the triangle shape (a variation of the straight, or tubular, silhouette) of the 1930s and 1940s reoccurred as the wide-shoulder, narrow-hip silhouette of the late 1970s. The widespread sociological change and rapid technological developments of recent decades, however, may have altered both the traditional life span and the sequence of these silhouettes.

Details

The individual elements that give a silhouette its form or shape are called **details**. These include trimmings, skirt and pant length and width, and shoulder, waist, and sleeve treatment.

Silhouettes evolve gradually from one to another through changes in detail. When the trend in a detail reaches an extreme, a reversal of the trend takes place. For example, dresses and suits featured wide shoulders with much padding in the 1940s and 1950s. This was reversed in the late 1960s and 1970s, when the look became casual and unstructured. This casualness reached such extremes that by the start of the 1980s, structured clothing was back in fashion and dress and suit shoulders began once again to grow wider as padding was inserted.

The spiked-heel, pointed-toe shoe of the 1950s gave way to the "clunky" flat shoe with broad toe of the late 1960s. Again, extremes were eventually reached and the heel went higher, first becoming a wedge and then, by 1980, a regular heel. Toes narrowed somewhat, and soon the American woman was reunited with her favorite shoe fashion—the classic pump.

Variations in detail allow both designer and consumer to freely express their individuality within the framework of the currently accepted silhouette. To emphasize a natural-waistline silhouette, for example, a slender woman might choose a simple wide belt, a heavily decorated belt, or a belt in a contrasting color to suit her personality and the occasion. To express his individuality, a man might emphasize the wide-shoulder look with epaulets or heavy shoulder pads.

Texture

One of the most significant components of fashion is texture. **Texture** is the look and feel of material, woven or nonwoven.

Texture can affect the appearance of a silhouette, giving it a bulky or slender look depending on the roughness or smoothness of the materials. A woman dressed in a rough tweed dress and a bulky knit sweater is likely to look larger and squarer than she does in the same dress executed in a smooth jersey and

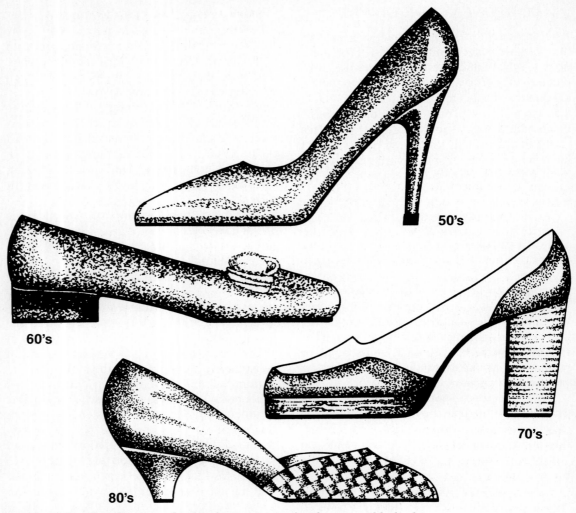

Designers alter the silhouette of a shoe by varying its details—toe width, heel width, and heel height.

topped with a cashmere sweater. When the bulky look is fashionable, popular textures include shaggy tweeds, mohairs, cable-stitched and other heavily ribbed knit fabrics, and rough-textured knit and woven materials. When sleek lines are the fashion, rough textures yield to smooth surfaces and simple flat weaves and knits.

Texture influences the drape of a garment. Chiffon clings and flows, making it a good choice for soft, feminine styles, while corduroy has the firmness and bulk suitable for more casual garments.

Texture affects the color of a fabric by causing the surface to either reflect or absorb light. Rough textures absorb light, causing the colors to appear flat. Smooth textures reflect light, causing colors to appear brighter. Anyone who has tried to match colors soon discovers that a color which appears extremely bright in a shiny vinyl, satin, or high-gloss enamel paint seems subdued in a rough wool, a suede, or a stucco wall finish. Pile surfaces such as velvet both reflect and absorb light; thus the colors of pile surfaces look richer and deeper than those of flat, smooth surfaces.

Color

Color has always been a major consideration in women's clothing. Since World War II, color in men's clothing has been regaining the importance it had in previous centuries. Today color is a key factor in apparel selection for both sexes. Color is important in advertising, packaging, and store decor as well.

Historically, colors have been used to denote rank and profession. Purple, for instance, was associated with royalty and in some periods could be worn only by those of noble birth. Black became customary for the apparel of the clergy and for members of the judiciary.

Color symbolism often varies with geographical location. While white is the Western world's symbol of purity, worn by brides and used in communion dresses, it is the color of mourning in India.

Color has been importantly affected by developments in technology. Better ways of tanning leather and dyeing and finishing fabrics have produced a wider variety of colors and color combinations than ever before for fashion designers to work with. Colors today are also more permanent, more resistant to fading or changing, and thus more acceptable to consumers. Colors change appearance depending on adjacent colors. Thus blues are brightened by nearby oranges or dulled by adjacent grays or blacks.

Today a fashion designer's color palette changes with consumers' preferences. In some seasons, all is brightness and sharp contrast, and no color is too powerful to be worn. In other seasons, only subdued colors appeal. Fashion merchants must develop an eye for color—not only for the specific hues and values popular in a given season, but also for indications of possible trends in consumer preference.

THE INTANGIBLES OF FASHION

A style is tangible, made up of a definite silhouette and details of design. But fashion is shaped by such intangibles as group acceptance, change, the forces at work during a specific era, and people's desire to relate to certain lifestyles.

Acceptance

Group acceptance or approval is implied in any definition of fashion. An article of clothing may be breathtakingly innovative and aesthetically flawless, yet it is not a fashion until it has been accepted and used by a substantial number of people.

Acceptance need not be universal, however. A style may be adopted by one group while other segments of the population ignore it. For example, the fashions shaped by big-city lifestyles are rarely popular with the suburban crowd. The carefree, nonconformist fashions on college campuses bear little or no relationship to those accepted by businesspeople.

A style may also be accepted and become a fashion in one part of the world while it is ignored or rejected elsewhere. Each of the following is considered fashionable by its own inhabitants: the igloo of the Inuit, the thatched hut of some African tribespeople, and the ranch-style house of many American suburbanites. Similarly, many ethnic and religious groups have distinctive styles of dress. In this country, the Amish and the Mennonites can be recognized by their apparel, as can male Hasidic Jews, Indians in saris, and both male and female members of the Hare Krishna sect.

Acceptance also means that a fashion is considered appropriate to the occasion for which it is worn. Clothes considered appropriate for big-business boardrooms would not be acceptable for casual weekends or outdoor living. Certain extreme styles that are accepted by college students for campus wear would not be considered appropriate for job interviews.

The group that adopts and rejects a specific

In the 1980s, the Hasidim, the Amish, and the Hare Krishna sects continue to wear their traditional modes of dress.

style influences and changes what is considered acceptable. When the term "white-collar class" was coined, the collar being referred to was white, high, and stiffly starched, and a man always wore it with a coat and tie in company. Today, fashions for men are much more relaxed, even in office wear. The stiff collar is gone. However, the traditional dark tailored suit is still the major "uniform" for men in most offices in the Northeast and Midwest, though in California and in the Sun Belt, a more relaxed mode of dress is quite acceptable in the business world. Casual jackets in brighter colors and patterns, along with the absence of ties, make up the look that often dominates those scenes. In the business world, the accepted style for working women was once a dark tailored suit or dress. Today casual separates are also widely accepted.

Regardless of practicality, a style is considered a fashion if it is accepted by the majority of a specific group at a given time and place for a specific occasion. Many fashions can and do exist side by side at any one time because of the varied preferences and activities of different consumer groups.

Change

Fashion is subject to never-ending change—sometimes rapid, sometimes gradual. Women's apparel has always shown the most rapid rate of change. Until recently, men's fashions changed more slowly. Fashion in home furnishings changes even more slowly, and architectural fashions more slowly still. Some people constantly seek the new and different, and when a fashion is fully accepted, it has already become too ordinary for them.

The rate of fashion change in women's clothing has greatly accelerated over the last century, and in men's clothing over the last 40 years. Much of this acceleration has resulted from the popularity of the sewing machine and the development of man-made fibers. These have given designers and manufacturers a faster means of producing garments and a much greater variety of materials to work with. New technology is constantly producing new fibers and blends of fibers. Each seems to offer more than the one before and encourages the discarding of the old. Also, the consumer finds the moderately priced, "off-the-rack" dress easier to discard than the more expensive hand-sewn or hand-knitted creation.

Modern communications play a major role in today's accelerated rate of fashion change. The mass media spread fashion news across the face of the globe in hours, sometimes seconds. Live TV coverage of events around the world enables us to see not only what people are doing but also what they are wearing. Our morning newspapers show us what fashion leaders wore to a party the night before. Even slight fashion changes are given faster and wider publicity than ever before. Consumers who like these changes demand them from merchants, who in turn demand them from manufacturers.

THE FUTILITY OF FORCING CHANGE.

Since fashion changes are outgrowths of changes in consumers' needs, it is seldom possible to force them or hold them back. Efforts have been made from time to time to alter the course of fashion, but they usually fail. Fashion is a potent force which by definition requires support by the majority.

As an example, in the late 1960s, designers and retailers decided that skirts had reached their limit in shortness and that women would soon be seeking change. So the designers designed and the retailers stocked and promoted the "midi," a skirt mid-calf in length. The designers and retailers were right in theory but wrong in timing and choice of skirt length. Consumers found the midi too sudden and radical a change and did not accept or buy the style in sufficient numbers to make it a fashion.

Occasionally, necessity and government regulation can interrupt the course of fashion. During World War II, the U.S. government controlled the type and quantity of fabric used in consumer goods. One regulation prohibited anything but slit pockets on women's garments to avoid using the extra material that patch pockets require. Skirts were short and silhouettes were narrow, reflecting the scarcity of material.

MEETING THE DEMAND FOR CHANGE.

After World War II, a reaction to these designs was to be expected. A new French designer, Christian Dior, caught and expressed the desire for a freer line and a more feminine garment in his first collection, which achieved instant fashion success. Using fabric with a lavishness that had been impossible in Europe or America during

After World War II, Christian Dior met the demand for change from the tailored short-skirted look of the early 1940s by providing women with the full-skirted, feminine "New Look."

the war years, he created his "New Look," with long, full skirts, fitted waistlines, and feminine curves.

Dior did not change the course of fashion; he accelerated it—from an evolutionary course to a revolutionary one. He recognized and interpreted the need of women at that time to get out of stiff, short, narrow, unfeminine clothes and into soft, free, longer, feminine ones. Consumers wanted the change, and the lifting of wartime restrictions made it possible to meet their demand.

Another example of a consumer demand for change occurred in menswear just before World War II. Year after year, manufacturers had been turning out versions of a style that had long been popular in England—the padded-shoulder, draped suit. A number of young men from very influential families, who were attending well-known northeastern colleges, became tired of that look. They wanted a change. They took their objections to New Haven clothing manufacturers, and the result was the natural-shoulder Ivy League suit that achieved widespread popularity for the next 15 to 20 years.

A Mirror of the Times

Fashions have always mirrored the times in which they occur. Because fashions are shaped by the forces of an era, they in turn reflect the way we think and live. The individualistic fashions of the 1980s are a true reflection of the new freedom of lifestyle and expression. The extreme modesty of the Victorian era was reflected in bulky and concealing fashions. The sexual emancipation of the flappers in the

1920s was expressed in their flattened figures, short skirts, and short hair.

Fashions also mirror the times by reflecting the values of each level of society in a given era. The peasant worker in Europe in the Middle Ages thought it necessary to have a strong, sturdy wife to help out with work in the fields. Such women were both needed and admired. The common fashions at that time combined puffy sleeves, laced bodices, and full skirts—details which made even slender women look plump and sturdy. While European peasant women wore this costume, the women of the wealthy classes were emphasizing their desired and admired delicacy with entirely different fashions.

Fashions mirror the times by reflecting the degree of rigidity in the class structure of an era. Although such ideas are difficult to imagine today, throughout much of history certain fashions were restricted to the members of certain rigidly defined social classes. In some early eras, royal edicts regulated both the type of apparel that could be worn by each group of citizens and how ornate it could be. Class distinctions were thus emphasized. Certain fashions have also been used as indications of high social standing and material success. During the nineteenth century, the constricted waists of Western women and the bound feet of high-caste Chinese women were silent but obvious evidence that the male head of the household was wealthy and esteemed.

Now, in the late twentieth century, social classes are far more fluid and mobile. Many fashions exist simultaneously, and we are all free to adopt the fashions of any social group. Only our incomes restrict us. If we do not wish to join others in their fashion choices, we can create our own modes and standards of dress. The beatniks of the 1950s and the hippies of the 1960s had their typical fashions, as did the bohemians of the 1920s, the liberated groups of the 1970s, and the punk rockers of the 1980s.

Fashions also mirror the times by reflecting the activities in which the people of an era participate. The importance of court-centered social activities in seventeenth- and eighteenth-century Europe was evidenced in men's and women's ornately styled apparel. Men's fashions became less colorful and more functional only when a new working class was created by the industrial revolution in the late eighteenth and early nineteenth centuries.

In the 1980s, wardrobes also vary according to lifestyle. If a businesswoman plays tennis each morning before going to the office, her closet probably contains fashions for both the business world and the tennis court, as well as leisure and formal attire. A working woman who also manages a home and family must see that her wardrobe contains fashions suitable for business and family-based activities.

PRINCIPLES OF FASHION

While the intangibles of fashion can be vague and difficult to chart, the five fundamental principles of fashion are tangible and precise. From season to season, year to year, these principles do not change. They provide a solid foundation for fashion identification and forecasting. As valid for today's fashion as for yesterday's, they will continue to apply for decades to come.

The five principles listed below are the foundations upon which the study of fashion is based, whether that study concerns the history of fashion, the dissemination of fashion, or the techniques relating to fashion merchandising. These principles will be referred to throughout this book; several have already been touched on in this chapter.

1. *Consumers establish fashions by accepting or rejecting the styles offered.*
   Contrary to what some believe, fashions are not created by designers, producers, or retailers. Consumers—customers—create fashions.

   A **customer** is a patron or potential purchaser of goods or services. Thus, a retail store's dress buyer is a customer of a dress

FASHION FOCUS

YVES SAINT LAURENT: KING OF HIGH FASHION

"When I was just starting out, I saw Mr. Christian Dior come and speak to students at the Sorbonne in Paris. I was very moved, and I thought to myself, 'I will do the same thing myself someday.'" So said Yves Saint Laurent in 1983 when he visited the Fashion Institute of Technology in New York to speak to the students.

While Saint Laurent was in New York to attend the opening of the Metropolitan Museum of Art's retrospective on his 26 years in the fashion business and to be feted and admired as the only active designer to be so honored, he still found time to speak to the fashion students. Saint Laurent summed up his fashion philosophy by saying, "I think that anguish is necessary for a creator. It is not very nice to have—it is a terrible thing—but when the result is good, one forgets immediately the anguish which preceded, and one is happy to be a part of this metier."[1]

Saint Laurent (often referred to simply by his YSL monogram) is a decidedly troubled, complex man who has spoken often about his unhappy childhood when, as a frail young boy who decided to dress up marionettes, he was often beaten up by schoolyard bullies. His interest in design began at the age of five when he was given

manufacturer, and the dress manufacturer is a customer of a fabric producer. The **consumer** is the ultimate user; the person who uses the finished fashion garment is the consumer. Consumers decide when a style no longer appeals, and they determine which new styles will be favored.

Designers create hundreds of new styles each season, based on what they think may attract customers. From among those many styles, manufacturers choose what they think will be successful. They reject many more than they select. Retailers choose from the manufacturers' offerings those styles they believe their customers will want. Consumers then make the vital choice. By accepting some styles and re-

jecting others, they—and only they—dictate what styles will become fashions.

2. *Fashions are not based on price.*

The price tag on an item of apparel or an accessory is no indication of whether the item is currently in fashion. Although new styles that may eventually become fashionable are often introduced at high prices, this is less often the case than it once was. At about the same time in 1982 two popular styles—back-blousing and down-filled outerwear—were introduced. Back-blousing did indeed originate in a high-priced salon, that of famous-name designer James Galanos. But down-filled outerwear had a humbler origin. It was modeled on the

a marionette stage. He made his own cardboard figures and dressed them with pieces of fabric.[2]

During the years that Saint Laurent has been a designer, he has dominated the world of fashion. First he served as an apprentice, then head of the House of Dior, then head of his own couture house and owner of 172 Rive Gauche boutiques around the world. Many of the designs he has produced are now considered classics, but were startling innovations in their time: the "trapeze" dress, the Mondrian-inspired wool skimmer, the "rich peasant" look, tailored "city pants" for women, the "little black dress" (a revival of a Chanel design), the classic military overcoat, and the safari jacket.

Despite his success over the years, YSL has had his share of anguish. He was drafted into the French army at the age of 22 and suffered a nervous breakdown. He was stridently criticized—and even ostracized—by the French press when he lowered hemlines at the wrong time (1958 and 1964).

Even though he is considered the undisputed king of high fashion, he cannot rest on his laurels because his rivals are always gaining ground. Saint Laurent reflected on his present situation in an interview with *Time* magazine. He compared his career to that of Maria Callas, the late opera star, of whom he was a great fan. " 'I would go to hear her every evening, particularly her last performances,' he remembered. 'The hall was waiting for her to make a false note, divided between those who wanted her to sing beautifully and the others who wanted her to hit the false note.' The analogy to his own lofty status does not require elaboration."[3]

However, resting on his laurels may never have occurred to YSL. He has made it to the top in the fashion business and stays there by continuing to discover and fill the needs and wants of customers. YSL bridges the gap between the Paris high fashion world, where instinct and intuition often rule, and the worldwide business that licenses his accessories and home furnishings, where the more traditional rules of marketing apply.

[1] Personal appearance at Fashion Institute of Technology, New York, December 7, 1983.

[2] E. J. Dionne, Jr., "A Salute to Yves Saint Laurent: The Man Behind the Myth," *The New York Times Magazine,* December 4, 1983, p. 161.

[3] Martha Duffy, "Toasting Saint Laurent, A New York Retrospective in Glamour and Luxury," *Time,* December 12, 1983, p. 98.

This Fashion Focus is based on information from the sources cited above.

---

warm, practical, multipocketed down vests that had been used for many years by hunters and fishermen to keep themselves warm.

Also, items that were originally introduced at high prices may be quickly made available in a variety of price lines if they appear to have considerable consumer appeal. A Paris dress style, for instance, may be introduced at a price over $6,000 for a custom-made, hand-sewn copy. A few weeks later, stores may offer ready-to-wear copies of that style in a wide range of prices, including budget prices. The fabric, trimmings, and workmanship will be different, but the style will appear essentially the same.

3. *Fashions are evolutionary in nature; they are rarely revolutionary.*

Throughout history there have probably been only two real revolutions in fashion styles. One of these occurred during the twentieth century: the Dior New Look of 1947 (see page 12). The other was the abrupt change of styles brought about by the French Revolution when the fashion changed overnight from voluminous full skirts, low-cut daring bodices, and ornate and glamorous fabrics to simple, drab costumes in keeping with the political and moral upheaval.

Fashions usually evolve gradually from one style to another. Skirt lengths go up or down an inch at a time, season after season.

Suit lapels narrow or widen gradually, not suddenly.

Fashion designers understand and accept this principle. When developing new design ideas, they always keep the current fashion in mind. They know that few people could or would buy a whole new wardrobe every season, and that the success of their designs ultimately depends on sales. Consumers today buy apparel and accessories to supplement and update the wardrobe they already own, some of which was purchased last year, some the year before, some the year before that, and so on. In most cases, consumers will buy only if the purchase complements their existing wardrobe and does not depart too radically from last year's purchases.

4. *No amount of sales promotion can change the direction in which fashions are moving.*
Promotional efforts on the part of producers or retailers cannot dictate what consumers will buy, nor can it force people to buy what they do not want. The few times that fashion merchants have tried to promote a radical change in fashion, they have not been successful.

As the women's liberation movement grew in the late 1960s, women rebelled against the constriction of girdles and bras. The overwhelming majority stopped wearing girdles and began wearing panty hose instead. Various "counterculture" looks were adopted by some and a more relaxed look was adopted by nearly everyone. Reflecting this change was the reemergence of the soft, no-seam natural bra. Regardless of promotion by the intimate-apparel industry, nothing could persuade the majority of American women to submit again to the rigid control of corsets and girdles.

Also, promotional effort cannot renew the life of a fading fashion unless the extent of change gives the fashion an altogether new appeal. This is why stores have markdown or clearance sales. When the sales of a particular style start slumping, stores know they must clear out as much of that stock as possible, even at much lower prices, to make room for newer styles in which consumers have indicated interest.

5. *All fashions end in excess.*
This saying is sometimes attributed to Paul Poiret, a top Paris designer of the 1920s. Many examples attest its truth. Eighteenth-century hoopskirts ballooned out to 8 feet in diameter, which made moving even from room to room a complicated maneuver. Similarly, miniskirts of the 1960s finally became so short that the slightest movement caused a major problem in modesty.

Once the extreme in styling has been reached, a fashion is nearing its end. The attraction of the fashion wanes and people begin to seek a different look—a new fashion.

REFERENCES

[1] *Webster's New Collegiate Dictionary*, G. & C. Merriam Company, Springfield, Massachusetts, 1973, p. 416.
[2] Paul H. Nystrom, *Economics of Fashion*, The Ronald Press, New York, 1928, pp. 3–7; and *Fashion Merchandising*, The Ronald Press, New York, 1932, pp. 33–34.
[3] Nystrom, *Economics of Fashion*, p. 7.

[4] James Laver, *Taste and Fashion*, rev. ed., George G. Harrap & Co., Ltd., London, 1946, p. 202.

[5] Agnes Brooke Young, *Recurring Cycles of Fashion: 1760–1937*, Harper & Brothers, New York, 1937. Reprinted by Cooper Square Publishers, Inc., New York, 1966, p. 30.

MERCHANDISING VOCABULARY

Define or briefly explain the following terms:

Classic	Fashion marketing
Consumer	Fashion merchandising
Customer	High fashion
Design	Marketing
Details	Mass or volume fashion
Fad	Silhouette
Fashion	Style
Fashion business	Taste
Fashion industries	Texture

MERCHANDISING REVIEW

1. What are the three most common misconceptions about fashion? Do you agree or disagree?
2. Describe several apparel styles that are named for the period of history in which they originated.
3. Describe several apparel styles (for men, women, or children) that are in fashion today and can be considered classics.
4. What are the four components of all fashions? Briefly explain their interrelationships.
5. Distinguish between (*a*) style and fashion; (*b*) style and design; (*c*) classic and fad.
6. What factors have contributed to the acceleration of fashion apparel change during the last 100 years? In your opinion, which factors have had the greatest impact, and why?
7. In what respects do fashions mirror the times? Give examples to illustrate your answer.
8. Is it possible to force an unwanted fashion on consumers? Defend your answer.
9. What are the five basic principles relating to fashion? Discuss the implications of any two of these principles for fashion merchants.
10. Name at least three types of consumer products, other than apparel or accessories, in which you believe fashion plays a dominant role today. What fashion elements or components are featured in each?

The following are statements from the text. Discuss the significance of each, citing specific examples to illustrate how each applies to the merchandising of fashion goods.

1. "Because they can come and go in a single season, fads have been called 'miniature fashions.'"
2. "Acceptance . . . means that a fashion is considered appropriate to the occasion for which it is worn."
3. "Today color is a key factor in apparel selection for both sexes."
4. Today "many fashions exist simultaneously."

2. THE ENVIRONMENT OF FASHION

Ever since a Roman emperor proclaimed that citizens who failed to cooperate with the census taker would be whipped and sold into slavery, the practice of periodically counting a country's people has been serious business.

The 1980 U.S. census produced 3 billion separate statistics about how many Americans there are, what they work at, where they live, and how they are doing as measured by income and creature comforts.[1] These seemingly dull statistics are a treasure of vital information, not only for government, but also for virtually every business interested in translating the data and projections drawn from them into new product and profit opportunities.

Used properly, census data provide us with all-important information about conditions that affect our lives and influence our actions. Collectively, the conditions under which we live are called our **environment**. Just as the environment of one nation or society differs from that of another nation or society, so the environment of one neighborhood differs from that of another. In fashion merchandising, it is important to be aware of the conditions that affect a particular target customer's environment and to know how the environment differs from one target group to another.

Four major environmental factors affect fashion interest and demand:

1. Demographics and psychographics.
2. The degree of economic development of a country or society.
3. The sociological characteristics of the class structure.
4. The psychological attitudes of consumers.

Each will be discussed in turn in this chapter.

DEMOGRAPHICS AND PSYCHOGRAPHICS

Manufacturers and retailers both try to identify and select target markets for their goods. They attempt to determine who their customer is, what that customer wants, how much the customers are willing to pay for goods, where these potential customers are located, and how many of the targeted customers there are. Today, demographic and psychographic data are a vital part of determining these important factors.

Demographics are studies that divide broad groups of consumers into smaller, more homogeneous target segments. The variables covered in a demographic study are: population distribution by regional, urban, suburban, and rural population; age; sex; family life cycle; race; religion; nationality; education; occupation; and income.

Psychographics are studies that develop fuller, more personal portraits of potential customers. Psychographic studies more fully predict consumer purchase patterns and distinguish users of a product. The variables covered in a psychographic study are: personality; attitude, interests, and personal opinions; and actual product benefits desired. These studies help greatly in matching the image of a company and its product with the type of consumer using the product. Psychographics help companies understand the behavior of present and potential customers.

ECONOMIC FACTORS

The growth of fashion demand depends on a high level of economic development, which is reflected in consumer income, population characteristics, and technological advances. In his book *On Human Finery*,[2] Quentin Bell underscored the relationship between economics and fashion. He showed that most economically sophisticated countries discard their national costumes long before other nations begin to abandon theirs. England, for example, which led the Western world into the industrial revolution, was the first country to stop wearing traditional national dress. Bell pointed out that Greece, Poland, and Spain, countries with little in common except for being in similar stages of economic development, retained their national costumes when countries with more industrialized economies—Germany, Belgium, Denmark, and Japan—were abandoning theirs.

An example of how countries moving swiftly in economic development also move ahead in fashion is the oil-rich Middle East. For centuries, the national costume—the classic Arab burnoose—was favored by both men and women. Today, among the largest purchasers of designer fashions are the Arab sheiks and businessmen, whose wealth is part of the economic growth ensured by oil or mineral resources.

Consumer Income

Consumer income can be measured in terms of personal income, disposable income, and discretionary income. Many groups of people use the amount of personal income as an indicator of "arriving" in their particular social set. The more personal income they have, the more socially acceptable they consider themselves to be.

Many U.S. families may presently be earning more personal income, but enjoying it less. Measurements have shown sharp increases in personal income in the past decade, but decreases in amounts of disposable and discretionary income.

PERSONAL INCOME. The total or gross income received by the population as a whole is called **personal income**. It consists of wages, salaries, interest, dividends, and all other income for everyone in the country. Divide personal income by the number of people in the population and the result is **per capita personal income**.

DISPOSABLE PERSONAL INCOME. The amount a person has left to spend or save after paying taxes is called **disposable personal income**. It is roughly equivalent to take-home pay and provides an approximation of the purchasing power of each consumer during any given year. As seen in Table 2-1, in 1972, direct federal taxes on the income of a family claimed 13 percent of earnings ($1,450 ÷ $11,152). In 1982, as a result of tax increases, the figure was more than 17 percent of income ($4,103

÷ $23,895). As a proportion of income, direct federal taxes peaked in 1981 at 17.7 percent ($3,697 ÷ $22,410), prior to the implementation of the tax cuts in the Economic Recovery Tax Act of 1981. This means that the median-income family of 1982 could buy about 12 percent fewer goods and services than the same family could purchase in 1972. This reflects the effects of double-digit inflation and an income tax structure that disproportionately burdened the middle class.

DISCRETIONARY INCOME. The money that an individual or family can spend or save after buying necessities—food, clothing, shelter, and basic transportation—is called **discretionary income**. Of course, the distinction between "necessities" and "luxuries" or between "needs" and "wants" is a subjective one.

TABLE 2-1 Median Family Incomes Before and After Direct Federal Taxes and Inflation 1972–1984

| YEAR | MEDIAN FAMILY INCOME* | DIRECT FEDERAL TAXES | | | AFTER-TAX INCOME | |
		Income tax†	Social security	Total	Current dollars	1972 dollars‡
1972	$11,152	$ 982	$ 468	$1,450	$ 9,702	$9,702
1973	11,895	1,098	632	1,730	10,165	9,569
1974	13,004	1,267	761	2,028	10,976	9,311
1975	14,156	1,172	825	1,997	12,159	9,451
1976	15,016	1,388	878	2,266	12,750	9,370
1977	15,949	1,466	933	2,399	13,550	9,355
1978	17,318	1,717	1,048	2,765	14,553	9,332
1979	19,048	1,881	1,168	3,049	15,999	9,221
1980	20,586	2,163	1,262	3,425	17,161	8,712
1981	22,410§	2,477	1,490	3,967	18,443	8,483
1982	23,895§	2,502¶	1,601¶	4,103	19,792	8,543
1983	25,329§	2,522¶	1,697¶	4,219	21,110	8,596
1984	26,848§	2,616¶	1,799¶	4,415	22,433	8,617

* Median income for all families with one earner employed full-time, year-round.
† Married couple filing joint return, two children.
‡ Adjusted by Consumer Price Index of the Bureau of Labor Statistics.
§ Estimated by Tax Foundation.
¶ Assumes no changes in current law.

Source: U.S. Department of Commerce, Bureau of Labor Statistics; Treasury Department, Internal Revenue Service; and Tax Foundation computations. Reprinted in *Consumer's Research,* November 1982, p. 25.

PURCHASING POWER OF A DOLLAR.

While Table 2-1 shows that income has gone up each year, this does not mean that people have had an equivalent increase in purchasing power each year. The reason for this is that the value of the dollar—its **purchasing power**, or what it will buy—has steadily declined over the years.

A decline in the purchasing power of money is caused by inflation. **Inflation** is defined as "an increase in the volume of money and credit relative to available goods resulting in a substantial and continuing rise in the general price level."[3] Inflation, therefore, is an economic situation in which demand exceeds supply. Scarcity of goods and services, in relation to demand, results in ever-increasing prices. As seen in Table 2-1, as the amount of federal taxes increased, the purchasing power of the median income family dropped. With inflation, a 10-year (1972–1982) increase of $10,090 in after-tax income became a loss of $1,159 when translated into 1972 dollars.

Because of inflation, the working time required to acquire the necessities of life—food, shelter, clothing, transportation—was far greater in 1982 than 10 years earlier. Table 2-2 shows that the typical manufacturing worker needed to work almost 13 hours a month just to pay ordinary electric and natural-gas bills, compared with only about 7 hours in 1972. Note, however, the increase was not uniform among the items.

In a **recession**, which represents a low point in a business cycle, money and credit become scarce, or "tight." Interest rates are high, production is down, and the rate of unemployment is up. People in the low- and fixed-income groups are the hardest hit; those with high incomes are the least affected. Yet these groups are small when compared with the middle-income group. It is the reaction of

TABLE 2-2 Impact on Paychecks Varies Widely		
	ESTIMATED WORKTIME REQUIRED TO PURCHASE*	
	1972	1982
New home (median price)	42 months	47 months
New car (average price)	25 weeks	28 weeks
Hospital room, semiprivate, per day	16 hours, 37 min.	23 hours, 54 min.
Week's groceries (family of 4)	12 hours, 3 min.	11 hours, 46 min.
Motor tuneup	8 hours, 9 min.	8 hours, 34 min.
Month's electric bill (750 kwh)	4 hours, 20 min.	6 hours, 34 min.
Month's gas bill (100 therms)	2 hours, 42 min.	6 hours, 23 min.
Tank of gasoline (18 gallons)	1 hour, 40 min.	2 hours, 43 min.
Physician's office visit	2 hours, 7 min.	2 hours, 37 min.
Man's haircut	43 min.	38 min.
Coffee (2 pounds)	29 min.	36 min.
Dry cleaning, man's two-piece suit	28 min.	31 min.
Movie admission, adult	32 min.	25 min.
Round steak (1 pound)	23 min.	21 min.
Six-pack of beer	22 min.	18 min.
Toothpaste (8 ounces)	16 min.	15 min.
Milk (1 gallon)	11 min.	8 min.

*Figures are based on average hourly wage in manufacturing—$3.82 in 1972 and $8.50 in 1982, and assume a 40-hour workweek.

Source: Reprinted from *U.S. News & World Report*, May 9, 1983; p. 129, 1983, U.S. News & World Report, Inc.

these middle-income people to any economic squeeze that is the greatest concern of the fashion merchant. For not only is the middle-income group the largest, it is also the most important market for fashion merchandise.

EFFECT ON

FASHION MARKETING.   Both inflation and recession affect consumers' buying patterns. Fashion merchants in particular must thoroughly understand the effects of inflation and recession when planning their inventory assortments and promotional activities. Manufacturers must also understand how consumers are affected by economic factors.

Most manufacturers are concerned with national trends. Retailers, however, must consider the impact of statistics in their local areas as well as the statistics from national studies. **Market segmentation** is the separating of the total consumer market into smaller groups. These are known as **market segments**. Through identifying and studying each market segment, producers and retailers are able to target their goods and services to their special markets.

Population

The majority of the population of the United States has some discretionary income and thus can influence the course of fashion. Two factors relating to population, however, have an important bearing on the extent of fashion demand:

1. The size of the total population and the rate of its growth.
2. The age mix of the population and its projection into the future.

SIZE OF POPULATION.   The size of the population relates to the extent of current fashion demand. The rate of population growth suggests what tomorrow's market may become. In 1920 the United States had a population of about 106 million. By 1950 that figure

had reached 151 million, and by 1980, 227.6 million. The U.S. Census Bureau has projected that by 1990 our population will reach the staggering figure of 249,731,000 people—a tremendous increase of well over 140 million people, or almost 58 percent, in 70 years.

AGE MIX.   The age mix and its projection into the future affect the characteristics of current fashion demand and suggest what they may be in the future. While the overall population continues to grow, the growth rate is not the same for all age groups or for both sexes. (See Table 2-3) Since each group has its own special fashion interests, needs, and reactions, changes in the age mix serve as vital clues to future fashion demand.

Today the largest and fastest-growing age group in the United States is the 25- to 44-year-old group. This is a new factor. The lower birthrate of the early 1970s is now reflected in the 1980 decline in the under-14 group. The resulting decrease in the number of 15- to 24-year-olds will be apparent in 1990. Although the 15- to 24-year-old group is not as large today as other age groups, it will probably continue to be the group most responsive to change and eager for the new. However, since this group will not show an increase until the year 2000, its impact on the current fashion scene is actually reduced.

Because of the longer life span of both men and women, the over-65 group is steadily growing in numbers. This group becomes increasingly important in the fashion world as their earlier retirement, and in some cases increased retirement incomes, allow them to spend many active years wherever and however they choose. Their interests and discretionary expenditures vary radically from those of their younger counterparts.

Technological Advances

In few if any countries has business competition been as keen and fast-growing as in the United States. The competition has fostered

				PERCENT CHANGE	PERCENT CHANGE
AGE	1980	1990	2000	1980–1990	1990–2000
<5	16,448	19,200	17,624	16.7	− 8.2
5– 9	16,595	18,599	18,758	12.1	0.9
10–14	18,227	16,776	19,519	− 8.0	16.4
15–19	21,123	16,957	18,950	−19.7	11.8
20–24	21,605	18,567	17,126	−14.1	− 7.8
25–29	19,763	21,503	17,380	8.8	−19.2
30–34	17,824	22,003	19,007	23.4	−13.6
35–39	14,126	20,004	21,736	41.6	8.7
40–44	11,752	17,841	21,982	51.8	23.2
45–49	11,047	13,973	19,753	26.5	41.4
50–54	11,687	11,418	17,341	− 2.3	51.9
55–59	11,619	10,451	13,285	−10.1	27.1
60–64	10,134	10,639	10,494	5.0	− 1.4
65–69	8,805	10,006	9,110	13.6	− 9.0
70–74	6,843	8,048	8,583	17.6	6.6
75–79	4,815	6,224	7,242	29.3	16.4
80–84	2,972	4,060	4,965	36.6	22.3
85 +	2,274	3,461	5,136	52.2	48.4
Total	227,658	249,731	267,990	9.7	7.3

TABLE 2-3 U.S. Population* by Age: 1980, 1990, and 2000†

* In thousands
† All figures are as of July 1, including the 1980 figures, which are *Current Population Survey* estimates based on 1980 census results.
Source: U.S Census Bureau. Reprinted in *American Demographics,* January 1983, p. 47.

countless technological advances, many of which have had impact on the fashion field. As technological advances have increased both the variety and availability of new products, the demand for new fashions has increased.

MANUFACTURING
EQUIPMENT AND PROCESSES. Improved spinning and weaving machines, which helped start the industrial revolution, were the first major advances in the fashion industry. The mechanical sewing machine was the next advance, in the mid-1800s. Today, almost every phase of fabric and apparel manufacture is mechanized or automated.

Modern sewing machines are powered to operate at high speeds; some specialized machines can produce 5,000 to 6,000 stitches a minute. High-speed knitting machines are equally efficient. Embroidery machines can be programmed to stitch different patterns at the turn of a dial and can produce a design on many pieces of cloth at one time. Hems can be power-stitched at high speed or even "welded" by ultrasonic waves. Bonding machines for welding two thicknesses of cloth are available. Some machines can also weld fibers into new types of nonwoven fabrics more supple and delicate than felt, the original nonwoven fabric.

New processes have burgeoned, too. These include ways to make and use a wide variety of man-made fibers, separately or in blends. The industry also is producing blends of man-made and natural fibers for improved quality, appearance, and performance. For example, a new finishing process, called Sanfor-Set, when used on a 100 percent cotton fabric "irons itself in the dryer." The advantages of the natural cotton fiber combined with the Sanfor-Set process make ironing unnecessary.

The development of new methods of treating

fabrics has made possible many fashions that could not have been introduced in the past. Bright colors were more readily accepted when they became resistant to fading from sun, rain, and laundry soaps. Pleats became more popular when they were treated to retain their creases through many washings or dry cleanings. Bulky fashions met less resistance when the bulk was achieved without weight.

AGRICULTURE. Agricultural developments have affected the fashion field most strongly in the areas of cotton, wool, fur, and leather. In general, improved agricultural techniques have resulted in more and better-quality products.

Improved seed strains and better control of insect pests and plant diseases have helped increase the quality and quantity of cotton grown on an acre. Mechanized equipment helps farmers plant the crop, tend it, and harvest it more efficiently and with less labor. Scientific breeding has produced sheep that yield increasingly better grades of wool and has increased the amount of wool that can be clipped from each animal. Improved methods of fur farming and ranching have contributed to better pelts and hides for the fur and leather industries.

COMMUNICATIONS. Not many years ago, news of every sort traveled more slowly. This meant that life moved more slowly and fashions changed more slowly. It took weeks or months for people in one section of the country to learn what was being worn in another part of the country. Fashion trends moved as leisurely as the news.

Our electronic age has changed all that. Today we enjoy rapid communication in ever-increasing quantities and infinite varieties. By means of Telstar and almost round-the-clock broadcasting, television brings the world to our homes. Thus it has become a most important medium for transmitting fashion information. Famous designers create special costumes for stars, and we all take note. Changes in the dress and hairstyles of our favorite newscast-

ers, soap opera characters, and talk show personalities have a great impact on us.

In 1983, the motion picture *Flashdance* caught the fancy of millions of young people. Soon the one-bare-shoulder look was seen all over. Then it was specially designed into dresses, blouses, and tops.

At the same time, the nationwide enthusiasm for exercise found new outlets, such as aerobic dancing, jazzercise, and the "workout." The enormously popular Jane Fonda Workout was promoted by the actress via exercise studios, a book, and cassettes. Special Jane Fonda workout fashions were created by renowned theatrical designer Theoni V. Aldridge. These totally practical reversible clothes could be used in the workout, for streetwear, or for dancing.

While television informs us about fashion on a national and international scale, radio also has its valuable place. Radio is an excellent medium through which local merchants can inform their audiences of special fashion events.

TRANSPORTATION. Improved trucks and superhighways and the growth of the air-freight business all bring the producer of fashion goods and the stores that sell them much closer together. Instead of weeks, the transportation of goods from vendor to store now takes days—sometimes only hours if the speed is worth the cost. Consolidated shipping, in which two or more shippers put together a truckload or carload, helps get merchandise to the stores more quickly and at reduced transportation costs.

Developments in transportation have also influenced fashions themselves. The earliest automobiles created a need for dusters, veils, and gauntlets. Today sports cars and motorcycles require practical dress such as jeans, pants, scarfs, and short or divided skirts. Air travel has made any part of the world and any climate accessible in a matter of hours. This, plus the new affluence of such a large segment of the population, has created a demand for

Developments in transportation continue to influence fashion. Early automobiles created a need for dusters and veils. Today different needs must be met.

travel and vacation clothes that grows every year.

The old "resort season," which took place only among the extremely wealthy in late December and January, has become a "fifth season," which begins in October and lasts until late March. Increasingly, retailers need to have appropriate fashions for warm or cold climates almost year-round. The demand for wrinkle-free, packable clothing also continues to grow.

SOCIOLOGICAL FACTORS

To understand fashion, one needs to understand the sociological scene in which fashion trends begin, grow, and fade away. The famous designer Cecil Beaton saw fashion as a social phenomenon that reflects "the same continuum of change that rides through any given age." Changes in fashion, he emphasized, "correspond with the subtle and often hidden network of forces that operate on society. . . . In this sense, fashion is a symbol." [4]

Simply stated, changes in fashion are caused by changes in the attitudes of consumers, which are in turn influenced by changes in the social patterns of the times. The key sociological factors influencing fashion today are leisure time, ethnic influences, status of women, social and physical mobility, and wars, disasters, and crises.

Leisure Time

One of the most important possessions of the average U.S. citizen today is leisure time—time that can be spent away from the workplace in any way desired. By the end of the 1970s, the number of work hours had shrunk to the point where some companies and government offices now enjoy a four-day workweek. This, in addition to paid holidays, paid vacations, and early retirements, has provided people with an increasing amount of leisure time as compared to the 1940s and 1950s.

The ways in which people use their leisure time are as varied as people themselves. Some turn to active or spectator sports; others prefer to travel. Many seek outlets for self-improvement, while growing numbers fill their time and enhance their standard of living with a second job. Increased leisure has brought changes to people's lives in many ways—in values, standards of living, and scope of activities. As a result, whole new markets have sprung up. Demand for larger and more versatile wardrobes for the many activities consumers can now explore and enjoy has mushroomed.

CASUAL LIVING.   A look into the closets of the American population of the 1980s would probably reveal one aspect that is much the same from coast to coast, in large cities and in small towns: Most would contain an unusually large selection of casual clothes and sportswear. The market for casual apparel developed with the growth of the suburbs in the 1950s, and has had a continuous series of boosts in the years since. The "do your own thing" revolution of the 1960s made a casual look for men and women acceptable in what had been more formal places and occasions. The 1970s saw a tremendous surge in the number of women wearing slacks and pantsuits and in the number of men and women wearing jeans just about everywhere. Even with the return to more formal styles in the 1980s, casual clothing remains an option for many people at work as well as at play.

ACTIVE SPORTSWEAR.   There is no doubt about it, the superstar of the fashion market in the 1970s and the 1980s has been sportswear. The sportswear growth has been phenomenal! While sports clothes have been around since the turn of the century, when they first appeared they were not particularly distinctive. Women's dresses for playing tennis or golf were not much different from their regular streetwear, and men's outfits similarly varied little from business suits. By the 1920s, consumers began demanding apparel that was appropriate for active sports or simply for relaxing in the sunshine. But it is the emphasis on health and self in the last two decades that has caused the fantastic growth of the active sportswear market. Sports-minded people play tennis in specially designed tennis fashions. Golfers want special golf-wear. Joggers want only jogging outfits. And bikers seem able to bike only in appropriate fashions. The same goes for skaters, skiers, runners, hang gliders, sky divers, and climbers. Health clubs, exercise classes, and workout gyms exploded in popularity in the 1980s and a whole new and vast world of leotards, exercise suits, warm-up suits, and other self-improvement fashions and accompanying accessories were born. Whatever the activity, the specialized fashions quickly followed and became a vital need.

RETIREMENT LEISURE. Unique to the twentieth century is a special and rapidly growing population segment—retired people. In the next century, those 65 and over will account for more than one of every five persons and will alter the way the United States lives and works. Medical advances, better nutrition, and earlier retirements all have contributed to the growth of the over-65 group. This group will be active much longer as medical advances reduce illness and disability.

By 2033, the U.S. Census Bureau expects life expectancy to increase by about four years to 74.4 years for men and 82.7 years for women. But many scientists feel that those estimates could be far too conservative.

In the marketplace, the burgeoning ranks of the elderly will require companies to meet the demand of older consumers for such items as package travel tours, cosmetic aids, and apparel that suits their ages, figures, and new interests. This formerly neglected market will offer new opportunities and challenges for marketers, especially in fashion.

Ethnic Influences

In recent years, minority groups in the United States, representing approximately one-eighth of the nation's total population, have experienced vast population increases and sociological changes.

The Spanish-speaking market within the United States is growing so fast that market researchers can't keep up with it. The 1980 U.S. Census Bureau counted 14,608,673 Hispanics. In addition, 6 million to 10 million undocumented Hispanics are estimated to be here illegally. Together, these groups form the fastest-growing minority in the United States and the world's fifth largest Spanish-speaking population, following only Mexico, Spain, Colombia, and Argentina.

Until 1930, immigration to the United States was almost exclusively from Europe. Then for the following three decades, Latin Americans, mostly from Mexico and Puerto Rico, comprised 15 percent of the immigrants. By 1970, that portion had grown to 40 percent, with an influx of Central and South Americans. Since 1980, an estimated 153,000 Haitians and Cubans have also sought refuge in the United States.[5] The Hispanic population has made its impact on the fashion scene with the introduction of fiery colorations, prints reminiscent of lush South American rain forests, and dance and music styles that have been accepted by the entire American public.

Blacks are better educated and hold higher-level jobs than they did in the past. With better education comes a stronger sense of oneself and one's heritage. Today many black people show the pride they feel in their African heritage by wearing African styles, fabrics, and patterns. Nonblacks have adopted these styles as well. Fashion companies have acknowledged the changes that have occurred among the black population and have reflected these changes in the products they market and the models they use. Today, cosmetics are available that emphasize rather than hide the beauty of dark skin. Black men and women have become world-famous modeling clothing at couture shows and advertising various items in magazines and on television.

The end of the Vietnamese war and the influx of thousands of refugees from Cambodia and Vietnam brought additional traditions and costumes to be shared. These refugees joined the other segments of Asians already part of our country: the Koreans, the Chinese, and the Japanese. This stimulated interest in some of the more exotic fashions of the East and in the everyday comfort of the Chinese sandal and quilted jacket. The early 1980s brought Japanese designers to the attention of the American fashion scene with the highly exaggerated Japanese look. These oversized, multilayered clothes were styled in materials of somber tones and with an old, worn look. The latter

The Japanese influence on fashion in the 1980s was marked by oversized, multilayered clothes.

was achieved by artfully designed "holes" actually cut in the garments and with edges left ragged. This "ragged" look was accepted by the most avant-garde of young women who had a large supply of self-confidence. To the majority of women, the influence of the Japanese designers was accepted only as it was translated into more subdued fashions.

Status of Women

In the early 1900s, the American woman was, in many ways, a nonperson. She could not vote, serve on a jury, earn a living at any but a few occupations, own property, or enter public places unescorted. She passed directly from her father's control to her husband's control, without rights or monies. In both households, she dressed to please the man and reflect his status.

Profound changes began to occur during World War I, and have accelerated ever since.

The most dramatic advances have happened since the mid-1960s and the advent of the women's movement. Women's demands for equal opportunity, equal pay, and equal rights in every facet of life continue to bring about even more change. These changes have affected not only fashion but the entire field of marketing.

JOBS AND MONEY. In early 1981, predictions were that by 1985, half of all American women over the age of 16 would be in the work place. At the end of 1981, that figure had already been reached and surpassed. The U.S. Department of Labor reported that the figure of all such working women was 52.3 percent. This represents a staggering increase of over 5 million women who have entered the work force since 1977, when the figure was 48.4 percent.

The dramatic increase in working women has led to a surge in fashion interest, because a woman who works is continuously exposed to fashion. It is everywhere around her as she meets people, shops during her lunch hour, or is on her way home. As a member of the work force, she now has the incentive, the opportunity, and the means to respond to fashion's appeal. New periodicals, such as *Ms.* and *Working Woman*, make this market reachable.

Finally, women in general today have more money of their own to spend as they see fit. Approximately four women in every six have incomes, earned and unearned, of their own. These women and their acceptance or rejection of offered styles have new importance in the fashion marketplace.

EDUCATION. Often the better educated a woman becomes, the more willing she is to learn new things. She is also more willing to try new fashions, which of course serves to accelerate fashion change. And with more women today receiving more education than ever before, the repercussions on fashion are unmistakable. Today's educated women have had wider exposure than their mothers or grandmothers to other cultures and to people of different backgrounds. Consequently, they are more worldly, more discerning, more demanding, and more confident in their taste and feel for fashion. Fashion marketers must recognize these new customers.

No wonder Edward Sapir, a leading social scientist, considered education a major factor in fashion change. "Fashion is custom in the guise of departure from custom," said Sapir.[6] To him, fashion is a resolution of the conflict between people's revolt against adherence to custom and their reluctance to appear lacking in good taste.

SOCIAL FREEDOM. Perhaps the most marked change in the status of women since the early 1900s is the degree of social freedom they now enjoy. Young women today are free to apply for a job, and to earn, spend, and save their own money. They are free to go unescorted to a restaurant, theater, or other public place. Women travel more frequently than they did in the past. They travel to more distant locations, at a younger age, and often alone. Many own their own cars. If they can afford it, they may maintain an apartment or share one with others.

Short skirts, popular in the 1920s, the early 1940s, and the 1960s, are commonly interpreted as a reflection of women's freedom. So, too, is the simplicity of the styles that prevailed in those periods: chemises, sacks, tents, shifts, other variations of loose-hanging dresses, and pants.

Different theories exist about why these changes came about. Some people believe that stiff, unyielding corsets went out with a stiff, unyielding moral code. Others believe that the changes had no particular social significance. They believe that women rejected inflexible corsets not because of a change in the moral code but because the new materials were simply more comfortable. Similarly, pants may be viewed as an expression of women's freedom or merely as suitable garments for hopping in and out of the indispensable automobile.

Whatever the reasons, the lifestyles of American women, and their opinions and attitudes about fashion, have changed radically in the past three decades. American women have gained hard-won freedoms in their social and business lives. They are just as definite about their freedom of choice in fashion. The thought of today's independent women accepting uncomfortable and constricting clothing or shoes just to follow the dictates of some fashion arbiter, as they did years ago, is ludicrous. Today's busy, active women, whether at home or at the office, have very carefully defined preferences for fashions that suit their own individual needs and comfort. The successful designers of the 1980s recognize these preferences and make sure that their drawing boards reflect them.

Social Mobility

Almost all societies have classes, and individuals choose either to stand out from or to conform to their actual or aspired-to class. Bell viewed fashion as the process "whereby members of one class imitate those of another, who, in turn, are driven to ever new expedients of fashionable change."[7]

Bell considered the history of fashion inexplicable without relating it to social classes. He is not alone in his thinking. Other sociologists have related fashion change to changes in social mobility and to the effort to associate with a higher class by imitation.

The United States is sometimes called a classless society, but this is valid only in that there are no hereditary ranks, royalty, or untouchables. Classes do exist, but they are based largely upon occupation, income, residential location, education, or avocation, and their boundaries have become increasingly fluid. They range from the immensely wealthy (self-made millionaires or their descendents—the Vanderbilts, Whitneys, and Rockefellers, for example) at the top through the very wealthy (mostly nouveau riche) through the many middle-income levels and finally to the low-

WOMEN

Macy's and Working Woman Magazine present a full report, Monday, September 10 through Friday, September 14 in Herald Square.

Join us for a complete look at the business of being a woman in 1984. You'll have the opportunity to ask questions and formulate your own opinions as experts from a wide variety of fields share their points of view. In Clubhouse, 3rd Floor, Herald Square.

A copy of Working Woman Magazine and a special Macy's/Working Woman gift, is yours while supplies last. Enter our Women Mean Business prize drawings.† And while you're here, visit The 34th Street Branch on 7, where you'll find a special section of books written by, for and about women today. Best bet: The Working Woman Report, Simon and Schuster, 16.95.

MONDAY
status report

An update on where we've been, where we are, and where we're going. Moderator: Kate Rand Lloyd, Editor-at-Large, Working Woman Magazine. Guest panelists: Dr. Adele M. Scheele, PhD, author and renown career strategist; Kay Wight, Vice President CBS Sports and Chairman of the NYC Commission on the Status of Women. 6pm

TUESDAY
entrepreneurial woman

A look at what it's like to start and run your own business. Moderator: Charlotte Taylor, contributing editor, Working Woman Magazine. Guest panelists: Julee Rosso and Shiela Lukins, co-owners of the highly successful gourmet food business, The Silver Palate; Jackie Markham, partner Markham/Novell Communications, Ltd. 1pm

mean

WEDNESDAY
balance of lifestyle

An overview: how to handle business and pleasure with style, grace and minimum stress. Moderator: Halcyone Bohen, PhD, and Director of Clinical Services, Family Therapy Practice Center, Wash., DC. Guest panelists: Gilda Marx, fitness authority, designer of exercise wear; Ina Yalof, author, medical sociologist, Newark-Beth Israel Medical Center. 1pm

THURSDAY
career & financial advancement

Your financial personality: what it is and how you can develop it for future successes. Moderator: Bonnie Siverd, contributing editor, Working Woman. Guest panelists: Susan Antilla, contributing editor, Working Woman, reporter for USA Today; Ann Dauberman, stockbroker, Merrill Lynch. 1pm

FRIDAY
working wardrobes

Linda Lee, Director of Macy's Buy Appointment, fashion consultants, presents the perfect working woman wardrobe. 1pm

BUSINESS

Events macy's

†Details in store. No purchase necessary. Macy's employees and their families not eligible.

Today, fashion works for the working woman, reflecting her higher status.

FASHION FOCUS

LIZ CLAIBORNE:
DARLING OF THE DESK SET

Unlike the designers who costume their clients as peasants or punk rockers, Liz Claiborne designs her fashions for the ever-increasing number of women who are members of the work force. And by offering the working woman moderately priced career clothes that wear well and pack easily, Claiborne has successfully emerged as the "darling of the desk set."

Claiborne has managed to capture the essence of the working woman better than most other designers because she designs clothes with her own needs in mind. The person she refers to as "'the Liz lady' is a white-collar woman who needs a versatile, long-wearing wardrobe that's fashionable without being freaky."[1] Instead of setting fashion trends, Claiborne has chosen to design clothes that the working woman will respond to and want to wear.

Born in Europe of American parents, Claiborne, who is now in her early fifties, got a very early start in the fashion-designing business. At the age of 17 she won a design contest sponsored by *Glamour* magazine. She studied at an art school in Brussels and the Académie in Nice, France, and at 21 she was hired as a sketcher at Tina Lesser, a sportswear house in New York City. Then came jobs with Junior Rite and the Rhea Manufacturing Company of Milwaukee, where she met her

income and poverty levels. At the very bottom are the so-called hard-core unemployed and those people who have no homes and whose possessions can be carried from place to place.

MIDDLE-CLASS GROWTH. Most fashion authorities agree that there is a direct relationship between the growth and strength of the middle class and the growth and strength of fashion demand. The middle class has the highest physical, social, and financial mobility. Because it is the largest class, it has the majority vote in the adoption of fashions. Members of the middle class tend to be followers, not

leaders, of fashion, but the strength of their following pumps money into the fashion industry. And the persistence of their following often spurs fashion leaders to seek newer and different fashions of their own.

The United States has a very large middle class with both fashion interest and the money to indulge it. It is growing in proportion to the total population, thanks to this country's efforts to bring the entire population up to a reasonable standard of living. This growth means a widespread increase in consumer buying power, which in turn generates increased fashion demand.

husband and business partner, Arthur Ortenberg. Claiborne's 16 years as a designer at Youth Guild, a division of Jonathan Logan, confirmed her reputation as a solid fashion professional.

In 1976, Claiborne and her husband, who then ran a small textile company, decided to start their own business, largely because they recognized that no firm was fully taking care of the career woman who has a limited budget. They knew that they could fill the gap. She invested $50,000 of her own and was able to raise an additional $200,000 from friends and relatives.

Because Claiborne's designs were already known in the large department stores, these stores were willing to retail Claiborne's own line. To her surprise, sales took off at such a rapid rate that the company was unable to keep up with the demand. The staff of six people often had to work seven days a week to process the orders for the 30 items, including jackets, blouses, and pants, that were offered for sale.

The first year, Liz Claiborne, Inc. did more than $2 million worth of business. And by 1982, billings were estimated at $160 million. The company now offers blouses, sweaters, pants, and jackets in more than 600 stores nationwide. When the company began, no item sold for more than $100; now the top figure is still a reasonable $150.

The growth of the company has been so rapid that in 1981 it went public and was offered for sale to customers on the over-the-counter stock market. However, Claiborne, her husband, and two other partners still maintain controlling interest in the company, which now has 700 employees and offers 175 items.

Claiborne is a feminist who employs many female managers, and she speaks to women's groups all over the country about her business. "Fashion is still a male-oriented business at the top," the company president says in her elegant New Orleans drawl. "Many women still don't realize what it takes to become an executive—being willing to move, to give up a good part of their personal lives."[2]

[1] Lynn Langway, "The Darling of the Desk Set," *Newsweek*, February 22, 1982, p. 79.
[2] Ibid.

This Fashion Focus is based on information from the article cited above and from these sources:
Fred Bratman, "Liz Claiborne and a Landmark," *The New York Times*, February 27, 1983, Sec. 11, p. L.I. 6.
Barbara Ettorre, "Working Woman's Dressmaker," *The New York Times*, July 6, 1980, Sec. 3, p. 7.
Karen Alberg Grossman, "Profile on People," *Fashion Accessories Magazine*, April 1981, pp. 6–12.
"Liz Claiborne, Inc. to Try Men's Wear," *The New York Times*, September 17, 1984, Sec. D, p. D3.
Lee Wohlfert-Wihlborg, "With Working Women in Fashion, Wall Street is Bullish on Designer Liz Claiborne," *People*, March 1, 1982, p. 74.

Physical Mobility

Physical mobility, like social mobility, encourages the demand for and response to fashion. One effect of travel is "cross-pollination" of cultures. After seeing how other people live, travelers bring home a desire to adopt or adapt some of what they observed and make it part of their environment.

Thus Marco Polo brought gunpowder, silks, and spices from the Orient, introducing new products to medieval Europe. In the nineteenth century, travelers brought touches of Asian and African fashions to Western dress and home furnishings. In the twentieth century, Latin American and pre-Columbian influences were introduced into North America, dramatically changing the direction and emphasis of fashion in this country.

In the United States, people enjoy several kinds of physical mobility. For example, the daily routine for many people involves driving to work or to a shopping center, often in a different city. Among the broad range of influences they are exposed to during their daily trips are the fashions of others and the fashion offerings of retail distributors.

A second form of physical mobility popular

among Americans is vacation travel. Whether the travelers are going to a nearby lake or around the world, each trip exposes them to many different fashion influences and each trip itself demands special fashions. Living out of a suitcase for a few days or a few months requires clothes that are easy to pack, wrinkle-resistant, suitable for a variety of occasions, and easy to keep in order.

A third form of physical mobility is change of residence, which, like travel, exposes an individual to new contacts, new environments, and new fashion influences. According to annual statistics of the U.S. Census Bureau, about one person in five changes residence in any given year. However, high interest rates and tight rental markets have lately curtailed this movement and increased the tendency to remodel or add on to existing homes. In the 1980s, 90 percent of the nation's population growth has centered in the Sun Belt, and for the first time in U.S. history, metropolitan centers grew at a slower rate than nonmetropolitan areas.[8]

Wars, Disasters, and Crises

Wars, widespread disasters, and crises shake people's lives and focus attention on ideas, events, and places that may be completely new. People develop a need for fashions that are compatible with their altered attitudes and environments.

Such changes took place in women's activities and in fashions as a result of the two world wars. World War I brought women into the business world in significant numbers and encouraged their desire for independence and suffrage. It gave them reason to demand styles that allowed freer physical movement. World War II drew women into such traditionally masculine jobs as riveting, for which they previously had not been considered strong enough. It put them in war plants on night shifts. It even brought women other than nurses into the military services for the first time in the country's history. All these changes gave rise to women's fashions previously considered appropriate only for men, such as slacks, sport shirts, and jeans.

The Depression of the 1930s was a widespread disaster with a different effect on fashions. Because jobs were scarce, considerably fewer were offered to women than had been before. They returned to the home and adopted more feminine clothes. And because money also was scarce, wardrobes became skimpier. A single style often served a large number of occasions. Women who did hold jobs felt pressure to look younger so they could compete with younger applicants. This caused an increased use of lipstick and other cosmetics.

In the late 1970s and early 1980s, a combination of the energy crisis and exceptionally cold weather brought a mass of warm clothing to the marketplace. Thermal underwear, formerly seen only in sporting goods catalogs, was featured in department and specialty shops. Retailers stocked up on sweaters, tights, boots, mittens, leg warmers, scarfs, coats, jackets, and vests with down fill. Not only the Northeast and West but the normally temperate Sun Belt was struck by bitter-cold weather. The record-breaking cold and unfamiliar snow and sleet created demand for warm clothing in areas formerly uninterested in such apparel.

PSYCHOLOGICAL FACTORS

''Fashion promises many things to many people,'' according to economist Dr. Rachel Dardis. ''It can be and is used to attract others, to indicate success, both social and economic, to indicate leadership, and to identify with a particular social group.''[9] Fashion interest and demand at any given time relies heavily on the prevailing psychological attitudes.

The five basic psychological factors that influence fashion demand are boredom, curiosity, reaction to convention, need for self-assurance, and desire for companionship.[10] These factors motivate a large share of people's actions and reactions in general.

People tend to become bored with fashions

too long in use. Boredom leads to restlessness and a desire for change. In fashion, the desire for change expresses itself in a demand for something new and satisfyingly different from what one already has.

Curiosity causes interest in change for its own sake. Highly curious people like to experiment; they want to know what is around the next corner and how color combinations, changes in line, and details affect the look of a garment. There is curiosity in everyone, though some may respond less dramatically than others to its prodding. Curiosity and the need to experiment keep fashion demand alive.

One of the most important psychological factors influencing fashion demand is the reaction to convention. People's reactions take one of two forms: rebellion against convention or adherence to it. Rebellion against convention is characteristic of young people. This involves more than boredom or curiosity: it is a positive rejection of what exists and a search for something new. However, acceptance by the majority is an important part of the definition of fashion. The majority tends to adhere to convention, either within its own group or class or in general.

The need for self-assurance or confidence is a human characteristic that gives impetus to fashion demand. Often the need to overcome feelings of inferiority or of disappointment can be satisfied through apparel. People who consider themselves to be well- and fashionably dressed have an armor that gives them protection and self-assurance. Those who know that their clothes are dated are at a psychological disadvantage.

The desire for companionship is fundamental in human beings. The instinct for survival of the species drives individuals to seek a mate. Humans' innate gregariousness also encourages them to seek companions. Fashion plays its part in the search for all kinds of companionship. In its broader sense, companionship implies the formation of groups, which require conformity in dress as well as in other respects. Flamboyant or subdued, a person's mode of dress can be a bid for companionship as well as the symbol of acceptance within a particular group.

IMPLICATIONS OF ENVIRONMENTAL INFLUENCES

Projections based on demographic and psychographic research can be used by manufacturers and retailers alike to determine their target customers. Projections for the second half of the 1980s indicate that consumers will be better-educated, more affluent or upscale, more mature, and more concerned with receiving greater value. Working women will be a prime target market segment, and this will influence both product style and distribution.

"We're seeing a 'smart shopper' mentality coming into place now," said Ann Clurman, vice president with Yankelovich, Skelly & White, New York. "That is not necessarily a

Rebel or conform? Teenagers often try both—here at the same time.

function of shoppers being better educated—although they are—but rather, it's because there's been a change in the value system. In the '70s the emphasis was on living for the moment, convenience at all cost. Increasingly, we are now becoming a society that is willing to spend time when it will result in greater value.

"The consumer is changing, and that will have implications for fashion marketers."[11]

REFERENCES

[1] Robert Levy, "Cashing in on the Census," *Dun's Business Month*, April 1983, p. 52.
[2] Quentin Bell, *On Human Finery*, The Hogarth Press, Ltd., London, 1947, p. 72.
[3] *Webster's Ninth New Collegiate Dictionary*, Merriam-Webster, Inc., Springfield, Mass., 1983, p. 620.
[4] Cecil Beaton, *The Glass of Fashion*, Doubleday & Company, Inc., New York, 1954, p. 335 and pp. 379–381.
[5] Udajan Gupta, "From Other Shores," *Black Enterprise*, March 1983, p. 51.
[6] Edward Sapir, "Fashion," *Encyclopedia of the Social Sciences*, Vol. VI, London 1931, p. 140.

[7] Bell, p. 72.
[8] "People on the Move: A Sensitive Growth Barometer," *Sales and Marketing Management*, May 16, 1983, p. 56.
[9] Rachel Dardis, "The Power of Fashion," *Proceedings of the Twentieth Annual Conference, College Teachers of Textiles and Clothing, Eastern Region*, New York, 1966, pp. 16–17.
[10] Paul H. Nystrom, *Economics of Fashion*, The Ronald Press, New York, 1928, pp. 66–81.
[11] Belinda Hulin-Salkin, "Special Report: Retail Marketing," *Advertising Age*, July 25, 1983, pp. M6–M32.

MERCHANDISING VOCABULARY

Define or briefly explain the following terms.

Demographics	Market segmentation
Discretionary income	Per capita personal income
Disposable personal income	Personal income
Environment	Psychographics
Inflation	Purchasing power
Market segments	Recession

MERCHANDISING REVIEW

1. What are the four major environmental influences on fashion interest and demand in any era?
2. Why is market segmentation so important to producers and retailers of fashion merchandise?
3. How does the size and age mix of a population affect fashion demand?

4. How has increased leisure time affected the fashion market?
5. How has the changing status of minority groups affected fashion interest and demand?
6. In what ways does a higher level of education affect fashion interest and demand?
7. What is meant by the term "social mobility"? How does the degree of social mobility affect fashion interest and demand? Give examples to illustrate your answer.
8. Why is it more difficult to identify social classes in this country than it is in many other countries? Upon what factors are classes in the United States largely based?
9. Name three kinds of physical mobility that people in this country enjoy today. How does each influence fashion demand?
10. Name the five basic psychological factors motivating much of human behavior. How does each affect fashion interest and demand?

MERCHANDISING DIGEST

1. Which is a more *significant* figure to fashion producers and marketers: discretionary income or disposable personal income? Why?
2. Discuss how technological advances in the following areas have affected interest and the rate of fashion change: (*a*) manufacturing equipment and processes; (*b*) transportation; (*c*) communications.
3. In what ways has the status of women significantly changed in the twentieth century? How has each of these changes affected fashion interest and demand?

3. THE MOVEMENT OF FASHION

Fashion is, in many ways, like a river.

A river is always in motion, continuously flowing—sometimes slowly and gently, other times rushing and turbulent. It is exciting, never the same. It affects those who ride its currents and those who rest on its shores. Its movements depend on the environment.

All of this is true of fashion, too. The constant movements of fashion depend on an environment made up of social, political, and economic factors. These movements, no matter how obvious or how slight, have both meaning and definite direction. There is a special excitement to interpreting these movements and estimating their speed and direction. Everyone involved in fashion, from the designer to the consumer, is caught up in the movement of fashion.

The excitement starts with the textile producers. Fully 12 to 18 months before they offer their lines to manufacturers, the textile people must choose their designs, textures, and colors. From 3 to 9 months before showing a line to buyers, the apparel manufacturers begin deciding which styles they will produce and in which fabrics. Then, 2 to 6 months before the fashions will appear on the selling floor, the retail buyers make their selections from the manufacturers' lines. Finally, the excitement passes on to the consumers, as they select the garments that will be versatile, appropriate, and suitably priced for their individual needs and wants.

How can all these people be sure their choices are based on reliable predictions? Because successful stylists, designers, manufacturers, buyers, and consumers have a good understanding of basic cycles, principles, and patterns that operate in the world of fashion.

THE CYCLING OF FASHION

All fashions move in cycles. The term **fashion cycle** refers to the rise, wide popularity, and then decline in acceptance of a style. The word "cycle" suggests a circle. However, the fashion cycle is represented by a bell-shaped curve. (See page 44.)

Some authorities compare the fashion cycle to a wave, which shows first a slow swell, then a crest, and finally a swift fall. Like the movement of a wave, the movement of a fashion is always forward, never backward. Like waves, fashion cycles do not follow each other in regular, measured order. Some take a short time to crest; others, a long time. The length of the cycle from swell to fall may be long or short. And, again like waves, fashion cycles overlap.

Stages of the Fashion Cycle

Fashion cycles are not haphazard; they don't "just happen." There are definite stages in a style's development that are easily recognized. These stages can be charted and traced, and in the short run, accurately predicted. Being able to recognize and predict the different stages is vital to success in both the buying and the selling of fashion.

Every fashion cycle passes through five stages: (1) introduction, (2) rise, (3) culmination, (4) decline, (5) obsolescence. A comparison of these stages to the timetable suggested by Laver in Chapter 1 would look like this:

Introduction	"indecent" "shameless"
Rise	"outré"
Culmination	"smart"
Decline	"dowdy" "hideous"
Obsolescence	"ridiculous"

The fashion cycle serves as an important guide in fashion merchandising. The fashion merchant uses the fashion cycle concept to introduce new fashion goods, to chart their rise and culmination, and to recognize their decline toward obsolescence.

INTRODUCTION. The next new fashion may be introduced by a producer in the form of a new style, color, or texture. The new style may be a flared pant leg when slim legs are popular, vibrant colors when earth tones are popular, slim body-hugging fabric texture such as knit jersey when heavy-textured bulky looks are being worn.

New styles are almost always introduced in higher-priced merchandise. They are produced in small quantities since retail fashion buyers purchase a limited number of pieces to test the new styles' appeals to targeted customers. This testing period comes at the beginning of the buying cycle of fashion merchandise, which coincides with the introduction stage of the fashion cycle. The test period ends when the new style either begins its rise or has been rejected by the target customer. Because there can be many risks, new styles must be priced high enough so that those that succeed can cover the losses on those that don't succeed. Promotional activities such as designer appearances, institutional advertising, and charity fashion shows, which will appeal to the fashion leaders of the community and also enhance the store's fashion image, will appear at this point.

RISE. When the new original design (or its adaptations) is accepted by an increasing number of customers, it is considered to be in its **rise stage**. At this stage, the fashion buyer reorders in quantity for maximum stock coverage.

During the rise stage of a new original design, many retailers will offer **line-for-line copies** or "knock-offs," as they are referred to in the fashion industry. These are versions of the original designer style duplicated by manufacturers. These copies look exactly like the original except that they have been mass-produced in less expensive fabrics. Because production of the merchandise is now on a larger scale, prices of the knock-offs are generally lower.

As a new style continues to be accepted by more and more of the customers, **adaptations** appear. Adaptations are designs that have all the dominant features of the style that inspired them, but do not claim to be exact copies. Modifications have been made but distinguishing features of the original, such as a special shoulder treatment or the use of textured fabric, may be retained in the adaptation. At this stage, the promotion effort focuses on regular price lines, full assortments, and product-type ads to persuade the customer of the store's superiority in filling his or her fashion needs.

CULMINATION. The **culmination stage** of the fashion cycle is the period when a fashion is at the height of its popularity and use. At this stage, also referred to as the **plateau**, the fashion is in such demand that it can be mass-produced, mass-distributed, and sold at prices within the range of most customers. This stage may be long or brief, depending on how extended the peak of popularity is. The quilted coat, which began as an expensive down-filled style in the late 1970s, reached its culmination stage when mass production in acrylic fill had made a quilted coat available to practically every income level. At the culmination stage, the high-price line fashion buyer ceases to reorder the fashion and begins stock reductions.

The culmination stage of a fashion may be extended in two ways:

1. If a fashion becomes accepted as a classic, it settles into a fairly steady sales pattern. An example of this is the cardigan sweater, an annual steady seller.

2. If new details of design, color, or texture are continually introduced, interest in the

fashion may be kept alive longer. Jeans are a perfect example. A more recent example is the continued fashion interest in running shoes, fostered by new colors, designs, and comfort innovations.

DECLINE. When boredom with a fashion sets in, the result is a decrease in consumer demand for that fashion. This is known as the **decline stage**. It is a principle of fashion that all fashion ends in excess. It is also true that excess ends all fashion.

As a fashion starts to decline, consumers may still be wearing it, but they are no longer willing to buy it at its regular price. The outstanding fashion merchandiser is able to recognize the end of the culmination stage and start markdowns early. At this point, production stops immediately or comes slowly to a halt. The leading fashion stores abandon the

Fashion ends in excess, as in this "zoot suit" from the 1940s. Or does the excess end the fashion?

style; traditional stores take a moderate mark-down and advertise the price reduction. This will probably be followed in a short while by a major price-slash clearance or closeout. At this stage the style may be found in bargain stores at prices far below what the style commanded in earlier stages.

OBSOLESCENCE. When strong distaste for a style has set in and it can no longer be sold at any price, the fashion is in its **obsolescence stage**.

Lengths of Cycles

Predicting the time span of a fashion cycle is impossible since each fashion moves at its own speed. However, one guideline can be counted on. Declines are fast, and a drop to obsolescence is almost always steeper than a rise to culmination. At this point, as they say in merchandising, "You can't give it away."

As the world moves closer and closer to the twenty-first century, the speed with which products move through their cycles is accelerating. Rapid technological developments and "instant" communications have much to do with this speedup, as do fast-changing environmental factors. The result is an intense competition among manufacturers and retailers to provide consumers with what they want and expect—constantly changing assortments from which to choose.

The cycle of innovation, demand, wide acceptance, and rejection occurs in most products, from home computers to automobiles to sports equipment, from women's apparel to menswear. The cycle starts with a new idea from a designer. This is introduced to the public as a product. It commands interest and begins to be accepted by the innovators in the buying public. The product gains in popularity and "everybody has to have it." And then, its popularity declines—sometimes because it has become too common, more often because people have been impressed by a newer idea. This is the pattern that all fashions follow. All that

varies is the speed of passing from one stage to the next, which dictates the lifetime of the cycle.

American society in the mid-1980s accepts as routine live TV pictures of astronauts working in outer space, of battles being fought in various parts of the world, and of personalities participating in social occasions at every point of the globe. Our appetite for constant newness and change seems to be insatiable. The vast choice of new styles that consumers are offered continuously by the fashion world provides them with an important role in the movement of fashion cycles. Consumers either give a new style enough acceptance to get it started, or they immediately reject it. Since more new fashions are always ready to push existing ones out of the way, it is no wonder that with each passing year the time required for a fashion to complete its cycle becomes shorter and shorter.

Breaks in the Cycle

In fashion, as in everything else, there are always ups and downs, stops and starts. The normal flow of a fashion cycle can be broken or abruptly interrupted by outside influences. The influence can be simply unpredictable weather or a change in group acceptance. Or it can be much more dramatic and far-reaching—war, worldwide economic depression, or a natural disaster, for example.

Although no formal studies have been made of the phenomenon of the broken cycle, manufacturers and merchants have a theory about it. They believe that a broken cycle usually picks up where it has stopped once conditions return to normal or once the season that was cut short reopens. Consider the effect that the shortage of petroleum has had on the movement of man-made fibers. Although the success of man-made fibers—with all their easy-care attributes—was tremendous, their availability was interrupted by petroleum shortages both in 1973 and again in 1979. However, when the petroleum supply increased, the popularity of these fibers returned to what it had been.

Widespread economic depressions also temporarily interrupt the normal progress of a fashion cycle. When there is widespread unemployment, fashion moves much more slowly, only resuming its pace with economic recovery and growth.

Wars also affect fashion. They cause shortages which force designers, manufacturers, retailers, and consumers to change fashions less freely or to restrict styles. People redirect their interests, and fashion must take a back seat. When fashion apparel is in a cycle break, interest in cosmetics usually picks up. Women switch cosmetics or use them differently to satisfy their desire for something new. After wars have ended, interest in fashion picks up and it flourishes once again.

Long-Run and Short-Run Fashions

The length of time individual fashions take to complete their cycles varies widely. **Long-run fashions** take more seasons to complete their cycles than what might be considered average; **short-run fashions** take fewer.

Some fashions tend to rise in popular acceptance more slowly than others, thereby prolonging their life. Some stay in popular demand much longer than others do. The decline in popular demand for some fashions may be slower than for others.

Silhouettes, colors, textures, accessories, classics, and fads may be classified as long-run or short-run fashions. The length of time each takes to complete a full demand cycle varies widely. As discussed in Chapter 2, the level of technological development, existing lifestyles, and psychological reactions to prevailing social and economic conditions also influence these timetables.

SILHOUETTES AND DETAILS. Three basic fashion silhouettes form the basis for all clothing, as noted in Chapter 1. Therefore, it is obvious that silhouettes are long-run fashions. They do not change drastically from one season to another. Instead, it is through a series of changes in detail that a silhouette changes. The changes may be so imperceptible that a year-old garment may not look out of fashion. However, as these subtle changes add up over a period of four or five years, older apparel may take on a look that seems badly proportioned and definitely dated. And when the same silhouette goes through more and more years of detail changes—it is then replaced by another silhouette. In her book, *Recurring Cycles of Fashion,* Young pointed out that approximately every 35 years the silhouettes changed completely.[1]

Since the more detailed an item of apparel is, the sooner it becomes dated, obviously the simple, understated styles will generally have a longer fashion life. Is it any wonder that many high-fashion designers here and abroad aim for styles that will remain fashionable for 10 to 15 years . . . or longer?

COLORS AND TEXTURES. Colors and textures were once thought of as secondary and short-run fashions. However, with new scientific studies about its potentially beneficial emotional and psychological effects, color has gained importance as an element of fashion. Thus color in fashions of the 1980s has taken on new meaning, and designers and retailers herald new seasons, silhouettes, and details with exciting new colors. The traditional white and pastels for summer and black for winter are limitations of the past.

Textures, too, are less seasonally oriented. Whether a fabric is smooth or nubby, crisp or soft, sheer or opaque, light or heavyweight has more to do with the fashion needs of the customer than of the season. This has become possible with the technological advances in man-made fibers and the new texture finishes for natural fibers.

ACCESSORIES. For many years shoes, handbags, jewelry, millinery, gloves, belts, scarfs, and cosmetics were thought of merely as finishing touches for apparel, with only seasonal or short-run fashion cycles. Today many accessories are regarded as apparel items and have full-run fashion cycles of their own. Handbag and shoe "wardrobes" are owned by many consumers and are used to prolong or change the fashion cycles of their basic apparel. Scarfs are also considered important fashion accents. Today's scarfs come in many sizes, lengths, fabrics, and colors. They are used as belts or sashes, head coverings, and blouse fill-ins, and in any other exciting or innovative way the customer wishes.

Jewelry moves in both long-run and short-run cycles. Pearls had a long cycle of popularity during the fifties and sixties but declined because of the unstructured and casual look of the seventies. In the eighties, with the return of the fifties look and the classic and extravagant look and feel of fashion in general, pearls have once again begun a fashion cycle.

CLASSICS. The longest-running fashions are classics—those fashions that seem permanently arrested in the culmination stage of their cycles. Classics are usually practical and universally appealing. The shirtwaist dress, cardigan sweater, plain pump, neutral hosiery shades for women, and oxford-type shoe and sports jacket for men are examples.

Classics change, but only superficially. Material, texture, detail, and even silhouette may vary, but the style itself continues in fashion. A woman's pump may be made of any leather, fabric, or plastic. It may have a blunt or a pointed toe and a high or low heel. It may be made in a single color or a combination of colors. Although it changes superficially to relate to current fashions, it remains a pump—not an oxford, a loafer, or a T-strap. Similarly, a shirtwaist dress, whatever its fabric, color, sleeve length, and skirt fullness, remains a shirtwaist.

FADS. The here-today-and-gone-tomorrow nature of fads qualify them as the shortest-lived of short-run fashions. Fads rise with meteoric speed and decline even more quickly. One need only think of platform shoes, baggy jeans, and feather accessories to recognize a typical short-run fad.

However, sometimes a fad does not behave in the expected way and then the fashion experts are fooled. The fad starts normally, with a limited and highly subjective group accepting it. But then, instead of following the usual pattern of rapid saturation and sudden death, the fad is accepted by the general public and leaves the "fad" category to become a legitimate fashion. In some cases the fad even becomes a classic.

When, in the early 1980s, jogging became the rage with health-conscious men and women, specially designed jogging shoes began to appear and became a major fad in footwear. Gradually, these comfortable shoes were used instead of regular shoes on the cities' hard sidewalks by business women of all ages and social levels. Finally, foot-easing sport shoes turned up in practically every woman's wardrobe and are now worn at all but the most formal occasions.

Consumer Buying and the Fashion Cycle

Every fashion has both a consumer buying cycle and a consumer use cycle. (See page 44) The curve of the consumer buying cycle rises in direct relation to that of the consumer use cycle. But when the fashion reaches its peak, consumer buying tends to decline more rapidly than consumer use. Different segments of society respond to and tire of a fashion at different times. So different groups of consumers continue to wear fashions for varying lengths of time after they have ceased buying them. While each group is using and enjoying a fashion, the producers and merchants serving that group are already abandoning the style and

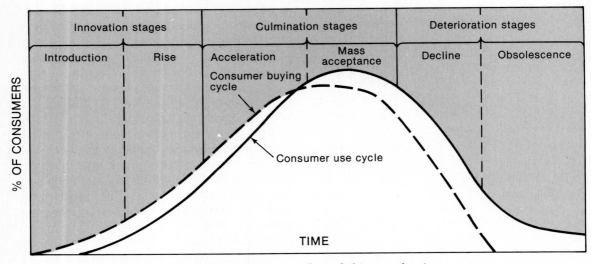

CONSUMER BUYING CYCLE
VERSUS CONSUMER USE CYCLE

Innovation stages		Culmination stages		Deterioration stages	
Introduction	Rise	Acceleration	Mass acceptance	Decline	Obsolescence

Consumer buying cycle

Consumer use cycle

% OF CONSUMERS

TIME

Consumer buying rises in relation to consumer use. After a fashion reaches its peak, buying declines and the two curves grow apart.

marketing something newer. Their efforts in this direction are most profitable when they anticipate, rather than follow, the trend of consumer demand.

Consumer buying is often halted prematurely. This happens because producers and sellers no longer wish to risk making and stocking an item they believe will soon decline in popularity. Instead, they concentrate their resources on new items with better prospects for longevity. This procedure is familiar to anyone who has tried to buy summer clothes in late August or skiwear in March.

FACTORS INFLUENCING FASHION MOVEMENT

At the beginning of this chapter, the movement of fashion was likened to the movement of a river. As Laver said, in comparing the fashion cycle to a force of nature, "Nothing seems to be able to turn it back until it has spent itself, until it has provoked a reaction by its very excess."[2] However, just as a river can swell to turbulent flood stage or be slowed or diverted by a dam, so the movement of fashion can be accelerated or retarded by a variety of diverse factors.

Accelerating Factors

There are seven general factors that speed up fashion cycles. These influences are, themselves, ever growing and accelerating as the pace of life in the last years of the twentieth century becomes more and more rapid and geographically all-encompassing. The accelerating factors are:

1. Increasingly widespread buying power.
2. Increased leisure.
3. More education.
4. Improved status of women.
5. Technological advances.
6. Sales promotion.
7. The changes of the seasons.

INCREASINGLY WIDE-SPREAD BUYING POWER. More widely diffused discretionary income means there are more people with the financial means to respond to a fashion change. The more consumers flock to a new fashion, the sooner it will reach its culmination. The more widespread the financial ability of consumers to turn to yet a newer fashion, the sooner the current fashion will plunge into obsolescence.

INCREASED LEISURE. In the past, long hours of work and little leisure permitted scant attention to fashion. More leisure time usually means more time to buy and enjoy fashion of many kinds. In the last 20 years, sharp decreases in working hours and increases in paid vacations have encouraged more use of at-home wear, casual clothes, sports apparel, travel clothes, and different types of ordinary business dress. Increased purchases of these types of apparel give impetus to their fashion cycles.

One result of today's increased leisure time has been the return to catalog buying. Catalog buying originally evolved because people in agrarian societies lived far from stores and had little leisure time for shopping. Today's leisure time has allowed people to add new physical and mental activities to their lives, such as sports and hobbies, leaving, once again, little time for shopping. Realizing that their customers are using leisure time in other pursuits, retailers are producing catalogs that come into the consumers' homes and can be read at night or during other spare time. Many department stores employ this technique for special events such as anniversary sales, white sales, Mother's Day, Father's Day, Easter, and Christmas.

MORE EDUCATION. The increasingly higher level of education in the United States helps to speed up fashion cycles in two ways. First, more people's horizons have been broadened to include new interests and new wants. And second, more people are equipped by education to earn the money to satisfy those wants. These two factors provide significant impetus to the adoption of new fashions.

IMPROVED STATUS OF WOMEN. In a society with few artificial social barriers, women with discre-tionary income can spend it as they choose. No law or custom prevents any woman from buying the newest and most prestigious styles in dresses, hats, or shoes if she can afford to—thus giving impetus to a fashion cycle in its earliest phases. Sex discrimination in the job market has steadily decreased, and social acceptance of women who manage both homes and jobs has steadily increased. As a result, today's women have more discretionary income and are influencing the speed of fashion cycles in the way they use that income.

TECHNOLOGICAL ADVANCES. Today we live in an "instant" world. The stunning advances in technology in almost every area have put us in immediate possession of facts, fantasies, and fashions. We see news as it happens around the world. Goods are sped to retail stores by land, air, and sea more rapidly than would have been dreamed of just a few decades ago. New fibers, finishes, and materials with improved qualities are constantly being developed, and reduced prices on many fashion goods have resulted. All of these technological advances combine to make goods available almost at the instant that the consumer is psychologically and financially ready to buy. Thus the cycle of fashion becomes more and more accelerated.

SALES PROMOTION. The impact of sales promotion is felt everywhere in the fashion world today. Magazines, television, newspapers, billboards, and direct mail all expose the public to new fashions in a never-ending procession. While there is no way to force consumers to accept new fashions, nor any way to save a fashion if consumers reject it, sales promotion can greatly influence a fashion's success by telling people it exists. Sales promotion can help to speed up acceptance of a new fashion or sometimes extend its peak or duration. The miniskirts of the 1960s, the jeans of the 1970s, and the classic look of the 1980s were looks made familiar to women through sales promotion. Promotion, therefore, can frequently assist a fashion to reach its culmination more speedily.

SEASONAL CHANGE. Nothing is so consistent in bringing change in fashions as the calendar. As the seasons change, so do consumer demands. After the months of winter, people want to shed their heavy, dark clothing for lightweight, colorful spring and summer fashions. In climates where there are radical seasonal changes, this is only natural, even though our homes, schools, cars, and places of business are kept at desired temperatures through central heating and air-conditioning. However, even in areas such as Florida and Hawaii, where the weather is moderate year-round, people change their wardrobes with the seasons. Even if the twenty-first century brings complete climate control, people will never accept the boredom of a year-round wardrobe.

Because people today are so geared to travel at all times of the year to all types of climates, the seasonal changes are accelerated and a kind of pre-season testing can go on. Resort wear appears in retail stores in time for selection by the public for January/February vacations in the tropical areas. The late-June appearance of the first fall fashions in leading stores makes it possible for the style-conscious to make their selections well in advance of the first cold wind. Consumer responses to these early offerings allow manufacturers and retailers alike to know what does and what does not appeal.

Retarding Factors

Factors that retard the development of fashion cycles either discourage people from adopting incoming styles or encourage them to continue using styles that might be considered on the decline. Retarding factors include the opposites of the accelerating factors; for example, decreased buying power during recessionary periods. Major retarding factors are habit and custom, religion and sumptuary laws, the nature of the merchandise, and reductions in consumers' buying power.

HABIT AND CUSTOM. By slowing acceptance of new styles and prolonging the life spans of those already accepted, habit and custom exert a braking effect on fashion movement. Habit slows the adoption of new skirt lengths, silhouettes, necklines, or colors whenever shoppers unconsciously select styles that do not differ perceptibly from those they already own. It is easy for an individual to let habit take over, and some consumers are more susceptible to this tendency than others. Their loyalty to an established style is less a matter of fashion judgment than a natural attraction to the more familiar.

Custom slows progress in the fashion cycle by permitting vestiges of past fashions, status symbols, taboos, or special needs to continue to appear in modern dress. Custom is responsible for such details as buttons on the sleeves of men's suits, vents in men's jackets, and the sharp creases down the front of men's trousers. Custom usually requires a degree of formality in dress for religious services. The trend toward similarity of dress for men and women in this country has permitted women to wear trousers, but custom still discourages men from wearing skirts.

A classic example of the influence of custom is the placement of buttons. They are on the right side for men, originating with the need to have the weapon arm available while dressing and undressing. And they are on the left for women, who tend to hold babies on that side and can more conveniently use the right hand for buttons. The stitching on the backs of gloves is another example; it dates back to a time when sizes were adjusted by lacing at these points.

RELIGION. Historically, religious leaders have championed custom, and their ceremonial apparel has demonstrated their respect for the old ways. In the past, religious leaders

In the 1920s, English women had abandoned national dress, while Italian women wore the more conservative dress that their tradition demanded.

tended to associate fashion with temptation and urged their followers to turn their backs on both. Religion today, however, exerts much less of a restraining influence on fashion. Examples of the new relaxation may be found in the modernization of women's dress in many religious orders and in the fact that women no longer consider a hat obligatory when in church.

In the 1970s and 1980s a countertrend arose to religion's diminishing impact on fashion. It is particularly evident in the dress adopted by the young followers of Hare Krishna and in the adoption of ancient dress by the followers of the revolution in Iran. In both cases, the religious leaders of these movements have decreed that modern fashions lead to temptation and corruption.

SUMPTUARY LAWS. **Sumptuary laws** regulate extravagance and luxury in dress on religious or moral grounds. Height of headdress, length of train, width of sleeve, value and weight of material, and color of dress have all at times been restricted to specific classes by law. Such laws were aimed at keeping each class in its place in a rigidly stratified society.[3]

Other laws, such as those of the Puritans, attempted to enforce a general high-mindedness by condemning frippery. An order passed in 1638 by the General Court of Massachusetts stated:

> *No garment shall be made with short sleeves, and such as have garments already made with short sleeves shall not wear same unless they cover the arm to the wrist; and hereafter no person whatever shall make any garment for women with sleeves more than half an ell wide.*[4]

And in the eighteenth century, a bill was proposed (but rejected) that stated:

> *All women of whatever age, rank, profession, or degree, whether virgin, maid, or widow, that shall impose upon, seduce, and betray into ma-*

trimony any of His Majesty's subjects by scents, paints, cosmetic washes, artificial teeth, false hair, Spanish wool, iron stays, hoops, high-heeled shoes, or bolstered hips, shall incur the penalty of the law now in force against witchcraft and the like demeanours, and that marriage, upon conviction, shall stand null and void.[5]

People have a way of ignoring local ordinances, however, if they conflict with a fashion cycle that is gathering strength. In New York during the 1930s, fines could be imposed if men or women appeared on the streets in tennis shorts, or if the shoulder straps of bathing suits were not in place on public beaches. What was considered indecent exposure then—shorts for streetwear, for example—is commonplace today.

NATURE OF THE MERCHANDISE.

Not all merchandise moves at the same pace through a fashion cycle. Often the very nature of the merchandise is responsible for the rate of movement. Over the years it has been accepted as normal that men's fashion cycles move more slowly than women's. In recent years, however, the changing lifestyles of the male population have resulted in accelerating menswear cycles. Women's apparel generally moves in slower cycles than accessories, though as was pointed out earlier in this chapter, some accessories now have full-run cycles comparable to those of apparel.

REDUCTIONS IN CONSUMERS' BUYING POWER.

Consumers' buying power has a powerful effect on the movement of fashion cycles. When buying power increases, fashion cycles often speed up. Decreased buying power, conversely, can retard the movement of fashion cycles. In 1982, the economic recession and resultant high unemployment sharply reduced American consumers' buying power. Many people made do with clothes they had, buying only necessities.

A similar caution is shown by consumers affected by strikes, inflation, high taxes, or interest rates. All these factors have a slowing influence on fashion cycles. The poorer people are, the less impact they have on fashion's movements. They become bystanders in matters of fashion, and as a result do not keep cycles moving. Laver emphasized the importance of buying power when he said that nothing except poverty can make a style permanent.[6]

RECURRING FASHIONS

In the study of fashion history, we see that styles reoccur, with adaptations that suit the times in which they reappear. Occasionally an entire look is reborn. The elegant, simple look of the late 1940s and early 1950s, for example, was born again for the generation of the 1980s. Nostalgia influenced choices not only in apparel, but also in hairstyles and makeup.

Sometimes a single costume component or a minor detail that had exhausted its welcome stages a comeback, like the "chandelier" earring in the mid-1980s. At other times, a single article of clothing, like the sandals of the ancient Greeks, returns to popularity.

An outstanding example of a recurring men's fashion is the T-shirt. T-shirts originated in France as cotton underwear. They were discovered during World War I by American soldiers who preferred them to their own itchy wool union suits. In the 1940s they reemerged as "tee" shirts for golfing and other active sports. In the sixties they became part of the women's fashion scene as well.

Today the T-shirt has put ego into fashion. T-shirts are bought for both fashion and anti-fashion reasons, and in both cases they announce to all what the wearer stands for. A T-shirt can project nationality (*Je suis Américaine*), affiliation (Boys Town), aspiration (Superman), or rock-star preference (the Rolling Stones). T-shirt wearers can identify themselves outright by names, initials, telephone numbers, or even blown-up photographs of themselves transferred onto the T-shirt.[7]

Research indicates that in the past, similar silhouettes and details of design in women's apparel have recurred with remarkable regularity.

In *Recurring Cycles of Fashion*,[8] Young studied skirt silhouettes and their variations in connection with her interest in theatrical costumes. From data she collected on the period from 1760 to 1937, she concluded that despite widely held opinions to the contrary, there were actually only three basic silhouettes: the bell-shaped, or bouffant; the bustle, or back-fullness; and the straight, or tubular. Her data indicated that these three basic silhouettes always followed each other in the same sequence, each recurring about once every 100 years. Each silhouette with all its variations dominated the fashion scene for a period of approximately 35 years. Having reached an excess in styling, it declined in popularity and yielded to the next silhouette in regular sequence.

The anthropologist A. L. Kroeber studied changes in women's apparel over the period from 1605 to 1936. His conclusions confirm Young's findings that similar silhouettes recur in fashion acceptance approximately once every 100 years. In addition, Kroeber found that similar neck widths recurred every 100 years, and similar skirt lengths every 35 years.[9] In more recent times, this rate of change has altered. There was the short skirt in the 1940s, the long skirt in the 1950s, the super-short skirt in the 1960s, the mid-length skirt in the 1970s; and now we have all skirt lengths in the 1980s.

PLAYING THE APPAREL FASHION GAME

According to Madge Garland, a well-known English fashion authority: "Every woman is born with a built-in hobby: the adornment of her person. The tricks she can play with it, the shapes she can make of it, the different portions she displays at various times, the cover-

The three basic silhouettes—(a) the bell, (b) the bustle, and (c) the straight—always follows each other in sequence recurring once every 100 years.

ings she uses or discards. . ." all add up to fashion.[10]

Many clothing authorities read a clear message into the alternate exposure and covering of various parts of the body—sex. J. C. Flügel cited sexual attraction as the dominant motive for wearing clothes.[11]

Laver explained fashion emphasis in terms of the sexuality of the body. "Fashion really began," he said, "with the discovery in the fifteenth century that clothes could be used as a compromise between exhibitionism and modesty."[12] Laver also suggested that those portions of the body no longer fashionable to expose are "sterilized" and are no longer regarded as sexually attractive. Those that are newly exposed are **erogenous**, or sexually stimulating. He viewed fashion as pursuing the emphasis of ever-shifting erogenous zones, but never quite catching up with them. "If you really catch up," he warned, "you are immediately arrested for indecent exposure. If you almost catch up, you are celebrated as a leader of fashion."[13]

Men's apparel has long played the fashion game, too, but, since the industrial revolution, in a less dramatic manner than women's. Women's fashions have tended to concentrate mainly on different ways to convey sexual appeal. Men's fashions have been designed to emphasize such attributes as strength, power, bravery, and high social rank. When a male style does emphasize sex, it is intended to project an overall impression of virility.

Pieces of the Game

The pieces with which the women's fashion game is played are the various parts of the female body: waist, shoulders, bosom, neckline, hips, derriere, legs and feet, as well as the figure as a whole. Historically, as attention to a part of the anatomy reaches a saturation point, the fashion spotlight shifts to some other portion.

In the Middle Ages, asceticism was fashionable. Women's clothes were designed to play down, rather than emphasize, women's sexuality. The Renaissance was a period of greater sexual freedom. Women's apparel during this period highlighted the breasts and the abdomen, particularly the latter.

By the eighteenth century, however, the abdomen had lost its appeal. Although the bosom continued to be emphasized, a flatter abdomen was fashionable, and heels were raised to facilitate upright carriage. The Empire period,

with its high waistline, also stressed the bosom. But the entire body was emphasized with sheer and scanty dresses—some so sheer they could be pulled through a ring. Some advocates of this fashion even wet their apparel so that it would cling to the figure when worn.

During the nineteenth century, fashion interest shifted to the hips, and skirts billowed. Later, the posterior was accented with bustles and trains.

Early in the twentieth century, emphasis switched from the trunk to the limbs, through short skirts and sleeveless or tight-sleeved dresses. Flügel interpreted accent on the limbs, together with the suggestion of an underdeveloped torso, as an idealization of youth. He foresaw continued emphasis on youth and boyishness as a result of women's participation in varied activities, the steady march of democracy, and increasing sexual freedom.[14]

In the 1960s, fashion interest was focused on short skirts and the legs. As the sixties drew to a close, interest shifted from legs to bosom. By the early 1970s, the natural look of bosoms was in. The unconstructed, natural look was followed by the "no-bra" look. This fashion reached its culmination and began its decline when bosoms were only slightly concealed beneath see-through fabrics or plunging necklines. As this excess led to obsolescence, the 1980s ushered in a reemergence of the 1950s bosom. Manufacturers of bras and inner wear are featuring soft-side bras, strapless bras, and molded sports bras to once again give a firmly supported look to the bosom.

THE FIGURE AS A WHOLE. According to Garland, the fashions of the 1950s and early 1960s showed off the entire figure:

> *The modern girl manages at the same time to bare her shoulders, accentuate her bust, pull in her waist, and show her legs to above the knees. It is a triumph of personal publicity over the taboos of the past and the previous limitations of fashion.*[15]

Fashions change as popular interest shifts to different parts of the female body. In the 1960s the figure as a whole was the focus of this then-daring swimsuit.

Until the late 1960s brought the "youth cult" and its attendant revolt against conventional sexual and political attitudes, previous fashion eras had centered attention only on parts of the body. The "triumph of personal publicity" achieved in the late 1960s and early 1970s broke all records for calling attention to just about every area of the human body. It was, indeed, an allover feast for the eye of the observer.

Rules of the Game

In the game of emphasizing different parts of the female body at different times, as in any game, there are rules.

The first and strongest rule is that fashion emphasis does not flit from one area to another! Rather, a particular area of the body is emphasized until every bit of excitement has been exhausted. At this point, fashion attention turns to another area. For example, as has been noted, when miniskirts of the 1960s could go no higher and still be legal, the fashion emphasis moved on.

The second rule of the fashion game may well be, as Garland suggested, that only certain parts of the body can be exposed at any given time.[16] There are dozens of examples throughout fashion history that back up this theory: floor-length evening gowns with plunging necklines, high necklines with miniskirts, turtlenecks on sleeveless fashions.

A third rule of the fashion game is that, like fashion itself, fashion attention must always go forward. "A fashion can never retreat gradually and in good order," Dwight E. Robinson said, "like a dictator it must always expand its aggressions or collapse. Old fashions never fade away; they die suddenly and arbitrarily."[17]

PREDICTING THE MOVEMENT OF FASHION

Producing and selling fashion merchandise to consumers at a profit are what fashion merchandising is all about. To bring excitement and flair to their segment of merchandising, producers and retailers must have a well-defined plan and must follow the movement of general fashion preferences.

The success of fashion merchandising depends upon the correct prediction of which new styles will be accepted by the majority of consumers. The successful forecaster of fashion must:

1. Distinguish what the current fashions are.
2. Estimate how widespread they are.
3. Determine at what point in time these fashions will appeal to the firm's target customer groups.

With information on these three points, projections—a prime requisite in successful fashion merchandising—become possible.

L. L. Bean
Outdoor Sporting Specialties

Summer 1984

FASHION FOCUS

L. L. BEAN: HOMESPUN COMPANY IN A COMPUTERIZED WORLD

When they hear the words "catalog sales," many people automatically think of Sears, Montgomery Ward, and JC Penney. But for the convenience of catalog shopping combined with the homespun touch of a past generation, there is no company quite like L. L. Bean, Inc.

The company was started in 1912 by Leon Leonwood Bean, an avid fisherman and hunter from the western part of Maine. At the age of 40, L. L. Bean was a partner in a small apparel shop. It seems that on his frequent hunting and fishing trips, L. L. was plagued by cold, clammy toes. In an attempt to solve his foot comfort problem, Bean designed a special hunting shoe that had a rubber sole and a leather upper. He was so pleased with his new hunting shoe that he produced and sold 100 more pairs in a short period of time. Unfortunately, the rubber was too light and it separated from the upper portion of the shoe. Of the 100 pairs sold, he took back 90 and refunded the $3.50 that each person had paid. (The company's liberal return policy remains in effect today.)

Despite this setback, L. L. was not discouraged. He borrowed $400 from his brother and headed for Boston, where he had the U.S Rubber Company craft a heavier, more durable rubber vamp for him. When the shoe was perfected, he set up a small manufacturing operation in the basement of the store and had a one-page circular prepared that proclaimed the virtues of his only mail-order product, his "Maine Hunting Shoe." He mailed the circular to holders of Maine hunting licenses, and orders started rolling in. This was the start of the famed L. L. Bean catalogs (now more than

Identifying Trends

A **fashion trend** is a direction in which fashion is moving. Manufacturers and merchants try to recognize each fashion trend and to determine whether it is moving toward or away from maximum acceptance. They can then decide whether to actively promote the fashion, to wait, or to abandon it.

For example, assume that short jackets have developed as a fashion trend. At the introduction and rise stages, retailers will stock and promote more and more short jackets. When customer response begins to level off, retailers will realize that a saturation point is being reached with this style and will begin introducing longer jackets into their stocks in larger

128 pages) which go out to 8 million customers around the world every season.

As of 1982 the company boasted a growth rate of about 25 percent a year and by 1983 had reached nearly $240 million in sales. L. L. Bean now employs a full-time staff of more than 1,400 and a part-time staff of up to 800 to process the more than 4 million mail orders each year. The U.S. Postal Service has even granted the company its own ZIP code.

In addition to the very successful catalog business, the company still operates its retail store, which stays open 24 hours a day, 7 days a week. It is a tourist attraction as well as a source of quality merchandise in wholesome, outdoor styles. This merchandise includes such items as soft flannel shirts, Mackinaw cruiser jackets, buffalo plaid woodchopper's vests, coats made from the same wool as Hudson Bay blankets, moose hide slippers, and of course, Maine Hunting Shoes. Much of the merchandise is manufactured in Bean's own 72,000-square-foot manufacturing building.

Although none of these items of merchandise are meant to be "fashion" items, many of them are sought after as chic. In fact, *Newsweek* called L. L. Bean's one of the most sought-after fashion labels.

What accounts for the phenomenal success of L. L. Bean, Inc.? The company ships orders quickly through a computerized system that allows them to process and ship within 72 hours. The merchandise is of high quality. In fact, no item of merchandise is sold by Bean unless it has been personally tested by Bean staff members. But speed and quality only partly explain Bean's success. The overriding factor in Bean's success is the fact that the customers are treated like human beings. The company, which is run by L. L. Bean's grandson Leon A. Gorman, stocks free replacement buttons for every item it sells. If a customer returns a product, a replacement or refund is sent with no questions asked. If you lose one shoe, Bean will special order you just one to replace it. If your feet are too big to fit into the shoes in the catalog, Bean will make you a pair to fit.

A Virginia physician summed up the feelings of many customers when she wrote a letter containing the following remarks to "whoever's at the head of the L. L. Bean company": "I feel that I must write you a love letter, because it is a joy just to know that organizations such as yours still exist. You're modern, and you have a computer, but you've kept your heart . . . you act as though you like your customers . . . you're out of this world."[1]

[1] Raymond J. Blair, "Hunting Boots and Chamois Shirts: The Growth of L. L. Bean," *The New York Times*, August 31, 1980, Sec. 3, p. 5.

This Fashion Focus is based on information from the article cited above and from these sources:
L. L. Bean, Inc., Department of Public Affairs, May 5, 1984.
Mary McCabe English, "Quaint, But Savvy," *Advertising Age*, January 18, 1982, p. 5.
Catherine Houck, *The Fashion Encyclopedia*, St. Martin's Press, New York, 1982, pp. 126–127.
Bill Riviere, *The L. L. Bean Guide to the Outdoors*, Random House, New York, 1981, pp. xi–xv (Introduction by Leon A. Gorman).
Laurence Shames, "The Maine Line—How L. L. Bean Sprouted from a Yankee's Ingenuity," *Gentlemen's Quarterly*, November 1981, p. 212.

and larger numbers. If the retailers have correctly predicted the downturn in customer demand for short jackets, they will have fewer on hand when the downturn occurs. And while some customers may continue to wear the short-jacket style, they will not be buying new short jackets, and certainly not at regular prices.

Sources of Data

Modern fashion forecasters bear little resemblance to the mystical prognosticators of old. Their ability to predict the strength and direction of fashion trends among their customers has almost nothing to do with what is often called a "fashion sense." Nor does it depend upon glances into the future via a cloudy crystal ball. Today's successful fashion forecasters depend upon that most valuable commodity—information. Good, solid facts about the willingness of customers to accept certain goods are the basis of successful merchandising decisions.

In today's computerized business world, merchants can keep "instant" records on sales, inventories, new fashion testing, and myriads of other contributing factors that aid the fashion merchandising process. In addition, wise merchants keep their eyes open to see what is being worn by their own customers as well as by the public as a whole. They are so familiar with their customers' lifestyles, economic status, educational level, and social milieu that they can determine at just what point in a fashion's life cycle their customers will be ready to accept or reject it. Merchants turn to every available source for information that will help ensure success. They use their hard-gained sales experience but don't just rely on their own judgment; they rely on the judgment of others too. From the producers of fashion, from resident buying offices, and from special fashion groups such as the predictive services I.M. International, Nigel French, and Here & There, they learn about the buying habits of customers other than their own. Successful merchants look at the large fashion picture to predict more ably just where their local scene fits in.

Interpreting Influential Factors

An old theater saying goes, "It's all in the interpretation." In other words, written or spoken words gain their importance by the way they are presented to the audience. That is where the special talents of the performer come in. The same is true of fashion forecasting. All the data in the world can be collected by merchants, producers, or designers, but this is of little importance without interpretation. That is where the forecasters' knowledge of fashion and fashion principles comes into the picture. From the data they have collected, they are

able to identify certain patterns. Then they consider certain factors that can accelerate or retard a fashion cycle among their target group of customers. Among these factors are current events, the appearance of prophetic styles, sales promotion efforts, and the canons of taste currently in vogue.

CURRENT EVENTS.   The news of what is going on in the country or the world can have a long-term or short-term influence on consumers and affect their response to a fashion. By 1984, for example, the media was reporting at length on the nomination of a woman Vice President for the country. Numerous papers and magazines discussed current events in the corporate business world with articles about the business opportunities for women at mid- and upper-management levels. Success in responsible positions in the business world demanded "dressing for success," and career-minded women responded by adopting the business-oriented suit look. By their very appearance these women indicated their determination to succeed in the still male-dominated world of business.

PROPHETIC STYLES.   Good fashion forecasters keep a sharp watch for what they call **prophetic styles**. These are particularly interesting new styles that are still in the introduction phase of their fashion cycle. Taken up enthusiastically by the socially prominent or by the flamboyant young, these styles may gather momentum very rapidly or they may prove to be nonstarters. Whatever their future course, the degree of acceptance of these very new styles gives forecasters a sense of which directions fashion might go in.

SALES PROMOTION EFFORTS.   In addition to analyzing the records of past sales, fashion forecasters give thought to the kind and amount of promotion that helps stimulate in-

This ad identifies certain patterns in the fashion news from London.

terest in prophetic styles. They also consider the kind and amount of additional sales promotion they can look forward to. For example, a fiber producer's powerful advertising and publicity efforts may have helped turn slight interest in a product into a much stronger interest during a corresponding period last year. The forecaster's problem is to estimate how far the trend might have developed without those promotional activities. The forecaster must also assess how much momentum remains from last year's push to carry the trend forward this year, and how much promotional support can be looked for in the future. The promotional effort that a forecaster's own organization plans to expend is only one part of the story; outside efforts, sometimes industrywide, also must be considered in forecasting fashions.

CANONS OF TASTE. According to Nystrom, fashions that are in accord with currently accepted canons of art, custom, modesty, and utility are most easily accepted.[18] Today's forecasters are careful to take current canons of taste into consideration as they judge the impact of new styles. In the 1960s, when it was "anything goes" in behavior and values for a large segment of the population, the subdued traditional styles had very little place in fashion. In the mid-1980s, while both ends of the taste spectrum can be found in the fashion world, the more conservative styles continue to dominate the fashion scene as a more moderate way of life continues to please more of the people more of the time. The development of good taste by the fashion merchant is a must. It comes from acquired merchandise knowledge as well as careful observation of people who possess good taste.

Importance of Timing

Successful merchants must determine what their particular target group of customers is wearing now and what it is most likely to be wearing a month or three months from now. The data these merchants collect enables them to identify each current fashion, who is wearing it, and what point it has reached in its fashion cycle.

Since merchants know at what point in a fashion's cycle their customers are most likely to be attracted, they can determine whether to stock a current fashion now, a month from now, or three months from now. For instance, in 1979, baggy jeans and trousers were a new style at the beginning of their cycle. Specialty shops that catered to young fashion leaders rushed to get these new pants into stock. Department stores, whose customers are a little more conservative, took note of this new style and began to add baggies to their inventories in small quantities. They waited until statistics and observations showed that the fashion was building and broadening in appeal. When acceptance was proved, the number and variety of baggies on the selling racks increased. Soon baggy styles were available in many textures, colors, and price ranges. Before long, however, demand for a more tailored, conservative pant style began to indicate that the time of the baggy was over, and by 1981, the style was in decline, and found on markdown racks.

REFERENCES

[1] Agnes Brooke Young, *Recurring Cycles of Fashion: 1760–1937*, Harper & Brothers, New York, 1937, reprinted by Cooper Square Publishers, Inc., New York, 1966, p. 30.

[2] James Laver, *Taste and Fashion*, rev. ed., George G. Harrap & Co., Ltd., London, 1946, p. 52.

[3] Pearl Binder, *Muffs and Morals*, George G. Harrap & Co., Ltd., London, 1953, pp. 162–164.

[4] Elisabeth McClellan, *History of American Costume*, Tudor Publishing Company, New York, 1969, p. 82.

[5] John Taylor, *It's a Small, Medium, and Outsize World*, Hugh Evelyn, London, 1966, p. 39.

[6] Laver, p. 201.

[7] Clara Pierre, *Looking Good: The Liberation of Fashion*, Reader's Digest Press, New York, 1976, p. 149.

[8] Young, p. 30.

[9] A. L. Kroeber, "On the Principles of Order in Civilizations as Exemplified by Change in Fashion," *American Anthropologist*, Vol. 21, July–September, 1919, pp. 235–263.

[10] Madge Garland, *The Changing Form of Fashion*, Praeger Publishers, New York, 1971, p. 11.

[11] J. C. Flügel, *The Psychology of Clothes*, International Universities Press, New York, 1966, p. 163.

[12] Laver, p. 200.

[13] Ibid., p. 201.

[14] Flügel, p. 163.

[15] Garland, p. 20.

[16] Ibid., p. 11.

[17] Dwight E. Robinson, "Fashion Theory and Product Design," *Harvard Business Review*, Vol. 36, November–December 1958, p. 128.

[18] Paul H. Nystrom, *Fashion Merchandising*, The Ronald Press, New York, 1932, p. 94.

MERCHANDISING VOCABULARY

Define or briefly explain the following terms:

Adaptations	Long-run fashions
Culmination stage	Obsolescence stage
Decline stage	Plateau
Erogenous	Prophetic styles
Fashion cycle	Rise stage
Fashion trend	Short-run fashions
Line-for-line copies	Sumptuary laws

1. Name and explain the five phases of a fashion's life cycle.
2. How do adaptations differ from line-for-line copies?
3. What are the two ways in which the culmination stage of a fashion can be extended?
4. What can disrupt the normal progress of a fashion cycle? Once disrupted, can the cycle be resumed? Cite examples to illustrate your answer.
5. Differentiate between long-run and short-run fashions and give examples of each.
6. What conclusions did Agnes Brooke Young reach in her study of skirt silhouettes from 1760 to 1937?
7. How does the consumer use cycle differ from the consumer buying cycle? What implications does this have for fashion merchants?
8. List the "pieces" with which the women's fashion game is played, according to Madge Garland.
9. What are the three basic rules that govern the fashion game, according to leading fashion authorities?
10. How does one predict fashion trends? From what resources can a fashion merchant collect data that will help determine fashion trends?

MERCHANDISING DIGEST

1. Discuss the various factors that tend to accelerate the forward movement of fashions through their cycles, giving at least one example of how each factor has an accelerating effect.
2. Discuss the factors that tend to retard the development of fashion cycles by discouraging the adoption of newly introduced styles. Give at least one example of how each factor exerts a braking influence on fashion development.
3. From your study and appraisal of currently popular styles in apparel, do you see any signs that indicate that a new and different silhouette is in the making? If so, what would that silhouette be? Give examples to defend your answer.

4. THE LEADERS OF FASHION

When Prince Charles and Lady Diana Spencer were married in London's St. Paul's Cathedral in 1981, hundreds of millions of people around the world watched the ceremony live on television, thanks to communications satellites. Prospective brides from Miami to Munich to Melbourne got their first look at Princess Di's wedding gown. And not many weeks later, many of these soon-to-be brides were preparing to drift down the aisle at their own weddings dressed in gowns that, to varying degrees, resembled the one created for the royal princess. Thus, they joined thousands of other women who were already imitating Princess Di's distinctive hairdo, her very feminine blouses, and her bare-shouldered evening gowns. This was a dramatic example of just how times have changed in regard to class distinctions and the dress restrictions associated with them throughout history. For in the last decades of the twentieth century, fashion moves at lightning speed and is available almost instantaneously to people of various income levels and widely different lifestyles.

Certainly, several factors are responsible for this changing scene. Probably the "instant" communication of television leads in importance. People "instantly" see what's new and, because more people are better educated than ever before, they understand, accept, and want these new things. Discretionary income also is now larger and more evenly distributed, enabling more people to purchase new things for their fashion appeal rather than just their utility. Constantly improving technology means that fashion goods can be mass-produced and mass-distributed. Finally, in the United States, particularly, the large middle class has more leisure time than ever before to select and enjoy new fashions. Consequently, they soon become bored with what they have and seek out newer styles.

But how do fashions begin? Who starts them, who sponsors them, and what influences consumers to accept them? Answers to these questions are complex and involve designers, manufacturers, retailers, and most of all, consumers.

The myth that every change in fashion is caused by some Paris designer seeking new ways to make money is, of course, not true. It is consumers who bring about changes in fashion. The needs and wants of consumers change. Their ideas about what is appropriate and acceptable change. And their interests in life change. These are all reasons for fashion designers and manufacturers to produce new and different styles for consumers' consideration. The charting, forecasting, and satisfaction of consumer demand are the fashion industry's main concerns.

BIRTH OF A FASHION

The current trends in consumers' ideas and attitudes are noted, analyzed, interpreted, and subsequently presented to consumers in the form of new styles. Designers and manufacturers influence fasl.ion by providing an unending series of new styles, from which consumers choose those that best express their individual lifestyles.

Many precautions are taken to ensure that designers are presenting what customers want. Even so, at least two-thirds of the new designs introduced each season by the fashion industry fail to become fashions. Some designs are introduced too early, before the public is ready to accept them. Other designs fail because they are too extreme for consumer acceptance. Still other designs fail to become fashions because although they are commonly accepted in many places, they meet pockets of resistance in certain areas of the country. What is worn in New York today is not necessarily what consumers in less urban areas of the United States are ready to accept. One has only to think of the hot pants of the early 1970s, the harem pants and peasant looks of the late 1970s, and the punk rock extremes of the early 1980s to find examples of looks that titillated New York and California but left the rest of the country unmoved and uninterested. The days of women and men jumping on each new fashion bandwagon were by the early 1980s a vague memory. Only a trend that reflects a nationwide mood will successfully cross the United States from ocean to ocean and affect the lives and wardrobes of all those in between. This does occur occasionally, and such a trend will be discussed later in this chapter.

THE DESIGNER'S ROLE

In the mid-1980s, one could think of the future as an empty page waiting for the sketches of a host of designers in every walk of life. Designers are everywhere, designing everything—fashions, furnishings, shopping centers, space-station family living quarters, even blood-flow patterns for artificial hearts. The potential open to the designer has never been greater, or more rewarding. The whole world of computers has opened countless new avenues for designs that are vital to projection of life in the twenty-first century. The days when a few designs created all the ideas for the general population are over. Today, the world of design offers ever-expanding opportunities for all those who have the ability to contribute to it.

In creating designs that will not only reflect consumer attitudes and needs but also give expression to artistic ideas, fashion designers are continually influenced and limited by many factors. Of particular importance are practical business considerations. All designs must be produced at a profit and within the firm's predetermined wholesale price range. Consequently, designers must consider the availability and cost of materials, the particular image that the firm wants to maintain, available production techniques, and labor costs. Great designers use their creativity to overcome all these limitations and to produce salable, exciting designs.

Designers must continually study the lifestyles of those consumers for whom their designs are intended. Because designers work far in advance of their designs' final production, they must be able to predict future fashion trends. Designers must be aware of the effects of current events, socioeconomic conditions, and psychological attitudes relating to fashion interest and demand.

Types of Designers

Most American designers who are using their artistic and innovative talents to design fashion-oriented merchandise fall into one of three categories:

1. High-fashion, or "name," designer.
2. Stylist-designer.
3. Freelance artist-designer.

HIGH-FASHION DESIGNER. A high-fashion designer is usually referred to in this country as a "name" designer. Because of the success and originality of their designs, name designers are well known to fashion-conscious customers. High-fashion designers are responsible not only for creating the designs but also for the choice of fabric, texture, and color in which each is to be executed. They may often be involved in development of the production model, as well as plans for the promotion of the firm's line. Some name designers work for fashion houses, as do Karl Lagerfeld for Chanel and Marc Bohan for Dior. Others like Bill Blass

Many "name" designers are so well known to fashion-conscious consumers that manufacturers of products other than apparel often contract with them for the use of their names. The sheets, pillowcases, and comforters shown here are from the Ralph Lauren collection.

and Yves St. Laurent own their own firms or are possibly financed by a "silent partner" outside the firm.

Until recently, designer names were associated only with original, expensive designs in apparel. Today, many designers whose names have come to be associated with what is new and original license their names to manufacturers of accessories, home furnishings, cosmetics, and fragrances.

STYLIST-DESIGNER. A second type of designer—the stylist-designer—uses his or her creative talents to adapt or change the successful designs of others. A stylist-designer must understand fabric and style construction as well as the manufacturing process because designs are usually adapted at lower prices. Stylist-designers usually create designs at the late rise or early culmination stage of the fashion cycle. They are usually not involved in details relating to either the production of the firm's line or the planning of its promotional activities, but must design within the limits of the firm's production capacity and capability.

FREELANCE ARTIST-DESIGNER. The third type of designer—the freelance artist-designer—sells sketches to manufacturers. These sketches may be original designs by the freelancer or adaptations, and may reflect the freelancer's own ideas or the manufacturer's specifications. The freelancer usually works out of a design studio and sells sketches and designs to the general apparel market. With the delivery of a sketch to the manufacturer, a freelancer's job ends.

Insight and Intuition

A designer takes a fashion idea and embodies it in new styles. Even the most creative designers, however, disclaim any power to force acceptance of their styles. Few have said so more effectively than Paul Poiret, one of the twen-

tieth century's great Parisian couturiers. He once told an American audience:

I know you think me a king of fashion . . . It is a reception which cannot but flatter me and of which I cannot complain. All the same, I must undeceive you with regard to the powers of a king of fashion. We are not capricious despots such as wake up one fine day, decide upon a change in habits, abolish a neckline, or puff out a sleeve. We are neither arbiters nor dictators. Rather we are to be thought of as the blindly obedient servants of woman, who for her part is always enamoured of change and a thirst for novelty. It is our role, and our duty, to be on the watch for the moment at which she becomes bored with what she is wearing, that we may suggest at the right instant something else which will meet her taste and needs. It is therefore with a pair of antennae and not a rod of iron that I come before you, and not as a master that I speak, but as a slave . . . who must divine your innermost thoughts.[1]

Insight and intuition always play a large part in a designer's success. Constant experimentation with new ideas is a must. As one fashion reaches the excess that marks its approaching demise, a designer must have new styles ready and waiting for the public.

On occasion a style takes such firm hold of consumers' affections that it continues to be popular for many seasons. Designers then give it apparent freshness each season by using new details or new materials.

For many years the blazer jacket has been widely accepted by both men and women. At many points in fashion history blazers were so widely accepted that they had become almost a uniform. Whenever this happened, designers added variety and a new look through changes in collar treatments, buttons, trims, and new fabrics. By 1983, for example, designers were fashioning blazers in just about every type of fabric: suede, linen, cotton, silk and blends, as well as the ever-popular flannel and velvet.

The blazer still continues to be demanded by the public. So, designers have met the need, in this case with a wide offering of fabrics to suit a multitude of occasions.

Sources of Design Inspiration

Where does the designer get ideas and inspiration for new fashion? The answer, of course, is: everywhere! Through television the designer experiences all the wonders of the entertainment world. In films the designer is exposed to the influences of all the arts and lifestyles throughout the world. Museum exhibits, art shows, world happenings, expositions, the theater, music, dance, and world travel are all sources of design inspiration to fashion designers.

THE 1980s LOOKED TO THE 1950s. In 1983, several factors converged to bring about the fifties rage that swept the country, a phenomenon that had been several years in the making. Leading the causes for the return to the 1950s was the state of the U. S. economy. For the first time since before World War II, many people were out of work. Young couples could not afford a home of their own. High school graduates found that money for college was hard to come by. People who had never hesitated to gratify instantly their material desires with the use of credit cards now found themselves watching their finances. Times were bad economically and the world political scene was even more depressing. So, as always happens in times of unhappiness and fear, people looked back to a time when everything was rosy (or so they thought)—the 1950s. And the entertainment world and the music world were ready.

For some years, television had been educating young people and reminding their parents about what life had been like in the 1950s. While *Happy Days* and *Laverne and Shirley* presented the 1970s version of the fifties, reruns of actual TV shows like *Father Knows Best, Leave It to Beaver*, and *Ozzie and Harriet* were brought back to show the actual styles of the times. A whole new group of people, born in the 1960s, were introduced to sock hops and hula hoops.

Meeting this television-inspired nostalgia for the fifties, the music world had its own special impact on the young. Disco music, which had commanded the scene since *Saturday Night Fever* in 1977, had run its course. Punk rock had limited appeal, but rock 'n' roll had never died. Now, some of the people who had starred in rock in its infancy—Frankie Avalon, Fabian, Del Shannon, the Beach Boys, Dion and the Belmonts—returned to lead the young of the 1980s into the biggest nostalgia trip ever seen. Department stores around the country staged hula hoop contests and sock hops, and brought some stars of the fifties in for personal appearances.

Fashion designers were ready! The looks of the 1950s were brought out and updated for the times and were seized upon by the young people and the not so young. The "little black dress" immortalized by Marilyn Monroe, the legend of the fifties, came back from coast to coast. Shortie gloves, button earrings, blouses and skirts, shorter hairdos, and fashions with form all added to the impact. The looks cut across all income levels, with adapted 1950s silhouettes from famous designers at one end of the scale and poodle skirts and toppers at the other. The only steady ingredient was nostalgia. In the troubled 1980s a highly romanticized picture of the more settled 1950s was a very comforting thing to think about, and, as far as possible through fashions and customs, to attempt to recreate.

THE 1980s LOOKED TO THE 1930s AND 1940s. Meanwhile, at this same time, another trend was under way in America, one that belonged to a more mature customer. Again, movies, television, music, and personalities had combined to give it impetus. The early 1980s saw the return of

In the early 1980s fashion looked back to a more elegant era. *Brideshead Revisited* was dramatized for television and people responded to the apparels of the 1930s luxe.

romance and femininity to the fashion and social scenes. Television programs such as *Brideshead Revisited* and *The Winds of War* evoked the 1930s and 1940s. Motion pictures added their impact with *An Officer and a Gentleman* and *Frances*, each reflecting the fashions, dreams, and customs of the period. Music of the 1930s and 1940s came back upon the American scene after two decades of rock, first led in by disco; then, as disco faded, by the rebirth of the Big Band sound. The emphasis was very definitely on the romantic.

Fashion responded with 1980s adaptations of the looks of the earlier years. Clothes once again had form. Soft fabrics and sweeping silhouettes evoked the mood. People began to dress up again for various functions and some of the niceties of life, such as debuts and proms, which had been subjected to ridicule in the turbulent 1960s and 1970s, were once again embraced by ever-larger groups. Designers reached for ways to provide elegance that was viable in the 1980s. Glittering productions on Broadway replaced the angry underside of life that had commanded the theater for the previous two decades. Hollywood once again

dared to film stories of hope and humor, and *E.T.* became the country's best friend from outer space. Romance novels, long derided as reading matter worthy only of the lowest intellects, were revealed as the nation's secret passion and the source of a huge multimillion-dollar industry. In the music world, the words and meaning of a song once again became important . . . even as the beat went on. The fashion world responded by translating the needs and wants of these romantically inclined customers into fashions and accessories that reflected the mood—and seemed to do it with almost uncanny speed and ease, proving, as ever, that fashion is the most fluid of all the industries.

Thus, it is the public that is the launcher of new trends. The designer reacts to those trends and creates styles that capture the public's ideas. While always alert to the new and exciting, fashion designers never lose sight of the recent past. They know that consumers need to anticipate something new each season. But they also recognize that whatever new style is introduced will have to take its place with what consumers already have in their wardrobes. No one starts with all new clothes each season. Rarely does a revolutionary new style succeed. Instead, it is the evolutionary new style that so often becomes the best-selling fashion.

THE MANUFACTURER'S ROLE

Manufacturers would agree with Robinson that "every market into which the consumer's fashion sense has insinuated itself is, by that very token, subject to [the] common, compelling need for unceasing change in the styling of its goods."[2]

Even in such prosaic items as paper napkins, the need for change has produced rainbows of pastels, brilliant deep shades, and whites with dainty prints. Similarly, in basics such as bedsheets or men's dress shirts, the once traditional white has yielded to a variety of colors, stripes, and prints. There is scarcely an industry serving consumers today in which the manufacturer's success does not depend in part upon an ability to attune styling to fashion interest and demand.

Types of Manufacturers

In general, manufacturers of fashion goods can be divided into three groups. One group is made up of firms that produce innovative, high-fashion apparel. This group is usually identified as the "better market." A second group of firms sometimes produces originals. But it usually turns out adaptations of styles that have survived the introduction stage and are in the rise stage of their fashion life cycle. This group of firms is usually identified as the "moderate-priced market." A third group of manufacturers makes no attempt to offer new or unusual styling. Rather, these firms mass-produce close copies or adaptations of styles that have proved their acceptance in higher-priced markets. This group is usually identified as the "budget market."

Fashion Influence

In the field of women's apparel, manufacturers are committed to producing several new lines a year. A **line** is an assortment of new designs with a designated period for delivery to the retailer. Some of these may be new in every sense of the word and others merely adaptations of currently popular styles. Producers hope that a few of the designs in a given line will prove to be "hot"—so precisely in step with demand that their sales will be profitably large. When such designs are reordered frequently, they are known as **Fords** in the industry.

Occasionally, manufacturers' styles may be too advanced for the fashion tastes of customers. Such producers neither accelerate nor retard fashion: their goods simply do not get wide distribution and have little or no impact upon the public.

For the most part, the fashion industries are made up of manufacturers whose ability to anticipate the public's response to styles is excellent. Those who do badly in this respect, even for a single season, usually reap small sales and large losses. Unless they are unusually well financed, they quickly find themselves out of business. In the fashion industry, the survival of the fittest means the survival of those who give the most able assistance in the birth and growth of fashions that consumers will buy.

THE RETAILER'S ROLE

Retailers are in much the same position as producers. They do not create fashion, but they can encourage or retard its progress by the degree of accuracy with which they anticipate the demands of their customers. They seek out in the market styles that they believe are most likely to win acceptance by these target groups.

Types of Retailers

There are many ways to classify retail firms. However, when firms are evaluated on the basis of their leadership positions, they tend to fall into three main categories.

First there are firms that are considered "fashion leaders." They feature newly introduced styles that have only limited production and distribution. These styles are usually expensive. A second group, called "traditional retailers"—by far the largest in number—features fashions that have captured consumer interest in their introduction stage and are in the late rise or early culmination stage of their life cycles. Since these styles are usually widely produced by this time, they are most often offered at moderate prices. A third group of retailers, often called "mass merchants," features widely accepted fashions that are well into the culmination phase of their life cycles. Since fashions at this stage of development are usually mass-produced, mass merchants can and do offer fashions at moderate to low prices.

Fashion Influence

Occasionally, retailers are so intuitive or creative that they are a step ahead of their suppliers in anticipating the styles their customers will accept. Such retailers accelerate the introduction and progress of new fashions by persuading manufacturers to produce styles that answer a latent demand. Product development is becoming more and more important for major retailers.

Normally, however, retailers simply select from what is offered by producers in the market. To do a good job, retailers must carefully shop the markets, selecting styles they feel sure will be of special interest to their customers. They must have the styles in their stores when customers are ready to buy. Retailers can hold back good incoming fashions by failing to stock styles that consumers would buy if given the opportunity. Conversely, retailers can make the mistake of exposing new styles prematurely— that is, before their customers are ready to accept them. No amount of retail effort can make customers buy styles in which they have lost

interest or in which they have not yet developed interest. Stocking such merchandise simply means lost sales and probable markdowns.

The more accurately a retailer understands his or her customers' fashion preferences, and reflects this understanding in the assortments purchased, stocked, shown, and promoted, the more successful the operation will be. And the more successful the operation, the more important the retailer's fashion role will be.

THEORIES OF FASHION ADOPTION

Fashions are accepted by a few before they are accepted by the majority. An important step in fashion forecasting is isolating and identifying those fashion leaders and keeping track of their preferences. Once these are known, the fashion forecaster is better able to forecast which styles are most likely to succeed as fashions, and how widely and by whom each will be accepted.

Three theories have been advanced to explain the "social contagion" or spread of fashion adoption: the downward-flow theory, the horizontal-flow theory or "mass-market" theory, and the upward-flow theory. Each attempts to explain the course a fashion travels or is likely to travel, and each has its own claim to validity in reference to particular fashions or social environments.

Downward-Flow Theory

The oldest theory of fashion adoption is the **downward-flow theory** (or the "trickle-

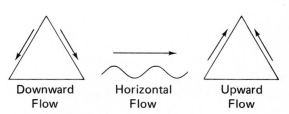

| Downward Flow | Horizontal Flow | Upward Flow |

The three theories of fashion flow.

DIANA, PRINCESS OF WALES: ROYAL FASHION QUEEN

Diana Frances Spencer was born on July 1, 1961, the third daughter of Viscount and Viscountess Althorp. Despite the fact that her family had held numerous royal appointments since the eighteenth century, Diana Spencer led a private and comfortable childhood. She was educated in nonacademic boarding schools, attended two English prep schools, and for one term studied at a Swiss finishing school.

In 1979 or early 1980, she might have been described as a sweet, shy, reasonably pretty young woman. She could be seen wearing a nondescript pullover, a boy's shirt, and a slightly unkempt medium-brown hairdo as she taught nursery school at the Young England Kindergarten in Pimlico, enjoyed a shopping spree, or even dropped by a pub if she felt like it.

Then, in the summer of 1980, Prince Charles began to show a great deal of interest in Lady Diana. By the time the Prince announced his engagement to her on February 24, 1981, Lady Diana Spencer's life had changed dramatically. Suddenly people from all over the world were watching her every move. She began to diet strenuously, streaked her hair, accumulated a spectacular wardrobe, changed her makeup colors, and,

down theory"). It maintains that in order to be identified as a true fashion, a style must first be adopted by people at the top of the social pyramid. The style then gradually wins acceptance at progressively lower social levels.

This theory assumes the existence of a social hierarchy in which lower-income people seek identification with more affluent people. At the same time, those at the top seek disassociation from those they consider socially inferior. The theory suggests that (1) fashions are accepted by lower classes only if, and after, they are accepted by upper classes, and (2) upper classes will reject a fashion once it has flowed to a lower social level.

Early economists, such as Roe in 1834 and Foley and Veblen at the turn of the twentieth century, were among the first to observe this type of social behavior and its effect upon fashion. In 1903, French sociologist Gabriel Tarde described the spread of fashion in terms of a social water tower from which a continuous fall of imitation could descend.[3] The German sociologist Georg Simmel, one of the first of his discipline to undertake a serious study of fashion, wrote in 1904:

Social forms, apparel, aesthetic judgment, the whole style of human expression, are constantly being transformed by fashion in [a way that] . . . affects only the upper classes. Just as soon as the lower classes begin to copy their styles, thereby crossing the line of demarcation the upper classes have drawn and destroying

with great style, became a fashion sensation as the wife of the future King of England. Their wedding took place on July 29, 1981, and was a worldwide media event.

Although royal etiquette dictates that her name is actually Diana, Princess of Wales, she is popularly known as Princess Di, and her fashion influence is the strongest since that of Jacqueline Kennedy Onassis. "She has made a little revolution," said Edith Locke, an editor who has followed fashion professionally since the 1950s. "Because of her youth, her looks, her attitude, she's charmed the world."[1]

From the moment she came to the attention of the public, women of all ages have sought clothes that have been popularized by Princess Di—pale stockings, small-heeled shoes, big white collars, stylish hats, and ruffles. And Princess Di haircuts can be seen throughout the world.

On her 1982 tour of Australia, Princess Di was such a sensation that twice as many people turned out to see her as had come to see Queen Elizabeth the year before. The crowd was so dense that older women were fainting as they lined up to see the new fashion sensation.

During her two recent pregnancies, the designs created for her maternity wardrobe were eagerly anticipated. And, as with her other fashion leads,

mothers-to-be throughout the world sought styles similar to those worn by Princess Di.

Naturally there are many women who choose not to emulate Princess Di, and some will even criticize those who do. But no matter which side one takes in the debate over the wisdom of copying the look of Diana, Princess of Wales, few people claim to turn the page when her picture appears on it. This type of charisma is appropriate for a young "fairy tale princess" who has become a fashion phenomenon.

[1] E. C. Anthony, "The Lady's Got Style!" *McCall's,* August 1983, p. 84.

This Fashion Focus is based on information from the article cited above and from these sources:
Michael Demarest, " 'Shy Di' Makes a Darling Debut," *Time,* March 23, 1981, p. 81.
"Lady Diana Spencer," *British Vogue,* May 1981.
"Queen Elizabeth and Diana—A Comparison of the Two Women in Prince Charles' Life," *Good Housekeeping,* February 1982, p. 122.
"Reveling in the Lap of Luxury," *People,* March 21, 1983, p. 64.
"The Joys and Problems of Being Married to Prince Charles," *Good Housekeeping,* February 1982, p. 121.
"The Princess of Wales," *Vogue,* August 1981, p. 470.

---

their coherence, the upper classes turn away from this style and adopt a new one. . . . The same process is at work as between the different sets within the upper classes, although it is not always visible here.[4]

The downward-flow theory has had among its twentieth-century proponents such authorities as Robinson, Laver, Sapir, and Flügel. Flügel, in fact, suggested that sumptuary laws originated with the reluctance of upper classes to abandon the sartorial distinctiveness that to them represented superiority.[5]

IMPLICATIONS FOR MERCHANDISING.

To some extent, this theory has validity. Some fashions may

appear first among the socially prominent. Eager manufacturers then quickly mass-produce lower-priced copies that many consumers can afford, and the wealthier consumers seek newer styles.

Because our social structure has radically changed, this theory has few adherents today. The downward-flow theory of fashion dissemination can apply only when a society resembles a pyramid, with people of wealth and position at the apex and followers at successively lower levels. Our social structure today, however, is more like a group of rolling hills than it is a pyramid. There are many social groups and many directions in which fashion can and does travel.

This altered pattern of fashion acceptance is

also a result of the speed with which fashion news now travels. All social groups know about fashion innovation at practically the same time. Moreover, accelerated mass production and mass distribution of fashion goods have broadened acceptance of styles. They are available at lower prices and more quickly than ever before.

INDUSTRY PRACTICE. For the reasons given above, those who mass-produce fashion goods today are less likely to wait cautiously for approval of newly introduced styles by affluent consumers. As soon as significant signs of an interesting new style appear, the producers are ready to offer adaptations or even copies to the public.

Horizontal-Flow Theory

A newer theory is the **horizontal-flow theory** (or mass-market theory) of fashion adoption. This theory claims that fashions move horizontally between groups on similar social levels rather than vertically from one level to another.

One of the chief exponents of this theory was Dr. Charles W. King. He proposed that the modern social environment, including rapid, mass communications and the promotional efforts of manufacturers and retailers, exposes new styles to the fashion leaders of all social groups at approximately the same time. King noted that there is almost no lag between the adoption of a fashion by one social group and another.[6] Paris fashions, for example, are now bought and copied for mass distribution sometimes even before the originals are available to the more affluent markets. Trade buyers at couturier openings purchase models, ship them home by air, and get copies into retail stores often before the custom client—whose garments are made to order by the same couturiers—has had a chance to wear the new clothes.

This horizontal flow also has been observed by some modern supporters of the older downward-flow theory. Robinson, for example, said that any given group or cluster of groups takes its cues from contiguous groups within the same social stratum. He claimed fashions therefore radiate from a center of each stratum or class.[7]

IMPLICATIONS FOR MERCHANDISING. The theory of horizontal fashion movement has great significance for merchandising. It points out the fallacy of assuming that there is a single, homogeneous fashion public in this country. In reality, a number of distinctly different groups make up the fashion public. Each group has its own characteristics and its own fashion ideas and needs. The horizontal-flow theory recognizes that what wealthy society people are wearing today is not necessarily what suburbanites, college students, or office workers will either wear tomorrow or wait until tomorrow to accept. This theory acknowledges that there are separate markets in fashion goods as in any other type of merchandise.

Retailers who apply the horizontal-flow theory will watch their own customers closely rather than be guided solely by what more exclusive stores are selling. They will seek to identify the groups into which customers can be divided in terms of income, age, education, and lifestyle. Among their customers, they will look for the innovators and their style choices as well as the influentials and their selections. King defined a **fashion innovator** as a person who is quicker than his or her associates to try out a new style. A **fashion influential** is a person whose advice is sought by associates. A fashion influential's adoption of a new style gives it prestige among a group. The two roles may or may not be played by the same individual within a specific group.

The news that socially prominent women are wearing plunging necklines in exclusive New York restaurants will have less significance for the retailers in a small Midwestern city than the observation that the leader of the country-club set in their community is abandoning bright colors for black on formal occasions. If the latter is a fashion influential in the community, she is a more important bellwether for them than the New York socialites.

INDUSTRY PRACTICE.   King drew a distinction between the spread of fashion within the industry itself and its adoption by consumers. A vertical flow definitely operates within the industry, he conceded: "Exclusive and famous designers are watched closely and emulated by lesser designers. Major manufacturers are studied and copied by smaller and less expert competitors."[8] And, as any reader of *Women's Wear Daily* knows, the hottest news in the industry concerns what the top designers and the top producers are showing.

King pointed out, moreover, that the innovation process in the industry represents a "great filtering system." From an almost infinite number of possibilities, manufacturers select a finite number of styles. From these, trade buyers select a smaller sampling. Finally, consumers choose from among retailers' selections, thereby endorsing certain ones as accepted fashions.

This process, King maintained, is quite different from the consumer reaction outlined by Simmel and other proponents of the downward-flow theory. The difference lies in the fact that today the mass market does not await the approval of the "class" market before it adopts a fashion.

Upward-Flow Theory

The third theory that attempts to explain the process of fashion adoption is relatively new. It reflects the enormous social changes that have occurred in the past decade or two and that continue to occur. Because the process of fashion dissemination that evolved in the 1960s and 1970s was exactly opposite of that which prevailed throughout much of recorded history, this theory has important implications for producers and retailers alike.

This theory of fashion adoption is called the **upward-flow theory**. It holds that the young—particularly those of low-income families and those in higher-income groups who adopt low-income lifestyles—are quicker than any social group to create or adopt new and different fashions. As its name implies, this theory is exactly the opposite of the downward-flow theory. The upward-flow theory holds that fashion adoption begins among the young members of lower-income groups and then moves upward into higher-income groups.

Between the late 1960s and early 1980s, a series of examples of the upward-flow theory was evident. Young people discovered Army-Navy surplus stores and were soon wearing khaki pants, caps, battle jackets, fatigues, and even ammunition belts. Led by the Hell's Angels, the motorcycle clubs introduced the fashion world to black leather—in jackets, vests, and studded armbands. The jet set soon favored black leather in long coats, skirts, and pants. Meanwhile, other young people were discovering bib overalls, railroad worker's caps, and all-purpose laborer's coveralls that were soon translated into jumpsuits.

Peasant apparel, prairie looks, and styles and designs from various minority groups have followed the same pattern. They begin as part of a young and lower-income lifestyle and are then quickly adopted among older people with different lifestyles and incomes. Perhaps nothing so dramatically illustrates this as the T-shirt. In its short-sleeved version, it has long been worn by truckers, laborers, and farm workers. In its long-sleeved version, it was the uniform of local bowling and softball teams. In the late 1970s, the T-shirt became a message board and sprouted a brand-new fashion cottage industry. T-shirts told the world a person's political views, spelled out the wearer's favorite rock group or ecological opinion, and were

The popularity of workers' overalls and caps dramatically illustrates the upward flow of fashion.

mass-produced by the tens of millions in sizes for everyone from the just-born to great-grandparents. Thus, the humble T-shirt moved with amazing upward flow into wardrobes from one end of the country to the other.

IMPLICATIONS FOR MERCHANDISING.
For producers and retailers, this new direction of fashion flow implies radical changes in traditional methods of charting and forecasting fashion trends. No longer can producers and retailers look solely to name designers and socially prominent fashion leaders for ideas that will become tomorrow's best-selling fashions. They also must pay considerable attention to what young people favor, for the young have now become a large, independent group that can exert considerable influence on fashion styling.

As a result, today fewer retailers and manufacturers attend European couture showings, once considered fashion's most important source of design inspiration. Now producers and retailers alike are more interested in ready-to-wear (prêt-à-porter) showings. Here they look for styles and design details that reflect trends with more fashion relevance for the youth of the United States.

INDUSTRY PRACTICE.
Apparently, fashion will never again flow in only one direction. Of course, customers will always exist for high fashion and for conservative fashion. But producers and retailers must now accept that they will be doing a considerable proportion of their business in fashions created or adopted first by the lower-income young and by those who choose to be allied with them.

FASHION LEADERS AND FOLLOWERS

As different as they may be, the three theories of fashion flow share one common perspective: they recognize that there are both fashion leaders and fashion followers. People of social, political, and economic importance here and abroad are seen as leaders in the downward-flow theory. The horizontal-flow theory recognizes individuals whose personal prestige makes them leaders within their own circles, whether or not they are known elsewhere. Finally, the important fashion role played by young, lower-income groups in the last half of the twentieth century is recognized in the upward-flow theory.

Fashion Leaders

The theories of fashion adoption stress that the fashion leader is not the creator of the fashion; nor does merely wearing the fashion make a person a fashion leader. As Bell explained: "The leader of fashion does not come into existence until the fashion is itself created . . . a king or person of great eminence may indeed lead the fashion, but he leads only in the general direction which it has already adopted."[9]

If a fashion parade is forming, fashion leaders may head it and even quicken its pace. They cannot, however, bring about a procession; nor can they reverse a procession.

INNOVATORS AND INFLUENTIALS. Famous people are not necessarily fashion leaders, even if they do influence an individual style. Their influence usually is limited to only one striking style, one physical attribute, or one time. The true fashion leader is a person constantly seeking distinction and therefore likely to launch a succession of fashions rather than just one. People like Beau Brummel, who made a career of dressing fashionably, or the Duchess of Windsor, whose wardrobe was front-page fashion news for decades, influence fashion on a much broader scale.

What makes a person a fashion leader? Flügel explained: "Inasmuch as we are aristocratically minded and dare to assert our own individuality by being different, we are leaders of fashion."[10] King, however, made it clear that more than just daring to be different is required. In his analysis, a person eager for the new is merely an innovator or early buyer. To be a leader, one must be influential and sought after for advice within one's coterie. An influential person, said King, sets the appropriate dress for a specific occasion in a particular circle. Within that circle, an innovator presents current offerings and is the earliest visual communicator of a new style.[11]

SOCIAL LEADERS. In today's world, "society" has replaced royalty in the role of fashion leader. Whether the members of "society" derive their position from vast fortunes and old family names or from new fame and recent wealth, they bring to the scene a glamour and excitement that draws attention to everything they do. Their pictures appear in newspapers and magazines; they appear on television, radiating success. The average person seeks to imitate these people in the only way available—by imitating their fashions.

In the past, fashion leadership was the province of royalty. New fashions were introduced in royal courts by such leaders as Empress Eugénie and Marie Antoinette. Until the advent of Princess Diana as a member of English royalty to be imitated in fashions and styles, few royal personages in recent years have qualified as fashion leaders. Despite the belief held by some that kings and queens and their royal relatives walk around wearing crowns and ermine, the truth is that modern royalty is a hard-working group whose day-to-day life is packed with so many activities that only a sensible and conservative mode of dress will do for most occasions.

As monarchies were replaced by democracies, members of the wealthy and international sets came into the fashion spotlight. Later, the families of political figures and industrialists made the best-dressed lists. Today, through the constant eye of television and the newspapers, the average person is able to find fashion leadership in a whole new stratum of society—the jet set. This unstructured group cuts across old, established social lines. It is not unusual, for example, to find a countess skiing with a rock star, an oil executive, or a news commentator.

What these socialites are doing and what they are wearing are instantly served up to the general public by the media. As far as fashion is concerned, these people are not just *in* the news; they *are* the news. Any move they make is important enough to be immediately publicized. What they wear is of vital interest to the general public. The media tell us what the social leaders wear to dine in a chic restaurant, to attend a charity ball, or to go shopping. Because they are trendsetters, their choices are of prime interest to designers and to the world at large.

This inundation of news about what social leaders wear of course influences the public. The average person is affected because so many manufacturers and retailers of fashion take their cue from these social leaders. Right or wrong, fashion merchants count on the fashion sense of these leaders. They know that the overwhelming exposure of these leaders in the media encourages people of ordinary means to imitate them—consciously or unconsciously.

PEOPLE IN THE NEWS. Fashion today takes its impetus and influence from people in every possible walk of life. These people have one thing in common, however: they are newsworthy. Because of some special talent, charisma, notoriety, or popularity, they are constantly mentioned and shown in fashion magazines and on the front pages of newspapers. They may or may not appear in the society pages.

In this group can be found presidents and princesses, movie stars and religious leaders, sports figures and recording stars, politicians and TV personalities. Because they are seen so frequently, the public has a good sense of their fashions and lifestyles and can imitate them to the extent of the public's means and desires.

Prominent individuals have been responsible for certain fashions that continue to be associated with them. Many times, however, these individuals are not what would be considered fashion leaders. In the nineteenth century, the semifitted, velveteen-collared coat style adopted by the earl of Chesterfield became known simply as a Chesterfield. It continues as such today. The short jacket adopted by General Dwight D. Eisenhower during World War II is still identified as the Eisenhower jacket. And although the cornrow braiding of hair had been practiced among blacks in Africa and America for decades, it only was adopted by many young black women after Cicely Tyson appeared with the hairstyle in the movie *Sounder* in 1972. In 1979, Bo Derek wore it in the film *10* and gave the style new impetus. Moreover, when Geraldine Ferraro was nominated as a candidate for Vice-President in 1984, her short, distinctive hairstyle became known as the "Gerry cut," and was adopted by women of all ages. When Nancy Reagan visited the royal family

in England to attend the wedding of Prince Charles and Princess Diana, she was photographed wearing plastic earrings instead of more formal precious jewel earrings. Overnight, "Reagan plastics" were seen in American stores and, more important, on the ears of the fashion-conscious all over the country.

Even if particular fashions or hairstyles associated with people in the news do not bear their names, the influence of famous people may be just as strong. In the 1930s, a tremendous impact was felt by an entire menswear industry when Clark Gable appeared without an undershirt in *It Happened One Night.* Practically overnight, men from all walks of life shed their undershirts in imitation of Gable. In the late 1930s, women dared to wear slacks after seeing Greta Garbo and Marlene Dietrich wearing them in the movies. In the early 1960s, when the then Mrs. John F. Kennedy appeared in little pillbox hats, both the style and the hat market blossomed under the publicity.

SPORTS PROFESSIONALS. Today there is strong emphasis on sports. And what prominent sports figures wear is of great importance to the people who seek to imitate them. Television has increased the public acceptance of several sports. For example, people have enjoyed going to baseball, football, or basketball games for years. But sports of a more individual nature, such as tennis and golf, were of minor interest. Now these sports are brought into the living rooms of an increasing number of viewers. As a result, fashions for participating in these sports have grown remarkably in importance. Tennis is now a very popular participation sport and has given rise to an entire specialized fashion industry. It is difficult to remember that a mere 30 years ago white was the only color seen on a tennis court and that women wore knee-length tennis skirts. When Gussie Moran, a professional woman tennis player, first appeared on the courts in 1949 with lace-trimmed panties under her shortened skirt, the furor shook the tennis world and reverberated throughout the sports world. Today, every aspiring tennis player has endless fashion styles, colors, and fabrics to choose from. A wide selection of fashions is also available for golf, jogging, running, swimming, skating, biking, snorkeling, and other sports.

Some fashions that appear in the media are embraced with unanimity by the public. They are quickly produced at every price and in every possible fabric and design and are seen everywhere. They may even become classics. Others are hailed by only a portion of the public. While their immediate impact may be great, they are soon gone from the fashion scene.

Fashion Followers

Filling out forms for his daughter's college entrance application, a father wrote of his daughter's leadership qualities: "To tell the truth, my daughter is really not a leader, but rather a loyal and devoted follower." The dean of the college admissions responded: "We are welcoming a freshman class of 100 students this year and are delighted to accept your daughter. You can't imagine how happy we are to have one follower among the 99 leaders!"

Most people want to be thought of as leaders, not followers. But there are many people who are followers, and good ones. In fact, followers are in the majority within any group. Without followers the fashion industry would certainly collapse. Mass production and mass distribution can be possible and profitable only when large numbers of consumers accept the merchandise. Though they may say otherwise, luckily, more people prefer to follow than to lead. The styles fashion leaders adopt may help manufacturers and retailers in determining what will be demanded by the majority of consumers in the near future. Only accurate predictions can ensure the continued success of the giant ready-to-wear business in this country, which depends for its success on mass production and distribution. While fashion leaders may stimulate and excite the fashion industry, the fashion followers are the industry's lifeblood.

REASONS FOR FOLLOWING FASHION.

Theories about why people follow rather than lead in fashion are plentiful. Among the explanations are feelings of inferiority, admiration of others, lack of interest, and ambivalence about the new.

Feelings of Insecurity. Flügel wrote, "Inasmuch as we feel our own inferiority and the need for conformity to the standards set by others, we are followers of fashion."[12] For example, high school boys and girls are at a notably insecure stage of life. They are therefore more susceptible than any other age group to the appeal of fads. A person about to face a difficult interview or attend the first meeting with a new group carefully selects new clothes. Often a feeling of inadequacy can be hidden by wearing a style that others have already approved as appropriate and acceptable.

Admiration. Flügel also maintained that it is a fundamental human impulse to imitate those who are admired or envied. A natural and symbolic means of doing this is to copy their clothes, makeup, and hairstyles. Outstanding illustrations of this theory have been provided by movie stars and models—Mary Pickford, "America's Sweetheart" of the 1910s; Clara Bow, the "It" girl of the 1920s; Veronica Lake and Ann Sheridan, the "Oomph Girls" of the 1940s; Doris Day and Marilyn Monroe in the 1950s; Twiggy in the 1960s; Farrah Fawcett in the 1970s; and Christie Brinkley in the 1980s. Their clothes and hairstyles were copied instantly among many different groups throughout this country and in many other parts of the world. On a different level, the young girl who copies the hairstyle of her best friend, older sister, or favorite aunt demonstrates the same principle, as do college students who model their appearance after that of a campus leader.

a. Mary Pickford

b. Marilyn Monroe

c. Twiggy

d. Christie Brinkley

Their clothes and hairstyles were copied instantly around the world.

Lack of Interest. Sapir suggested that many people are insensitive to fashion and follow it only because "they realize that not to fall in with it would be to declare themselves members of a past generation, or dull people who cannot keep up with their neighbors."[13] Their response to fashion, he said, is a sullen surrender, by no means an eager following of the Pied Piper.

Ambivalence. Another theory holds that many people are ambivalent in their attitudes toward the new; they both want it and fear it. For most, it is easier to choose what is already familiar. Such individuals need time and exposure to new styles before they can accept them.

VARYING RATES OF RESPONSE. Individuals vary in the speed with which they respond to a new idea, especially when fashion change is radical and dramatic. Some fashion followers apparently need time to adjust to new ideas. Merchants exploit this point when they buy a few "window pieces" of styles too advanced for their own clientele and expose them in windows and fashion shows to allow customers time to get used to them. Only after a period of exposure to the new styles do the fashion followers accept them.

FASHION AS AN EXPRESSION OF INDIVIDUALITY

As the twentieth century entered its eighth decade, a strange but understandable trend became apparent across the nation. People were striving, through their mode of dress, to declare individuality in the face of computer-age conformity.

People had watched strings of impersonal numbers become more and more a part of their lives—ZIP codes, bank and credit card account numbers, employee identification numbers, department store accounts, automobile registrations, social security numbers, and so on. An aversion to joining the masses—to becoming "just another number"—began to be felt. So while most people continued to go along with general fashion trends, some asserted their individuality. This was accomplished by distinctive touches each wearer added to an outfit. A new freedom in dress, color and texture combinations, use of accessories, and hairstyles allowed people to assert their individuality without being out of step with the times. Most social scientists see in this a paradox—an endless conflict between the desire to conform and the desire to remain apart.

We have all known people who at some point in their lives found a fashion that particularly pleased them. It might have been a certain style dress, a certain shoe, or a hairstyle. Even in the face of continuing changes in fashion, the person continued to wear that style in which she or he felt right and attractive. This is an assertion of individuality in the face of conformity. Although superbly fashion-conscious, the late famous actress Joan Crawford never stopped wearing the open-toed, sling-back, wedge shoe of the 1940s. When the pointed toe and stiletto heel of the fifties gave way to the low, chunky heel of the sixties, she continued to wear the same style. She was perfectly in step with fashion when the wedge shoe finally returned to popularity in the early 1970s. Woody Allen achieved special recognition for wearing—anywhere and everywhere—sneakers! At formal occasions he conforms by wearing appropriate formal attire. But his feet remain sneakered, and Woody retains his individuality.

Most people prefer to assert their individuality in a less obvious way, and today's ready-to-wear fashions lend themselves to subtle changes that mark each person's uniqueness. No two people put the same costume together in exactly the same way.

Fashion editor Jessica Daves summed up the miracle of modern ready-to-wear fashion. It offers, she said, "the possibility for some women to create a design for themselves . . . to choose the color and shape in clothes that will present them as they would like to see them-selves."[14]

The Paradox of Conformity and Individuality

For decades, experts have tried to explain why people seek both conformity and individuality in fashion. Simmel suggested that two opposing social tendencies are at war: the need for union and the need for isolation. The individual, he reasoned, derives satisfaction from knowing that the way in which he or she expresses a fashion represents something special. At the same time, people gain support from seeing others favor the same style.[15]

Flügel interpreted the paradox in terms of a person's feelings of superiority and inferiority. The individual wants to be like others "insofar as he regards them as superior, but unlike them, in the sense of being more 'fashionable,' insofar as he thinks they are below him."[16]

Sapir tied the conflict to a revolt against custom and a desire to break away from slavish acceptance of fashion. Slight changes from the established form of dress and behavior "seem for the moment to give victory to the individual, while the fact that one's fellows revolt in the same direction gives one a feeling of adventurous safety."[17] He also tied the assertion of individuality to the need to affirm one's self in a powerful society in which the individual has ceased to be the measure.

One example of this conflict may be found in the off-duty dress of people required to wear uniforms of one kind or another during working hours, such as nurses, police officers, and mail carriers. A second example is seen in the clothing worn by many present-day business executives. Far from the days when to be "The Man in the Gray Flannel Suit" meant that a man had arrived in the business world, today executives favor a much more diversified wardrobe. While suits of gray flannel are still worn, so are a wide variety of other fabrics and patterns. And some top executives favor a more relaxed look altogether, preferring to wear appropriately fashioned separate jackets or blazers with their business slacks.

Retailers know that although some people like to lead and some like to follow in fashion, most people buy fashion to express their personality or to identify with a particular group. To belong, they follow fashion; to express their personality, they find ways to individualize it.

Fashion and Self-Expression

Increasing importance is being placed on fashion individuality—on expressing your personality, or refusing to be cast in a mold. Instead of slavishly adopting any one look, today's young person seeks to create an individual effect through the way he or she combines various fashion components. For instance, if a young woman thinks a denim skirt, an ankle-length woolen coat, and a heavy turtlenecked sweater represent her personality, they will be considered acceptable by others in her group.

Forward-looking designers recognize this desire for self-expression. Designers say that basic wardrobe components should be made available, but that consumers should be encouraged to combine them as they see fit. For instance, they advise women to wear pants or skirts, long or short, according to how they feel, not according to what past tradition has considered proper for an occasion. They suggest that men make the same choice among tailored suits, leisurewear, and slacks, to find the styles that express their personalities.

Having experienced such fashion freedom, young people may never conform again. Yet despite individual differences in their dress, young experimenters have in common a deep-rooted desire to dress differently from the older generations with whom they live and associate.

Most people—particularly those who lack the time, funds, and flair for combining different components into a strictly personal look—

still tend to accept a fashion or effect as a whole. A touch of novelty in accessories, color, line, or texture within the framework of prevailing fashion is enough to create the feeling of individuality that the average consumer craves.

REFERENCES

[1] Quentin Bell, *On Human Finery*, The Hogarth Press, Ltd., London, 1947, pp. 48–49.

[2] Dwight E. Robinson, "Fashion Theory and Product Design," *Harvard Business Review*, Vol. 36, p. 129, November–December 1958.

[3] Gabriel Tarde, *The Laws of Imitation*, Henry Holt and Company, New York, 1903, p. 221.

[4] Georg Simmel, "Fashion," *American Journal of Sociology*, Vol. 62, p. 545, May 1957.

[5] J. C. Flügel, *The Psychology of Clothes*, International Universities Press, New York, 1966, p. 139.

[6] Charles W. King, "Fashion Adoption: A Rebuttal to the Trickle-Down Theory," *Proceedings of the Winter Conference*, American Marketing Association, New York, December 1963, pp. 114–115.

[7] Dwight E. Robinson, "The Economics of Fashion Demand," *The Quarterly Journal of Economics*, Vol. 75, p. 383, August 1961.

[8] King, pp. 114–115.

[9] Bell, p. 46.

[10] Flügel, p. 140.

[11] King, p. 124.

[12] Flügel, p. 140.

[13] Edward Sapir, "Fashion," *Encyclopedia of the Social Sciences*, Vol. VI, 1931, p. 140.

[14] Jessica Daves, *Ready-Made Miracle*, G. P. Putnam's Sons, New York, 1967, pp. 231–232.

[15] Simmel, pp. 543–544.

[16] Flügel, p. 140.

[17] Sapir, p. 140.

MERCHANDISING VOCABULARY

Define or briefly explain the following terms:

Downward-flow theory
Fashion influential
Fashion innovator
Fords

Horizontal-flow theory
Line
Upward-flow theory

MERCHANDISING REVIEW

1. What practical obstacles act as limitations to fashion designers? What other factors must be considered in preparing each fashion design?
2. Name the three types of designers most commonly serving the American fashion industry today. What are the responsibilities of each?
3. What are the major sources of inspiration for many fashion designers? Give an example of how the designs of a modern apparel designer have been influenced by one such source.

4. Into what three groups may fashion manufacturers be classified? Indicate the identifying characteristics of each.

5. What are the three groups of classifications into which most fashion retail firms fall? What are the basic identifying characteristics of each?

6. How valid is the downward-flow theory of fashion adoption today? Why?

7. Discuss the implications for modern merchants of (a) the horizontal-flow theory of fashion adoption, and (b) the upward-flow theory of fashion adoption.

8. Why are the following prime candidates for positions of fashion leadership: (a) social leaders, (b) people in the news, (c) sports professionals?

9. For what four reasons do most people follow, rather than lead, in matters relating to fashion? Elaborate on each.

10. How can an individual use fashion as a means of self-expression?

MERCHANDISING DIGEST

1. Discuss the implications of the following quotation from the text: "Rarely does a revolutionary new style succeed. Instead, it is the evolutionary new style that so often becomes the best-selling fashion." Cite examples to support your answer.

2. The text states, "Famous people are not necessarily fashion leaders, even if they do influence an individual style." Discuss this statement and its implications for the fashion industry. Name at least one recently famous person who has not been a fashion leader or influential and at least one who has been a fashion leader or influential. Name a specific style for which the latter is famous.

3. Discuss why people today seek both conformity and individuality in fashion. Discuss the implications this has for the fashion retailer.

4. Discuss the statement "you're only as good as your last collection" in regard to fashion designers.

5. THE BUSINESS OF FASHION

Fashion leads, fashion follows, and fashion moves. We have seen how fashion is affected by a myriad of factors and how, in turn, fashion affects everything and everyone it touches. The study of fashion involves elements of psychology, sociology, art, history, and religion. In addition, it involves the economic principles that govern and shape all business. For fashion is a business—a big business—that involves all the same principles used in the automobile industry, the steel industry, and the electronics industry.

Business is the activity of creating, producing, and marketing products or services. The primary objective of business is to make a profit. **Profit,** or net income, is the amount of money a business earns in excess of its expenses. Consequently, in this country, **business** can be defined as the activity of creating, producing, and marketing products or services for a profit.

If a business does not make a profit, it remains stagnant. If it can no longer be a vital, contributing, expanding entity that employs people and supports the economic growth of the community, it goes out of business! Therefore, profit is the lifeblood of any business.

ECONOMIC IMPORTANCE OF THE FASHION BUSINESS

The fashion business is one of the largest employers in this country. This business encompasses four different levels. One level is concerned with the production of the raw materials. A second level is concerned with the manufacture of the finished product. A third level is concerned with the distribution and retailing of fashion products. Finally, a fourth level, known as the auxiliary level, is concerned with the use of all avenues of advertising and promotion as they relate to the other three levels.

The growth and development of mass markets, mass-production methods, and mass distribution have contributed to the creation of new opportunities in the fashion industry—not only in the production area, but in design and marketing jobs. Young people are entering the fashion business in greater numbers each year and are having a marked effect on the business. Innovation and change have become important factors in the economic growth of the fashion business.

SCOPE OF THE FASHION BUSINESS

The fashion business is composed of numerous industries all working to keep consumers of fashion satisfied. A special relationship exists among these industries that makes the fashion business different from other businesses. The four different levels of the fashion business—known as the primary level, the secondary level, the retail level, and the auxiliary level—are composed of separate entities, but they also work interdependently to provide the market with the fashion merchandise that will satisfy consumers. Because of this unique relationship among the different industries, some students of economics find the fashion business unusually exciting.

The Primary Level

The **primary level** is composed of the growers and producers of the raw materials of fashion—the fiber, fabric, leather, and fur producers who function in the raw materials market. The earliest part of the planning function in color and texture takes place on the primary level. It is also the level of the fashion business that works the farthest in advance of the ultimate selling period of the goods. Up to two years' lead time is needed by primary-level companies before the goods will be available to the consumer. Primary-level goods may often be imports from third world emerging nations, where textiles are usually the earliest form of industrialization.

The Secondary Level

The **secondary level** is composed of industries—manufacturers and contractors—that produce the semifinished or finished fashion goods from the materials produced on the primary level. On the secondary level are the manufacturers of women's, men's, and children's apparel and accessories. Manufacturers who function on the secondary level may be based in America or overseas. Fashion goods are now produced in the Far East, the Caribbean countries, South America, and Europe. Secondary-level companies work from 1½ years to 6 months ahead of the time goods are available for the consumer.

The Retail Level

The **retail level** is the ultimate distribution level. On this level are the different types of retailers who buy their goods from the secondary level and then supply them directly to the consumer. In many cases the retail level works with both the primary and secondary levels to ensure a coordinated approach to consumer wants. A vertical interrelationship exists between the primary, secondary, and retail levels. Retailers make initial purchases for resale to customers from 3 to 6 months before the customer buying season.

The Auxiliary Level

The **auxiliary level** is the only level that functions with all the other levels simultaneously. This level is composed of all the support services that are working constantly with primary producers, secondary manufacturers, and retailers in order to keep consumers aware of the fashion merchandise produced for ultimate consumption. On this level are all the advertising media—print, audio, and visual—and fashion consultants and researchers.

Diversity of Firms

A wide diversity of kinds and sizes of firms operate on each level of the fashion business. Giant firms (national and international) and small companies (with regional or local distribution) exist side by side as privately or publicly owned corporations, partnerships, or sole proprietorships. Fashion-producing companies may also be part of conglomerates, which own, for example, publishing or entertainment companies, oil wells, or professional athletic teams.

Whether large or small, the different types of producers have one need in common—the need to understand what their ultimate customer will buy. Only through complete understanding and cooperation can the four levels of the fashion business be aware of new developments in fashion and apply them to satisfy the wants of their customers. This cooperation aids them in having the right merchandise at the right price, in the right place, at the right time, in the right quantities, and with the right sales promotion for their customers.

FORMS OF BUSINESS OWNERSHIP

Ownership of a fashion business—or of any business—may take many different legal forms, each carrying certain privileges and responsibilities. The three most prevalent forms of ownership are the sole or single proprietorship, the partnership, and the corporation. The sole proprietorship and the partnership are both unincorporated businesses that have no existence except through their owners. The corporation is an incorporated business that continues to exist even when one or more of its owners leaves or dies. The franchise also deserves mention.

The Sole Proprietorship

The sole proprietorship is the most common form of business in the United States, as well

Giant firms and small businesses exist side by side.

as in many foreign countries where the economics of the nation depend upon the small shopkeeper.

In the **sole proprietorship,** the individual owns the business, assumes all risks, and operates the business for his or her own personal interest. Although this type of ownership dominates in the number of businesses, it represents less than 15 percent of the dollar volume of all business transactions. The sole proprietorship is known as an unincorporated or common-law form of business organization. This is because minimum authorization from federal, state, or local government is required to begin or terminate legal operations. Today sales tax authorizations, and for some businesses, licenses, must be obtained. Also, the business name must be registered. In addition, local zoning laws must be obeyed. Some areas do not permit any businesses to operate, and other areas restrict the types of business.

There are many examples of the sole proprietorship in all areas of the fashion business—in designing, contracting, retailing, advisory service, and manufacturing. For example, Helen Galland, former president of Bonwit Teller, decided to leave that position and form her own consulting and advisory firm. She formed a sole proprietorship and, using the experience and expertise gained through her years of working for large corporations, built a most sought-after fashion service.

ADVANTAGES. The advantages of the sole proprietorship are ownership of all profits, personal satisfaction, freedom and flexibility, tax savings, and ease and low cost of organization and dissolution.

Ownership of All Profits. The sole proprietorship allows the owner to receive 100 percent of the profits earned in the business—that money in excess of expenses and business taxes. These profits also represent the salary of the owner, since no salary is allocated for the owner in a sole proprietorship. Personal income tax must be paid on this account.

Personal Satisfaction. The concept of being one's own boss may be the most significant incentive for establishing the sole proprietorship. The individual has a sense of responsibility and accomplishment that cannot be matched when the person works as an employee for someone else.

Freedom and Flexibility. The sole proprietor does not have to get the permission of other parties in making day-to-day decisions. However, the sole proprietor often consults with an accountant or a lawyer. As a result, the proprietor can make decisions promptly and take action at the opportune moment.

Tax Savings. Special taxes that are levied against the corporation are not levied against the sole proprietorship. However, the proprietor is not exempt from normal individual and business taxes, such as those imposed upon payroll, property, and income.

Ease and Low Cost of Organization and Dissolution. A prime advantage of this form of ownership is the ability to enter into a business agreement with little red tape. Though some types of sole proprietorships require licensing by the city or state, most can operate without that approval. Dissolution of the business is also accomplished quite easily, as few legal procedures are needed. These involve mainly leases, payment of debts, and taxes.

DISADVANTAGES. The disadvantages of the sole proprietorship are unlimited liability, limited financial resources, difficulties of management, lack of opportunity for employees, and lack of continuity.

Unlimited Liability. The individual owner is legally liable for all the debts of the business, and if his or her original investment in the business cannot satisfy these debts or obligations, the proprietor's personal and real property may be attached and taken by creditors. The unlimited liability of a sole proprietor can mean financial ruin to the owner if the business fails.

Limited Financial Resources. Because the individual is the sole owner of the business, the entrepreneur must rely on his or her own ability to borrow in order to finance the operations of the business. Banks and other lending institutions may hesitate to lend large sums of money to sole proprietors. Also, creditors might be unwilling to sell large quantities to a firm having just one owner.

Difficulties of Management. According to Dun and Bradstreet, which issues credit ratings, most failures of sole proprietorships are specifically attributed to a lack of managerial capabilities—the ability to plan, organize, direct, coordinate, and control the business.

Lack of Opportunity for Employees. Because ambitious employees may be unwilling to stay for an extended period of time in a business where the opportunities are so limited, the sole proprietor may be unable to keep highly qualified individuals. This may be the case even though he or she offers good salaries and fringe benefits.

Lack of Continuity. Extended illness, death, insanity, imprisonment, or bankruptcy of the owner of a sole proprietorship will terminate the business. Many firms have dissolved because the business is profitable only as long as the owner is able to run it.

The Partnership

A **partnership**, as defined by the Uniform Partnership Act, "is an association of two or more persons to carry on as co-owners of a business for a profit." Except for the same legal responsibilities noted under the sole proprietorship, a partnership is also comparatively free from government regulations. However, some states do levy various regulations, and partnership information is required by the Internal Revenue Service. A contract between or among partners is needed to ensure understanding of the obligations and rewards that each partner agrees to and shares.

The original form of business ownership of famous retail establishments such as Abraham

Brooks Brothers is a retail establishment that started as a partnership.

SUCCESS OF THE NAKASH BROTHERS: THE JORDACHE LOOK

When Joe Nakash arrived in the United States from Israel in 1962, he had $25 in his pocket. He slept in bus stations until he found a job as a stock clerk on New York's Lower East Side that paid $40 a week. By 1967, his salary was up to $110 a week and he had saved enough money to bring his two brothers, Ralph and Avi, to America. Saving $150 a week among them, they opened a jeans store in Brooklyn in 1969, and expanded to four stores within four years.

When they decided to manufacture their own jeans, they scouted all over the world for an innovative new style. And in 1977, Ralph designed a tight-fitting jean with pocket stitching that got second looks from jeans manufacturers. The brothers were able to put together $300,000 and the Jordache Company was born. Jordache is an acronym derived from the names Joe, Ralph, and Avi.

The first major company decision was to hire the best sales reps the company could find. When their orders reached the $1 million level, bankers were willing to loan the company the money it needed for advertising. By placing expensive local

and Straus and Lord & Taylor was the partnership. Today, many manufacturing firms are partnerships with two partners having different expertise working together. The most usual combinations are a person with factory and manufacturing know-how partnered with a creative design person or a person with outstanding sales ability.

TYPES OF PARTNERS. Partners' duties and obligations may differ with respect to such factors as management practice, sharing of profits, and extent of liability. Although there are many variations, the following are the most important types.

General Partner. A general partner is an individual who has unlimited liability and who

may be called upon to furnish additional money from his or her own personal assets to pay the debts of the partnership.

Limited Partner. A limited partner is an individual whose liability extends up to the amount of his or her investment and who is not permitted to take an active part in the management of the business. The limited partner, of course, shares in a smaller way in any profits from the business.

Silent Partner. A silent partner is an individual who does not take an active role in the business, but who is known to the public as a member of the partnership.

Secret Partner. A secret partner is an individual who does take an active role in the part-

commercials ($6,000 for a 30-second spot on *60 Minutes* and similar news programs) Joe Nakash attracted both retailers and consumers. The ads made the company seem much bigger than it was. Soon Jordache was shipping about 200,000 pairs of jeans a month.

Today the company has expanded beyond jeans manufacture to include the manufacture and licensing of children's clothes, handbags, menswear, active wear (sneakers, running suits, and other athletic apparel), and junior separates. Despite their phenomenal growth, the Nakash brothers' business methods remain relatively unchanged. Joe, officially chairman, handles advertising and financial arrangements. Ralph is in charge of production and merchandising. And Avi is responsible for operations such as inventory control. The three brothers usually do most of their planning during their hour-long commute by car to and from their Queens residences, and promotion is still considered all-important. Joe Nakash personally oversees this area and the company spends 8 percent of its budget on advertising in an industry where the norm is 5 percent.

Jordache is still a private corporation, although

a huge, successful one. The Nakash brothers have gradually made some changes that have improved the efficiency of the company. They have delegated some of their duties to their top executives, set up more easily managed divisions within the company, and automated inventory control, credit information, cash flow, and accounts receivable.

Whenever Joe Nakash is interviewed about Jordache, the word "fun" is likely to crop up again and again in the conversation. But it is quite evident that while they are "having fun" with their business, the Nakash brothers have shown a remarkable entrepreneural spirit that has made Jordache and the "Jordache look" a huge success.

This Fashion Focus is based on information from these sources:

"The Jeaning of America," *Newsweek*, October 6, 1980, pp. 83–85.

"Jordache's New Executive Look," *Business Week*, November 2, 1981, p. 121.

"The Jordache Story." A press release from Jordache Enterprises, Inc.

"Topless Jeans Fake the Scene," *Time*, September 10, 1979, p. 74.

nership affairs, but who is not known to the public as a member of the firm.

Senior and Junior Partners.   These terms apply in partnerships where distinctions are drawn between individuals on the basis of their investment, business experience, and share in the firm's profits.

ADVANTAGES.   The advantages of the partnership are ease of organization, employee incentive, capital, ease of expansion, management benefits, and tax savings.

Ease of Organization.   Although a partnership is more difficult to organize than a sole proprietorship, essentially all that is needed is an agreement between the partners in the form

of a contract. This contract can be written or oral, but should be written because of all the problems that arise in running any business. The dissolution of a partnership is also a relatively simple matter.

Employee Incentive.   In a partnership, unlike a sole proprietorship, a talented or loyal employee can be made a partner, thus providing the incentive for better work.

Availability of Capital.   Because a partnership has more than one owner, more sources of **capital** (money, property, and other assets) are available than under the sole proprietorship. Usually banks are more willing to loan money when two or more people are responsible for the repayment of the loan.

Ease of Expansion. Since a greater amount of capital is available, the partnership can expand the business more readily than the sole proprietor can. Multiple owners can also supervise more employees and oversee larger facilities than could a single individual.

Management Benefits. Each partner may handle or supervise different functions of the business. This pooling of talent is of tremendous value to the business, as it enables the partnership to operate with a variety of specialists.

Tax Savings. There are no specific additional taxes levied against the general partnership's business income other than sales taxes and social security. Just as in the sole proprietorship, the partners pay income taxes as individuals on their share of the profits, which also represent their salaries for the work they performed.

DISADVANTAGES. The disadvantages of the partnership are unlimited liability, complicated decision making, and lack of continuity.

Unlimited Liability. If the assets of the partnership are not sufficient to meet its obligations, the creditors may choose to sue any or all of the partners to satisfy the debt. Partners are liable not only for debts incurred by joint decisions, but also for any debts made by a partner when acting for the firm.

Complicated Decision Making. Because the partnership deals with two or more individuals, decision making takes longer, and if a stalemate should occur on a vital decision, the only solution to the problem may be to dissolve the partnership.

Lack of Continuity. The partnership is a temporary form of business and can be terminated by the partners themselves, by court decree, or in the event of the death, bankruptcy, or insanity of any partner. The death of any partner leaves his or her heirs no authority to interfere in the affairs of the partnership or to try to carry on the business. Therefore, it is obvious that the more people involved in a firm, the greater the chances of dissolution, causing the partnership to be the least permanent form of the three types of business ownership. Insurance on the life of each partner carried by the other partner or partners often lends stability to the partnership.

The Corporation

The third form of business ownership is the corporation. A **corporation** is defined by law as "an artificial being, invisible, intangible, and existing only in contemplation of law." The corporate form of organization comprises a relatively small percentage of the total number of business organizations. However, large corporations represent the most powerful segment of the national economy. In the 1980s, many fashion businesses incorporated or became part of large diversified national corporations. Today it is sometimes difficult for small fashion businesses to compete against the large corporations.

Not all corporations are giants; some are relatively small. However, there are two forms of ownership of corporations. The most common form of ownership is public ownership. A **public corporation** sells shares of its stock on the open market to the public. Anyone can buy a share of stock in the business and become a part owner. (See Table 5-1.) Some corporations are privately owned. In a **private corporation** no shares of stock are sold on the open market and the ownership is usually held by a few owners. The public cannot buy shares in this type of corporation.

CORPORATE STRUCTURE. Three groups comprise the corporate structure: the stockholders, the board of directors, and the officers of the corporation. Size is *not* an indicator of form of ownership. There are small corporations that are publicly owned just as there are giant corporations that are privately owned.

Stockholders. The **stockholders** are the owners of the corporation. They are individuals who bought shares of stock that give proof of ownership. The stockholder becomes a part owner of the business whether he or she owns one share or the majority of shares in the firm. This is true in both public and private corporations.

Board of Directors. The **board of directors** is the chief governing body of the corporation. Because the individuals who comprise the board hold a position of great trust, directors may be held personally liable to the stockholders for gross negligence, fraud, or the use of corporate assets for their personal gain to the detriment of the company. They cannot be held liable for normal mistakes in business judgment.

Officers. The **officers** of the corporation are elected by the board of directors and are directly responsible to the board for carrying out the business objectives of the firm. The board usually appoints a president, executive vice president, secretary, and a number of additional vice presidents who are responsible for various divisions of the firm.

ADVANTAGES. The advantages of the corporation are limited liability, transfer of ownership, continuity, capital formation, and management specialties.

Limited Liability. In the corporation, unlike the sole proprietorship and the partnership, the problem of unlimited liability for individuals does not exist. The stockholder can lose no more than the value of his or her original investment. The creditors cannot look beyond the assets of the corporation to settle their debts because the corporation is a separate entity and the firm, rather than the owners, owes the debt.

Transfer of Ownership. Unlike the other two forms, the corporation permits ease in transfer of ownership. Stockholders are able to buy and sell shares of stock in the public corporation through brokers in organized markets known as "stock exchanges." The value of these shares fluctuates daily. Therefore, owners may gain or lose money on the sale of their stock.

Continuity. Unlike the sole proprietorship or partnership, the corporation can be dissolved in only three ways: by court order, by the approval of the majority of the stockholders, or by the expiration of the corporate charter. Since corporations are rarely dissolved, they may possess an extremely long life. However, corporations may be merged with or taken over by other corporations by the exchange or sale of shares.

Capital Formation. Because the corporation can divide its ownership into shares of small denominations, it can attract capital from a few to thousands of individuals of varying incomes. It can also expand as long as investors are willing to purchase additional shares of stock.

Management Specialties. Because the corporation is usually larger than the sole proprietorship or partnership, it can be staffed with specialists to a greater degree. Stock incentive plans and stock bonuses offer greater incentive motives for employees than the other forms of organizational ownership usually do.

DISADVANTAGES. The disadvantages of the corporation are cost of organization, legal restrictions, taxation, lack of owners' personal interest, impersonality, and federal and state regulations.

Cost of Organization. The corporation must secure state approval and legal assistance in forming this type of ownership. Requirements vary from state to state, but all states require a minimum number of stockholders, a minimum amount of capital, and a payment of incorporation fees and taxes.

Legal Restrictions. The charter is the basis of the corporation's transactions and permits it

TABLE 5-1 Leading Diversified Apparel Manufacturers That Are Public Corporations

MANUFACTURERS	SALES (000)	LOCATION	PRODUCTS	SELECTED TRADEMARKS OR BRAND NAMES
Levi Strauss	$2,572,172	San Francisco	Designs, manufactures, and markets diversified line of apparel for men, women, and children	Levis, Oxxford, Koret of California
Interco	2,566,606	St. Louis	Designs, manufactures, and distributes branded and private-label sportswear for men and women	Queen Casuals, Londontown, Pant-Her, Devon, John Alexander, Florsheim, Thayer-McNeil
Northwest Industries	2,306,600	Chicago	Produces and markets men's and children's underwear and knit shirts	Fruit of the Loom, B.V.D., Underoos
Chesebrough-Pond's	1,623,190	Greenwich, Conn.	Manufactures and markets children's clothing	Health-Tex, Bass, Weejuns
Blue Bell	1,292,220	Greensboro, N. C.	Manufactures westernwear, sportswear, and casual clothes for men, women, and children	Wrangler, Blue Bell, Maverick, Jantzen
U.S. Industries	971,367	Stamford, Conn.	Manufactures and distributes men's, women's, and children's apparel	Not available
VF Corp.	879,528	Wyommissing, Pa.	Designs, manufactures, and markets men's, women's, and children's jeanswear and casual apparel, women's intimate apparel	Lee, Vanity Fair

to engage in only those activities that are stated or implied in that document.

Taxation. A corporation must pay federal income taxes in the same manner as an individual. Double taxation of corporate income results, because the net profit is taxed as well as that portion of the profit distributed to the stockholders as individual income (dividends). An exception to the double taxation rule is the

MANUFACTURERS	SALES (000)	LOCATION	PRODUCTS	SELECTED TRADEMARKS OR BRAND NAMES
Cluett, Peabody	$875,620	New York	Designs, manufactures, and markets a variety of apparel and related items for men, women, and children	Arrow, Lady Arrow, Sanforized, Gold Toe, Halston for Men, Donmoor, Ron Chereskin
Hartmarx	863,231	Chicago	Designs, manufactures, and markets apparel for men. Recently added some women's apparel	Hart Schaffner & Marx, Jack Nicklaus, Christian Dior, Austin Reed, Johnny Carson, Hickey Freeman, Handmacker, Country Miss
Genesco	664,805	Nashville	Designs, manufactures, and distributes footwear and men's apparel	Aquascutum, Kilgour, French & Stanbury, Donald Brooks, Chaps, Hardy Amies, Oleg Cassini, Johnson & Murphy, Sock Works
Fuqua Industries	607,480	Atlanta	Designs, manufactures, and distributes uniforms, sports hats, and athletic hosiery	Hutch Sporting Goods, Pioneer Cap, Willow Hosiery (NFL and Major League Baseball licenses)

Source: Fairchild's Tenth Annual Textile & Apparel Financial Directory, 1983.

"Subchapter S corporation." A Subchapter S corporation is a corporation with 10 or fewer stockholders initially and 25 or fewer after five years that elects to be taxed in the same manner as a partnership.

Lack of Owners' Personal Interest.   Because corporations have several to thousands of owners who usually own a very small part of the business, each one has little interest in the day-to-day management of the firm. Normally, their interest is in the amount of dividends they will receive and the increase in the value of their stock, which results from good management.

Impersonality. The separation of those running the firm (management) from those owning the firm (stockholders), together with the often large size of the corporation, leads to an impersonal atmosphere that is not found in either the partnership or the sole proprietorship.

Federal and State Regulations. Both federal and state governments require that the corporation file various reports and financial statements each year, causing the expenditure of money, time, and effort on the part of the company's managers.

The Franchise

A rapidly growing business arrangement is the **franchise**. This arrangement is a contract that gives an individual (or group of people) the right to own a business while benefiting from the expertise and reputation of an established firm. In return, the individual, known as the **franchisee**, pays the parent company, known as the **franchisor**, a set sum to purchase the franchise and royalties on goods or services sold. Franchises may be organized as sole proprietorships, partnerships, or corporations, although the form of business organization that the franchisee must use may be designated in the franchise contract.

Franchises generate one-third of all retail sales in the United States today. The franchise arrangement is widespread among automobile dealers, soft drink bottlers, fast-food restaurants, and convenience stores. While still small in the fashion business, the franchise is spreading rapidly. Franchises can be found at many levels of the fashion business, especially in retailing, where franchises include Stretch and Sew stores, Lady Madonna maternity shops, and the Athlete's Foot stores (specializing in leisure and athletic shoes).

ADVANTAGES. Franchising offers advantages to both the franchisee and the franchisor. The franchisee can get into business quickly, use proven operating methods, and benefit from training programs and mass purchasing offered by the franchisor. The franchisee is provided with a ready market that identifies with the store or brand name, thus assuring customer traffic. The franchisor has a great deal of control over its distribution network, limited liability, and less need for capital for expansion. Expansion is therefore more rapid than would be possible without the franchising arrangement. Royalty and franchise fees add to the profits of the parent company, and the personal interest and efforts of the franchisees as owner-managers help to assure the success of each venture.

DISADVANTAGES. Franchising also has drawbacks for both parties. The franchisee may find profits small in relation to the time and work involved, and often has limited flexibility at the local level. In addition, there is the risk of franchise arrangements organized merely to sell franchises, rather than for their long-range profitability to all parties involved. The franchisor may find profits so slim that it may want to own stores outright rather than franchise them. Attempts to buy back franchises often lead to troubled relations with the remaining franchises.

GOVERNMENT REGULATION OF BUSINESS

The right of government to regulate business is granted by the U.S. Constitution and by state constitutions. Although business originally operated in a **laissez-faire** economy, which in business terms refers to a government policy of noninterference with business, the development of trusts and monopolies in the late nineteenth century created the need for regulation. There are three basic categories of legislation that affect the fashion industry:

TABLE 5-2 Key Federal Laws Affecting the Fashion Industry

LAWS AFFECTING COMPETITION	PURPOSE AND PROVISIONS
Sherman Antitrust Act—1890	Outlawed monopolies. Outlawed restraint of competition.
Clayton Act—1914	Same purpose as Sherman Act but reinforced Sherman Act by defining some specific restraints—e.g., price fixing.
Federal Trade Commission (FTC) Act—1914 (Wheeler-Lee Act of 1938 amended the FTC Act.)	Established the FTC as a "policing" agency. Developed the mechanics for policing unfair methods of competition, e.g., false claims, price discrimination, price fixing.
Robinson-Patman Act—1936	Designed to equalize competition between large and small retailers (i.e., to reduce the advantages that big retailers have over small retailers—outgrowth of 1930 depression and growth of big chain retailers in 1920s). Examples of provision of law 1. Outlawed price discrimination if both small and large retailers buy the same amount of goods. 2. Outlawed inequitable and unjustified quantity discounts (e.g., discounts allowable if (a) available to all types of retailers and (b) related to actual savings that vendor could make from quantity cuttings or shipments). 3. Outlawed "phony" advertising allowance monies—i.e., advertising money must be used for advertising. 4. Outlawed discrimination in promotional allowances (monies for advertising, promotional displays, etc.)—equal allowances must be given under same conditions to small and large retailers alike.

PRODUCT AND LABELING LAWS DESIGNED TO PROTECT CONSUMERS	PURPOSE AND PROVISIONS
Wool Products Labeling Act—1939	Protects consumers from unrevealed presence of substitutes or mixtures. FTC responsible for enforcing law.
Fur Products Labeling Act—1951	Protects consumers and retailers against misbranding, false advertising, and false invoicing.
Flammable Fabrics Act—1953	Prohibits manufacture or sale of flammable fabrics or apparel.
Textile Fiber Identification Act—1958	Protects producers and consumers against false identification of fiber content.
Fair Packaging and Labeling Act—1966	Regulates interstate and foreign commerce by prohibiting deceptive methods of packaging or labeling.
Care Labeling of Textile Wearing Apparel Act—1972	Requires that all apparel have labels attached that clearly inform consumers about care and maintenance of the article.

1. Federal laws affecting competitive practices.
2. Federal product and labeling laws designed to protect consumers.
3. State and local laws affecting marketing activities.

Table 5-2 lists the key federal laws that affect and/or regulate the fashion industry.

BUSINESS GROWTH AND EXPANSION

Statistics show that our largest corporations control much of the nation's wealth. The rise of the corporate giants started in the early 1930s, continued into the 1980s, and will undoubtedly continue into the next century.

Expansion can occur in a variety of ways—internal growth, mergers, or integration. Various forms of licensing are also contributing to business growth. The growth of corporate giants in the fashion business has changed some of the old methods of doing business, and has led to the demise of old-time famous-name sole proprietorships, partnerships, and small incorporated companies that could no longer compete.

Internal Growth

A company's ability to grow internally determines its ability to offer more service and broader assortments of merchandise, and to increase profits. This is true because internal growth is real growth, in terms of creating new products and new jobs. Internal growth can be accomplished through horizontal and/or vertical means. When a company has horizontal growth it expands its capabilities on the same level it has been successfully performing. An apparel company could add new lines to diversify its product offerings; a retail store could open new branches. When a company has vertical growth it expands its capabilities on other levels than its primary function. An apparel company could begin to produce its own fabric, or could retail its manufactured goods in stores that the apparel company owns.

Mergers and Integration

Merger is the most common form of growth by acquisition. In a **merger**, a sale of one company to another company occurs, with the purchasing company usually remaining dominant. Companies merge to form a larger corporate organization for many reasons. They may wish to take advantage of a large corporation's greater purchasing power, or they may want to sell stock to obtain the financial resources needed for expansion. The desire to constantly increase sales is often able to be fulfilled only by a merger.

Operating economies can often be achieved by combining companies. Many times duplicate facilities can be eliminated, and marketing, purchasing, and other operations can be consolidated. **Diversification**, the addition of various lines, products, or services to serve different markets, can also be a motive for a merger. For example, the merger of Levi Strauss, noted for the manufacture of jeans, with Koret of California, a sportswear manufacturer of women's garments, broadened the markets for both types of clothing.

HORIZONTAL MERGERS OR INTEGRATION.
In a horizontal merger or integration, two companies with the same type of business are combined. An outstanding example of this type of integration was the purchase of Caldor's and Loehmann's by the Associated Dry Goods Corporation. ADG, a corporation that owns traditional department and specialty stores, such as Lord & Taylor, that have the middle-to-upper-income customer as their target audience, looked to expand its impact on the retail scene. Surveying the retail market, the officers of the corporation determined that a large and lucrative audience existed in the discount store customer and in the off-price fashion customer. In order to enter these fast-growing markets quickly, the corporation merged with Caldor's, a New England discount store chain, and Loehmann's, the original off-price fashion retailer. Using the method of horizontal

integration, ADG was able to penetrate two new areas of retailing.

VERTICAL MERGERS OR INTEGRATION.

In a vertical merger or integration, a company expands by either absorbing or merging with companies at other levels of business. For example, a fiber company could expand into the production of yarn and also into the production of fabric. Textile companies, such as Burlington and J. P. Stevens, have expanded through combinations of mergers and acquisitions to bring all levels of yarn and fabric production into one corporation.

CONGLOMERATES.

A **conglomerate** is a company consisting of a number of subsidiary companies in *unrelated* industries. In a conglomerate merger, two companies in unrelated lines of production or industry are combined. A conglomerate in the fashion world might have one company in the apparel business and own businesses with unrelated product lines. Batus, a British firm, owns the Brown and Williamson Tobacco Company; the Wilkinson Blade Company, maker of razor blades; and Saks Fifth Avenue, Gimbels, and Marshall Field's, famous retail firms.

One reason for conglomerate mergers is to diversify a company's sources of income so that economic pressures on one line of business do not seriously jeopardize the entire business. Another reason is that the government has severely restricted vertical and horizontal mergers in the interest of free competition. However, a major disadvantage of the conglomerate has been management difficulties in managing so many unrelated types of business.

Some textile companies have expanded to bring all levels of production into one company.

Licensing

Although not a form of business ownership, licensing is an increasingly popular method of expanding an already existing business. **Licensing** is an arrangement whereby firms are given permission to produce and market merchandise in the name of the licensor. The licensor is then paid a percentage of the sales, usually from 5 percent to 7 percent, for permitting the name to be used. This practice grew tremendously in the late 1970s and early 1980s, with sales of all licensed merchandise reaching an estimated $21 billion in 1983. Of that total, apparel and accessories account for about one-third of sales, and represent the largest single category of licensed goods sold.[1]

The first designer to license his name to a manufacturer was Christian Dior, who lent his name to a line of ties in 1950. Today, many of the best-known women's apparel designers are licensing either the use of their original designs or just their names without a design for a wide variety of goods, from apparel to luggage, from housewares to chocolates. Among the many American designers involved in licensing ar-

Pierre Cardin

In a licensing arrangement, the merchandise is identified with a reputation for quality. This montage shows Cardin's wide range of licenses identified by year.

rangements are Gloria Vanderbilt, Calvin Klein, Halston, and Bill Blass.

The licensing phenomenon is not limited to name designers. Popular movies and T.V. shows like *Star Wars* and *Flashdance* have spawned apparel and other products based on their themes or characters. Comic or greeting-card characters like Strawberry Shortcake and Snoopy are also frequently licensed, as are most professional sports teams and many players or athletes. Yet fashion designers pull in the greatest share of licensing dollars: a full one-third of all the licensed goods sold in the United States are designer clothes or accessories.[2]

The advantage of a licensing arrangement to a manufacturer is that the merchandise is identified with a highly recognizable name, which also generally connotes high quality. This recognition factor can be valuable to retailers in presenting their own fashion image. And to consumers, the designer name not only indicates a certain quality of merchandise, but symbolizes status or achievement as well. Because of that built-in appeal, stores have stocked up on designer goods from socks to fragrances and even jewelry.

RETAIL PROGRAMS. As an example of how strong a designer name is as a selling point at the retail level, Ralph Lauren opened his own freestanding store for his products in the early 1970s. By 1983 the number of stores had expanded to 30.

A more recent trend is the direct licensing of designer names by established retailers. For instance, Federated Department Stores, Inc., the parent company of department stores including Foley's in Houston, Bloomingdale's in New York, Burdine's in Miami, and Filene's in Boston, entered into an exclusive licensing agreement with Cacharel. Similarly, JC Penney, traditionally known as a budget retailer or mass merchandiser, created a licensing program with Halston for an exclusive "Halston III" collection for the national chain. Under the agreement, Halston created a line of moderately priced apparel, which could be used by JC Penney to upgrade its budget image and reposition itself as a fashion retailer.

INTERNATIONAL PROGRAMS. Licensing is also crossing international borders, as an increasing number of American designers are making licensing agreements with foreign producers. At the end of 1979, Oscar de la Renta signed licenses transferring the production of his entire Miss O line, with an annual volume of about $2.5 million, from New York to Hong Kong. Other designers have simply created new programs for foreign markets. For instance, in 1983 Calvin Klein awarded an exclusive license for apparel to one firm in Brazil, which projected it would do a wholesale volume of $2.5 million per month by the end of its first year. In 1982, Ralph Lauren began building a licensing network in Europe and Japan, which he was working to turn into a $50 million wholesale business by late 1983.[3]

At the same time, some American manufacturers have contracted to license and market goods by foreign designers. An example is George Masket, Ltd., a New York manufacturer that signed a licensing agreement with French designer Guy Laroche to produce a collection of women's suits, blazers, skirts, pants, and coats. Although apparel by Guy Laroche was already being sold in the United States through designer boutiques, the firm wished to broaden its American market through American-made goods sold to better department and specialty stores.

REFERENCES

[1] Susan K. Reed, "What Does BIll Blass Know About Chocolates?," *Savvy,* May 1983, p. 56.
[2] Ibid.
[3] Susan Alai, "Lauren Seeks to Widen Foreign Role," *Women's Wear Daily,* November 10, 1982, p. 50.

Define or briefly explain the following terms:

Auxiliary level
Board of directors
Business
Capital
Conglomerate
Corporation
Diversification
Franchise
Franchisee
Franchisor
Laissez-faire
Licensing

Merger
Officers
Partnership
Primary level
Private corporation
Profit
Public corporation
Retail level
Secondary level
Sole proprietorship
Stockholders

1. What is the primary objective of all business? Why?
2. What are the four levels of the fashion business? List, briefly describe, and give one example of each.
3. In what way does the auxiliary level differ from the other levels of the fashion business?
4. Name the five key reasons why an individual would go into business as a sole proprietor. What might the reasons be for that individual subsequently to take a partner in the business?
5. What does the term "liability" mean to the sole proprietor?
6. There are several types of partners that may own a business. List and briefly describe each one.
7. The corporate form of business ownership has certain disadvantages. Name five of them. What is the key advantage to this type of business when the firm decides to expand?
8. Name five laws and regulations that would affect a national chain of shoe stores. Which would probably *not* affect a small, privately owned dress shop?
9. Differentiate between the following: horizontal mergers or integration and vertical mergers or integration.
10. What is the advantage of a licensed designer name to the manufacturer? to the retailer? to the consumer?

1. Discuss some of the initial decisions that need to be made by an individual or group of individuals seeking to form a company in regard to the form of ownership of the proposed organization that will best benefit themselves.
2. Discuss the major differences between private and publicly owned corporations. Indicate how these differences would affect you as an officer of the corporation.
3. List some recent mergers and acquisitions in the fashion business that were not mentioned in the text. (The information might be found in *Women's Wear Daily, Newsweek, Business Week, U.S. News & World Report,* and so on.)

PROJECT 1.

EXPLORING
THE DYNAMICS
OF FASHION

There seem to be definite correlations between fashions and the times. As times change, so do fashions, and when a fashion changes, the *total look* changes. Accessories, makeup, and hairstyles are all part of this total fashion look. When styles are revived, they are revived in new forms, adapted for new lifestyles and occasions.

Study the following chart; then answer the questions about it.

1. Find examples (draw, sketch, photograph, cut and paste) of one or more of the fashion items listed in the right-hand column of the chart.

2. What similarities in fashions and their causes can you find in the decades listed?

3. What environmental changes within the last two decades do you feel will have lasting effects over the next 10 to 20 years?

4. What examples from the decades listed can you find to support the theory that fashion is evolutionary?

5. During what time period was fashion closest to being revolutionary?

6. What additions can you make to the information in any of the decades listed?

7. From your interpretation of the information on past decades, what conclusions can you draw about the evolution of fashions and their relationship to current events?

SOCIAL AND ECONOMIC INFLUENCES IN FASHION IN THE UNITED STATES (1920–1989)

ERA	EVENTS TAKING PLACE	PUBLIC REACTIONS	INTERPRETATION IN APPAREL AND DRESS
1920s	Post World War I, Paris influence Voting rights for women Increasing prosperity Modern art, music, literature Birth of sportswear	Daring looks and behavior Freedom for the body Short hair styles Women begin to smoke Dancing (Charleston)	Chemise dresses, short skirts T-strap shoes, cloche hats Luxurious fabrics: silks, satins, crepes Costume looks, long strands of beads
1930s	Depression era Unemployment, little money Hollywood influence: stars & designers Rayon and acetate fabrics Big bands, swing music	Frugality, conservatism "The little woman" Make do	Soft looks: loose, light fabrics Long hemlines, bias cuts Big hats, big brims The housedress Fox, fur-collared coats, wraps
1940s	World War II: Government restrictions Exit France as fashion source Shortage of materials Emergence of American designers Radio, records Crooners: Crosby, Sinatra Dior—1947 "New Look"	Women take men's jobs Glamour, pinup girls Strong nationalism Common cause philosophy	Tailored, mannish suits, peplum jackets Padded shoulders Knee-length straight skirts Soft, shoulder-length hair (pageboy) Rolled hair Small hats, perched in front Pants for women
1950s	Population increasing; baby boom Korean war Firms expand, go public, diversify Move to suburbs Incomes rising More imports Improved transportation; communications: TV Development of more synthetics, finishes Birth of rock 'n' roll	Buy new homes, appliances, furnishings Conformity Improve quality of family life Use of increased leisure time for sports and recreation The station wagon	Classics: shirtwaist dress At-home clothes Mink coats Sack dress (too quickly copied) Sportswear Ivy League look, gray flannel suit, skinny ties, buttondown shirts Car coats Wash 'n' wear fabrics
1960s	Rise of shopping centers: boutiques New technology: stretch fabrics, new knitting methods Big business expansion; prosperity Designer names Civil rights movement Vietnam war: youth rebellion, antiwar movement London influence: the Beatles, Twiggy, Mod, Mary Quant, Carnaby Peacock revolution, rock music, youth cult	New sexual freedom Experimentation in fashion Antiestablishment attitudes Generation gap Identity seeking, new values Divorce, singles Drug experimentation	Street fashions: jeans Vinyls, synthetics, wet-look Miniskirts Wild use of color patterns Knits, polyester Ethnic clothing and crafts Unisex clothes Fun furs Long hair, wigs Men: turtlenecks, wide ties. Nehru jackets, golf coordinates, nylon printed shirts
1970s	Equal rights, women's liberation movement Women working outside the home Watergate, disenchantment with politics Recessions Ecology, conservation; energy crisis Stabilizing economy End of Vietnam war Disco dancing, clubs Consumerism Hostage crisis in Iran	Individualism Return to sanity, reaction to 1960s chaos Back to nature, health foods, natural fibers New conservatism Urban renewal, interest in cities & their problems Equal Rights Amendment Minority organizations	Pantsuits (women) leisure suits (men) Maxi and longuette (1970s disaster) Jeans: bell bottoms, straight leg, tapered leg, peg leg. Jeans acceptable for dress and casual wear T-shirts, tank tops, boots Eclecticism Classic look: blazers, shirts, investment clothing Separates, not coordinates Romantic look: soft, feminine
1980s	Computer explosion Music videocassettes Nuclear weapons buildup in Europe Yuppy (Young Urban Professional) Recession and unemployment Wars in Central America, Middle East Movies: *Fame, E.T., Flashdance* First black presidential and first woman vice-presidential candidates Japanese fashion explosion Executive-level women; Two-income families New baby boom	Buy home computers Michael Jackson, youth hero Nuclear freeze movement Entrepreneurship Immigration legislation Day-care centers Graffiti art London influence: Punk— Boy George and Culture Club Patriotism flourishes Convertibles return	Return of the chemise Punk hairdos Androgynous dressing Tailored suits and classic dressing for men and women Torn clothes fad Return to pants in mid-decade Hats return for everyone Furs

THE PRODUCERS AND MARKETERS

Fashion is products—products with a past. The past of a product includes all the industries and all the people involved in making it what it is and in overseeing its distribution. These are the producers and marketers of fashion.

Behind every product there is a story that begins with the raw materials of fiber or fabric, leather or fur, and those who are responsible for their production. Unit 2 starts with a discussion of these, the primary suppliers.

The steps necessary to convert these raw materials into the fashions that draw the customers into the stores make up the subsequent episodes in the life of a product. This is the business of the secondary suppliers, and there are all kinds of them. There are industries that produce men's, women's, and children's apparel. There are industries that specialize in accessories—shoes and handbags, hosiery and gloves. There are businesses that engage in the production of intimate apparel. And there are companies that fo-

cus on cosmetics. The history and development and the organization and operation of each of these industries is discussed in Unit 2.

Next, products have to be presented and sold to fashion buyers—the people responsible for getting them into the retail stores. This takes place at market centers, places where new fashions and buyers are brought together. The domestic fashion market is discussed in one of the chapters of Unit 2. Another chapter takes us to major fashion markets around the world.

Each of the industries involved in these processes is affected by the laws relating to fashion discussed in Unit 1. Specific applications of these general principles are taken up in Unit 2.

It is important to understand the interrelated roles played by the different fashion industries. Anyone interested in a career in the field needs a working knowledge of the producers and marketers of fashion.

6. TEXTILES— FIBERS AND FABRICS

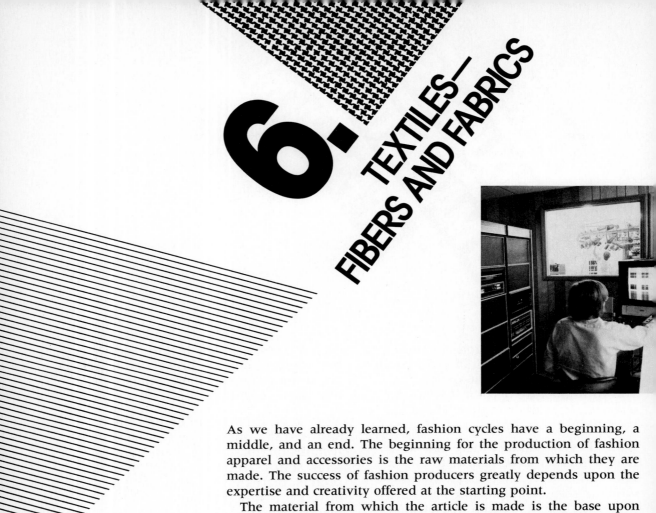

As we have already learned, fashion cycles have a beginning, a middle, and an end. The beginning for the production of fashion apparel and accessories is the raw materials from which they are made. The success of fashion producers greatly depends upon the expertise and creativity offered at the starting point.

The material from which the article is made is the base upon which others in the fashion industry build. The designer creating a style at the drawing board must consider the material best suited for the particular silhouette and details of design. The fashion apparel manufacturer also considers the various weights and patterns currently desired as well as the cost factors. Finally, the retailer must select fashions made of those materials considered appropriate and desirable by the specific target customer.

In the manufacture of fashion apparel, textiles, or fabrics, are used more than any other material. The textile, or fabric, industry is composed of related industries using different raw materials. Fashion textiles are the end product of close collaboration among these related industries. **Primary suppliers** are industries that produce the fibers and fabrics that make up the fashion textile world. There are two kinds of primary suppliers: the textile fiber industry and the textile fabric industry. The textile fiber industry produces both natural and man-made fibers. The textile fabric industry knits or weaves yarns made of these fibers into various finished products.

The process by which natural fibers (from animal, vegetable, or mineral sources) or fibers made from chemicals ultimately become a fashionable item of apparel is a remarkable one. In the past few years there have been more and more newsworthy developments in the fashion textile industry, affecting every step of the fashion process. To understand these processes, one must know something about the many producers involved as the product moves along toward its ultimate destination—the fashion customer. As Christian Dior, the world-famous haute couture designer, commented, "Fabric not only expresses a designer's dreams but also stimulates his own ideas. It can be the beginning of an inspiration. Many a dress of mine is born of the fabric alone."[1]

THE TEXTILE FIBER INDUSTRY

Garments are made from fabrics. Most fabrics are made from yarns, and yarns are made from fibers. A single **fiber,** then, is the smallest part of the fabric. It is extremely fine and hairlike in appearance. Although tiny, fibers have a great influence on fashion. When spun into yarn and knit or woven into fabric, it is the fibers that will have a great deal to do with the color, weight, texture, durability, and care qualities of the finished product.

Fibers are divided into two broad categories: natural and man-made. **Natural fibers** are derived from plant or animal sources. **Man-made fibers** are produced in chemical factories; however, not all are truly synthetic. Rayons, for example, are pure cellulose restructured into fiber from wood or cotton linters.

With today's wide array of textile fibers, it is hard to realize that much of what we are now accustomed to has come into existence only in recent decades. Polyester, the most widely used man-made fiber in the world, was first produced by E. I. du Pont de Nemours in 1953. Nylon, the man-made fiber with the second-highest use, is also a Du Pont product and was introduced in 1939. Rayon, the first man-made fiber, was produced by the American Viscose Company in 1910, and today is the third most used of the man-made fibers.

In contrast, natural fibers have been with us from the beginning of time and have been used extensively over the centuries. However, during the 1950s, 1960s, and 1970s, the use of natural fibers declined while the growth of man-made fibers exploded. By the 1980s, the demand for all the characteristics of natural fibers and concern for our ecology and environment created consumer awareness of and renewed interest in fashions made of natural fibers in sophisticated urban U. S. markets.

Originally the natural fibers were not given special finishes and properties that we find in them today. Advanced technology and innovative chemical processing changed that, and we are able to give natural fibers many of the advantages and characteristics of man-made fibers that make natural fibers equal in care and wear properties to man-made fibers.

History and Development

The fiber industries are of vastly different ages and backgrounds. The natural fiber industry has had a very long history of slow development, while the man-made fiber industry has had a short history of very rapid development. These differences have resulted in some different operational and organizational forms, even though the ultimate goal of both groups is to produce fibers that fill consumer needs.

THE NATURAL FIBER INDUSTRIES. The natural fiber industries are so old that they predate written history. Even primitive human beings are believed to have gathered flax (the fiber in linen) to make yarns for fabrics. The slow development of natural fibers has accelerated only in recent years. The most important natural fibers are cotton, wool, silk, and flax. The natural fiber industry is dependent on animals and plants. Therefore, the production of natural fibers depends on climate and geography, and in most cases, small farmers

MOHAIR

Fibe sheared from the angora goat twice a year.

Because natural fibers come from plants and animals, small farmers and herders of sheep and goats are prime movers in the industry.

and small herders of sheep produce the majority of our natural fibers.

Cotton.   Cotton, the most used of all the natural fibers, is the vegetable fiber attached to the seed of the cotton plant. Because the cotton plant grows best in warm climates, the Southern states of the United States cultivate and grow the largest amount of cotton and have become known as the "Cotton Belt." The Cotton Belt stretches from the Southeast (the Carolinas, Georgia, and Alabama) through the Mississippi Delta (Arkansas, Mississippi, and Louisiana) to the Southwest (Texas and Oklahoma), and more recently to the West (New Mexico, Arizona, and California). Brazil, Mexico, Peru, China and the Soviet Union are other producers of cotton.

Because cotton fibers are composed primarily of cellulose, they have good durability and a pleasing feel in the hand. The cotton fiber absorbs moisture quickly. It also dries quickly, giving a cooling effect which makes cotton a good fiber for warm or hot weather. This is why most T-shirts are made of cotton. Cotton fabrics can be washed or dry-cleaned and never produce the undesirable static electricity generated by other fibers.

The cotton boll provides a multitude of products. The longest and finest fibers (up to 2½ inches) are more suitable for spinning than are shorter fibers and so are used for sheer cotton fabrics; the shorter fibers are used for coarser goods. The very short fibers, called linters, are used in the manufacture of rayon and such nonfashion items as paper and absorbent cotton pads. The cottonseed itself is processed into cottonseed oil, which is used in cooking, and cottonseed meal, which becomes feed and fertilizer. The fertilizer goes into the ground to start the cotton crop all over again.

Wool. **Wool** is the fiber that forms the coat of sheep. Being an animal fiber, it is mainly composed of protein. By far the greatest amount of wool comes from Australia, New Zealand, and Russia. However, a considerable number of sheep are also raised for wool in the Western United States, England, Scotland, South Africa, and Uruguay. Good grazing lands in moderate climates are suitable for the growth of higher-quality wool coats. In colder climates, sheep develop coarser wool coats more suitable for carpets than apparel. However, many cold-climate sheep have developed a thick downlike wool ideal for apparel, for example, Icelandic and Shetland wools.

In the late 1600s, the first woolen mill in the western hemisphere was set up in Massachusetts. Most American woolen mills built since that time have been located in the Northeast and Southeast. The American sheep ranches, which provide the wool, are mostly located in the good grazing areas of Utah, Colorado, and Montana. Part of the history of the Old West records the range wars between cattle ranchers and sheep ranchers. Most of the West had originally been settled by the cattle ranchers. They fought bloody range wars attempting to keep sheep herders and ranchers from allowing their sheep to graze on cattle land.

Wool shorn from live sheep is called "fleece wool" or "clipped wool" and is considered superior in quality. Wool removed from sheep already dead from disease or slaughter is called "pulled wool" and is not considered as good a grade. This is due to chemical and mechanical damage from pulling.

There are over 200 grades of sheep. Wool produced by merino is considered to be the best grade of wool because it has the softest hand, the most crimp and resiliency, the best elasticity, and can be spun into the thinnest yarns. The least desirable wool comes from mongrel sheep. It has the least elasticity and strength and is used mainly for low-grade clothing and carpets.

Wool produces warm fabrics because it has a natural crimp that facilitates the production of bulky yarns, which trap air to form insulating barriers against the cold. Just the opposite of cotton, wool absorbs moisture slowly and dries slowly. Since excellent crimps can also be produced in thermoplastic fibers, these fibers are also excellent for insulating garments when so engineered.

Silk. Silk, too, goes far back in history. It is said that silk was discovered in 2640 B.C. by a Chinese princess who was studying the formation of the silkworm cocoon. Ever since its discovery, silk has been considered a most important fiber for fashion fabrics. In fact, the ancient Chinese guarded the production of silk and decreed death to anyone who revealed the secret.

The silkworm forms **silk** by forcing two fine streams of a thick liquid out of tiny openings in its head. These fine streams harden into filaments upon contact with the air. The worm then winds the silk around itself. It thus forms a complete covering, or cocoon, as protection during its change from worm into moth. Amazingly, up to 1,600 yards of this continuous fiber are wound into a cocoon by the silkworm. To keep this silk in one continuous length, most of the worms are intentionally killed by heat before they are ready to leave their cocoons. A few moths are allowed to break out of the cocoon, however, to produce eggs for the next crop of silk. Because of the exclusive mulberry-leaf diet and the climate preferences of the cultivated silkworm, China, Japan, and Italy are the world's principal producers of silk fiber.

Silk fabrics all but disappeared from the United States during and after World War II but have recently made a dramatic comeback. Consumers once again yearn for the luxurious look and feel of silk. Many consumers are willing to forgo the easy-care advantages of other fabrics for the glamorous and luxurious qualities that are to be found only in real silk.

Flax. **Linen** is a fabric made from fibers contained within and processed from the stem of the flax plant. Only after the flax fiber is spun into yarn and/or woven or knit into fabric is it actually called linen.

Flax is generally considered to be the oldest known textile fiber, having been used in the Stone Age. It may have been first cultivated for its food value but was soon used for its fiber as well. Materials made of linen were used by the ancient Egyptians to wrap mummies.

The cultivation of flax spread throughout Europe into Asia and to the Americas. During colonial times, flax was a popular crop in this country. It dwindled rapidly in importance after the invention of the cotton gin made cotton cheaper to produce. Today, flax for linen fiber is grown mainly in Ireland and Belgium. In the United States flax is grown primarily for the oil yielded by its seeds.

Flax, which is mainly composed of cellulose, has a fiber length that averages from 6 to 20 inches. This means that linen fabrics are lint-free because there are no short fibers. Flax is the strongest of the vegetable fibers (twice as strong as cotton) and, like cotton, absorbs moisture and dries quickly. This makes linen, too, a good fabric for hot weather apparel, but one that requires a good deal of care.

THE MAN-MADE FIBER INDUSTRIES.

Unlike natural fibers, which can be traced back thousands of years, the oldest of the man-made fibers will not reach its one. hundredth birthday for some years to come.

There are three broad classifications:

1. Cellulosic
   Rayons

2. Cellulose esters
   a. Acetate
   b. Triacetate

3. Noncellulosic
   a. Petroleum plastic
      (1) Nylon
      (2) Polyester
      (3) Acrylic
      (4) Olefin
      (5) Modacrylic
      (6) Spandex
   b. Mineral
      (1) Fiberglass
      (2) Carbon fiber
      (3) Asbestos

Cellulosics, Cellulose Esters, and Noncellulosics.

Cellulose is the main constituent of all plant tissues and fibers. The fiber industry derives most of its cellulose from spruce pulp and other soft woods. **Cellulose esters** are plastics derived from cellulose; for example, acetates. **Noncellulosic** fibers are made from chemical derivations of petroleum, like nylon and polyester, or from minerals, like Fiberglass.

All man-made fibers, cellulosic and noncellulosic, start out as thick liquids. Fibers of continuous, indefinite lengths are produced by forcing the liquid through the tiny holes of a mechanical device known as a **spinnerette.** This is much the same way that spaghetti is made out of dough, or that the silkworm produces its fibers. These fibers are called **filaments.** Filament fibers may be cut into short lengths and spun into yarn, as are natural fibers, or may be directly drawn together into a

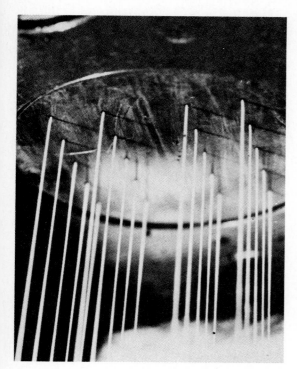
Manmade fibers are produced by forcing thick liquids through a spinnerette.

yarn. In the latter case, filament fiber and yarn production are therefore simultaneous.

The growth of the man-made fiber industry in the United States has been rapid and provides an outstanding example of technological advancement. The total textile consumption figures for fibers in the United States from 1962 through 1987 (projected) forecast an increase in consumption by 100 percent in a 25-year period—from 7 billion pounds in 1962 to 14 billion pounds in 1987.[2] These test-tube fibers have changed the face of fashion. They have also helped change the living habits of the entire American public.

Organization and Operation

Because of the vast differences in the origin and characteristics of various fibers, the fiber industries do not have uniform patterns of organization or operation. Although there may be similarity within groups, the practices of the natural fiber industry differ markedly from those of the man-made fiber industry.

THE NATURAL FIBER INDUSTRIES.

There are four major areas of cotton production in the United States: the Southeast, the Mississippi Delta, the Texas-Oklahoma Panhandle, and the far Southwestern states of New Mexico, Arizona, and California.

Nearly all cotton growers sell their product in local markets, either to mill representatives or, more likely, to wholesalers. The cotton wholesalers then bargain at central markets in Memphis, New Orleans, Dallas, and Houston. Many of these transactions may also take place in New York and Chicago, although the actual cotton goods are not on hand.

The wool produced in this country comes from relatively small sheep ranches in the Western states. But Boston remains the major central marketplace for wool, both domestic and imported.

Both cotton growers and sheep ranchers have been greatly affected by the advent of man-made fibers. Consumers have become accustomed to fabrics made of fibers specifically created to provide whatever qualities they demand. Cotton and wool producers now must pay close attention to consumers' needs and wants. They attempt to develop and promote in their products those characteristics that will command the best prices in the marketplace. Cotton farmers try to grow more cotton and cotton of a better quality on each acre. Sheep farmers try to develop hardier breeds that will produce larger quantities of high-quality wool per clipping.

As man-made fibers continue to grow in usage, the cotton- and wool-fiber industries continue to compete.

THE MAN-MADE FIBER INDUSTRIES.

Obviously, climate and terrain have nothing to do with the production of a man-made fiber. Indeed, chemical plants are extremely adaptable, requiring only supplies of raw chemicals, power, and labor. Chemical companies have thus erected their plants in every part of the United States—up and down the East Coast, in the South, the Midwest, and increasingly on the West Coast. Operations are located wherever companies have found raw materials or railroads and waterways for convenient shipment of those materials. Most of these plants are huge.

With man-made fibers, it is also possible for the producing plant to serve as its own market. It purchases fibers from chemical companies, spins them into yarn and then knits or weaves the yarn into fabric. Burlington Industries, J. P. Stevens, Dan River, and Milliken are just a few of the giants that consolidate all operations, from spun yarn manufacture to finished fabric.

Fiber Development. Limited quantities of a new or modified man-made fiber are usually first produced in a pilot plant on an experimental basis. If research indicates that both industry and consumers will accept the new product, additional plant capacity is allocated. New applications of the fiber are then explored and new industries are consulted and encouraged to use it.

While this procedure is going on in one chemical company, there is always the possibility that another company may be working along similar lines to develop a competitive fiber. The company that is first to develop a new fiber has no assurance that it will have the field to itself for long. There are many brands of such man-made fibers as nylon, rayon, and acetate on the market and a roster of companies producing various acrylics and polyesters. For example, acrylic fibers are produced by Du Pont as Orlon, by Monsanto as Acrilan, by American Cyanamid as Creslan, and by Badische as Zefran. These various companies all have unique specialty variants of the basic acrylic.

Consumer products in which textile fibers are incorporated are required by federal law (the Textile Fibers Products Identification Act of 1960) to bear labels specifying their fiber content by generic name and percentage of each that is used. The brand name or trademark of any of the fibers contained may also be stated, although this is not required by law.

Fiber Distribution.   There are three ways in which producers of man-made fibers usually sell their fibers to fabric manufacturers:

1. As unbranded products, with no restrictions placed on their end use and no implied or required standards of performance claimed.
2. As branded or trademarked fibers, with assurance to consumers that the quality of the fiber has been controlled by its producer, but not necessarily with assurance as to either implied or required standards of performance in the end product.
3. Under a licensing agreement, whereby the use of the fiber trademark concerned is permitted only to those manufacturers whose fabrics or other end products pass tests set up by the fiber producer for their specific end uses or applications.

Licensing programs set up by different fiber producers and by processors of yarn vary considerably in scope. The more comprehensive programs entail extensive end-use testing to back up the licensing agreement. They exercise considerable control over fabric products that have been licensed and offer technical services to help correct a fabric that fails to pass a qualifying test. Trademarks used under such licensing agreements are referred to as **licensed trademarks.** Celanese's Fortrel is an example of a licensed trademark.

Licensing programs may involve wear tests as well as laboratory tests. They also may specify blend levels, requiring, for example, that a minimum percentage of the designated fiber be contained in the yarn to qualify the product for licensing. Checking products periodically through retail shopping is not unusual.

TABLE 6-1 Man-made Fibers and Major Trade Names

Acetate	Nylon	Olefin	Polyester (cont.)
Acetate by Avtex	A.C.E.	Herculon	Strialine
Ariloft	Anso	Herculon Nouvelle	Trevira
Avron	Antron	Marvess	Ultra Glow
Celanese	Blue "C"	Patlon	Ultra Touch
Chromspun	Cadon		
Estron	Cantrece	**Polyester**	**Rayon**
Loftura	Caprolan	A.C.E.	Absorbit
	Captiva	Avlin	Avril
Acrylic	Celanese	Caprolan	Avsorb
Acrilan	Cordura	Crepesoft	Beau-Grip
Bi-Loft	Courtaulds Nylon	Dacron	Coloray
Creslan	Cumuloft	Encron	Courcel
Fi-lana	Eloquent Luster	Fortrel	Courtaulds HT Rayon
Orlon	Eloquent Touch	Golden Glow	Courtaulds Rayon
Pa-Qel	Enkacrepe	Golden Touch	Durvil
Remember	Enkalon	Hollofil	Enkaire
So-Lara	Enkalure	Kodaire	Enkrome
Zefkrome	Enkasheer	Kodel	Fibro
Zefran	Lurelon	KodOfill	Rayon by Avtex
	Multisheer	KodOlite	Zantrel
Aramid	Natural Luster	KodOsoff	
Kevlar	Natural Touch	Lethasuede	**Spandex**
Nomex	Shareen	Matte Touch	Lycra
	Shimmereen	Natural Touch	
Modacrylic	Softalon	Plyloc	**Triacetate**
SEF	T.E.N.	Polyextra	Arnel
	Ultron	Shanton	
	Zefran	Silky Touch	**Vinyon**
	Zeftron		Vinyon by Avtex

Source: Man-Made Fibers—A New Guide, Man-Made Fiber Producers Association, Inc., 1984, p. 6.

Merchandising and Marketing Activities

No matter how familiar fashion fabric and apparel producers and consumers may be with the qualities of each fiber, there is always the need to disseminate information about the newest modifications and their application to fashion merchandise. To do this, producers of both natural and man-made fibers make extensive use of advertising, publicity, and market research. They also extend various customer services to manufacturers, retailers, and consumers.

Usually a producer of man-made fibers, such as Celanese or Monsanto, undertakes these activities on behalf of its own individual brands and companies. The Man-Made Fiber Producers Association also carries on a very active program of consumer education about man-made fibers in general. Producers of natural fibers, on the other hand, carry on related activities through trade associations, each presenting a particular natural fiber. Examples are the National Cotton Council (the central organization of the cotton industry), Cotton Incorporated (the group specializing in promoting the use of cotton by designers and manufacturers), the American Wool Council, the Wool Bureau, and the Mohair Council of America.

ADVERTISING AND PUBLICITY. Both man-made and natural fibers are advertised and publicized, but man-made fiber producers put considerably more dollars into the merchandising effort than do natural fiber trade associations. They maintain a continuous flow of competitive advertising and publicity directed at both the trade and consumers. Sometimes an advertising and publicity effort will concern the entire range of textile fibers made by a single producer. Sometimes it will concentrate on a single fiber and its characteristics.

Among the trade publications used by the man-made fiber producers are *Women's Wear Daily, M,* and the *Daily News Record.* Serving as consumer media are mass-circulation magazines and newspapers as well as radio and television. Some giant man-made fiber producers use national television to publicize their brand name and get their fashion message across to consumers.

Since the names of major fibers are relatively well known today, an increasing number of man-made fiber producers now emphasize the qualities of their products rather than the names of fibers. An outstanding example is Monsanto. The company has used almost every medium including television to publicize its "Wear-Dated" licensed trademark program. The basis of this program is a guarantee that not only the fabric, but also the buttons, belts, buckles, zippers, lining, padding, thread, and all other appurtenances used in the construction of a garment labeled "Wear-Dated" will give satisfactory normal wear for one full year, or Monsanto will provide the customer with either a refund or a replacement.

Although natural fibers are not advertised and promoted as aggressively as man-made fibers, some natural-fiber groups are putting more effort and money into campaigns to combat the growing domination of man-made fibers. Because these campaigns are mainly handled by trade groups, they promote the fiber itself, not the products of an individual natural fiber producer. One of the most eye-catching campaigns is that of Cotton Incorporated. The ads and posters not only underline cotton's advantageous characteristics as a fiber but also point to the cotton industry's importance in the economy and to cotton's ecological appeal.

Fiber sources also provide garment producers and retailers with various aids that facilitate mention of their fibers in consumer advertising. This adds impact to the recognition already achieved by the fiber producer's name, trademark, slogan, or logotype. For example, the Wool Bureau encourages the use of its ball-of-yarn logotype in producer and retailer advertising of all-wool merchandise, as well as in displays.

To facilitate mention of fashion and fiber in the media, producers and trade associations continually provide the press with newsworthy information, background material, and photographs for editorial features. Some of this publicity effort is accomplished by direct contact with the press; some of it is done by supplying garment producers and retailers with glossy photographs and swatches to enhance the efforts. A familiar example of fashion publicity on behalf of a natural fiber is the National Cotton Council's annual Maid of Cotton program. A beauty queen is selected to make appearances throughout the United States in a fashionable cotton wardrobe designed by famous designers.

Another form of fiber advertising and publicity is the development of seasonal fashion presentations for use by retail stores. Publicity kits and programs specially prepared for local markets are developed. The objective is to support promotions during peak retail selling periods.

Advertising is also undertaken by fiber producers in cooperation with fabric and garment manufacturers and retailers. Such **coopera-**

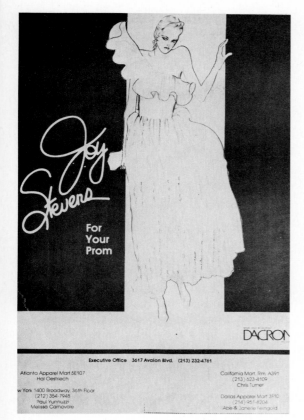

Garment producers and retailers often choose a fiber that offers them cooperative advertising.

tive advertising, for which the costs are shared by a store and one or more producers on terms mutually agreed to, benefits the fiber in two ways. First, consumers begin to associate the fiber name with other names already familiar, such as the name of the fiber source or the name of the retail store selling the garment. This is particularly important when a fiber is man-made and still new. Second, fabric and garment producers as well as retailers are encouraged to use and promote the fiber because of the fringe benefit they get in the form of subsidized local or national advertising.

RESEARCH AND DEVELOPMENT.
Both natural fiber producers and man-made fiber producers are constantly seeking ways to improve their products. The large man-made fiber producers handle research and development mainly on an individual company basis. The natural fiber producers, because of the small size of the average company, often work through group efforts.

The research facilities of the giant chemical companies engineer both existing and new fibers to meet the fashion and performance demands of their expanding and varied markets. The producers of man-made fibers are particularly active in instructing the fabric industry in the manipulation of new yarns, in developing optimum blends and constructions, in improving dyeing and finishing techniques, and in evaluating consumer reaction to the fabrics made from their fibers. Technical bulletins on the proper methods of processing their fibers are issued to the trade. These are supplemented by available expert advice on specific problems relating to yarn, fabric, or garment production.

Producers of natural fibers have increased their research activities in recent years in attempts to impart to their fibers, yarns, and textiles such qualities as dimensional stability, crease retention, wrinkle resistance, luster or matte finish, washability, and any other characteristics that improve their acceptance. For example, some man-made fibers offer dimensional stability, or shrink and stretch resistance. Wool and cotton can also offer this characteristic when they are woven into cloth if the fabric is preshrunk. Similarly, wash-and-wear and crease-resistant properties, formerly found only in fabrics made from certain man-made fibers, can now be offered in fabrics made of cotton, wool, and flax, primarily as the result of topical chemical finishes.

CUSTOMER SERVICES.
All major producers of man-made fibers and many smaller firms offer a number of services to direct and secondary users of their products. Producers of natural fibers, working through their associa-

tions, also offer many such services. These include:

- Technical advice to yarn and textile mills as well as to garment producers.
- Assistance to textile and garment producers and retailers in locating sources of supply.
- "Libraries" of fabrics that can be examined by manufacturers, retailers, and the fashion press, with information supplied about where to buy these fabrics, what to pay for them, and what delivery to expect.
- Fashion advice and information to the textile industry, retailers, and the public.
- Fashion exhibits, sometimes open to the public, for manufacturers and retailers.
- Extensive literature for manufacturers, retailers, educators, and consumers about fiber properties, use, and care.
- Fashion experts and clothing and textile home economists to address groups of manufacturers, retailers, or consumers, staging appropriate fashion shows and demonstrations.
- Educational films and audiovisual aids for use by the trade, schools, and consumer groups.
- Assistance to retail stores in staging promotions of garments in which one or more of the promoted fibers are used.
- Textile processing experts to help solve problems involving fabric production; similarly qualified experts to help solve problems in the production of apparel and accessories.

Trends in the Fiber Industries

The relative importance of different fibers in the total production of textiles has changed gradually but significantly in recent years.

Even among man-made fibers, it is becoming increasingly clear that the man-made synthetics have a more promising future than man-made cellulosics. However, the growth of the industry will be in technological advances concentrated in innovation and improvement for already existing fibers rather than in brand-new generic fibers.[3]

Many market executives agree that the United States must become more competitive in world markets in order for the fiber industry to survive. This conclusion is based on the belief that world apparel needs in 1985, projected to be 7 billion pounds greater than in 1979, will originate *primarily outside* the United States.[4]

THE TEXTILE FABRIC INDUSTRY

Americans use textiles! We consume nearly 60 pounds of textile products a year—each of us! This is about twice what the Western Europeans use and as much as 10 times that of other countries around the globe. We depend on textiles for clothing, for home furnishings, for transportation, for industry, for defense, for health care, for space exploration, and for recreation.

The range of apparel uses in the United States, however, is far greater than just fashion apparel. Doctors, nurses, and medical technicians must have sanitary gowns. Workwear uniforms are a very large business. Garage mechanics, steelworkers, restaurant waiters and waitresses, and airline flight attendants, to name a few, all have functional, and in many cases stylish, attire.

Midway between the fiber and the finished fashion apparel is the fabric, the basic material out of which the garment or accessory is made. **Textile fabric** is cloth or material made from yarn by one of the following methods: weaving, knitting, braiding, crocheting, knotting, laminating, or bonding. Each method may go through a period of popularity; however, today most textile fabrics are either woven or knitted.

The production of most fabrics begins with the production of yarn from fibers. **Yarn** is a continuous thread formed by spinning or twisting fibers together. Fibers cannot be made into fabrics; they must first be made into yarn (exceptions to this are the process of felting and the production of nonwovens such as Pellon interfacing). Yarns are made into **greige goods,** or unfinished fabrics. Greige goods (pronounced "gray goods") are converted into finished fabrics for industrial or consumer use.

History and Development

The earliest step toward mechanization in the textile fabric industry was in the production of yarn, when the spinning wheel was introduced into Europe from India around the sixth century. Even with this, spinning remained a slow, tedious process and a home occupation for centuries thereafter. Then in the eighteenth century, the British worked out mechanical methods of spinning cotton fibers into yarn. By 1779, Hargreaves, Arkwright, and Crompton each had made a contribution toward the modern factory production of yarn.

When the British worked out machine methods of spinning fibers into yarns, they were confronted with quantities of yarn much larger than hand-operated looms could use. Mechanization of the loom, which weaves the yarn into cloth, became necessary. The first power loom was invented by an English clergyman, Dr. Edward Cartwright, and patented in 1785. It used water as a source of energy.

The same sequence of mechanization was

Before the days of mechanization, hand looms like the one shown top left wove the yarn into cloth.

true on this side of the Atlantic. In 1790, Samuel Slater established a yarn mill in Pawtucket, Rhode Island. A present-day giant in the textile field, J. P. Stevens and Company, is descended from Slater's famous mill. For some time, however, fabric production remained both a hand operation and a home industry, totally inadequate to meet the demand for apparel fabrics. Then, Francis Cabot Lowell, a New Englander, visited a textile factory in England and memorized the detailed specifications of its power-operated machinery. In 1814 Lowell built the first successful power loom and the first textile fabric mill in the United States.

The demands of a rapidly growing country provided an eager market for the output of U. S. textile mills, and the young industry flourished. Automation and mechanization techniques developed both here and abroad have greatly advanced production procedures. Today it is possible for a single operator to oversee as many as 100 weaving machines if the fabric is plain.

Organization and Operation

Textile companies are highly diversified. Many are large corporations employing thousands of workers while even more are small operations with only a few dozen employees. In total, there are over 6,000 separate firms and 7,200 plants. Many of these plants are located in small towns or even out in the countryside.[5] See Table 6-2.

In 1981, annual sales of all textile products amounted to the staggering figure of $47.3 billion. Of the 900,000 people employed in the textile industry, 17 percent are minorities, compared to a national average of 11 percent in all manufacturing. Women number 47 percent of the work force, as opposed to 31 percent in all manufacturing.[6]

Textile mills are widely dispersed throughout the country. The industry has tended to seek areas where labor and land costs are low. There has also been little advantage in concentrating production in any one area through the construction of giant mills or complexes. A small mill can operate about as efficiently as a large one, since textile machinery has a long useful life and output can be increased by having two or three shifts. There used to be some concentration of textile mills in the northeastern states, but in recent years the southeastern part of the country has offered cheaper labor and land.

Because commitments to specific weaves,

TABLE 6-2 The 10 Largest Publicly Held U.S. Textile Companies	
NAME	ANNUAL SALES (MILLIONS OF DOLLARS)
Burlington	$2,876,205
J. P. Stevens	1,814,315
West Point Pepperell	1,110,573
Springs Industries	874,512
Collins & Aikman	669,122
Cone Mills	608,201
United Merchants & Manufacturers	561,446
M. Lowenstein & Sons	536,650
Dan River	519,124
Fieldcrest Mills	491,018

Source: "Fortune 500 Industrial Corporations," *Fortune*, May 2, 1983, pp. 228–246.

colors, and finishes must be made far in advance, the textile fabric industry is extremely well informed about fashion and alert to incoming trends. Information about these trends comes from fashion designers, predictive services, fashion directors for fiber or yarn companies, and advance textile shows throughout the world. But because they are geared to mass-production methods, most mills are reluctant to produce short experimental runs for individual designers.

The market centers for textile fabrics are not at the mills but in the fashion capital of the country, New York City. There, on the doorstep of the garment industry, every mill of importance has a salesroom. A fabric buyer or designer for a garment maker, or a retail store apparel buyer or fashion coordinator, only has to walk a block or two to obtain firsthand information on what the fabric market offers.

TYPES OF MILLS.   Some mills sort and select the fibers to be used, spin them into yarn, then weave or knit them and finish the fabric. Finishing may include dyeing, napping, adding fire retardants, glazing, waterproofing, and pressing. It may also include treating the fabric to ensure such attributes as nonshrinkage and permanent press. Fashion influences decisions every step of the way.

Some mills produce only the yarn. Others weave or knit fabric from purchased yarn but do not carry the process beyond the greige state. There are also plants that bleach, dye, preshrink, print, or in other ways impart desired characteristics to fabrics produced by other mills. The plants that handle the various stages may or may not be under common ownership, and may or may not be geographically close.

For deeper and richer color, yarns may be dyed before being woven or knitted (yarn-dyed). However, most fabrics are knitted or woven first and then dyed (piece-dyed) because this process gives manufacturers maximum flexibility for a given color as fashion requires.

Many mills no longer limit themselves to working with yarns made of a single fiber. Fibers may be used alone or with other fibers, as demand dictates. Any of the types of mills described above may combine a natural fiber with another natural fiber, or, more commonly, a natural fiber with a man-made fiber, to achieve a desired effect. Examination of the fiber content labels on garments will show how widespread the man-made fibers are.

THE CONVERTER.   It is probably correct to say that the textile converter is the real middleman of the textile industry. **Textile converters** buy greige goods from the mills, have the goods processed to order by the finishing plants, and then sell the finished goods to garment makers. Therefore, textile converters must be on top of trends in colors, patterns, and finishes. They must fully understand fashion and must be able to anticipate demand. Converters work very quickly since they come on the production scene toward the end of the operation, and are primarily interested in the finish and texture applied to the greige goods.

In recent years, converters' know-how has helped American textile producers meet the competition of foreign textile producers who offer more fashion-oriented goods in small yardages. Converters can supply apparel producers with fewer yards of selected fabrics than can larger fabric mills. The latter must produce tremendous yardages of a designated pattern or design in order to maintain a profitable operation. While many converters are truly small operators, others, such as Everfast, Cohn-Hall-Marx, and M. Lowenstein, are large.

Merchandising and Marketing Activities

It is said that fabric precedes fashion. This means that dress designers, for example, cannot create a garment unless they find just the right cloth. It must drape the way they want

America's Freedom Fabric

Visa

Fabric that cares for itself. And you.

FORTREL® polyester

FASHION FOCUS

FORTREL POLYESTER FIBER AND VISA FABRIC: A TALE OF TWO PROMOTIONS

Man-made fiber and fabric manufacturers maintain a flow of competitive advertising directed at both the trade and consumers. Two recent campaigns, one for a single fiber and one for a fabric, illustrate the extensive (and expensive) nature of such advertising and promotion.

An example of fashion publicity on behalf of a man-made fiber was the method Celanese used in 1982 to upgrade the image of its polyester fiber, Fortrel. Seeking to bury the double knit image of polyester, Celanese fashioned a consumer education program that included an advertising and publicity campaign whose theme was "Look what polyester is doing now." Such outstanding fashion designers as John Weitz, Vera Maxwell, Dimitri, and Don Simonelli praised polyester as a wonderful fiber with which to work. Celanese also used Nolan Miller, costume designer for pop-

it to and have the colors and textures needed to give the desired form to the design.

Since the textile fabric industry must work several seasons ahead of consumer demand, it must be early in recognizing the direction that fashion is taking. Textile firms employ staffs of fashion experts who attend market openings around the world. They work with designers to create fabrics in those weights, textures, colors, and patterns that they anticipate consumers will want. And they do this two to three seasons, or some 12 to 18 months, before the garments made of those fabrics will appear in stores.

Many textile fairs are held throughout the world. Two textile fairs of worldwide importance are the Interstoff Textile Fair, held in Frankfurt, West Germany, and the Ideacomo, held in Como, Italy. These fairs are held semiannually and show and project trends in texture and color for the upcoming two years. Other well-known foreign textile fairs are Pre-

miere Vision, held in Paris, and Texitalia, held in Milan, Italy. For the past few years, fabric producers from individual countries have shown in America, among them the British Woolens Fair Show and the Japan Wool Exhibition.

The importance of identifying the dominant trend at a major textile fair becomes more important each year as competition becomes more keen, not only between competitors within this country, but from foreign textile companies all over the world. Failure by textile producers to identify and act upon a trend seen at a major textile fair can mean that retailers and apparel producers will be unable to supply the fashions consumers want.

ADVERTISING AND PUBLICITY. Large fabric manufacturers advertise lavishly. Their advertising features the brand names of their products and frequently the names of specific apparel manufacturers that use their goods. Ei-

ular television shows such as *Dynasty* and *The Love Boat*, to be the Celanese spokesperson to plug Fortrel polyester in public appearances on radio and television. Celanese also set up the Meridian Award as part of its promotion. The award was presented to successful women who regard polyester as an integral feature in their lifestyle, and the first so honored were Liza Minnelli, Barbara Walters, Liv Ullmann, and Jeane Kirkpatrick, United States ambassador to the United Nations.

An example of fabric advertising and publicity was the promotion by the Milliken Company for its Visa fabric in 1983. Based upon the research study undertaken in 1980–1981, Milliken determined that consumers were concerned about the impact of foreign goods on American manufacturers and were becoming more conscious of "Made in America" labels. New labels for Visa, calling it "America's Freedom Fabric," were distributed to all manufacturers that used Visa fabric. This was done in conjunction with Du Pont,

whose Dacron fiber was used in the manufacture of Visa fabric. Commercials featuring apparel made of Visa fabric appeared on all the TV networks and stations. Information-filled print advertising of all products of Visa appeared in magazines such as *Family Circle, People, Woman's Day,* and *Sports Illustrated*.

The success of both the Celanese Fortrel fiber and Milliken Visa fabric promotions depended heavily on getting each company's message across to the ultimate consumers. It is because the manmade fiber and fabric industries recognize the importance of keeping consumers aware of the innovations of their industries that they devote vast amounts of money to advertising and promotion.

This Fashion Focus is based on information from these sources:

Marvin Klopper "Polyester" *Women's Wear Daily,* November 8, 1983, p. 6.

"Polyester Out to Sport New Image" *Advertising Age,* November 8, 1983, p. 56.

ther with the cooperation of fiber sources or on their own, these fabric houses sponsor radio and television programs, run full-color advertisements in a wide variety of mass-circulation magazines and newspapers, and share the cost of brand advertising run by retail stores. Their advertising generally makes consumers aware of new apparel styles, the fabrics of which they are made, and often the names of retail stores where they may be purchased.

Fabric producers compete among themselves for the business of apparel producers. They also compete for recognition among retail store buyers and for consumer acceptance of products made of their goods. They publicize brand names and fabric developments, and stage seasonal fashion shows in market areas for retailers and the fashion press. They provide hang-tags for the use of garment manufacturers. These tags may bear not only the fabric's brand name but also instructions relating to its care. In accordance with federal reg-

ulation, fabric producers also supply manufacturers with the required care labels that must be permanently sewn into all garments. Many fabric firms supply information to consumers and the trade press. Many also make educational materials available to schools, consumer groups, and retail sales personnel.

RESEARCH AND DEVELOPMENT. Fabric producers, like fiber producers, now devote attention to exploring the market potential of their products and anticipating the needs of their customers. Success in the fashion industry depends on supplying customers with what they want. Swift changes are the rule in fashion. Anticipation of such changes requires close attention to the market and a scientific study of trends.

Many of the large fabric producers maintain product- and market-research divisions. Their experts work closely with both the trade and consumer markets in studying fabric performance characteristics. Many fabric producers provide garment manufacturers with sample runs of new fabrics for experimental purposes. The market researchers conduct consumer studies relating to the demand for or acceptance of finishes, blends, and other desired characteristics. Such studies also help fabric and garment producers to determine what consumers will want in the future, where and when they will want it, and in what quantities.

CUSTOMER SERVICES. Today's well-integrated and diversified textile companies speak with great fashion authority. They also employ merchandising and marketing staffs whose expertise in fashion trends is available to apparel manufacturers, retailers, the fashion press, and frequently to consumers. Fashion staffs attend fashion forecasts. They conduct in-store sales training programs, address consumer groups, and stage fashion shows for the trade and press. They help retail stores arrange fashion shows and storewide promotions featuring their products, and they assist buyers in locating merchandise made from their fabrics.

TRENDS IN THE TEXTILE INDUSTRY

The decade of the 1990s will produce much change in the textile industry. Some of it is predictable, but a great deal will depend on political and economic climates that are difficult to predict.

The consumption rate of textiles is increasing over the years and most economists forecast this trend to continue and surpass even the great growth of the last decade. The role of textiles in the U.S. economy is a very important one. The fiber/textile/apparel industries employ one out of every nine Americans working in manufacturing. The earning power of these employees has been estimated at $100 billion each year. The impact of this earning power on other industries in turn is also great—on food, housing, transportation. This alone

makes textiles one of the nation's most essential economic resources.

World conditions are uncertain, and within the U.S. textile industry there is concern about proliferating imports of foreign goods and burgeoning federal regulations for employee safety and environmental protection. (Of course, from the standpoint of labor and the general population, these regulations can be seen as positive measures.)

Expanded mechanization and automation have changed the industry from a labor-intensive to a capital-intensive one. Increased foreign operations, increased international trade, and greater diversification of products will be needed in order for the U.S. textile industry to increase its share of the world market and economy in the 1990s.

Expanded Mechanization and Automation

The trend toward the use of more machinery and less labor is apparent at all levels in the production of textile fibers and fabrics.

In the cotton fields, a new mechanical picker can harvest 500 times as much cotton lint as a worker who picks the lint from the plants by hand. In the mills, machinery has been re-equipped with more efficient motors, and new machines are bought on the basis of low energy consumption as well as high production speeds. Automated weaving and knitting machines operate at increasingly higher speeds and require fewer operators.

The dawn of the 1980s saw the computer revolutionize the dyeing and printing of fabrics. One incredibly fast system transfers the computerized designs from a television screen directly onto the fabrics. Other electronic systems make it possible for a firm's management to determine the cost price of fabrics before they are knitted or woven.

During the 1980s, innovations and experimentations in robot efficiency and production proved to the industry that there was a place and a need for the added efficiency and time-saving abilities of the new robotic technology. Looking toward the 1990s, robots are expected to enter the work force in all segments of the textile industry.

All of this means a reduction in labor costs, in human errors, and in production time. It means improved productivity per work hour, greater standardization of product, and better quality control.

Increased Foreign Expansion

Another trend, limited to fabric producers, is toward the acquisition or establishment of mills abroad. Such foreign-based mills may be wholly owned by a U.S. firm or may be jointly owned by a U.S. firm and a host-country firm. Most mills are located close to the fiber sources. The engineers may be American or American-trained, but the rest of the staff usually consists of local workers who are paid according to local wage scales. Advantages to the host-country firm are the availability of the facilities, the fashion knowledge, the technical skill of the U.S. owners or part owners, and increased employment opportunities for its citizens. By producing some goods abroad, domestic manufacturers are able to defend themselves against the competition of foreign-made fabrics. They can also put themselves in a more favorable position to sell in countries where tariff walls limit or keep out goods made in the United States.

Another trend involves foreign business firms buying into fabric or finishing plants here. Some of these firms are becoming partners in, or sole owners of, new facilities being built here. One of the world's largest chemical companies—larger even than Du Pont—is the West German-owned Hoechst Group. This company employs 9,000 Americans in 19 states and registers over $900 million in sales here. It makes a diversified group of products, from the polyester fiber Trevira to Foster Grant Sunglasses.

Increased International Trade and Exporting

Directing efforts toward more international business is seen as the key to survival for the American textile industry. A number of corporate strategies for the years ahead include:

- Increasing focus on foreign markets and operations for apparel fabrics, since most studies indicate that the major growth in apparel markets will be outside the United States.

- Developing overseas manufacturing operations, or exploring licensing in conjunction with foreign mills, in order to attain a stronger foothold on the international scene.

- Devoting increased resources to market research.

For example, the United States is currently a world leader in home furnishing textiles, offering more diversified products than any other country. In an attempt to expand this trade, the U.S. textile industry is focusing more of its manufacturing and marketing activities abroad on fabrics for home furnishing and industrial end uses, which are projected to gain larger market shares in the future. The recently enacted Trading Companies Act should significantly assist in increasing export opportunities for the U.S. textile industry. This act was designed to protect American exporters from world currency fluctuations when competing internationally.[7]

Greater Diversification of Products

Today, the textile industry produces a more diversified range of fibers and fabrics than ever before. The specialization that once divided the industry into separate segments, each producing fabrics from a single type of fiber, has all but faded. To meet the needs of consumers, it is often necessary to blend two or more fibers into a yarn or to combine a warp yarn of one fiber with a weft yarn of another. Mills are learning to adjust their operations to any new fiber or combination of fibers. Illustrating the importance of blends is the trademark developed by Cotton Incorporated that is used on fabrics containing 60 percent or more cotton fiber but not 100 percent cotton. The Wool Bureau introduced a trademark for fabrics made of a fiber blend of at least 50 percent wool. (See page 104.)

Two of the largest firms in the field illustrate how the industry is moving toward greater product diversification. Burlington, originally a rayon mill specializing in bedspreads, now produces and sells spun and textured yarns of both natural and man-made fibers. Its products include a wide variety of finished woven and knitted fabrics, some unfinished fabrics, and hosiery for men, women, and children. It also produces a wide variety of domestic and home furnishings, from bed linens to rugs and furniture. Under the J. P. Stevens banner are both cotton and woolen mills. Some produce spun and textured yarns, others produce finished fabrics for both over-the-counter sales and apparel manufacture, and still others produce women's hosiery. Both companies use the major natural fibers and a large number of the man-made fibers available in this country.

Increased Government Regulation

One of the biggest impacts on the textile industry in the last decade has been the intervention of the federal government in every aspect of the industry: health and safety, noise levels and chemical pollution, consumer product liability, environment, and hiring practices.

Until recently, federal regulation of the textile industry was mainly concerned with the fiber content labeling of fabrics and products made of those fabrics. In 1954, the Flammable Fabrics Act was passed, but it served to ban from the market only a few very ignitable fabrics and apparel made from them. The increasing strength and direction of the consumerism movement, however, resulted in more government regulation of the textile industry, on both the federal and state levels.

This fabric label shows the type of care this 100% lambswool fabric requires. It uses international care symbols and many languages.

In July 1972, two important changes in federal textile regulations became effective: the FTC's rule on Care Labeling of Textile Wearing Apparel, and the revision of the Flammable Fabrics Act. The FTC's care-labeling rule requires that all fabrics—piece goods as well as apparel and accessories made of fabric—be labeled to show the type of care they require. The label must indicate whether the fabric can be hand washed or machine washed or should be dry-cleaned. If the fabric can be washed, the label must indicate the temperature at which it should be washed and whether bleach can be used. The label must also indicate whether ironing is required, and if so, at what temperature. The manufacturer must sew a permanent label into each garment.

The following trends in the textile industry are a result of government environmental and consumer regulations:

- Fibers and textile products will be made by larger producers with a resulting decrease in the number of small concerns and marginal operations. This will result primarily from the higher production costs related to complying with the new government regulations and the greater capital investment required to stay competitive in a period of continually rising costs.
- Manufacturing operations will function at higher efficiencies, recycling as much material as possible and converting waste to energy.
- Fibers with built-in environmental disadvantages will slowly give way to more suitable replacements, or new processing techniques will be devised to allow their continued use.
- Transfer printing may be an important way to reduce some of the dye-house stream-pollution problems.
- Consumers will be increasingly protected, with particular emphasis on children's apparel and home furnishings.
- Consumers will be better advised on the characteristics of their purchases.

REFERENCES

[1] Jane Dorner, *Fashion in the Forties and Fifties*, Arlington House, New Rochelle, N. Y., 1975, p. 38.
[2] D. V. Parikh and Shridhar V. Parikh, "Natural vs. Man-made," *America's Textiles*, March 1982, p. 26.
[3] Martha de Llosa, *American Fabrics and Fashions*, Spring 1981, p. 13.
[4] Eileen B. Brill, "Recovery Under Way," *Women's Wear Daily*, April 5, 1983, p. 27.
[5] "The U. S. Textile Industry Is the Largest in the World and Intends to Remain So," *America's Textiles*, August 1982, p. 32H.
[6] Ibid., p. 32D.
[7] Stu Campell, "Study Tells Textile Industry to Pursue International Business," *Daily News Record*, November 22, 1982, p. 12.

MERCHANDISING VOCABULARY

Define or explain each of the following terms:

Cellulose
Cellulose esters
Cooperative advertising
Cotton
Fiber
Filaments
Greige goods
Licensed trademarks
Linen
Man-made fibers

Natural fibers
Noncellulosic
Primary suppliers
Silk
Spinnerette
Textile converters
Textile fabric
Wool
Yarn

1. Why does a student of fashion merchandising need a basic knowledge of textile fibers and fabrics and of their respective industries?
2. Compare and contrast natural and man-made fibers on the basis of the following: (*a*) relative size of their producers, (*b*) location of production facilities, (*c*) predictability of supply, and (*d*) consistent uniformity of product.
3. Trace the steps or stages through which a completely new or newly modified man-made fiber goes from its conception to its general availability.
4. Name and explain the three ways in which producers of man-made fibers usually sell their products to fabric manufacturers.
5. Outline the merchandising/marketing activities of (*a*) producers of both natural and man-made fibers; (*b*) producers of textile fabrics.
6. What are the two most common methods used for transforming fibers into fabrics today? Outline the processes that fibers usually go through in being converted to fabrics.
7. What is the function of a textile converter? What are the advantages of dealing with a converter for (*a*) a fabric mill and (*b*) the apparel trade?
8. What are the trends that are changing the textile industry?
9. Name and describe the provisions of two government regulations that had an important effect on the American textile industry in the past 20 years.
10. What part does the consumer play in the textile industry?

1. What is the role of trade associations in the marketing of fibers and textile products?
2. When Halston designed his Halston III collection for J C Penney, he went directly to the textile mills with specifications for his fabrics in regard to width, pattern repeats, and so on. Can most designers do this? Why or why not?
3. Discuss the relationship of the designer and the manufacturer of fashion merchandise to the textile industry.
4. Discuss the current trends in the textile industry relating to (*a*) expanding use of mechanization and automation, (*b*) increased foreign expansion, and (*c*) greater diversification of products.

7. LEATHER AND FUR

As the twentieth century draws to a close, it is interesting to note that two of today's most up-to-the-minute fashion materials are the very first ones that prehistoric people used—fur and leather. Those earliest "cave people," surviving in a cold and hostile world, soon discovered that the animals they killed for food served yet another purpose. When the animals' skins were removed and cleaned, they were found to provide warmth on the fur side and protection against the elements on the leather side. Soon these prehistoric people not only wrapped themselves in animal skins, but used them as coverings for cold cave floors and for soft bedding.

Today, leather and fur are enjoying an even greater place in the fashion picture. Leathers, which have long been vital to the fashion accessory business for handbags, shoes, and gloves, today are being used for a wide range of high-fashion apparel. New processes have made possible fine leathers so thin and supple that America's designers fashion them into everything from bikinis to blouses to evening wear, in every color of the rainbow!

Meanwhile, the fashion fur industry, after a decade of decline due to changing lifestyles and environmental pressure, has recently experienced a dramatic revival. The demand for fur garments in the United States has never been greater—ranging from the most elegant minks and sables to the 1980s sports and "fun" furs, which appear as jackets, sweaters, vests, or other items of apparel.

THE LEATHER INDUSTRY

Leather making is a time-consuming and very highly specialized process. Because of this time factor, the leather industry has always had to anticipate and predict trends in advance of other fashion material suppliers. Leather producers must decide on which production methods to use to obtain the desired colors, textures, and finishes from 8 to 16 months before the leather is used by apparel and accessory manufacturers. The coordination of colors, textures, finishes, and other fashion variables is vital to the leather industry for a number of reasons. Other fashion producers often look to the leather industry for leadership in color. They also look to this industry in many instances for long-range forecasts relative to textures and finishes.

The process of transforming animal skins into leather is known as **tanning.** The term "tanning" comes from the Latin word for oak bark, the material used in the earliest known treatment of animal skins. Tanning is the oldest craft known. Primitive people not only killed animals for food, but also devised ways to treat the skins for use as body covering. The modern tanning industry receives almost all of its hides as by-products of the meat-packing industry. After these animals have fulfilled their primary function, tanners convert the hides to leather.

History and Development

In the many years that Indian tribes roamed the North American continent, long before the arrival of the first European colonists, the tanning of leather was an important part of tribal life. Indians used deerskins to make clothing, soft yet sturdy moccasins, and tepee homes. By today's tanning standards, their methods would be considered limited and primitive, yet the techniques they used to transform raw animal hides into a variety of products certainly served them well.

In 1623, not long after the arrival of the Pilgrims to Massachusetts, the first commercial tannery in the American colonies was established in Plymouth by an Englishman with the fitting name of Experience Miller. Later Peter Minuit, Governor of New Amsterdam, invented the first machinery used for tanning in the colonies. His invention was a horse-driven stone mill that ground the oak bark then used in converting animal skins into leather.

Many years passed before more important mechanization of the leather industry took place. But in 1809, a giant step was taken. Samuel Parker invented a machine that could split heavy steer hides 25 times faster than men could do by hand. These more rapidly split hides produced a lighter and more supple leather, just what the people wanted for their shoes and boots and other clothing.

Today there are new machines that do much of the manual work formerly required to stir hides and skins as they soaked. Other machines dehair and deflesh them. Still others split the skins and emboss patterns on them. Machinery has taken much of the human labor

Modern machinery has taken much of the heavy labor out of the processing of leather.

out of the processing of leather. In addition, chemistry has provided new tanning agents that reduce the time required to transform hides and skins into leather, and that achieve a greater variety of finishes.

However, even this mechanization has had little effect in reducing the total amount of time needed for the actual tanning process. Prolonged exposure to a series of treatments is a must in the transformation of hides and skins into leather. For example, the production of kid leather takes weeks of actual tanning and finishing. This is in addition to the time required to purchase the skins, ship them to a tannery, receive and inspect them, and start them on their way through the tanning process. The final fashion product, though, reflecting the rich beauty that belongs only to fine leather, certainly proves that all the time taken to achieve that beauty was time well spent.

Organization and Operation

Tanning was once a household industry, and in some of the less developed areas of the world it still is. Today tanning has become a relatively big business in the United States. Nearly 21,000 workers are employed in this country's tanneries, turning out $2 billion worth of leathers a year for widely divergent uses.

The mergers, consolidations, and affiliations prevalent in the textile industry during and immediately following World War II had parallels in the leather industry. In 1870 there were 4,500 tanneries in operation in the United States; today there are fewer than 500. The trends toward mergers and fewer and larger plants continue.

The processes involved in tanning are basically the same as they have been for thousands of years. Although the grease and brains of an animal are no longer used to treat its pelt, tanners still soak pelts to soften them, remove any flesh or hair that may adhere to them, and treat them to retard putrefaction. As recently

as a century or two ago, tanners still relied principally on such natural materials as oak or hemlock bark to process skins. But today tanners have a vast range of chemical and natural agents at their disposal: chrome salts, synthetic tanning agents, and oils, for example. As a result, the variety of colors, textures, and finishes available to the fashion industries today is infinitely greater than it was even 50 years ago. This is true even though the variety of animals whose skins are used has decreased. Some animals have been placed on state, national, and international endangered-species lists and their commercial uses restricted or banned.

ORGANIZATION.   The leather industry in this country is divided into three major types of companies: regular tanneries, contract tanneries, and converters. **Regular tanneries** purchase and process skins and hides and sell the leather as their finished product. **Contract tanneries** process the hides and skins to the specifications of other firms (mainly converters) but are not involved in the final sale of the leather. **Converters** buy the hides and skins from the meat packers, commission the tanning to the contract tanneries, and then sell the finished leather. However, in recent years, converters have been buying finished leather from both regular and contract tanneries.

The leather industry is highly specialized because the methods and materials used vary according to the nature of the hides or skins being treated and the end product for which each is intended. Tanners of calfskin do not normally tan kidskins; tanners of glove leathers do not normally produce sole leather.

Leather is largely a by-product of the meat packing industry in the United States. Its cost has therefore been lower than it would have been had the animals been raised for their skins alone. Some recent developments in world economics, however, have begun to change this. Because of an expanding market for hides in other countries, the trend toward smaller herds of cattle in the United States, and the growing use of leather in apparel and home furnishings markets, U.S. leather hides are becoming very expensive. This is leading to imports of less expensive foreign leather.

Most U.S. tanneries are located in the northeast and north central states. In these regions are also clustered the industry's major customers: shoe, apparel, and accessory manufacturers. Like textile producers, however, most leather firms maintain sales offices or representatives in New York City for the convenience of their customers.

SOURCES OF LEATHER SUPPLY.

Almost all leather comes from cattle. But the hides and skins of many other animals from all parts of the world are also used in fashion. Kid and goatskins come from Europe, Asia, Africa, and South America; capeskin comes from a special breed of sheep raised in South Africa and South America; pigskin comes from the peccary, a wild hog native to Mexico and South America; buffalo comes from Asia.

The variety of glove leathers alone illustrates how worldwide are the sources of leather:

- *Cabretta* from South American sheep
- *Calfskin* from young calves of the United States and elsewhere
- *Goatskin* from South America, South Africa, India, and Spain
- *Kidskin* from Europe
- *Pigskin* from Yugoslavia, Mexico, and Central and South America
- *Buckskin* from deer and elk in Mexico, South and Central America, and the People's Republic of China
- *Mocha* from Asian and African sheep

Over the next few years, the U.S. tanning and leather finishing industries will show a decline in value of shipments, due mainly to lower raw materials prices. The U.S. Commerce Department predicts that total employment in leather-related fields will gradually decline by approximately 5 to 7 percent.

LEATHER PROCESSING. The leather trade divides animal skins into three classes according to weight. Animal skins that weigh 15 pounds or less when shipped to the tannery are referred to as **skins**. Calves, goats, pigs, sheep, and deer are among the animals producing skins. Animal skins weighing from 15 to 25 pounds, such as those from young horses and cattle, are referred to as **kips**. Animal skins weighing over 25 pounds, such as those from cattle, oxen, buffalo, and horses, are referred to as **hides**.

The process by which skins, kips, and hides become leather is a lengthy one. This is one of the many reasons why the leather industry has to work well in advance of demand. Three to six months is usually required for the vegetable tanning of hides for sole leather and saddlery. The time is shorter for kips and skins, but the processes are more numerous, requiring more expensive equipment and more highly skilled labor. Leather for shoe uppers, garments, and accessories is tanned and finished in 3 to 6 weeks. These are chrome-tanned and are overwhelmingly made of cowhide.

Tanning may involve the use of minerals, vegetable materials, oils, or chemicals alone or in combination with other tanning agents. The choice of agent depends mainly upon the end use for which the leather is being prepared.

Minerals. There are two important tanning methods that use minerals. One uses alum; the other uses chrome salts. Alum, used by the ancient Egyptians to make writing paper, is rarely used today. Chrome tanning, introduced in 1893, is now used to process nearly two-thirds of all leather produced in this country. This is a fast method that produces leather for shoe uppers, gloves, handbags, and other products. Chrome-tanned leather can be identified by the pale, blue-gray color in the center of the cut edge. It is slippery when wet. It is usually washable and can be cleaned by sponging.

Vegetable Materials. Vegetable tanning, which is also an old method, uses agents such as tannic acids from the bark, wood, or nuts of various trees and shrubs and from tea leaves. Vegetable tanning is used on cow, steer, horse, and buffalo hides. The product is a heavy, often relatively stiff leather used for the soles of shoes, some shoe uppers, some handbags and belts, and saddlery. Vegetable-tanned leather can be identified by a dark center streak in the cut edge. It is resistant to moisture and can be cleaned by sponging. Vegetable tanning is the slowest tanning method and takes months to complete. Because it is so labor-intensive, there is relatively little vegetable tanning done in the United States.

Oil. Processing with oil is one of the oldest methods of turning raw animal skins into leather. A fish oil—usually codfish—is used. Today, oil tanning is used to produce chamois, doeskin, and buckskin—relatively soft and pliable leathers used in making gloves and jackets.

Chemical. Formaldehyde used in a relatively new process is the most widely used chemical for tanning. This is the quickest method of tanning. The leather is white when tanned and thus can be dyed easily. Leather tanned by formaldehyde is washable and is often used for gloves and children's shoe uppers.

Combinations. It is possible to combine tanning agents. A vegetable and mineral combination, or "retanning," is used for products such as work shoes and boots. Combinations of alum and formaldehyde, and oil and chrome, give leather different qualities.

Merchandising and Marketing Activities

Because of problems in coordinating leather with textile fashions, leather producers do not merely stay abreast of fashion; they must keep ahead of it. As a result, they are among the best and most experienced forecasters in the fashion business. They have to be—especially those who work with the skins or hides of foreign animals. Months before other fashion industries have to commit themselves on matters of color and textures, leather producers have already made their decisions. They have started the search for precisely the right dyes

TABLE 7-1 Special Finishes for Leather	
FINISHES	**CHARACTERISTICS**
Aniline	Polished surface achieved with aniline dyes
Matte (mat)	Flat, eggshell-surface look
Luster or pearl	Soft, opaque finish with a transparent glow
Antiqued	Subtle, two-toned effect like polished antique wood
Burnished	Similar to antiqued, but with less shadowing
Metallic	Surface look of various metals—copper, gold, silver, bronze
Waxy	Dulled, rustic look, as in waxy glove leathers
Patent	Glossy, high-shine finish
Napped	Buffed surface such as in suede or brushed leathers
Suede	Leather finish that can be applied to a wide variety of leathers

Source: William A. Rossi, "What You Should Know About Leathers," *Footwear News Magazine*, June 1982, p. 16.

and treatments to produce what they expect will be in demand in a given future period. The time it takes to transform skins, kips, and hides into leather requires that tanneries project fashion demand several seasons into the future.

FASHION
INFORMATION SERVICES.
Having made their assessments of fashion trends very early, leather tanners, like fiber and fabric producers, share their conclusions with their customers. Individually or through industry associations, tanners retain fashion experts to disseminate this information. These experts advise manufacturers, editors, and retailers on future fashion trends in leather.

A typical activity of leather producers is the preparation of fashion booklets for distribution to manufacturers, retailers, the press, and other interested persons. Such booklets are sometimes available a year or more before consumers are likely to wear or use the leather products described. The booklets include comments on general fashion trends. They describe the leather colors and textures suitable for classics, boutique merchandise, and promotional use. Finally, they include samples of important textures and looks in leather.

Another typical activity of individual producers and industry associations is the assignment of a fashion expert to work with retailers, manufacturers, and the press to help them crystallize their fashion thinking. This service might take the form of individual conferences, of participation on a committee of producers or retailers, or of fashion presentations to industry, retail, or consumer groups.

Yet with all this activity, individual tanners are not known by name to the public. A fashion editor describing a leather garment, glove, or shoe is not likely to mention the leather producer. Nor are leather producers likely to be named in retail store advertising or in the advertising placed by the manufacturers of the finished products. As a result, a consumer who could recall names of several fabric and fiber producers would probably have a hard time naming even one tanner.

TRADE ASSOCIATIONS. Tanners work together to promote their products, through associations that disseminate technical and fashion information to producers, consumers, and the press. Some associations, like the Sole Leather Council and the Auto Leather Guild, strive to promote a particular kind of leather. Others, such as the Tanners' Council, function on an industrywide basis, working to promote all kinds of leather.

Formerly such associations were primarily concerned with serving segments of the market that were already customers. Today their major effort is to broaden the market for all types of leathers. Markets that once used only leather, such as the shoe industry, are now using other products as well, making it necessary for the

Trade associations like the Tanners' Council work to promote the leather industry.

leather industry to defend its frontiers. Markets that traditionally used little leather, such as dresses, skirts, and coats, now are being widely cultivated by the leather industry.

At the retail level, the leather industry's associations are a valuable source of information in fashion planning and selection. They are also an important source of fashion and technical information for salespeople. For consumers, the industry associations provide fashion and technical material which is made available to schools, distributed with merchandise purchased in retail stores, and publicized through the fashion press.

RESEARCH AND DEVELOPMENT. The leather industry retains and expands its markets by adapting its products to fashion's changing requirements. Before World War II, relatively few colors and types of leather were available in any one season, and each usually had a fashion life of several years. Today, a major tannery may turn out hundreds of leather colors and types each season, meanwhile preparing to produce more new colors and textures for the next season.

To protect and expand their markets, leather producers constantly broaden their range of colors, weights, and textures. They also introduce improvements that make leather an acceptable material where it formerly had either limited use or no use at all.

Leather has the weight of tradition behind it; people have regarded fine leather as a symbol of luxury for centuries. But today leather shares its hold on the fashion field with other and newer materials. Through product research and development, producers are attempting to meet the competition not only of other leathers but also of other materials. The Tanners' Council Research Laboratory at the University of Cincinnati and the Eastern Regional Research Laboratory of the U.S. Department of Agriculture in Philadelphia have expanded research efforts on behalf of the in-

dustry. The Tanners' Council has contracted with the U.S. Bureau of Mines for research on chromium in the tanning industry. The objective is to develop improved technology to recycle or recover chromium from tanning wastes.

Industry Trends

Until just a few decades ago, the leather industry concerned itself primarily with meeting consumer needs in relatively few fashion areas—mainly shoes, gloves, belts, handbags, luggage and small leather goods. The use of leather for apparel was restricted largely to a few items of outerwear, such as jackets and coats. These were stiff, bulky, and primarily functional in appeal.

Today, the leather industry is changing. These changes are the result of several trends: enlarging market opportunities, increased competition from synthetics, and increased foreign trade.

ENLARGING MARKETS. Improved methods of tanning are turning out better, more versatile leathers with improved fashion characteristics. In general, these improvements fall into two categories:

1. The new leathers are softer and more pliable. Much of this new suppleness is due to tanners' splitting full-grain leather thinner and thinner.

2. The new leathers can be dyed more successfully in a greater number of fashion colors.

Because of these new characteristics, the markets for personal leather goods and leather furniture continue to have the most growth potential. In cowhide leathers, the demand is high for the lighter-weight, mellow, natural-looking, full-grain leathers. Especially desirable are the glazed, rich-colored, aniline-dyed types that accentuate the natural beauty of the grain. These are used predominantly in luggage, portfolios, and furniture. The sheep and lamb tanners are very encouraged by the sustained growth of and demand for glazed and suede leathers in the leather apparel market.

INCREASED COMPETITION FROM SYNTHETICS.

Some of the potential market for leather is being taken away by synthetic materials. For instance, synthetics are replacing leather in some shoe parts. The traditional leather heel lift is now almost always made of plastic. Synthetics are also replacing leather in other accessories. Synthetics are used in making handbags that look and feel like leather but are less susceptible to scratches and can be cleaned more easily. Synthetics are even taking over some of the potential leather apparel market. Today fabrics made of natural and man-made fibers look and feel like various types of leather but are easier to clean and care for. An outstanding example of a synthetic that has replaced leather and suede in fine clothing is Ultrasuede. Famous designers such as Halston and Yves St. Laurent are using Ultrasuede in almost all of their collections. Many menswear designers and manufacturers have adopted Ultrasuede for many of their designs, and today consumers feel that Ultrasuede is a fine-quality fabric—even though it is a synthetic.

INCREASED FOREIGN TRADE.

The demand for leather throughout the world continues to increase. American packers and hide dealers, able to get higher prices for their hides from tanneries in countries where demand outstrips supply, have sharply increased their export of hides.

Domestic leather-products manufacturers have been severely affected in the last two decades by imported products. This in turn has prompted domestic tanners to concentrate on exploiting foreign markets more fully. Developing foreign markets for U.S. leather products represents growth potential for this industry. Impetus may come from government programs designed to stimulate export expansion for small businesses.

INDUSTRY GROWTH FACTORS.

Factors that can contribute to the growth of the leather industry over the next 5 years are:

- Consumer demand for products manufactured from genuine, natural-looking leather, which, in contrast to synthetic materials, symbolizes quality and value to the consumer.
- A supply of raw cowhide large enough to allow for real growth in production.
- Strong industry efforts to develop foreign markets and increase exports.
- Success of industry and governmental efforts to secure relaxation or elimination of foreign trade barriers on U.S. leather.
- Expanded research and development to raise the levels of technology.

THE FUR INDUSTRY

People in ancient civilizations not only wore fur; they spread it on the floor as rugs and used it to decorate walls. Fur was also used as a valuable item of trade with other countries. In the Middle Ages, sable, marten, ermine, and fox were favorite trimmings on the clothes of the rich and noble in England. By this time, furs were well established as visible signs of prestige and were more precious than any cave dweller could have imagined. Italian cardinals wore ermine as a symbol of purity; English nobles wore it as a symbol of power. In Northern Europe furs were valued more than gold and silver, which were cold comfort in that harsh climate.

Centuries later, beaver skins were highly valued and became the common currency in North America. In Canada in 1733, one beaver pelt could buy one pound of sugar or two combs or six thimbles or eight knives. Four beaver pelts were enough to purchase a gallon of brandy or a pistol. Fur was still as good as gold as late as 1900, when Chile banked chinchilla skins as security for a loan.

History and Development

It was the search for the fabled Northwest Passage, a way to get from the Atlantic to the Pacific through a northern route, that led to the establishment of North America as a prime source of fur wealth.

Jacques Cartier, a French explorer, sailed to the New World in search of such a passage and arrived at the mouth of the St. Lawrence River in 1534. He traded for furs with the Indians there and returned to France to tell of his discovery. The next year he sailed even farther up the St. Lawrence and found a vast wealth of fur-bearing animals.

In 1604, another Frenchman, Champlain, made his first voyage up the St. Lawrence River and down the New England coast. Word of his adventures reached the English and Dutch, who had explorers of their own. In 1606, King Charles I of England gave the first patent rights to the Virginia Company. And in 1609, the Dutch, who had already been trading along the coast, sent an Englishman, Henry Hudson, to find a waterway to the Orient. What he found was the river that bears his name. He, too, reported on the tremendous wealth of furs in North America. The Dutch soon set up trading posts on the Hudson River at Albany and on lower Manhattan Island.

More and more trading posts were set up as the English and Dutch organized companies to trade with the Indians who supplied furs. These trading posts extended westward and became centers of colonization that grew into such cities as St. Louis, Chicago, Detroit, St. Paul, and Spokane.

The plentiful supply of furs was a boon to the colonists in many ways. They were able to export furs and use the revenue to purchase from Europe those articles they could not yet produce. In addition, furs were used for apparel and furnishings. Daniel Boone's coonskin cap and the bearskin rug are two examples of the early use of fur by settlers in the New World.

But it was, and still is, the beaver and its fur that deserve a special place in the history of North America. So important was the beaver trade that place names such as Beaver Creek, Beaver Falls, and Beaver Lakes commemorate it. And the beavers, which bred in many regions of North America, were never in danger of extinction. Beaver furs today account for approximately 25 percent of all furs sold. While mink still accounts for almost 60 percent of all furs sold today, fashion tastes do change. Fifty years ago a famous Hollywood star looking for a smashing fur to wear to a premiere would be likely to buy an ermine cape, while today an ermine cape would more likely turn up as a theatrical prop or be found in a secondhand clothing store.

Today, the list of popular furs is long and varied. The category of "sport" or "contemporary" furs includes raccoon, fox, beaver, coyote, muskrat, Tanuki (Asian raccoon), and nutria. Raccoon is the fastest-growing fur in popularity because the letting-out technique (described on page 136), formerly used only on expensive furs such as mink, is now widely used to eliminate the bulky look of raccoon. However, each season brings many new popular favorites to the fashion front, and each year many other furs await their turn in the fashion spotlight.

Organization and Operation

The fur industry in the United States can be divided into three groups: (1) the trappers, farmers, and ranchers who produce the pelts; (2) the fur-processing firms; and (3) the firms manufacturing fur products for consumers.

OBTAINING THE PELTS. The first step in the production of fur merchandise is to obtain the necessary pelts. A **pelt** is the skin of a fur-bearing animal. Trappers are the major source of wild animal pelts, which must be taken only

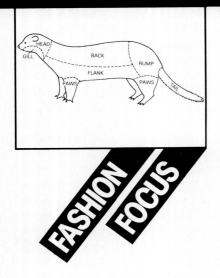

HEAD
GILL
BACK
RUMP
FLANK
PAWS
PAWS
TAIL

FASHION FOCUS

KEY TERMS IN THE FUR INDUSTRY

Nothing makes its wearer feel more glamorous and pampered than a fur. Because a fur—coat, jacket, stole, scarf, or hat—is often the largest single investment in that type of garment one makes, potential buyers must become familiar with certain key terms used in the fur industry.

BLEACHING   Chemically whitening or lightening the natural color of fur. White furs may be bleached to enhance their whiteness and eliminate yellow spots. Darker furs may be bleached to lighten them before dyeing them a lighter color. Because bleaching has a drying effect on the leather side of the fur, the quality of the pelts is somewhat reduced by this process.

DYEING   Changing the natural color of a fur by chemical means. In general, a dyed fur will not wear as well as a natural fur because dye, like bleach, weakens the leather. However, Persian lamb and Alaskan fur seal last longer dyed. If dyed, fur and skin will be the same color; if natural, they will be different.

FEATHERING   A process in which let-out long-haired furs have strips of leather or ribbon sewn in at intervals to accentuate the diagonal lines and give a textured effect. See also "leathering."

at the coldest season of the year to be of prime quality. The trapper sells pelts to nearby country stores or directly to itinerant buyers. In some areas, collectors or receiving houses accept furs for resale on consignment from trappers or local merchants. When enough pelts have been gathered, a fur merchant may export them or send them to an auction house. Private sale or sales through a broker may also take place.

A fairly recent development in the fur industry, and an increasingly important source of pelts, is **fur farming**, or the raising and breeding of furbearing animals under con-

GLAZING   The final processing step, glazing brings out the natural luster and sheen of a fur by drawing the oils to the surface. Different furs are glazed differently, but the process usually involves steaming and ironing. After cleaning a customer's fur, a furrier also glazes it.

GUARD HAIR   The longer, coarser outer hair of the fur that protects the underfur from the elements. Flat furs, such as otter, do not have guard hair. Others have more appeal when the guard hair is sheared or removed by plucking.

LEATHERING   Separating fur strips with insertions of leather, suede, or ribbon that is not visible in order to create visual effects. Leathering is done to make a long-haired fur lighter and less bulky.

LETTING-OUT   Slicing a single pelt down the center, then into diagonal strips (⅛ inch to ³⁄₁₆ inch wide), and then sewing them together again into a single longer, narrower strip. This costly process is used for better garments because it reduces bulk and permits greater variety in drape, design, and style.

PIECED FURS   Fur garments made from small pieces of fur such as paws, tails, and pieces left over when pelts are let out or cut to fit a pattern. The pieces are then recut and sewn together into "plates," or lengths of fur from which the garment is cut. The leather side must be carefully reinforced to keep the seams from splitting. Even if this is done, pieced furs tend to open at the seams; however, pieced furs cost about one-fourth the price of unpieced ones.

PLATES   Lengths of fur made from pieced furs.

PLUCKING   Removing the guard hairs by pulling them out to improve the texture of the fur.

PROCESSING   Any method, such as bleaching, dyeing, or shearing, that changes the color or texture of the fur pelts.

SHEARING   Cutting the underfur to an even, plush, velvety texture. The guard hair on furs such as nutria, beaver, opossum, Alaska fur seal, and raccoon is plucked before shearing, but on furs where the guard hair is less coarse, shearing is done without plucking.

SKIN-ON-SKIN   Sewing pelts together without changing their shape or size other than cutting them to fit a pattern. Small, relatively inexpensive furs, such as muskrat, rabbit, and squirrel, are worked this way.

UNDERFUR   The soft, dense fur next to the skin. The colder the climate the animal lives in, the more compact and dense the underfur will be.

---

trolled conditions. This began in 1880 with silver-fox fur farming on Prince Edward Island, off the eastern coast of Canada. Chinchilla, Persian lamb, fox, and nutria farms as well as mink ranches have grown rapidly throughout the United States during the past 50 years. By careful breeding, strains most likely to win fashion and financial success have been evolved. Some of the most beautiful and exotic colors in fur pelts today are the result of breeding to develop colors and markings that meet the changing demands of fashion. Fur farmers and ranchers usually sell their pelts directly to auction houses.

FUR AUCTIONS. Today fur pelts are still sold at auctions much as they were back in the thirteenth century. At auctions, fur buyers and manufacturers bid for the pelts, which are sold in bundles. Those who plan to make garments seek bundles of matched skins similar in color and quality which will make up a garment of uniform beauty. Recently, there has been great competition among buyers at auctions to buy the "top bundle"—the lot that brings the highest price. Many times this is used for publicity and has resulted in fur garments costing $100,000 and over being sold on the strength of the claim that the coat was made from the "top bundle."

The auction trail is an international one. It attracts U.S. fur buyers to England, Scandinavia, China, and Russia, as well as to various fur market centers in the United States and Canada. Fur buyers from all over the world visit auction houses in New York, Seattle, and Toronto to obtain pelts of animals native to North America. Except for London, and more recently Tokyo, each auction center handles primarily the pelts of its own country.

FUR PROCESSING. After manufacturers of fur goods buy the pelts at auctions or from wholesale merchants, they contract with fur-dressing and fur-dyeing firms to process the pelts.

The job of fur dressers is to make pelts suitable for use in consumer products. First the pelts are softened, both by soaking and by mechanical means. Then the "flesher" removes with a blade any unwanted substances from the inner surface of the skin. For less expensive furs, this process may be performed by roller-type machines. At this point, the pelts are treated with solutions that tan the skin side of the pelt into a pliable leather. Also at this stage, the fur side of the pelt may be processed. This involves either plucking unwanted guard hairs or shearing the underfur to make the fur lighter in weight and the pelt still more pliable. Finally, the pelt is cleaned again. Although fur dressing has traditionally been a handcraft industry, modern technology has turned it into a more mechanized process.

After dressing, the pelts may go to a dyer. Fur dyes once were derived from vegetable matter, but today they consist largely of complicated chemical compounds. New dyes are constantly being developed, making it possible to dye fur more successfully and in more shades than ever before.

MANUFACTURING OF FUR GOODS. Manufacturing of fur goods is basically a handcraft industry, made up mainly of small, independently owned and operated shops. This is because of the nature of the basic material with which the industry works. No two animals are quite alike, and neither are any two pelts. Moreover, a pelt varies in hair color and quality from one section of the body to another.

Because of the skills and judgments required in working with pelts, the production of fur garments lends itself neither to mass-production methods nor to large-scale operations. After the processing that all fur pelts undergo, the following steps are required to transform pelts into finished garments:

1. Sketching a design of the garment.

2. Making a canvas pattern of the garment.

3. Cutting the skins to conform to the designer's sketch, to exhibit the fur to its best advantage, and to minimize waste.

4. Sewing the cut skins together.

5. Wetting the skins and nailing or stapling them to a board so that they dry permanently set.

6. Sewing the garment sections together.

7. Lining and finishing.

8. Inspection.

Nearly all the above steps are done by hand, with consideration for each pelt's peculiarities and the differences in color and hair quality in the various parts of each skin. This is in sharp

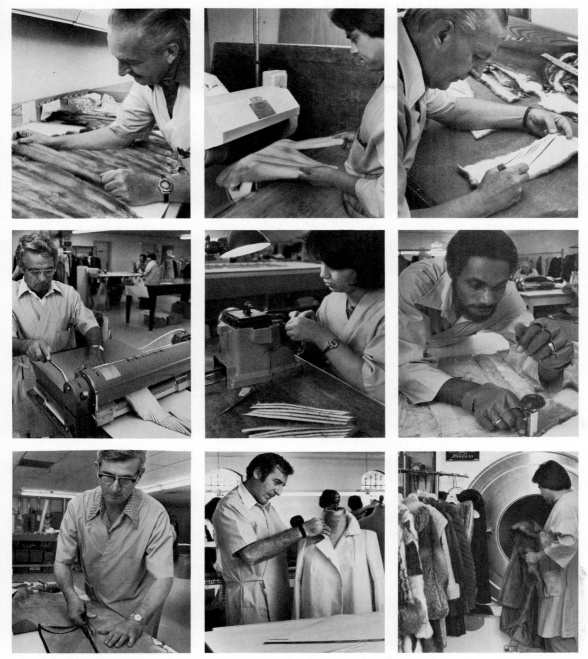

Top—the skins are matched, glazed, and sliced into strips by hand. Center—a machine slices the skins, the slices are sewn together, and wet skins are stapled to the pattern to dry. Below—the leather is cut, a canvas model is fitted, and finally—the cleaning machine.

contrast to the mass-production methods of apparel makers who cut and sew fabrics.

For some more luxurious furs, the cutting operation may be extremely complex in order to **let out** short skins to a length adequate for garment purposes. Letting out mink, for example, involves cutting each skin down the center of the dark vertical stripe (the "grotzen stripe"). Each half-skin is then cut at an angle into diagonal strips ⅛ inch to ³⁄₁₆ inch wide. Then each tiny strip is resewn at an angle to the strips above and below it in order to make the skin longer and narrower. The other half-skin is resewn in like manner. The two halves are then joined, resulting in a longer, slimmer pelt that is more beautiful than the original. Ten miles of thread may be needed to join the strips let out for a single coat. The nailing process may require as many as 1,200 nails.

RETAIL
DISTRIBUTION OF FUR GARMENTS. The line between manufacturing and retailing is less clear in furs than in other industries. Retail fur merchants may maintain an assortment of finished garments to show or sell to customers who buy off the rack. But they will also have a supply of skins and a fur workroom so that they can make up custom garments as well.

Most fur garments are retailed in one of two ways: through leased departments or through consignment selling. Both types of operation permit a retail store to offer its customers a large selection of fur accessory and garment types without tying up vast quantities of capital in inventory.

A **leased department** is one that is ostensibly operated by the store in which it is located, but which is actually run by an outsider who pays a percentage of sales to the store as rent. In a leased department, the operator or lessee owns the stock. The lessee may also run departments in other stores and can, if necessary, move garments and skins from one location to another. The lessee, a retailer of a

special kind, is usually well capitalized and has expert knowledge of both furs and retailing. In **consignment selling,** a manufacturer places merchandise in a retail store for resale but permits any unsold portion to be returned to the wholesale source by a specified date. In consignment selling, the garment producer in effect lends stock to a store. If not sold, the furs are returned to the producer for possible sale elsewhere. When the economy dips and there are high interest rates, consignment selling is reduced considerably.

An important change started in the early 1980s that is expected to become even more pronounced in the coming years is the increased role fur manufacturers are taking in their retail business. Although wholesale furriers have catered to a retail trade for decades, the practice never used to account for more than a small percentage of their total volume. However, in 1983, a random survey showed that retail operations represented 50 to 75 percent of some fur manufacturers' total volume.[1] The fur manufacturers' bid for local retail fur business is just part of a larger movement in the fur industry away from traditional channels of distribution, such as department and specialty stores.

Merchandising and Marketing Activities

The fur industry is made up almost entirely of small firms. Thus, it relies to a considerable extent upon group efforts rather than those of individual entrepreneurs for its merchandising and promotional activities. In some instances, the labor unions, fur traders, dressers, and garment producers all work together to encourage the public's acceptance of furs.

TRADE ASSOCIATIONS. The fur industry relies mainly on the efforts of its trade associations to impress upon consumers the fashion and luxury values of its product. Trade associations also assist retailers in promoting fur to the public. The American Fur Industry, Inc.

TABLE 7-2 Furs and Their Characteristics

FUR	CHARACTERISTICS	YOU SHOULD LOOK FOR
Badger	Very heavy, warm, and durable.	Long silvery-gray guard hair over dense white or tan underfur.
Bassarisk	Brownish yellow, touched with gray. The belly and flank are paler yellow, shading to light brown.	Density of fur and color, depending on markings.
Beaver		
Sheared	Soft, plushy texture.	Silky texture. Well-matched pelts, evenly sheared.
Natural	Long guard hairs over thick underfur.	Lustrous sheen of guard hairs and thickness of underfur.
Calf	Short, sleek, flat hairs. It comes in many natural colors and patterns and may be dyed.	Lustrous, supple pelt with bright luster. Markings should be attractive.
Chinchilla	A short, dense, very silky fur. Originally from South America, but now wholly ranch-raised.	Lustrous slate-blue top hair and dark underfur, although mutation colors are now available.
Coyote	A long-haired fur, often pale gray or tan in color. Durable and warm.	Long guard hair and thick, soft underfur.
Ermine	Very silky guard hair and thick downy underfur.	Pure white color and dense, silky texture.
Fisher	Color shades from brown to blackish tones.	Silky guard hair, thickness of underfur, and richness of color.
Fitch	Long guard hairs over woolly light underfur. Color ranges from ecru with black markings to orange.	Silky texture and clarity of color.
Fox	The widest range of natural mutation colors of any fur except mink: silver, blue, white, red, cross, beige, gray, and brown. May also be dyed.	Long, glossy guard hairs and thick soft underfur. Also clarity of color.
Kid	Short, flat, silky fur from China, Ethiopia, South America.	Even, silky fur. May be patterned similarly to broadtail.
Lamb		
American Processed	Pelts of fine wool sheep sheared to show the pattern near the skin. Naturally white but may be dyed.	Silky, lustrous moire pattern, not too curly.
Broadtail	A natural (unsheared) flat moire pattern. Color may be natural browns, gray, black, or dyed.	Silky texture and uniformity of pattern.
Mongolian	Long, wavy, silky hair. May be natural off-white, bleached, or dyed.	Silky texture, with wavy—not frizzy—hair.
Mouton	Pelts are sheared, hairs are straightened for soft, water-repellent fur, generally dyed brown.	Uniformity of shearing.
Shearling	Natural sheepskin, with the leather side sueded and worn outside. The fur side is often sheared.	Softness of leather side and even shearing.

TABLE 7-2 Furs and Their Characteristics (continued)

FUR	CHARACTERISTICS	YOU SHOULD LOOK FOR
Lamb (continued)		
Persian Lamb	From karakul sheep raised in Southwest Africa, Afghanistan, U.S.S.R. Traditionally black, brown, and gray, new mutation colors available; also dyed.	Silky curls or ripples of fur and soft, light, pliable leather.
Lynx	Russian lynx is the softest and whitest of these long-haired furs, with the most subtle beige markings. Canadian lynx is next, while Montana lynx has stronger markings. Lynx cat or bobcat is reddish black fading to spotted white on longer belly hairs.	Creamy white tones and subtle markings.
Marmot	Hair tends to be coarse although fur is thick.	The best marmot has a bluish cast. Often dyed.
Marten		
American	Long guard hair and dense underfur. Color ranges from blue-brown to dark brown.	Clarity of color and soft texture. This is the least expensive marten.
Baum	Softer and silkier than American marten.	High luster and silky texture.
Stone	The finest marten, very soft and thick.	Soft, thick texture and bluish-brown cast with pale underfur.
Mink	Soft and lightweight, with lustrous guard hairs and dense underfur.	Natural luster and clarity of color. Fur should be full and dense.
Mutation	Most colors of any natural ranched fur, from white to grays, blues, and beiges.	
Ranch	Color ranges from a true, rich brown to a deep brownish black.	
Wild	Generally brown in color.	
Pieced*	Color and pattern depends on pieces used. This is the least expensive mink.	Pattern and well-made seams.
Mole	Soft, short, dense fur. Always dyed.	Well-matched skins in color and hair height.
Muskrat		
Jersey	Fur is full and thick, with a dark grotzen or black stripe and paler beige sides.	Density of fur and well-matched skins.
Northern	Strong guard hairs and dense short underfur. Sides and bellies of silver shades often worked skin-on-skin. Backs are darker, with longer top hair and heavier underfur.	Clarity of color and density of fur.
Southern	Flat with little underfur.	Pale color and uniformity of relatively sparse guard hairs.
Nutria	Similar to beaver.	
Sheared	Plush texture, lighter than beaver.	Evenness of shearing and color.
Natural	Long, sleek guard hairs and thick underfur. Color is lustrous brown. When ranched, bluish-beige in tone and slightly coarser. Nutria may be dyed.	Uniformity of color and texture.

TABLE 7-2 Furs and Their Characteristics (continued)

FUR	CHARACTERISTICS	YOU SHOULD LOOK FOR
Opossum		
Amer-ican	Long guard hair with dense underfur. From silver-gray to gray-black.	Uniformity of color.
Aus-tralian	Short, dense, plushlike fur, ranging from yellow-gray to blue-gray.	Soft texture with woolly underfur. The best is blue-gray in color.
Otter	Sleek flat fur, naturally brown; also dyed.	Sleek flat texture, lustrous in color.
Pahmi	Also known as Asian ferret badger. Has dark guard hair and light, dense underfur. May be plucked and sheared.	Clarity of color from brown to silver-gray over orange-yellow underfur.
Rabbit	Generally long hair in a variety of natural colors, including 14 natural mutation colors in ranch rabbit. May be sheared and grooved.	Silky texture and uniformity of color. Ranch rabbit sheds less.
Raccoon	Long silver, black-tipped guard hairs over woolly underfur. May also be plucked and sheared and dyed.	Silvery cast. Plenty of guard hair with heavy underfur.
Sable	Member of marten family. Crown sable is brown with a blue cast. Golden sable, an amber tone, is less expensive.	Soft, deep fur in dark lustrous brown, with silky guard hairs.
Seal		
Alaska or Fur Seal	Short fur, always plucked to remove long, coarse guard hairs. Dyed black, brown, and other colors.	Density of fur, luster, and velvet texture.
Hair	Hair is short, shiny, and flat with no underfur, more like coarse hair than fur. Naturally gray or spotted. Also dyed.	Sheen of hair and pliable leather.
Skunk	Underfur is thick and long, keeping guard hairs exact. Stripe may vary in length and width.	Blue-black color, fineness of white marking, thick texture.
Zorina	South American skunk, similar to North American skunk.	Flatter fur with silkier texture.
Squirrel	Heavily furred, lightweight, with lustrous guard hairs. Only clear-gray pelts left natural. Best squirrel comes from U.S.S.R., next from Poland, Finland, and Canada. The last has a flatter brown cast.	Dense fur and silky texture.
Tanuki	Also called Japanese raccoon. Color is closer to red fox with distinctive cross markings.	Clarity of color and dense, full texture.
Weasel	Similar to mink but shorter. May be dyed.	Soft, lightweight texture.

* The same piecing technique can be used for almost any fur. The most common pieced furs are mink, sable, marten, fox, Persian lamb, raccoon, and beaver.

Source: Furs Naturally by Edythe Cudlipp for The American Fur Industry, Inc., New York, pp. 20–22. Reprinted with permission.

does this for the industry as a whole. Individual types of furs are promoted by such specialized associations as EMBA (organized as the Eastern Mink Breeders Association and now nationwide), GLMA (the Great Lakes Mink Association, a much smaller group than EMBA, specializing in ranch mink), and ECBC (the Empress Chinchilla Breeders Cooperative). By far the biggest and most important of these trade groups is EMBA. It disseminates publicity and produces educational booklets for retailers, schools, and the general public. Both mink associations have heavily advertised slogans for prospective customers. "Wrap yourself in something special," say EMBA ads. Ads sponsored by GLMA ask, "What becomes a legend most?"

LABELING.   To capitalize on consumers' interest in whatever furs are currently fashionable, the industry finds ways to treat one type of fur so that it resembles another more desirable or more expensive one. For consumers' protection, the Federal Trade Commission issued the Fur Products Labeling Act of 1952 and various rules since then. These have established definite requirements for the labeling of articles made of fur.

By law, the following must be stated, both on a label attached to the merchandise and in all advertising of fur products:

1. The English name of the animal.

2. The country of origin.

3. The type of processing, including dyeing, to which the pelts may have been subjected.

4. If paws or tails have been used or if parts from used garments have been reused.

Thus, a customer who buys a Persian lamb coat made from the most desirable sections of the pelts and a customer who buys a coat made of paws alone both know exactly what they are paying for. What was labeled "Hudson seal" generations ago would be labeled "Dyed muskrat" today.

Industry Trends

Demand for furs is generally related to a country's economic conditions. During the Depression of the 1930s, fur sales dropped off drastically. In the period immediately following World War II, when the public had money and very little consumer merchandise was available, fur sales boomed.

In the early 1970s, conservationists were in full swing, newly aware of the diminishing wildlife resources of an increasingly civilized planet. As a result, coats made of fake fur and petrochemical synthetics were replacing the genuine articles in the closets of the fashion-buying public.

Since then, the fur industry has made an incredible comeback. Furs remain a desirable item among consumers in bad times as well as good. During the recession of 1981–1982, contrary to past economic history, the U.S. retail fur industry produced sales topping $1 billion for the first time in history, rising from $944 million in 1980.[2] In 1972, fur sales were $361,500,000 and by 1982 had risen to $1,078,000,000.[3]

Although the number of furriers today is half what it was 10 years ago, the fur industry looks forward to a time of growth and of challenge. On the one hand, new fashion interest, increased foreign trade, new legislation, and new channels of retail distribution are the major trends influencing the growth of the fur industry. On the other hand, such issues as low-cost imports, management/union relations, rising overhead, and a high retirement rate among fur workers, coupled with a shortage of skilled workers entering the field, give the fur industry many new challenges to face.

FASHION INTEREST.   Once worn only by the rich or for formal occasions, furs are now bought and worn by everyone on a variety of occasions. Changing fashion demand in recent years has led to an increase in the variety of fur garments, from casual and sporty to elegant and classic to faddish and trendy.

The fur business is booming at the retail level.

Increased interest in fur apparel is found not only among older customers—once the traditional market for furs—but also among young customers and career women. Nor is it limited to women: the use of fur coats and accessories by men has greatly increased and now accounts for 20 to 25 percent of retail fur volume in some large retail stores. Furs for men have gained popularity because of their acceptance by many male sports figures and celebrities.

There are fur vests, fur jackets, fur suits, fur-trimmed sweaters and dresses, and all types of fur accessories. Fur has been feathered, ribbed, and crocheted.

Famous French and American designers such as Christian Dior, Yves St. Laurent, Givenchy, Bill Blass, Halston, Oscar de la Renta, Pauline Trigere, and Calvin Klein are now designing especially for the fur industry. Italian fur designers such as Fendi and Soldano use innovative techniques. As a result, many people are thinking of buying fur fashion garments. And the demand outweighs the supply.

INCREASED FOREIGN TRADE. In 1982, export sales (wholesale) of raw, dressed pelts and manufactured goods were $350 million compared to only $281 million in imports—a very favorable balance of trade.[4] European, South American, and Far Eastern furriers buy in the United States, not only because of the high quality of U.S. pelt dressing, but also for the variety available here. Europeans come here primarily for mink, muskrat, beaver, raccoon, and fox.

Because of this trend, the first Amercian International Fur Fair was held in New York in March 1979. Attendance was estimated at well over 5,000 people. Exhibiting at the fair were 70 American manufacturers and 55 foreign companies from 11 different countries, including France, England, Italy, Sweden, and Finland. Buyers attending from Germany, Japan, South America, Switzerland, and Canada reflected the importance of the fair to the international market. Today this annual fur fair is held in different cities throughout the United States.

NEW LEGISLATION. The Federal Trade Commission and the fur industry are perpetually engaged in discussion about changes in the fur labeling rules. The most important fur legislation of recent years, however, concerned "endangered species," or those species of animals in danger of becoming extinct. In 1973, the Endangered Species Act was passed, forbidding the importation or transportation across state lines of a variety of animals or products made from those animals. Among the species classified as endangered are a number formerly used in making fur products. These include most varieties of leopard, tiger, ocelot, cheetah, jaguar, vicuna, and a few types of wolf.

NEW CHANNELS OF RETAIL DISTRIBUTION. As with other manufactured fashion apparel items, new retail options are appearing that enable manufacturers to deal more directly with the buying public. In the fur industry, "hotel sales" are held almost every weekend in New York and other large cities. At these sales the buying public is invited to buy directly from the fur manufacturer, choosing from a large stock of furs displayed in a midtown hotel. Or they may shop manufacturer-leased fur departments in discount stores, such as the Oceanside Coat Factory, Filene's, Syms, and Loehmann's.

More retailers are selling furs through mail-order catalogs. The special Spiegel fur catalog, called "Ambience," shows 35 to 40 fur items, compared to its main catalog, which shows about a dozen coats. JC Penney has also been showing furs in its catalog.

Manufacturers are also opening freestanding stores outside of New York and retail storefronts within the fur market itself. A major fur manufacturer has launched a franchising and licensing operation that it hopes to introduce throughout the country.

LOW-COST IMPORTS.   An increasingly serious problem to the industry is the importation of fur garments produced mainly in the Far East and Canada. The industry estimates that 25 percent of the dollar volume of furs sold at retail in this country are of imported fur garments, and that by the end of the decade this may increase to 65 percent. For the past few years imports of fur garments have increased tremendously. In 1976 they were $23 million and by 1982 they had reached $131.8 million.[5] For now, domestic manufacturers point out the lower quality of the imports and hope that through advertising and educational publicity the buying public will look for American-made quality garments.

RISING OVERHEAD.   Rents in top buildings in the New York fur market area have tripled over what most furriers have been accustomed to paying. Although Seventh Avenue between Thirtieth Street and Twenty-third Street has long been considered ''the Fur Market'' and rather out-of-the-way for other types of business firms, businesses with no relation to the fur industry are moving into fur building lofts, where the rents are relative bargains compared to garment-center and uptown rents that are much higher.

**LACK OF SKILLED
WORKERS AND MANAGERS.**   Each year fewer and fewer American-born people opt to become fur workers. At the same time, many manufacturers in their sixties and older are thinking about retirement, and in the face of rising costs, are expected to retire earlier and thus close their factories. Therefore the usual smooth balance of younger workers replacing retirees in the industry has been threatened. Offsetting this problem somewhat is the fact that new immigrants, primarily from Greece, are entering the trade increasingly as both skilled and unskilled labor. Another problem is the lack of trained middle-management people for both fur manufacturers and fur retailers.

The fur industry recognizes these major problems and has pledged to support and maintain a fur program at the Fashion Institute of Technology in New York. The F.I.T. program is aimed at encouraging young people to enter the fur business and preparing them for it. Students are trained in fur design, pattern making, merchandising and sales, retailing, production, breeding and wildlife management, and other related skills. Courses in the Continuing Education Division at F.I.T. enable current industry workers to learn new skills and to update current ones.

REFERENCES

[1] *Women's Wear Daily*, January 1, 1983, pp. 16–17.
[2] Ibid.
[3] Jess Chernak of The American Fur Industry, Inc., August 31, 1983. (Personal correspondence.)
[4] Ibid.
[5] Ibid.

MERCHANDISING VOCABULARY

Define or briefly explain the following terms:

Consignment selling	Leased department
Contract tanneries	Let out
Converters	Pelt
Fur farming	Regular tanneries
Hides	Skins
Kips	Tanning

1. In what ways have technological advances in machinery and chemistry benefited the leather industry?
2. Why does specialization prevail throughout the leather industry in this country? Give examples of such specialization.
3. Name five major agents or methods used for tanning leather. Briefly describe the characteristics of leather tanned by four of these agents or methods. For what consumer products is each of these best suited?
4. Describe the fashion information services provided by leather producers and/or their trade associations.
5. Why is product research and development so important today in the leather industry? What specific benefits to the consumer have resulted from such product research and development?
6. Describe the history and development of the fur industry in this country.
7. Into what three groups is the fur industry divided? Briefly describe the function of each.
8. Why is the manufacturing of fur goods considered a handcraft industry rather than one suited to mass-production methods?
9. Outline the steps in transforming processed fur pelts into finished garments.
10. Differentiate between "leased departments" and "consignment selling" as these terms apply to retail distribution of fur garments. What major advantages does each have for retail merchants?

1. Discuss the following statement from the text and its implications for leather merchandising: "Leather producers do not merely stay abreast of fashion; they must keep ahead of it."
2. Discuss current trends in the leather industry that relate to: (a) enlarging markets, (b) competition from synthetics, (c) increased foreign trade.
3. Discuss: (a) provisions of the Fur Products Labeling Act of 1952 and how it protects the consumer, and (b) recent legislation relating to furs.
4. Discuss current trends in the fur industry as they relate to (a) fashion interest, (b) increased foreign trade, (c) new channels of retail distribution, (d) low-cost imports, (e) rising overhead, (f) lack of skilled workers and managers.

8. WOMEN'S APPAREL

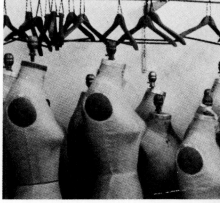

If visitors from another planet were to land their spaceship in the middle of New York City's "Garment District," they would surely be baffled by their discovery. They would think that they had discovered a world in which people were engaged in just one activity from morning to night—making women's apparel. What's more, they would be pretty much right!

The manufacturing of women's fashion apparel *is* a world of its own. It is a giant, multibillion-dollar industry, with a hub of activity concentrated in an area of New York City less than 10 blocks square. The women's apparel industry is so important, and employs so many workers, that the health of the entire nation's economy has come increasingly to depend on it. The women's apparel industry includes all categories of apparel in these size ranges: women's, misses, junior, and petite.

The women's apparel industry is no place for the fainthearted. The production of ready-to-wear that will please today's fashion-wise customers is a constantly challenging and exciting task. Competition can be so fierce that the business is often called "cutthroat"; certainly "exhausting" is an accurate description. But for the thousands and thousands of people involved in it, the manufacturing of women's apparel is the only game in town.

Considering the huge size and importance of this segment of the fashion business today, it is hard to realize that the women's ready-to-wear industry was little more than a young-ster until after World War I. Since that time, it has grown constantly and made tremendous advances. And today it continues to grow and change. The "instant" capabilities of the computer, the emergence of new world markets, the up-and-down economic picture around the globe—all indicate that in the years remaining to the year 2000, the women's apparel industry will keep shifting, adapting, and evolving. Whether it's called the "rag business," the "cutting-up trade," the "needle trade," or any other nickname, the women's apparel industry not only welcomes change; it thrives on it.

HISTORY OF THE WOMEN'S APPAREL INDUSTRY

Historically, the making of apparel for the entire family was a household job, usually the responsibility of the women. This has been true in most cultures ever since the family home was a cave and garments were animal skins, sewn together with leather thongs.

Although women traditionally did the sewing, men were the first industrial producers of apparel. For many centuries, professional tailors have made a business of producing custom-made clothes for men. It was only a few centuries ago that professional dressmakers began producing custom-made women's apparel. Today, the demand for custom tailoring and dressmaking has been overshadowed by the demand for less expensive, factory-produced ready-to-wear in great variety.

Growth of Ready-to-Wear

The term **ready-to-wear** (RTW) refers to apparel made in factories to standard size measurements. This is in contrast to custom-made apparel produced by professional dressmakers or by home sewers to the exact measurements of the individual who will wear the garment.

During the first half of the 1800s, apparel manufacturing was limited to men's clothes.

Only after the Civil War did women's apparel begin to be made on a commercial basis. The first ready-to-wear garments turned out were cloaks and mantles, which, unlike most women's garments, did not require a careful fit.

By the turn of the century, limited quantities of women's suits, skirts, and blouses were being made in factories. Within a decade, some manufacturer had the idea of sewing a blouse and skirt together, and the first ready-to-wear dresses were produced.

By the end of World War I, the women's apparel industry—today the heart of the fashion business—had passed the $1 billion mark in produce value. By 1982, the factory value of all shipments made by the U.S. women's apparel industry (not including furs, shoes, or hosiery) totaled close to $18 billion.[1]

Unionization

An important factor in the growth of the women's ready-to-wear industry in this country was that the right kind of labor was available at the right time and in the right place. In the nineteenth and early twentieth centuries, millions of Europeans sought refuge in the United States, particularly in big cities along the eastern seaboard. They needed to earn a living. Many, trained as dressmakers or tailors in their homelands, turned naturally to the growing apparel industry for jobs. However, working conditions in the apparel trades at the turn of the century were appalling. Hours were long, pay was little, and factories were overcrowded, dark, unsanitary, and unsafe.

In 1900, workers formed the International Ladies' Garment Workers' Union (ILGWU), the major union in the women's apparel trade today. Strikes in 1909 and 1910 helped pave the way for collective bargaining in the women's garment trade. The tragic Triangle Shirtwaist Factory fire of 1911, which killed 146 workers, rallied support around the workers and eventually led to stricter building codes and revised labor laws.

Characteristic of today's union activities is

A label for the ILGWU.

the ILGWU's participation in joint employer-union committees to set prices for piecework on individual garments. These prices depend on the elements of work involved in each style.

However, the ILGWU has developed into more than a collective bargaining agency. This union has contributed funds for promoting New York City as an industry fashion center. It has helped develop schools to train technical workers, designers, and other skilled employees needed in the industry. In addition, the ILGWU has subsidized housing and vacation resorts and has provided other benefits, making it easier and more pleasant for employees to remain in the city and to stay in the garment industry.

CREATION OF WOMEN'S APPAREL

Much work and planning goes into women's apparel long before it reaches the retail store racks. As the ready-to-wear business has grown, planning and organization at the manufacturing level has necessarily become more sophisticated, enabling the industry to better meet the demand of fashion-conscious con-

sumers for quality apparel. The position of the merchandiser is becoming more important in manufacturing because it is the responsibility of the merchandiser to predict the fashion wants of the consumer and to see that these are reflected in the line the manufacturer presents.

To a degree probably never matched before, manufacturers are concerned about style and fashion at the earliest stages of production, and they depend heavily on staff or outside designers to create new looks based on upcoming trends. These designers may also be charged with maintaining a sense of continuity from season to season and year to year, based on the image the apparel producer wants to project to the public.

At the same time, manufacturers are constantly looking for better and more efficient methods of producing their apparel. Over the years, a number of new technologies have been developed that allow various operations to be performed more quickly and accurately, saving manufacturers time, money, and labor. As the industry has matured, all the stages that go into the actual design and production of women's apparel have settled into a basic cycle that repeats itself more or less unchanged from season to season.

Developing a Line

Two to four months before the apparel for a specific selling season reaches a retail store, the store's buyers are in the wholesale markets. Here they view the lines of manufacturers and make their selections. From 3 to 12 months before that time, manufacturers begin creating their future seasonal lines. This means that the development of a line may begin as much as a year and a half before consumers have their first look at new seasonal merchandise on a store's selling floor. (See Table 8-1.)

First, the designer charged with creating the line reviews all available information on trends, materials, and previous fashion successes and failures. From these, the designer

TABLE 8-1 Manufacturer's Line Planning Calendar for the Fall Season for Pants, Shirts, and Tops

June *(start)*	1. Establish piece goods reserves with domestic mills.
July	

August	1. Define and submit product category concept as to:
	   a. Customer.
	   b. Body fit/silhouette.
	   c. Fashion direction.
	   d. Unit volume goals.
	   e. Marketing objectives.

September	1. Establish gross margin goals. 2. Approve merchandiser's SKU (stock keeping unit) of volume. 3. Get final approval of volume by brand. 4. Get commitment from retailer on quantities required.
October	1. Make initial forecast of basic program (style and color). 2. Develop preliminary marketing plan. 3. Prepare master schedule for basics. 4. Compare master schedule with production availability (fashion production must fit balance). 5. Make initial commitment for 50% of basic fabrics. 6. Make initial domestic fabric purchase of fashion piece goods.
November	1. Approve basics. 2. Implement fabric commitment on balance of basics. 3. Make initial imported fabric purchases on confined goods.
December	1. Complete imported fabric purchases. 2. Hold merchandising meeting. 3. Submit advertised features to marketing division. 4. Make final commitment for domestic and imported fabrics. 5. Approve ads and mailer.
January	1. Submit plans for new or special labels, hangers, buttons, packages, supplies, etc.
	2. Increase commitments for advertised fabrics. 3. Complete costing of new models made in own plants. 4. Outline swatching procedures. 5. Issue sample orders for in-house production. 6. Review construction and packaging of new models. 7. Finalize new trimmings. 8. Review acceptance of costing/new models/own plants. 9. Issue sample orders with complete specification sheets. 10. Cut model lines (for sales staff). 11. Get acceptance of cost structure for contracted items, if any. 12. Review line for breadth sampling.
February	1. Develop marketing plan by model/pattern (total quantity required plus regional plans according to quotas). 2. Complete final review, cost contracting. 3. Conduct gross profit test. 4. Complete updated master schedule for finished goods. 5. Synchronize sales plans, marketing plans, master schedule, and manufacturing plans. 6. Conduct final line and pricing review at merchandise meeting of executives. 7. Issue final marketing plan. 8. Conduct gross profit test (final). 9. Distribute merchandise bulletin and swatch cards. 10. Ship samples. 11. Hold sales meeting. 12. Follow up on shipment of late samples.
March	*Put on sale for delivery to stores in May, June, and July.*

forms some idea of what the coming season's line should include. Each design is first sketched or developed in muslin. The design is then considered both on its own merits and for its suitability in the line as a whole. Many designs may be discarded at this point.

Designs that seem most likely to succeed are then made up into finished garments. This is done by a **sample hand**, a designer's assistant who is an all-around seamstress. Various executives of the firm (sales, purchasing, and production heads, cost experts, and others) then examine the samples. At this point, several more designs may be discarded while others may go back to the design room for modification.

Producing a Line

When a design has survived these preliminary challenges, a pattern maker makes a production pattern in whatever garment size the firm uses for its samples. From this pattern, one or more samples are cut and sewn. If the sample is acceptable, its production costs are carefully figured and wholesale price is determined. The design is given a style number and becomes part of the manufacturer's line.

After buyers have viewed a line and placed their orders, the manufacturer usually finds that some style offerings have received considerable buyer interest while others have not. Those in the first group are scheduled for production; those in the second group are usually dropped from the line.

For every style that is to be produced, the original pattern is **graded** or sloped to adjust it to each of the various sizes in which the style will be made. Next, the pieces of the pattern in all its sizes are carefully laid out on a long piece of paper, or **marker**, which is placed on top of the fabric to be cut.

CUTTING.   One of the most important processes in the mass production of apparel is that of cutting through many thicknesses of material in one operation. The success of the cutting process depends on the accuracy with which

each layer of material is placed on top of the one directly underneath. A "laying-up machine" carries the material back and forth along a guide on either side of the cutting table, spreading the material evenly from end to end. On top of this pile of laid-out material, which may be anywhere from 50 to 100 layers in depth, the marker is laid to serve as a cutting pattern. On this paper are traced the outlines of each piece of a pattern for every size in which the style will be made. Then the material and marker are secured by clamps at either end and at intervals along the material's selvaged edges.

Among the more revolutionary pieces of machinery to come along in recent years was the computerized pattern maker "Camisco." This computerized system for designing and producing patterns eliminated manual labor and increased the speed and accuracy of designing and producing the patterns. It also reduces fabric needs up to 9 percent by allowing fabric to be cut to much closer tolerances.

Cutting the material around the edges of individual pieces of the pattern's marker is done by electric knife or, increasingly, by laser beam. Individual pieces of each pattern, such as sleeves, collars, fronts, and backs of blouses, still with the paper marker on top, are then tied up in bundles according to size. They are then passed along to the sewing operators in the same plant or in a contractor's shop.

SEWING.   Much of the sewing function has also benefitted from new technologies. For instance, a robotic-hemmer/unit stacker was introduced several years ago, which automatically hems the back pockets of jeans and casual slacks. Requiring no operator, the machine is capable of hemming 1,200 pockets an hour.

After the sewing process is completed, the garment is finished, pressed, inspected, and finally shipped to retailers. As the season progresses, retailers reorder popular numbers, and manufacturers may recut them to meet demand. However, producers recut only the hottest, best-selling numbers in their lines. They

New computerized systems design the pattern.

drop any others for which there have been only scattered reorders.

ORGANIZATION AND OPERATION OF THE WOMEN'S APPAREL INDUSTRY

The women's apparel industry was, until very recently, made up of small, family-oriented businesses. There were no giants in this industry comparable to General Motors or Ford in the automotive industry.

This all began to change at the end of the 1960s. Many marginal firms went out of business, and many mergers took place. The ownership of apparel manufacturing businesses by such conglomerates as Gulf & Western became economically desirable.

These changes necessarily brought some restrictive measures to an industry noted for its flamboyant methods of operation. While it is still possible to respond quickly to changing demands in fashion, more planning is now involved. As the apparel industry moves into the pattern of big business, it cannot contract or expand its facilities at a moment's notice. Starting an apparel business with minimum capital in hopes that a particular item will catch on and skyrocket into the fashion success story of the year is today the exception, not the rule.

Although the advent of mergers has affected the women's apparel industry, certain aspects of operation remain the same. Firms within the industry are highly specialized in terms of their production. Not all producers of apparel actually perform all the processes necessary to turn out finished garments. And new lines, or assortments of styles, are developed for each selling season of the year.

Types of Producers

The fashion apparel industry consists of three types of producers: manufacturers, jobbers, and contractors. A **manufacturer** is one who performs all the operations required to produce apparel, from buying the fabric to selling and shipping the finished garments. An **apparel jobber** handles the designing, the planning, the purchasing, usually the cutting, the selling, and the shipping, but not the actual sewing operation. A **contractor** is a producer whose sole function is to supply sewing services to the industry, where it is sometimes called an **outside shop**.

MANUFACTURERS. The greater New York area in general and New York City in particular are home to many of the women's apparel manufacturers. More than 60 percent of the women's apparel produced in this country is made in the greater New York area.

In recent years, some manufacturers have set up sewing plants of their own or begun to work with contractors far from New York City. Where people with sewing skills are available for employment—including upstate New York, New Jersey, Pennsylvania, and Alabama—smaller plants have been built. Having an abundant labor supply available is both a practical and economical way of expanding a manufacturer's sewing operations. The training, supervision, and planning requirements of the smaller plants are minimal compared with those of a main plant. However, even when a manufacturer moves production facilities out of New York, designers and the major showroom usually remain in the city.

A manufacturer, by definition, is a producer who handles all phases of a garment's production. The staff produces the original design or buys an acceptable design from a freelance designer. Each line is planned by the company executives. The company purchases the fabric and trimmings needed. The cutting and sewing are usually done in the company's factories. On certain occasions, however, a manufacturer may use the services of a contractor if sales of an item exceed the capacity of the firm's sewing facilities and if shipping deadlines cannot otherwise be met. The company's sales force and traffic department handle the selling and shipping of the finished goods. One great advantage of this type of operation is that close quality control can be maintained. When pro-

ducers contract out some part of their work, they cannot as effectively monitor its quality.

APPAREL JOBBERS. Apparel jobbers handle all phases of the production of a garment except for the actual sewing and sometimes the cutting. A jobber firm may employ a design staff to create various seasonal lines or may buy acceptable sketches from freelance designers. The jobber's staff buys the fabric and trimmings necessary to produce the styles in each line, makes up samples, and grades the patterns. In most cases, the staff also cuts the fabric for the various parts of each garment to be produced. Jobbers, however, do not actually sew and finish garments. Instead, they arrange with outside factories run by contractors to perform these manufacturing operations. The sales staff takes orders for garments in each line, and the shipping department fills store orders from the finished garments returned by the contractor. (Note that apparel jobbers are involved in manufacturing, whereas most other ''jobbers'' buy finished goods and sell them to small users who are not able to place large orders.)

CONTRACTORS. Contractors usually specialize in just one phase of the production of a garment: sewing. In some cases contractors also perform the cutting operation from patterns submitted by a jobber or a manufacturer. Contractors developed early in the history of the fashion industry, with the beginning of mass-production techniques. Contractors serve those producers who have little or no sewing capability of their own as well as those whose current business exceeds their own capacity.

If a contractor is used, cut pieces of the garment are provided by the manufacturer. For an agreed price per garment, the article is sewn, finished, inspected, and returned to the manufacturer for shipment to retail stores.

In the mass production of ready-to-wear, a single sewing-machine operator rarely makes

TABLE 8-2 Leading American Designers

Adolfo	Oscar de la Renta	Bill Kaiserman	Giorgio Sant'Angelo
Adri	Louis Dell'Olio	Norma Kamali	Arnold Scaasi
Gil Aimbez	Florence Eiseman	Donna Karan	Harriet Selwyn
John Anthony	Perry Ellis	Herbert Kasper	Adele Simpson
Richard Assatly	Luis Estevez	Calvin Klein	Willi Smith
Bill Atkinson	Jack Fuller	Don Kline	George Stavropoulos
Dominick Avel-lino	James Galanos	John Kloss	Charles Suppon
	Rudi Gernreich	Ralph Lauren	Viola Sylbert
Scott Barrie	Mady Gerrard	Ron Leal	Gustave Tassel
Geoffrey Beene	Betsy Gonzalez	Mary McFadden	Bill Tice
Bill Blass	Bill Haire	Anthony Muto	Jacques Tiffeau
Donald Brooks	Halston	Leo Narducci	Pauline Trigere
Stephen Burrows	Cathy Hardwick	Frank Olive	Joan Vass
Albert Capraro	Holly Harp	Mollie Parnis	Diane Von Fursten-berg
Bonnie Cashin	Stan Herman	Dominic Rompollo	
Oleg Cassini	Carol Horn	Clovis Ruffin	Ilie Wacs
Sal Cesarani	Betsey Johnson	Gloria Sachs	Chester Weinberg
Aldo Cipullo	Robin Kahn	Fernando Sanchez	John Weitz
Liz Claiborne			Harriet Winter

Source: Anne Stegemeyer, *Who's Who in Fashion,* Fairchild Books, 1980, unpaged.

a complete garment. Each operator sews only a certain section of the garment, such as a sleeve or a hem. This division of labor, called **section work**, makes it unnecessary for an operator to switch from one highly specialized machine to another or to make adjustments on the machine. Any change or adjustment in equipment takes time and increases labor costs. In the fashion trade, time lost in making such changes also causes delays in getting a style to consumers. Delays in production could mean the loss of timeliness and sales appeal before an article reaches its market.

A contractor may arrange to work exclusively with one or more jobbers or manufacturers, reserving the right to work for others whenever the contractor's facilities are not fully employed. Such agreements are necessarily reciprocal. If a contractor agrees to give preference to a particular jobber's or manufacturer's work, the jobber or manufacturer gives preference to that contractor when placing sewing orders. The major advantages of the contractor system are as follows:

- Large amounts of capital are not required for investment in sewing equipment that may soon become obsolete.

- Difficulties in the hiring and training of suitable workers are minimized.

- The amount of capital necessary to meet regular payrolls is greatly reduced.

- By providing additional manufacturing facilities in periods of peak demand, contractors help speed up delivery of orders.

The contractor system has the disadvantages common to most assembly-line productions. No individual has full responsibility for the finished product, and so the quality of workmanship and inspection may tend to be uneven.

Once, most contractors were located in the metropolitan New York City area. Today, contractors may be located anywhere in the world where labor is abundant, where wages, taxes, and land costs or rents are lower, and where modern facilities and good transportation are available. For example, it now sometimes proves more profitable to ship fashion goods from New York to contractors in Mexico or Puerto Rico for sewing and finishing, then return them to New York for shipment to customers, than to sew and finish those same goods in the metropolitan New York area.

Size of Producers

Throughout the history of the industry, many of the firms producing women's apparel have been relatively small. For instance, in the early 1970s, there were some 5,000 firms making dresses. Their total output amounted to $3 billion. In contrast, the industry producing radios and television sets had an equal output achieved by only 300 firms.

However, during the last two decades a number of large apparel companies have emerged, each doing over $100 million in annual sales volume. The largest is Levi Strauss, with a $3 billion annual volume. Another large firm is Jonathan Logan, Inc., which more than quadrupled its sales to nearly half a billion dollars from the early 1960s to the early 1980s. (See Table 8-3 for a list of its divisions.) Cluett, Peabody is another example of a corporate apparel giant. It began in the 1850s as a privately held company making men's collars, and expanded by public stock offerings in the 1920s. Finally, after World War II, Cluett, Peabody expanded further through horizontal integration by acquiring new businesses or segmenting its own into various categories of men's and women's wear.

Currently, the trend is toward giantism, in part because the economics of the times demand it. The 10 largest apparel companies in the United States today represent over 20 percent of total domestic volume, and continue to grow at a rate faster than the total industry.[2] This trend, which is expected to continue at least through the decade, means that more and more small or medium-sized firms will disappear or be bought up by larger firms.

TABLE 8-3 A Large Apparel Company and Its Divisions: Jonathan Logan, Inc.	
DIVISION	PRODUCTS
Act III	Women's sportswear
Alice Stuart	Women's blouses
Amy Adams	Half-size dresses
Butte Knitting Mills	Women's apparel
Etienne Aigner	Women's & men's leather goods
Fabric Masters	Unused piece goods—wholesale
Harbor Masters	Raincoats
Imerman	Children's sleepwear
Kollection	Women's wear
Misty Harbor	Raincoats
Modern Juniors	Junior sportswear
R & K Originals	Women's apparel
Rose Marie Reid	Women's swimwear
Trebor Knitting Mills	Girl's underwear, sportswear
The Villager	Sportswear

Source: *Directory of Corporate Affiliations*, 1984, Macmillan, New York, p. 598.

Specialization by Product

Traditionally, women's apparel firms were divided into distinct groups according to (1) types of apparel, (2) size ranges, and (3) price zones. A blouse manufacturer seldom made dresses as well. A dress manufacturer seldom turned out both women's and juniors' sizes. A coat and suit manufacturer rarely produced both expensive and popular-priced lines.

Today, however, the industry is much less specialized. An increasing number of firms are developing diversified lines and crossing previously established price and product lines. Again, Jonathan Logan, originally a house for junior-sized dresses, is a typical example. It has diversified its product mix to include R & K Originals, a misses' dress company; Modern Juniors, a company for junior sportswear; Rose Marie Reid, a bathing suit company; and

FASHION FOCUS

CALVIN KLEIN: KING OF UNCLUTTER

Calvin Klein has been called the "King of Un-clutter" by *British Vogue*.[1] An American women's wear designer, he feels that when clothes are simple and beautiful, they permit the sense of the woman wearing them to come through. His clothes enhance the woman who wears them; they don't dominate her. He also says that fashion is not so much a matter of buying the right clothes as keeping your body in shape to wear them. And Klein practices what he preaches by working out regularly in his own gym.[2]

A native New Yorker, he graduated from the New York High School of Art and Design and the Fashion Institute of Technology. Today he is a member of F.I.T.'s board of directors as well as a visiting critic for the school's fashion students.

Klein's first job was as a copy boy for *Women's Wear Daily*; then he went to work as an apprentice to a coat maker. After 5 years of experience with several coat and dress makers, Klein and his boyhood friend Barry Schwartz set up Calvin Klein, Inc. Klein's first collection in 1968 consisted of just three dresses and six coats, but they did enable him to earn an appointment with the president of Bonwit Teller. Klein personally rolled his collection the whole 23 blocks from his Seventh Avenue workshop to the department store in midtown Manhattan. One of the wheels on the rack even broke on the street, but this didn't discourage Klein, who managed to receive his first

Etienne Aigner, a leather handbag, belt, and shoe company.

Another example is Jordache, which began its fashion empire on a base of designer jeans. (See the Fashion Focus on page 84.) Today, the company produces a full range of apparel including outerwear, shoes, and intimate apparel, as well as accessories from handbags to sunglasses. (These other Jordache products are actually produced by other manufacturers under a licensing arrangement.)

Designer Ralph Lauren has also greatly diversified from the original Polo line of mens-wear to include apparel for women and children, and an entire collection of merchandise for the home, from sheets to furniture. (See the illustration on page 60.)

Nevertheless, both producers and retail buyers still have to think and work in terms of product specialization. For instance, a producer will choose an inexpensive fabric for a popular-priced line and a more expensive fabric for a better-priced line. A retail buyer will shop one group of producers for sportswear, another group for coats, and still another for bridal wear.

order from Mildred Custin, Bonwit Teller's president at that time.

Calvin Klein and Barry Schwartz have been tremendously successful partners for almost two decades now, with Klein supplying the fashion inspiration and Schwartz managing the business expertise. Calvin Klein has always credited his friend and business manager with being the reason for his success. This may well be true if Schwartz was responsible for initiating the advertising campaign that helped to catapult Calvin Klein jeans to the top of the American fashion scene.

When Klein bought $5 million in TV time and hired Brooke Shields to pose in skintight jeans and proclaim, "You know what comes between me and my Calvins? Nothing!" the ad created such a sensation that it was banned from stations nationwide. Despite—and perhaps in part because of—the uproar, Calvin Klein jeans managed to take over the number one position in the jeans market that was formerly held by Murjani's Gloria Vanderbilt jeans.

Subsequent Calvin Klein ads have capitalized on the image established by the Brooke Shields ads. They have featured tight close-ups on sexy young jeans-clad women who confide in the viewer about subjects totally unrelated to jeans. The voice-over simply says "Calvin Klein jeans."

In *The Fashion Makers*, Klein is quoted as saying, "It's easier to get to the top than to stay there. People are hungry for anything good and will encourage you on the way up. To be consistent is the trick."[3] According to the book's authors, "His clothes are consistent. They are never way out . . . one season's collection grows out of the one before."[4] "Unpretentious about his work, he has always said, 'I make clothes people like to wear.' "[5]

Calvin Klein is as well known for his tailored suits and evening dresses as he is for his sportswear, and he is the youngest designer to be elected to the Coty Hall of Fame. New Calvin Klein products include "men's style" underwear for both men and women, menswear, cosmetics, and accessories. Career women especially like his designs, and many feel that because of the variety of styles and consistent quality of design, they need only look for the Calvin Klein label to be assured of being properly outfitted for any and all occasions.

[1] Ernestine Carter, *Magic Names in Fashion*, Prentice-Hall, Englewood Cliffs, New Jersey, 1980, p. 190.
[2] Catherine Houck, *The Fashion Encyclopedia*, St. Martin's Press, New York, 1982, p. 113.
[3] Barbara Walz and Bernadine Morris, *The Fashion Makers*, Random House, New York, 1978, p. 145.
[4] Ibid.
[5] Ibid., p. 144.
This Fashion Focus is based on information from the sources cited above and from this source:
"Suslow Joins Klein, Schwartz as Partner," *Women's Wear Daily*, January 19, 1984, pp. 1, 6.

CATEGORIES. The following are the traditional basic categories in women's apparel and the types of garments generally included in each:

1. *Outerwear*—Includes coats, suits, rainwear, jackets.

2. *Dresses*—Includes one- or two-piece designs and ensembles (a dress with a jacket or coat).

3. *Sportswear and separates*—Includes active, contemporary; town-and-country and spectator sportswear, such as pants, shorts, tops, swimwear, and cover-ups; bathing caps; beach bags; sweaters; skirts; shirts; jackets; tennis dresses; casual dresses; pantsuits.

4. *After-five and evening clothes*—Consists of dressy apparel.

5. *Bride and bridesmaid attire.*

6. *Blouses*—Includes both dressy and tailored.

7. *Uniforms and aprons*—Includes housedresses and sometimes career apparel.

8. *Maternity*—Includes dresses, sportswear.

SIZE RANGES. Women's apparel is divided into several size ranges. Unfortunately, the industry has not yet developed standard industrywide size measurements for each of these ranges, although exploratory work has been undertaken in this direction. This is why one manufacturer's misses' size 12 is likely to fit quite differently than another manufacturer's misses' size 12. The traditional size ranges are:

1. *Women's*—Includes even-numbered half-sizes 12½ to 26½ and straight sizes 36 to 52.
2. *Misses'*—Includes regular even-numbered sizes 6 to 20, tall sizes 12 to 20, and sometimes sizes as small as 2.
3. *Juniors'*—Includes regular sizes 5 to 17 and petite sizes 1 to 15.
4. *Petites'*—Includes regular even-numbered sizes 2 to 16 and junior sizes 1 to 15.

There is a growing number of customers in this country who wear clothes that are petite or large sizes. But most department stores, specialty stores, mass merchants, and apparel chains prominently display and sell a great proportion of their total sales in the misses' and juniors' size ranges. Less space and display are devoted to petite sizes, large sizes, and maternity wear.

WHOLESALE PRICE ZONES. Women's apparel is produced and marketed at a wide range of wholesale prices. Major factors contributing to the wholesale price of a garment are (1) the quality of materials used, (2) the quality of workmanship employed, and (3) the amount and type of labor required in the production process.

Within this wide range of prices, however, there are certain **price zones**, or series of somewhat contiguous price lines that appeal to specific target groups of customers. The women's apparel market has traditionally been divided into the following four price zones:

1. *Designer* (usually the higher prices; sometimes referred to as the "prestige" market)—Includes lines of name designers, such as Bill Blass, Ralph Lauren, and Oscar de la Renta.
2. *Better* (usually the medium to high prices)—Includes lines such as Liz Claiborne, Evan-Picone, and Jones New York. Also includes some of the better-known national brand names, such as Izod-LaCoste, and department stores' private-label lines, as well as "boutique" lines produced by the prestige designers.
3. *Moderate* (usually the medium prices)—Includes lines of nationally advertised makers, such as Jantzen, Catalina, Lady Manhattan, Koret of California, and Pant-Her. Sold usually in chain stores or in main-floor departments in department stores.
4. *Budget* (usually the lower prices; sometimes referred to as the "promotional" or "mass" market)—Includes some national brand names, such as Wrangler and Huckapoo.

A development of the early 1980s that is expected to reach even greater proportions through the remainder of the century is the appearance of a growing number of **"off-price" apparel stores**, selling name-brand and designer merchandise at prices well below traditional department store levels. These off-price outlets, such as Marshalls and T. J. Maxx, are putting increasing pressure on all the traditional price zones, and are especially affecting the moderate to better goods.

MERCHANDISING AND MARKETING ACTIVITIES

Most fashion producers sell directly to retail stores rather than through intermediaries. The pace of fashion in all but a few staple items is much too fast to allow the selling, reselling, or warehousing activities of wholesale distributors or jobbers.

Women's apparel producers aim their sales promotion efforts at both retailers and consumers. Such efforts take the form of advertising, publicity, and promotional aids available to retailers who buy their products.

Advertising

Today, much retail advertising of women's fashion apparel carries the name of the apparel producer. As recently as the 1930s, however, nearly all retailers refused to allow any tags or labels other than their own on the fashion goods they offered. A series of governmental regulations, in addition to merchandise shortages during World War II, helped reverse this situation. Today, most merchants capitalize on the producers' labels that are attached to the goods, feature producers' names in their own advertising and displays, and set up special sections within their stores for individual producers' lines.

The apparel manufacturing industry spends less than 1 percent of its annual sales total on advertising, but the exposure given to its products is impressive. After all, that 1 percent is often based on very healthy sales figures. For example, in the first quarter of 1982, manufacturers of women's sportswear spent $20,683,500 to advertise their apparel on television and radio, and in newspapers and magazines.[3] Both fashion and general-interest magazines are prime outlets for advertising exposure for all apparel firms, as are trade publications to reach retailers. Another important source of exposure is cooperative advertising with retail stores.

Publicity

Whether they spend money on advertising or not, apparel producers have many opportunities to familiarize the public with their brand names through publicity. To obtain maximum publicity, producers sometimes hire a public relations person or firm. These publicity firms distribute photographs of best-selling styles to newspapers and magazines. They also may supply TV and sports personalities with items of apparel in an attempt to attract public attention.

In addition to the individual efforts of firms to secure publicity, the major women's designer firms located in New York City show their collections at semiannual press weeks. There are two press weeks each January and two each June. One is organized by the New York Couture Group, the public relations arm of the New York Couture Business Council. The other is called the American Designers Showings and is an activity of the public relations firm Eleanor Lambert, Inc. Both give the country's fashion editors (newspaper, magazine, radio, and television) an opportunity to examine the latest designer collections. Both also provide photographs, prepared stories, and interview opportunities that editors need to tell the fashion story to their audiences.

Press weeks once exhibited merchandise lines that ran the entire gamut of price levels. Gradually, however, lower-priced merchandise was eliminated. In recent years, New York press weeks have featured almost exclusively the lines of higher-priced producers. In addition, the press is able to preview the new original lines of individual international designers, as they hold fashion show extravaganzas to model their high-fashion creations.

Promotional Aids

To assist retailers and to speed the sale of their merchandise, many apparel manufacturers provide a variety of promotional aids. The range is vast, and a single firm's offerings may include any or all of the following:

- Display ideas.
- Display and stock fixtures.
- Advertising aids.
- Suggestions for departmental layout and fixturing.
- Reorder forms and assistance in checking stock for reorder purposes.
- Educational booklets for salespeople and customers.

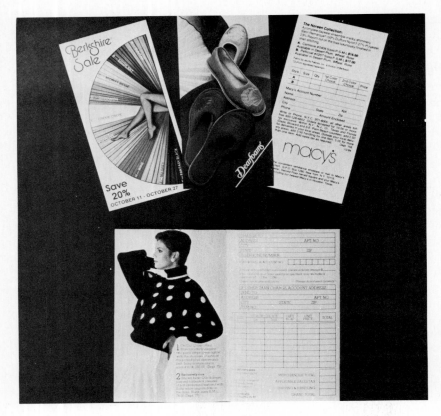

Promotional aids from manufacturers include statement enclosures like these that retailers can send to their charge customers.

- Talks to salespeople by producers' representatives.
- Assistance from producers' fashion experts in training salespeople, staging fashion shows, and addressing customers.
- Statement enclosures or other mailing pieces for stores to send to customers.
- Special retail promotions to tie in with producers' national advertising campaigns.
- Advertising mats for smaller stores.

The following is typical of what can be achieved by close cooperation between producers and retailers. A sportswear producer offered assistance to any store that would stage a travel promotion using the firm's merchandise. A major airline joined in the effort. Its flight attendants were available in the store to show customers how to pack and to advise them on clothing needs in vacation spots served by that airline. The producer's fashion experts planned minimal wardrobes to meet maximum travel demands. The producer, the store, and the airline all contributed to the promotion, and each profited by the interest generated.

More recently, one apparel producer showed a 20-minute color videotape featuring its current line to sales personnel of its retail store customers. The taped fashion show used four live models, and the producer provided the commentary. The purpose of the videotape was to help educate the fashion sales personnel about fabrics, colors, silhouettes, and skirt lengths in the producer's line, as well as the accessories necessary to complete this fashion message. Videotapes of this kind are sometimes also shown on the selling floor to customers of the retail store.

Another effective promotion is a trunk show. A **trunk show** is a showing of samples of most of the producer's line to a retail store's customers. Accompanying the samples is the producer, the designer, or a special representative of the firm. A fashion show is usually part of the trunk show, with the producer or the producer's representative on hand to deliver the commentary, meet customers, and discuss actual garments. The retail store's customers may then order any of the items shown.

Everyone benefits from these special events. Customers see fashions that they might never otherwise see, and experience the glamour of the fashion world. The retailer enjoys a dramatic influx of customers who come to see the show and place their orders. And finally, the manufacturer has an opportunity to see which of the styles shown are hot. If customer response is enthusiastic, the manufacturer also sees these products attain a new status in the eyes of the retailer.

INDUSTRY TRENDS

There is no question that through the rest of this century, the U.S. women's apparel industry and the U.S. apparel industry as a whole face dramatic change. While American designers have finally succeeded in rivaling Paris designers as definers of high fashion, American manufacturers are facing their toughest challenges from competitors in other parts of the world.

After decades of dominating the apparel manufacturing world, in recent years the American wholesale apparel market has been continually eaten into by massive imports from countries where labor wages are low. These imports, increasingly higher in quality, leapt from 6 percent in 1967 to over 22 percent in 1980. They are currently estimated to be from 22 to 28 percent of the market, and are projected to reach more than 40 percent by 1993.[4]

The apparel industry, however, is not taking this threat lying down. Instead, it is continuing to take steps enabling it to compete more ef-fectively in an increasingly international marketplace. Some of these tactics include:

- Placement of more emphasis on licensing, with its broad-based appeal.
- Internationalization of apparel marketing (increased exports).
- Decentralization of production facilities to take advantage of favorable labor costs and tariffs.
- Diversification of product lines to meet new market demands.
- Decreasing of emphasis on seasonal lines.
- Automation of more aspects of production in order to manufacture goods efficiently and competitively.

In looking ahead to the future of the fashion apparel industry, it is necessary to realize that this fast-moving, complex industry has consistently adjusted to the changing tastes and preferences of consumers. It may be that this very ability to respond to change will result in the emergence of a more successful apparel industry than ever before.

Licensing

Licensing, described in detail in Chapter 5, has experienced tremendous growth in the early 1980s, with sales of all licensed merchandise reaching an estimated $21 billion in 1983. Of that total, apparel and accessories account for about one-third of these sales, and represent the largest single category of licensed goods sold.[5] The advantage of a licensing arrangement is that the merchandise is identified with a highly recognizable name.

Internationalization of Apparel Marketing

American apparel manufacturers are increasingly thinking in international terms, because the industry in general has become increasingly international in scope. The appeal of American garment styling knows no boundaries, as evidenced by the worldwide popularity of the Western look and other classic American looks.

Yet despite that international appeal, the U.S. apparel trade deficit reached a record high in 1982, with imported apparel totaling $7.2 billion more than exported apparel.[6] This deficit has led both the apparel industry and the government to increase their emphasis on the opportunities for American apparel firms to export their goods to foreign countries.

The U.S. Department of Commerce has fostered a Textile and Apparel Export Expansion Program. Its purpose is to help strengthen the international competitive position of the textile and apparel industries. New evaluations of market potentials, manufacturing competition, distribution practices, and markets for major apparel product categories are being compiled and reviewed to provide new and greater opportunities for apparel manufacturers.

In 1982, the Commerce Department assigned it first director for textile/apparel export programs in Europe. This official, who is based in Europe, serves two main functions: (1) to aid individual exporters who want to break into the lucrative European market, and (2) to help coordinate the Commerce Department's European-based export programs.

In another effort toward internationalization, a number of individual designers have begun tapping foreign markets, not only through new licensing programs, but by marketing directly to consumers in other countries. Both Ralph Lauren and Calvin Klein have established their own boutiques overseas to sell their goods. Others, including Liz Claiborne, Oscar de la Renta, and Gloria Vanderbilt, have concentrated their efforts on arousing foreign retailers' interest in carrying their collections. Gloria Vanderbilt for Murjani went so far as to back its launch in England with some $3 million in advertising.[7]

In 1981, the New York Apparel Industry sponsored its first prêt-à-porter (or ready-to-

Liz Claiborne sells these American fashions overseas.

wear) show of fashion apparel designed by Americans. The purpose of the exhibition (patterned on the French prêt-à-porter shows) was to increase apparel exports to Europe, the Orient, and South America. In the same spirit, the U.S. Department of Commerce, in cooperation with the U.S. Apparel Council, sponsored a series of three international overseas exhibits for U.S.-made apparel, from November 1982 to February 1983. The exhibitions were held for markets in the Middle East, Japan, and Europe.

Foreign countries themselves have also initiated exchanges with the purpose of increasing their American imports. In 1983, China invited designer Pierre Cardin and his 540 worldwide licensees to participate in a special trade fair. The fair was aimed at acquainting the Chinese with the Western fashion industry, and to increase trade with the West.

Decentralization of Production Facilities

A few years ago, an industry survey reported that the present 15,000 apparel-manufacturing plants in the United States will be reduced to 10,000 by the end of this century. While some of the decrease will probably be caused by mergers and bankruptcies of small firms, the most significant factor will be the number of firms that move their production facilities out of the country.

Offshore production is being used increasingly by American apparel firms to lower their costs of production and thereby enable them to better compete with low-cost imports. **Offshore production** is the production of American goods in foreign cheap-labor countries, with the foreign producers using production specifications furnished by the American firms. Some people view this practice as a threat to the health of American labor. Others regard offshore production as a necessary tool for facing competition, but they didn't always feel this way. As recently as the beginning of the 1970s,

American manufacturers refused to put their brand names on what they considered to be low-quality products made abroad with cheap labor. But by the beginning of the 1980s, more and more apparel manufacturers were importing goods, either from their own apparel plants operating in cheap, labor-rich foreign areas, or through long-term supply arrangements with foreign producers.

A factor that helps make offshore production beneficial to U.S. manufacturers is a special tariff advantage under Section 807 of the Tariff Classification Act of 1962. Section 807 works like this: An American apparel manufacturer designs the patterns and cuts the fabric in its U.S. plant. This material is then shipped to the offshore country for sewing, after which it is returned to the United States for finishing and packaging. The company thus takes advantage of cheap labor for the most labor-intensive aspect of the apparel manufacturing process and pays duty only on the value added to the garment by the work done abroad.

An apparel industry analysis prepared by Werner Management Consultants in 1983 reported that some manufacturers predict even more dramatic changes in production in the U.S. apparel industry. Part of that prediction is that the dominating firms of the mid-1990s will manufacture totally offshore, or will directly import lines that are styled, merchandised, and marketed from their U.S. offices.[8] However, most industry watchers do not foresee the total disappearance of a domestic manufacturing segment.

Factors that are expected to work in favor of domestic production include a number of variables on the world scene. First, improved technology in this country is increasing productivity and allowing many manual tasks to be completed in less time and at lower cost than ever before. In addition, wage scales in many foreign countries are rising rapidly. For example, in Taiwan, apparel industry wages have risen more than 1,180 percent since 1967, compared with a 265 percent increase in the United States.[9] Although wages in that country still represent only 25 percent of American wages, a continuing upward spiral could help make domestic manufacturing an increasingly viable alternative to offshore production.

Diversification of Product Lines

Traditionally, as mentioned earlier, women's apparel producers were specialized in terms of the types, size ranges, and price zones of apparel they produced. Today, producers are broadening their offerings. For instance, Blue Bell, maker of Wrangler jeans, has broadened its base through acquisition and new product development. It has expanded its lines to include shirts, sports coats, and slacks. Interco, Inc., formerly the International Shoe Company, began diversifying in the late 1960s, when footwear was the first apparel industry to feel the sting of imports. Since then, Interco has purchased more than a dozen apparel producers, including London Fog raincoats and College Town sportswear.

In addition, manufacturers of women's apparel have been reevaluating their size ranges in recent years, and have been offering greater selections or new lines designed for the larger- and smaller-size markets. Orit Corporation's Gitano division, for example, introduced a new line of proportionately sized women's jeans, designed in three lengths for short-, regular-, and long-waisted women. The company's strategy was based in part on the findings of a national Gallup poll that reported that 50 percent of women surveyed have held back from many sportswear purchases because of problems with sizing.

A further indication of the growing emphasis on size was the First International Special Size Fashion Fair, held in New York in 1982. The 4-day exposition featured medium- and higher-priced collections of women's apparel and accessories in petite sizes, large sizes, half sizes, tall sizes, and maternity wear.

PETITES. According to the National Center for Health Statistics, 55 percent of the female population in the United States is under 5'4". That represents about 37 million potential customers for apparel in the petite size category, and a burgeoning market for manufacturers of that special-size apparel.

Petite apparel can be worn by both junior and misses' customers, but it is proportioned for short, small-boned women who wear sizes 0 to 8. A number of manufacturers, including Jones New York, Liz Claiborne, The Villager, and Levi Strauss, have added petite lines to their regular assortment. Evan-Picone, Inc. created a whole separate division for its petite-sized apparel in 1980, which within 2 years reached an annual sales volume of over $27 million.[10]

The first show that displayed only petite sizes was held in January 1979 by the California Mart. Approximately 500 buyers viewed some 20 manufacturers' lines at that show. Today, a growing number of department and specialty stores are catering to their petite customers with boutiques devoted specifically to smaller sizes in apparel. Marshall Field's in Chicago doubled its sales of petite clothing in just the first year after it opened its Petite World shop. Other stores have opened that carry nothing but petite sizes, such as The Great American Short Story, a multiunit chain headquartered in Temple City, California.

LARGE SIZES. Research figures show that approximately 25 percent of all women in the United States wear large sizes—sizes 16 to 20, $12\frac{1}{2}$ to $26\frac{1}{2}$, and 36 to 52. Although we as a nation have been diet- and figure-conscious for many years, there still has always been a substantial number of large-sized women in this country. However, apparel in these sizes has made up only a small proportion of apparel production. In recent years, more attention is being paid to the larger size, and fuller-figure fashions are gaining in importance at the man-

Clothes for women who wear large sizes are receiving more attention at both the manufacturing and retail levels.

ufacturing level. Many top-name manufacturers have established special divisions devoted to designing and producing large-sized apparel. In the past few years, many of the regional apparel markets have been sponsoring special market weeks for the large-size market.

Retailers also are beginning to place more emphasis on offering fashion to larger-sized woman customers. Specialty stores, such as The Forgotten Woman chain, are devoted exclusively to large sizes in apparel. Traditional full-line retailers are also giving more attention to the needs of this customer group. JC Penney, for one, ran a special try-on session for large women customers at its Milwaukee catalog center. Over the course of a week, 49 women tried on and critiqued about 300 garments, including blazers, coats, dresses, blouses, and pants. The women's comments and opinions were then taken into consideration by JC Penney merchandising and marketing staff in order to create a better-fitting line of apparel for large women. The newest development in this market is that styling and promotion are geared toward young large-sized customers in contrast to the previous nearly exclusive focus on the over-40 customer.

MATERNITY. The area of maternity clothing is receiving new emphasis from both manufacturers and retailers, in part because of the growing number of expectant mothers who are working outside the home. They have created a demand for more tailored, businesslike maternity outfits, and the demand is being met by apparel producers and specialty stores.

The tremendous market for maternity wear is illustrated by one company, Mothers Work, which began in 1981 selling cotton knit dresses by mail order. Response was so great that the company expanded its line to include business suits, tailored dresses, and jumpers with matching jackets. Another well-known name in the field is Lady Madonna, which began with one store in New York in 1969 and by 1983 grew to more than 90 franchises, with retail sales of $20 million.[11]

LADY MADONNA
M A T E R N I T Y

Let the season begin

Lady Madonna introduces a dramatic new season
of the finest fall couture fashions. The stylings of
Lady Madonna are bold and gentle. Tasteful. Imaginative.
And appealing. Come and see a completely new couture line
designed to look as graceful and stylish at the
beginning of your pregnancy as it does at the end.
Please phone or write for your free copy of our
full colour Lady Madonna Fall & Winter Collection Catalogue.

Maternity wear is receiving new emphasis as more expectant mothers work outside the home.

Decreasing of Emphasis on Seasonal Lines

Traditionally, women's apparel producers created two lines a year—one for the spring–summer season and one for the fall–winter season. Rarely were new styles available until the next semiannual line was introduced. Buyers simply reordered those styles that sold well.

However, because of consumer demand, producers gradually began introducing minor seasonal lines (such as holiday, resort and cruise, and transitional wear) between regular semiannual lines. These helped stores bring new styles and new interest to their selling floors throughout the year.

The trend away from strictly seasonal lines is continuing. Although producers of better apparel still tend to develop strictly seasonal lines, producers of moderate-priced apparel keep adding new styles to their lines throughout each season. Producers of popular-priced apparel have just about dropped seasonal lines. They concentrate instead on producing a continuous series of lower-priced items that are copies or adaptations of higher-priced popular styles.

Automation of Apparel Production

The most radical change taking place in the apparel industry today is its belated transformation, through automation, from a labor-intensive industry to a capital-intensive one. Long after every other major industry, the apparel industry is finally responding to the technological explosion of the 1960s and 1970s. The most important changes involve refinements in traditional cutting and sewing machinery. Applications of new technologies— lasers, computers, or both—have revolutionized production processes and improved management methods. Increased productivity, reduced labor costs, better standardization of product, and better quality control have resulted. (See Chapter 6 for additional information.)

CUTTING AND SEWING PROCEDURES. Laser-beam systems for cutting fabric were first introduced in the menswear manufacturing industry. They have now been adapted for use in the production of women's apparel, where the cutting work is more complicated. A laser beam can cut fabric more quickly and more accurately than an electric knife. Since in this method cuts are made by burning, raw edges that might unravel are eliminated.

Equipment has been developed, using a computer, that automatically lays out a pattern so that the least amount of fabric is used. This allows maximum usage of each bolt of fabric.

Also in use is equipment that records apparel patterns on electronic tape. The patterns can thus be stored easily and safely and can be located quickly. Some equipment in experimental use makes sample duplicates at the same time the original pattern is made.

More automation is also being used in sewing plants. Electronic scanners optically guide sewing-machine heads to stitch the pieces of a cut pattern according to programs. Conveyor belts carry the pieces of a garment from one machine to another in the order in which they are to be sewn together. Machines have been introduced that fuse seams by heat instead of by stitching, thus saving time and eliminating raw edges. Other machines, which fit a section of tubular fabric over a three-dimensional metal form, heat-set the fabric, and then cool it, have reduced the labor once involved in sewing by 30 to 40 percent.

The use of industrial robots to perform some of the functions of apparel production is still a number of years away, although the robot is seen as another useful technological tool for increasing efficiency. Robots are already being used effectively in the automotive industry, and it is predicted that by 1990, American industry will employ 120,000 of the computerized machines.[12] Japan's apparel industry has already begun a development program that uses robots heavily, and which is being implemented over a 7- to 10-year period at a cost of $60 million.[13]

SALES AND INVENTORY REPORTS. Computer printouts have become extremely important to the entire fashion industry, from the fiber houses to the manufacturers to the retailers. More and more producers of women's apparel are using daily or weekly computer printouts to keep their inventories of piece goods in better balance with unit sales for each style number.

Printouts also provide producers with up-to-date information on the number of units—by style, size, and color—that are on hand, in the process of being produced, and on order from each of their retail store customers. Computerized reports can also tell producers the dollar volume of business they are doing in the current year compared to that in previous years with each of their retail accounts.

Some larger retailers and producers are experimenting with daily or semiweekly transmittal of sales information. Store sales are fed into store computers and sorted by style and producer. Producers are then sent a rundown on the activity of their styles. This enables both stores and producers to keep close track of changes in consumer demand.

For instance, with such current information at their fingertips, producers can update production plans and fabric commitments to correspond with demand trends. Their design departments can keep close track of the acceptance or rejection of individual styles and can use this information in their planning of new styles. Their sales staffs can be given more complete information to use in telling store buyers about the firm's best-selling styles, fabrics, and colors.

DEVELOPMENT FORECASTS

The women's fashion apparel industry is not immune to the effects of an economy in recession. New York, which produces $17 billion worth of apparel each year, lost some 31,000 apparel and textile jobs in the years between 1977 and 1982, about 6,200 of which were in women's apparel.[14] At the same time, unemployment in the nation's apparel industry hit 16 percent in 1982, according to the ILGWU.[15] Yet that same year, women's apparel outpaced most other apparel categories in retail sales.

Coping with a poor economy is just one more challenge that American apparel firms have faced creatively. They have found solutions in targeting new retail markets, new price points, and new customers and sizes. This type of expansion will undoubtedly continue in the coming years, just as designer and manufacturer expansion into the international fashion arena will continue through increasingly sophisticated licensing and export programs.

In a special report called "Outlook for the Apparel Industry," prepared in January 1983 by the management consulting firm Kurt Salmon Associates, the coming years were predicted to be a time of change and challenge for the apparel industry. According to the report, the next decade will see increasing competition from imports, and a continuation of the trend toward big companies getting bigger. National brand names and designer labels will establish themselves further as their recognition grows in both the national and international markets. Additional applications of computer technology will continue to impact on production and management, creating an ever more efficient factory and inventory system for apparel manufacturers and retailers.

In short, the changes going on in the American apparel industry make this an exciting and challenging time to be in the field of women's apparel. For those producers that approach the market creatively and take advantage of the opportunities open to them, the potential for success has probably never been greater.

REFERENCES

[1] International Ladies' Garment Workers' Union.
[2] "Outlook for the Apparel Industry," *The KSA Perspective for Apparel Management*, No. 29, Kurt Salmon Associates, New York, January 1983, unpaged.
[3] Jo Ann Paganetti, "Quality Will Take Fashion Forward," *Advertising Age*, September 6, 1982, p. M-13.
[4] "Outlook for the Apparel Industry," unpaged.
[5] Susan K. Reed, "What Does Bill Blass Know About Chocolates?," *Savvy*, May 1983, p. 56.
[6] "Apparel Deficit Hit $7.2B Peak in '82," *Women's Wear Daily*, May 25, 1983, p. 32.
[7] Megan McGuire, "The Tide Turns Slowly," *Advertising Age*, September 14, 1981, p. S-6.
[8] Mary T. Scannapieco, "TexScope USA—Decision '87," *Apparel Industry Magazine*, March 1983, p. 28.
[9] Helen Burggraf, "Panel Advises New Look at U.S. Production Cost," *Women's Wear Daily*, April 6, 1983, p. 52.
[10] "Small Clothes are Selling Big," *Business Week*, November 16, 1981, p. 152.
[11] Elaine Louie, "A Ballooning Industry," *Working Woman*, October 1983, p. 174.
[12] Marvin Klapper, "Eisen: Robots Are Answer to Import Woes," *Women's Wear Daily*, December 1, 1981, p. 14.
[13] Wesley Stilwell, "Robots Unready to Take Over," *Daily News Record*, May 31, 1983, p. 10.
[14] Nancy Josephson, "NY Apparel, Textile Jobs Show Decline for 5 Years," *Women's Wear Daily*, May 4, 1983, p. 28.
[15] Nancy Josephson, "ILGWU Puts Apparel Industry Unemployment at 16% in '82," *Women's Wear Daily*, January 7, 1983, p. 8.

MERCHANDISING VOCABULARY

Define or briefly explain the following terms:

Apparel jobber
Contractor
Graded
Manufacturer
Marker
Off-price apparel stores
Offshore production

Outside shop
Price zones
Ready-to-wear
Sample hand
Section work
Trunk show

1. Discuss the growth and contributions of the ILGWU to the apparel industry.
2. Outline the steps in the development and production of a line of women's apparel.
3. What are the major advantages of the contractor system? What is the key disadvantage?
4. List the traditional basic categories of women's apparel, giving types of garments in each category.
5. Into what size ranges is women's apparel traditionally divided?
6. List and describe the four major price zones into which women's apparel is divided. What are the major factors contributing to the wholesale price of garments?
7. Why do most fashion producers sell directly to retail stores rather than through wholesalers?
8. Discuss the merchandising activities of women's fashion producers today.
9. How does a manufacturer or designer benefit from attending a trunk show in a retail store?
10. Discuss the internationalization of apparel marketing, including the challenges faced by American manufacturers and the attempts of the industry and the government to meet those challenges.

1. Discuss the advantages and disadvantages of standardization of women's apparel sizes.
2. What are the repercussions of a name-brand or designer manufacturer selling current-season apparel to off-price outlets as well as to department and specialty shops?

9. CHILDREN'S APPAREL

Two very important events, occurring close together, had a dramatic effect on the children's wear industry. First, World War II ended, bringing men back to their homes after years away. Second, television came into America's living rooms.

The result of the first of these occurrences was a tremendous postwar "baby boom" during which millions of babies were born in the United States after a 4-year period of very low birth rate. The result of the second was that by the time these babies were toddlers, T.V. viewing was a big part of their lives. And many of the things they saw advertised on television, they wanted. So for the first time in history, children began to make their wants known—as to what cereal they would eat, what toys they had to have, and finally, what clothes they wanted to wear.

This was a giant step away from the way children had traditionally acted. In the 1900s children were expected to be "little adults" and were dressed accordingly, usually in scaled-down versions of adult apparel. By the 1930s, children's clothes were purchased by their parents with no thought of asking the child's opinion. Children simply went along to try on the clothes chosen for them in order to guarantee the correct fit.

In the 1950s, children's wear manufacturers were quick to act upon the new demand for clothes that children wanted. They responded with "child-oriented" styles that reflected the individuality of the youngest generation as opposed to the adult look of their parents. At the same time, they recognized the need for "active" styles and carefree fabrics to go with the new freedom of children.

In the 1970s there was a movement in the United States and other nations for "zero population growth." The resulting low birth rate was reflected in the children's wear market for several years. However, the 1980s brought a return to the traditional ideas of family. This trend, of course, can only mean a continued growth pattern for the children's wear industry.

Despite the dour view of the total population growth during the eighties and nineties, children under 14 years of age are likely to become more numerous; this is the projection, based upon statistical information, of the Census Bureau.[1] About 4 million babies can be expected to be born each year up to 1991, for a total that will at least come close to the 41.6 million born during the baby-boom decade of 1955–1965. That means a children's wear market expansion of 20 to 29 percent, which will be a result of the baby-boom babies having their own families. Even though they will be having fewer babies per family, the impact will be explosive since the newcomers will greatly outnumber the children who will be growing up and out of children's sizes.[2]

Dr. Joyce Brothers, the celebrated psychologist, has reported that clothes play a major role in forming a child's self-image. One of the discoveries she made is that throughout a child's growing years, clothing plays a key role in shaping and guiding the emerging self. With an understanding of the role clothing plays during the different stages of children's growth, parents can help ensure that a child's appearance will enhance his or her strivings to become a mature, self-confident adult.[3]

It is therefore important to look at the children's wear industry not only from the historical view, but also toward the future view. In this chapter we will deal with children's wear—girls' wear and boys' wear. Although boys' wear is considered a separate part of the menswear industry at the production level, we will consider it as part of the total children's wear industry in this chapter.

HISTORY OF THE CHILDREN'S APPAREL INDUSTRY

As a commercial activity, the children's wear industry is largely a phenomenon of the twentieth century. Prior to this time, the production of infants' and children's clothing was almost entirely a cottage industry. The special needs associated with children's activities, and the changing proportions of their growing bodies, were not considered in making children's clothing. While boys' and girls' clothing was different, there was little distinction within either boys' or girls' wear. All little girls, for example, dressed in the same few styles. Clothes were made large enough so that a child could grow into them and sturdy enough to be handed down to younger or smaller children.

Although a few designers specialized in higher-priced children's wear, it was not until after World War I that the commercial production and distribution of children's wear became a recognized industry. This followed in the wake of a developing women's apparel industry, discussed in Chapter 8.

The same technological, sociological, and economic changes that were responsible for the development of the women's clothing industry were responsible for the development of the children's wear industry. As more women were working outside the home, they had less time to sew. And a rapidly increasing juvenile population created new markets. These factors encouraged existing companies to expand their operations, brought new companies into the field, and encouraged special-

This 1874 engraving shows children wearing miniature versions of adult apparel.

ization of products. The development of snaps, zippers, and more durable sewing made more functional apparel possible for children as well as adults.

After World War I, attention was directed toward developing standard size measurements in clothing for immature and growing physiques. Since then, commercial standards of sizing have been developed for infants' and children's knit underwear, for toddlers' apparel, and also for girls' and preteens' apparel and boys' wear.

Changes in the American way of life since the end of World War II have brought about changes in American children. Rare is the child who accepts homemade clothing or clothes bought by parents to suit *their* tastes.

Today's children are customers in their own right. They are in the store at the time of purchase, know what they want, and do not hesitate to express their wishes. They live, more than their predecessors, in the adult world. They are exposed to advertising on television, on radio, and in printed media; they are targets of programs and publications. Children are encouraged to express their individuality. And many of them do.

ORGANIZATION AND OPERATION OF THE CHILDREN'S APPAREL INDUSTRY

The majority of children's wear firms are small and in many cases family-owned. Exceptions are such giant companies as Carter's and Health-Tex, as well as the children's wear divisions of large-scale apparel producers, such as Danskin, Russ-Togs, Levi Strauss, White Stag, Blue Bell, and Interco.

Similar in structure to the women's and men's apparel industry, the children's wear industry is categorized by price, size, and type of merchandise. In terms of price, again as in adult clothing, the industry is made up of producers of budget-, moderate-, and better-priced goods. By far the greater share of the children's wear business is done by producers of budget-priced and moderate-priced goods. Because of the rising costs of operation, many former producers of budget-priced lines are moving into the moderate-price range. Most of the real budget-priced goods are being produced out of this country in low-wage foreign countries.

The children's wear industry specializes in six basic size ranges. The age group and sizes included in each category are given below:

1. **Infants'**—Two sizing systems are used. One system uses sizes 3 to 24 months. The other uses sizes newborn, small, medium, large, and extra large.

2. **Toddlers'**—Worn by young children who are learning to walk. Sizes range from T1 to T4 (the "T" stands for toddler).

3. **Children's**—Includes sizes 3 to 6X for girls and 3 to 7 for boys. Worn by girls and boys between ages 3 and 6.

4. **Girls'**—Includes sizes 7 to 14, corresponding to the growth and development of girls as they enter their teens.

5. **Preteen**—Includes sizes 6 to 14, developed in recent years to provide the more sophisticated styling required by some girls.

6. **Boys'**—Includes sizes 8 to 20, corresponding to the growth and development of boys as they enter their teens and mature. **Young men**, **student**, or **teen sizes** have been developed in recent years to provide more sophisticated styling requested by some young men.

Another area of specialization within the industry is by type of product. For example, one producer will make only girls' knits, another dresses, another sportswear, another sleepwear, and still another coats. Frequently, however, a producer will make a single type of product in more than one size range—sportswear or dresses in toddlers' through girls' sizes, for example, or in sizes 2 to 14. The same is true in boys' wear.

The same design and production methods that apply to adult apparel are used in the children's wear industry, except that in the latter they are less elaborate.

Four size ranges of children's apparel are featured in this ad.

The children's wear business has never been more fashion-oriented than today. Although it is more obvious in the large metropolitan areas, the influence of fashion looks is being felt in even the most rural areas of the country.

Even the most "basic" lines of children's wear reflect, in one way or another, those fashion trends that are first appearing in European or American adult clothing. This fashion interest has been growing for several years and is probably most noticeable today in the designer jeans and designer clothing being produced for girls and boys. However, the children's wear business is a *fashionable*, as opposed to a *fashion*, business. What is the difference?

The children's wear industry produces fashionable clothing that mirrors many of the trends that appear in the women's and men's apparel industries. But the children's wear market is not a fashion business because, generally speaking, it does not operate on a ready-to-wear production and design schedule.

For one thing, children's wear companies for the most part operate on the one line/one season method of production. This means that most manufacturers come out with a maximum of four lines during the year, timed according to season. Once the particular line is shown, however, that is it. The most exciting, new, hot look or designs might appear mid-season, but most manufacturers would not be able to produce them until the following season, probably after the demand has begun to decline. Of course, there is no question that the children's wear business has changed considerably from several years ago, when a style popular in the adult market would work its way down to children's wear a year later. Now the time lag is more like one season. Still, very few children's wear manufacturers go into production on an item the moment it appears on the scene.[4]

MARKET CENTERS

Most of the children's wear firms are located in the North Atlantic states, particularly in New York City. As is the trend in the women's and men's apparel industries, some factories have moved farther south in order to obtain lower production costs. In many cases goods are produced in foreign countries—the Far East primarily for outerwear, jeans, woven shirts, and sweaters; Greece, Spain, and Israel for infants' knits and apparel items. (See Chapter 8.) These countries offer lower production costs than do France, Italy, and Switzerland, which produce prestige merchandise. But the design, sales, and distribution centers of such firms remain in New York City. While New York continues to be the most important market center for children's wear, many producers maintain permanent showrooms in the large regional apparel marts and schedule showings there for seasonal lines.

MERCHANDISING AND MARKETING ACTIVITIES

Many of the features and activities of the children's wear industry are similar, if not identical, to those of the women's and men's apparel industries. Sales promotion and advertising activities for children's wear, however, are considerably more limited.

The few giants in the industry—Carter's, Health-Tex, and Danskin—advertise aggressively to consumers. Smaller firms—the majority of firms producing budget and moderately priced children's wear—leave most consumer advertising to retailers. Firms producing higher-priced, name-designer merchandise do a limited amount of consumer advertising. The high cost of this advertising is often shared with textile firms.

In general, the industry limits its advertising to the trade press. Specialized publications that are concerned solely with children's wear include: *Earnshaw's Infants; Girls and Boys Wear Review; McCall's Children's Wear Merchandiser;* and *Kids Fashion*. Trade publications that report on adult fashions, such as *Women's Wear Daily* and *Daily News Record*, also carry children's wear industry advertising and news re-

The newest beat. Clothes with flair.

OUR·GIRL®
Girls' sizes 7 to 14 from Health-tex®

Our Gang™
Boys' sizes 8 to 20 from Health-tex®

© 1984 Health-tex Inc. 1411 Broadway, New York, N.Y. 10018

Health-tex is one of the giants in the children's wear market. These clothes are clearly fashionable!

ports of interest to retailers on a regular, weekly basis.

In October 1979, sponsors of the National Fashion and Boutique Show inaugurated a national showcase for the children's wear industry and called it the National Kids' Fashion Show. Now a tri-annual event, featuring over 350 children's wear lines, it is held in New York City. The range of categories shown includes infants', toddlers', boys' sizes 4 to 7 and 8 to 20, girls' sizes 3 to 6X, 7 to 14, and preteen garments.

Designer Labels

Children's designer-label clothing and accessories are now highly visible in stores countrywide. The appeal of these items seems to rise above income levels. Designer labels are available in stores geared to middle-income customers as well as stores that cater to high-income customers.

Although designer wear for children has been around for some time—Izod introduced its boys' line in the late 1960s—the explosion in designer-label children's wear started in 1978–1979 with the designer jean craze.[5] Today, because they have designer-name status, some long-term children's wear designers are receiving celebrity treatment, including Ruth Scharf and Florence Eiseman.

One of the phenomena of this designer craze is the "I can dream, can't I?" customer, who is usually a mother who can't afford a $1,500 Yves St. Laurent outfit for herself and wouldn't have anywhere to wear it if she could. For $40 she can deck out her little daughter in a delectable YSL party skirt and blouse, indulging her fantasy of *someone* in the family wearing famous designer clothes.

Status names are also changing the shape of the boys' wear industry. It is difficult to tell which came first—boys' demand for designer clothes or designers' efforts to enter the boys' wear business. Whatever the case, well-known fashion designers are now competing for space alongside traditional branded merchandise in boys' wear departments

Because of the increasing interest in fashion, boys' wear has become a prime area for both European and American name designers. Jeans and other items of apparel bearing the labels of Pierre Cardin, Yves St. Laurent, John Weitz, Ralph Lauren, Calvin Klein, and Sasson illustrate this point.

Licensing

Licensed characters, always favorites in children's wear, now are proliferating at such a fast pace that one can hardly keep track of all of them and of who is the most popular one at any given time. Strawberry Shortcake, the Smurfs, Miss Piggy, Cabbage Patch dolls, and E.T. join old-timers like Snoopy, Yogi Bear, and Mickey Mouse as favorites in character licensing each year. Royalties for character licenses average 5 to 6 percent, although the creators of both Snoopy and E.T. get between 10 and 20 percent from their licensors.

Licensed characters dominate in T-shirts, sweatshirts, and sleepwear. They are also strong in accessories and in sportswear. Their impact is rather small in dresses, suits, and outerwear.

According to industry sources, while the hit or miss of a licensed character in children's apparel is unpredictable, there are two successful ways to spark its advance. These are:

1. Tie-in of a major licensing company (like American Greetings) with a major toy company (like Kenner), which will put millions of dollars into giving a character (like Strawberry Shortcake) national exposure.
2. Getting a character on a T.V. cartoon program. The Smurfs had been around for more than 2 years, but sales of Smurfs' products did not explode until the Smurfs went on television in September 1981.[6]

The active sports field is another major source of licensing in children's wear. Some 30

Licensing of favorite TV characters is proliferating in children's wear.

million kids 6 years to college age participate in organized sports outside their schools, and some 6 million (2 million girls) participate in interscholastic sports competition in high school.[7] Because of this, sports figures have an instant recognition factor that makes them appealing to boys and girls. Names of hockey, tennis, football, and baseball teams are licensed to manufacturers so that their products will bear the name of the team. Also, individual sports stars have licensed their names to be used on active sportswear such as jogging and running suits, tennis outfits and accessories, and sports equipment.

INDUSTRY TRENDS

Like women's apparel manufacturers, children's wear producers are constantly on the lookout for ways to increase productivity and reduce or at least minimize current costs, while still maintaining quality. Many producers have found that the way to keep their business flourishing is through complete and total modernization, with computerized systems operating throughout the entire production process.

The clear distinction that once existed between budget-, moderate-, and better-priced children's wear has been eroded by continuing inflation. Some of the once-major producers of moderate-priced sportswear and dresses, such as Pandora and Girlstown, went out of business because of inflation and rising operating costs. To have stayed in business under such conditions, they would have been forced to raise their prices beyond the upper limits of the moderate price range. This would have placed them in competition with already well-established producers of higher-priced apparel, a much smaller segment of the children's wear market.

FASHION FOCUS

FLORENCE EISEMAN: MATRIARCH OF CHILDREN'S FASHION

Hand-me-downs are sometimes looked upon with scorn by the younger siblings, cousins, and friends' offspring who receive them. And mothers who dress their children in recycled garments often do so out of economic necessity. But not so with Florence Eiseman designs: the recipients treasure the clothes for their timeless styling, and the well-to-do mothers who pass them on are often reluctant to part with them. Florence Eiseman herself enjoys seeing children in clothes that were part of a collection of 10 or 15 years ago because it reaffirms the basic tenet of her design philosophy—that good taste does not change.

The distinguished doyenne of children's wear designs has been producing kids' clothing since the mid-forties, when she sold her first order of organdy pinafores to Marshall Field's. She began sewing small items of clothing for the sons and daughters of friends when a doctor suggested that she might calm her nerves by keeping her hands busy. She moved from her original location—a corner of her husband's toy factory—to larger and larger quarters as the company grew. Then her husband Laurie joined her in the business, doing most of the traveling to present the line to retailers across the country. The business is still very much in the family, with sons Robert and Laurie, Jr., current heads of the firm.

Although Mrs. Eiseman is now in her eighties and no longer works full-time, she manages to stay involved in the business that bears her name. Boarding a bus in front of her apartment on Lake Michigan in Milwaukee, she travels to the factory

In order to fill the vacuum thus created in the moderate price range, many budget producers are trading up. The vacuum thus created in the budget market is now being filled to a large extent by offshore production in countries with lower labor costs.

Producers' associations and labor unions such as the International Ladies' Garment Workers' Union both continue to apply pressure on U.S. government agencies, demanding greater curbs on imports. According to these groups, burgeoning imports—particularly those involving textiles and apparel—are a potential threat to the survival of the American fashion industries. Trends indicate that industry and labor will continue to demand curtailment of such imports. The government, on the other hand, will view the import-export situation in

3 days a week and still exercises veto power over the designs. She is very outspoken if she sees something she doesn't like, such as too much trim on a dress. She is as particular about the quality of the finished product as she is about simplicity of design, and she still insists that all finishing touches on seams, buttonholes, and hems be hand-worked with meticulous care. This demand for perfection has earned Florence Eiseman's designs an excellent reputation among retailers. According to one Bergdorf-Goodman buyer, her line is one of the few that requires no inspection before going to the selling floor.

When Florence Eiseman began her designing career in the forties, garments for young people were fashioned to make them look like undersized adults. There was no concession made for the actual shape of children's bodies, pastels predominated, and excessive decoration was the norm. Florence Eiseman changed all that. Two of her favorite sayings are "Children have bellies, not waists," and "You should see the child, and not the dress, first." When she gave children their own clothes, featuring bright primary colors, she eliminated the restrictive waistband. She banished fussy frills and unnecessary embellishments. Instead, she often added fanciful appliqués of flowers, fish, vegetables, and animals—touches that have come to be associated with Florence Eiseman clothes and that are so often copied by other manufacturers.

Florence Eiseman clothes have always been moderately expensive to expensive. They are found in prestigious stores such as Neiman-Marcus and Marshall Field's and in the most exclusive children's specialty stores. But if the money spent on children's clothes by wealthy and indulgent parents and grandparents borders on the excessive, they have never complained about not getting their money's worth in terms of both status and quality. Suits for boys and dresses are made of the finest European fabric, and the playclothes line (established in the mid-fifties) is well known for being comfortable as well as attractive. Mrs. Eiseman has always updated her designs to incorporate the new fabrics—knits for the more moderately priced playclothes line in the late fifties and stretch nylon from France for swimsuits and stretch pants in the sixties—that are well suited to active children.

Mrs. Eiseman has stated that she hates change, but ironically, it is she who has done more than almost any designer to change the shape and style of children's clothes in America in the past 50 years. Her all-time best-selling A-line jumper and T-shirt outfit for girls—and the subsequent copies—are such a fact of life in America that it is hard to imagine a preschool or elementary-school class picture without at least one little girl dressed in this classic. Most importantly, Florence Eiseman has succeeded in doing what she set out to do in the beginning: she has dressed children so they look like children.

This Fashion Focus is based on information from these sources:
Paul Marla, "Florence Eiseman: Small Wonder," *Women's Wear Daily,* July 12, 1982, pp. 5–6.
E. P. Shipp, "The Woman Behind the Eiseman Look," *The New York Times Magazine,* August 14, 1984, pp. 72–75.

---

terms of what is best for the country as a whole.

Buying foreign-made merchandise has as many pitfalls as pluses. Very early commitment is necessary, giving about 8 to 9 months' lead time, and usually there is no opportunity for reordering. However, most buyers feel that they can better satisfy consumer demand for both price and quality when they buy foreign-made merchandise. Not only do retail buyers seek merchandise overseas, but many children's wear manufacturers are seeking foreign contractors to produce merchandise to their specifications in order to meet the competition of the direct purchasing abroad by the retailers.

Children's wear producers are increasingly aware of the importance of the right fashion and styling in their products. This is particularly noticeable today with the licensing of such famous American designer names as Sasson, Calvin Klein, and Gloria Vanderbilt to jeans and other sportswear items for children. Similarly, licensing arrangements with such top French designers as Yves St. Laurent, Pierre Cardin, Givenchy, and Christian Dior permit producers to offer exclusivity of product to their retail store customers and help sell designer clothes for children.

Another important trend is that as children grow into their teens, they are looking to their peers and the young adult group—not to their parents—for their fashion direction. To be successful, children's wear producers must be alert not only to the trends and fads of their own target customers, but also to hot items and product styling in the young adult market, and must style their products accordingly.

There is a gradual trend away from producing only two lines a year and toward introducing additional styles on a continuing basis. Many children's wear manufacturers are now producing "items" rather than complete lines. For example, manufacturers may produce T-shirts rather than polo shirts or sweatshirts. Within that T-shirt category, one style may be a best-seller or "hot item"—a T-shirt with a current saying, for example. While often involving a fad rather than a full-blown fashion, early identification and production of a single hot item can spell the difference between a red and a black bottom-line figure for a producer.

More and more children's wear producers of name-brand lines are increasing their volume of business by developing unbranded goods or additional brands for their discount store customers. Many have already had success in making up goods to the exact specifications of chain organizations. The chains merchandise these goods under their own brand names, thus developing exclusivity of product.

REFERENCES

[1] "Merchandising the Major Departments: Girls' and Infants' Wear," *The Discount Merchandiser*, June 1982, p. 87.
[2] Lewis Spaulding, "New Strategies for a Growing Market," *Stores*, August 1980, p. 43.
[3] Joyce Brothers, "How Clothes Form a Child's Self-Image," *Earnshaw's Infants*, November 1979, p. 48.
[4] Deborah Feengold, "Kids Industry Working Harder to Keep Pace With Fashion," *Kid's Fashions*, November 1979, pp. 41–42.
[5] Susan Ferraro, "Hotsy Totsy," *American Way*, April 1981, p. 61.
[6] Angela Cuccio, "Licensing for Kids: Sales with Character," *Women's Wear Daily*, August 9, 1982, p. 34.
[7] "Getting the Most from the Sports Dollar," *Earnshaw's Infants*, September 1981, p. 60.

MERCHANDISING VOCABULARY

Define or briefly explain the following terms:

Boys' sizes
Children's sizes
Girls' sizes
Infants' sizes

Preteen sizes
Toddlers' sizes
Young men, student, or teen sizes

MERCHANDISING REVIEW

1. Describe how children were dressed at the turn of the century.
2. In what three main ways is the children's wear industry categorized? Explain each briefly.
3. Where are most budget-priced children's goods produced today?
4. How does design of children's wear today relate to trends in the adult apparel market? Give two examples, one with girls' wear, one with boys' wear, to illustrate your answer.
5. Explain the statement, "The children's wear business is a *fashionable*, as opposed to being a *fashion*, business."
6. Where are most of the domestic children's wear firms located?
7. How do sales promotion and advertising activities in the children's wear industry differ from those in the men's and women's apparel industry? Discuss.
8. What are the key trade publications of the children's fashion industry?
9. What are the key trends affecting the children's wear industry today?
10. Why is private labeling of children's wear important to today's chain merchandising organizations?

MERCHANDISING DIGEST

1. Discuss the importance of licensing in today's children's wear market. How does the licensing system work? Why is it particularly popular with children?
2. Discuss the growing importance of foreign-made children's wear. What are some of the advantages and disadvantages?
3. What trends do you see in the young adult market today that have filtered into the design of children's clothing? How do these trends relate to Florence Eiseman's philosophy of design for clothing for children?

10. MEN'S APPAREL

The 1960s brought the rock music explosion, hippies, trips to the moon, and social, moral, and academic revolution to American life. This decade also introduced a fashion revolution in the styling and color of men's apparel, as well as radical changes in the production and selling practices that had prevailed for over 150 years in the menswear industry.

Today, it is almost impossible to believe that for years and years, the majority of businessmen dressed alike: dark gray flannel suit, white shirt, subdued tie, dark socks, black shoes. So definite a uniform was this look that in the 1950s a book and movie about the pressure on men to conform in order to succeed were called *The Man in the Grey Flannel Suit*.

The menswear industry, which began during this long conservative period, was very slow in making any changes in men's styles or in production methods. So men's fashions had the same look year after year, while women's fashions seemed to change daily.

It was not always this way. Until the time of the industrial revolution, men's fashions reflected the dominance that the male sex enjoyed. As elsewhere in nature, among human beings the male's "plumage" was far more stylish and colorful than the female's. Men's clothing, throughout history, reflected certain things. As discussed in Chapter 3, in earlier times a person was at the mercy of royal decree or custom regarding the clothing to be worn by members of his or her social class. In medieval times, men's clothing symbolically depicted strength and manliness—the bravery of knight. Later, in the seventeenth and eighteenth centuries, men of the French royal courts displayed the most intricate curled wigs, the most lavish laces and ribbons, and the brilliant colors of the rainbow in silk and satin coats and breeches.

But a fashion turning point was precipitated by the French Revolution. It changed everything, including the social role of men and the way they dressed. Sartorially, according to Flügel in *The Psychology of Clothes,* the French Revolution was an event that caused the ''Great Masculine Renunciation.''

It was a time, wrote Flügel, when ''man abandoned his claim to be considered beautiful. Hitherto, man had vied with women in the splendor of his garments. Henceforward, to the present day, woman was to enjoy the privilege of being the only possessor of beauty in the purely sartorial sense. With the new ideals of the Revolution, a man's most important activities were passed, not in the drawing room, but in the workshop, the office, places which had long been associated with a relatively simple costume.''[1]

HISTORY AND DEVELOPMENT OF THE MENSWEAR INDUSTRY

The menswear industry is the oldest of the domestic apparel industries, having gotten its start in the late 1700s and early 1800s. Moreover, menswear is the industry in which custom tailoring retained its importance the longest. Yet it is also the industry that gave women's and children's ready-to-wear industries their start.

Until the late 1700s, men's apparel was custom-tailored, meaning it was made to individual measurements. The rich patronized tailor's shops. Those who could not afford tailor-made clothing wore clothing made at home.

Then this began to change. The industrial revolution began. Machinery was introduced that quickly replaced human hands in the making of goods. Industry boomed and soon produced a new group of men—the industrialists. These men gained power, wealth, and influence, things that had previously belonged only to the upper classes by reason of inheritance. But these newly rich and powerful men had achieved their success by hard work and ability. They had a strong work ethic and an aversion to using elegant clothing to flaunt their wealth. They were sober and conservative, and they chose to dress soberly and conservatively.

Many decades later, men who worked in offices or in various service industries began to adopt this same form of dress. The mood of the times indicated to them that conservative clothing was practical clothing. They probably also felt that it was to their best interests to conform to the times and to the dress of the times. And so the years passed. For over 150 years, men were locked into their conservative look-alike clothing and so relinquished their former fashion-plate roles to women. A man would stand proudly by his elegantly dressed wife and daughter, secure in the knowledge that the beautiful fashions they wore clearly showed the world that *he* was a success.

The first ready-to-wear clothing produced here probably was made by tailors in ports in the Northeast. Seamen off ships stopping in these ports needed city clothes to wear onshore, but they lacked the time or money to spend on tailor-made clothes. To meet the seamen's needs, a few tailors in waterfront cities such as New Bedford, Boston, New York, Philadelphia, and Baltimore began anticipating sales. They made suits to roughly standard size measurements in advance so that sailors could put them on as soon as they stepped onshore. A number of Southern plantation owners regularly ordered these ready-made garments for their slaves.

These first ready-to-wear shops were called **slop shops,** and in comparison with today's

Dressing for success in the nineteenth century, complete with tightly-furled umbrella and top hat.

apparel, the name was appropriate for the products they sold. These ready-to-wear suits offered none of the careful fit and detail work found in custom-tailored suits. However, sailors at that time seldom wore anything except homemade clothes, and the prices were right, so the ready-to-wear suits were acceptable.

Some of today's leading menswear retail organizations got their start in those early days. For instance, Brooks Brothers' first store was a shop opened by Henry Brooks in 1818 in downtown New York. Jacob Reed's Sons' first store was opened by Jacob Reed in 1824 near the waterfront in Philadelphia.

During this period, industrialization resulted in a population movement to urban areas, where people settled around or near factories.

Often the adults and older children of a family worked in a nearby factory. Factory work left neither time nor anyone at home to make the family's clothing. However, it often provided enough income so that the head of the house could buy a ready-made suit.

Industrialization also created a rapidly growing new middle class of white-collar factory supervisors, managers, and junior executives. These newcomers to the middle class did not have the income to pay for custom-tailored clothes, but they did want wardrobes that would show off their new class status. To meet this new demand, tailors improved the quality, fit, and variety of ready-to-wear apparel.

Soon the slop shops became respectable men's clothing stores. By the mid-1800s, wealthy people still would not consider buying clothes off a rack, but the middle class—always most important in terms of fashion acceptance—patronized these stores.

The sewing machine, invented by Elias Howe in 1846, helped speed up production of men's ready-to-wear. The Gold Rush of 1848 increased the demand for male ready-to-wear. One name connected with menswear during the Gold Rush is Levi Strauss. He went to the gold fields of California with heavy fabric to sell to miners for tents. Instead, he turned it into pants and overalls, which the miners needed more than tents. The Civil War increased the demand for ready-to-wear even more, this time in the form of uniforms. In addition, the specifications given factories for the production of Civil War uniforms gradually led to the development of standard measurements and a better fit in men's ready-to-wear.

Store-bought clothes succeeded in breaking the final class barrier near the end of the 1800s. Several financial crises during that period caused men who had formerly worn only custom-made clothes to patronize ready-to-wear clothing stores. Their patronage helped ready-to-wear to gain widespread acceptance throughout the American society. Even though custom tailoring remained a vital part of the industry until recently, it gradually declined to its present status as a minor segment of the menswear industry.

Following World War I, little if any lifestyle change took place. However, when the Great Depression occurred, demand for all types of consumer products declined precipitously. During World War II, the entire apparel industry was subject to restrictions as to design and use of fabric. Once the war was over these restrictions were lifted, and higher styling again became possible. Servicemen returning home were eager to get out of their uniforms, and the menswear industry had to gear itself up to meet the accelerated demand for civilian clothes. For the first few years after the war the primary aim of manufacturers was to produce enough goods to fill orders from retailers. Stores needed merchandise, and their customers were demanding mainly conventional tailored clothing.

An exception was Southern California, where suburban living and the climate created a developing demand for sportswear. This was the first time such a need had been perceived. This new demand for sportswear was filled by a small group of mainly former New York manufacturers who gave not only Californians but eventually the whole nation casual wear and colorful weekend and off-duty attire. The "California market," as it came to be known, got its real start in the late forties when buyers from such large stores as Chicago's Marshall Field's, Detroit's Hudson's, and New York's Macy's and Lord & Taylor began attending the spring showings held each October in Palm Springs.

New York manufacturers did not wait long to take a cue from what was happening on the West Coast, and by the mid-1960s sportswear was as much a part of the Eastern market as tailored clothing, outerwear, and furnishings.

What became later known as the "name designer concept" of the seventies had its roots in the fifties when such Hollywood motion-picture designers as Don Loper, Orry-Kelly, Howard Greer, and Milo Anderson styled lines for California sportswear makers. At the same time, Oleg Cassini and Adrian began licensing agreements with New York neckwear producers.

The advent of the "Ivy League look" and the "Continental" theme, as well as the lack of marketing and merchandising expertise, stunted the growth of the designer concept. This concept reemerged in the late sixties with such names as Pierre Cardin and John Weitz.

Men's fashions developed slowly but surely through the fifties, sixties, and seventies. The colorful Edwardian look was followed first by Mod, which swept the country after the American debut of the Beatles, and then by the short-lived Nehru look. Perhaps the first time technology influenced fashion since the advent of the sewing machine was the knit boom of the early seventies, when a man could outfit himself almost entirely in knit styles—a double-knit suit, circular knit shirt, knit tie, interlock knit underwear, and jersey knit socks—everything except for his leather belt and shoes. In the eighties the punk look vies with the classic three-piece suit as the fashion successes.

Dual Distribution

One operating policy connected with the men's ready-to-wear industry since its early history has been **dual distribution,** which refers to manufacturers' policy of selling goods at both wholesale and retail. This practice has been far more prevalent in the menswear industry than in women's apparel.

Dual distribution of menswear got its start in the early and middle 1800s, when the ready-to-wear business was expanding along with the country's population. New ready-to-wear factories were concentrated in the North, but since population was growing rapidly in the South, particularly in port cities, good business was to be found there.

At first, ready-to-wear clothing manufacturers were content to sell goods to independent

HICKEY-FREEMAN

The sleeve of your Hickey-Freeman coat is hand-cut on a subtle arc so there are no twists or wrinkles and more comfort.

THE BOARDROOM COLLECTION. FOR· THE PROFESSIONAL PERFECTIONIST.

Perfection is achieved through consistency and innovation. It's the way you run your business and the way you dress. You depend on the excellence and style of the Boardroom Collection. Fashioned for you—the professional perfectionist. *Hickey-Freeman*® By Hickey-Freeman.

Every Hickey-Freeman garment is inspected by a master craftsman to assure that a consistently high level of excellence was maintained throughout each stage of assembly.

For the Hickey-Freeman dealer nearest you, call 1-800-231-2211; Nebraska, call 1-800-742-9900.

© 1984 Hart Services, Inc.

The Hickey-Freeman brand is produced by Hartmarx, a dual distributor.

clothing stores in the South. However, producers soon decided that it would be doubly profitable to own some of those Southern retail outlets. By the 1830s, a number of New York manufacturers had outlets in New Orleans, then the second-largest port in the United States, and in other Southern population centers. At the same time, other manufacturers continued to sell goods on a wholesale basis to independent clothing stores where they did not have outlets of their own.

Interest in dual distribution waned in the last half of the nineteenth century. It again became a popular trend in the boom years following World Wars I and II. Each time, interest lasted for a few years, then sagged.

The most recent interest in dual distribution occurred in the latter half of the 1960s. One reason for the proliferation of dual distribution during this period was a desire on the part of manufacturers to ensure their franchises with stores. This prompted Hartmarx Corporation, Botany Industries, Phillips Van Heusen, and Cluett, Peabody to purchase specialty stores.

By the mid-1970s, however, the trend had passed. One reason for this was the economic situation. The pattern was holding true: in good times, dual distribution has been attractive, and in bad times it has been dangerously costly. Another reason (which probably will keep manufacturers from ever again becoming involved with dual distribution) was the increasing possibility of violating federal antitrust laws, which rule against one-company domination of any specific segment of an industry. The number of stores owned and operated by menswear producers has never been large, nor is it now, in comparison with the total number of menswear retail outlets.

Today, one of the most successful dual distribution manufacturers of men's tailored suits is Hartmarx Corporation. This company manufactures men's clothing, outerwear, and sportswear, and retails them in its over 350 retail outlets, producing close to $1 billion in annual sales.[2] In addition to its own brand,

Hart Schaffner & Marx, the firm produces many different lines of menswear, such as Hickey-Freeman and Austin Reed, as well as the American-made suits and coats that are licensed by Christian Dior, Pierre Cardin, and Nino Cerutti. Although the firm functions under the dual distribution system, its lines are also sold to independent specialty and department stores.

Contractors

As the men's ready-to-wear business grew, so did its attractiveness as a profitable investment. But going into business as a menswear manufacturer required considerable capital in terms of factory construction, equipment, and labor costs. This situation led to the birth of the contractor business, described in Chapter 8. By hiring a contractor to do the sewing and sometimes the cutting as well, manufacturers eliminated the need for their own factories, sewing machines, or labor force. They could function with just a showroom or space for shipping.

Early contractors of menswear operated in one of two ways. Usually, they set up their own factories where the manufacturing was done. But sometimes they still distributed work to operators who would work at home, either on their own machines or on machines rented from the contractors. These workers were paid on a piecework basis.

Right after the Civil War and for the next two decades or so, menswear was manufactured in three different ways: (1) in **inside shops,** or garment factories, owned and operated by manufacturers; (2) in contract shops, or contractors' factories, where garments were produced for manufacturers; and (3) in homes, where garments were made usually for contractors but sometimes for manufacturers.

A contractor's most important value for apparel manufacturers is the ability to turn out short runs of a style quickly and inexpensively. A **short run** is the production of a limited number of units of a particular item, fewer than would normally be considered an average number to produce. Because short runs are a contractor's specialty, contracting has remained an important factor in women's apparel manufacturing. However, it was gradually abandoned by menswear manufacturers until recently, when it again became important in the production of sportswear because of the impact of faster moving fashion cycles in menswear.

Traditional menswear manufacturers turned away from contractors and stayed away until recently for several reasons. First, the menswear industry had a pattern of very slow style change, and contracting was not as economical as inside-shop production. Second, improved equipment and cheaper electric power helped make production in inside shops more practical and efficient. Third, as quality became increasingly important, menswear manufacturers found it easier to control work within their own factories than in the contractors' factories.

Because of escalating labor costs in this country, in the 1970s many menswear manufacturers, including those producing designer collections, returned to the use of contractors, particularly in Hong Kong and Korea. Of late, Hong Kong is favored by better makers, more for quality standards than for cost.

Unions

As the menswear market and industry grew, so did competition among manufacturers. Factory employees became the victims. To produce ready-to-wear clothing at competitive prices, manufacturers and contractors demanded long hours from workers and yet paid low wages. In addition, factory working conditions, which had never been good, deteriorated further. Contractors were particularly guilty, and their factories deserved the names **sweat shops** or "sweaters" that were given to them. According to an official New York State inspection report of 1887:

The workshops occupied by these contracting manufacturers of clothing, or "sweaters" as they are commonly called, are foul in the ex-

treme. Noxious gases emanate from all corners. The buildings are ill smelling from cellar to garret. The water-closets are used by males and females, and usually stand in the room where the work is done. The people are huddled together too closely for comfort, even if all other conditions were excellent.[3]

The outcome was inevitable. Workers finally rebelled against working conditions, hours, and pay.

Local employee unions had existed in the industry since the early 1800s, but none had lasted long or wielded much power. The Journeymen Tailors' National Union, formed in 1883, functioned (and still functions today) mainly as a craft union. A union representing all apparel industry workers, the United Garment Workers of America, was organized in 1891, but it had little power and soon collapsed. Finally, in 1914, the Amalgamated Clothing Workers of America was formed. It remained the major union of the menswear industry until the 1970s, when it merged with the Textile Workers of America and the United Shoe Workers of America to form the **Amalgamated Clothing and Textile Workers Union.**

Workers in tailored-clothing plants make up the backbone of the Amalgamated, and the union is a strong force in menswear manufacturing in the North. However, its influence in factories producing men's work clothes, furnishings, and sportswear in the South and other parts of the country was almost nonexistent until the mid-1970s. It was then that a drive to organize support in the South gave the union its first toehold in these areas.

The famous strike during the early 1970s at the El Paso, Texas factory of the Farah Company, the largest manufacturer of men's pants and work clothes, was part of a long and bitter fight. The company had resisted the attempt of the union to organize the Farah workers for many years, and only after a long court battle were the plant and its workers unionized.

ORGANIZATION AND OPERATION OF THE INDUSTRY

The menswear industry traditionally has been divided into firms making five kinds of clothing:

1. *Tailored clothing*—Includes suits, overcoats, topcoats, sports coats, and separate trousers.
2. *Furnishings*—Includes shirts, neckwear, sweaters, knit tops, underwear, socks, robes, and pajamas.
3. *Heavy outerwear*—Includes jackets, snowsuits, ski jackets, parkas, and related items.
4. *Work clothes*—Includes work shirts, work pants, overalls, and related items.
5. *Other*—Includes uniforms, hats, and miscellaneous items.

For many years, the Federal Bureau of Labor Statistics did not recognize these divisions within the industry. Instead, all production was grouped under the general heading of "men's apparel" or "men's garments." Since 1947, however, because of strong urging from tailored-clothing firms, the federal government has used these five classifications. In the trade, **tailored-clothing firms** are those producing structured or semistructured suits, overcoats, topcoats, sports coats, and separate slacks in which a specific number of hand-tailoring operations are required. Tailored-clothing firms once dominated the menswear market, both in unit production and in sales. However, in recent years there has been a steady decline in demand for tailored clothing. On the other hand, there has been a steady growth in demand for sportswear, or more casual apparel that is less structured and involves fewer (if any) hand-tailoring operations.

Sportswear and casual wear were the fastest-growing segment of the menswear industry during the 1970s. Changes in lifestyles, resulting in a demand for leisure looks, as well as men's increasing interest in more variety and fashion in their apparel, all contributed to this growth.

As we move through the eighties, however, demand has risen for **suit separates**. These consist of suit jackets, trousers, and vests that can be mixed and matched for size and color, much like coordinates for women. This appears to represent a shift toward the expression of more individualized taste, as well as a response to economic limitations and apprehensions. The suit separates are usually machine-made and significantly lower-priced than most traditional tailored suits. Because a mix of sizes can be bought, the customer also avoids expensive alterations. However, the success of separates is not limited to just popular-priced goods but applies to better-priced goods as well. One authority believes that people who buy separates are more fashion-aware than those who need the reassurance of a preassembled look, such as that of suits. Less expensive suit separates are sometimes referred to as "instant suits" because the purchaser can walk out of the store with his suit coat (which can double as a sports coat) and exact size pants.

A phenomenon of the eighties is the rapid growth of the sector of sportswear known as **active sportswear**. This includes casual attire (i.e., running shorts and tops, jogging suits, tennis and racketball clothes, and athletic footwear) that men often wear for after-work and weekend activities. Also included are those activities that have little to do with physical exercise. Literally millions of men who want to look like runners, even while ambling down to the store for the Sunday paper, or flopping on the sofa to watch the ball game, want to do these activities dressed in the correct active sportswear. One of the most outstanding influences of active wear on the menswear market has been the use of color. Perhaps the majority of men have always been a bit shy about outspoken coloration in clothing, even in sports coats, sweaters, and furnishings; but many men have found that active sportswear allows

Bonnie & Arnel® are *Active Everywear.*

Bonnie's warm-up suit is comfortable and classy in Action Suede of Celanese Arnel® Triacitate and nylon by Fab Industries. Bonnie Sportswear, Inc.; 2425 S. Hill St., Los Angeles, CA 90007; (213) 746-5202.
AT MAGIC: NH2010-NH2011

This ad for active sportswear reflects the phenomenal growth of that sector of sportswear. Note the mention of the fabric name and the reference to the MAGIC trade show.

them to break loose and show off a colorful side.

Size and Location of Manufacturers
Traditionally the manufacture of menswear, unlike that of women's apparel, is dominated by large firms. In 1983, manufacturers of menswear and boys' wear shipped an estimated $17.6 billion at wholesale costs.[4]

For the past few years Levi Strauss, Blue Bell, Cluett, Peabody, and Interco have been the four largest manufacturers of menswear and boys' wear. Their combined volume accounts for approximately one-third of the total volume of the top 30 firms. Because of diversification, mergers, and acquisitions by top menswear producers in the past few years, it is more difficult to ascertain the size and production figures of each firm.

Although there are menswear manufacturers in almost every section of the country, the largest number of plants are in the mid-Atlantic states. New York, New Jersey, and Pennsylvania form the center of the tailored-clothing industry, and traditionally over 40 percent of all menswear manufacturers have been located in this area.

However, the industry's center is gradually moving south. A number of northeastern manufacturers have set up plant facilities in the South, where both land and labor are less expensive. These include not only apparel manufacturers from the mid-Atlantic states but also some men's shoe manufacturers, once found almost exclusively in New England.

Some menswear manufacturers have always been located in the South. For instance, firms manufacturing separate trousers—a segment of the tailored-clothing industry—have always been centered in the South, as have many manufacturers of men's shirts, underwear, and work clothes.

The number of firms located in the West and the Southwest is also steadily growing. Most of these plants produce sportswear or casual attire. The Northwest and Upper Midwest are important for outerwear.

The sportswear and casual-wear output within the industry is not clearly defined, because many manufacturers who produce sportswear, including active sportswear, are also involved either primarily or secondarily with other merchandise categories. Also, because official government sources (mainly the U.S. Bureau of the Census) do not specifically report on many important items of sportswear and casual wear, the size and production fig-ures relating to these types of apparel are difficult to estimate.

Designing a Line

For generations, tailored-clothing manufacturers in the United States were known as slow but painstakingly careful followers, rather than leaders, in menswear styling. The typical tailored-clothing manufacturer had a staff of designers or bought freelance designs. Designers' names were known only within the trade and were seldom considered important by consumers.

Traditionally, the leading fashion influence was English styling. Designers in this country would study the styles currently popular in England, decide which might be acceptable here, and gradually develop a line based on those styles. Production was a slow process because of the amount of handwork involved in producing tailored clothing. Usually, a full year passed from the time a style was developed until a finished product was delivered to a retail store.

The first signs of male rebellion against traditional styling came during the late 1940s and early 1950s. As described earlier, year after year manufacturers had been turning out versions of a style that had long been popular in England—a draped suit with padded shoulders, based originally on the broad-chested uniform of the Brigade of Guards. A number of young men attending well-known northeastern colleges became tired of the traditional look. They took their objections to New Haven clothing manufacturers, and the result was the natural-shoulder, Ivy League suit.

Importance of Name Designers

However, it was the radical shift in attitudes in the 1960s that brought about men's willingness to wear suits as fashion. The antiwar protests, student activism, and the black power and other minority movements all encouraged

American men to express themselves in a non-mainstream manner. They led to the era of the "Peacock Revolution," when men, as in days long ago, once again took a great pride in their appearance. Some favored long hair, bold plaid suits, brightly colored shirts, wide multicolored ties, and shiny boots. Others dressed, even for work, in Nehru and Mao jackets, leisure suits, white loafers, polyester double knits, and the "California look"—shirts unbuttoned to the waist and gold necklaces in abundance hung around their necks.

By the late sixties, designer names in the menswear industry mushroomed. Most of them were women's wear designers, mainly from Europe, who decided to exploit their renown by trying their creativity in the men's field. So popular was the European designer image that even an American designer like Bill Kaiserman gave his firm an Italian name, Raphael.

Among the first American designers who made no bones about being American were John Weitz, Bill Blass, and Ralph Lauren. In fact, Bill Blass, who has been designing menswear since 1965, won the first Coty Award ever given for menswear design, in 1968.

Since most of these designers were famous as designer's of women's apparel, there was a question about whether men would buy their designs. However, the movement of men into fashion during the sixties and seventies dispelled that doubt. As reported in *The New York Times,* "The idea that men would wear clothes designed by a women's apparel designer was never considered seriously, and one thing that men have arrived at today is that being interested in clothes does not carry a stigma."[5] The fact that much menswear, particularly furnishings and sportswear, is bought by women for men also aided acceptance of name designer styles. Women are familiar with the names and have confidence in the designers' taste.

Although the first foreign country that influenced the design of menswear was England, French and Italian designers became as important in menswear as the traditional English. Pierre Cardin signed his first contract for men's shirts and ties in 1959 and did his first ready-to-wear men's designs in 1961. Christian Dior, Yves St. Laurent, and other famous women's designers followed his example. One important menswear designer who did not come from the ranks of women's wear is Ralph Lauren. He began his career in menswear, designing for women well after he became successful and famous designing for men.

Today, an entirely new world of menswear has emerged in which designer labels are promoted as heavily as well-established brand names used to be. Famous foreign and domestic name designers of women's apparel are now actively engaged in entering into licensing agreements for the production of menswear bearing the famous designer's label. A designer who licenses his name in suits may also license men's jeans, shirts, jackets, or ties. The manufacturer pays for the design or name of the designer in royalties based on gross sales. Royalties average from 5 to 7 percent on men's suits and 5 percent on men's sportswear, according to industry sources.

Manufacturing companies that license "names" usually establish separate divisions and in many cases allocate separate manufacturing facilities for them. In licensing agreements, the extent of designer involvement varies; designers are not necessarily responsible for all the designs that bear their name.

Today the "name game" is big business in all segments of the menswear industry. While there are no hard figures on the amount of designer business done at wholesale, the best market estimates for retail sales are over $1 billion for all categories combined.

With their spectacular rise to popularity in the 1970s, designer clothes offered much more than a unique look. Men developed confidence in certain labels, no matter where they might be sold. Labels also gave items an aura of qual-

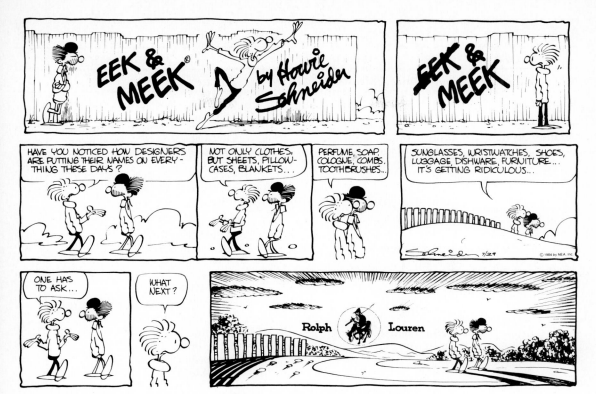

Licensing of "name" designers is spreading dramatically in menswear as in every area of apparel, accessories, and home furnishings.

ity, and even if the quality was questionable, some designer goods also conveyed a look of privilege. Thus, status became the major merchandising tool in the mid-seventies.[6]

Today, designer labels are more easily promoted than the familiar brands of former decades. This is so for a number of reasons, other than the fashion and prestige associated with the label:

- Designers are visible. Their names are household words; their faces appear in newspapers and magazines. They lend themselves to the fantasy of the customer who is longing for a life of wealth and excitement.

- Designers have more exposure because their names often appear in different categories of merchandise in different shops or departments.

- Designer labels often allow retailers to put a higher markup on merchandise because of the fashion mystique associated with the name.

A large number of European and American designers have thus begun to fulfill the desires of the newly fashion-conscious American man. Industry fashion leaders classify leading menswear designers as follows:

- *The Old Guard*—Bill Blass, Ralph Lauren, Nino Cerutti, Pierre Cardin, Christian Dior, Geoffrey Beene.

- *The New Guard*—Giorgio Armani, Basile, Gianni Versace, Yves St. Laurent.

TABLE 10-1 Leading Menswear Designers

DESIGNER	COMPANY	CLASSIFICATION
Giorgio Armani	Groupo Finanziario Tessili (GFT)	All categories
Jeffrey Banks	Lakeland Corporation Oxford Industries	Outerwear, sportswear, active wear, tailored clothing
Geoffrey Beene	Joseph & Feiss Chesa International Mannor Corp. Randa Coberknit Jacqueline Cochrane	Clothing Sportswear Slacks Neckwear Active wear Toiletries
Bill Blass	PBM After Six Malcolm Kenneth Gates Shirts J. S. Blank Buxton Revlon Royal Robes	Clothing Formal wear Coats, rainwear Dress, sport shirts Neckwear Small leathers Toiletries Robes
Pierre Cardin	Intercontinental Apparel Harry Irwin, Inc. Eagle Shirtmakers Smerling Swank Jaqueline Cochrane Sheridane Roytex Breezy Point Gilbert Hosiery	Clothing Coats, dress shirts Sportswear Footwear Belts, leathers Toiletries Neckwear Robes Active wear Hosiery
Oleg Cassini	Phoenix Clothes Burma Bibas Auerback Robes CBS Apparel Crown Clothing Jarman Lyntone Belts Jovan	Clothing Dress shirts, sportswear, outerwear, neckwear Robes Active wear Rainwear Footwear Belts Toiletries
Christian Dior	Hartmarx Corporation Gleneagles Hathaway Cisco Thane Stern-Merritt State O'Maine Host Pajamas Camp	Clothing Rainwear Dress shirts Sportswear Sweaters Neckwear Robes Sleepwear Hosiery

TABLE 10-1 Leading Menswear Designers (continued)		
DESIGNER	**COMPANY**	**CLASSIFICATION**
Christian Dior (continued)	Destino	Leathers, jewelry
	Liberty	Umbrellas
Jean-Paul Germain	Bidermann Industries	All categories
Halston	J. Schoenemann	Clothing
	Van Heusen Co.	Dress, sport shirts
	Pacesetter	Neckwear
	Halston Fragrances	Toiletries
	Weldon	Loungewear
Daniel Hechter	Bidermann Industries	All categories
J. G. Hook	George Weintraub & Sons	All categories
Alexander Julian	Arrow Co.	Shirts, knitwear
Calvin Klein	Bidermann Industries	All categories
Ralph Lauren	Polo Fashions	Clothing, sportswear, neckwear
	Trylon	Robes
	Acme Boot	Boots
	Chaps—Greif	Clothing
	Chaps—Hathaway	Shirts, sportswear
	Chaps—Warner/Western	Fragrances
	Polo Western Wear	Western apparel
Oscar de la Renta	K-R Men's Apparel	Clothing
	Champion	Slacks
	Excello	Shirts
	Wembley	Neckwear
Gianfranco Ruffini	Cluett, Peabody	Sportswear, knitwear
Yves St. Laurent	Bidermann Industries	Clothing, shirts, sportswear
	Manhattan Accessories	Neckwear, belts, leathers
	Harwyn	Footwear
	Charles of the Ritz	Toiletries
Valentino	Groupo Finanziario Tessili (GFT)	All categories
John Weitz	Palm Beach	Clothing
	Casualcraft	Outerwear
	Excello	Shirts
	Glen Oaks	Slacks
	State O'Maine	Swimwear
	Host Pajamas	Pajamas
	Imperial Handkerchief	Handkerchiefs
	Storm Hero Umbrella	Umbrellas
	John Weitz Toiletries	Toiletries
	Camp Hosiery	Hosiery
	Gemini	Footwear

- *The New Breed*—Jeffrey Banks, Jhane Barnes, Lee Wright, Sal Cesarani, Ron Chereskin, Calvin Klein, Vicky Davis, Alexander Julian, Perry Ellis, Robert Stock, Andrew Fezza.
- *The Oriental Wave*—Issey Miyake, Yohji Yamamoto, Yashie Inaba, Irie of Studio V, Mitsuhiro Matsuda.

Table 10-1 lists today's leading designers of menswear and the classifications of products appearing under their labels.

Producing a Line

A generation ago, it might have been possible to identify tailored clothing as office or formal wear, and sportswear as weekend or vacation wear. Today, the only real difference between the two types of apparel lies in their construction, rather than styling, colors, or fabrics.

A tailored sports coat is "three-dimensional," or "structured." Its construction involves many different hand-tailoring operations. These give it a shape of its own even when not being worn. A sports jacket is "unstructured." Its construction involves few if any hand-tailoring operations. It often lacks padding, binding, and lining. It takes its shape, in part, from the person who wears it.

For this reason, two distinctly different production methods are currently used to produce menswear. One is the older, tailored-clothing method. This segment of the menswear industry has traditionally been slow to react to consumer demand. The other is the newer sportswear method, developed specifically because it can respond quickly to demands for style change.

TAILORED-CLOTHING PRODUCTION.
The production of tailored clothing in general and of suits in particular has long been considered the backbone of the menswear manufacturing industry. Suits made by tailored-clothing firms are graded according to the number of hand-tailoring operations required for their production. The grades, from lowest to highest, are 1, 2, 4, 4+, 6, and 6+. The grade 1 suit represents the lowest quality of tailored suit carried by a store that features popular prices. A **grade 6+** suit, which requires between 120 and 150 separate hand-tailoring operations, is the top line of tailored suits carried in a prestige store. Oxxford and Hickey-Freeman produce top-of-the-line, 6+ suits.

However, a revolution has been under way in the production workrooms of the menswear apparel industry. The introduction of the polyester double knit in the 1960s led to new automation processes, including that known as **fusing**. In this process, various parts of the suit can be melded together under heat and pressure rather than stitched. Other new machinery made it possible to produce suits with "cookie-cutter" speed and precision. Today, as a result, a lower-quality, high-volume suit known as a **grade X suit** can be produced in 90 minutes with only 90 stitching and pressing operations.

The average retail price of the grade X suit is about $150, while the grade 6+ suit costs about $475 and up.

There is a distinct difference between the fit of a traditional suit and that of a designer suit. Designer suits are usually sized on what is called the "7-inch drop." The term **drop** refers to the difference between the waist and chest measurements of the jacket. For example, a designer suit jacket measures 38 inches around the chest and 31 inches at the waist. Traditional suits are usually styled with a 6-inch drop, which gives the suit jacket a completely different look and fit. However, in some jackets for young men and other customers who work at keeping in shape, the drop may be even greater than 7 inches. **European styling** usually features more-fitted jackets that hug the body, have built-up shoulders and a high armhole.

Production of tailored clothing is usually a relatively long and complicated process. After selecting the styles to be featured in the next line, a manufacturer orders the fabric in which the various styles are made up. Once the line is set up, the manufacturer shows it to store buyers. Delivery of the fabric may take up to 9 months. Even after the fabric is delivered, however, the manufacturer does not start to cut a style until enough store orders are accumulated for that style to make its production profitable. This is because making up a single style in a man's suit, for example, involves cutting a great many sizes—considerably more than are involved in producing a woman's dress style.

Men's tailored clothing is produced in the following proportioned sizes:

1. *Shorts*—Includes sizes 36–44.
2. *Regulars*—Includes sizes 35–46.
3. *Longs*—Includes sizes 37–48.
4. *Extra longs*—Includes sizes 38–50.
5. *Portlies*—Includes sizes 39–50.
6. *Portly shorts*—Includes sizes 39–48.
7. *Big sizes*—Includes sizes 46, 48, 50.

While it is unlikely that a manufacturer will receive orders that require a single style to be cut in this entire range of proportioned sizes, it is likely that the most popular styles will have to be cut in at least half of them.

Even after the cutting is done, the work goes slowly. For instance, a grade 6 + suit may require as many as 15 hours of an experienced tailor's time. This is why the cost of labor makes up approximately two-thirds of the entire cost of producing a tailored-clothing item.

SPORTSWEAR PRODUCTION. In contrast, many sportswear firms use contractors in exactly the same way and for the same reasons that women's apparel producers do. Sportswear manufacturers, unlike tailored-clothing manufacturers, are interested in short runs and quick response to customer demand. The quality of workmanship is much less important in this area than having the styles, colors, and fabrics that customers want when they want

them. It is the style, color, and fabric of a sports jacket that sells it, not the way its lapel is constructed.

In addition, unstructured sportswear, regardless of what kind of firm produces it, is likely to be made up in a much narrower size range than tailored clothing. For instance, a sport shirt is not produced in the wide variety of neck sizes, sleeve lengths, and collar and cuff styles in which a dress shirt is made. Instead, a sport shirt is usually produced in four basic sizes (small, medium, large, and extra large) and sometimes with a choice between short and long sleeves.

This is the kind of production work that contractors handle most successfully. When contractors are used, the sportswear manufacturer may be the designer, or a designer may be hired, or a design may be bought from a freelancer. The manufacturer buys the needed fabric. Then sometimes the cutting and all of the sewing are done by the contractor, as in the women's apparel field. Finally, the finished goods are returned to the manufacturer, who handles the distribution.

Contractors' plants are located wherever production costs can be kept low. There are many in different locations in this country, and an increasing number of American sportswear manufacturers are using contractors in other countries. The use of the contractor system allows the sportswear manufacturers to provide a steady flow of new styles at moderate prices.

Contemporary Apparel

Contemporary menswear, like sportswear, has not yet been recognized by the Bureau of the Census as a separate category of men's clothing. A product of the 1970s, this category has only recently appeared on the apparel scene. The term **contemporary menswear** relates to a special type of styling that is often also referred to as "updated," "better," or "young men's." It applies not only to coats and suits but to all categories of apparel, from outerwear to furnishings. Although there is no precise definition of the term, it can best be described as new fashion, better fashion, or fashions at the mid- to late-rise stage of their cyclical life span. Although contemporary apparel is not ultrafashionable or way out in terms of styling, it is often distinguished by the use of bright colors.

The typical contemporary menswear customer is usually a young man in his late 20s or early 30s. He is a college graduate and is working at a good job with a promising future. He is a sports enthusiast, if not an active participant, and is at least somewhat active in social, business, and community affairs.

Contemporary merchandise is produced by both tailored-clothing and sportswear firms. It is usually produced under a name designer's licensing agreement, rather than being styled by a manufacturer's in-house or freelance designer. When this type of merchandise is produced by a firm already making other types of apparel and furnishings, new operating divisions are usually created to handle the product, to give it identity, and to enhance its marketability.

Contemporary suits are usually produced in the following sizes:

1. *Shorts*—Includes sizes 36–40.
2. *Regulars*—Includes sizes 36–42.
3. *Longs*—Includes sizes 38–44.

BRIDGE DEPARTMENTS. In the mid-1980s, the menswear industry tried to replace names like "contemporary," "better," "young men's," and "updated" with "bridge." **Bridge** defines the area that spans young men's and men's collections, that services aging baby-boom customers who have grown out of young men's but can't afford designer prices. Bridge customers are between 25 and 40 and have sophistication and style.

The menswear market offers some guidelines for a bridge department: "Bridge has style approximating (and sometimes surpassing) men's collections, and price points approximating (but never abutting) young men's."[7]

Early retail innovators to develop the bridge concept were Robinson's in California, Dayton's in Minneapolis, and Barney's in New York. New resources appeared—Sahara Club, Generra, Charlie, USA, Dweedo, and Ruffini, among others—that merchandised and marketed to attract the bridge customer.

Retailers that are developing bridge departments seek to balance fashion with price. Such bridge departments are usually bought by separate buyers reporting to young men's divisional merchandise managers.

MARKET CENTERS

New York is the traditional and still by far the largest market center for all kinds of menswear, including tailored clothing, sportswear, contemporary lines, and furnishings. Regional markets in other parts of the country—Chicago, Los Angeles, and Dallas, for example—are growing in importance. But the biggest shows and the largest number of permanent showrooms are still located in New York.

The Clothing Manufacturers Association, the trade association of the tailored-clothing industry, holds two market weeks a year in New York. Fall lines are shown in February, and spring lines in late August or early September.

The National Association of Men's Sportswear Buyers, a membership organization founded by sportswear buyers but now including independent store owners, retail buyers, and merchandise managers, holds two week-long showings a year in New York. Fall lines are shown in late March or early April, and spring lines in October. These showings include lines from manufacturers of all types of menswear, including tailored-clothing as well as sportswear and contemporary lines. It is claimed that these showings bring together the offerings of more menswear producers than any other show in the world.

In addition, numerous small regional shows are held around the country. Nearly every area has a Men's Apparel Club (MAC), which stages regular seasonal showings in regional market centers as well as in various cities throughout each region. These clubs are run by and for salesmen. Their market weeks are known as "MAC markets."

MERCHANDISING AND MARKETING ACTIVITIES

Menswear producers, like women's apparel producers, back their offerings with both advertising and publicity. Various fiber firms and associations often cooperate in these endeavors, as discussed in Chapter 8. Advertising is usually done by individual producers or by producers working in cooperation with fiber firms or associations. Publicity is handled mainly by various trade associations.

Advertising

Men's apparel producers turned to advertising in the latter 1800s, using trade advertising to establish direct contacts with retailers. As a result, the business relationships between manufacturers and stores soon became very strong and stable. In most large towns and small cities, each major menswear retailer had an exclusive arrangement with a separate manufacturer. That tie often continued for generations. As a result of this long relationship, most menswear manufacturers in general and tailored-clothing firms in particular have not felt it necessary to do much national consumer advertising. Instead, they have tended to put advertising money into cooperative programs with established retail accounts. This remains the trend among many long-established firms. Today, tailored-clothing firms prepare newspaper and magazine ads for use by retail store customers. Some provide the necessary material for radio and television commercials as well.

The sportswear houses, however, are relatively new and have not yet built strong retail ties. Sportswear manufacturers have to compete for retail accounts much as women's apparel manufacturers do. Thus they use little

cooperative advertising. Instead, they concentrate on building brand recognition and acceptance by advertising nationally. Some of the ads are aimed at consumers. Others, placed in the trade press, are aimed at retail stores.

Publicity

While most large menswear manufacturers have publicity departments, the major publicity efforts in the menswear industry are organized and carried out by trade groups: the Men's Fashion Association of America (MFA), the National Association of Men's Sportswear Buyers (NAMSB), the Men's Apparel Guild in California (MAGIC), the Clothing Manufacturers Association (CMA), the Big and Tall Associates, The Menswear Retailers of America (MRA), and The Father's Day Council, Inc.

MFA. The Men's Fashion Association of America (MFA) represents all segments of the menswear manufacturing industry. The MFA was established in 1955 as the public-relations arm of the menswear industry. Manufacturer members contribute a percentage of their volume to support the assocation. The association aims its publicity and public relations efforts at consumers by providing consumer media with information about the menswear industry. Its program, which has resulted in much greater coverage of men's fashions in the consumer print and broadcast media, includes press preview weeks at which fashion editors are briefed as to the coming season's trends.

The MFA holds three major press preview weeks a year. In January or February, it holds a press preview week for the spring–summer season. This is usually held in a major southwestern or west coast city, such as Dallas, Houston, or Los Angeles. In June, it holds a press preview week in the New York area to cover fall–winter trends. The third press preview week is held in the Southwest or on the West Coast in September or October. It is not uncommon for more than 300 editors and commentators to attend these press preview

JOHN WEITZ: DESIGNER OF MANY TALENTS

If you were to visit the public library in search of information about the designer John Weitz, you would probably be surprised at how many people seem to share the name John Weitz. In the *Reader's Guide to Periodical Literature* you would probably find information about John Weitz the photographer, John Weitz the well-known author, and John Weitz the fashion designer. But on further investigation, you would learn that all of these men are the same John Weitz.

"John Weitz is exactly what you would never imagine a successful clothing designer to be. He used to race cars—he once served on the British Morgan team—and he also designed his own car. Besides designing watches, raincoats, suits, socks, he is the author of two novels."[1]

Weitz was born in Berlin, Germany in 1923, the son of a prosperous ready-to-wear clothing manufacturer. His family emigrated to London in the early 1930s. Weitz attended St. Paul's School and, at the young age of 16, he entered Oxford. At St. Paul's he had starred on the varsity rugby team, but at Oxford he found it increasingly difficult to blend in socially with the other sophisticated 18- to 24-year-olds who were his classmates. On one of his weekend visits to London to escape the social atmosphere at Oxford, he met his friend from St. Paul's, John Cavanaugh, who was an apprentice to a couturier. Cavanaugh convinced Weitz to join him on weekends "because there were lots of pretty girls around." There he learned how to cut and sew clothes. Shortly thereafter, the noted designer Molyneaux asked Weitz to go to Paris for three months to apprentice as a dressmaker/tailor.[2]

When World War II broke out, Weitz fled to Shanghai, China, where he waited for a U. S. visa and played on the rugby team that won the 1941

weeks. Recently, women's wear has been added to the showings as many menswear manufacturers, particularly in the tailored-clothing segment, have added women's lines.

Each press preview week lasts between 4 and 5 days. It consists of fashion shows, slide presentations, seminars, and other events intended to tell media representatives about major trends in menswear fashions. In addition, the MFA arranges interviews with designers and manufacturers, sends out regular publicity to the media, and semiannually issues press

Chinese championship. He became a naturalized American citizen in 1943, and several months later he joined the United States Army. During the next 3 years he was promoted from private to captain in the Office of Strategic Services, where he worked as an intelligence operative.

When the war was over, Weitz moved to New York City, where he began designing women's clothes derived from men's attire. At the encouragement of Dorothy Shaver, president of Lord & Taylor at the time, he produced a style to meet the needs of active living that could be recognized as American by its casual, sporty look. After working for various apparel firms, Weitz founded John Weitz Designs, Inc. in 1954. He was designing about 1,500 styles a year by 1960 and had accounts with Amco of Norvet, Inc., Montgomery Ward, and White Stag, among others. His wearable clothes included maternity outfits, children's wear, baby garments, uniforms for Cities Service gas station attendants, and two one-of-a-kind sportswear collections sold at Henri Bendel, the posh New York clothing store. It was during this period of time that he wrote his first book, *Sports Clothes for Your Sports Car.*

Because he was bored by the off-the-rack menswear he was able to buy in department stores and specialty shops throughout the country, Weitz began to design menswear in 1964. His styles were then and still are the kind of clothes he would personally like to wear. All-weather coats have extra padding for warmth, driving jackets are made to keep you warm but are short enough so you don't have to sit on them, and sports clothes are made in colors that don't get filthy when they are used. He is also recognized for his talent in designing shirts, trousers, jackets, and shoes for middle-aged professionals who need to add a bit of imagination and color to their conservative business attire.

John Weitz still produces functional, classic styles that he himself wears. But John Weitz Designs, Inc. is also big business. He has sold the rights to his name and designs to over 60 manufacturing companies, which produce more than $250 million worth of John Weitz products each year, including furniture, luggage, shoes, towels, umbrellas, and accessories.

Designing is only one part of John Weitz's life, and he has managed to make "a very nice living out of it." But this aspect of his life is by no means all that he is interested in. His second book (and first novel), *The Value of Nothing,* was published in 1970. It is the story of a young man who rises from an unlikely background to become a fashion designer. In 1974 he wrote *Man in Charge,* a guide to executive grooming. And in 1983 he again published a novel. This one, entitled *Friends in High Places,* is a globe-circling tale of a Nazi officer who is caught up in the activities of Hitler's Germany. Later he is ashamed and begins to work on his redemption.[3]

"I've a very low threshold for boredom," says Weitz. "I'm bored with too much work or too much free time. I'm up at 5:30, and I'm so furiously organized that I have great gobs of free time."[4] Few people could question whether John Weitz has made constructive use of his free time.

[1] Andre Leon Talley, "John Weitz," four-page interview distributed by John Weitz Designs, Inc. (no date).
[2] Becky Homan, "Designing Men—John Weitz," *St. Louis Post-Dispatch,* September 4, 1983, Feature Sec., p. 1.
[3] Kathy Larkin, "The Designer Book," New York *Daily News,* November 29, 1982, Manhattan Sec., p. 1.
[4] Francesca Stanfill, "Weitz-Cracking," *Women's Wear Daily,* March 6, 1979 p. 8–9.

This Fashion Focus is based on information from the sources listed above and from this source:
Current Biography, 1979, "John Weitz," p. 424.

kits, which include written forecasts and visuals. It also prepares slide presentations, which are available to clubs, schools, and organizations.

The Cutty Sark Awards presentation, sponsored by the Scotch brand of the same name, is a highlight of the June press week. Unlike the Coty Awards, the Cutty Sark Awards are made to menswear designers only, and are international in scope. Also included are awards presented to promising students in the field of menswear design.

The MAGIC Show, specializes in sportswear with the "California look."

NAMSB. The National Association of Men's Sportswear Buyers (NAMSB) is a retail membership organization. It stages three market weeks annually in New York. The association was founded in 1953 by a group of New York menswear buyers conscious of the burgeoning sportswear market.

Currently, NAMSB shows have more than 1,200 exhibitors and attract over 25,000 buyers and retailers. Exhibitors include resources from over 30 countries, and the buyers and retailers come from more than 60 countries.

Shows are held in October and March, with an "interim" show in January. The October and March market show weeks are held at the New York Coliseum and the January show is held at the Statler Hotel in New York. When the proposed New York Convention Center is completed, NAMSB plans to hold all market events there.

In addition to its show weeks, NAMSB also provides members with a steady stream of pertinent information about developments within the menswear industry. For instance, it distributes a detailed monthly newsletter about fashion trends in menswear to association members. Twice a year, it prepares fashion-trend slide kits that members can rent for a nominal fee for use in their merchandising and marketing efforts. NAMSB also has a college scholarship program for children of retail members and their employees, intended to encourage young people to consider menswear retailing as a career.

MAGIC. What is now known as the Men's Apparel Guild in California (MAGIC) was established before World War II as the Los Angeles Menswear Manufacturers Association. After membership was extended to San Francisco producers, the name was changed. However, the name remained MAGIC even when manufacturers based elsewhere in the country were admitted.

Since 1979 the MAGIC show has been a national men's show with emphasis on sportswear. The success of the "California look" has drawn retailers to the show from all over the United States. Today the show is held at the Los Angeles Convention Center.

The MAGIC semiannual market events are now similar in character to those of the NAMSB, both in exhibitors and in site. While many retailers attend both shows, economics and geography often dictate which of the two will be omitted, since both are regarded as national market events.

CMA. The Clothing Manufacturer's Association was originally formed by producers of tailored clothing to represent them in negotiations with the union. Although CMA is still doing this, its activities have been greatly expanded. It coordinates and publicizes New York market weeks, and twice a year, in January and July, it publishes a trade periodical for international distribution. Another association function is to compile and distribute to members statistical and technical reports on developments in the tailored-clothing industry.

BIG AND TALL ASSOCIATES. Founded in 1971, this association of approximately 60 menswear manufacturers and 40 merchants concentrates on the less than 5 percent of the nation's males who are over 5'11" tall and/or who have a chest measurement of over 48". The association has a semiannual market week program.

MRA. The Menswear Retailers of America (MRA) is a national trade association of independent menswear stores, and is based in Washington, D.C. Originally called the National Association of Retail Clothiers and Furnishers, it began as a lobbying organization for the menswear retail community.

Today, the MRA is no longer in the showing business, having reached an agreement with the NAMSB to work with and join with it in that regard. Instead, its major programs are MRA national conventions, regional meetings, and such projects as its annual Executive Menswear Management Institute seminars for young retail executives, held at New York's Fashion Institute of Technology. The MRA's services to its members also include a monthly newsletter containing fashion and economic reports and an important annual business survey.

THE FATHER'S DAY COUNCIL INC. This is essentially a nonprofit organization for promoting Father's Day as a gift-giving holiday. Today there are almost as many Father's Day gifts being bought as Christmas gifts. The council estimates that Father's Day retail volume was $4 billion in 1983 and expects it to grow to $9 billion by 1990.[8]

The council is supported by manufacturers and major department stores. It was started in 1931 and was associated with the MRA. However, today it is a separate organization.

One of the major functions of the council is to prepare a noncommercial poster and to send it out with a promotional kit for the stores to build their own promotion around. For over 40 years, the council has selected National Fathers of the Year from all walks of life—sports, medicine, politics, theater, and film.

INDUSTRY TRENDS

After more than 150 years, men are once again fashion-conscious. As a result, the menswear industry is finally doing what the women's apparel industry has been doing for years. A wide range of choices in color, fabrics, and styles is now available to men of all ages.

The dynamics of population growth as well as developments in the economy today tend to favor certain segments of the menswear market over others. The fastest-growing age group at the present time includes men 25 to 44 years of age. A large percentage of men in this group have upward mobility in their careers and are interested in projecting the correct image through their fashion selections. Because of

this, contemporary styling and tailored separates may benefit in the 1980s. The growing numbers of higher-income, quality-conscious, mature males should create markets for an increasing number of diversified products. Other trends include a greater emphasis on the automation of production processes, an increase in both foreign production and sales, and a growing awareness of factors currently influencing the marketplace.

Diversification of Product

Many menswear manufacturers are increasing the types of apparel they offer. Traditionally, a firm in this industry produced only a single type of garment and sometimes only a single grade of that garment. Now menswear producers are beginning to ignore the tradition of product specialization that both manufacturers and retail stores have followed for so long.

For example, some of the biggest changes have taken place in an area that once was the most rigid: work clothes. For generations, firms like H. D. Lee and Levi Strauss turned out overalls, work pants, and work shirts in approximately the same patterns and the same fabrics, season after season. Now casual clothes have become popular, and the big-name producers of work clothes have found themselves producing fashion goods. In addition to jeans, which had almost completely saturated the market by the mid-1970s, these manufacturers are also producing a wide range of slacks, casual pants, and jackets. They are available in different styles, colors, and fabrics, all carefully selected to sell to today's sportswear-conscious male—and female. By the late 1970s, H. D. Lee and Levi Strauss were as much interested in style sales reports as they were in unit sales reports.

Suits are another example. In the past, manufacturers of traditional suits turned out a selection of styles in one or two grades. Today, the trade calls the traditional tailored suit a "suit-suit," because so many other types of suits have made gains in fashion importance.

Styling

The blazers, vests, and slacks produced by such giant firms as Levi Strauss, Haggar, and Farah helped introduce separates to the casual menswear market. Popular-priced sportswear was at the forefront of the separates movement in the late 1970s. Today, however, separates in the category of better-priced tailored clothing are beginning to have an increasingly pronounced influence on the marketplace.

Some manufacturers and retailers see separates as a bridge between sportswear and traditional menswear. One retailer sees separates as the trend of the future, satisfying the American consumer's need for instant gratification by allowing a suit to be bought and taken home immediately.[9] Most likely, however, separates will continue to have major impact in the popular-priced merchandise categories (approximately $175 to $195 at retail) and a less significant effect on the $350 to $400 suit market.

How separates will affect the sales of coordinates in the decade of the eighties is an open question. This will be an important trend to watch.

Traditionally, men's long-sleeved dress shirts have been made in neck sizes 14½" to 17", graduated in half-inches. Each size has also been available in a choice of sleeve-length sizes 32" to 35", graduated in inches. In an effort to reduce inventory levels and increase stock turnover at both the manufacturing and retailing levels, manufacturers have resorted recently to making dress shirts in only two sleeve lengths—regular (32"–33") and long (34"–35"). Half-inch neck sizes have been retained, however. Today more than 50 percent of all men's dress shirts are being produced in regular and long sleeve lengths. This percentage is expected to increase considerably in the future.

Automation of Production

Advances in technology have affected every industry. In menswear, new equipment and systems are helping manufacturers combat one of the most serious problems faced by all apparel producers today: the slow but steady dwindling of an available labor force. Every year it becomes increasingly difficult to find a sufficient supply of workers. Turnover in the industry is tremendous, averaging between 60 and 70 percent in recent years. The time required to train workers has become a crucial factor in estimating productivity.

One way that major companies are handling the labor problem is by establishing clusters of plants in the South and other areas where land costs are low and labor is relatively cheap. A large central plant turns out the main segments of a garment, such as various parts of a shirt. Bundles of those parts are then trucked to small satellite plants in nearby communities for machine-stitching. Since the more intricate work has already been done in the central plant, the work handled at the satellite plants is simple, and the labor cost is relatively low. The satellite plants attract workers because they provide a hometown source of income, with minimum training required. Workers do not have to travel long distances each day, as they would be required to do in order to earn slightly more at more distant plants.

It is in the central plant of such a cluster, and in other large apparel manufacturing plants, that automation is beginning to be developed. This is being achieved through the installation of equipment that (1) does jobs by machine that formerly had to be done by hand, (2) cuts down on the number of workers needed to do a specific job, and (3) cuts down on the amount of training and skill that workers need.

For instance, "pocket-setters" sew a pocket on a shirt automatically. "Sequential buttonhole sewers" stitch all buttonholes on a shirt in a single automated operation. "Collar-makers" reduce the number of workers needed to make a collar on a production-line basis from eight to two. Since the equipment is programmed to follow a set pattern of operations

Combatting foreign competition through advertising.

and only a few simple tasks are left to the operators, these workers can be trained to run such collar-making equipment in 2 weeks instead of the 10 to 12 weeks once required to teach workers to handle manual collar-making operations.

Automation has also invaded the labor-intensive, better-tailored-clothing industry. In the past, 1 to 1½ hours were required to hand-press a man's grade 6 or 6+ suit. Today that time is reduced to a matter of minutes by means of a computer-controlled, automated system that steam-presses each part of the suit.

In general, the industry is gradually becoming more machine-oriented than operator-oriented. This is a vast change for an industry that, throughout most of its history, prided itself on the individual workmanship that went into many of its products.

Foreign Production

Price competition is very strong in the menswear market. A very important factor in setting prices at wholesale is the cost of labor. Because of this, an increasing number of menswear producers, particularly sportswear firms, are building plants or contracting to have work done in areas outside the country, where land and labor costs are lower.

The amount and type of work done outside the country vary greatly. Some firms handle everything except the sewing in their domestic plants and contract to have the sewing done in plants outside the United States. Some have both the cutting and sewing done outside the country. Some ship greige goods to one country for dyeing and finishing and then ship these goods to another country for cutting and sewing. Some buy fabric outside the country and have the garments cut and sewn outside the country. In such cases, producers never actually see the products in any form until the finished goods are delivered to this country for distribution.

The disadvantages of foreign production include uncertain quality control and a longer wait for delivery of finished garments. Advantages, as discussed in earlier chapters, include lower production costs because of lower building or renting costs and lower costs of labor. This enables manufacturers to charge lower wholesale prices and retailers to pass on savings in lower retail prices. However, since goods produced in foreign countries are subject to import duties, savings are possible only when import duties are relatively low. In the 1980s, increasingly worried by the amount of foreign production in the menswear industry, menswear production workers in this country continued to demonstrate to get duties raised on imports of menswear from several key areas of foreign production, such as Taiwan, South Korea, and China.

Current Influencing Factors

That designer talents and labels add significant value to women's apparel has now been well established. To what degree this may hold true for the menswear industry will be determined in the 1980s. National brands, together with a good store name, are another factor that will assure the menswear customer of good value.

Imports continue to make inroads in the menswear market. Spiraling prices for domestic production, quality considerations, and the desire for exclusivity are causing more and more retail menswear organizations to build up their direct-import programs, as well as to buy indirect imports (clothing made abroad for U.S. manufacturers).

Another example is the increase in retail-advertising funding by manufacturers. In some cases, this funding has enabled retailers to send out specialty men's mailers and catalogs. Many specialty retailers and, of course, large department stores, have begun to enter into the hallowed institution of mail-order cataloging. Today's catalogs provide merchandise that features styling, price, or exclusiveness, and ease in buying. Specialty catalogs in menswear have proven to be very successful for the stores that do thorough market research, and offer to their customers exactly what they want.

The number of menswear stores rapidly increased in the 1960s and decreased in the early 1970s. However, shops featuring clothing and accessories for men are again proliferating in all areas of the country. Shops featuring active sportswear for jogging, running, tennis, and so on are especially popular.

However, economic situations sometimes force fashion-conscious men to seek shops where their fashion demands are compatible with limited finances. They thus shop in "pipe-rack" discounters, where "fashion at a low price" is the motto. Examples of discounters in the East are Syms, BFO (Buyer's Factory Outlet), and NBO (National Brands Outlet); in Houston and Dallas, Kuppenheimer Clothing Discount Centers and The Men's Wearhouse; in Los Angeles, C. & R. Clothiers, Inc.; in Detroit, National Dry Goods; and in Chicago, The Suitery. All are retailers catering to this new need in the menswear industry, similar to the "off-price" stores in women's apparel.

REFERENCES

[1] J. C. Flügel, *The Psychology of Clothes,* International Universities Press, New York, 1966, p. 111.
[2] Sidney Ruthberg, "Gore Sees Good 1984 for Hartmarx," *Daily News Record,* October 27, 1983, p. 12.
[3] Quoted in Harry A. Cobrin, *The Men's Clothing Industry,* Fairchild Publications, Inc., New York, 1970, p. 67.
[4] Extrapolated from statistics provided by John Mediarete of the American Apparel Manufacturers Association, April 2, 1984.
[5] Barbara Ettore, "Businessmen and Buttonholes," *The New York Times,* October 28, 1979, p. F1.
[6] "The Designer Syndrome," *Men's Wear,* January 28, 1980, p. 48.
[7] Jane Golden Reilly, "The View from the Bridge," *Men's Wear,* October 25, 1982, p. 49.
[8] T. Edward Popper, *Gift Behavior, Attitudes and Patterns,* The Father's Day Council, New York, 1981.
[9] Lynn Rothman, "Separates—New Tailored Separates Sales Spell Success," *F.I.R.E.,* February/March 1980, p. 56.

MERCHANDISING VOCABULARY

Define or briefly explain the following terms:

Active sportswear
Amalgamated Clothing and Textile Workers Union
Bridge
Contemporary menswear
Drop
Dual distribution
European styling
Fusing
Grade 6+ suit
Grade X suit
Inside shops
Short run
Slop shops
Suit separates
Sweat shops
Tailored-clothing firms

1. What effect did the industrial revolution have on male apparel? What socioeconomic factors were responsible for the drastic changes that occurred?
2. What four developments in the nineteenth century were largely responsible for the development of the men's ready-to-wear industry in this country? How did each help to accelerate those developments?
3. Discuss the development of sportswear and casual wear in the men's market and the influence they have had on the menswear industry as a whole.
4. Name and describe the three ways in which menswear was manufactured in this country in the latter part of the nineteenth century.
5. For what three reasons did early manufacturers of men's tailored clothing give up the use of contractors?
6. Name the different segments into which the menswear industry is subdivided, on the basis of the type of product lines each produces. What specific products are produced by each segment?
7. Describe the differences between a tailored sports coat and a sports jacket, from a manufacturing standpoint.
8. Contrast the advertising policies of men's tailored-clothing firms with those of firms producing sportswear.
9. Besides advertising, in which merchandising and marketing activities do menswear producers and trade associations participate?
10. What is the single greatest problem facing producers of menswear today? How are producers attempting to alleviate this problem?

1. Discuss the following statement from the text and cite examples to illustrate it: "Until the time of the industrial revolution, men's fashions reflected the dominance that the male sex enjoyed . . . the male's 'plumage' was far more stylish and colorful than the female's."
2. Discuss and give examples of how diversification of product lines, as an increasingly important industry trend, has affected (a) menswear production and (b) the retailing of menswear.
3. Discuss the increased use of foreign production facilities as a trend in the menswear industry. What are its advantages? Disadvantages?

11. ACCESSORIES

Clothes may make the man or the woman, but accessories make the clothes! If life in the fashion apparel world is challenging and exciting, life in the accessories world is really the "fast lane." Manufacturers of fashion accessories must constantly forecast changes in ready-to-wear, and must make sure that their accessories are right for these new fashions. A fashion accessory may be all the rage one year and completely out the next. It is only through constant alertness to trends and degree of customer acceptance that fashion accessory designers and manufacturers succeed. So sensitive is the fashion accessory business to fast changes that a really successful manufacturer can adapt or change a style or even an entire line right in the middle of a season. That's really life in the fast lane!

ACCESSORIES AND CLOTHING COORDINATION

There has always been a strong relationship between fashion accessories and the clothes with which they are worn. Accessories must be designed to be worn with new fashions and also to update fashion apparel already owned. Thus manufacturers of fashion accessories must be prepared to produce styles that blend, follow or lead, and innovate. Manufacturers must be aware of the fashion trends in color, silhouette, texture, and design so that retailers and consumers can be offered accessories to complete a total fashion look.

The fashion accessories industries must be highly responsive to fashion and quick to interpret incoming trends. Very often, consumer reactions to fashion accessories come first and can signal changes and trends in apparel fashions. Many times an accessory item becomes very successful with customers early in a season. Other industries take advantage of this early selling success by manufacturing similar or identical items. When this occurs, the hot item will be stocked and sold in many different departments of a store. Past examples of this are shawls, sunglasses, headwear, tops, and bodywear. All have been sold both in accessories departments and in many apparel departments at the same time.

The practice of showing accessories lines during fashion apparel market weeks enables merchants to coordinate the apparel and accessories they purchase. Thus the assortments they display and advertise will reflect the total fashion look they wish to present to their target customers.

Retailers have traditionally viewed accessories as **impulse items**—items that customers buy on an impulse rather than as a result of planning. Impulse items are bought because of color, excitement, or newness, or because customers simply want something new to give their spirits and wardrobes a lift. Most large department stores position the fashion accessories departments on the main floor near the front of the store because of this impulse buying pattern. A trend now is to have accessory department "outposts" throughout the store, adjacent to fashion apparel departments. This merchandising technique has proved very successful in helping customers achieve a coordinated look.

Some departments also feature total coordination in accessories and apparel. Often these departments feature name designers' apparel and accessories, allowing one-stop shopping. The concept of one-stop shopping is growing rapidly, because more and more women are entering the work force and have

less free time for shopping. Retailers and manufacturers are working hard to coordinate fashions so that customers can buy more in less time. The current success of career shops for women, where coordinated fashions and accessories are sold, prove that this is what shoppers want.

Many successful boutiques and specialty stores feature fashion accessories. Shoe stores, handbag and hosiery stores, millinery stores, and cosmetics stores are becoming more popular because of the new interest of customers and retailers in fashion accessories. The association of famous designer names with fashion accessories is another reason for this growing popularity.

Among European fashion leaders, fine accessories have long been a status symbol and have been considered indispensable to a fashion wardrobe. Americans, however, have just recently become aware of the versatility and uniqueness of fashion accessories. Fashion accessories have now become a major part of fashion in this country and an essential segment of the fashion industry.

The impact of foreign-made merchandise has been very evident in the fashion accessories industries. Whether the foreign merchandise is made to specification for U.S. manufacturers or retailers or is sold directly by importers to retailers, its percentage of total merchandise sold has grown tremendously. In some of the industries, notably shoes, handbags, and neckwear, sales of foreign-made accessories have risen to well over 50 percent of all merchandise sold.

The rise of accessories as a dynamic force in fashion only came about in the past few decades. Although this force diminished for a time, accessories regained a starring role in the mid-1980s and once again play an important part in the look of fashion. Many major stores devote entire banks of windows and create small shops on their main floors to focus on accessories. Leading fashion apparel designers, American and foreign, have begun showing their collections with accessories an integral part of the design. Not one apparel outfit was shown without the right shoe, handbag, hat, gloves, scarf, and jewelry. The impact of fashion accessories grows stronger each year.

SHOES

Feet, the base upon which our bodies stand, have been wrapped, covered, or left uncovered since the beginning of time. Primitive people wrapped their feet in fur, and later people strapped them into sandals.

Customs concerning footwear have differed since the early Greeks and Romans donned sandals and boots. The Greeks generally went barefoot in the house. Romans rarely did so, regarding the wearing of footwear as a mark of superior class.

Making shoes was once a painstaking handicraft. But the commercial production of shoes has developed into an industry providing over 300 variations in shoe lengths and widths and over 10,000 different shapes and styles. Most shoe styles originated in Europe, keeping pace with the growth of European fashion. However, a classic shoe style that originated in America is the moccasin. Favored by both men and women and adored by most children, the moccasin style of shoe still retains its popularity and stands as one of the first examples of a unisex fashion.

Organization and Operation

Shoemaking in America was once exclusively a Yankee industry. The major center for footwear production in the United States is still in New England, where the industry had its origin. But another large center of production today is the St. Louis, Missouri region. The westward movement of the industry came when the Midwest was recognized as an important source of hide supplies and cheaper labor. Brown Shoe Company, the largest

The sandal, a classic since the days of ancient Greece, has been reinterpreted for the 1980s.

American producer of name-brand footwear, is based in St. Louis.

For each type and size of shoe in a producer's line, there must be a **last.** Lasts were originally wooden forms in the shape of a foot, over which the shoes were built. Today most modern factories, American and foreign, make lasts of plastic or aluminum. Lasts made from these materials provide more exact measurements, and are more expedient to handle than the old wooden lasts. The variety of lasts, the quality of materials, and the number and type of manufacturing operations required determine the quality and price of the finished shoe. As many as 200 to 300 operations may be performed by highly skilled workers in the making of an expensive, high-quality shoe.

The range of sizes that shoe manufacturers must produce is enormous. The normal range of women's shoe sizes involves 103 width and length combinations. And this does not include sizes shorter than 4, longer than 11, or wider than D. Inventories, production problems, and capital investments are tremendous compared with those of other fashion-related industries. Thus it is not surprising that giant companies dominate the industry. Among the fashion industries, only cosmetics has a higher percentage of production by giant companies.

Market Centers

As with most fashion industries, New York City is the major U.S. market center for shoes. Most producers maintain permanent showrooms there, regardless of where their manufacturing plants may be located. Foreign footwear producers employ selling agents in the United States who also have showrooms located in this market center. This is also true for U.S.–based importers. Twice a year, seasonal lines are shown to store buyers and the fashion press. These shows are known as the National Shoe Fairs. The semiannual National Shoe Fair, which is usually held in New York City, is so gigantic that in addition to shows at the New York Coliseum, it has to be segmented in several major New York hotels. These shows make it easy for buyers, store owners, and other fashion-related people to view the whole market. Capsule shoe showings are also held quarterly in regional markets such as Dallas, Miami, Chicago, and Los Angeles for the benefit of area buyers and merchants.

Merchandising and Marketing Activities

The shoe industry has an active national trade association known as the National Shoe Manufacturers Association. Together with the National Shoe Retailers Association, it disseminates technical, statistical, and fashion trend information on footwear. In addition, the leather industry and its associations operate as sources of fashion information for shoe buyers and other retail store executives.

Brand names are a major part of the footwear industry, and manufacturers advertise extensively in national fashion magazines and on national television.

In contrast with most other fashion industries, many of the larger shoe manufacturers operate retail chain organizations of their own. This practice is known as "dual distribution." The other industry that practices dual distribution is the menswear industry. (See Chapter 10.) An outstanding example of dual distribution in the shoe industry is the Brown Group, which manufactures Buster Brown shoes for children, Naturalizer and Air Step shoes for women, and Roblee and Regal shoes for men. The Melville Corporation, which manufactures Thom McAn shoes, is another example. All of these shoe brands are sold in retail stores owned by the shoe manufacturers. Frequently these shoe chains also stock related accessories, such as handbags and hosiery.

Some shoe manufacturers also operate in the retail field through leased departments in retail stores. Because of the tremendous amount of capital required to stock a shoe department

FASHION FOCUS

JOSEPH FAMOLARE: FASHION FOOTWEAR INNOVATOR

If you were to ask a dozen people what came to mind when they thought of "the excitement of fashion," you would be lucky to find one who answered "shoes." Yet Joseph Famolare (pronounced "Fa-mo-la-ray") has captured the excitement of fashion combined with the wisdom of anatomically correct design to create a thriving fashion footwear company.

Shoemaking is a tradition in the Famolare family. As a boy growing up in Boston, Famolare learned the trade from his father, who serviced the shoe manufacturing industry with his shoe-design and pattern-making company. Yet Famolare decided to major in drama when he attended Emerson College. Later he was able to combine his talent with shoes and his interest in the theater when he joined Capezio Dance, where he designed footwear for stage productions.

His next position was with Marx and Newman, a large shoe company, where he was appointed executive vice president. In 1970, after 9 years with Marx and Newman, he decided to open his own shoe company. He began by manufacturing molded clogs, and in 1973 won the Coty Award for his jeweled wood-and-plastic clog. Then, in the mid-1970s, Famolare developed a shoe that established Famolare Shoes as a fashion innovator. The Get There was an anatomically beneficial shoe with a wavy sole. The four waves in the sole acted as shock absorbers as the wearer walked, passing along the force of walking from one wave to the next, and the contoured leather interior properly supported the foot. Although many people doubted this strange new shoe would sell (including the quarter of Famolare's own sales force who quit when the shoe was introduced), it was largely responsible for lifting the compa-

and the expertise needed to fit and sell shoes, many department and specialty stores lease their shoe departments to shoe manufacturers. Surveys made by the National Retail Merchants Association have repeatedly shown that women's shoe departments are among those most commonly leased by its member stores. Examples of manufacturers of shoes who operate leased shoe departments in stores are the U.S. Shoe Corporation and the Brown Shoe Company. Morse Shoe Company and Edison Shoe Company are chain store retailers that

ny's sales from $15 million to almost $100 million in just 5 years.

After the Get There came the Hi There, which was a high-heeled wedge with a wavy sole. Then, in 1982, Famolare introduced another unique shoe, called the Plosive. This one featured four "islands" called Plosives that were built into the sole of the shoe to cushion the foot and provide for increased circulation.

Throughout his career as a shoe designer, Joe Famolare has never forgotten his interest in the theater, and his dramatic talents have made him a master of promotion. Early in his career as a company president, he toured the country with a dozen Sardinian dancers and musicians to draw publicity for the company. When the Get There was first introduced, he commissioned a rock group to create and record a song called "Get There," and he gave away a complimentary record with each pair of shoes. The "Get There" was also a dance, and he encouraged stores to stage dance promotions for Get There shoes.

Other promotional events have included hot-air balloon races, foot races, 3-day festivals, and the use of a clown-magician who pulls shoes out of hats in the otherwise quiet shoe departments of retail stores. At one time Famolare himself even did a roller-skating performance on top of a float in a Minneapolis parade.

Famolare's "Footloose and Famolare" ads, which are seen in magazines and newspapers nationwide, feature a tight close-up of his bearded, smiling face, and his hand holding his shoes. This innovative advertising campaign has made Famolare something of an instant celebrity and created a "folksy and fun" image for his shoes and his company.

In 1982, Famolare went a step further in innovative advertising—into television. His ads, which feature himself, were the first TV ads to be signed for the deaf.

The company, which makes shoes in Italy, Brazil, and the United States, introduced three new lines in 1984: the Sports line of casual shoes, the Dance There line for the increasing number of people interested in dancing for fitness, and the Bibiana line of boutique shoes. To these new fashions, Famolare has added Dance There clothing.

"Famolare, who has a Boston accent, loves to talk, is decidedly not shy, and has definite opinions about shoe retailing . . . As for creating the shoes that will make customers flock to the stores, that calls for 'a creative company that will make a shoe the world has never seen before,' says Famolare."[1] Joe Famolare has brought excitement to the footwear industry by creating just that type of shoe, over and over again.

[1] Ulana Blyznak, "Joe Famolare: No Business Like Shoe Business," *Footwear Focus*, February 1983, p. 15.

This Fashion Focus is based on information from the article cited above and from these sources:

"Famolare Shoes Take First Steps into T.V.", *Advertising Age*, January 25, 1982, p. 38E.
Bernice Kanner, "Famolare's Flair Builds a $100M Shoe Biz," New York *Daily News*, February 24, 1981, p. 10.
Bernadine Morris and Barbara Walz, *The Fashion Makers*, Random House, New York, 1978, pp. 73–74.
Meg Rottman, "Famolare Again Wins Ms. Liberty Award," *Footwear News*, April 11, 1983, p. 22.
Personal telephone interview with Bibiana Famolare on March 7, 1984.
Steven Solomon, "A Ride to Golconda in a Wavy Shoe Sole," *Fortune*, July 30, 1979, pp. 104–106.

import shoes and also operate leased shoe departments in other stores.

WOMEN'S SHOES.

For centuries, little attention was paid to the styling of women's shoes. Their purpose was regarded as purely functional, and it was considered immodest to expose the feminine ankle. Since the 1920s, however, women's feet have been plainly visible, and shoes have developed both in fashion importance and variety. When fashion invaded the shoe industry after World War II, the black or brown all-purpose shoes that were to be worn with any wardrobe disappeared. New and varied leather finishes, textures, plastic and fabric materials, and ranges of colors provided shoe styles that not only kept pace with changes in fashion but in many cases originated fashion trends. Styles have run the fashion gamut from pointed to squared toes, from high to flat heels, and from naked sandals to thigh-high boots.

MEN'S SHOES. A shift in thinking and lifestyles on the part of American men has had a dramatic effect on the merchandising of men's shoes. Dress shoes were once the most important sales category in men's shoe departments in retail stores. They are now being replaced by dress/casual and casual shoes. Casual shoes were once considered appropriate only for the 18 to 25 age group, but now are preferred by men of all ages. The return in the 1980s of the classic look, the three-piece suit, and narrower ties has revived interest in loafers, moccasins, and dressier, classic slip-ons.

Although the sales volume for men's shoes is increasing, it is moving at a slower rate than the sales volume for women's shoes.

CHILDREN'S SHOES. Until they are approximately 10 years old, boys and girls take more interest in their shoes than anything else they wear. Maybe this is due in part to the influence of children's stories—*The Wizard of Oz, Seven League Boots,* and *Cinderella,* for example—in which shoes have magical powers.

Also, boys and girls must be taken along when shoes are bought and are involved in the purchase decision. From an early age they are taught that the correct fit and look of their shoes are important. This early training leads children to view shoes as the mainstay of a fashion wardrobe.

Industry Trends

In the United States in 1982, shoe retail sales reached a peak of $19.7 billion, a slight gain over 1981. Unit sales of men's, women's, children's, and athletic footwear increased by 30 million in 1982, to 979 million pairs. By the mid-1980s, sales were projected to reach over 1 billion pairs.[1]

Over 60 percent of shoes sold in the United States are imported from the following countries: Italy, Taiwan, Brazil, Korea, and Spain. Italy and Taiwan contribute the greatest number; however, Brazil is making great strides in shoe exports to the United States, according to mid-1980s statistical reports.

Among women's fashion shoes alone, 80 percent of the shoes sold were imported, and this figure is rising slightly every year. This shows a drastic decline in domestically manufactured shoes and a tremendous increase in the volume of imported shoes. The number of manufacturing plants in the domestic shoes industry has dropped from 950 in 1969 to about 350 in the early 1980s. The industry now has as many foreign as domestic producers. One of the primary reasons for this rise in footwear imports is the continually rising cost of production in the United States.

Domestic manufacturers are experimenting with new and upgraded computer technology to aid in the design and manufacturing of shoes. Producers are thus attempting to meet the problems of foreign competition and to enlarge their market potential. The U.S. Department of Commerce's Footwear Revitalization program, in operation since July 1977, is also providing impetus. This program has been of aid to many domestic manufacturers who have used grants of money to update their operations so that the new technology can be used in their U.S. factories. The government also extracted shoe quotas on shoe exports from Taiwan, Korea, and other foreign producers. With the expected increase in more advanced technology in manufacture and with the styling and know-how of American shoe designers, the domestic shoe industry is trying to increase exports of American-made shoes to the rest of the world.

Americans are participating in a greater variety of sports than ever before. This has brought about a proliferation of styles in athletic footwear. Athletic shoes have also become fashion items for people who want to look like athletes, even though they may not participate in any sport. An estimated 90 percent of athletic shoes sold are not strictly used for the purposes for which they were designed but for comfort and style. This phenomenal boom in athletic footwear is to a large extent the result of foreign fashion leadership. The success of the Adidas and Puma lines from West Germany and the Tiger line from Japan led American manufacturers to update and restyle their existing athletic footwear lines. One outstanding American producer of athletic footwear is Nike, Inc. of Beaverton, Oregon.

There is a strong relationship between shoes and the clothes with which they are worn. Greater emphasis on fashion continues to be the major trend in the footwear industry. Shoe designers and manufacturers regularly attend European apparel openings, as do shoe buyers from retail stores, gathering information on international trends in styling. More and more, apparel fashions influence both the styling and color of footwear. Skirt lengths, silhouettes, pants, and sporty or dressy clothes are the fashion keys to shoe designs. It is therefore essential for retailers to coordinate shoes and apparel wherever and whenever they can.

HOSIERY

People have been wearing stockings and socks for centuries. The ancient Greeks wore cloth legwear. By the late 1500s, European men and

Apparel fashions influence the styling of footwear. Manufacturers coordinate the two whenever they can.

women wore stockings made from a single piece knitted flat, with the two edges sewn together to form a back seam. This technology remained essentially unchanged for centuries.

Until World War I, women's legs were concealed under floor-length skirts and dresses, and were rarely, if ever, seen. When skirt lengths moved up and women's legs became visible, interest in adorning them increased and the hosiery industry began to grow. Today creative designers, using new and advanced technology in fibers and production techniques, are able to provide stunning new designs and styles for this important focal point of interest: legs!

History and Development

It was not until the introduction of nylon that hosiery as we know it today became a fashion accessory. Before the introduction of nylon in 1938, women wore seamed silk, cotton, or rayon stockings. Because of its easier care and durability, the new nylon hosiery was eagerly accepted despite its high price.

With the entry of the United States into World War II, nylon production was restricted to war purposes and silk was unavailable. Because the hosiery that was available was heavy and unattractive, women began to go bare-legged and used leg makeup to give the effect of sheer stockings. The bare-legged look became very popular, and when nylon became available again, the industry developed sheerer weights (deniers) and seamless hosiery that would give this look.

Fashion first entered the hosiery picture in the 1950s with the introduction of colors other than black or flesh tones. But it was not until the 1960s that hosiery became a major fashion accessory. To accessorize the shorter skirt— eventually evolving into the miniskirt and micromini—colors, textures, and weights of stockings were created in great variety. It was at this time in fashion history that panty hose were introduced and became a fantastic success.

The great popularity of panty hose brought about the introduction of seamless panty hose and figure-control panty hose. In the 1970s, when the popularity of pants for women was at its peak, knee-high and ankle-high hosiery became popular. Together with panty hose, they captured the major share of the hosiery business. In the 1980s changes in lifestyle produced different customer needs and wants. The great interest in athletics by men, women, and children spurred the hosiery industry to innovations in yarn, textures, and manufacturing procedures. These new needs and wants were met with textures in panty hose and tights, socks in ribs and knits, leg warmers from knee-to thigh-high, and a revitalized category of athletic socks.

Organization and Operation

The hosiery industry consists primarily of large firms, many of which are divisions of huge textile or apparel conglomerates. The largest concentration of hosiery plants is found in the Southern states, with more than half of them in North Carolina.

Most hosiery mills perform all of the steps necessary for the production of finished hosiery. Some smaller mills may perform the knitting operation only, contracting out the finishing processes.

Full-fashioned seamed hosiery is flat-knit to size and length specifications on high-speed machines. These machines shape the hosiery as it is knitted. The outer edges are then stitched together on special sewing machines, after which the hosiery is dyed. Each stocking acquires permanent shape through a heat-setting process called **boarding.** Then the stockings are carefully matched into pairs. Their welts are stamped with a brand name or other appropriate information, and the pairs are packaged.

Seamless hosiery and panty hose are circular-knit to size and length specifications on high-speed machines. Again, these machines shape the item during the knitting process. Subsequent steps are dyeing, boarding, pairing, stamping, and packaging, as for full-fashioned hosiery.

Since hosiery is knitted in the greige (unfinished) state, most manufacturers can produce branded and unbranded hosiery in the same mill. The greige goods are then dyed, finished, stamped, and packaged to specification for national brand, private brand, or unbranded customers.

Market Centers

Although most hosiery is produced in the South, New York City is the market center where manufacturers maintain permanent showrooms. Retail buyers visit these showrooms semiannually. Here they view seasonal lines and find out about the national advertising programs of the big producers. Smaller mills frequently employ the services of selling agents. These agents maintain offices in New York City for closer contact with retail and fashion markets.

Merchandising and Marketing Activities

Traditionally, the women's hosiery industry concentrated its merchandising activities almost exclusively on the promotion and sale of nationally advertised brands. Recently, however, the industry has been merchandising its products for private labeling or for sale in vending machines and from self-service displays in supermarkets and drugstores. Designer labeling has also become increasingly important in hosiery merchandising.

NATIONAL BRANDS. Major hosiery producers sell their brand lines to a wide variety of retail stores across the country. The producers aggressively advertise these lines on a national basis in magazines and newspapers and on television. They also usually supply coop-

erative advertising, display aids, and fashion assistance to help promote these national brands at the store level. Major national brands include Hanes, Burlington, Round-the-Clock, and Kayser-Roth.

DESIGNER-LABEL BRANDS. Because designer labeling adds an aura of couture and prestige to any item, designer labels have appeared on a variety of hosiery items, including panty hose, socks, and leg warmers. Many hosiery manufacturers upgrade their designer-label collections with superior yarns and production techniques. Almost all of the designer-label hosiery produced is the result of licensing agreements between the designer and manufacturers of national brands. In hosiery and panty hose, Hanes uses Oleg Cassini and Round-the-Clock uses Givenchy; in socks, Bonnie Doon uses Geoffrey Beene, Camp Company uses Christian Dior and John Weitz, and Hot Sox uses Ralph Lauren. Many companies try to identify their hosiery designer with the apparel style of the particular designer to capture the patronage of that particular customer.

PRIVATE BRANDS. Chain organizations, groups of retail stores, and some individual stores have developed their own **private or store brands** or labels in competition with or in addition to nationally advertised brands of hosiery. There are many advantages to a private label for the retailer. The cost of the hosiery is usually less because there is no built-in charge for advertising as there is for national brands. The private brand can be made up in colors and construction that will match customer profile specifications. Because the private brand is not available elsewhere, price promotions are easier. Customer shopping loyalty can also be built upon the exclusivity of the private brand. Some private-label brands are Sears' Best, Macy's Supremacy and Marchioness brands, Lerner's own brand, and I. Magnin's Magninique.

These days bodywear makes fashion news.

MASS-MERCHANDISED BRANDS. More and more self-service stores such as supermarkets, discount stores, and drug chains are beginning to carry packaged hosiery. With this change in the channels of retail distribution, hosiery manufacturers are developing low-priced, packaged hosiery that can be profitably sold in these stores. Each of these brands offers a good choice of styles and colors. Each manufacturer supplies attractive, self-service stock fixtures and promotes its brand through national advertising. Examples of mass-merchandised brands are L'eggs panty hose, made by Hanes Hosiery, and No Nonsense panty hose, made by Kayser-Roth.

BODYWEAR. The interest of the buying public in health and bodybuilding activities has produced a new fashion category—**bodywear,** which consists of coordinated leotards, tights, and wrap skirts. Also, sweatsuits, exercise outfits, leg warmers, and shorts and T-shirts used for aerobics are part of the bodywear classification. Because bodywear has price and brand-name advantages over competing merchandise in swimwear, active sportswear, and junior sportswear departments, sales in this category have boomed in many hosiery departments. In fact, by the mid-1980s, many stores were selling bodywear in separate shops or boutiques.

Interest in dance as a way of keeping fit and healthy has added impetus to the bodywear business. Long-time bodywear manufacturers, Danskin and Flexotard, introduced new, exciting leotards just for dance wear. Manufacturers noted for producing other accessories, Aris and Evan-Picone, entered the bodywear field with Isotoner Fitnesswear and Highstepper Leotards, respectively.

Industry Trends

Fashion trends have a tremendous influence on sales in the hosiery industry. For example, when skirts are shorter or have leg-revealing silhouettes, texture and color in hosiery become more important. "All-in-ones"—panty hose with built-in-panties—are the answer when tight-fitting pants and skirts are the fashion look. Apparel manufacturers have recently worked with hosiery manufacturers to design panty hose that are both texture- and color-coordinated to their sportswear. The hosiery is displayed with the apparel to convey a total fashion look.

Hosiery manufacturers are devoting more time and money to new developments in product manufacturing and research. The industry is becoming more fashion-oriented and is working closely with apparel manufacturers to offer customers a coordinated fashion look.

The inventory of most hosiery departments includes conventional stockings, panty hose, casual legwear, leg warmers, bodywear, and casual footwear. Bodywear and casual footwear are relatively high-priced retail items, while packaged hosiery is low-priced. As a result, some stores have made separate departments out of these two different categories.

The varying needs and wants of hosiery customers have prompted hosiery manufacturers to design entirely new items. Control-top panty hose, support hose, queen-sized panty hose, and "all-in-ones" are examples. Silk hosiery, which had not been glimpsed on legs since the mid-forties, returned to the fashion picture. But it came back updated to a 1980s lifestyle, in the sportswear look of silk knee-highs and socks. Expansion plans in this category include silk metallic socks and silk panty hose. The industry feels that if it continues to be innovative and do exciting new things with color, texture, and fashion involvement, hosiery will continue to be important, and the industry will never go back to "basic beige."

With the increasing importance of new distribution channels, such as mass merchants and supermarkets, hosiery manufacturers have developed new packaging and marketing strategies for these markets. The success of the L'eggs and No Nonsense brands has prompted the industry to look to more innovative and technologically advanced methods for introducing and marketing hosiery fashions.

Men's, women's, and children's hosiery sales are predicted to steadily increase. Athletic, sport, and work socks are exploding in the men's area; knee-highs, tights, leg warmers, and new textures and colors in panty hose are fueling the women's area; and children are emulating their parents in their requests for sport socks, tights, and leg warmers.

In the past decade, innovations in yarn, marketing, and manufacturing have transformed a labor-intensive business into a semiautomated, very competitive industry producing over $4.6 billion in retail sales. It is estimated that by the year 2000, the domestic hosiery industry will be about 40 percent larger in terms of number of units produced. However, the output will be manufactured by an industry with only one-half as many firms, employing two-thirds as many people as today.[2]

HANDBAGS

The ways in which people carry their belongings reflect the times in which they live. For many centuries, small sacks vied with pockets as places to keep belongings. The modern handbag has become more than a receptacle for needed coins or personal possessions. It is now a fashion item that is used to reflect a person's personality and style.

Handbags are used for different needs, moods, fashion statements, and occasions. They are part of the total fashion look. Handbag styles vary from the most casual to the most formal. Shapes may be small or large, pouch or tote, draped or boxlike. In general, they are designed to suit the size of the wearer and the currently popular apparel silhouette. Well-dressed women use their handbags to dramatize, harmonize, or contrast with their fashion apparel. For example, a woman may choose a leather briefcase for wear to the office with her tailored suit, a small delicate fabric or beaded evening bag to harmonize with her filmy and feminine dance or party dress, and a lightweight vinyl or canvas tote to carry her things to the exercise spa or dance class.

Organization and Operation

Compared with other fashion industries, the handbag industry is quite small. The number of domestic firms producing handbags is diminishing each year, as imports of handbags made in Europe, South America, and the Far East increase. In just two years, from 1979 to 1981, the number of domestic firms dropped from about 400 to roughly 380, and during the same period, the number of production workers fell from an estimated 19,000 to 18,000. This drop was from a high of over 600 firms

in 1963.[3] Domestic firms producing handbags are concentrated in New York and New England. More and more frequently, the smaller firms, employing from 20 to 30 people, are closing. The remaining firms are becoming larger and more diversified in order to obtain a larger share of the consumer market.

Market Centers

The handbag market center is in New York City, close to the major garment industries. Permanent showrooms are maintained there, and seasonal lines may be viewed at least twice a year with the seasonal showings of fashion apparel.

Merchandising and Marketing Activities

Although manufacturers' brand names are relatively unimportant in the handbag industry, there has been tremendous growth in designer-name handbags. Famous fashion de-

This handbag showroom is located in the market center, New York City.

signers such as Pierre Cardin, Bill Blass, Calvin Klein, and Diane Von Furstenberg have entered into licensing agreements with handbag manufacturers.

Few handbag manufacturers are large enough to advertise on a national basis in newspapers or on television. The customer's impression of what is new and fashionable in handbags is gained primarily through stores where they are coordinated and displayed with fashion apparel. ''Total look'' advertising in newspapers and magazines also keeps the customer up-to-date on handbag fashion.

Industry Trends

Faced with severe competition from foreign imports, many domestic handbag manufacturers have themselves become importers of foreign-made handbags. These importers employ experienced American designers to create styles and then have the handbags manufactured in countries where the wage scale is much lower. In the mid-1980s, almost 50 percent of all handbags sold in the United States were imported. The industry's trade association—the National Handbag Association—is lobbying for tighter import restrictions and for financial adjustment assistance to domestic firms hurt by foreign competition.

Some of the larger manufacturers have recently diversified their lines to include styles for men. Still others are adding luggage, small leather goods such as wallets and key cases, and coordinated belts to their product lines. The handbag industry is attempting to provide a complete wardrobe of fashion handbags to fashion-conscious men and women through continued improvements in styling, the use of new and exciting textures and colors, and total coordination with fashion apparel.

JEWELRY

Jewelry, as the symbol of wealth and importance, has been worn by the nobility for centuries. Laden with gold chains, their clothing encrusted with gems, their fingers covered with rings, they carried on their persons the immense fortunes of their ruling houses. In those times to wear one's fortune on one's back was perhaps the best way both to keep it safe and to show off one's possessions. The beautiful women who still live for us in the ancient frescoes obviously loved jewelry very much. They are shown with long, thin necklaces that encircle the neck two and three times, gold earrings, strands of pearls braided in their hair, and engraved belts made of precious stones set in gold. Medieval noblemen displayed heraldic symbols or emblems of knighthood, while military men made a great display of their decorations, all jewel-encrusted. By the 1800s, the gold or silver watch became an accessory of great importance. The chains and medallions worn by some fashion-conscious men in the last decade are no great departure from the protective amulets worn by men in ancient Rome as necklaces. Since the earliest civilizations, jewelry has played a significant and varied role in people's lives.

Organization and Operation

Modern methods of making jewelry may be less arduous than those of earlier times, but essentially they involve the same steps. Modern jewelry makers melt and shape metal, cut and carve stones, and string beads and shells. Jewelry designers still use enamel, glass, ceramic materials, and natural mineral formations to express their creative ideas.

The jewelry industry in the United States is divided into two groups, primarily on the basis of intrinsic value or quality of product. One group is referred to as **fine jewelry;** the other is termed **costume** or **fashion jewelry.**

FINE JEWELRY.   The counterpart of haute couture apparel is fine jewelry. Only precious metals such as gold and all of the platinum family (palladium, rhodium, and iridium) are used to make fine jewelry. Silver is also considered a precious metal but is not used as widely as gold and platinum. Precious metals are too soft to be used alone. They are therefore combined with one or several other metals to produce an alloy hard enough to retain a desired shape and to hold stones securely.

Stones used in fine jewelry are known as **gemstones** to distinguish them from those stones suitable only for industrial use. Gemstones are natural stones and are classified as either precious or semiprecious. **Precious stones** include diamonds, emeralds, rubies, sapphires, and real, or oriental, pearls. **Semiprecious stones** include amethysts, garnets, opals, jades, and other natural stones that are less rare and costly, but still beautiful. In recent years, chemists have succeeded in creating synthetic rubies, sapphires, and diamonds that are chemically identical to the genuine gemstone. These synthetic stones are now used in combination with 14-karat gold and silver. The most popular is the cubic zirconia, which has the dazzle of a diamond at a fraction of the cost.

The fine-jewelry industry is essentially a handcraft industry. A lapidary, or stonecutter, is an artisan who transforms dull-looking stones into gems of beauty by cutting, carving, or polishing them.

In the creative fine-jewelry houses, as in haute couture apparel houses, design, production, and retail sales all usually take place under one roof and one management. Many fine-jewelry firms sell only the merchandise they manufacture, much of which is custom-designed.

COSTUME JEWELRY. Costume or fashion jewelry may be compared to mass-produced apparel. Materials used in the manufacture of costume jewelry are plastics, wood, glass, brass, and other base metals (such as aluminum, copper, tin, and lead). Some of these materials may be coated with costlier metals like gold, rhodium, or silver. Stones and simulated pearls used in costume jewelry are made from clay, glass, or plastic. While attractive and interesting in surface appearance, they are less costly and have none of the more desirable properties of natural stones.

Before the 1920s, most jewelry worn by both men and women was made from gold and was often set with precious or semiprecious stones. Silver was seldom used as a jewelry metal because it was too soft to hold stones securely. It also quickly tarnished. Rarely was jewelry in those days designed to accessorize or complement apparel styles of a period. Coco Chanel has been credited with changing this. In the 1920s she introduced long strands of frankly fake pearls to be worn with the widely popular short, sleeveless, collarless, elongated-torso dresses of that period. It is interesting to note that Chanel not only introduced this jewelry style but wore it herself throughout the rest of her life. Long strands of pearls became her trademark. The new type of jewelry was aptly called "costume," since its design was originally intended, and still continues, to be influenced by the neckline, bodice, and sleeve details of apparel design. In the 1960s, Kenneth Jay Lane designed costume jewelry that looked so real that social and other fashion leaders preferred to wear it rather than their own authentic jewels. In the 1980s the smaller costume jewelry designers are making a strong impact with their versions of frankly fake jewelry. Eva Graham, Catherine Stein, Carol Daiplaise, and Van Allen are but a few of the designers in small companies who are making a large contribution to costume jewelry.

Most of the large, popular-priced costume-jewelry houses employ stylists who design seasonal lines or adapt styles from higher-priced lines. Most of this jewelry is produced in New England and the Middle Atlantic states, with Providence, Rhode Island, as the major production center of the costume-jewelry industry. Facilities concentrated there produce jewelry to the specifications of individual firms, much the same as apparel contractors work with apparel manufacturers and jobbers. Mass-

American costume jewelry designers sometimes buy materials from importers who import from foreign suppliers.

production methods prevail. In contrast to the hand-shaping of metal used in fine jewelry, the metal used in costume jewelry is usually cast by melting it and then pouring the molten metal into molds to harden. Finally, designs may be applied to the hardened metal by painting its surface with colored enamel or etching the metal by machine.

A great portion of costume jewelry is mass-produced by large companies such as Monet, Marvella, Swank, Accessocraft, and Bergere. But there is also a trend toward smaller manufacturers in this market. Individuals with creative talent open small retail and/or wholesale operations catering to customers interested in individualized styling and trend-setting fashions. This is an outgrowth of the handcraft movement of the 1960s and 1970s, when single entrepreneurs designed, created, and sold their own designs and merchandise.

BRIDGE JEWELRY DEPARTMENTS. With the dramatic increases in the price of gold and silver in the 1980s, jewelry designers and retailers sought ways to meet the public's demand for reasonably priced authentic jewelry. A solution was the creation of "bridge" lines and "bridge" departments. A **bridge jewelry department** is a department that forms a bridge—in price, materials, and newness—between costume and fine jewelry.

The recognition of sterling silver as a precious metal and the boom of Native American turquoise jewelry from 1970 to 1975 also prompted some of the larger department and specialty stores to create bridge departments for these new categories. Today, bridge jewelry departments are those in which merchandise is classified on the basis of one of the following: (1) prices, (2) precious metal, (3) fashion newness, (4) karat of gold.

Stores such as Marshall Field's, Neiman-Marcus, Broadway Department Stores, and the May Company have bridge departments that carry gold-filled, vermeil, sterling silver, and some 14-karat fashion jewelry. Ivory, tur-quoise, coral, and other semiprecious stones set in high-fashion designs are also part of bridge departments' inventories.

Market Centers

New York City is the principal market center for both fine and costume jewelry. Major firms maintain permanent showrooms there as a convenience to store buyers and also to keep in close contact with developments in other segments of the fashion industry. New York now has a permanent showroom facility located in the Park Avenue Atrium. Known as the Worldwide Business Exchange (WBE), this 5,000-square-foot showroom features 600 illuminated display modules that national and international buyers can shop. Los Angeles also has a fast-growing jewelry center that has become an important source of Asian jewelry, particularly jade and pearls.

Seasonal showings, held semiannually, are sponsored by the industry's trade association, the Jewelry Industry Council.

The Manufacturing Jewelers and Silver-smiths of America, Inc., another industry trade group, sponsors annual shows in New York and Los Angeles and hosts a delegation of American companies at the European Watch, Clock, and Jewelry Fair in Basel, Switzerland. Retailers of both fine and costume jewelry attend these trade shows to preview fashion trends for the coming season, to keep abreast of developments in the industry, and to buy for their seasonal needs.

Merchandising and Marketing Activities

Fine-jewelry manufacturers traditionally have concentrated on providing a wide range of fairly basic items, such as diamond rings and watches. They provide their store customers with a wide range of services and, in many cases, some form of advertising assistance. With the exception of watches, brand names are relatively unknown in this branch of the jewelry industry.

Leased jewelry departments are fairly common in the merchandising of fine jewelry. A large amount of capital is required to provide adequate assortments, and specialized knowledge is needed to sell this merchandise. Therefore, large-scale operators, who in many cases are also manufacturers, provide retail stores with stock, trained personnel, and advertising. They return a percentage of sales as rent to the host store. An example is the Zale Company, which operates leased departments in many stores.

The larger costume jewelry firms offer seasonal lines so broad that they can easily adapt to whatever direction fashion may be taking. Because they contract the production of most of their merchandise, emphasis can swiftly be switched from less popular items to those in greater demand. The larger firms also market much of their merchandise under brand names and advertise widely in national consumer publications.

Some of the larger costume jewelry firms offer advertising assistance in the form of advertising mats or cooperative advertising allowances. Some firms help to plan and maintain retail store assortments. Others supply display fixtures. Still others offer fashion guidance and traveling representatives to help train retail salespeople and to serve customers on the retail selling floor.

Industry Trends

Today, all branches of the jewelry industry are placing greater emphasis on producing designs that complement current apparel fashions. As an example, when turtlenecks became popular, jewelry producers began designing and offering long chains and pendants that looked graceful on high necklines. When sleeveless apparel is in fashion, bracelets are prominent in producers' lines. When prints are popular in apparel, more tailored jewelry styles are usually featured.

Some fine-jewelry firms are broadening their lines. Traditionally known for prompt service, fine workmanship, and high prices, several such firms today also offer costume jewelry of original design and excellent quality at modest prices.

Some of the larger costume jewelry manufacturers, especially in the men's field, have begun to diversify, although this is not yet a general industry practice. For example, Speidel, traditionally a watchband producer, has had excellent response to its line of men's colognes. Swank, traditionally a producer of men's cuff links, tie tacks, tie clasps, and related jewelry items, has diversified into colognes, sunglasses, travel accessories, and a variety of men's gifts.

Designer jewelry has become a major factor in better costume jewelry, and it is through the impact of the designer name that jewelry sales figures have had an upward trend. Mary McFadden, Yves St. Laurent, Christian Dior, Givenchy, Pierre Cardin, and Anne Klein are some of the apparel designers who have made the move into jewelry via the licensing of their names to jewelry manufacturers.

GLOVES

People have used hand coverings in various forms since earliest recorded history. Crude animal-skin coverings preceded mittens, which, in turn, preceded gloves with individual fingers. Primitive men and women covered their hands with animal skins to protect them and to keep them warm. Leather gloves were worn by the Egyptians and were discovered along with the mummies in ancient Egyptian tombs. During the era of knighthood, gloves were a sign of good luck. A knight might wear his lady's glove on his arm in battle. In the exchange of property, giving a glove once symbolized good faith in the transaction. Gloves have also been used to denote rank or status. Prior to the sixteenth century, for instance, only men of the clergy or of noble rank wore gloves. In times past, for one man to slap another across the face with his glove was an invitation to a duel.

The development of gloves as a fashion item occurred early in the history of fashion. During certain periods of history, gloves were embroidered lavishly and trimmed with fringe, lace, stones, and tassels.

Today, gloves are worn both as a costume accessory and for protection and warmth. To be in fashion, gloves must closely relate in styling, detail, and color to current apparel fashion. For example, fashions in women's glove lengths are largely determined by the fashionable length of sleeves, particularly coat and suit sleeves. Just as there are classic styles in apparel, so, too, are there classic styles in gloves. Examples are the untrimmed, white, wrist-length glove for wear on dress occasions, and the "suit" glove, which extends a few inches beyond the wrist, for more general wear.

Gloves come and go as an accessory. They are less important when the trend is to casual clothes, more important when suits and classics return.

Organization and Operation

In the early days of the twentieth century, fashion interest focused on the well-gloved hand, and the glove business flourished in the United States. The glove material most favored by fashion at that time was leather. Today, however, knit and woven fabric gloves dominate the field.

In the production of leather gloves, most of the manufacturing operations are hand-guided. In some cases, they are done completely by hand. As a result, glove factories have remained small, few machines are required, and comparatively few workers are employed in any one factory. Moreover, producers tend to specialize, performing just one manufacturing operation, such as cutting or stitching. The other operations are farmed out to nearby plants, each of which performs its own specialty.

In contrast to the methods employed in the production of leather gloves, much of the production of fabric gloves is mechanized. The most favored and durable glove fabric used today is a double-woven fabric. It is possible to use almost any fiber in producing this particular type of fabric. Knit gloves are usually made of woolen, acrylic, or cotton string yarns.

Today fabric gloves are produced in various parts of the country. Gloversville, New York, however, remains the major production center for both fabric and leather gloves, with several plants producing both types.

Market Centers

The major market center for both leather and fabric gloves is in New York City. Here many glove firms maintain permanent showrooms where they show seasonal lines to buyers. The typical glove firm offers a very wide and versatile assortment of both domestic and imported gloves in a wide range of prices.

Some better-known glove resources are Hansen, Kayser-Roth, and Aris Glove. Kayser-Roth produces gloves at many prices, including expensive designer lines under the Halston label. Aris Glove manufactures fine leather gloves and the Isotoner glove. A special construction and fabric cause the hand to be "massaged" during the wearing of the Isotoner glove.

Merchandising and Marketing Activities

In general, the merchandising activities of the women's glove industry have tended to lag behind those of other fashion accessories industries. Compared with the dollars spent on consumer advertising by other segments of the fashion industry, outlays for glove advertising are quite modest. Only a few large producers with nationally distributed brand lines have actively promoted their products or offered even limited merchandising services to their retail store customers. In recent years, however, because of stagnating sales and competition from imports (particularly of leather

When glamour reappeared, hats came, too. But bubble gum and glamour don't mix.

gloves), many glove producers have begun to reevaluate their merchandising techniques. For example, some producers are now packaging many styles of stretch gloves that can be sold from self-service fixtures. Another technique is the packaging of matching gloves, hats or caps, and scarfs in sets for self-service sales. This is a means of increasing the market for glove manufacturers as well as building volume. To help reduce the amount of inventory, many store departments carry knit gloves in small, medium, and large sizes only and have many styles in stretch fabrics where one size fits all.

To add interest and variety to the glove selection, many manufacturers now produce gloves lined with fur, silk, and cashmere. They are also designing and manufacturing styles for specific sports—ski gloves and mittens, golf gloves, tennis gloves, and driving gloves, for example.

Although most of the larger producers of women's gloves employ fashion stylists, few make their services available to retail store accounts except on rare occasions. Sales-training aids have been limited mainly to color charts.

For years the glove industry has maintained a trade association known as the National Association of Glove Manufacturers, with headquarters in Gloversville, New York. This association's activities, however, have focused mainly on tariff questions and federal agency regulations and rulings rather than on industry and product publicity.

Industry Trends

Sales of domestically produced leather gloves have suffered considerably in recent years from the competition of less expensive imports. To meet this challenge, the industry is trying to improve manufacturing procedures in order to reduce costs. In addition, improved materials are resulting from product research and development in the leather industry. These are expected to increase the market potential of domestically produced leather gloves. For example, many leather gloves today are hand-washable and come in a wide range of colors.

MILLINERY

An old saying goes that whatever is worn on the head is a sign of the mind beneath it. Since the head is one of the most vulnerable parts of the body, many hats also have a protective function. The man's hat of the nineteenth and twentieth centuries in Europe, which was derived ultimately from the medieval helmet, protected its wearer both physically and psychologically. The heavy crown kept the head safe from blows, and the brim shaded the face from strong sunlight and close scrutiny. In America, the hat was a status symbol of a special kind. This was the time of European immigration, and as boatload after boatload of hatless peasants landed, those who wanted to make it plain that they were of a higher class origin than most immigrants took care to wear hats.[4]

After decades of prosperity and popularity, the millinery industry began to collapse in the years following World War II. Because of the more casual approach to women's dressing and the popularity of beehive and bouffant hairstyles, millinery sales hit bottom in 1960. During the freewheeling 1960s and 1970s a hat was worn only on the coldest days, and strictly for warmth, not for fashion. Millinery departments turned to selling wigs to gain sales volume, but wigs also enjoyed only a few seasons' popularity.

During that time, the millinery industry and its active trade association, the National Millinery Institute, researched, publicized, and campaigned in an extensive effort to reverse the trend, but with little success. This was an example of the fashion principle that no amount of sales promotion can change the direction in which fashion is moving.

With the return of glamour and the classic looks in the mid-1980s, the situation in millinery began to change. In fashion shows on both sides of the Atlantic, models paraded the runways with hats adorning their heads! Hats with big brims and little brims; hats decorated with jewels, feathers, veilings; hats made from velvet, felt, and satin—all worn for flattery or fun rather than practicality. The versatility of the new hats is attributed to a new breed of designer. The number of established milliners in New York declined sharply over the past three decades, but the millinery field now is attracting fresh young design talent. Young designers are bringing to the industry a vibrant and young appeal to headwear and are successfully interpreting the needs of the new headwear customers. They are the prime reason for the steady growth and success of the "new" millinery industry.

Once upon a time a person wasn't considered well-dressed unless he or she was wearing a hat. The industry is hoping that "once upon a time" has returned!

OTHER FASHION ACCESSORIES

Other fashion accessories include neckwear, belts, small leather goods, handkerchiefs, sunglasses, umbrellas, and wigs. While once some of the industries producing these accessories were quite large, today they are relatively small. The output of industries producing these accessories tends to fluctuate in direct relationship to the fashion importance of each to the current popular look. The main showrooms of the producers are in New York City, although much of the merchandise in these categories is manufactured in foreign countries.

One innovative and successful approach to merchandising these fashion accessories has been to group them all together into one store department. This department is usually called the "dress accessories department" and features the merchandise in current fashion in each of these classifications. Depending upon the accepted fashion of the season, one or more dress accessories may be prominently featured. When the emphasis is on neck and shoulders, scarfs become important. When emphasis is on the waistline, belts are featured.

In the past few years sunglasses have become big business and in some stores separate counters or even a separate department has been devoted to fashion-inspired sunglasses. To better service this growing consumer demand, the sunglasses industry has expanded its facilities and introduced new styles. A leading indicator of renewed and added interest in sunglasses is the growing impact of designer names in both direct manufacture and licensing.

Another fashion accessory recently in the spotlight is the umbrella. Far from being merely a device for shielding against sun or rain, the umbrella now is a fashion-right item available in vivid colors and prints, and with exciting and exotic handles to please fashion customers.

REFERENCES

[1] Statistics furnished by Jack Tepper, a leading shoe industry consultant, October 14, 1983.
[2] Delphi Survey of the United States Hosiery Industry, conducted by Kurt Salmon Associates, Inc. and the National Association of Hosiery Manufacturers, December, 1978.

[3] *Women's Wear Daily*, March 4, 1983, p. 21.
[4] Alison Lurie, *The Language of Clothing*, Random House, New York, 1981, p. 177.

MERCHANDISING VOCABULARY

Define or briefly explain each of the following terms:

Boarding	Impulse items
Bodywear	Last
Bridge jewelry department	Precious stones
Costume or fashion jewelry	Private label or brand
Fine jewelry	Semiprecious stones
Gemstones	Store brand

1. Why is the accessories department usually on the main floor of a store near the main entrance? What is the value of accessories "outposts"?
2. What are the main locations in the United States for the production of shoes?
3. Discuss the merchandising activities of the domestic shoe industry in terms of (*a*) advertising, (*b*) maintenance of retail outlets, and (*c*) leased departments.
4. How do changes in lifestyle and activities affect the shoe industry? Give examples.
5. Name and briefly describe four methods of merchandising women's hosiery.
6. Give examples of fashion trends that have influenced hosiery.
7. Discuss the fashion importance of handbags. Of what materials are handbags made?
8. Why are shoe and fine-jewelry departments often leased?
9. What are the major materials used in the production of gloves? Give several examples of how women's apparel fashions influence glove fashions.
10. What categories of merchandise are usually to be found in fashion accessories departments today? Discuss the current fashion importance of each category.

1. Discuss the following statements and their implications for retail merchants of fashion accessories: "The rise of accessories as a dynamic force in fashion only came about in the past few decades. Although this force diminished for a time, accessories regained a starring role in the mid-1980s and once again play an important part in the look of fashion."
2. Discuss the current importance of bodywear. How important do you feel it will be in the future? Why?
3. List each of the currently important fashion accessory items and discuss why they are important to the total fashion look today. At which stage of the fashion cycle is each item, and why do you feel this is so?

12. INTIMATE APPAREL AND COSMETICS

THE INTIMATE APPAREL INDUSTRY

The wearing of undergarments probably began as the wearing of a soft material next to the body to protect it from the chafing of harsh animal skins. As civilization advanced, other demands were made upon these hidden garments, and although they increased in variety and use, public mention of them, much less display, was avoided discreetly for centuries. Today, however, because of the great variety, fashion interest, and widespread usage of the various types of women's undergarments, their production has attained industry status and they are widely advertised and promoted.

Intimate apparel, sometimes referred to as "inner fashions" or "body fashions," is the trade term for women's foundations, lingerie, and loungewear. Originally these products were commercially produced by three separate industries: the foundations industry, the lingerie industry, and the robe industry. In recent years, however, as a result of business mergers, widespread diversification of products, significant technological advances in fibers and fabrications, and the close fashion relationship that exists between the three types of garments and women's ready-to-wear, a single industry has evolved known as the intimate apparel industry. This industry produces goods for three market segments, namely the foundations market, the lingerie market, and the loungewear market.

Foundations

Classified as **foundations** are such undergarments as brassieres, girdles, panty girdles, garter belts, corsets, and corselettes (one-piece garments combining a brassiere and a girdle).

HISTORY AND DEVELOPMENT. The foundations industry began with the factory production of corsets just after the Civil War, when Warner Brothers opened its first plant in Bridgeport, Connecticut. At that time, the bell-shaped silhouette was at the height of its popularity. To achieve the tiny waist required by the fashionable bell silhouette (and its successors, the bustle-back silhouette and the Gibson Girl look), women wore foundations of sturdy, unyielding cotton. These were reinforced with vertical stays of whalebone or steel. Front or back lacing permitted varying degrees of waist constriction to achieve the desired effect.

The foundations market experienced a drastic change in customer demand in the 1920s, when the fashion shifted to straight, loose styles in apparel. These required little corseting but did demand flattening of the bosom. Bandagelike bras were worn to minimize the bust, while girdles controlled any conspicuous bulges below the waistline. Sometimes women used girdles whether or not these garments were needed to control the flesh. Some women who wore girdles were so slim that the girdles bruised their hipbones. Still, women considered girdles essential, if only because the attached garters held up their stockings.

In the 1930s, the silhouette again became more feminine and softly curved. Women coaxed their figures into the appropriate lines with two new types of foundations, more comfortable than anything available before: the two-way stretch girdle and the cup-type brassiere. These innovations heralded a trend toward foundations that molded the figure gently while permitting freedom of movement. They also reflected the fashion for easy fit in outerwear, with definite but not exaggerated curves.

In the past three decades, further technological advances have enabled foundations firms to produce softer, more comfortable, and lighter-weight undergarments. These garments come with better shape-retention properties and in a wider assortment of styles for various figure types, made possible by the development of spandex and other fibers with elastic characteristics.

Brassieres are a good example of the radical style changes that have occurred in foundation garments in the last 50 years. During this period, brassiere styling has evolved from the original bandage type, to cup form, to fiber-filled, to wire-supported, to the "no-bra" (or unconstructed) bra, to the molded (rather than seamed) bra.

Today, foundation garments coax or mold a body; they do not harness it. Moreover, they can be comfortable, light, soft, and pretty, all at the same time.

MERCHANDISING AND MARKETING ACTIVITIES. Brand names have always been important in foundations, and most of the merchandising activity has been directed toward their promotion. The major foundations producers widely advertise their brand names—such as Lily of France, Playtex, Maidenform, Bali, Formfit-Rogers, and Warner—in both trade and consumer publications. Ads in consumer publications often mention the names of retail stores that stock the featured merchandise. In addition, many firms offer cooperative advertising arrangements to their retail store customers. Merchants use such cooperative allowances to stretch their own advertising budgets and to tie in at the local level with national advertising of the brands they carry.

Historically, foundations firms have supplied many services to their retail store customers. Producers have helped train retail salespeople and have offered retail store buyers assistance in planning assortments and controlling stocks. Innovative display fixtures are becoming more

Today intimate apparel is often displayed on self-service fixtures, some of which emphasize the brand name.

and more available from manufacturers. Hanging bra fixtures have allowed retailers to better identify bra styles and permit customers to quickly locate their correct size. Such self-service fixtures were first introduced in 1949 by the Loveable Bra Company. Working with retailers, Playtex has developed a fixture that holds bras in packages. The Playtex package, with pictures and description, is readily accepted by customers and the fixture is self-contained for stockkeeping and inventory control purposes.

Lingerie and Loungewear

Lingerie is the undergarment category that includes slips, petticoats, panties of all types, nightgowns, and pajamas. Slips, petticoats, camisoles, chemises, and panties are considered "daywear," while nightgowns and pajamas are classified as "sleepwear." **Lounge-wear** is the trade term for the category that today includes robes, negligees, bed jackets, at-home wear sets, and housecoats (sometimes referred to as dusters). However, some lingerie firms have expanded and diversified their product lines to include loungewear items, and some lingerie and loungewear firms have merged. It is therefore sometimes difficult to draw a clear-cut line between the two intimate-apparel categories.

HISTORY AND DEVELOPMENT. Until the 1930s, most mass-produced lingerie and loungewear were purely functional, with little variety in style or seasonal change. Cotton was the principal fabric, but wool was also used in extremely cold climates. Silk appeared only in luxury styles. In the 1930s, rayon began to be used extensively and remained a basic fabric material throughout the 1940s. During all of this time, lingerie and loungewear were considered staple items, relatively untouched by fashion and produced in limited styles and colors.

The introduction of easy-care, man-made textile fibers in the 1950s revolutionized the intimate apparel industry, and lingerie and loungewear entered the fashion spotlight. Nylon tricot was to the 1950s what rayon was to the 1930s. Previously, only the largest companies had sent fashion experts to the Paris openings to report on the lines and colors featured in new apparel styles. As fashion interest began to center around a total look or fashion theme, women began to develop a feeling for color and design harmony in everything they wore. Consequently, lingerie and loungewear firms became increasingly aware of the need to keep in touch with the total fashion picture.

Creative lingerie firms today employ top designing talent, often recruiting them from the apparel field. Styling in all three categories— daywear, sleepwear, and loungewear—closely follows that of apparel. For example, when slim, body-hugging skirts are important, slip and petticoat producers cut their slips slim also. When vibrant colors and explosive prints predominate in apparel, slips, sleepwear, robes, bras, and panties are featured in matching or contrasting colors and prints.

MERCHANDISING AND
MARKETING ACTIVITIES. Brands are as important in lingerie and loungewear as they are in foundations. In fact, store purchases of lingerie and loungewear are often made in terms of brand resources rather than categories of merchandise. Like foundations firms, lingerie and loungewear firms widely advertise their branded lines in both trade and consumer publications. Most firms also offer cooperative advertising arrangements to their retail store customers. While some lingerie and loungewear brands, such as Vanity Fair, Barbizon, Lady Lynne, Miss Elaine, and Olga (formerly a foundations designer), continue in popularity, merchandising activities today focus on styling, color, fabric, and well-known designer names.

Most American loungewear and lingerie firms cover the major U.S. and European fashion markets today. They provide stores with seasonal color and style charts and suggestions for relating intimate apparel styles and colors to those of ready-to-wear. Some firms offer assistance in planning and controlling retail assortments. Some of them also help in staging retail sales-promotion events, often in cooperation with a textile fiber or fabric producer.

Market Centers for the Intimate Apparel Industry

The principal market center for foundations, lingerie, and loungewear is New York City. The major firms maintain permanent showrooms in that city, as well as in most of the major regional marts, and publicize market weeks in January and June. Since many store buyers purchase all three types of merchandise, concurrent market weeks enable them to plan and coordinate purchases and promotions simultaneously. If stores employ separate buyers for each category, those buyers usually work closely with one another in the market, coordinating their purchases and promotional plans for the coming season.

Headquarters of the industry's trade associations, the Associated Corset and Brassiere Manufacturers, the Intimate Apparel Council of the American Apparel Manufacturers Association, and the Lingerie Manufacturers Association, are also located in New York City. All three organizations schedule activities for the January and June market weeks.

Industry Trends

Fashion continues to be the major competitive strategy in the marketing of intimate apparel. Nevertheless, vast quantities of intimate apparel are still sold on the basis of function and in slowly changing styles. These involve minimum risk for producers and retailers and minimum price to consumers. But in the medium-

Lingerie firms widely advertise their brands in trade publications, here emphasizing price and delivery.

to upper-price brackets, fashion rather than intrinsic value is the motivating element. It is in these categories that the work of name designers is beginning to appear. Halston, Diane Von Furstenberg, Christian Dior, Geoffrey Beene, Clovis Ruffin, and Givenchy have all designed or sponsored the design of women's intimate apparel.

MARKET SEGMENTS. Most manufacturers are trying to reach segment markets on the basis of lifestyles. Manufacturers recognize there are different age groups and attitudes they must address. Loungewear is the most talked-about growth segment of the intimate apparel business. With a rapidly increasing number of women now employed outside the home, a whole new category of clothing for after-work and at-home wear is being born. Greater use of such fabrics as sweatshirtings,

flannel, and flannelettes that will inject a sportswear spirit into these types of clothes is a recent trend.

CATALOGS. In addition to major redesigning of fixtures and presentations of intimate apparel at the retail level, new attention is being paid to heightening the fashion focus on each category. And as an increasingly important sales- and image-building strategy for sales of intimate apparel, the special catalog or booklet is fast becoming an essential merchandising technique for many stores. Today many department stores send out special intimate apparel catalogs, and regularly include high-fashion intimate apparel in their seasonal catalogs. *Private Lives* by Spiegel, the giant mail-order house, marked that company's entrance into the intimate apparel specialty-catalog field. Other innovators in this new area include Hanover House, *Intime* by Brownstone Studio, Victoria's Secret, and many traditional department stores such as Hudson's, The Broadway, Bloomingdale's, and Macy's. There is even a specialized catalog—Lady Annabelle—with lingerie and sleepwear for large-size women.

MERGERS. Trends in foundations are similar to those of other fashion-related businesses. The trend toward mergers, however, did not develop in the intimate apparel field until the late 1950s. At that time, customers began demanding color-coordinated foundation garments. Many small firms that made either brassieres or girdles saw an advantage in joining with one another to produce matched colors. In time, many such collaborating firms merged their ownership and operations in order to meet the competition of larger firms. Some merged with lingerie producers, such as Form-fit-Rogers. Others explored the advantages of merging with ready-to-wear producers. Since the introduction of figure-control features in bathing suits, some foundations firms have merged with swimsuit makers or set up their own swimsuit divisions. In addition, some are making "body suits"—control garments that are completely made of stretch material, with a panty-type bottom and a T-shirt or camisole-type top. Although intended as undergarments, if done in attractive materials the body suits closely resemble ready-to-wear "body shirts" and often can be used as such.

Trends in the production of lingerie and loungewear parallel those in the foundations industry. There have been increasing numbers of mergers, both between lingerie and loungewear firms and between these firms and foundation producers. There also has been an increasing emphasis on fashion-oriented styling and use of luxury fabrics such as chiffon, satin, and panne velvet.

DIVERSIFICATION. Another trend has been the strong diversification and expansion of product lines. Daywear has now been expanded to include body shirts, chemises, camisole tops, "teddys," and packaged "little nothings." The latter are bras, panties, and bikinis that are "nonconstructed," in contrast to the more conventional "constructed" brassieres and foundations. They are often packaged for sale on self-selection racks in both conventional and mass-merchandising stores. Manufacturers of sleepwear have added travel sets of matching robes and gowns. Manufacturers of loungewear have added matching robes and lounging pajamas, some of which can be worn outside the home as well as for at-home occasions.

THE COSMETICS AND FRAGRANCE INDUSTRIES

Beauty may be only skin-deep, but how avidly men and women have worked to enhance that thin veneer of the face and body! For thousands of years people have smeared themselves with lotions and potions of every description in the hope of making themselves more attractive. Cleopatra rubbed her face with lemon rinds, took milk baths, and set her hair with mud. Shakespeare described the sails of Cleopatra's royal barge as "so perfumed that the winds were lovesick with them." Galen, the great physician of Greece in the second century A.D., invented cold cream. Eighteenth-century kings and queens powdered their faces as well as their wigs. So did American revolutionaries. Today the cosmetics industry is big business, turning out hundreds of products made from scores of natural and synthetic ingredients.

The relationship between cosmetics and fashion apparel grows stronger each year. Many designers are introducing cosmetic, skin-care, and fragrance lines under their own names. These top fashion designers are also moving into the creative segment of the cosmetics industry. They work with manufacturers to develop and forecast the color, design, line, and textures of coming fashions. The cosmetics industry then manufactures and promotes exciting new colors to coordinate with the new season's fashion apparel. As changing lifestyles influence the design of apparel, so do they prompt the development of new products by the cosmetics industry.

History and Development

Historically, the pursuit of beauty has been the prerogative of the rich and privileged. Special beauty aids were concocted in the temple, the monastery, the alchemist's cell, or the kitchen. Only in the past 55 years or so has the age-old pursuit of beauty found its way into modern laboratories. The Federal Trade Commission defines **cosmetics** as articles other than soap that are intended to be "rubbed, poured, sprinkled or sprayed on, introduced into, or otherwise applied to the human body for cleansing, beautifying, promoting attractiveness or altering the appearance without affecting the body's structure or functions."[1] Today the enhancement of appearance is no longer the privilege of the select few. It is now the necessity of the many. Innovative products created through research and development, together with outstanding advertising, package design, and mass production, have made cosmetics widely available to consumers of different ages, lifestyles, and economic levels.

Until recently the cosmetics industry sold dreams. Now the industry also sells science, thus shifting its advertising thrust to stress the functional value of products. "Nourish," "protect," "erase," and "renew" are the new watchwords of the industry. Twenty years ago there was one watchword—"moisturize." The ad copy now sounds scientific. You take a "daily dose" of this product. Another one promotes "cell renewal." Yet another is "pH-balanced." Today cosmetic counters in department stores don't just let you select the color of makeup; they have diagnostic centers where trained technicians test your skin and prescribe the correct formula.

In the 1970s, "natural" (without synthetic ingredients) cosmetics were introduced. Lines using aloe vera, honey, musk, almonds, henna, and other natural substances have proved to be successful.

The cosmetics industry has undergone a significant change in recent decades. It was once made up of many small firms, none of which owned a significant share of the market. Now a relatively small number of firms command major market shares. Although there are close to 600 companies in the cosmetics industry, the top eight firms account for 50 percent of total shipments. Although a number of firms have remained autonomous, a large number of national-brand cosmetics companies are now part of large drug conglomerates. This relationship between the drug and cosmetics industries continues to grow.

Another change has been the passing of the individual giants of the industry. A few flamboyant personalities helped to shape the scope and direction of the entire cosmetics industry. Elizabeth Arden, Helena Rubinstein, Charles Revson, and Max Factor were all legends in their own time and individual rulers of their own special beauty empires. Less well known but equally innovative, were Dorothy Gray and Harriet Hubbard Ayer. The drive, intuition, foresight, and promotional abilities these entrepreneurs brought to the field known as the "beauty business" is still felt in the industry today. The success of these pioneers has rarely been duplicated in any other fashion accessories industry. Today, only Estée Lauder still operates her "beauty empire" (still privately owned) with the personal drive and decision-making skill of the original innovators. The companies of the other cosmetics giants have become public corporations or divisions of multinational conglomerates. However, a new group of farsighted entrepreneurs have begun to take their place in the industry. Adrien Arpel, Madeleine Mono, Christine Valmy, Georgette Klinger, Merle Norman, Irma Shorell, Flori Roberts, and Don Bochner of Perfumer's Workshop are just a few among this new breed.

MARY KAY ASH: BEAUTY BUSINESS BONANZA

When Mary Kay Ash retired in 1963, she started to write a book about her business experiences. When she finally finished her book 17 years later, she had written about a whole new set of business experiences—and she had built a $235 million cosmetics empire. Mary Kay, as she is known by everyone including her great-grandchildren, is the modern empress of entrepreneurship who started a business from scratch and persevered despite everyone's advice to give up on a scheme that supposedly wouldn't work. When she first started to write her book in her "retirement," she took two yellow legal pads and wrote down all the good things that had happened to her during her working career on one; then she wrote down all the problems on the other. As a kind of intellectual exercise, she tried solving the problems and when she finished she realized she had formulated a unique marketing plan that would give women an opportunity to do all the things she had been prevented from doing when she was working.

She had devised a marketing strategy in which women could sell directly to other women at Tupperware-like parties in the home of a hostess. Then she chose cosmetics as the product because that was something women would feel comfortable selling. She further narrowed her product line by concentrating on skin care so that she could avoid direct competition with Avon, whose broad line of personal care items encompasses more than just cosmetics for women. She purchased formulas for products she herself had been using for years, had a chemist prepare them, packaged the products in pink, and set out to sell them. Her first demonstration was a disaster. She sold $1.50 worth of skin care products. Only after

Organization and Operation

All large, nationally advertised cosmetics firms produce hundreds of items. For sales and inventory purposes, products must thus be divided into broad categories. The typical order form of one large firm, for example, lists all the company's products, in the various sizes or colors available, under such end-use categories as skin care, facial makeup, nail care, bath preparations, hair care, fragrances, eye products, body care, and so on. If a firm produces men's as well as women's cosmetics, each of

the party was long over did she realize she'd forgotten to hand out order cards. At her next demonstration, she gave out the cards as the women walked in the door.

Today, Mary Kay Cosmetics, Inc. has over 150,000 sales representatives ("beauty consultants") in North America, Central America, and South America. These saleswomen (there are no sales*men*) conduct skin care demonstrations, show how to apply makeup, and sell $75 to $100 worth of merchandise per party. The sales force is able to realize a high profit on sales because the wholesale discount (all products are purchased in advance) can be as high as 50 percent with a 90 percent buy-back guarantee on unsold merchandise.

The beauty consultants are motivated by the sales directors, who get 9 to 13 percent of the consultants' volume as well as an 8 percent recruitment commission. They are also motivated by Mary Kay herself, whose sales philosophy permeates the organization. She conducts the annual inspirational meetings at the home base in Dallas and hands out the awards—medals, ribbons, certificates, mink stoles, diamond pins, and the famed "Mary Kay pink" Cadillacs to achievers and superachievers. She and her sales staff always stress confidence building and consider the phrase "constructive criticism" an absolute contradiction in terms. The consultants' selling methods reflect the company's employee motivation strategy. During a demonstration they emphasize the advantages of the Mary Kay system, show the women how it can benefit them, and most important, attempt to inspire a feeling of self-confidence that is purported to be the direct result of using Mary Kay cosmetics.

Mary Kay products are not available anywhere except through the sales reps, whose contact with new and repeat customers is essential to Mary Kay's success. The firm's advertising expenditures are quite small in comparison to those of most major cosmetics manufacturers, although the personal promotion and public relations expertise of the famous founder cannot be discounted.

Mary Kay Cosmetics has not had one long, uninterrupted successful flight since its beginnings in 1963. One month after she began selling, Mary Kay's husband/partner died and she was advised to scrap the fledgling firm. The company ran into problems again when sales growth fell below the rate of inflation in the 1974–1977 period. Mary Kay's son, Richard Rogers, president of the company, has said that they ignored the warning signals of inflation for too long and had to overhaul their compensation structure and raise prices in order to regain their competitive position. Mary Kay Cosmetics, Inc. is currently in the pink financially and Rogers expects $500 million in sales per year in the eighties.[1]

In 1981, Mary Kay Ash finished her book, an autobiography titled simply *Mary Kay*. The publication publicity improved company sales and increased recruitment. It took her a long time to write that book, but she was doing a few other things in the meantime.

[1] Howard Rudnitsky, "The Flight of the Bumblebee," *Forbes,* June 1981, pp. 105–106.

This Fashion Focus is based on information from the article cited above and from these sources:

David Einhorn, "Dynamo of Direct Sales: Mary Kay Capitalizes on the Feminine Mystique to Create a Beauty Business Bonanza," *Marketing Communications,* February 1982, pp. 12–14.
Jamie Laughridge, "Start Your Own Business," *Harper's Bazaar,* March 1983, p. 242.

the two lines is given its own distinctive brand name, and separate sales and inventory records are kept for each brand line.

Because of fashion and product obsolescence, as well as customer boredom, manufacturers are constantly updating and shipping new items to keep cosmetics customers buying new products and/or new colors. Manufacturers update formulas when they become aware of new technology and new ingredients to improve their products.

A system of product returns, unique to the

cosmetics industry, aids the retailer in keeping the inventory current. The industry refers to this system as **rubber-banding.** Rubber-banding means that cosmetic products not sold within a specified period of time are returned to the manufacturer and are replaced with others that will sell. It guarantees that the cosmetics retailer will never have to take a mark-down on this merchandise. However, if a cosmetics company is not going to produce any more of an item, it will permit markdowns by the store instead of accepting returns on the discontinued item. (Other industries allow returns to vendors for damages, overshipments, or wrong shipments only.)

PRIVATE-LABEL MANUFACTURERS. Although dominated by giant producers of nationally advertised brand lines, the industry has many **private-label manufacturers,** which produce merchandise to specification under the brand name of chain stores, mass merchants, department stores, or small independent stores and hair salons. Examples of private-label cosmetics are Henri Bendel's "Beauty Checkers" line; and fragrance private-label lines, such as "Volage," sold by Neiman-Marcus, "Bloomies," sold by Bloomingdales, and "Fireworks," sold by Bergdorf Goodman.

Some of the better-known private-label manufacturers are Kolmar Laboratories of Port Jervis, New York, and Private Label Cosmetics of Fair Lawn, New Jersey. Kolmar sells mass quantities to large users, but not all private-label producers are big enough to meet large order requirements. Smaller private-label manufacturers, such as Orlin (a division of the House of Westmore), supply smaller distributors. A beauty salon owner can walk into a private-label distributor's office, and in less than 10 days and for about $500 can have a complete private-label line in his or her shop. However, this line is based on what the private-label house has been manufacturing. Private-label manufacturers do not do "develop-ment work" for new items for individual clients.

Retailers get little help from their private-label suppliers. Private-label firms never share advertising costs, do not provide gift-with-purchase offers, and never accept returns.

A serious threat to the private-label industry is posed by federal ingredient-label requirements. Packaging is usually kept to a minimum by private-label firms in order to keep cost prices low. However, to get an ingredient label on a small lipstick, an unnecessary package will be required. Through its lobbying group, the Independent Cosmetic Manufacturers and Distributors Association, the private-label industry is fighting labeling requirements. At present, consumers may ask for ingredient lists at retail stores. These lists are supplied to the store by the manufacturers.

TRADE ASSOCIATIONS. The Cosmetic, Toiletry, and Fragrance Association (CTFA) is the major cosmetics trade association. Its membership markets 90 percent of all cosmetics, toiletries, and fragrances sold in the United States. The CTFA coordinates the industry's commitment to scientific and quality standards. It is the industry vehicle for information exchange about scientific developments among association members, consumers, and those who regulate the industry at federal, state, and local government levels. The CTFA also keeps members informed on government regulations and offers advice on interpretation and compliance.

Federal Cosmetics Laws

The major ingredients of cosmetics in any price range are fats, oils, waxes, talc, alcohol, glycerin, borax, coloring matter, and perfumes. Because chemicals are the basis for most cosmetic products, the Food and Drug Administration is the federal agency that polices and regulates the cosmetics industry. Manufacturers are prevented by FDA regulations from using potentially harmful ingredients and from making exaggerated claims regarding the efficacy of their products.

The Federal Food, Drug, and Cosmetic Act, effective in 1938, was the first federal law controlling cosmetics in the United States. It prohibits adulteration and misbranding of cosmetics. When the act was updated in 1952, new amendments made it more stringent. Additional amendments were enacted by Congress in 1960, requiring government review and approval of the safety of color additives used in cosmetics.

The Fair Packaging and Labeling Act was passed by Congress in 1966 to prevent unfair or deceptive methods of packaging and labeling. This act covers many consumer industries besides the cosmetics industry. All cosmetics labeled since April 15, 1977, must bear a list of their ingredients, listed in descending order by weight.

Constant surveillance by consumer and industry groups and advisory boards keeps the cosmetics industry sensitive to product liability. A formal regulatory program for cosmetics is expected to be passed and implemented in the 1980s. This legislation will require manufacturers to register their products and formulations and to establish their safety before selling to the customer.

New Market Segments

Today the cosmetics industry is serving four new major market segments, in addition to the traditional women's market with its many segments. These new market segments are the male cosmetics market, the ethnic market, the international market, and the fragrance market.

THE MALE COSMETICS MARKET. The market for male cosmetics is expanding today and is expected to experience above-average growth in the future. Changing male images are opening up new and larger markets in hair care, face and body care, and fragrances. Men are buying more diversified products, such as moisturizers, cleansers, and skin toners. These products are being designed to give a healthy look throughout the year and to keep the skin naturally healthy. Men, like women, are concerned about aging. Unlike women, they have done little about it until now. It is gradually becoming socially acceptable for men to treat their skin to retard the aging process.

Because men have been influenced by the national preoccupation with youthful appearance and bodily fitness, installation of complete men's cosmetics sections in department and specialty stores is a growing trend. Bloomingdale's and Saks, among others, have expanded their men's cosmetics areas. Menswear specialty stores are adding cosmetics areas, and mail-order catalogs are devoting more space to men's grooming aids.

THE ETHNIC MARKET. The 1980 census finding that over 10 percent of the U.S. population is Spanish-speaking came as no surprise to cosmetics and toiletries makers, who have been actively wooing these relatively high-spending consumers. Another ethnic group, black consumers, totals slightly higher than Hispanics, and has become a large market for specialized products.

These separate groups, often called collectively "the ethnic market," total almost 40 million people. The ethnic market is growing at a rate of 17 percent each year. Retail sales to blacks and Hispanics in cosmetics, toiletries, and fragrances are estimated to be one of the fastest-growing sectors of the business. Sales to Asian Americans also have increasing potential.

The market for special beauty products for blacks is thriving. The 26 million blacks in the United States, who represent 12 percent of all U.S. consumers, are growing not only in num-

Male images changed and the cosmetics industry got itself a profitable market segment. This ad in a trade journal heralds the change.

bers, but in their desire for beauty, grooming, and fashion aids as well.[2] By the year 2000, black women are expected to be spending $2 billion each year on cosmetics.[3]

Differences in skin shades, skin tones, and hair texture among black women have stimulated the growth of special products for the black market. In the 1960s, companies such as Libra and Astarte pioneered in producing special lines for black women. However, of the early pioneers only Flori Roberts, producer of the first prestige cosmetics line for blacks, is still an important factor in the market. Flori

Roberts, which was started by a white woman by that name, claims to have been the first company to offer a fragrance within a major black line, the first to present in-store seminars on careers for black women, and the first to introduce demonstrations for black women at cosmetics counters in department stores.

Most major companies started to recognize the potential of this market in the late 1960s. Helena Rubinstein ran a makeup ad featuring white and black models in 1969. Today, some traditionally "white" cosmetics marketers have begun to pick up on the black market.

Revlon is advertising its line of Polished Ambers with a black model, as did Maybelline with its Blooming Colors Boutique. Estée Lauder claims it carries lip and foundation shades "suitable for the Black woman."

Flori Roberts, Fashion Fair, Zuri, and Moisture Formula are the current successful specialized companies that have targeted black women as their audience. These companies attribute their success to marketing that educates black consumers and the line personnel who serve them.

THE INTERNATIONAL MARKET. The foreign market for most cosmetics is growing faster than the U.S. market. The best markets for U.S. exports of cosmetics are South America, the Middle East, Japan, Canada, the Far East, and South Africa. Although cultural differences exist, basically the same types of cosmetics and toiletries are in demand worldwide. As major companies have discovered, overseas sales are good business. Little or no adjustment needs to be made in formulas or packaging of items popular in the United States to make them best-sellers worldwide. This applies primarily to fragrances, body-care, skin-treatment, and hair-care items, but it does not apply to shaded makeup items.

The U.S. Commerce Department suggests that smaller cosmetics companies initiate exports to some of the more affluent third world countries where per capita expenditures on cosmetics products are growing rapidly. Direct distribution, private-label products produced for foreign firms, and licensing specialties for foreign production are considered to be the most productive options for the international market.

THE FRAGRANCE MARKET. Total U.S. fragrance sales were $1.5 billion in 1980. All fragrance sales have increased nine times since 1960, basically tripling each decade.[4]

The term **fragrance** includes cologne, toilet water, perfume, spray perfume, after-shave lotions, and environmental fragrances. Some interesting changes have occurred in this market over the past 20 years. For example, after-shave lotions declined from roughly 70 percent of total men's fragrance sales to 30 percent today, spurred by a dramatic rise in use of colognes by men. In the women's market, sales of perfumes, which once amounted to 30 percent of women's fragrance sales, have declined to less than 20 percent today. Again, colognes and toilet waters have replaced perfumes in the public's fancy, primarily because of price and new forms of spray colognes.

Continual innovation in fragrances is necessary to maintain growth in a fashion-conscious market. A fragrance is usually offered as both a perfume and a lower-priced cologne. The latter is intended to entice the customer who may be hesitant about experimenting with an expensive product. The success of a perfume or cologne depends in part on attractive packaging and aggressive promotion.

When a perfumer creates a fragrance, he or she generally has in mind the type of person who would wear it. The success of advertising in conveying the image of this kind of person to the public can be an important factor in the success of the fragrance. This was the case with Revlon's Charlie. The ads for Charlie were "lifestyle" types of ads and burst upon the public at exactly the right time. The ads were clever, but the fragrance was successful because it appealed to its targeted market.

Perfumes are worn predominantly by women between 25 and 44 years of age, because this group is both fashion-conscious and affluent enough to purchase these expensive items. Toilet waters and colognes are worn more informally than perfumes. They are lower in price because the perfume oils are diluted with alcohol. These items are popular with younger women. It appears that market growth of fragrances should remain very strong through 1990. An important factor in this growth will be the increasing number of working women, particularly in white-collar

Paloma Picasso

THE FIRST FRAGRANCE BY PALOMA PICASSO.

The right bottle and the right name—it's often the package that sells the perfume.

jobs, where lighter fragrances are preferable to the heavy perfumes they may wear in the evening. The concept of a ''wardrobe'' of fragrances to suit the various roles a women assumes is being promoted and has boosted demand.

Over the past 10 years, fragrances have proliferated in the marketplace. Today's consumer selects a fragrance not only for its scent, but also for its packaging, its promotion, and where it can be bought.

Looking ahead to the year 2000, industry forecasters speculate that fragrances then will be more highly individualized, perhaps varying with specific skin biochemistry or changing with one's moods. The wearer might have more control over the formulation itself or the gradual release of the fragrance.

Environmental Fragrances.   Many industry authorities feel that home, or environmental, fragrances will be the next major breakthrough in the fragrance industry. The public's growing awareness of fragrance is not restricted to personal use but includes their homes as well. Many consumers are gaining satisfaction from enhancing their environment, and are taking in-home activities, such as gourmet cooking and home entertaining, more seriously.[5]

Many famous fashion designers worldwide are interested in environmental fragrances. Designers have already produced scented candles, silk flowers, paperweights, and holiday gifts.

Two of the largest prestige cosmetic and fragrance manufacturers, Estée Lauder and Charles of the Ritz, are already producing products in this area. Charles of the Ritz introduced a plastic record injected with fragrance oil in 1983 through its home fragrance subsidiary, Environmental Technologies. Estée Lauder produced a line of environmental products in Cinnabar, White Linen, and Youth Dew scents in 1981. The New York–based Fragrance Foundation put the market total for all home/environmental fragrances at $350 million annually—an amount equal to air-freshener retail market sales.[6]

Merchandising and Marketing Activities

The cosmetics, toiletries, and fragrance business is a highly visible one. The products are used nearly every day by millions of people. In the prestige cosmetics market, competition for restricted distribution to quality department and specialty stores is keen. All of the prestige brand manufacturers want to sell their lines in the most prestigious store in each town. They offer these stores exclusives, specials, and co-operative advertising to guarantee that their products will receive prime locations in these stores. Limiting the stores, or "doors," where their products are available adds to the aura of exclusivity and uniqueness the manufacturer of each line wishes to convey to its target customers. Such merchandising techniques are used by most prestige cosmetics brands, including Estée Lauder, Elizabeth Arden, Clinique, Lancôme, Borghese, Ultima II, and Irma Shorell.

DISTRIBUTION. The structure of distribution techniques in the cosmetics area is both distinctive and complex. Issues involved include class versus mass distribution, limited versus popular distribution, and the use of counter brand-line representatives.

Class versus Mass. Another name for "class" is "franchise," so the proper matchup of terms is "franchise versus mass." In **franchise distribution,** the manufacturer or exclusive distributor sells directly to the ultimate retailer. "Ultimate" means the only and final vendor to the customer. No wholesalers, jobbers, diverters, rack jobbers, or intermediaries of any kind are involved. Each vending retailer is on the books of the manufacturer or distributor as a direct receivable account. A good example of this is Estée Lauder, who sells directly to stores such as Neiman-Marcus and Saks. In **mass distribution** third-party vendors, such as wholesalers, diverters, and jobbers, are often interposed. These third parties may sell to any one of a number of retailers of any type. No control can be exercised over these intermediaries. Manufacturers may not know their retailers. Furthermore, area, territory, or other definable exclusivity does not run from the manufacturer to the retailer in mass distribution as it does in the franchise or class relationship. A good example of this is Revlon's Natural Wonder line, which is sold in "variety," drug, chain, or mass merchandise outlets.

Limited versus Popular. "Limited" and "popular" are terms that apply to the franchise or class end of the distribution business. They do not apply to mass distribution, since in mass distribution retailers have no contractual exclusivity with manufacturers and are selected by wholesalers or jobbers. In the industry, 5,000 doors is considered to be the dividing line between limited and popular.

Counter Brand-Line Representatives. Since there is a need to inform and educate cosmetics customers, prestige cosmetics companies place their own **brand-line representatives** behind the counter as "line" salespeople. These line salespeople, also called "beauty counselors," are well equipped to perform this important function. They are trained in the end use of the hundreds of items carried in each specific line. In many instances, the salaries of these salespeople are paid by the cosmetics company directly. Sometimes the store shares in the payment of their salaries. These salespeople are also responsible for stock inventory. They keep detailed records that show what items are and are not selling. The cosmetics companies constantly keep their brand salespeople informed about new items, new colors, and new promotions through updated training and materials. As might be expected, the limited class stores have the best-trained sales people.

ADVERTISING AND SALES PROMOTION.

National advertising budgets of cosmetics companies are immense, and seem even higher when related to percentage of sales. However, the dollar amount is small when compared to the mass advertising budgets used by cereal, soup, and soap companies. Television and print advertising for cosmetics were close to $1 billion in the early 1980s and continue to show growth.[7] But advertising in national media is not the only type of sales promotion in which cosmetics firms are engaged. A new product or visiting company specialist or authority is often promoted through editorials in newspapers and magazines.

The standard cosmetics promotion entices customers into buying a new color or treatment item with "an offer they can't refuse"—usually a "gift-with-purchase" or a "purchase-with-purchase" offer. The concept for "gift-with-purchase" was started by Estée Lauder, and now most cosmetics and/or fragrance companies use this type of promotion. The items offered in these promotions run the gamut from cosmetic "paint boxes" to umbrellas, tote bags, scarfs, or samples of new cosmetic products. A promotion combining a direct-mail piece, television and newspaper exposure, and a point-of-purchase item, such as makeup artists and beauty authorities from a cosmetics company, can result in three times the business usually generated by a particular product in any given week.

A promotional tool used by exclusive lines is the creation of separate promotional privileges for various limited class stores. The pur-

A trained cosmetic consultant demonstrates her product in the customer's home.

pose of this promotion is to keep individual retail establishments feeling exclusive.

The various forms of direct mail are generally vendor-funded. They most commonly include order forms in four-color vendor mailers, bill insertion leaflets, and remittance envelope stubs. Because of the breadth and depth of its reach, many stores are finding direct mail to be one of the most successful forms of advertising for both promotions and regular price. Estimates of sales volume from mail-order average about 2 percent of all cosmetics sales per year.

Beyond vendor-sponsored promotions, retailers have found other ways to maintain a reasonable level of regular-price business. One way is to create an atmosphere of exclusivity by featuring unique product lines. Another is to emphasize personal service. All of these merchandising activities are widely used to promote the image and sales of prestige cosmetics companies in department and specialty stores.

The mass-distribution cosmetics market involves drugstores, discount stores, variety stores, and large national chains such as Sears, JC Penney, and Montgomery Ward. The volume of business done in these stores is growing. As they have become increasingly interested in distribution to these types of retail outlets, large cosmetics companies have planned and implemented new merchandising activities. Until a few years ago, the mass-distribution outlets were limited to selling lines such as Cover Girl, Maybelline, or a store's own label line. At the present time, large, nationally advertised brands such as Max Factor and Revlon are introducing their medium-priced lines into these outlets. This enables customers to select products more easily and thus increases sales. Mass-market retailers are turning to open-access display systems and mass-marketing displays. Max Factor is now selling its Pure Magic line from pegboards. Revlon's Natural Wonder line has been repackaged for distribution to the mass-market outlets, as

have Coty, Aziza, and L'erin. A recent suggestion is that following the lead of the food and drug industries, a generic line of cosmetics that is properly packaged, attractively displayed, and advertised by the stores themselves could make even more selection and variety available to the mass-market customer.

The cosmetics industry is attempting to personalize the sale of its products through point-of-purchase information and the greater use of samples. More companies are using computerized displays with a scientific approach to assist customers on correct choice of makeup and treatment products. Both prestige and mass-distribution lines are using these merchandising activities.

Department and specialty stores are now offering services for hair, skin, and body care. This is a trend that is growing each year. Sales floor salons in department stores, featuring such cosmetic lines as Lancôme, Orlane, Payot, and Adrien Arpel, offer customers advice on complete beauty care and treatment. Beauty regimens, which in the past were favored mainly by European women, have today been simplified and modernized to fit American lifestyles. Both products and regimens are becoming more personalized as more and more lines offer analyses of individual needs and tailor their products to these needs.

Industry Trends

The sales volume for cosmetics reached $13.7 billion in 1982, a 48.9 percent increase from 1978, and sales are projected to be more than $20 billion by 1990.[8] Some key factors influencing this continuing sales growth in the cosmetics industry are:

- An increased percentage of women in the heavy-spending age group of 25 to 44.
- A growing number of women in the work force.
- Introduction of new and upgraded products, especially skin care products.

- An expanded market for male cosmetics.
- The growth of the ethnic markets.
- The growth of home/environmental fragrances.

Competition is very keen in the cosmetics industry, and product obsolescence is rapid. Large research and development departments employed by cosmetics manufacturers are constantly working to improve the quality and performance of their products. The cosmetics business depends upon repeat business, and so a well-made product that performs as claimed means repeat sales and loyal customers. In the prestige cosmetics market, the influence of high-fashion and prêt-à-porter designers continues to grow. This results in a closer tie between beauty and fashion in seasonal color statements. Department and specialty store retailers who are anxious to maintain product exclusivity will be the beneficiaries of this trend toward cosmetics marketed under high-fashion designers' labels.

Fashion has prompted a growing use of cosmetics by both men and women of all ages.

Preoccupation with self-image and health will continue to stimulate sales growth. Pollution, especially where populations are highly concentrated, has prompted consumers to become more aware of the protective aspect of face creams and cosmetic preparations. Facial skincare products are the fastest-growing classification in the cosmetics business, reflecting the emphasis placed on care of the skin by all segments of the buying public. Products carrying a "treatment," or therapeutic, image will continue to grow. Growing affluence also affects the cosmetics industry. More consumers are willing to spend more money in the pursuit of health and beauty and are able to afford complete skin and body care. It is interesting to note that in periods of economic downturn or recession, sales of cosmetics have traditionally been far less affected than have sales of clothing or most other apparel accessories. The reason may be that for only a small investment consumers can still keep in step with new fashion looks and thus can gain a greater feeling of self-assurance and confidence in their appearance.

REFERENCES

[1] Definition, Federal Trade Commission.
[2] *Women's Wear Daily,* January 25, 1981, pp. 12–13.
[3] *Soap/Cosmetics/Chemical Specialties,* March 1982, p. 31.
[4] *Product Marketing: Cosmetics and Fragrance Retailing,* Vol. 12, No. 6, p. 38, June 1983.
[5] Ibid.
[6] Ibid.
[7] *Product Marketing: Cosmetic and Fragrance Retailing,* Vol. 12, No. 8, p. 22, August 1983.
[8] Ibid., p. 9.

MERCHANDISING VOCABULARY

Define or briefly explain the following terms:

Brand-line representatives
Cosmetics
Foundations
Fragrance
Franchise distribution
Intimate apparel

Lingerie
Loungewear
Mass distribution
Private-label manufacturers
Rubber-banding

1. How has the foundations industry responded to the trend toward a soft, natural look in ready-to-wear?
2. Describe the various merchandising and marketing activities currently engaged in by the intimate apparel industry.
3. How does the intimate apparel industry relate to the ready-to-wear industry?
4. Why is market segmentation by lifestyle important in the intimate apparel industry?
5. Discuss the recent trends in the intimate apparel industry.
6. How does the cosmetics industry relate to the ready-to-wear industry?
7. Summarize the Food and Drug Administration's laws in regard to cosmetics.
8. Outline the major distribution methods used by the cosmetics industry.
9. Describe the various merchandising and marketing activities currently engaged in by the cosmetics industry.
10. Briefly discuss the most significant trends in the cosmetics industry today.

1. Discuss current trends in the intimate apparel industry as they relate to (*a*) mergers, (*b*) diversification of product lines, and (*c*) styling.
2. Discuss the recent growth in men's cosmetics and ethnic cosmetics lines.
3. Cosmetics salespersons, or brand-line representatives, exercise much more control over the products carried in their stock than do salespeople in other departments in a store. Discuss the system used, and its advantages and disadvantages.

13. DOMESTIC FASHION MARKETS

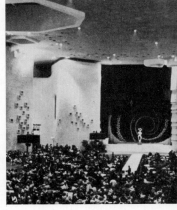

MARKET TERMINOLOGY

Markets, marts, trade shows—what's the difference? To add to the confusion, these terms are often used interchangeably! In a discussion of domestic fashion market centers, however, certain trade terms must be differentiated so that concepts can be discussed without confusion or misunderstanding.

Market

In the trade, this term has several meanings when used as a noun. "Market" may refer to the total demand for any given product. For example, it may refer to the extent of demand for active sportswear or for petite-sized women's apparel. A **market** also refers to a location where buyers and sellers meet for the purpose of trading ownership of goods at wholesale prices. This is the definition that is meant in this chapter. The term **domestic market** refers to a fashion market center located within the United States. Well-known domestic fashion markets include New York City, Los Angeles, and Atlanta. **Foreign markets** are those located outside the United States.

Market Center

A **market center** in the fashion industry is a geographic center for the creation and production of fashion merchandise, as well as for exchanging ownership. In market centers, buyers view lines of merchandise on-site in factory showrooms or in centralized locations where space is shared by locally based producers as well as sales representatives of competing firms headquartered outside the area. Each market center is usually known by the name of the dominant city within the trading or geographic area. In the United States, market centers are located in New York City, Los Angeles, Dallas, and Miami, while such locations as Atlanta, Chicago, and Denver are considered to be markets only, since they are not major apparel-*production* centers.

Mart

A **mart** is a building or building complex housing both permanent and transient showrooms of producers and their sales representatives. Examples of marts include the Atlanta Apparel Mart, the Denver Merchandise Mart, and the Dallas Apparel Mart.

Market Weeks

Organized by an association of manufacturers or salespeople or by the mart staff, **market weeks** are scheduled periods throughout the year during which producers and their sales representatives introduce new lines for the upcoming season to retail buyers. Each market center and mart plans several market weeks each year, with a concentrated agenda of activities for the buyers. The majority of retailers plan their market trips to coincide with scheduled market weeks, as they know they can view the widest variety of lines during these periods.

Fashion market weeks take place several months in advance of the dates on which stores can expect to receive delivery of purchase orders. For domestically produced goods, the lead time can be 2 to 8 months. On some foreign-produced goods and men's tailored clothing, the lead time can be 6 to 10 months.

Trade Shows

Trade shows are periodic merchandise exhibits staged in various regional trading areas around the country by groups of producers and their sales representatives for the specific purpose of making sales of their products to retailers in that area. Trade shows are usually held in hotels or civic centers. For example, the New York Coliseum hosts the semiannual show of American and foreign-made shoes. Periodic "mini-shows" are then held in various locations around the country.

THE DEVELOPMENT OF REGIONAL FASHION CENTERS

The American apparel industry is as geographically concentrated as it is highly competitive. New York City has from the beginning been the center of American fashion. But, as the country grew, the population expanded, and lifestyles unique to individual parts of the country developed, the demand for regional fashion centers outside of New York was created.

The New York Market

The American apparel industry originated in New York City at the turn of the century. All the factors were right: New York was the largest, most cosmopolitan and fashion-conscious city in the country. The Port of New York received fashion news from Europe as well as materials and trims for the industry. The city was near the textile mills in New England. Perhaps the most important of all was the endless supply of immigrants who came through this port—Jewish, Italian, and later Hispanics—many either skilled in the needle trades or anxious to learn.

Design and production clustered together in

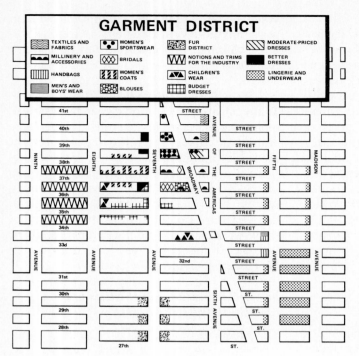

GARMENT DISTRICT

▨ TEXTILES AND FABRICS	⬡ WOMEN'S SPORTSWEAR	▦ FUR DISTRICT	▨ MODERATE-PRICED DRESSES
▰ MILLINERY AND ACCESSORIES	⬡ BRIDALS	⋙ NOTIONS AND TRIMS FOR THE INDUSTRY	■ BETTER DRESSES
⫼ HANDBAGS	▨ WOMEN'S COATS	▲▼ CHILDREN'S WEAR	▨ LINGERIE AND UNDERWEAR
▤ MEN'S AND BOYS' WEAR	▦ BLOUSES	⊞ BUDGET DRESSES	

In New York, apparel, design, and production are clustered together in the Garment District. Study the map to learn what can be found where.

an area of the city that quickly became known as the **Garment District,** the center of the women's apparel market. (See Chapter 8.) Factories soon set up showrooms where retail buyers could view their seasonal lines in comfort. New apparel and accessory manufacturers, as well as suppliers for fabrics, notions, and trims, tried to locate as closely as possible to existing firms to appeal to buyers who went from showroom to showroom on foot. The lack of an overall master plan for the industry, however, resulted in a jumble of buildings throughout the Garment District.

The Role of the Sales Representative

For years, traveling sales representatives (reps) from the larger apparel manufacturers toured the country with sample garments and accessories, a major link between many retailers and the market in New York City. Traveling at first by train, later by automobile, sales reps would mail advance notices to key customers in each city, announcing the date of their arrival.

Prior to the expansion of the suburban shopping center concept following World War II, most retail stores in a town were located in the central downtown area. Often groups of salesmen would travel in a group, allowing buyers to view several lines at once as they went from one adjoining hotel room to another where goods were displayed. Eventually, groups of sales reps began pooling their resources and renting space for a few days in a large hotel ballroom or exhibit hall.

The role of the sales representative was an important one. Few buyers could afford the time and expense of frequent trips to New York. Some buyers in larger stores managed to visit New York twice a year; smaller mom-and-pop operations often relied entirely on the sales reps. They brought fashion news and information on sales results for specific garments in comparable stores in other cities, as well as sample garments in the line. The early sales reps carried only one manufacturer's line, but soon many who worked for the smaller companies began to expand their offerings, showing several noncompeting lines at once.

The Growth of Regional Markets
Despite New York's undisputed position in the fashion industry, additional centers of creative production have developed to meet specific needs. California, with its unique lifestyle and climate, has become famous for sportswear and casual wear, and is the largest market center outside of New York.

Dallas is the apparel market center of the Southwest, producing fashions that are particularly suited to life in the Southern states. Finally, the Miami market has made its contribution in design and production of children's wear, resort wear, and cruisewear.

The Growth of Regional Marts
The Chicago Merchandise Mart, built in the early thirties, was the first major mart building in the country, exhibiting everything from apparel and accessories and footwear to home furnishings, toys, and gifts. Then, in 1964, Dallas opened the Apparel Mart building, a permanent location for men's, women's, and children's apparel and accessory lines in the Dallas Market Center. That same year, the California Mart opened in Los Angeles, and soon regional mart buildings were springing up throughout the country: Atlanta, Seattle, Miami, Chicago, Denver, Pittsburgh, Charlotte, Kansas City, Minneapolis. Sales reps still tour the country between shows, but the majority of their orders are written at the marts.

Organization of Markets and Marts Today
Every major regional fashion center outside of New York City—Los Angeles, Dallas, and Miami—has a central mart building or building complex. Not all manufacturers show in the mart buildings, however; some still prefer factory showrooms or hotels near the mart complex. Most fashion marts today are owned and operated by independent investors. A permanent staff directs the operation of the mart, with additional temporary employees, such as typists, models, and a larger maintenance crew, brought in during market weeks and shows. Some marts are operated by civic organizations, and at least one—the Carolina Trade Mart in Charlotte—is operated by a trade association.

Some marts have a large percentage of showrooms leased on a yearly basis, with the balance being rented only during specific shows. Other marts utilize their space extensively for a variety of other events in between apparel shows.

SERVICES OFFERED BY REGIONAL MARKETS AND MARTS

Keeping buyers and sellers happy, so that an increasing amount of orders will be written, is the mission of both the national markets and of the regional marts. All services and facilities are planned to make doing business at the markets and marts more pleasant and profitable for both the producers and the retailers. Newer marts have been especially constructed to offer maximum convenience to buyers.

Facilities
Mart buildings are constructed by real estate operators who create their buildings especially to attract manufacturers to open showrooms in these structures. Therefore, these marts usually offer both showroom space and support services under one roof, allowing a store buyer to see a wide diversity of fashions in a short time with a minimum of effort. Marts are usually arranged by category of apparel and accessories. For example, they have handbags, small leather goods, and jewelry in one area;

women's sportswear in another area; and lingerie in still another area.

Manufacturers rent or lease space in the building ranging from 8- by 10-foot open booths to spacious, fully equipped permanent showrooms. Some of these showrooms are open, at least on a limited basis, almost year-round, while others are open only during shows or market weeks. The marts will assist manufacturers' reps in renting or leasing showcases and fixtures and in setting up their space. Maintenance services are provided by the mart's owners.

Other facilities include both large and small rooms and theaters for fashion shows, seminars, and other meetings, as well as restaurants where buyers and sales reps can stop for a quick meal. Many marts have offices, complete with desks and calculators, where buyers can take a few moments to summarize and plan before moving on to view the next line.

Publications

Each mart produces several publications on a regular basis, as well as many special promotional pieces. A **buyer's directory** lists manufacturers and sales reps and also lists merchandise by category and by location within the mart, as well as giving specific information concerning services offered by the mart, scheduled events, and other items of importance to the buyer. Many marts produce their own trade newspapers, calendars of market weeks, and special newsletters promoting specific market week highlights.

Publicity

Each mart does a considerable amount of institutional advertising directed toward potential manufacturers and retail buyers, urging them to show their lines and shop at that particular mart: "Be Dazzled in Dallas," "Write Here in California!," "The Denver Merchandise Mart: Marketing Power!" In addition, special buyers' breakfasts, luncheons, and cocktail parties accompany many fashion shows produced by the marts.

Fashion shows at a mart are particularly hectic, because no one really knows exactly what will be featured until 1 or 2 days prior to the show! The mart's fashion director must contact sales reps to determine what items they want in the show, arrange for fittings and accessorizing, get an accurate description of each garment, including the name of the rep and the price, and rehearse the show. All this must be done during the times when the showrooms are closed, as the garments must be available for buyers to view during regular market hours.

Services During Market Weeks

The marts make an almost endless list of services convenient to buyers and sales reps. Most marts have hotel facilities either on-site or close by, with shuttle services provided. Hotels offer special rates for those registered at the show. Travel agencies are ready to assist with problems or changes in schedule. Security precautions are maintained 24 hours a day during markets to protect valuable merchandise. Screening of participants assures both retailers and sales reps that only authorized buyers and exhibiting manufacturers will be present, thus avoiding the problem of nonparticipating manufacturers stealing style ideas and attempting to lure buyers away from the organized show. Legal, accounting, telex, secretarial, printing, courier, and check-cashing services are handy, as well as models to assist in showrooms and during fashion shows.

Education

During market weeks, special seminars are held to assist buyers in keeping up-to-date on the latest trends in fibers and fabrics, colors, sales training methods, advertising and promotion, and other merchandising techniques. Orientation programs are held for new buyers. Consultants are on call on an individual basis to discuss specific problems.

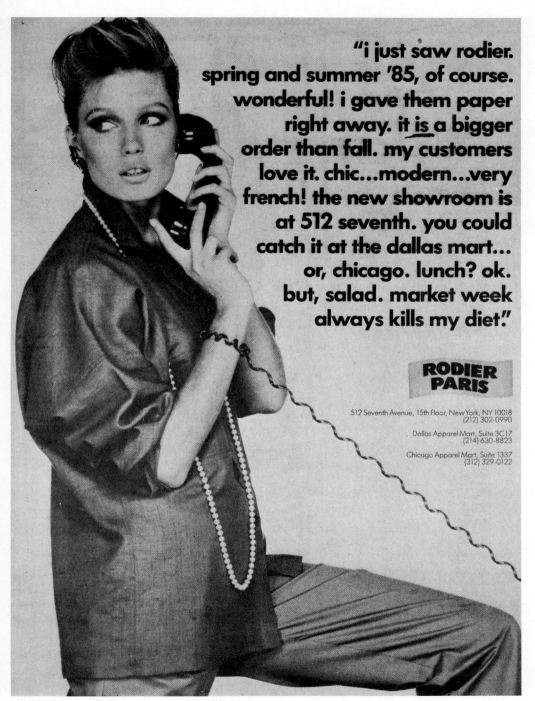

"i just saw rodier. spring and summer '85, of course. wonderful! i gave them paper right away. it _is_ a bigger order than fall. my customers love it. chic...modern...very french! the new showroom is at 512 seventh. you could catch it at the dallas mart... or, chicago. lunch? ok. but, salad. market week always kills my diet."

RODIER PARIS

512 Seventh Avenue, 15th Floor, New York, NY 10018
(212) 302-0990

Dallas Apparel Mart, Suite 3C17
(214) 630-8823

Chicago Apparel Mart, Suite 1337
(312) 329-0122

This advertiser claims its line is very French. But buyers may see it in New York, Chicago, or at the Dallas Mart.

FASHION FOCUS

HOW TO "WORK THE MARKET"

A typical buyer spends a great deal of time prior to market week preparing buying plans and setting appointments with key resources. Advance notices, listing schedules and special events, are mailed to each buyer, so that planning can maximize the effectiveness of each market trip.

A buyer may choose to arrive early at a regional mart for premarket educational seminars. New-buyer orientation programs may be held before a market opens. Premarket guidance sessions are held by resident and corporate buying offices for the benefit of member retail organizations.

After registration at the mart, buyers begin a back-to-back schedule, moving from one showroom to another, taking notes, making quick sketches, checking their projected needs against market offerings. At noon there may be a simple sandwich and coffee, or perhaps a fashion show and luncheon, giving the buyers an opportunity to relax—even though the note taking may continue—while viewing a capsule showing of the current offerings. A buyer may perhaps pick up valuable information at these shows on a new resource that he or she had not planned to visit. Then, it's back to the showrooms, continuing until 6 o'clock.

Between Shows

According to the needs and policies of each mart, various services may be offered between shows. The Miami International Merchandise Mart, for example, has a sizable group of permanent tenants who are open for business on Monday Market Days. The California Mart advertises that it is open 5 days a week, 52 weeks a year. Some of the marts have resident buying offices, both independent and store-affiliated, housed in the building. And publicity and public relations to encourage patronage of the mart are, of course, ongoing processes, as is advance planning for future shows.

Market Calendar for the Year

Generally, four or five market weeks are held for women's wear and children's wear, three to five for men's and boyswear, and two to five for shoes. Separate market weeks are held in many marts for accessories, infants' and children's wear, lingerie, western wear, sportswear, or bridal merchandise classifications. Summer markets are held in January, early fall markets in the latter part of March or in April, late fall markets at the end of May and the first part of June, resort markets in August and early September, and spring markets in late October or early November.

In the evening, a cocktail party sponsored by the mart or by a group of major manufacturers may be a highlight. This may be accompanied by a fashion show. Usually, the buyer has dinner, sometimes ordered in the hotel room, and subsequently an hour or so is devoted to organizing and regrouping a myriad of notes taken that day.

The next morning may begin at 7:30 A.M. with a breakfast fashion show. Then it's on to the showrooms for more appointments, more lines to be viewed, more notes, and more sketches. Valuable contacts are made with noncompeting buyers from other cities, and buyers may share ideas and tips on promising new lines. Throughout the day, mini-workshops may be held showing buyers how, for example, to pull together the looks of the season, or how to coordinate cosmetics with current fashions. Several marts even feature foot massages for worn-out feet!

A typical market week usually lasts 5 to 6 days, although the smaller marts often feature between-season mini-market days over a weekend and Monday. At the end of the market week, out-of-town buyers may attend postmarket analysis seminars at the mart, sponsored by resident and corporate buying offices, then devote time back home in their offices to making final decisions and writing orders.

Working the New York Market is quite differ-ent because no central mart building exists. Generally, however, similar-quality apparel and accessories items are grouped together, either within buildings or in those that are in close proximity to each other. The women's wholesale market, for example, traditionally has two identities: the couture or higher-priced lines, which are situated primarily on Seventh Avenue in buildings containing elegant showrooms, and the moderate-priced lines and sportswear firms, which are housed either in adjacent buildings or across the street or around the corner on Broadway. Valuable time therefore can be saved by careful planning and by making advance appointments with key resources so that all calls in one building may be grouped together. In this way, the buyers avoid retracing steps in going from one building to another and back again.

Despite the most careful planning, covering any market is always exhausting, not only because of the physical effort, but also as the result of the excitement and mental effort involved in viewing so many new items and trying to determine just the right mix for the individual buyer's customers.

This Fashion Focus is based on a conversation with Gayle Smith, owner of Gayle's of Houston, Texas.

THE NEW YORK MARKET

New York, which produces $17 billion worth of apparel each year, is truly the Fashion Capital of the World.[1] Although plans have been in the development stage for several years for an enormous central fashion mart to be erected on the West Side of New York between 40th and 42nd Streets, these plans are not final.

Manufacturers of women's and children's apparel have generally opposed the concept of a central mart, arguing that the Garment District is in itself an apparel mart. They question whether the huge selection of merchandise—over 5,500 women's and children's lines alone—could possibly be condensed into a single building.[2]

Retailers are somewhat in favor of the central mart concept, but many feel the idea is unrealistic. Many manufacturers also fear that such a mart could become a central showroom for foreign goods, at a time when American producers are struggling to meet competition from abroad. Whether or not a central mart ever materializes, the city of New York will continue to provide strong support for the apparel industry, which is one of the largest employers in the city.

The Trading Area and Economic Impact of the New York Market

The Fashion Institute of Technology (F.I.T.) was founded in 1944 specifically to provide training for fashion designing, production, and merchandising. The Metropolitan Museum of Art has one of the finest collections of historic fashions in the country. In 1973, the industry and New York City government renamed Seventh Avenue "Fashion Avenue," and the city launched a campaign to become known as the "Fashion Capital of the World."

Literally thousands of showrooms displaying various types and price lines of men's, women's, and children's apparel, accessories, intimate apparel, and cosmetics are housed in high-rise buildings in the Midtown area of the city, bounded on the north by 59th Street, on the south by 28th Street, on the west by Ninth Avenue, and on the east by Madison Avenue. Many of these showrooms are maintained on a permanent basis by domestic manufacturers whose production facilities are located in the Greater New York area. Others are maintained on a permanent basis by manufacturers whose headquarters and/or production facilities are located elsewhere in the United States. Some of the latter only show their lines in New York during scheduled market weeks. Those producers consider it essential to be represented in the city during market weeks because so many out-of-town retailers travel to New York for major market showings. An increasing number of foreign fashion producers also maintain showrooms and/or sales reps in the New York Market Center area.

Unique Features Today

Because retail merchants and buyers have limited time to spend away from their stores, many find it advantageous to be able to do all their purchasing in one city. The New York Market Center can provide this one-stop shopping advantage, saving the merchants both time and travel expense. Most major fiber and fabric producers, publishers of consumer and trade publications for the fashion industry, a variety of fashion support services, and trade associations maintain offices and/or showrooms in New York City.

Retailers who have New York offices visit New York to interact with their alter egos and to get the latest news about fashion trends. Store buyers often come to New York, not only to see complete and varied lines of fashion goods, but also to keep up with the latest trends in theater and opera presentations and in museums and art galleries, and to visit the headquarters of the large stores that are making fashion news: Macy's, Bloomingdale's, Lord & Taylor, Bergdorf Goodman, Bonwit Teller, and Saks Fifth Avenue. Small stores specializing in international fashion merchandise, such as Givenchy, Hanai Mori, and Kenzo are places to visit for new ideas. Fashion showings by The Fashion Group also attract out-of-town buyers.

To retail merchants, the major disadvantage of the New York Fashion Market Center is the fact that there is no central mart for housing showrooms, and the legwork involved in adequately shopping a single given market is both strenuous and time-consuming. Many producers also are finding problems with the New York Market. There is a dearth of adequately trained workers. Labor costs are high and escalating, while production in the city is declining. Buildings housing production facilities are old and rapidly deteriorating. Space rentals for workrooms and showrooms are escalating. Streets in the market area are so crowded that transportation of incoming and outgoing goods has become a real and very expensive problem. Taxes and living costs are among the highest in the country.

For these reasons, many manufacturers have already moved or are moving both their headquarters and production facilities out of the city to other areas of the country, namely the South, Mid-south, Southwest, and West Coast. In these areas labor is more plentiful and less costly. Space is available on which to build modern, more productive plants. There are good transportation facilities. Lower taxes and living costs prevail.

As producers move out of New York production facilities, most establish reputations in the local regional market to which they have moved. Many also seek representation in other regional market areas where their retail customers are located. In turn, retail merchants, eager to reduce their market trip expenses in an uncertain economy, are finding that with producers' expanded regional market coverage they can buy most, if not all, of their merchandise requirements in a market closer to home at considerably reduced costs, as well as needing less time spent away from their stores.

Major Market Openings

The New York Market, as has been mentioned, is actually open year-round, but specific times are still set aside for major showings. Two to five major lines are shown each year, with producers concentrating their efforts on presenting the majority of their goods during these times. (See Chapters 8–12 for listings of New York Market showings by industry.)

REGIONAL MARKETS

Many smaller retailers seldom if ever attend the New York Market weeks, preferring instead to patronize regional markets closer to home. Travel costs are lower, less time is spent away from their stores, and they are on a first-name basis with sales reps in the showrooms. If the local market meets all of their buying needs, why struggle through a grueling week in New York? Other retailers have reduced the number of New York trips and are filling in with trips to regional markets in Los Angeles, Dallas, or Miami.

The Los Angeles Market

Much of California's fashion success stems from its ability to promote a certain lifestyle approach to fashion. Since the 1930s, when California designers introduced pants for women, West Coast trends have been important nationwide. Culottes, the bikini, and blue jeans are all "California looks." Today, sales of the sportswear-oriented California look are booming as Americans grow more leisure-conscious and the population moves toward the Southern and Southwestern states known as the Sun Belt. Because of this success, California has become the second-largest apparel manufacturing state in the country, behind only the New York/New Jersey complex in gross output.

Apparel design, production, and distribution actually spreads out along the entire West Coast, but is heavily concentrated in the Los Angeles and San Francisco areas. In California, over 125,000 people work in apparel, including about 90,000 in the Los Angeles basin. The state produces 10 percent of the apparel industry's annual output, with Los Angeles generating about 75 percent of that total.[3] Its apparel producers have experienced a phenomenal growth rate, in part through their relationship with the California Mart, a major regional apparel mart located in the center of downtown Los Angeles. The mart is open 52 weeks a year, 5 days a week, with permanent showrooms and temporary exhibit space for market weeks. Not only California lines are represented, but also New York and Dallas lines, as well as a number of foreign producers.

Even then, all California producers do not show in the mart building. In addition to those producers who exhibit at the mart or in nearby hotels during market weeks, a number of the better women's apparel lines that are located in the Los Angeles area hold open house in their factory showrooms, rather than in the mart. They find that buyers who consider them a major resource are not reluctant to go the extra distance to see the lines on-site. The *California Apparel News* covers this important market, acting as the West Coast's answer to *Women's Wear Daily*.

The Dallas Market

The Southwestern United States today is one of the fastest-growing areas of the country in terms of population, industry, and wealth. It is also the home of several minority groups, chief among which are American Indians and Mexican-Americans. The cultural contributions to fashion made by these groups are evident in some of the regional dress items and accessories that are widely accepted today. The prevailing climate in the Southwest is conducive to more casual lifestyles, and the preferred apparel for such lifestyles is sportswear.

With the rapid growth in the Southwest, Dallas has become both an apparel production center and a very important domestic fashion market center. It is the third-largest market center in this country and advertises itself as the place "where New York and California meet." Dallas-produced fashions are shown alongside those from New York, California, and a number of foreign countries.

Besides the Apparel Mart and the Menswear Mart, five other buildings comprise the Dallas Market Center Complex, including the World Trade Center, the Trade Mart, Market Hall, the Decorative Center, the Home Furnishings Mart, and the INFOMART. Opened in January of 1985, the INFOMART houses a million square feet of showrooms of computer and high tech electronics firms. Each merchandise category is placed in an area of its own to conserve the buyer's time and energy. Adjacent to the Market Center are several hotels, including one hotel on the property.

The Miami Market

Miami, long known as the fun and sun capital of North America, has changed its image. No longer is it merely a playground for people escaping chill winds and snowdrifts. The new Miami has taken on a decidedly business-oriented flavor. Its location is a great advantage in attracting business from Central and South America and the Caribbean, and it has capitalized on that advantage by aggressively pursuing the Latin American market, as well as buyers from the Southeastern portion of the United States.

Estimates are that Latin American buyers represent about 15 percent of the traffic in the mart and 25 to 30 percent of the buying, and the numbers are growing each year. By 1986, the mart expects Latins to represent 50 percent of its business in apparel, accessories, gifts, and decorative accessories.[4]

Design and production in the Miami market has centered around cruise and resort wear, budget and moderate-priced sportswear, and children's wear. The great majority of merchandise is shown at the mart, although, like Los Angeles, the Miami area still hosts a number of shows in nearby locations, such as the Florida Children's Wear Manufacturers' Guild shows held at the Doral Country Club.

REGIONAL MARTS

In recent years, a growing number of both large and small regional marts have been built in a number of larger cities and have become important regional trade centers. Little design and production takes place in the areas surrounding these marts, especially when compared with New York, California, Dallas, and Miami. Yet they play a vital role in bringing fashion goods to the stores surrounding them. Many buyers in larger stores in the area supplement regular trips to New York and the West Coast with trips to their local regional mart. (See Table 13-1 for a list of the regional marts in the United States as well as the regional markets in Dallas, Los Angeles, and Miami.)

Like the larger market areas already described, these regional marts house the permanent showrooms of local, national, and some foreign producers. Regularly scheduled market weeks are also held in these marts. These weeks are usually sponsored by the

Dallas claims to be the place where New York and California meet and boasts a
spectacular new market center to house the encounter.

TABLE 13-1 Regional Markets and Marts in the United States

LOCATION	NAME OF FACILITY	SQUARE FEET	NUMBER OF APPAREL LINES (SHOWROOMS)	NUMBER OF MARKETS EACH YEAR	PRIMARY TRADE AREA	OTHER FACTS
Atlanta	Atlanta Apparel Mart	1.2 million	5,000 (1,000)	4 men's and boys' 5 women's 4 children's 2 activewear 1 ski	11 states in SE U.S.	Opened 1979. Serves 25,000 buyers. Six-story Atrium Fashion Theater seats over 1,200.
Boston	Bayside Merchandise Mart & Expo Center	200,000	2,400 (200)	5 women's 3 children's	New England states	Opened 1983. Additional 6,000 sq. ft. planned. Serves 10,750 buyers.
(Woburn)	North East Trade Center	200,000	2,000 (165)	3 men's and boys'	New England states	Serves 5,000 buyers. Also houses gifts, electronics, furniture, and housewares markets.
Charlotte	Carolina Trade Mart	250,000	2,800 (576)	5 women's	N. & S. Carolina, Virginia, W. Virginia, Tennessee	Opened 1972. 20,000 buyers. Owned and operated by Carolina-Virginia Fashion Exibitors. Publishes *The Roadrunner*.
	Charlotte Merchandise Mart	450,000	2,000 (400)	4 men's 5 children's 2 Western Wear	N. & S. Carolina, Virginia, W. Virginia, Tennessee	20,000 buyers. Gift, jewelry, and housewares shows also here.

City	Mart	Size	Showrooms (permanent)	Types of showrooms	Region served	Notes
						Also 13 Belk Stores Services Shows for buyers of 350+ Belk Leggett organizations.
Chicago	Chicago Apparel Center	2.2 million (includes retail stores, hotel, & exhibit hall)	6,000 (850)	5 women's and children's 4 large-size 2 bridal 2 footwear and accessories 2 menswear	20-state Midwestern region and Canada	Opened 1978. Located across from Chicago Merchandise Mart. Annual "Chicago Is" promotion reviews creations of the growing group of Chicago designers and manufacturers.
Dallas	The Apparel Mart	1.8 million	14,000 (2,000)	5 women's and children's 2 shoes 2 bridal 2 active sportswear	Texas, Oklahoma, Louisiana, New Mexico, Arkansas, Colorado, Mississippi, Kansas	Opened 1964. Spring markets, held in October, have been declared International Market Weeks by U.S. Dept. of Commerce. Over 100,000 buyers
	The Menswear Mart	400,000	700 + (250)	4 men's		

TABLE 13-1 Regional Markets and Marts in the United States (continued)

LOCATION	NAME OF FACILITY	SQUARE FEET	NUMBER OF APPAREL LINES (SHOWROOMS)	NUMBER OF MARKETS EACH YEAR	PRIMARY TRADE AREA	OTHER FACTS
Denver	Denver Merchandise Mart	679,000	2,000 (400)	5 women's and children's 2 shoes and accessories 3 men's and boys 1 Western Wear	Rocky Mountain/ Central Plains region	Opened 1965. International Western Apparel and Equipment Market draws buyers from all over the U.S. and 30 foreign countries.
Kansas City	Kansas City Apparel Mart	327,640 (includes gift mart and exhibit hall)	1,000 (175)	5 women's and children's 4 men's and boys' 2 shoes 2 Western 2 sportswear	Missouri, Kansas, Nebraska, Iowa, Oklahoma, Arkansas	Opened in 1979. 3,200 buyers.
Los Angeles	The California Mart	3 million	10,000+ (2,000)	5 women's 4 children's 2 men's 4 young men's 6 shoes 1 textiles 1 swim/active-wear	All of U.S. especially Southwest Many buyers from Orient	Opened 1964. Serves 75,000+ buyers Houses over 30 buying offices Publishes *Fashion West* magazine 5 times/year
Miami	Miami International Merchandise Mart	520,000 Note: Adjoining Miami Expo Center adds 65,000 sq. ft.	6,000 (525)	5 women's 3 men's and boys' 3 infants' and children 4 handbags, jewelry and accessories	Southeastern U.S., Central and South America and Caribbean	Opened 1969. Serves over 125,000 buyers. 2 major gift shows

City	Mart	Total Sq. Ft.	Number	Markets	Territory	Remarks
Minneapolis	Hyatt Merchandise Mart	196,000	5,000 (437)	6 women's and children's 5 men's and boys'	Minnesota, N. and S. Dakota, Iowa, Wisconsin	5,600 buyers. Adjoins Hyatt Hotel in downtown Minneapolis.
Pittsburgh (Monroeville)	Pittsburgh Expo Mart	80,000	1,000 (200)	5 women's 5 children's 4 men's and boys' 3 shoes	Central and W. Pennsylvania, Ohio, W. Virginia, W. New York, W. Maryland	Opened 1975. 12 miles east of Pittsburgh. Also houses gifts and decorative accessories.
Portland	Portland Galleria	66,000	300	5 women's and children's	Oregon, Washington, Idaho, N. California	Located in downtown Portland.
Salt Lake City	Expo Mart	170,000	1,750 (225)	5 women's and children's 3 men's	Utah, W. Wyoming, S. Idaho, Central Nevada	Opened 1982. 2,500 buyers. Additional 40,000 sq. ft. planned for 1986, plus a hotel.
San Francisco	San Francisco Apparel Mart	375,000	1,400 (430)	10 women's, men's, children's, and textiles	N. and C. California, Nevada	Opened 1981 in restored turn-of-century building in Bay Area. 6,500 buyers. Holds composite markets for tenants, as well as separate markets for sales rep associations. Many new firms from area show only here.

TABLE 13-1 Regional Markets and Marts in the United States (continued)

LOCATION	NAME OF FACILITY	SQUARE FEET	NUMBER OF APPAREL LINES (SHOWROOMS)	NUMBER OF MARKETS EACH YEAR	PRIMARY TRADE AREA	OTHER FACTS
Seattle	Seattle Apparel Center	340,000	4,500 (310)	5 women's 3 men's 2 shoes	Pacific North-west, Alaska, Idaho, Mon-tana, Oregon, Washington	Opened in 1970s. Holds 2 winter sportswear and sports equip-ment shows and one yarn and apparel show.

Sources:

Atlanta: Atlanta Merchandise Mart press releases. *Stores*, April 1983, p. 46; telephone interviews with mart management.

Boston: Telephone interviews with mart management.

Charlotte: Brochures from Carolina Trade Mart; interview with Zeb Burnette, manager of Charlotte Merchandise Mart; interview with Beckey Moser of Belk's in Charlotte.

Chicago: Mart brochures and press releases.

Dallas: Apparel Mart Press Releases and telephone interviews and correspondance with Richard H. Murry, Director of Public Relations, Dallas Market Center.

Denver: Mart brochures, buyer's manuals, and press releases.

Kansas City: *Fashion Showcase Retailer*, May 1983; press releases from the Kansas City Market Center and interview by phone with mart management.

Los Angeles: The California Mart press releases and correspondance and telephone interviews with Karen Witynski at the California Mart.

Miami: "Mart Facts" published by the Miami International Merchandise Mart in 1982, pp. 2-3, correspondance and telephone interviews with Leslie Goldman, Director of Advertising and Buying Services, Miami International Merchandise Mart.

Minneapolis: Brochures and correspondence with Hyatt Mart and trade associations.

Pittsburgh: Expo Mart brochures and press releases and telephone interview with mart management.

Portland: Telephone interview with ex-director of sales reps association.

Salt Lake City: David D. Hansen, General Manager of Expo Mart (telephone); *California Apparel News*, Feb. 18, 1983, p. 18.

San Francisco: Mart brochures, buyer's manuals, press releases, telephone interview with mart management.

Seattle Trade Center: Brochures, press releases and buyer's manuals, interview with mart management via telephone.

marts in cooperation with various sales representatives' associations, such as the Shoe Travelers' Association, the Carolina-Virginia Fashion Exhibitors, the San Francisco Children's Wear Association, and the California Handbag Guild.

TRADE SHOWS AND ASSOCIATIONS

Trade shows were previously described as merchandise exhibits in various regional trading centers around the country. They are sponsored by **trade associations** (professional organizations for manufacturers or sales representatives) who are active in the geographic area in which the trade show is held. They take place periodically in cities that are in key business centers near a major market. For example, trade shows may be held in Des Moines, Iowa, which is in the area covered by the Chicago and Kansas City markets.

These shows are limited versions of the market center's regional market weeks, with fewer lines and styles being shown than at the major markets. Trade shows, lasting 2 to 4 days, take place in a public facility such as a major hotel or motel, civic center, or exhibit hall. Temporary booths or displays in hotel rooms are used to display samples. Often two seasons' markets are combined, resulting in fewer showings each year. Spring and summer or fall and winter showings might be combined, for instance.

Markets held at the Birmingham Civic Center are a good example of trade shows. The Birmingham Apparel Market sponsors five 3-day shows a year for women's and children's wear in the 130,000-square-foot Civic Center in downtown Birmingham. The shows were first organized in the early 1930s, when they met in hotels in the city. Today, despite the fact that Birmingham is only a 2-hour drive from Atlanta and the Atlanta Merchandise Mart, the women's and children's markets draw between 900 and 1,000 buyers to view lines shown by 225 sales representatives. The

BAMA Men's Apparel Club of Alabama holds three shows a year in the Civic Center, with some 125 sales representatives hosting between 350 and 500 buyers at each show. Retailers come from Alabama, Tennessee, northern Mississippi, Georgia, and the Florida Panhandle.[5]

For the smaller retailer, the trade shows are a real boon. Sales reps are personally familiar with the needs of each buyer, and many smaller producers display their lines only at trade shows. Boutique shows in Los Angeles, for example, feature many unique and unusual items from new designers and smaller manufacturers who do not display at the marts. The trade shows offer the smaller retailer the convenience of a close-to-home show complete with exhibitor directories. Travel costs and time away from the store are lower than if the retailer attended one of large regional marts. However, the big disadvantage lies in the limited number of lines and styles available, as well as in the lack of permanent showrooms for between-market trips and resource contacts.

Professional associations for both producers and sales reps continue to grow in importance as the fashion business becomes more and more complex. Their importance in organizing the first central market week shows outside of New York City cannot be overemphasized. Today, professional associations are major sponsors of trade shows and market weeks throughout the country, and serve in an advisory capacity on the governing boards of every major mart in the country.

A survey of the Bureau of Wholesale Sales Representatives, the largest organization for independent sales reps in the apparel business, revealed that over 60 locations throughout the United States—in hotels and civic centers—are used for regional markets, each of which is held several times a year.[6] The efforts of professional associations result in more efficient, profitable buying and selling in fashion markets throughout the United States.

Spring. California Mart/Pacific Coast Travelers
Los Angeles Market Week. November 2-6

California is warming up for Spring '85. This year will be better than ever as the California Mart premieres the new 8th floor designers area.

Up to $75.00 Airfare Rebate
Airfare rebate offers you savings of 50% off your airline ticket up to a maximum of $75.00 with airline ticket, validated passports and positive identification. You must shop two of the following three days to be eligible for the rebate program: Friday, November 2; Saturday, November 3; Sunday, November 4. Rebate check is given to you at the end of your second day of shopping.

Reservation Information
American Airlines, the official airline carrier for California Mart/Pacific Coast Travelers Market Week, offers special discounts of up to 30% off the coach fare for November 2-6, 1984 Market Week.
For reservations, please call American's Convention Desk, 1-800/433-1790 and provide them with your Special Market Week "S.T.A.R." identifier #S5086. From Alaska, Call 1-800/421-4206.

Added Incentives
Local buyer gas coupons.
Discount luncheon coupons.
Hospitality Suites.
Validated parking.

Market Events
Friday, November 2
New Buyer Orientation, 8:30 a.m.
Market Mezzanine Room 2

Friday, November 2
Cocktail Party, 6:00 p.m.
Galleria; 8th Floor Collections Show; 6:30 p.m.
Fashion Theatre; 8th Floor Champagne Reception, 7:30 p.m.

Saturday, November 3
Bridal Fashion Show/Breakfast,
8:30 a.m. Galleria

Saturday, November 3
Cocktail Party, 6:00 p.m.
California Designer Fashion Show,
6:30 p.m. Fashion Theatre

Sunday, November 4
Pacific Coast Travelers
Fashion Show/Breakfast, 8:00 a.m.
Fashion Theatre

Sunday, November 4
Cocktail Party, 6:00 p.m. Sandy Baldanza,
Fashion Show, 6:30 p.m. Fashion Theatre

Monday, November 5
TAG (The Accessory Group) Seminar and
Continental Breakfast, 8:00 a.m., Fashion
Theatre, "Spring Accessories; The New
Directional Trends."

Monday, November 5
"Get Out The Vote Election Eve"
Cocktail Party, 6:00 p.m.
Fashion Theatre

California Mart
110 EAST NINTH STREET, LOS ANGELES, CA 90079 (213) 620-0260

Trade associations like the Pacific Coast Travelers co-sponsor market weeks in regional fashion centers.

TRENDS

Among the most important trends in fashion marketing is the expansion and modernization of existing mart facilities. Almost without exception, either the original facilities of every mart have been expanded, or plans are on the boards for future expansion. The popularity of the regional marts has created demand for larger facilities that offer more buyer services and show more lines more frequently.

New mart buildings are opening throughout the country to serve the smaller retailer closer to home: Salt Lake City, Boston, Portland, and Honolulu are but a few examples. And, there is a growing demand for between-market openings, with many marts having Monday Market Days, and more and more mart facilities opening their showrooms, at least on a limited basis, year-round. With consumers buying closer to need (closer to the time they need to wear the garment), the retailers are responding with buying trips closer to need, resulting in more frequent visits to local marts.[7] Between market openings as well as during market weeks, the sales representative continues to be important, bringing midseason offerings directly to many stores and servicing individual accounts.

Growing numbers of off-price retailers are also having an impact on fashion markets today. By coming into the market with incentive cash for early commitments before regular season openings, they have caused slight distortions in the traditional buying periods in both women's and men's goods. And, by daily covering wholesale and retail sources, off-price retailers are reducing the usual sources of special-purchase merchandise their competitors have come to rely on to enhance seasonal promotions.

International participation at regional marts is increasing, with some marts devoting whole floors or sections of the building to imported merchandise. Special trade shows for foreign goods are becoming more and more popular, like the Italian Leathergoods show held in New York City, sponsored by the Italian Ministry of Foreign Trade and the Italian Leathergoods Association. Specialized trade shows are also growing in importance, such as special shows for stout men and for licensed goods. As consumer demands change, fashion producers and retailers will continue to change their marketing strategies to meet those new demands in the marketplace.

REFERENCES

[1] Bernadine Morris, "Sportswear Makes City a World Fashion Leader," *The New York Times,* April 11, 1983, p. B3.

[2] "Marts and Markets: What's Happening Around the Country and in New York," *Stores,* April 1983, p. 47.

[3] Andrew Jaffe, "Cal Mart Avoids Apparel Industry Recession," *Los Angeles Herald Examiner,* May 9, 1982; and the *California Mart Directory and Yellow Pages,* July 1982.

[4] Faye Melton, "Region's Marts Pursue Latin American Buyers," *Apparel South,* September 1981.

[5] Based on information received from Sarah Scruggs, Executive Secretary, Southern Fashion Exhibitors, and from Jack Mann, BAMAC Secretary/Treasurer, telephone conversations, September 22, 1983.

[6] *Bureau News,* September 12, 1983, pp. 5–7 (Published by the Bureau of Wholesale Sales Representatives, 1819 Peachtree Road, Suite 600, Atlanta, Georgia 30309).

[7] Marjorie Axelrad, "Timing Tactics," *Stores,* April 1983, pp. 44–45.

MERCHANDISING VOCABULARY

Define or briefly explain the following terms:

Buyer's directory

Domestic market

Foreign markets

Garment District

Market

Market center

Market week

Mart

Trade association

Trade shows

1. What criteria must be met for an area to be considered a market center?
2. What conditions created the demand for regional fashion centers outside of New York City?
3. Describe the role of the sales representative in the early days.
4. Describe the organization of a typical mart.
5. What services are offered by a typical mart to buyers and manufacturers?
6. What services are offered between market weeks?
7. Why is New York City considered the major fashion market center in the United States?
8. Compare the major advantages and disadvantages of the New York Market as opposed to regional fashion markets.
9. Where are three fashion market centers located in this country outside of New York? Three fashion marts? Discuss four of these market centers, indicating the distinctive characteristics and services that each offers to retail store buyers.
10. What is the role of trade associations in the distribution of fashion merchandise today?

1. Describe a typical buyer's schedule during market week. How does working the New York Market differ from working the regional marts?
2. What market center serves the retailers in your city? If your city is not in the New York City area, discuss the advantages to local retailers who use your regional mart.

14. FOREIGN FASHION MARKETS

World War II had profound effects far from the battlefields. These effects were felt strongly in the fashion industry. Until the outbreak of the war, the industry had always looked to Paris as the center of the Western fashion world. When France fell to the Nazis and was occupied, Paris designers, along with all the rest of the French people, were cut off from the Western world until the end of the war. As a result, people turned to designers in their own countries to satisfy their fashion needs. Wartime shortages of materials forced these designers to be truly innovative in creating new fashions. Because they succeeded, and the people adopted these new fashions from their own designers, new fashion centers were born.

When the war ended, these new national fashion images helped many countries to rebuild their war-shattered economies. By the export of its new fashion image, a country could interest the rest of the world in learning more about the realities behind the image. Consumers who until then knew little about a certain country wanted to learn more about its customs, its natural resources, and just what designs and materials were characteristic of that country.

Since World War II, many nations have gained independence from colonial powers. Many other nations, which had been severely underdeveloped, began to emerge as producers of goods. These emerging countries found that through exporting their goods they could gain increased technological and economic status.

Two types of goods that these emerging countries have been producing and exporting are textiles and apparel. Both of these industries require a large supply of labor and little machinery. The emerging countries are very able to satisfy the requirement for labor. The producers of these fashion goods are often subsidized by their governments in order that these exports can be made more competitive and more attractive in the world marketplace. To further aid emerging and underdeveloped nations and help them become economically more independent, the United States offers lower custom duties on their merchandise.

All of these things have combined to encourage fashion development everywhere. So in the mid-1980s, fashion centers and fashion innovations are to be found all around the globe.

SHOPPING FOREIGN MARKETS

Because American consumers have become fashion-oriented and because American buyers are constantly trying to meet the needs and wants of these consumers, the buyers shop fashion centers worldwide to find exciting, innovative, and fashion-right apparel and accessories. Foreign fashion merchandise and designs are becoming more and more important in the assortments offered to consumers. Merchandising these fashion assortments from all over the world gives customers a wider choice both in design and price.

Methods Used for Buying Foreign Fashion Merchandise

To guarantee that they have the best possible coverage in worldwide fashion markets, buyers use many different shopping methods. The five methods most used for buying foreign fashion merchandise are through:

1. Buyers' visits to foreign fashion markets.
2. Foreign commissionaires or agents.
3. Store-owned foreign buying offices.
4. Foreign exporters at import fairs or with showrooms in the United States.
5. American importers.

BUYERS' VISITS TO FOREIGN FASHION MARKETS. This method ensures that stores' foreign fashions will suit the special needs of their target customers. Many times, foreign production and styling have to be adjusted to suit American requirements. Thus the approach to foreign merchandise must be creative. Preparations at home and development work abroad by its buyer helps a store maintain an individual approach. Most stores encourage their buyers to spend time investigating the cultural, economic (including retail), and social climate of each foreign country visited. This flavor can then be translated to their customers in the form of imports.

FOREIGN COMMISSIONAIRES OR AGENTS. These people are used by retailers to represent and assist their buyers in a foreign country. A **commissionaire** (pronounced ko-me-see-ohn-air) organization is usually located in a major city of a foreign market area. It is staffed by market representatives, each of whom specializes in a particular category of merchandise. These market representatives constantly keep abreast of market developments. They work with visiting retail buyers who want to locate specific types of goods or who simply want to see what the market has to offer. The commissionaire does not make purchases for its store clients, however, unless authorized to do so by an appropriate store executive. The store pays the commissionaire a fee that is usually a percentage of the **first cost** (the wholesale price in the country of origin) of any purchase made. The commissionaire then follows up to make sure that the merchandise deliveries are made, and made on time, since this is critical in fashion merchandising, and has often been a major problem with imports.

STORE-OWNED FOREIGN BUYING OFFICES.

These offices work year-round, advising buyers about new trends and items. They also function as a follow-up service to ensure prompt delivery and quality control of the foreign merchandise bought in each country. Most large stores and chains maintain a foreign buying office in each of the large fashion capitals of the world, such as Paris, Rome, London, Hong Kong, and Tokyo. Examples of the type of company that maintains a store-owned foreign buying office are:

- Large department store organizations, such as Macy's, Allied Stores, BATUS, and the May Company department stores.
- The big general-merchandise chains, such as Sears and JC Penney.
- Large resident buying offices, such as Frederick Atkins, and the Associated Merchandising Corporation.

FOREIGN IMPORT FAIRS PRODUCED IN THE UNITED STATES.

Another way that buyers can shop foreign markets is to attend the foreign import shows produced in the United States. The New York Pret—a semiannual event in New York City—is one of the largest and most prestigious of these U.S.–produced import shows. Many foreign countries now participate in such shows or stage their own fashion fairs in the United States. The importance of these shows grows each year because at these shows American buyers and foreign producers are able to work together to ensure quality and styling adapted for the American consumer. Buyers and retailers unable to make trips to these countries can view fashions and talk to the designers and manufacturers of each country. France, Italy, Greece, Germany, Israel, Brazil, and Hong Kong are some of the countries that participate in such foreign import fairs.

AMERICAN IMPORTERS.

American importers offer another method of covering foreign fashion markets. Many small retailers do not make overseas trips or use any of the other methods of foreign buying. Shopping the lines of American importers gives them the opportunity to purchase foreign fashion merchandise that would not otherwise be available to them. Although this method limits the opportunity for individualized styling available through the other methods, it allows smaller retailers to offer their customers some of the excitement of foreign styling and merchandise.

FRANCE

France emerged as an all-important European center of culture and learning during the late thirteenth century. Steadily growing for 400 years, France's reputation for fashion inspiration peaked during the reign of Louis XIV (1643–1715). The court of Louis XIV was a showcase of luxury, and the elaborate clothing preferred by his court was widely copied by the royal and wealthy throughout Europe. The splendor of the court of Versailles created a need for beautiful fabrics, tapestries, and lace. Textile production in Lyons and lace works in Alençon were established to meet these needs. This was the beginning of France's fashion industry, and of Paris as the fashion capital of the world.

As an artistic center, Paris was considered ideal by creative apparel designers. Skilled seamstresses were abundant and luxury fabrics were readily available. The court, nobility, and wealthy merchants, along with international visitors to Paris, all supported the growth of the fashion industry in France.

Paris is still considered the cradle of the fashion world. The major fashion changes are usually born there. They are then seen, reported on, adopted, and adapted throughout the rest of the world.

Historically renowned for original and trend-setting high-fashion collections, today

Paris is also an important fashion center for innovative ready-to-wear apparel. In fact, the traditional differences between the world of haute couture and ready-to-wear are fading. Today foreign fashions are selected from one of two categories: haute couture and prêt-à-porter.

Haute couture, originally a French term, pronounced "oat-koo-tour" literally means "fine sewing" but actually has much the same meaning as our own term "high fashion." That is, it includes original styles or designs accepted by a limited group of fashion leaders. These designs are often very expensive, one-of-a-kind creations made for particular customers. The term "haute couture" is generally used in connection with those design houses that combine luxury fabrics and fine handiwork to create original and trend-setting styles.

Prêt-à-porter, also originally a French term, pronounced "pret-ah-por-tay," means "ready-to-wear," and is similar to our domestic ready-to-wear. Both categories of fashions will be discussed in detail throughout the chapter.

Paris Couture

France has been a fashion leader from the year 1858, when the house of Charles Frederick Worth, generally regarded as the father of the Paris couture, opened its doors. Following Worth and beginning about 1907, Paul Poiret, another French couture designer, contributed to and continued the great fashion legend that was Paris. Poiret was the first to stage fashion shows. His oriental balls were part of the opulence that characterized Paris as the center of the fashion scene. He was also the first to branch out into the related fields of perfume, accessories, fabric design, and interior decoration.

From the middle of the nineteenth century until about 20 years ago, haute couture designers in Paris were the undisputed arbiters of fashion throughout the world. Ready-to-wear may have flourished in the United States and elsewhere, but all over the world women aspired to go to France to have their clothes made to order—at least their most important ones. Haute couture itself is considered by the French people to be one of its national treasures and monuments and, as such, is given special prestige and support rarely found in other countries.

A **couture house** is an apparel firm for which a designer creates original designs and styles. The proprietor or designer of a couture house is known as a **couturier** pronounced "koo-tour-ee-ay" (if male) or **couturiere** "koo-tour-ee-air" (if female). Most Paris couture houses are known by the names of the designers who head them—Yves St. Laurent, Givenchy, Ungaro, and Cardin, for example. Sometimes, however, a couture house may keep the name of its original designer even after the designer's death. For example, Marc Bohan designs under the Dior name, and Karl Lagerfield under the Chanel name.

CHAMBRE SYNDICALE. In 1868, an elite couture trade association called the *Chambre Syndicale de la Couture Parisienne* came into being. Membership in the **Chambre Syndicale** (pronounced "Shahmbrah seen-dee-kahl") was by invitation only and was restricted to couture houses that agreed to abide by strict rules. For membership in the *Chambre Syndicale* today:

- A formal written request must be presented to and voted on by the body.

- Workrooms must be established in Paris. (It is preferred that the creative production be based in Paris also.)

- Collections must be presented twice a year on the date in January and July established by the *Chambre Syndicale*.

- A collection should consist of 75 or more designs.

- Three models must be employed by the house throughout the year.

Pierre Cardin is a member of the *Chambre Syndicale de la Couture Parisienne.* Major changes are often born in Paris, the "cradle of the fashion world."

- A minimum of 20 workers must be employed in the couture operation.

The *Chambre Syndicale* has remained strong in France by providing many needed services for the entire French fashion industry—for ready-to-wear as well as couture. For the ready-to-wear designers there is the *Fédération Française de la Couture du Prêt-à-Porter des Couturiers et des Créateurs de Mode,* part of the official *Chambre Syndicale.* In 1984 an autonomous section was created for the noncouture designer and designer-firm members, those involved only with ready-to-wear. This group includes 18 of the Chambre's 39 members. These 18 designers have been designated "*créateurs*" as opposed to "*couturiers.*" They include, among others, Jean-Paul Gaultier, Angelo Toulaggé, Dorothee Bis, Thierry Mugler, and Claude Montana.

Many services are provided by the *Chambre Syndicale:*

- It represents all members and advises on law, taxes, and many aspects of employment.
- It lobbies by carrying on negotiations with the various branches of government.
- It polices the industry itself to prevent misuses of creative design.
- It registers designs and serves as the protection agency against design piracy. A garment made by a *Syndicale* member is photographed from the back, front, and sides. The design is registered with the *Chambre Syndicale.* If a registered design is copied in France, the act is punishable by law.
- It coordinates openings, setting the dates and hours to avoid an overlapping of showings.
- It issues credentials for authorized buyers and the French and foreign press.
- It establishes the delivery dates of merchandise ordered by trade buyers. Merchandise is usually shipped 30 days after its showing.

HOW TO SEE A FASHION SHOW IN PARIS

Imagine yourself at a Paris haute couture fashion show: The beautiful models parade one after another down the runway. There is a restrained excitement in the air. The salon is filled with flowers and palms and elegant women who speak in hushed voices, quietly expressing their enthusiasm for the display that unfolds before them. Above all else there are the clothes: splendid, seductive, completely luxurious. Nowhere else in the world can you see this richness of fabric, this incredible workmanship, this imaginative design. This is *la haute couture Parisienne.*

And, believe it or not, you don't have to be Princess Caroline or Queen Noor of Jordan to see one of these fantastic shows. With advance planning just about anyone can see a high-fashion style show in Paris. The French are as anxious for visitors to Paris to view their beloved couture as they are for these same tourists to see the Eiffel Tower or the Louvre. To them, haute couture is not just the producing of apparel, but the creation of a work of art. It is a national treasure, like their wine, and as such is regulated by the trade association (the *Chambre Syndicale de la Couture Parisienne*), which requires couture houses to have a minimum of two monthlong showings twice a year. The excitement and effort that is part of the production of these showings has often been compared to that of producing a Broadway show.

Before the collection is presented—usually the last week in January for the spring–summer line and the last week in July for the fall–winter line—the designers spend long hours working on their

- It regulates press release dates, which are set approximately 6 weeks after showings. This gives the buyers of expensive models time to receive them and have copies manufactured.

COUTURE SHOWINGS. The major Paris couture houses show their semiannual haute couture collections in late January (for spring–summer) and in late July (for fall–winter). Four types of customers attend:

1. *Private customers*—They may select a model (garment) from a designer's collection and have it made to measure.

2. *Retail store buyers*—They may buy models from a collection for resale to their own customers or, in many cases, so they can

creations in their workrooms (*ateliers*). They may make sketches or prepare mock-ups in plain white muslin (the *toile*). The expense of the fabric—the satin, fine cashmere, embroidered lace, beaded silk—does not allow for mistakes. Only after the sample is perfected is the fabric cut. When the garment has been hand-stitched together, the *paruriers* (literally "adorners") add the buttons, sequins, beads, mink trim, feathers. If the designer wants a tailored garment, it is constructed by the *tailleurs,* experts so specialized that one may cut the jacket for a suit, another the skirt.

A designer's regular showings begin a week after the grand opening and the first weeks are usually very busy, so the best time to schedule your trip to Paris would be either in the middle or end of March or in August. Some couture houses even arrange showings for tour groups, but if you're on your own, simply telephone for the always necessary reservations (the receptionist will speak English) or have your hotel concierge call for you. Some houses will call back to confirm that you are in fact registered. The regular showings are free, usually start at around 3 P.M., and last an hour. Remember to take your passport with you (there is an attempt made to keep out copyists and a charge for people in the fashion industry) and remember to leave your checkbook back at the hotel if you are even slightly susceptible to impulse buying (the clothes are *incredibly* expensive: $1,500 for a blouse, $3,000 for a simple dress, $6,000 for a suit, and $15,000 for an evening gown). The salons are elegant, but simple, designed not to detract from the show, and can seat anywhere from 20 to 150 patrons. Some houses—Yves St. Laurent, Emanuel Ungaro, and Hanae Mori, for instance—show their collections on videotape in order to save money and because they feel they cannot recapture the excitement of the first showings in months of subsequent presentations. If the salon is not too busy, you may be assigned a *vendeuse* (a saleswoman who acts as an adviser).

The profits from these one-of-a-kind clothes are very small when compared to what the designers make from ready-to-wear, cosmetics, and perfumes, and they only continue to produce haute couture because it allows them to experiment. Pierre Cardin, Yves St. Laurent, and Emanuel Ungaro have all called their couture their "laboratory."

If you are so filled with fear and trembling at the mere thought of entering such an exalted establishment that you think your knees will buckle in the vestibule when the uniformed doorman says *"Bonjour,"* remember that while the main purpose of these showings is to sell clothes, the designer is also anxious to promote goodwill. After all, you may go back to your hometown and buy something from the ready-to-wear collection, and you may already be wearing the designer's perfume. *Bonne chance.*

This Fashion Focus is based on information from these sources:

Carrie Donovan, "Made to Influential Order," *The New York Times Magazine,* February 26, 1984, p. 61.
Hebe Dorsey, "Couture: The Splendid Craft," *Vogue,* October 1982, p. 292.
Bernadine Morris, "Passport to Paris Fashion," *The New York Times,* November 29, 1981, p. D-29.

---

have the model copied or adapted into exclusive ready-to-wear.

3. *Ready-to-wear producers*—They may buy models for inspiration or adaptation when designing styles for their own lines.

4. *Pattern manufacturers*—They may buy models or paper patterns of models for reproduction as patterns for home sewers.

Private customers and the press are admitted free, although the latter have to apply for admission passes. (See the Fashion Focus above.) Retailers and manufacturers, who must also apply for admission, are charged a stipulated caution. A **caution** is a fee charged for viewing a couture collection to prevent copying without buying. The caution may be stated as a dollar fee, or as an agreement to purchase a certain number of models, or as an agreement to purchase a certain number of paper patterns, or any combination of these three requirements. The amount of the caution usually varies with the importance of the couture house; less well-known houses usually require lower cautions than do more famous ones.

Other Couture Business Activities

While the traditional haute couture collections continue to make fashion news, actual sales volume has steadily declined in recent years. More and more, private customers whose wardrobes might once have consisted almost entirely of exclusive, couture-made garments are now turning to ready-to-wear. This has occurred partly because

- Many private customers have become impatient with the numerous and lengthy fittings couture garments require.

- The figures of potential private customers now tend to be so slender and well-cared-for that they can easily be fitted with ready-to-wear garments.

- General economic trends have made many longtime private customers balk at the money required to be dressed by the couture.

- An increasing number of talented designers are creating ready-to-wear.

COUTURE BOUTIQUES. Boutique, pronounced ''boo-teek,'' is a French word for ''shop.'' The term has come to mean a shop associated with one- or few-of-a-kind merchandise. The first step in meeting the challenge of couture customers' buying more ready-to-wear was the creation of couture boutiques, usually located on a lower floor of the same building that houses the couture showrooms. Most well-known Paris couture houses now have their own couture boutiques. They feature unusual and exclusive fashion accessories as well as limited lines of apparel. Boutique items are usually designed by members of the couture house staff, are sometimes made in the couture workrooms, and all bear the famous label.

COUTURE READY-TO-WEAR. Couture is exclusive and so expensive to produce that all of the couture designers have now begun to design ready-to-wear. Styling of these lines was originally the responsibility of the design staff of a couture house. But today couture designers say they design their most outrageous, creative, and innovative designs for ready-to-wear, with the haute couture collection serving as prestige earners.

Some couture ready-to-wear is sold in special shops operated by the couture house in major cities around the world. Large quantities are sold to department and specialty stores, which often set aside special departments or areas for displaying and selling couture-designed ready-to-wear and accessories. Modern couture designers create lines that fall between what most people are actually wearing and the designer's own private imaginings of how people might be persuaded to clothe themselves. Fashion for them combines fantasy and fact. Rather than widening the gap between the past glories of haute couture and the vitality of ready-to-wear, these designers have worked to join the two.

Ready-to-wear operations have become major money-makers for many couture designers. Yves St. Laurent with his partner, Pierre Berge, launched the firm St. Laurent–Rive Gauche in 1964. Through a licensing arrangement with Rive Gauche, Didier Grumbach produced and distributed apparel and accessories under the Rive Gauche label. There are now more than 200 Rive Gauche boutiques worldwide, and annual income is estimated at about $150 million.[1] However, all the boutiques, except those owned personally by Berge and Yves St. Laurent, are franchised operations.

COUTURE LICENSING AGREEMENT. A number of couture designers not only sell their own accessories and ready-to-wear lines but also license the use of their names on a wide variety of other producers' goods. These goods range from apparel and accessories to bed, bath, and table linens, to home furnishings, and more.

In 1983, Pierre Cardin was the undisputed king of couture licensing, with over 620 licensing agreements. Some 150 products bear his name and are sold in 80 countries. His name appears on such diverse products as chocolates, T-shirts, bed sheets, and furniture.[2] Jean-Claude Givenchy, brother of Hubert and business manager of the couture house, was quoted as saying: "That we continue in couture is often a condition of the licensee contracts that we sign—and through these licenses, the couture can pay for itself."[3]

French Ready-to-Wear

The ready-to-wear operations of Paris couture houses represent only a part of the burgeoning French ready-to-wear industry. The ready-to-wear houses in Paris began attracting world attention around 1960 by emphasizing change. The major change involved throwing out the conventions set by couture houses in favor of a natural way of dressing. This attracted the new, young generation of fashion-oriented consumers who were intent upon making their own fashion image. Through the sixties and seventies, French ready-to-wear turned out designs that were kicky, funky, antiestablishment, and just as good-looking as those that the couture showed. Sometimes they were better-looking. As the customers increased, all designers viewed the ready-to-wear business as more creative and free, and the concept of French ready-to-wear grew.

The strength and importance of the French ready-to-wear industry is obvious today. More than 30,000 trade buyers attend the showing of the prêt-à-porter collections. And the press gives more coverage and attention to these showings than to the couture showings.

DESIGNERS. Paris ready-to-wear showings are increasingly more important to American fashion merchants as a source of fashion inspiration. New, young, innovative Paris designers, such as France Andrevie, Thierry Mugler, Sonia Rykiel, Karl Lagerfeld, and Kenzo Takado, are making big fashion news with their trend-setting styles. French ready-to-wear firms, such as Cacharel, MicMac, Dorothee Bis, and Chloe, have become very important fashion resources for American fashion retailers. (See Table 14–1.)

TRADE SHOWS. In March and October, two large Paris trade shows take place simultaneously:

1. The showings of those known as fashion leaders and innovators—the more famous prêt-à-porter designer names, who also produce couture, and
2. The many mass-producing, ready-to-wear firms and boutiques.

These semiannual trade shows draw thousands of store buyers and apparel manufacturers from all over the world. They also attract approximately twice the number of press representatives as their nearest competitors—the ready-to-wear shows in Milan and London.

The two groups do not exhibit in the same place. Traditionally the couture designers' shows are held throughout the city. Since 1979 the couture designers have held their fashion shows in huge tents erected in a centrally located area of Paris known as Les Halles (literally "The Hole"). Once the site of the Paris food market, this area is being redeveloped as a shopping and cultural center. Adjacent is a recently completed multilevel building, the Forum des Halles, one level of which is reserved for showrooms of leading Paris designers. Nearby are facilities for boutique' showrooms.

The group of mass-producing designers has traditionally exhibited at the Porte de Versailles Exhibition Center. Their trade show, known as the *Salon du Prêt-à-Porter Féminin*, is held in the Palais Sud building in the Porte de Ver-

TABLE 14-1 Selected Foreign Designers		
CANADA	**GERMANY**	**HONG KONG**
Leo Chevalier	Wolfgang Joop	Tenny Cheung
Wayne Clark	Caren Pfleger	Diane Freis
Claire Haddah	Uta Raasch	Ragence Lam
Norma Lepofsky	Edith Sonanini	Eddie Lau and John Cheng (Jopej)
Linda Lundstrom		Jenney Lewis
Pat McDonogh	**GREAT BRITAIN**	Kai-Yin Lo (jewelry)
Alfred Sung	Hardy Amies	Judy Mann (Cheetah)
John Warden	Sheridan Barnett	Hannah Pang (Fulion)
	Monica Chong	Viviene Tam
FRANCE	Jasper Conrans	Florence Tse
France Andrevie	Wendy Dagworthy	
Dorothee Bis	Edina and Lena	**ITALY**
Marc Bohan	David and Elizabeth Emanuel	Giorgio Armani
Jean Cacharel	Betty Jackson	Claude Montana (Complice)
Pierre Cardin	Emmanuelle Khanh	Fabiani
Chloe	Jenni Ku	Fendi
André Courrèges	Stephan Linard	Giovanna Ferragamo
Christian Dior	Mulberry	Gianfranco Ferre
Givenchy	Jean Muir	Galitzine
Alix Gres	Megumi Ohki and Barbara	Muriel Grateau
Philippe Guibourge	Kennington (Lumiere)	Mariuccia Mandelli (Krizia)
Daniel Hechter	Bruce Oldfield	Andre Laug
Karl Lagerfeld	Arabella Pollen	Tai and Rosita Missoni
Guy Laroche	Wendy Regg	Emilo Pucci
MicMac	Zandra Rhodes	Heinz Riva
Hanae Mori	John Richmond	Luciano Soprani (Basile)
Thierry Mugler	Belleville Sassoon	Tiziani
André Oliver	Stevie Stewart and David	Mario Valentino
Jean Patou	Holah (Body Maps)	Gianni Versace
Gerald Pipart	Kojix Taksuno	
Paco Rabanne	Jan Vanvelden	**JAPAN**
George Rech	Janice Wainwright	Kensho Abe
Sonia Rykiel	Vivienne Westwood	Yoshki Hishinuma
Yves St. Laurent	Dexter Wong	Shin Hoskokawa
Kenzo Takado		Hitoshi Imai
Emanuel Ungaro		Rei Kawakubo
Philippe Venet		Matsuhiro Matsuda
		Issey Mikaye
		Sosuke Oguri
		Koshin Satoh
		Thisato Tsumori
		Kansai Yamamoto
		Yohji Yamamoto

sailles. This trade fair brings together more than 1,000 exhibitors, not only from France but from all over the world.

The strength and importance of French ready-to-wear is growing each season, with more and more trade buyers attending the shows. But the haute couture is also regaining some of its former importance and prestige with the revival of romance, elegance, and sophistication. The fit and construction of clothing is once again important, and elegant clothes design still has its finest practitioners in the haute couture.

The semiannual men's ready-to-wear show, *Salon de l'Habillement Masculin* (S.E.H.M.), is held in February and September and is as important to the men's industry as prêt-à-porter is to women's wear. It is also held at the Porte de Versailles while the designers hold their special shows in their showrooms or in large salons around the city. The *S.E.H.M.* itself is international, and all of the leading European menswear designers can be seen there. The show covers every aspect of men's clothing, from the most casual to the most elegant, including suits, dress shirts, ties, and accessories.

EXPORT EFFORTS. In an effort to promote the export of more ready-to-wear for both men and women, French apparel manufacturers formed a trade association in the early 1970s. Called *Féderation Française des Industries de l'Habillement,* this is roughly the equivalent of the American Apparel Manufacturers Association. In order to carry on its work, this association maintains offices in major countries throughout the world. When the French Apparel Center opened in New York in 1972, its main function was to help the federation publicize and promote French ready-to-wear to the American market. This Center plays a major role in helping member firms find agents for their products. It also assists in planning retail store promotions featuring French apparel products and carries on a number of other related activities.

Many major French designers and ready-to-wear firms—including Yves St. Laurent's Rive Gauche, Daniel Hechter, Cacharel, and MicMac—now have their own offices in New York. This enables them to handle the volume of business done in the United States and to reach those buyers who do not travel to Paris.

ITALY

Although not as large or as prestigious in the fashion world as France, Italy has come a long way in the past decade and is now considered a major fashion market. In the past few years, new and extremely innovative designers, such as Tai and Rosita Missoni, Giorgio Armani, and Gianni Versace, have made the Milan showings a must on the European fashion tour. The Milan showings have had a major impact on worldwide fashion trends and now generate an excitement and fashion newness that once emanated only from Paris.

In addition to providing a major market for women's apparel in the Milan showings, Italy has also achieved outstanding fashion leadership in menswear, fine knitwear, and leather accessories. Today, when one thinks of fine leather handbags and shoes, beautifully designed and handsomely crafted, Italian designers such as Ferragamo and Gucci come to mind. In the last few years, the growth in exports of Italian-made and -designed men's apparel to the United States has rivaled that of Italian-made women's wear. Italian menswear designers responsible for this growth include Basile, Giorgio Armani, and Gianni Versace. Fendi's innovative designs and expert execution of fur fashions have made this name an international synonym for exciting and creative fur designs.

Italian Couture

Like France, Italy has long had couture houses named for the famous designers who head them—Galitzine, Pucci, Valentino, Heinz Riva, Tiziani, Fabiani, and Andre Laug, for example. These houses are all members of Italy's couture trade association known as the *Alta Moda Italiana.* Unlike French couture houses, however, Italian houses are not all located in a single city. Many are in Rome, but others are in Milan, and a few are in other Italian cities.

Both Italian and French couture heavily depend on Italian fabric and yarn design. Much

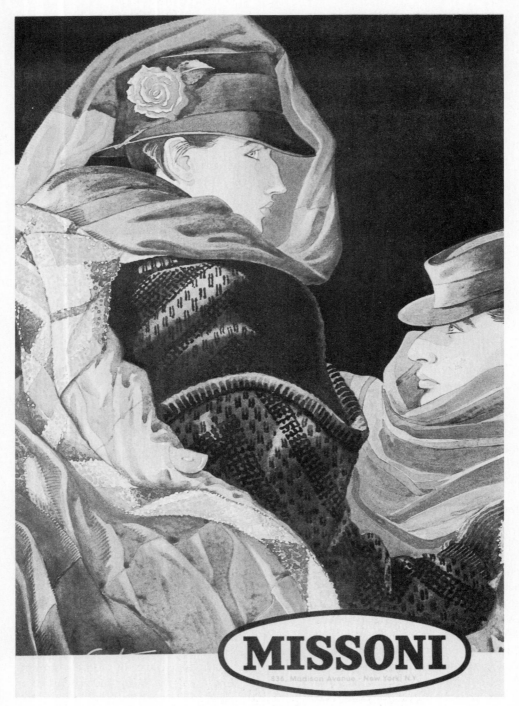

Italy too has couture houses named for the designers who head them.

of the innovation in print and woven textile design is created and produced in the fabric mills of Italy. Innovation also characterizes both the yarn mills (note the international importance of the *Pitti Maglia,* and the Italian Yarn Show) and the knitters who buy the yarns and produce the world-famous Italian knits.

COUTURE SHOWINGS. Members of the *Alta Moda* show their high-fashion collections semiannually in Milan and Rome to private customers, retailers and manufacturers, and the press. The showings are scheduled to take place just before the Paris couture-collection showings, so that foreign visitors can cover both important fashion markets in a single European trip. Italian couture houses not participating in the Milan showings usually arrange to show their collections either in their own salons or in some other location during the same period, also for the convenience of foreign visitors.

As in Paris, buyers and manufacturers are required to pay a caution to attend the Italian couture showings. Private customers and the press are admitted free, although cards of admission are required for the latter.

OTHER COUTURE
BUSINESS ACTIVITIES. Many Italian couture houses, like their Paris counterparts, have set up boutiques for the sale of exclusive accessories and limited lines of apparel. The designs are usually those of the couture house staff, and the apparel and accessories are sometimes made in the couture workrooms. All items offered in the boutique bear the couture house label.

In addition, many Italian couture houses now have high-fashion, ready-to-wear lines. These are sold either in their own shops or to retail distributors throughout Europe, in the United States, and, to an increasing extent, in Japan. For example, Valentino's ready-to-wear is sold in more than 20 stores in the United States and is also distributed in Japan.

More and more Italian couture designers also have licensing agreements with foreign producers. Some design and produce uniforms for employees of business firms, such as airlines. Some accept commissions to create designs for a wide range of fashion products, from menswear to home furnishings.

Italian Ready-to-Wear
Italy began to develop both its women's and men's ready-to-wear industries, separate from that of haute couture, earlier than France did. As a result, it started exporting earlier, and today its economy relies heavily on its exporting program. Much of this exported merchandise is in the medium-high price range, especially in knitwear and accessories.

DESIGNERS. Innovative Italian ready-to-wear designers make their shows as exciting as the Paris ready-to-wear shows have become. Among the better-known Italian designers who may work for one or more ready-to-wear firms are Mariuccia Mandelli, Claude Montana, Luciano Soprani, Gianni Versace, and Muriel Grateau. Among widely known designers who head their own firms are Giorgio Armani, Giovanna Ferragamo, and Rosita and Tai Missoni. Among well-known Italian ready-to-wear firms are Krizia, Gianfranco Ferre, Basile, Callaghan, Ken Scott, Cadette, Mirsa, Tiktiner, and Fendi. (See Table 14-1.)

TRADE SHOWS
AND MARKET CENTERS. Preparing a calendar of Italian showings of women's ready-to-wear was a fairly simple matter until the late 1960s. As interest in ready-to-wear grew and Paris initiated its semiannual prêt-à-porter showings, Italian ready-to-wear producers followed suit. Since many of these producers were located in Florence—a city that already had an established reputation as a fashion center—regular, semiannual showings of both ready-to-wear and accessories began to be held

in both the Pitti and Strossi palaces in Florence. The showings were scheduled for the week before the prêt-à-porter showings in Paris, for the convenience of foreign visitors.

Along with the exhibits and showings of regular ready-to-wear lines, both the Florence and the Milan shows include some ready-to-wear collections of Italian couture houses. These collections are known as the *Alta Moda Pronto*. In addition to the couture and ready-to-wear shows, the more volume-oriented knitwear show (*MAIT*) is held in Florence in February. This is well attended by American buyers because of its importance in sweater design.

Men's ready-to-wear shows are held in Florence in February and in September. Since 1980, *Uomo Modo*, the twice-a-year show of Italian Menswear Manufacturers, gives American and Canadian buyers a preview of these manufacturers' spring designs before they are shown in Italy. These shows are increasing in importance with the growing number of talented designers producing menswear apparel and furnishings.

Accessories

Italy has always been a fashion leader in the design and manufacture of leather accessories. Shoes, handbags, gloves, and small leather goods are a major part of Italy's fashion industry. Other accessories that are world-famous are silk scarfs and knitted hats, scarfs, and gloves. Because of the Italian finesse in designing these accessories they have become major exports to the rest of the world.

The importance of accessories to the well-dressed European public is well known, and this message has been carried to the United States by buyers shopping Italian fashion markets. Today, well-designed accessories are a fashion must for the well-dressed, fashion-conscious American public. Because of the importance of Italian fashion accessories, many accessories fairs are held all over Italy. The most famous of them are held in Lake Como, Florence, Milan, Bologna, and Rome.

Mipel is the name of the trade show for Italian-produced handbags and other accessories such as luggage, belts, umbrellas, hats, and scarfs. This important show is held in Milan twice each year, in January and in June. The *Mipel* show is sometimes too late to allow some American buyers to place orders and be sure of receiving delivery by the start of the coming season. For this reason, an earlier show, called *Europel*, was instituted in 1974. This show concentrates on handbags and small leather goods and features exhibitors from all over Europe, as well as Italian producers. Although originally sponsored by Italian handbag manufacturers, *Europel* has held shows in Paris, Düsseldorf, and Berlin, as well as in Rome and Florence.

The famous shoe show held in Bologna in March is considered very important by foreign buyers because of the importance of Italy's shoe industry and the large quantity of shoe exports. Among famous Italian shoe manufacturers are Ferragamo and Gucci. The glove industry, centered around Naples, is represented in many fashion fairs, as is women's neckwear, produced mainly in the Lake Como and Milan areas.

Another interesting fashion fair is the famous *Ideacomo*, held at Lake Como in early May. It is here that the Italian fashion fabric producers show new designs and fabric textures for use in the following year's fashion apparel and accessories.

GREAT BRITAIN

For many years, London was for menswear what Paris has been for women's apparel—the fountainhead of fashion inspiration. In recent years its dominance has diminished, and Italy has become the main source of European-styled menswear. But London still remains the major fashion center for impeccably tailored custom apparel for men.

Britain's most important fashion strength, however, lies in tweeds, woolens, and knitwear for both men and women. The materials for these garments come not only from the mills of the Midlands of England but also from Scotland and Northern Ireland. Britain is also a growing market center for leather apparel for both women and men.

London Couture

The British Fashion Council, which was formed in 1982 by Britain's fashion industry, is supported by the Clothing Export Council, the British Clothing Industry Association, and the Fashion in Action group. It is working to boost London as an international fashion center. The B.F.C., as it is known, has given top priority to making London a fashion mecca again, reminiscent of the sixties. It was during these years that London's mods and rockers, with their wide ties and miniskirts, set the fashion tone for the youth revolution. In conjunction with London Fashion Fair, the B.F.C. produces a diary of all events that take place during London Fashion Week, including designer shows, and all the leading events that are associated with London Fashion Fair at Olympia Exhibition Center.

The Individual Clothes Show was established in 1977 as a platform for young designers who at that time were not able to exhibit in major exhibitions. Since then, the I.C.S. has shown at Olympia within a specially designed pavilioned area, and in a short time has become one of the important groups of designers in Britain. In 1984, 49 young designers presented under the Individual Clothes Show/ Clothes Show Collection banner at Olympia.[4]

British Ready-to-Wear

England was long a nation in which people relied heavily on made-to-measure apparel. Its ready-to-wear industry was of minor fashion importance both at home and abroad until after World War II. The British government is given credit for having played an active role in its growth. In fact, the British government has for many years been engaged in nurturing its apparel industries. According to one of England's best-known fashion authorities, Britain's Board of Trade has been "the fairy godmother to whom is due the survival of their couture and the rapid development of their large and excellent ready-to-wear trade."[5]

WOMEN'S APPAREL. Like its American and continental counterparts, British ready-to-wear for women is divided into three categories: high-fashion (usually high-priced), moderate-priced, and mass-produced (popular-priced). High-fashion ready-to-wear is usually the product of couture houses in Britain, but has rarely been considered trend-setting. British moderate- and popular-priced ready-to-wear was considered of little fashion importance until the 1960s.

Early in the 1960s, however, a London designer named Mary Quant recognized an emerging youth trend and began designing clothes for the young. Other London designers quickly followed her lead, and almost overnight London became the world's fashion market center for junior apparel.

The fashion trend in the early 1970s, however, moved toward longer, softer, more romantic styles. When the British ready-to-wear industry failed to follow, London began to lose fashion importance again. But backed by the British government and led by three London designers—Jean Muir, Zandra Rhodes, and Ossie Clark—who had sprung to prominence in the 1960s, a new group of young designers began to exert impact on the London fashion scene. By 1983 London had become fashionable again, as it was in the 1960s. New, young, innovative designers, products of England's famous design schools, such as the Royal College

London Fashion Headlines

Showing for Spring/Summer '84   October 9–12

JAN VANVELDEN

EDINA
AND LENA

MEGUMI OHKI AND BARBARA KENNINGTON
FOR LUMIERE

JENNI KU

ROLAND KLEIN

ARABELLA POLLEN

MONICA CHONG

WENDY DAGWORTHY

MULBERRY

DAVID AND ELIZABETH EMANUEL

Forces are at work to boost London as an international fashion center.

of Art, the London College of Fashion, and St. Martin, were once again shocking, teasing, and tempting the fashion world with their outrageous designs. Vivienne Westwood, Stephan Linard, Janice Wainwright, Bruce Oldfield, Belleville Sassoon, and Jasper Conrans are all new talents sparking the fashion scene in Great Britain. The English are very individual in their approach to fashion. Many of the designs of these new, innovative talents are being bought by United States stores such as Bloomingdale's, Macy's, and Henri Bendel.

London is the center of Britain's women's ready-to-wear industry, and the major manufacturers' trade associations have headquarters there. Most permanent showrooms of ready-to-wear producers are located there, although there also are showrooms in the Midlands and in Scotland. The major ready-to-wear shows take place in London. The International Fashion Fair, sponsored by the Clothing Export Council of Great Britain, is held each April and October. However, English designers sadly attribute their inability to capitalize on their design talents and ideas to the hopeless number of production problems of the domestic industry, and the rather unspectacular way collections are presented to international buyers and to the press.[6]

MENSWEAR.   Both London and Harrogate are important market centers for menswear. The major trade associations are located in London. So are many of the permanent showrooms of menswear producers, although others are located elsewhere in England and Scotland. One important trade show, the International Men's and Boys' Wear Exhibition, has some 200 British and continental firms exhibiting and is held in London in February. However, a bigger menswear show, the Menswear Association Convention and Exhibition, is held in Harrogate in September. At this show, about 300 exhibitors (90 percent British and 10 percent from the Continent, Australia, Japan, and Yugoslavia) show their lines. For the American customer, the major British menswear designers and manufacturers can be seen at the previously referred to S.E.H.M. show in Paris. The best-known companies also have showrooms or representatives in the United States to work with their customers in this country.

Savile Row.   Savile Row is both the name of a historic short London street and also an adjective that, when used to modify the word "suit," conjures up visions of impeccably tailored men's suits. Savile Row is a wonderful place where each suit is handcrafted for its new owner, a process that can take 6 to 10 weeks. Many shops require at least three individual fittings. All this effort adds up to high prices— as much as $1,000 a suit. However, a Savile Row suit is expected to last 20 to 50 years. It has long been predicted that because of its high prices and time-consuming tailoring, and the change in male fashions and tastes, Savile Row is doomed. But somehow it hasn't disappeared.

SCANDINAVIA

While the four Scandinavian countries—Norway, Sweden, Denmark, and Finland—each has its own fashion industries and specialties, these countries do form a single identifiable market center. This is partly because they tend to have the same basic materials with which to work: leather, fur, some wool, an increasing amount of textiles made of artificial fibers, some gold, and silver. However, the main reason is that the four countries, while they do make individual marketing efforts, hold major trade fairs and maintain permanent showrooms in one central location: Copenhagen. This is the dominant center of the Scandinavian fashion world.

Fashion Products
Conservative, high-style wool apparel, including coats, dresses, and suits, has long been the

specialty of the Danish apparel industry. Prices are generally high.

Moderate-priced apparel is particularly strong among the Swedish, Finnish, and Norwegian offerings. Some is cotton knit, but man-made fibers and cotton blends are more common. Styling is often youthful; a Swedish sportswear producer is among those who claim to have introduced the string bikini to the United States in the fall of 1973.

Leather apparel, primarily in menswear, is a popular Swedish product. Both Sweden and Norway are among the important suppliers of mink and other furs to countries around the world. Birgir Christiansen is a leading furrier.

Scandinavia offers some interesting textile designs. Both American producers and retail buyers, interested in finding unusual fabrics to have made up for special promotions, watch the Scandinavian textile offerings very closely, especially the offerings of Finland's Marimekko.

Excellent jewelry in all price ranges is available in Scandinavia. The area has long been known for its clean-cut designs in gold and silver. Today, an increasing amount of costume jewelry and ''fun jewelry'' is being produced there, particularly in Sweden.

Trade Shows

Each Scandinavian country holds its own national fairs in the city that is considered its trade center. However, the major market center for the whole of Scandinavia is Copenhagen. It is here that Bella Centrat is located; the international Scandinavian trade fairs are held in Bella Centrat. The apparel fairs are organized by the Scandinavian Clothing Council, headquartered in Copenhagen and made up of representatives from the national clothing associations of each Scandinavian country. The important women's apparel fair, called the Scandinavian Fashion Week, is held semiannually, usually in March and September. The Scandinavian Menswear Fair is also held twice a year, usually in February and in September. Both draw exhibitors from all the Scandinavian countries and from a number of other countries as well.

WEST GERMANY

The Federal Republic of Germany is better known to American producers than to American retail buyers. The huge *Interstoff* textiles fair, held in Frankfurt each May and November, is a very important place to find and buy new fabrics and new fashion ideas. Frankfurt is also one of the four big fur auction centers of the world, and its Fur Fair is held in April.

Up until the mid-1980s most Americans who followed international fashion usually skipped West Germany. Few German designers were well-known outside Western Europe. But a new wave of high-fashion designers who brought their collections to the giant *Igedo* fashion fair started to make this country a forward force in world fashion. *Igedo* is Germany's international fair for fashion. Held in Düsseldorf and scheduled to show six times a year, it is the largest fashion fair for women's ready-to-wear, accessories, and intimate apparel in Europe. It has more than 2,200 exhibitors representing 24 countries in its 1.25-million-square-foot fair space, similar to the Porte de Versailles in Paris. In 1983 over 22,300 buyers attended *Igedo*.

Germany is just beginning to increase its apparel exports beyond Europe. The West German fashion designers are attempting to target the better-designer American market by coming to New York and staging celebrity-studded shows of German high fashion. Their plan is to continue these shows over the next few years; the plan is backed by most members that show at *Igedo*.

The center of Germany's women's ready-to-wear industry is Düsseldorf. Here four fairs a year are held. There is also a fashion fair in Munich each March, and an Overseas Export Fair in Berlin every September. The center of

Igedo is the largest European fashion fair for women's ready-to-wear.

the menswear industry is Cologne, where major menswear fairs are held in February and August. There are numerous accessories fairs: the most important is the Leathergoods Fair held in Offenbach in February and August.

LATIN AMERICA

French and Italian have been the traditional foreign languages of fashion. By the mid-1970s, however, Spanish and Portuguese, spoken in Latin American accents, had been added to the list. Fashion merchants began visiting such market centers as Rio de Janeiro, Buenos Aires, São Paulo, and Bogotá.

Two factors encouraged fashion merchants in the United States to pay attention to Latin America, which includes Central America, South America, and the Caribbean area. One factor was inflation. The other was the level of achievement reached by the developing nations of Latin America.

Inflation in the 1970s cut sharply into American fashion merchants' traditional sources of textiles, apparel, and accessories. Because of inflation, Japan was temporarily priced out of its textile and textile products export business. American producers and retailers had to look elsewhere for goods at more reasonable prices.

Many countries of Latin America have reached a level of development where they can offer foreign buyers the goods they want at attractive prices. These countries have important raw materials, such as cotton, wool, leather, and the materials for man-made textiles, and have built networks of industries that are eager for export opportunities so that they can expand. These industries are being encouraged by their governments, because additional exports mean both an increase in gross national product and an increase in international trade status. These industries also have a good labor supply. Because the standard of living in these countries is not as high as elsewhere, the cost of this labor is not as high.

Fashion Products

As a result, Latin America has emerged in recent years as a market center for three different kinds of fashion goods. First, its most advanced countries already have industries producing a variety of fashion-right goods. Second, many countries in this geographic area offer increasingly greater quantities of unusual fashion goods that reflect each country's national heritage in arts and crafts. Third, the countries' production facilities and labor can turn out a variety of fashion goods to the specifications of American producers and retailers at relatively low prices.

Important industries producing both women's and men's apparel already exist in Argentina, Brazil, Colombia, and Uruguay. Argentina and Uruguay are probably the largest South American producers of apparel in both the moderate- and upper-price ranges, wool being a very important fabric. Brazil is particularly strong in sportswear. Colombia is an important market center for menswear. Together with the Dominican Republic and most of the Central American countries, Colombia produces popular-priced lines of men's sport shirts, particularly of the shirt-jac variety. Bolivia has a somewhat smaller apparel industry than the other three major countries of South America, but it offers some unusual styles of excellent quality.

Handbag buyers are likely to go to Argentina for better-quality goods, to Brazil for moderate-quality goods, and to Colombia for lower-quality goods. Uruguay is another source of handbags, producing moderate- to high-quality goods.

Perhaps the single most important market center for shoes in Latin America is Brazil. Brazilian shoe manufacturers concentrate on producing well-styled merchandise in lasts that fit North American feet. For belts and small leather goods, some of the major market centers are in Brazil, Argentina, and the Dominican Republic.

For costume jewelry, the major center is Brazil. A number of Latin American countries produce silver and gold jewelry of native design, with Ecuador and Peru having some of the most interesting offerings.

Fashion Production

For those producers or retailers who are interested in having contract work done in Latin America, there are many possibilities. Considerable contract work is already being done in Mexico, El Salvador, Costa Rica, and Haiti. Contract work is also being done in free trade zones in Latin America. **Free trade zones** are secure areas, usually located in or near customs ports of entry, that are regarded as legally outside a nation's customs territory. The primary purpose of these zones is to facilitate manufacturing for export or transshipment without compliance with customs laws. The Dominican Republic has five free trade zones, and contract work for U.S. fashion merchants is being done in each one of them. There is also a free trade zone in Colombia, where one Japanese firm has a plant employing 600 workers.

Most of the countries mentioned above have facilities that specialize in high-volume, moderate-quality, low-price goods. However, there are also opportunities for those who want to have top-quality work done. Ecuador, for instance, can only handle a small amount of contract work, but it specializes in producing top-quality goods.

As traditional Far East manufacturing sources such as Hong Kong, Taiwan, and South Korea become more expensive and quotas become more restricted, American apparel firms are looking for new sources for offshore production. Increasing numbers of American garment companies are looking at the Caribbean area for offshore manufacturing as a means of competing effectively in the United States against low-cost imported garments from the Orient.

The countries that make up the Caribbean basin offer American garment manufacturers many incentives that make manufacturing in the Caribbean very attractive: hourly wages that average between $.60 and $1.00, no import quota restrictions, liberal tax incentives, proximity to the United States, and governments ready to assist foreign investors. Kurt Salmon Associates completed a survey in 1984 that concluded that the Caribbean will become one of the fastest-growing offshore manufacturing regions.

Under **Item 807 of the U.S. Tariff Schedule,** apparel firms can ship cut fabrics overseas, have them assembled into finished garments, and import the garments into the United States at minimum (or added-value) duty rates. Much of Item 807 manufacturing is done in the Caribbean basin. Because of the proximity of the area, turnaround time for U.S. apparel makers is shorter, and the use of American-made textiles is easier than dealing with Europe or the Far East. Although many apparel manufacturers are just beginning to make major commitments to Item 807 manufacturing, textile companies have been active since 1982. West Point Pepperell, Dan River, and J. P. Stevens are all producing apparel in the Caribbean basin under Item 807.

Trade Shows

Probably the single most important market center in South America is São Paulo, Brazil. An international textile and textile products fair is held there every January and June, with exhibitors not only from Latin America but from other areas of the world as well. This trade show draws some 60,000 buyers from around the world.

Other important international fairs featuring textiles and textile products as well as fashion accessories are held in Bogotá, Colombia; Lima, Peru; and San Salvador, El Salvador. All three are annual fairs.

CANADA

The Canadian fashion industry may be something that most people haven't known or thought about when the word "fashion" is used. Most buyers automatically look to European-designed garments for fashion direction. But the fashion industry is the fifth largest employer in Canada. And with the growing importance of a larger market for Canadian designers and manufacturers, fashion newness and fashion importance are coming increasingly from Canada. The Canadian ready-to-wear look is typically described by designers and buyers as combining American fit and commercial sense with European styling and flavor.

Outerwear, of course, has long been a Canadian specialty. The history of the country is intertwined with the history of fur and skin trading in the New World. And the Canadian Outerwear Fashion Fair (C.O.F.F.), whose annual show is held in Winnipeg, Manitoba, is the largest such convention in North America. Manufacturers exhibit furs, leathers, skiwear, heavy knitted goods, and down and wool coats at this show.

In both Montreal and Toronto, ready-to-wear designers agree that the future of the fashion industry is in exporting if they are to make news in the world market. Well-known female Canadian designers of women's wear include Pat McDonogh, who got her start designing clothes for Diana Rigg in the *Avengers* TV series and now designs contemporary high-fashion ready-to-wear; Norma Lepofsky, who designs better-priced novelty-knit jackets and sweaters; Claire Haddah, who designs outer loungewear; and Linda Lundstrom, who designs and sells moderate-priced dresses, separates, and patented, adjustable jeans. Elen Henderson designs children's wear. Among the well-known male designers in Canada are Leo Chevalier, Alfred Sung, Wayne Clark, and John Warden. Canadian designers are well-known for high-fashion, well-made clothing designs and are selling well in the United States.

Much of the current recognition of Canadian fashion designers has been due to the inspiration set by Fashion Canada, *Mode du Canada*. As an association chartered by the Canadian Federal Government in 1973–1974, it instituted a fashion scholarship program and fostered a marketing program using effective advertising and publicity to aid the worldwide recognition of Canadian fashion designers.

THE FAR EAST

In the past, the mention of Far East merchandise conjured up an image of cheap, poorly made merchandise usually found in inexpensive shops in the United States. In general, since the 1950s, the Far East has been the source of low-price, low-quality, high-volume merchandise. American buyers came to depend upon the Far East as a source of low-cost production.

However, the highly developed Asian countries, such as Japan and Hong Kong, have become important participants in the mainstream of fashion and sophistication. As they took on Western standards of living, technology, and customs, their fashion direction turned more and more to designing and creating rather than to copying.

When fashion buyers refer to the Far East, they are talking about a large group of countries, each known for its styling and workmanship in different price points and qualities. For fashion buyers, the major countries of the Far East are Japan, Hong Kong, Korea, Taiwan, Sri Lanka, India, Singapore, Malaysia, China, and the Philippines.

The United States imports more apparel from the Far East than from any other area in the world. However, the major portion of these imports has been low-priced, high-volume merchandise, and hardly any of the apparel would have qualified as "designer merchandise." There are definite signs that this situation is beginning to change, and now fashion buyers can find exciting, innovative styles offered by new design-oriented Asian stylists.

Elen Henderson   CANADA

SPRING-SUMMER 1985

Ken Rosenthal Sales
112 West 34th Street
New York, NY 10120
U.S.A.
(212) 564-3890

Canadian designers' work is increasingly popular in the American market.

Buyers have used certain countries in the Far East as a market in which to have fashions they saw in the European fashion centers copied and adapted. A fashion buyer needs to know which areas in the Far East are best equipped to handle specific types of manufacturing. Japan and Hong Kong were once the two major contract or copyist countries. But these countries have upgraded their fashion images, so that today they are outstanding fashion producers of high-styled, high-priced fashion apparel.

Japan

The success of the Japanese in marketing automobiles and consumer electronics is legendary. The Japanese have cornered the market in these areas. Now, they are applying the same effort and skill to the apparel and textile markets with high hopes for similar success.

Apparel accounts for more than half of the finished goods that Japan exports to the United States, and in medium- to high-priced clothing the Japanese are making a significant impact on the U. S. fashion industry. Kalman Ruttenstein, vice-president and fashion director at Bloomingdale's, says Japan's current renaissance in fashion reminds him of "London in the '60s, when street fashion a la Carnaby Street became a major influence."[7]

Many Japanese boutiques in Tokyo have their own design staffs, who create exciting new looks. The Tokyo boutiques are very individualistic, and because of their ability to turn their fashion goods very quickly, the Tokyo fashion scene is often 6 months to a year ahead of other fashion centers.

JAPANESE READY-TO-WEAR. In the 1950s and 1960s the Japanese faithfully copied Western trends. In the 1970s individualistic Japanese designers began to emerge, first in Paris, where designers such as Hanae Mori, Kenzo Takada, Issey Miyake, and Kansai Yamamoto became design sensations with their prêt-à-porter showings that rivaled those of young French designers. In fact, for almost a decade these daring, avant-garde designers were thought of as part of the Paris fashion scene, not of a Japanese fashion world.

Today, Japan has many famous designers, all world-famous for innovative, experimental, and flamboyant designs. The trends in Japanese design have little to do with the Western concept of clothing that reveals those parts of the body considered fashionably erotic while distorting or concealing others. Such considerations as length of hemline or position of waistline are considered irrelevant. Japanese design encourages mobility and comfort.

DESIGNERS. The outstanding exponents of the new Japanese design are Issey Miyake, Rei Kawakubo of Comme des Garçons, Yohji Yamamoto, and Matsuhiro Matsuda. Matsuda opened a boutique in New York in 1983 and designs from Comme des Garçons were given boutiques of their own in Henri Bendel and Bloomingdale's. In late 1983 a Comme des Garçons freestanding boutique opened in Soho, a chic, sophisticated shopping area in New York City. Display windows of the leading fashion stores in New York, Dallas, and San Francisco all feature Japanese designers in their fashion presentations.

Japanese designers specialize in vertical-integration operations. Kansai Yamamoto, for instance, designs, manufactures, wholesales, and retails both in Japan and all over the world. In Japan, he has 200 retail outlets and four freestanding stores, and leases space in 40 department stores. He employs and trains for these leased departments much the way our cosmetics companies train line salespeople. Overseas, he wholesales to 350 accounts in Europe, 200 accounts in America, 50 in Australia, and 10 in South Africa, as well as opening his own stores.[8]

FASHION TRADE SHOWS. Since the mid-1970s, Japan has sponsored a Tokyo Fashion Week. This semiannual fashion fair is held in January and July and is the combined effort

By 1980 Tokyo was being hailed as the fashion frontier of the 1980s.

of over 150 Tokyo fashion apparel producers. By 1983, Tokyo was being hailed as the fashion frontier of the 1980s. Fashion buyers and fashion editors headed to the East to sample Japanese fashion, Japanese culture, and Japanese customs at the source. The Tokyo fashion scene blended Japanese art with American graphics, ancient traditions with microtechnology.

Hong Kong

Hong Kong has made a dramatic shift from carrying out copying and contracting work to creating and producing its own fashion designs. Hong Kong sponsors a fashion week each year, inviting buyers from all over the world to come to Hong Kong and view the exotic fabrics and fashions of its designers and manufacturers. Hong Kong has also presented fashion shows here in the United States, taking them from coast to coast to show American buyers innovative and exciting styling and designs. In 1984, at the NRMA Convention, the Hong Kong fashion presentation was one of the highlights of this convention of retailers.

In 1981, Hong Kong had a fashion pavilion at the ready-to-wear exposition at the Porte de Versailles. Eighty-eight manufacturers spent more than $1 million reproducing a Chinese village and staging a fashion show of 220 styles meant to demonstrate to fashion apparel buyers that Hong Kong can produce more than knitwear and blue jeans. In addition to trying to interest foreign designers in using their production facilities, the Hong Kong manufacturers are trying to interest buyers in their original designs and styles.

Hong Kong manufacturing facilities are used by Calvin Klein and Oscar de la Renta from the United States, as well as by Pierre Cardin, Givenchy, and Dior from Paris. Currently, Hong Kong is the world's largest exporter of fashion apparel, but its strength has been in production, not in the introduction of new designs. It is the hope of the fashion industry in Hong Kong that with more shows presented worldwide, and more young innovative designers working with fine fabrics and fine workmanship, the fashion future of Hong Kong will lie not only in its fine production facilities, but also in its fine designs.

Korea

With much the same design history as the Japanese, Korea has some exciting young designers creating for the Korean fashion-conscious market. One of them, Maria Kim, has also established a successful volume-priced knitwear business in the United States.

Much of the production of ready-to-wear in Korea is still contract work. But because of the fashion design movement among young Koreans, this is slowly beginning to change.

Taiwan

In Taiwan there is a definite upgrading in the quality of work being produced. Taiwan closely follows Hong Kong in the variety and innovation of knitwear technology. To stimulate and build a more fashion-oriented and higher-priced market, the Taiwan Textile Federation was established. Under its aegis, young Taiwanese designers and technicians are being trained in fashion design and execution. In addition, *Garmen Taipei,* an interesting showcase of what is being produced in Taiwan, is held in Taipei each October.

India

The traditional fabric designs and garments of India have had a profound impact on world fashion. Gauze, madras, and the native *kurta* (tunic worn over easy-fitting pants) had a tremendous influence on American fashion in the mid-sixties and seventies and are increasing in importance in the eighties.

People's Republic of China

In the future, the People's Republic of China may become one of the most interesting market centers of the Far East. As yet, only a small amount of fashion buying by American retailers is taking place in China. But many retailers expect Chinese–U. S. trade to increase tremendously, especially since the United States reestablished diplomatic and trade relations in 1978. For example, in 1980, Bloomingdale's launched a $10 million promotion featuring Chinese imports.

The People's Republic of China holds a very important semiannual trade fair in Guangzhou (formerly Canton). But admission is by invitation only, and just a few hundred foreign firms are invited. Today, more American buyers and producers are being invited to visit China, with the long-range purpose of establishing a flourishing trade.

REFERENCES

[1] Carrie Donovan, "A Salute to Yves," *New York Times Magazine,* December 4, 1983, p. 160.

[2] Susan Heller Anderson, "The Sun Never Sets on His Empire," *The New York Times,* September 6, 1981, p. F5.

[3] Bernadine Morris, "Fashion Report," *The New York Times,* April 9, 1979, p. 8.

[4] *Women's Wear Daily,* March 16, 1984, p. 31.

[5] Madge Garland, *The Changing Form of Fashion,* Praeger Publishers, New York, 1971, p. 73.

[6] Christopher Petkanas and Caroline Hunter, "London," *Women's Wear Daily,* December 22, 1982, p. 6.

[7] "Now Japan Unveils High Fashion," *Business Week,* June 14, 1982, p. 85.

[8] *News Flash Tokyo,* The Fashion Group, Inc., February 24, 1983, p. 2.

MERCHANDISING VOCABULARY

Define or briefly explain the following terms:

Boutique

Caution

Chambre Syndicale

Commissionaire

Couture house (or "house")

Couturier, couturiere

First cost

Free trade zones

Haute couture

Item 807 of U.S. Tariff Schedule

Prêt-à-porter

MERCHANDISING REVIEW

1. What are the five different methods that American retail stores may employ when shopping for foreign goods?
2. Distinguish between a store's own foreign buying division and a commissionaire organization.
3. Name and describe the four different types of customers who attend the showings of couture designers.

4. Give four reasons why the sales volume of European couture houses has declined in recent years.
5. How have most Paris couture houses attempted to meet the growing challenge and competition of a rapidly developing ready-to-wear industry? To what extent has each of these business efforts been successful?
6. Name the fashion products for which each of the following countries or group of countries is noted: Canada, Italy, Scandinavia.
7. Discuss the developments of the British ready-to-wear industry. What designer was credited with making London the world's fashion market center for junior apparel?
8. Discuss the importance of West Germany as a fashion center.
9. What countries are included in the geographic area referred to as Latin America? The Caribbean? Name and discuss several reasons why these areas have become important fashion market centers in recent years.
10. Discuss the growing importance of Japan as a fashion center.

1. The reputation of Paris as a prime source of fashion inspiration began to develop several centuries ago as the result of many interrelating factors. Identify those factors and discuss their importance in the development of any major fashion design center.
2. What major countries make up the Far East? Discuss the importance of that geographic area to producers and retailers of fashion goods.

EXPLORING THE MARKETS OF FASHION

For this project you will research and study an American apparel manufacturer who is broadly recognized under a brand name or designer label. (You may choose a women's wear, menswear, or children's wear manufacturer.) The following information must be included:

1. Name of company.

2. History of the company. Include pertinent and human-interest material about how the company got started and how it developed to its present status.

3. Where is the company located? Include headquarters, sales office, out of town locations, and factory locations.

4. Describe the company's manufacturing setup. Is the company an inside or outside shop, or both? Does it participate in dual distribution?

5. Does the company have a designer? Is the designer an owner? Is there a design staff?

6. Does the company or designer have licensees who produce products other than the major items manufactured by the firm? If so, include the names of the licensees and what products they produce.

7. Who is the target audience for this manufacturer? Give a customer profile.

8. Is the line considered to be a pacesetter or advanced fashion line or mostly a mainstream fashion?

9. Does this company import any of the products it sells? If so, from what countries does this company import?

10. Who are the major retail clients of this company?

11. Is the company privately or publicly held? Was it always structured the way it is now?

12. What is the company's sales volume (most currently published figures)?

UNIT 3. THE MERCHANDISING OF FASHION

Fashion has many faces—different faces for different places, different looks for different years. . . .

It is the merchandisers of fashion who are constantly updating and refining the way the faces of fashion are presented to the consumer.

Because there are many types of consumers, there are many styles of merchandising, all kinds of retail establishments, and all sorts of different ways of presenting goods to the consumer.

Retailers must be consumer-oriented. They have to anticipate and react to changes in the marketplace. They have to seek out information about the societies in which they operate.

Unit 3 examines fashion retailing and then discusses the auxiliary services that aid the retailer in learning and meeting the needs and wants of the consumer. The four chapters discuss the following:

- The retail distributors of fashion— the different types and their history and development; merchandising and store policies; and how retailers organize themselves for buying and for selling.

- Trends in fashion retailing—ever-changing consumerism; increased competition; emerging forms of retail distribution; and various patterns of buying.

- Resident buying offices—how they got started and how they developed; the different types of offices, organizations, and services; and changing patterns and trends.

- Auxiliary fashion services—fashion magazines; trade publications; consumer and general publications; the broadcast media; advertising; publicity; public relations; fashion consultants; and market research agencies.

Fashion has a face for every taste. The merchandising of fashion involves knowing the right face for today's taste and understanding where and how to present it.

15. FASHION RETAILING

The nation's fashion retailers, who have faced constant changes since the turbulent 1960s, encountered economic storms in the early 1980s. Day by day they counted the beats of the nation's economic pulse for signs of recovery. As the most flexible of American industries, fashion retailing was, for the most part, able to adjust to the ever-fluctuating buying mood. Fashion retailers were able to see that for the United States, as for the world, the era of conspicuous consumption was over. Value received for money paid was demanded. If anything was obvious in the mid-1980s to fashion retailers— department stores, specialty stores, coast-to-coast chains, and discounters alike—it was that the market was a buyer's market. And the buyers were an increasingly knowledgeable and demanding public whose loyalty had to be first earned and then constantly renewed.

HISTORY AND DEVELOPMENT OF FASHION RETAILING

The term **retailing** refers to the business of buying goods from a variety of resources and assembling those goods in convenient locations for resale to consumers. **Fashion retailing** is the business of retailing fashion-oriented merchandise.

As mentioned in Unit 1, the term merchandising refers to the planning necessary on the part of a retailer in order to have the right merchandise at the right time, in the right place, in the right quantities, and at the right price (that is, at a price that the firm's customers are both willing and able to pay), and with the right promotion. It logically follows, therefore, that "fashion merchandising" refers to this planning where fashion-oriented merchandise is concerned. The merchandising function is the most important function in all retail organizations because in almost all cases, sales are the sole source of a store's revenue. In this chapter we will explore how various forms of retailing have developed and the means by which modern retail organizations seek customer patronage.

Early Retailing

History does not record the very first retail sale made in the world, though it is safe to assume that even in the dawn of civilization someone had something someone else wanted to own. It's possible that early people soon found it increasingly hard to fight to gain possession, and began to look for something to trade. We do know that the bazaars of the Orient and the marketplaces of the eastern Mediterranean, prototypes of today's shopping centers, represented the beginning of what today is called retailing.

Sailing ships and desert caravans brought rich silks and exotic spices from the East to be sold in early centers of population. Other traders brought pottery, foodstuffs, and precious metals. As all these goods—a lavish selection of many different types of merchandise—were gathered by a merchant to be sold in one location, the first "department" stores and "variety" stores were born. The first actual department store was opened in Paris in 1850 when the Bon Marché was created.

Other early traders actually produced the goods they offered for sale to customers. These were the master craftsmen—weavers, potters, goldsmiths—who often worked and maintained shops in their homes. They were also usually responsible for the training and maintaining of a number of apprentices, who learned and perfected their skills before opening shops of their own. Usually, makers of one kind of merchandise stayed in one loaction on a street or in an area. Customers therefore knew just where to go to find the producers of any particular product. These early shops were forerunners of today's specialty shops.

In early times, though most of the population clustered around the cities with their shops and bazaars, there were many who lived in sparsely settled areas at far distances from the cities. Their needs were looked after by yet another type of trader—the peddler. Peddlers were roving retailers who carried their wares on their backs, on pack animals, or in wagons. They covered many miles on a regular circuit to resell the goods they bought from traders to their isolated customers.

Development of Fashion Retailing in the United States

When the early explorers of the fourteenth, fifteenth, and sixteenth centuries returned from their first contact with the New World, they brought back to Europe a wealth of goods that bedazzled that already mature continent. Along with the Spanish conquistadors' gold came the highly prized furs and skins brought back by French and English explorers. Demand in Europe for these furs and skins proved to be so great that the various royal courts sponsored further exploration in the northern areas of the New World.

On the eastern coast of North America, where the majority of newly arrived people from Europe settled, new towns sprang up that reflected as closely as possible those the immigrants had left behind. Philadelphia, New York, and Boston were soon populous centers of commerce and culture. Their shops and stores were patterned after those of London and Paris, and soon the areas became quite sophisticated.

But along the ever-widening frontiers to the west, and in sparsely settled farming areas, other forms of retailing developed. The most important retail distribution center was the general store, which carried a wide assortment of consumer goods. For those in isolated areas, peddlers took on a role of great importance as they went from farm to farm and hamlet to hamlet with their always welcome varieties of merchandise. Later on, when mail service became more reliable, mail-order selling took its place as yet a third method of distributing consumer goods to the rural areas.

GENERAL STORES.

The rugged frontier and the widely scattered farming areas of North America created the need for a special kind of retail establishment. Thus was born the **general store**, carrying stocks of utilitarian items that the frontiersmen and women needed, from salt pork to saddles, from lamp oil to ladies' bonnets. Soon the general store became the community social and economic center, as well as the gathering place for political debate. Since money was a scarce commodity on the frontier, bartering became an important way of doing business; the general store took goods as well as cash in payment. As the frontier pushed westward and attracted more farmers and ranchers and their families, general stores began adding new kinds of goods to their assortments, such as basic dress fabrics and sewing notions.

Then, as settlers grew more prosperous, many sent away to stores on the East Coast for their fashion purchases—new dresses or shawls for the ladies, for example, and even "dress-up" suits for men. They also patronized the local specialty shops that appeared as the frontier towns grew. In the rural areas, however, the general store continued to thrive. To this day, it exists on a reduced scale as a focal point of many communities in rural areas of the South, West, and Northeast.

Gradually, the general stores turned from a barter system to a cash-only system. They thus became strictly dispensers of merchandise. Such were the beginnings of many of the nation's great general-merchandise and department stores. An outstanding example is Meier & Frank Co. in Portland, Oregon.

PEDDLERS.

Even with trading posts scattered along the frontier and general stores in towns, there was need for another kind of retailer. Remote homesteads, far from towns or well-traveled roads, welcomed the peddlers with their packs full of necessities and luxuries.

In the peddler's pack were pots and pans, shoes and boots, pins, thread, combs, ribbons, and laces. The peddlers also brought news, including information on the latest fashions in the cities back East. And the peddler took orders along the way for items to be delivered on the next trip, although the peddler's route was often so long that a year might pass in the meantime. The peddler also reported back to producers in the East about the items that pleased or displeased customers. Thus peddlers became the first "market analysts."

Peddlers disappeared as the nation grew. They were replaced by traveling salesmen, who took samples of merchandise to stores and shops along their route for the purpose of soliciting orders for at least some of the sampled merchandise. Door-to-door or in-house selling techniques are used to this day, but only for certain types of fashion merchandise. Cosmetics are probably the number-one fashion product sold in this manner today.

Yet it was one of those early peddlers who founded one of the country's largest retail organizations. Adam Gimbel, tired of a life of travel, set down his peddler's pack and opened a retail store in Vincennes, Indiana, in 1842. From this beginning grew the giant retail dynasty that later encompassed all Gimbel Brothers, Inc., stores as well as the prestigious and fashionable chain of stores known as Saks Fifth Avenue.

MAIL-ORDER SELLERS. Certainly no aspect of the retail business has had a more remarkable, ongoing role in the buying activities of the American people than mail-order selling. The mail-order business was begun in the late 1800s specifically for the millions of rural Americans who could not get to a store. It was made possible by the introduction of Rural Free Delivery of mail to far-flung points across the nation, and Parcel Post, which allowed packages of goods to be delivered by mail.

The first **mail-order company**—that is, a company that does the bulk of its sales and deliveries by mail—was Montgomery Ward, founded in 1872. It was followed in 1886 by Sears, Roebuck, and the mail-order business was soon in full swing.

The mail-order catalog brought a new world to the lives of rural Americans. Hundreds of fashion items, furnishings for the home, and tools for the farm were illustrated, described, and priced. The fashions were not necessarily exciting. But the variety and prices delighted rural women, who had been limited to the scant provisions of the general store or the peddler's pack. A whole new world of fashion was opened to these women, and they eagerly responded. By 1895, only 9 years after its first issue, the Sears, Roebuck catalog boasted 507 pages. The fledgling company posted sales at three-quarters of a million dollars that year.

By the 1920s, the presence of the automobile was felt even in rural areas. Mail-order companies began to open retail stores in these areas to meet the competition of city stores now accessible by automobile. By the 1930s, mail-order companies began to open catalog centers. Here customers could come and write up their own orders. Salespeople were available to help them in selecting merchandise from the catalog. In addition to catalog centers, each of the Big Three general-merchandise chains—Sears, Roebuck, JC Penney, and Montgomery Ward—today maintains a catalog desk in its retail stores. Here customers may place orders for catalog items that are not carried in

In the latter part of the nineteenth century, the Montgomery Ward catalogs opened a whole new world of fashion to rural Americans who lived far away from shopping centers.

that store's stock, and they can do this in person, by mail, or by telephone.

The convenience of shopping at home by mail order is still widely used today. Once the province of rural dwellers, mail ordering has gained new customers in the nation's cities. Today department and specialty stores direct a considerable amount of money and effort to generating business through their catalogs and other forms of direct mail, which have become increasingly more elaborate and more frequent. The phenomenal growth of this type of retailing, as well as its future trends, is discussed in Chapter 16.

The Retail Scene Today

The function of retailers is to meet the needs and wants of their target customers. Just as the success of a style depends upon customer acceptance, so the success of retailers depends upon customer acceptance of the goods and services they offer. The success or failure of even the greatest and most prestigious of retailers depends upon the level of customer satisfaction they generate. In the words of the late Marshall Field, "Give the lady what she wants!" In today's retailing, however, it is not only the lady, but the man and child as well.

Various types of retailers have evolved from the early days of retailing. They each have unique organizations and methods of operation that enable them to give their customers what they want. There are retailers who stock many different types of merchandise and retailers who specialize in limited types of merchandise. There are retailers who serve those who casually spend large sums of money for their fashions and retailers who concentrate on customers who carefully watch every dollar. There are retailers who own no retail outlets of their own but operate departments in the stores of others.

Today there are hundreds of thousands of retail organizations of various kinds in the United States that specialize in apparel and accessories for men, women, and children. There are almost as many general-merchandise organizations that include apparel and accessories among their offerings. Many specialized retail firms also handle limited varieties of fashion merchandise. Examples are the food stores and drugstores that also sell hosiery, toiletries, cosmetics, and prepackaged T-shirts.

The forces of change are reshaping the retail trade. At one time, each type of retailer had a different organizational structure and hence a distinctive appeal to customers. However, retailers have had to change their retailing strategies in response to the changing environment. Clear-cut differences and distinctions that existed among retailers 20 or 30 years ago are now blurred. Most of today's successful retailers are characterized by their alertness to changes in the environment and in customer buying habits.

ORGANIZATIONAL STRUCTURE OF RETAIL FIRMS

The organizational structure of retail firms does not follow the clear-cut lines of authority and responsibility that are often found in other types of business firms. This is one of the strengths of retail firms. Management recognizes that retailing is a "people business"—a service to a firm's customers. A tightly structured and rigid organizational system could inhibit the creative awareness retailers need.

Organization Chart

An **organization chart** is a visual presentation of the manner in which a firm delegates responsibility and authority within the organization. A retail organization may adopt an organizational structure with anywhere from two to six major functions or areas of responsibility. Each of these functions is headed by a top-management executive. This person is responsible to the chief executive of the firm, usually called the general manager, the executive vice president, or the president.

The organizational structure of most medium-sized department stores today is based on a four-function plan, as follows:

1. *Finance and control division*—Responsible for the credit department, accounts payable, and inventory control.

2. *Merchandising division*—Responsible for buying, selling, merchandise planning and control, and usually fashion coordination.

3. *Sales promotion division*—Responsible for all advertising, display, special events, publicity, and public relations.

4. *Operations division*—Responsible for maintenance of all facilities, store and merchandise protection, customer services, receiving and marking, and personnel.

The number of major functions established by a retail firm as a basis for its effective operation depends upon its sales volume, the number of employees, and the number of store units it operates. The smaller the sales volume and the fewer the employees, the more varied are the responsibilities of each of its employees, including executives. The larger the sales volume and number of employees, the more specialized become the responsibilities of each employee.

In the smallest retail firms, an owner, a part-time bookkeeper, and a salesperson or two may handle all the work necessary to keep the firm operating successfully. In somewhat larger firms, an owner or manager is often responsible for both the sales promotion and merchandising activities, but turns over responsibility for financial and operational activities to one or two others in the firm who have experience in these fields.

Retail firms with larger than medium sales volume, a larger number of employees, and perhaps several branches usually find it necessary to increase their major functions from four to five. They remove responsibility for personnel from the operations division and elevate it to major functional status under the direction of a personnel executive. When this is done, a **personnel division,** as a separate function or division within a retail firm's organizational structure, is responsible for employment, training, employee records, executive recruitment and development, and related activities.

Retail firms with the largest sales volume and number of employees, and usually operating more than six branches, often add a sixth major function to their operating structure: a **branch store division.** The executive responsible for this function serves as the link between parent and branch store executives and sees that the firm's merchandising, personnel, and public relations policies are carried out in the branches. The organization chart of a retail operation is shown on page 308.

A chain's organizational structure is much more extensive than that of even the largest branch-operating retail firm because of the more complex nature of its activities. For example, in a branch-operating retail firm, transportation and warehousing activities are usually part of the operations function. But in a chain, these two activities are usually considered a major top-management function under the direct supervision of a top-management executive.

Overlapping authority and responsibility occur frequently in the retailing field. For example, salespeople are trained by the personnel department in ringing up sales, writing up sales checks, and handling delivery requests. But they are given merchandise and fashion training by their buyer and sometimes by the fashion coordinator.

Where there are several branches, overlapping can become even more complex. In an effort to adapt the merchandise assortments and presentations of each individual branch to the preferences of the community each serves, branch-operating stores can develop relationships within their organizational structure that defy charting. For example, in branch stores, department managers are assigned to supervise the merchandise assortments and selling activities in one or more merchandise areas. They also are responsible for reporting to the appropriate parent-store buyers the customer reaction to departmental assortments in their assigned areas. A department manager's immediate superior in the branch store may be a group manager or the branch store manager, but he or she also works with and receives directions from the parent-store buyer of each department managed.

TYPES OF RETAILERS OF FASHION MERCHANDISE

Many different types of retail stores sell fashion merchandise. There are small, independently

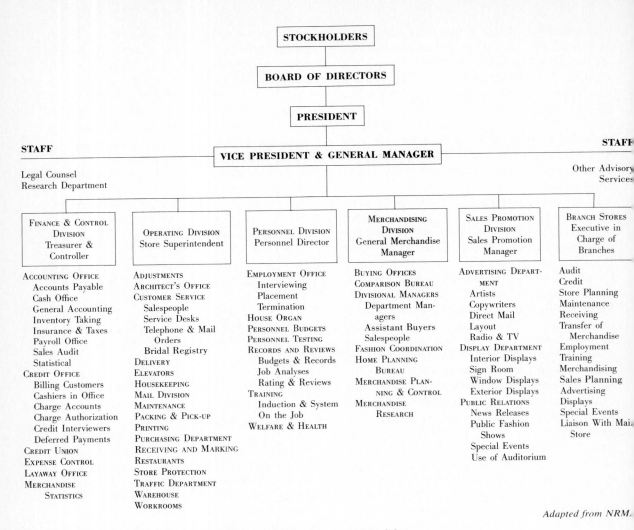

```
                          ┌─────────────────┐
                          │  STOCKHOLDERS   │
                          └─────────────────┘
                                  │
                          ┌─────────────────┐
                          │ BOARD OF DIRECTORS │
                          └─────────────────┘
                                  │
                          ┌─────────────────┐
                          │   PRESIDENT     │
                          └─────────────────┘
                                  │
STAFF        ┌────────────────────────────────────────┐                 STAFF
             │   VICE PRESIDENT & GENERAL MANAGER      │
Legal Counsel└────────────────────────────────────────┘          Other Advisory
Research Department                                                     Services
```

FINANCE & CONTROL DIVISION Treasurer & Controller	OPERATING DIVISION Store Superintendent	PERSONNEL DIVISION Personnel Director	MERCHANDISING DIVISION General Merchandise Manager	SALES PROMOTION DIVISION Sales Promotion Manager	BRANCH STORES Executive in Charge of Branches
ACCOUNTING OFFICE	ADJUSTMENTS	EMPLOYMENT OFFICE	BUYING OFFICES	ADVERTISING DEPARTMENT	Audit
Accounts Payable	ARCHITECT'S OFFICE	Interviewing	COMPARISON BUREAU	Artists	Credit
Cash Office	CUSTOMER SERVICE	Placement	DIVISIONAL MANAGERS	Copywriters	Store Planning
General Accounting	Salespeople	Termination	Department Managers	Direct Mail	Maintenance
Inventory Taking	Service Desks	HOUSE ORGAN	Assistant Buyers	Layout	Receiving
Insurance & Taxes	Telephone & Mail Orders	PERSONNEL BUDGETS	Salespeople	Radio & TV	Transfer of Merchandise
Payroll Office	Bridal Registry	PERSONNEL TESTING	FASHION COORDINATION	DISPLAY DEPARTMENT	Employment
Sales Audit	DELIVERY	RECORDS AND REVIEWS	HOME PLANNING BUREAU	Interior Displays	Training
Statistical	ELEVATORS	Budgets & Records	MERCHANDISE PLANNING & CONTROL	Sign Room	Merchandising
CREDIT OFFICE	HOUSEKEEPING	Job Analyses	MERCHANDISE RESEARCH	Window Displays	Sales Planning
Billing Customers	MAIL DIVISION	Rating & Reviews		Exterior Displays	Advertising
Cashiers in Office	MAINTENANCE	TRAINING		PUBLIC RELATIONS	Displays
Charge Accounts	PACKING & PICK-UP	Induction & System		News Releases	Special Events
Charge Authorization	PRINTING	On the Job		Public Fashion Shows	Liaison With Main Store
Credit Interviewers	PURCHASING DEPARTMENT	WELFARE & HEALTH		Special Events	
Deferred Payments	RECEIVING AND MARKING			Use of Auditorium	
CREDIT UNION	RESTAURANTS				
EXPENSE CONTROL	STORE PROTECTION				
LAYAWAY OFFICE	TRAFFIC DEPARTMENT				
MERCHANDISE STATISTICS	WAREHOUSE				
	WORKROOMS				

Adapted from NRM.

This organization chart shows how this large department store delegates responsibility and authority.

owned and operated stores. Others are part of large corporations that have many stores. The stores that dominate the fashion retail world today are those known as general-merchandise stores and specialty stores.

General-merchandise stores are retail stores that sell a number of lines of merchandise—apparel and accessories, furniture and home furnishings, household linens and dry goods, hardware and appliances, and small-wares, for example—under one roof. Included in this group are stores commonly known as mass merchandisers, department stores, discount stores, variety stores, general-merchandise stores, or general stores.

Specialty stores carry only limited lines of related merchandise. They define their customers more specifically—in terms of age range, size range, or common interests. Specialty stores differ from general-merchandise stores in that their customer groups are more homogeneous, at least in respect to the particular merchandise that the store offers.

The general-merchandise and specialty store groups account for the greater share of fashion retailers. But modern retailing has also seen the rise of leased and franchise departments and stores, catalog showroom stores, and the broad realm of nonstore retailing. The latter includes mail-order operations of all kinds, door-to-door or in-home selling, fashion merchandise offerings to credit card customers, automatic vending-machine merchandising, and the use of telecommunications in the sale and delivery of merchandise.

MERCHANDISING POLICIES

Merchandising policies are guidelines established by store managment for merchandising executives to follow in order to win the patronage of specific target groups of customers. Each type of retail organization has its own characteristic merchandising policies. Top management must consider many essential elements in establishing merchandising policies; including fashion cycle emphasis, quality, price ranges, depth and breadth of assortments, brand policies, and exclusivity. Each of these elements fit together to project the store image.

Fashion Cycle Emphasis

The emphasis on which stage of the fashion cycle each store selects in the introduction of its fashion assortments is an individual one. A store must choose whether to emphasize fashion assortments at the introduction or late rise, early culmination, or peak stages of the fashion cycle.

The timing of fashion emphasis is an important element of policy. The decision whether to undertake fashion leadership, be a close second, or wait until a trend becomes an accepted fashion is a major factor in fashion cycle emphasis. Naturally the store's choice must be directly related to the targeted customer's wants and needs.

Quality

The quality of the merchandise to be carried can be defined as one of the following:

- The finest materials and workmanship.
- The most serviceable materials and workmanship consistent with low price lines.
- Materials and workmanship in between the finest and the most serviceable.

Store merchandising policies may exclude anything except perfect goods or, depending upon its customer segmentation, may permit "irregulars" to be offered.

Price Ranges

Consumer income is a major factor in market segmentation; therefore, pricing policies are an important merchandising policy. Although there is no direct correlation between prices and quality, price ranges do generally interact with quality standards. A "top quality" policy usually calls for high price ranges whereas a "serviceable" quality standard generally puts a limit on the bottom price lines to be carried. Stores that emphasize the "cheapest" prices generally do not set quality standards.

Depth and Breadth of Assortments

There are two types of fashion assortments used by retailers. One is known as "narrow and deep" and the other is known as "broad and shallow." A **narrow and deep assortment** is one in which there are relatively few styles, but these styles are stocked in all available sizes and colors. A **broad and shallow assortment** is one in which there are many styles but only limited sizes and colors are carried in each style. Since space and money are major limiting factors, a policy of broad assortments usually limits the average depth to which items can be stocked; and conversely if depth is desired, variety must be limited.

Broad and shallow assortments presenting a large variety of styles, colors, and sizes, but not a large stock of any of these, are fairly characteristic of prestige stores and departments. In stores catering to the middle group of customers, assortments are usually broad and shallow early in the season when new styles are being tested, but relatively narrow and deep later in the season, once the trend of demand has become clear. Mass merchandisers concentrate on narrow and deep assortments of proven popular styles. Some large stores, with the space to carry wide assortments, may have broad and shallow stocks in the outer fringes of demand and narrow and deep stocks where demand is clearly defined.

Brand Policies

A **brand** is a name, trademark, or logo that is used to identify the products of a specific maker or seller and to differentiate the products from those of the competition. Some brands or names, especially those that are sold at very high prices, become associated with status symbols.

A **national brand** is one that identifies the producer of that product and is generally found in many stores across the country. In order to minimize competition from other local stores that feature the same brands, some stores may seek items from branded lines that will be **confined,** or exclusive with them in their own communities. National brands can give stores and customers alike a consistent standard of quality and are the backbone of the assortments in many stores.

Today the names of fashion designers have become so well known to the public, because they are featured on labels, in advertising, and in the media, that they can be considered national brands. For many customers, their "names" have a value quite distinct from the intrinsic value of the products themselves.

A **private or store brand,** meeting standards specified by the retailer, is an identification that belongs exclusively to that store and is often used to meet price competition and/or to achieve exclusivity of a product.

Different types of retailers have different policies pertaining to brand name merchandise. For example, prestige stores tend to feature their own store labels and designer names,

whereas nationally branded merchandise is dominant in the assortment of department stores. Although national brands are sometimes offered by mass merchandisers, as a rule these stores tend to emphasize either unbranded merchandise or their own private brands.

Exclusivity

Exclusiveness of merchandise is a feature that all stores would like to have but is very hard to obtain. Some retailers consider exclusives so important that their merchandising staff is expected to work with manufacturers toward this end. A store may attain exclusive merchandise in several ways:

- By prevailing upon vendors to confine one or more styles to their store for a given period of time and/or within their trading areas.
- By becoming the sole agent within their trading area for new, young designers.
- By buying domestically or abroad from sources of supply not yet tapped by competitors.
- By buying from producers who will manufacture goods to the buyer's special design and other specifications. Specification buying, however, imposes the necessity of placing large enough initial orders to ensure profitability for the producer.

DEPARTMENT STORES

Department stores are the type of retailer most familiar to the buying public. Department stores in large cities all over the world are often among the most famous landmarks. Few people visit New York without seeing Macy's or Bloomingdale's, for example. Such stores as Marshall Field's in Chicago, Hudson's in Detroit, John Wanamaker in Philadelphia, Lazarus in Columbus, Rich's in Atlanta, The Broadway in Los Angeles, Eaton's in Montreal, Harrods in London, and Galeries Lafayette in Paris are other well-known names. Department stores may be single-unit, branch-operating, or units of a chain organization. See Table 15-1 for the top department stores in the United States.

Department stores are so named because they present each of their many different kinds of merchandise in a separate area or department. A department store usually leads other types of stores in terms of overall status and importance in a community. It usually serves a larger segment of the local population than do other types of stores because its merchandise covers a wide range of categories and prices.

In addition, department stores are always very interested in finding ways to serve their local communities. If a department store can stage a fashion show for a local charity or lend space for an art show or club meeting, for instance, it usually does so willingly. Such community service generates goodwill. It also creates an awareness of the store and its merchandise that enhances the efforts that the store makes specifically to publicize and sell its merchandise.

Definition

A **department store** is defined by the U.S. Bureau of the Census as an establishment that normally employs 25 or more people and is engaged in selling general lines of merchandise in each of three categories:

1. Furniture, home furnishings, appliances, and radio and TV sets.
2. General lines of apparel and accessories for the entire family.
3. Household linens and dry goods (an old trade term meaning fabrics and sewing notions).

Organization for Buying and Merchandising

In department stores, various categories of related merchandise are grouped together into departments—sportswear, dresses, men's clothing, or furniture, for example. In most cases, a separate buyer is assigned to purchase all stock for each department. In the very largest of the department stores, each category may

In department stores, merchandise is grouped into different departments where it is arranged on open racks for the customer's inspection.

be more specifically defined and departmentalized. In some sportswear departments, for example, the categories become blouses, skirts, pants, and so on, with a separate buyer and department number for each category.

In nonchain retail organizations with only a few branches that are located relatively nearby, a departmental buyer is usually headquartered in the parent, or "main," store. This buyer is responsible for purchasing stock for all branches as well as for the parent store. In addition, the buyer is responsible for departmental sales in all locations, for the merchandise training of all departmental salespeople, and for the profitable operation of the department in all stores.

In department stores with numerous branches, particularly those that have a large annual sales volume and/or are located at a considerable distance from the parent store, buyer responsibility for sales and training supervision becomes impossible. In such cases departmental buyers' responsibility is limited to the merchandising and replenishment of stock in all stores. See Table 15-2 for a discussion of the merchandising policies of department stores.

Store Policies

After a business has defined and profiled its targeted group of customers and established its merchandise policies and assortments, it must then formulate **store policies,** that are guidelines that affect areas other than merchandising, such as customer services, selling services, promotional activities, and fashion coordination. These store policies enhance merchandising policies. There is no phase of the business of fashion merchandising that needs such careful consideration as the development of sound store policies since they form the business' personality.

CUSTOMER SERVICES.   Department stores were pioneers in offering customers charge and return privileges. This willingness to accept merchandise returns was one of the foundations on which the late John Wanamaker built his business. His first store, opened in Philadelphia in 1876 in an old freight station, was a men's clothing store. A year later he had added such departments as ladies' goods, household linens, upholstery, and shoes, making a total of 16 departments. Wanamaker advertised that any article that did not fit well, did not please "the folks at home," or for any other reason was unsatisfactory could be returned for cash refund within 10 days.

Today, department stores offer an increasing number of services because of increased competition for customers. The more familiar customer services include a variety of credit plans, free local delivery, free parking at suburban branches, and alterations. New customer services may include travel bureaus, ticket agencies, post office facilities, art and needlework instruction, child-care centers, expanded telephone-order facilities, and extended shopping hours.

SELLING SERVICES.   Modern department stores may offer a variety of selling services within a single store. This depends upon the nature and sometimes the price level of the merchandise involved. In prestige apparel departments, a salon type of selling service often prevails. In this type of service, merchandise other than that used for display purposes is kept out of sight. A salesperson chooses styles from the stockroom to bring out for individual customers' inspection. Self-selection is the type of selling service most commonly employed by department stores today, however. Merchandise is arranged on open racks, counters, or shelves for the customer's inspection. Salespeople are available to assist customers by providing information about the merchandise and by completing the sales transaction once a customer has reached a buying decision. A few department stores offer self-service with checkout counters for certain types of merchandise, but this is the exception rather than the rule.

TABLE 15-1 The Top 25 Department Stores in the United States

COMPANY/DIVISION	AFFILIATION	NUMBER OF STORES	VOLUME* (MILLIONS)
1. Macy's New York	(RHM)	17	$1,125†
2. Bamberger's, New Jersey	(RHM)	23	1,125†
3. Macy's California	(RHM)	22	1,000†
4. Broadway Southern California	(CHH)	40	865
5. Dillard's, Little Rock	(Ind)	66	847.5
6. Bloomingdale's, New York	(Fed)	13	787.9
7. Abraham & Straus, Brooklyn	(Fed)	15	731.8
8. Hudson's, Detroit	(DH)	20	728.0
9. May Co. California	(May)	34	725.1
10. Marshall Field's, Chicago	(Bat)	21	700
11. Lord & Taylor, New York	(ADG)	40	650
12. Burdine's, Miami	(Fed)	25	630.3
13. Foley's, Houston	(Fed)	15	625.9
14. Bullock's Southern California	(Fed)	28	588.9
15. Emporium-Capwell, San Francisco	(CHH)	21	580
16. Dayton's, Minneapolis	(DH)	16	514.3
17. Rich's, Atlanta	(Fed)	17	509.1
18. J. W. Robinson's, Los Angeles	(ADG)	21	485
19. Hecht's, Washington, D. C.	(May)	23	477.3
20. Jordan Marsh, New England	(All)	16	470
21. Gimbels East, New York	(Bat)	20	450
22. The Bon, Seattle	(All)	36	425
23. Lazarus, Columbus	(Fed)	17	420.4
24. Famous-Barr, St. Louis	(May)	16	419.1
25. Woodward & Lothrop, Washington, D.C.	(Ind)	16	403.6

† Four quarters ended Jan. 31, 1984

* All figures without a decimal are estimates; others are sales reported in company financial reports or other public statements.

Affiliation code: ADG, Associated Dry Goods; All, Allied Stores; Bat, Batus Retail Group of Batus Inc.; CHH, Carter Hawley Hale; DH, Dayton-Hudson; Fed, Federated Department Stores; Ind, Independent; May, May Department Stores; RHM, R. H. Macy & Co., Inc.

Source: Reprinted from *STORES Magazine,* (c) National Retail Merchants Association, 1984.

PROMOTIONAL ACTIVITIES. Department stores engage in a moderate amount of promotional activity. For this reason, they generally are referred to as "semipromotional stores." This means they regularly feature individual items in their advertising and displays. They also do a moderate amount of "special sale" and "special purchase" promotion, such as anniversary sales, end-of-month clearances, and traditional seasonal events such as white sales and back-to-school promotions.

FASHION DIRECTION. Department stores usually place only a moderate emphasis on coordination of fashion accessories with apparel, other than in fashion shows and in window and interior displays. However, as competition increases, particularly from specialty stores and discount stores, department stores are placing emphasis on the coordination of their fashion assortments as a means of creating a distinctive fashion image. Salespeople are urged to suggest accessories with every purchase.

MACY'S: PROFITS BY CHANGING AND BUY APPOINTMENT

Need a special gift for a special person? A whole new wardrobe custom-coordinated to fit your wants and needs? Too busy to shop? Call Linda Lee and her consultants at Macy's Buy Appointment in New York City. They'll help you choose an appropriate present or aid you in selecting outfits and accessories adapted to your lifestyle and budget.

Although Macy's is not the first store to offer a personal shopping service, it has become the most conspicuous of the major U.S. department stores to do so. Macy's print ads invariably remind customers about its shopping service. Whether or not shoppers take advantage of this offer of assistance, it has come to symbolize the "new" Macy's upscale image and its concern for the customer.

For years stores in the Macy's chain were dreary bargain-hunters' haunts—especially the huge Herald Square store. But that has changed, and the old flagship store at 34th Street is a tourist attraction that has inspired their slogan, "If you haven't seen Macy's you haven't seen New York." The turnaround for the Macy's chain began in the sixties in the New Jersey Bamberger's division, where young executives, led by Edward S. Finkelstein, now chairman and chief executive officer, overhauled the flagging Cherry Hill and Newark stores. The bright-eyed young retailers then

SPECIALTY STORES

Specialty stores vary widely in both size and type. They range from the tiny **mom-and-pop store**, run by the proprietor with few or no hired assistants, to huge departmentalized institutions that resemble large department stores. Some are single-unit stores; some are units of chains; some are suburban branches of central-city stores or branches of a parent store located in a distant city.

From a numerical standpoint most specialty stores in this country are individually owned, have no branches, and are not units of chains.

The composite sales of these single-unit stores, however, represent less than half the total sales volume of all specialty stores. The larger share of business is done by multiunit specialty stores or local, regional, or national chains. Robinson's is an example of a Los Angeles–based multibranch specialty store. For other examples of multiunit chain operations with units throughout the country, see Table 15-1.

Definition

According to the Bureau of the Census, a **specialty store** is one that carries limited lines of

moved on to San Francisco, where they experimented with several marketing innovations that proved successful and strengthened the California division. They brought several California concepts back East to the New York division, first turning the dismal Herald Square basement into "The Cellar," a shiny collection of separate departments selling housewares, gourmet foods, and gifts. The redecoration moved upward in the multistory emporium. The main selling floor was turned into an array of individual boutiques, and the balcony overlooking this floor was connected by a marble staircase matching the original marble and bronze columns, which have been restored. By 1983, when Macy's celebrated its 125th anniversary, the entire Herald Square store had been refurbished. While the contractors and decorators were at work on the interior of the 34th Street building, Finkelstein and company were busy revitalizing the Atlanta (Davison's) and Missouri (Midwest) divisions and opening a new branch in Stamford, Connecticut.

As a result of this update of its marketing strategy, Macy's now tops the list of retail stores coast-to-coast in earnings per square foot of retail space. The most highly visible reason for the turnaround and the increase in profit is the show-business-like visual displays Macy's uses to present merchandise, but the reasons for Macy's success are not all as apparent as these varied presentations based on color and theme. Chairman Finkelstein's policy of constantly building up the chain's executive-training program to make well-rounded executives is one reason; overstocking, even when other stores are reducing inventory, is another reason. Finkelstein has said he doesn't worry about duplication of stock or of buyers' responsibilities, although both have always been considered risky. There are always risks, he says, but the important thing is the entrepreneurial consideration.

Macy's has proclaimed its Herald Square store to be "the world's largest store," and plans are in progress to make the entire chain even larger. Finkelstein plans to build 10 new stores in Florida and Texas in the eighties, and this move may be the toughest challenge yet, especially in light of the economic stagnation in the Sun Belt. And, if Finkelstein needs appropriate clothing for commuting to the South to observe the progress on the new Macy's stores and is too busy to shop, he can always call Linda Lee at Macy's Buy Appointment.

This Fashion Focus is based on information from these sources:

Isadore Barmash, "Macy's Profits by Going Its Own Way," *The New York Times*, May 15, 1983, p. C1.
Ralph DiGennaro, "Pressed into Personal Service," *The New York Times Magazine*, November 28, 1982, p. 124.

apparel or accessories or home furnishings. A shoe store, a jewelry store, or a store handling only women's apparel and accessories is classified as a specialty store. In the trade, however, retailers use the term "specialty store" to describe any apparel and/or accessories store that exhibits a degree of fashion awareness and that carries goods for men, women, and/or children.

Organization for Buying and Merchandising

In large specialty stores, as in department stores, merchandise is usually grouped into separate departments. In these stores, a buyer is assigned to purchase stock for each department and has the same responsibilities as does the buyer for a single or multiunit department store.

Smaller specialty stores, however, may not be departmentalized. In this case, all merchandise is usually bought by the owner or store manager, sometimes with the help of one or two assistants.

Like department stores with few branches, specialty stores generally merchandise their branches from the parent store. Specialty stores with great numbers of branches use the chain-store type of organization. Specialty-store branches enjoy the same advantages over local competition that department store branches do: a skilled fashion merchandiser who directs the operation from the parent store and a large stock from which to draw styles, colors, and sizes.

Store Policies

CUSTOMER SERVICES.   Customer services offered by specialty stores tend to be fairly similar in both type and number to those offered by department stores with equivalent sales volume.

SELLING SERVICES.   Self-selection selling is used in specialty stores where it is appropriate, but there is likely to be more emphasis on personal selling than in department stores. In the medium- to higher-priced specialty stores, emphasis is placed on remembering what individual customers and their friends have purchased. The accent in such stores is on personal service.

PROMOTIONAL ACTIVITIES.   Advertising and display activities of specialty stores tend to be less promotional than those used by department stores. Rather than featuring individual items, moderate to higher-priced specialty store ads and displays usually feature designer collections and looks and trends in coordinated apparel and accessories. Lower-priced specialty stores, and particularly those that are units of a chain, tend to feature in both their ads and displays the fashion-rightness of the styles carried in their assortments.

FASHION COORDINATION.   In most specialty stores, accessories are carefully related to apparel, and fashion coordination is stressed in ads, displays, and selling services.

Moderate to higher priced specialty stores often feature items from designer collections.

CHAIN ORGANIZATIONS

Chains that deal in fashion merchandise may be national, regional, or local. They may be department store chains, with only a portion of assortments devoted to fashion goods. They may be mass-merchandise chains that emphasize the quality and durability of their fashion goods and distribute impressive quantities of merchandise. Or they may be general-merchandise chains known for selling fashion goods at low prices. There are specialty store chains that deal exclusively with fashion merchandise at high prices or at discount prices. There are also apparel specialty chains that focus on a special size, age, or income group.

Outstanding examples of department store chains are The Broadway and Bloomingdale's. Well-known mass-merchandising chains include JC Penney, Sears, Roebuck, and Montgomery Ward, while outstanding examples of general-merchandise chains are K-Mart and Zayre. Saks Fifth Avenue, Neiman-Marcus, and Lord & Taylor are examples of prestige specialty chains; Loehmann's is an example of a discount specialty chain. The Limited, The Gap, and Lerner Stores are examples of women's apparel specialty chains appealing mainly to junior customers, while Lane Bryant caters to women customers who need larger sizes.

Definition

According to the Bureau of the Census, a **chain organization** is a group of centrally owned stores, each handling somewhat similar goods and merchandised and controlled from a central headquarters office. The difference between a chain organization and a department or specialty store organization with multiple branches is that the former is merchandised and controlled from a central office, while the latter is merchandised and controlled from a parent store.

Organization for Buying and Merchandising

Centralized buying, merchandising, and distribution of fashion assortments prevail among retail chain organizations. The majority of chain stores are departmentalized. But a chain buyer located in a central buying office is usually assigned to purchase only a specific category or classification of merchandise instead of buying all categories carried in a single department, as a nonchain buyer does. This practice is called **category buying** or **classification buying**. For example, a sportswear buyer for a department or specialty store might be responsible for **departmental buying**; that is, buying all the various categories of merchandise usually carried in a typical sportswear department, such as swimwear, tops, jeans, sweaters, and slacks. In contrast, one chain organization buyer might be assigned to purchase swimwear, another to purchase sweaters, and so on. Category buying, rather than departmental buying, is necessary because of the huge quantities of goods in each category that are needed to stock all the individual units of a chain. These units sometimes number in the thousands.

Centrally purchased merchandise is usually distributed to the units of a chain from central or regional distribution centers. Most larger chains have set up elaborate systems of supervision and reporting so that their central-office buyers are kept informed at all times of what is selling and what remains in stock at each of their many units.

Unlike single-unit or multibranch department or specialty store buyers, central buyers are not directly responsible for sales. Sales are the responsibility of the store manager of each unit in the chain and the appropriate department manager. Neither are central buyers responsible for the merchandise training of salespeople in each unit. However, they do supply trend and other information to chain units about the merchandise distributed to them. And, since central buyers are usually responsible for providing stock in only one or a few merchandise categories, they are not responsible for the profitable merchandising of a department as a whole.

Store Policies

CUSTOMER SERVICES. Customer services are usually more limited in chain organizations than in most nonchain stores. Free delivery of fashion merchandise is rarely provided. The usual credit plans prevail, with greater emphasis on installment plans. Chain organizations may take the lead or follow the lead of other prominent stores in the community in establishing business hours.

SELLING SERVICES. With rare exceptions, selling services in department store and low- to moderate-priced specialty store chain organizations are usually of a self-selection type. Clerks simply answer questions and ring up sales. Higher-priced specialty store chains, however, tend to place more emphasis on personal selling techniques.

The three major mass-merchandise chains supplement floor sales in their retail outlets with catalog sales. A special catalog desk or counter is usually maintained in each retail store unit. Customers may phone, mail, or come in person to order merchandise not regularly carried in that store's stock.

Each chain prepares seasonal catalogs—as many as five or six a year. Selection of fashion merchandise for catalog selling has to be done much further in advance than selection for store floor sales, because of the time required to develop and print catalogs. Central buyers for each chain's retail stores may assist in the planning and buying of catalog merchandise.

Today's catalogs differ vastly from those of 20 to 50 years ago, especially in the case of fashion merchandise. More pages are now devoted to apparel and accessories for men, women, and children. Merchandise is more closely related to current fashion trends, and illustrations are usually in full color.

PROMOTIONAL ACTIVITIES. Promotional activities of most chain organizations are coordinated with their central buying activities. The advertising staff at a chain's central or regional headquarters prepares advertising layouts and provides display suggestions for all chain units. These are designed to promote the fashion merchandise purchased by the central buyers for the various units.

Department store chains concentrate mainly on item advertising of fashion goods, with fre- quent off-price promotions. Specialty store chains that carry higher-priced fashion merchandise usually follow the promotional pattern of nonchain specialty stores operating at the same price level; they feature looks and trends in ads and displays.

FASHION COORDINATION. Larger department and specialty store chains may employ the services of a fashion coordinator or director. This person is an experienced fashion professional who searches both domestic and foreign markets for new fashion trends and for unusual styling that can be adapted or incorporated into their private-label merchandise offerings. In the largest chains, a fashion coordinator has a staff of assistants. Each assistant is made responsible for a specific type of fashion apparel, such as dresses, sportswear, menswear, or children's wear.

The fashion coordinator of a chain, working closely with the central buying and merchandising staffs, is also responsible for periodic fashion reports to the managers and staff of each unit. These highlight current fashion trends and coordination possibilities in apparel and accessories for the coming season.

DISCOUNT STORES

After World War II, the service men and women returning home had a well-thought-out agenda for their lives: get married, buy a low-cost home in the newly emerging suburbs, and start a family on little money. This scenario, multiplied millions of times over, led to almost "instant" new homes and an accompanying need for "instant" furnishings and appliances. This need in turn led to the birth and rapid growth of discount retailing.

The first discounters ran a weekend operation, usually operating outside the jurisdiction of town or city government agencies. Each Saturday and Sunday they would offer the buys of the weekend—this weekend discounted G.E. toasters, next weekend bath towels, and

```
Filene's  BASEMENT

2 PC. SUIT

SIZE 14

┌DEPT┐
>802            E4F
┌SKU┐
307 9312     SELLING
┌PRICE┐       ┌DATE┐
$75.00        12/10

AUTOMATIC
┌MARK DOWN┐
$56.25        12/25
$37.50        01/10
$18.75        01/25
CHARITY       01/30
```

Buy now or take a chance? This tag from a discount store includes a schedule for markdowns.

so on. The young couples, using the time as a family outing, brought their toddlers along as they added yet another valued possession for their homes, at a price well below that which the department stores were charging. There was not much of a selection to choose from, but the price was right!

Gradually this word-of-mouth discount type of business operation grew and expanded. Many discounters moved into deserted factory or warehouse buildings, especially in New England, which the textile companies had fled to resettle in the South. Others opened for business in vacated storefront or loft space. All operated on a policy of low overhead, sought only low-rent areas, and provided plain surroundings with no services. Cash-and-carry was the rule—acceptable to the newly created "car generation" in view of the low prices. During this time, discounters continued to devote the bulk of their attention to items, usually small appliances, that were listed with the government as Fair Trade goods. This meant that it was illegal to sell such items at less than the manufacturer's suggested retail or "list" price.

By the time the Fair Trade Law was abolished, in the mid-1970s, the discounters had established themselves in many parts of the country and were selling all kinds of merchandise, from toasters to toothbrushes to tablecloths to tennis balls. Facilities were minimal, service was nonexistent, and a central cashier handled all sales.

Gradually recognizing the sales potential of fashion merchandise, the discounters began to improve their housekeeping and increase their services. Most important of all, they have vastly increased and upgraded their advertising and visual merchandising to provide the store with a definite fashion image. One of the most dramatic examples of this is Alexander's in New York City, which operates with great success across the street from Bloomingdale's.

Possibly on the principle that "if you can't lick them, join them," several large retailers and large ownership groups have entered the discount field by opening wholly-owned discount operations as separate divisions of the parent firm. For example, Target Stores is the discount operation of the Dayton-Hudson department store group; K-Mart is the highly successful discount chain operation of the now defunct S. S. Kresge variety chain.

Today, it is estimated that over 50 percent of all fashion goods are sold at discount. There are almost as many names for discounting stores as there are stores—"discount stores," "off-price stores," "mass merchandisers," "promotional department stores"—the list is endless. No matter what the name, discounters have a tremendous stake in fashion retailing in the future.

Definition

Discount Merchandiser, the magazine of the discount industry, defines a **discount store** as a departmentalized retail establishment using many self-service techniques to sell hard goods, health and beauty aids, apparel and other soft goods, and/or other general merchandise. Such a store operates at unusually low profit margins, has a minimum annual volume of $500,000, and has a size of at least 10,000 square feet. A discount store may be an independent store or a unit of a department, specialty, or variety-store chain.

Organization for Buying and Merchandising

In departments owned and operated by a chain discount organization, buying and merchandising activities are basically the same as those previously described for chain organizations. Centralized buying prevails. Discount store buyers, however, are usually responsible for buying for several departments rather than for only a single category of merchandise. The nonchain discount stores, which are far less numerous than chains, follow the same basic buying and merchandising pattern as that of similar-volume nonchain department or specialty stores.

Early discounters searched the market for closeouts and special-price promotions. In many cases, their inventories consisted almost entirely of this type of merchandise. Today, however, the fashion stocks of many discounters consist of either regular goods bought in the low-end open market or special lines made up exclusively for discount operations by producers who sell their regular lines to conventional stores. Most conventional retail firms will not allow their buyers to purchase fashion goods from producers who sell the same goods to mass-merchandised operations. Many producers, however, have found it profitable to create a second line for such mass merchandisers because of the huge quantities of fashion goods they can use.

Store Policies

CUSTOMER SERVICES. Transactions in discount operations are usually made for cash,

although a number of such stores today accept checks or bank credit cards or offer credit plans of their own. Refund policies are generally liberal: money back if the goods are returned unused in a specified number of days. Delivery service, if available, is usually restricted to bulky items and often involves an extra charge. Limited fitting-room service for trying on apparel may sometimes be found. Paperwork is kept to a minimum. The cash-register receipt often serves as a sales slip, and refunds are usually made in cash, eliminating credit slips and extensive bookkeeping.

SELLING SERVICES. In discount store selling, frills are eliminated. Merchandise is stocked on racks or tables and customers help themselves. Self-service prevails. Employees are present only to direct customers and straighten the stock. Customers make their selections and then take them to a cashier's desk where sales are rung up.

PROMOTIONAL ACTIVITIES. Today, discount stores are highly promotional. They are heavy users of all types of advertising, including newspaper, radio, and direct mail. Advertising always emphasizes low price and, in many cases, comparative prices.

Interior displays are used mainly to identify the location of merchandise; they play a relatively minor role in the store's promotional efforts. Window displays in some leading discount chains, however, are well planned and attractive.

FASHION COORDINATION. In spite of the gradual upgrading of some merchandising techniques, there is little evidence that discount stores try to coordinate their fashion apparel and accessories offerings.

VARIETY STORES

Variety stores once referred to themselves as "limited price variety stores," to underscore the fact that they carried a wide range of merchandise in a limited number of low-price lines. Some literally were 5-and-10-cent stores, with all merchandise priced at either a nickel or a dime. Others sold goods priced up to a dollar. Fashion merchandise was represented in their assortments only by such utilitarian articles as socks and underwear, ribbons and buttons, and simple hair and dress ornaments. Chain operations dominated the field.

In the 1930s, the larger variety chains began to broaden their assortments and extend their price ranges. They grew into what are now known as general-merchandise stores.

Definition

A **variety store** carries a wide range of merchandise in a limited number of low or relatively low price lines. Some variety stores are independent organizations but most are units of chain organizations.

Organization for Buying and Merchandising

Since most variety stores are units of a chain, their buying and merchandising techniques are identical with those described for chain organizations. (See page 317.) These include centralized buying and distribution handled by headquarters office personnel.

Store Policies

CUSTOMER SERVICES. The earlier variety stores had bare wooden floors, no fitting rooms, and few, if any, customer services. Today, modern units of such variety chains as F. W. Woolworth Company and S. S. Kresge are well lighted, air-conditioned, and carpeted or surfaced with resilient floor coverings. However, only the larger chains offer such customer services as charge privileges, delivery, and a basic kind of ready-to-wear fitting room.

SELLING SERVICES. Self-service generally prevails in variety stores, although some limited personal selling may be provided. Well-labeled merchandise is packaged, binned, or hung for customers' quick and easy inspection and selection.

PROMOTIONAL ACTIVITIES. Variety stores seldom, if ever, advertise fashion goods. Their promotion of fashion goods is largely limited to displays. Though mainly functional, these attempt to emphasize the important fashion points of the merchandise.

FASHION COORDINATION. Variety stores make no attempt to coordinate fashion assortments since the styles they feature are already widely accepted. In units of the larger chains, however, a concerted effort has been made to feature coordinated apparel and accessories both in window and in interior displays.

Because the fashions that are featured have already proved successful before appearing in these stores, and also because of their low pricing policies, variety stores make their major appeal to lower-income customers who are fashion followers.

LEASED DEPARTMENTS

Department stores tend to lease both merchandise and service departments, as do chain and discount organizations. Specialty stores usually restrict leased operations to services.

Services commonly leased include the beauty salon, shoe repair, and jewelry repair. Glemby Company and Seligman and Latz lease many of the beauty salons found in department, specialty, and chain stores throughout the country.

Merchandise departments most frequently leased include millinery, shoes, fine jewelry, and furs. There are also some leased departments that handle women's apparel. But these

TABLE 15-2 Merchandising Policies of Various Types of Firms That Sell Fashion Merchandise

MERCHAN-DISING POLICIES	NONCHAIN DEPARTMENT STORE	NONCHAIN SPECIALTY STORE	CHAIN ORGANIZA-TION	DISCOUNT ORGANIZA-TION	OFF-PRICE RETAILER	FIRM USING DIRECT MAIL
Fashion cycle emphasis	Mainly late rise and early culmination; early rise in prestige departments; full to late culmination in budget departments	Particular stage of cycle favored by majority of its customers	Mainly culmination stage; some specialty chains feature styles in earlier stages of cycle	Styles well into the culmination of their fashion cycles	Same as department and specialty chains	Particular stage of cycle favored by majority of its customers
Quality	High quality in prestige departments; quality at a price in moderate or budget departments	Highest quality as to materials and workmanship	Serviceable quality consistent with price	Quality may vary; "irregulars" and "seconds" may be carried	Varies from highest quality to serviceable depending on price	Quality consistent with targeted group of customers
Price ranges	Mainly moderate; high in prestige departments; low in budget departments	Mainly moderate but depends on stage of fashion cycle its customers prefer	Department store chains: lower and promotional pricing; some specialty chains: moderate to high price ranges	Lower than conventional retailers	Moderate- to high-priced	Mainly moderate but depends on stage of fashion cycle its customers prefer

are likely to be found in discount stores, and they usually concentrate on lower-priced goods. Marcus and Co. is an outstanding example of a leased fine jewelry department; they have leased departments in all the Gimbels East stores.

Definition

As indicated in Chapter 7, a leased department is merchandised by an outside organization rather than by the store itself. That organization owns the department's stock, merchandises and staffs the department, pays for its

MERCHAN-DISING POLICIES	NONCHAIN DEPART-MENT STORE	NONCHAIN SPECIALTY STORE	CHAIN OR-GANIZA-TION	DISCOUNT ORGANIZA-TION	OFF-PRICE RETAILER	FIRM US-ING DIRECT MAIL
Depth and breadth of assort-ments	Broad and shallow at start of new sell-ing sea-sons; nar-rower and deeper as customer preferences become known	Typically broad and shallow	Department store chains: narrow range of proven styles in considera-ble depth; moderate-to high-priced spe-cialty chains: broader and shal-lower	Mainly broad and shal-low	Broad and shallow	Narrow range of proven styles in considera-ble depth
Brand poli-cies	National brands em-phasized	Major em-phasis on own store labels or designer labels	Own private labels em-phasized	Unbranded; own brand or with brand label removed	Designer la-bels em-phasized, with many national brands also	Major em-phasis on own brand or national brands
Exclusivity	Use of store brand or label in-sures some exclusivity	Uses con-fined goods—es-pecially designer or home la-bels—to gain exclu-sivity	Mainly spec-ification buying and "store own" mer-chandise	No exclusiv-ity unless bought by specifica-tion	No exclusiv-ity	Much exclu-sivity be-cause goods are produced for them alone

Source: Reprinted from STORES Magazine, July 1984, p. 29 (c) National Retail Merchants Association, 1984.

advertising, is required to abide by the host store's policies, and pays the store a percentage of sales as rent. In general, the operator of a leased department is an expert in some mer-chandise or service that a retail store finds un-profitable to handle directly.

Organization for Buying and Merchandising

The operator of a leased department may be a local person functioning in a single store or a giant organization doing business in hundreds of stores across the country. Central buying and

This ad, directed at retailers, promotes a company that leases specialized departments in department stores.

merchandising prevail. In larger operations, traveling supervisors regularly visit their various locations to confer with both the host-store management and the department manager, to help them cope with problems that may arise, and to plan for future growth.

Leased-department operators are in a unique position with respect to the fashion industries. They are usually in daily contact with their markets and are sometimes established in a wide variety of stores. They can give impetus to incoming styles or clear producers' stocks of declining styles, according to the merchandising policies of their host stores. The successful, long-established operators sometimes know their industries better than the producers themselves. Such operators are equipped to give fashion guidance to their sources of supply as well as to the stores they serve.

Merchandising Policies

The fashion merchandising policies of a leased department are dictated by the terms of its lease and must conform to the policies of the store in which it operates. Assortments and services must be on a level with those of all other departments in the host store, so that customers have no indication that the depart-

ment is not owned and operated by the host store.

Some larger leased-department organizations are extremely flexible in their approach to individual store policies and can function on almost any level of fashion and service that may be required. Others limit themselves to narrow fields, such as popular-priced shoes. These seek connections only with stores whose merchandise and service policies are compatible with their own.

FRANCHISES

As explained in Chapter 5, franchising is fast becoming an important means of retailing fashion. During the 1970s franchised retail operations began to pop up with merchandise usually associated with department stores. Bath shops, cookware, fabrics, unfinished furniture, sewing supplies, maternity and bridal shops, as well as electronics and computers, all became highly successful franchises. Athletic footwear, tennis apparel, and men's active sportswear soon followed.

Branded apparel franchises are definitely on the increase. Today there are Polo Shops franchised by Ralph Lauren, worldwide Calvin

Klein shops, Rive Gauche shops with the Yves St. Laurent franchise, Lady Madonna maternity franchises. In the future, off-price retailers may prove suitable as franchises.

In a relatively short time, franchising has permeated every type of business, from fast food to car dealerships to hair salons—even professions such as law and dentistry. It is constantly entering new areas. Fashion retailing seems likely to be the next area of tremendous growth.

BOUTIQUES

The turbulent 1960s gave the United States an important and ever-growing form of retailing—the boutique. Boutiques, or "shops," had for many years been part of the great French couture houses, as small, intimate departments that sold perfumes or accessories that carried the couturier's label. But it was the antiestablishment attitudes of the 1960s that gave the boutiques their beginning in London, followed by their adoption and rapid growth in the United States.

Boutiques have come to be recognized as sources of highly specialized merchandise often presented in a distinctive and nontraditional way. The customer an individual boutique wishes to attract is generally well-defined as to age, status, and outlook. Some boutiques feature designer clothes; others favor the homespun look. One boutique may have as its target customer only the way-out young in search of the newest trends. Another will find its success by relying on the moneyed person of more mature years.

In the 1960s many large department stores, eager to win the young customers who had given their loyalty to boutiques, began to create specialized shops right on their selling floors. These in-store boutiques generally offered customers a total look in apparel and accessories.

Boutiques offer highly specialized merchandise presented in a distinctive way. This is a new Givenchy boutique in New York.

Today, small independent boutiques continue to proliferate. Often they are opened by highly creative people eager to promote their own fashion enthusiasms. Their chosen customers are generally people who share their social and political viewpoints as well as their creative ones. Some boutique owners design their merchandise; some buy and sell other people's designs. The avant-garde merchandise that is too risky and narrow for department stores to handle successfully forms the backbone of boutiques. Everything in a boutique, from decor and fixtures to merchandise displays, is generally highly creative and uninhibited, giving the boutique an air of special individuality.

The great designers of the 1980s have joined in the boutique method of retailing. First, such famous European designers as Cardin, Valentino, St. Laurent, and Givenchy selected stores in the United States to create boutiques in which to sell their apparel and accessories. American designers quickly followed suit— boutiques for Calvin Klein, Halston, Ralph Lauren, and others are to be found in major stores throughout the country. The boutique concept in America is still quite young in years, but as a desired method of retailing it has had phenomenal growth and projects a rosy future.

DIRECT-SELLING RETAILERS

In **direct selling**, merchandise is sold by its producer in one of two ways: either by contacting customers door-to-door or via in-home parties. These nonstore forms of retailing are modern versions of the early peddler. This form of selling is discussed in greater depth in Chapter 16.

CHANGING RETAIL PATTERNS

A theory expounded by Dr. Malcolm P. McNair, retailing authority and professor emeritus at Harvard University Business School, suggests that many retail organizations originate as low-priced distributors of consumer goods, with strictly functional facilities, limited assortments, and minimum customer services. As time goes on, each successful firm begins to trade up in an effort to broaden its consumer profile. Facilities are modernized. Store decor is made more attractive. Store assortments become more varied and higher in quality. Greater emphasis is placed on promotional efforts and more customer services are introduced.

In this process of trading up, considerably greater capital investment in physical plant, equipment, and inventory is required. Operating expenses spiral. As a result, retailers are forced to charge higher prices to cover the increased costs of doing business.

As retail organizations move out of the low-priced field and into the moderate- or higher-priced fields, a vacuum is created at the bottom of the retailing structure. This vacuum does not exist for long, however. Enterprising new firms move quickly into the vacated and temporarily uncompetitive low-priced area to meet the demands of customers who either need or prefer to patronize low-priced retail distributors. The pattern keeps repeating itself, with successful retail firms trading up and new firms moving into the bottom level of the retail price structure.

This pattern of movement is very obvious in today's retail scene. Department and specialty stores are expanding their facilities, services, assortments, and price-line offerings. Discount stores are trading up. As a result, a vacuum has appeared at the bottom of the retail price structure. As far as fashion goods are concerned, this vacuum is presently being filled by low-priced imports, retailers dealing solely in off-price merchandise, and factory outlet stores. These and other current trends in fashion retailing are discussed in detail in the next chapter.

Define or briefly explain the following terms:

Branch store division
Broad and shallow assortment
Category buying or Classification buying
Chain organization
Confined
Department store
Departmental buying
Direct selling
Discount store
Fashion retailing
General-merchandise stores
General store
Mail-order company

Merchandising policies
Mom-and-pop store
Narrow and deep assortment
National brand
Organization chart
Personnel division
Private or store brand
Retailing
Specialty store
Store policies
Variety store

MERCHANDISING REVIEW

1. What are considered the modern retail versions of the following types of early retail distributors: (*a*) outdoor bazaars of the Orient and marketplaces of the Mediterranean, (*b*) tradespeople who purchased goods from traders for purposes of resale rather than producing such goods themselves, (*c*) medieval craft or guild shops, and (*d*) peddlers?

2. Name and briefly explain the characteristics and importance of three early forms of rural retail distribution in this country.

3. Describe the organizational structure of most medium-size department stores and the responsibilities of executives in charge of each major function.

4. How did department stores originally get their name? What are four major responsibilities of a departmental buyer for an independent retail firm with fewer than 12 branches?

5. Who is responsible for establishing merchandising policies? What important purposes do they serve?

6. Compare and/or contrast the merchandising policies of department and specialty stores in regard to the depth and breadth of assortments during a selling season.

7. Compare and/or contrast the responsibilities of nonchain departmental buyers with those of central buyers for chain organizations.

8. What stage or stages of the fashion cycle would most likely be emphasized in the fashion assortments of: (*a*) a small or medium-size department store; (*b*) a higher-priced specialty store; (*c*) a department store chain; (*d*) a discount store?

9. In which major type of retail store would you be most likely to find the following emphasized in its merchandise assortments: (*a*) nationally advertised brands, (*b*) private brands, (*c*) low-price branded or unbranded goods?

10. What is a leased department and how does it operate? Name the departments in a retail store that are frequently leased.

MERCHANDISING DIGEST

1. "The number of major functions established by a retail firm . . . depends upon its sales volume, the number of employees, and the number of store units it operates." Discuss this statement from the text, citing specific examples of how these three factors affect not only the organizational structure of a firm but also the responsibilities of its various employees.

2. Compare and contrast the fashion coordination efforts of (*a*) department stores, (*b*) specialty stores, (*c*) department and specialty store chains, (*d*) discount stores, (*e*) variety stores.

3. What examples in your community can you cite which support Dr. McNair's theory of "trading up" by retailers?

16. TRENDS IN FASHION RETAILING

As the last decade of the twentieth century approaches, it must seem to many fashion retailers that they are already in 2000 A.D., fighting Star Wars of their own. Never has the world of fashion retailing, long marked by staid and stable department stores and mammoth chain operations, been so caught up in whirlwind change and so in peril of fragmenting. The forces within this country and outside its borders have, since the mid-1960s, changed the buying attitudes of the American public not once and for all, but on a fast-paced continuing basis.

RETAILING TODAY

For fashion retailers of the future, success will depend on their ability to anticipate and adapt to never-ending changes. This ability will in turn depend upon organizational flexibility coupled with rapid internal communications, so that managers can monitor shifts in demographics and accompanying changes in customer preferences.

More and more, consumerism exercises vast control over a store's operation policies and procedures. What consumers want and need has replaced what a store wanted to sell. Until recently, retailers considered product quality, variety, and pricing their main concerns. Today, consumers demand product information and safety. They expect to be recompensed for purchases they find unsatisfactory. Equally a part of retailers' responsibility are electronic systems for the transfer of funds. In the mid-1980s, there appears to be no aspect of a store's operation that doesn't somehow concern itself with the consumer's wants and needs.

Fashion retailing in the coming years will be aided by a growing trend toward bigness. This bigness, coupled with heightened efficiency and awareness, will govern the size and scope of the organization and the breadth of its assortments. Department stores and specialty stores, chain stores and discount stores, as well as mail order and franchising, all will participate in the same trend. They will be joined by the biggest new trend of all in fashion retailing—the use of the computer for selecting merchandise at home.

Consumerism

One of the fastest-growing aspects of the American business world today is **consumerism**, which means the efforts of consumers to protect their own interests. Consumer affairs offices are part of the federal government, state governments, and, certainly, most city governments across the country. In many areas the media, led by TV and newspaper "action lines," aid in consumer protection. New consumer-protection regulations are being added at state as well as federal levels, and the interpretation and implementation of these laws is an ever-increasing responsibility of business as well as government.

Consumers of the 1980s are more educated than ever before to demand information on expected product performance, and on guarantees and warranties. Safety has become a big consumer-interest issue (since the early 1960s efforts for flame-retardant children's sleepwear), as have product care and estimated product life. Retailers who were slow to support the consumer protection laws in earlier days have now increased their education of both buyers and sellers. One off-price retail chain, Syms, has as its slogan "An educated consumer is our best customer." In the fashion world, information is disseminated by all concerned—fiber houses, finishers, manufacturers, and retailers.

Certainly, consumerism is very much a part of our world today and will be even more important in the future. The beneficial effects of consumerism on retailing can be tremendous. Being able to fill customers' wants without disappointments in performance and quality of service must surely be the desired goal of retailing. For in addition to satisfying customers, retailers also free themselves from the cost of wrong choices and expensive replacements. Consumerism is, therefore, a valuable addition to everyone's way of life—buyers and sellers alike.

Organizational Flexibility

Retail fashion distributors face a great challenge in the next two decades—the challenge of monitoring the demographic shifts of consumers and their constantly changing merchandise preferences. Retailers need to rethink and reevaluate merchandising decisions made in the sixties and seventies and update their marketing strategies for new target markets. Retailers will need to use better planning methods and tighter inventory and expense controls in the coming years if they are to survive and grow. More professional management structures, better communication with consumers, and specialization of channels of distribution and merchandise will also be some of the methods used. For many years, retailers and small entrepreneurs thought of themselves

Consumers of the 1980s tend to shop more carefully and intelligently than ever before.

as "merchants," not as managers. With increased competition and more complex distribution problems, large and small retailers have found that the need for professional, well-trained, and educated managers is growing.

Increased Competition

Growing chains, specialized retailers, and the increased sophistication of shoppers have made competition more keen. The era of the "loyal" customer has passed. No longer do customers shop in only one store or expect that only one store will satisfy their needs. No longer do customers shop without checking to see what other stores are selling. Today's customers are alert observers of what is offered in the marketplace and choose to shop where they believe they will get the most for their money. (See Table 16-1, which indicates that changing tastes and prices are key factors in

the shift in shopping habits.) Therefore it is imperative for management to continually reevaluate the wishes of customers and to keep themselves competitive in all areas. Only with professional management and well-structured organizations will retailers be able to keep themselves abreast of consumer wants and needs.

Growth of Large-Scale Fashion Retailing

Both department and specialty stores in their early history were primarily single-unit, independent, and family owned. In the 1930s, a trend toward bigness and mergers began. Federated Department Stores, Allied Stores, and other corporate ownership groups were formed and began acquiring stores that had formerly been independent. At that time the Macy interests owned several stores, each in a

TABLE 16-1 Where Customers Buy

PRODUCT	DEPARTMENT STORES	SPECIALTY STORES	MASS MERCHAN-DISERS*	DISCOUNTERS†	OFF-PRICE RETAIL-ERS	OTHER
	%	%	%	%	%	%
Jeans	28.3	23.3	21.2	16.3	4.9	6.0
Athletic shoes	13.6	50.3	14.2	16.6	2.4	2.9
Active wear	35.5	14.0	19.4	23.7	4.4	3.0
Infant sleepers	30.8	9.9	33.0	25.3	—	1.0
Man's dress shirt	31.9	29.3	27.6	6.9	1.7	2.6
Bra-panties set	43.2	9.8	26.4	12.8	4.0	3.8
Man's fashion underwear	43.4	15.1	20.7	13.2	5.7	1.9

Source: Developed by the author based on statistics from *Chain Store Age—General Merchandise Edition*, December 1983, p. 26.

*Sears, Roebuck; Montgomery Ward; JC Penney.

†K-Mart and other discounters.

different city, as did the Gimbel family and May Department Stores. This trend has not only continued but accelerated. By the mid-1970s, only a few of this country's largest stores were still independently owned.

During the late 1920s and early 1930s, companies that had formerly been exclusively mail-order houses began opening store units. These retail units represented the entry of chain organizations into the retail distribution network.

MERGERS AND ACQUISITIONS. In the mid-1980s, it is difficult to realize that until the late 1930s, most retail stores in the United States were independently owned (most by the families whose names they bore). For over a century the advertising of one such retailing giant, Rich's of Atlanta, bore the slogan "Atlanta born, Atlanta owned, Atlanta man-aged"—putting particular emphasis on the local nature of the company. Other independently owned giants included Gimbels, Marshall Field's, John Wanamaker, and Hudson's. But in the last 40 years or more, mergers and acquisitions have made the independent retail department store almost a dim memory. For the most part, however, the image of the acquired store or chain remains unchanged as far as the public is aware. That, at least, is generally the desired objective.

Therefore, to its customers, Rich's is still Rich's, although it is now owned by Federated Department Stores, which also owns such giants as Bloomingdale's in New York, Bullock's on the West Coast, Filene's in Boston, and Foley's in Texas. John Wanamaker in Philadelphia now joins Neiman-Marcus and Bergdorf Goodman under the Carter Hawley Hale corporate ownership, along with such diverse holdings as the Walden bookstore chain.

VOLUNTARY ASSOCIATIONS. On another level, there is a growing trend among smaller stores to affiliate loosely with one another on a voluntary basis. The purpose of this is to exchange information as well as to secure certain group-buying advantages such as early delivery and sometimes lower prices.

In **voluntary associations**, each store retains its own identity, and owners retain complete control of their stores. No financial joining is involved. However, the heads of stores that are affiliated in this manner get together regularly to compare methods and results. They believe such meetings result in better and more profitable storekeeping for all concerned.

Affiliations of this type are often organized and guided by an accounting firm or by a management consultant firm that specializes in the retail field.

CHAIN EXPANSION. The giant chain organizations such as Sears, Roebuck, F. W. Woolworth, JC Penney, and Montgomery Ward continue to expand their operations. Older, smaller units are replaced by larger, newer stores with greater fashion assortments. To keep abreast of the new wants and needs of customers, stores move into fashion classifications they have never carried before, enter into new trading areas, and attempt to follow

Giant chain organizations continue to expand their operations. JC Penney grew dramatically from the 1950s to the 1980s.

their customers into new areas of the country. In addition to the growth of the chains in the United States, they continue to expand abroad. Travelers will feel right at home when shopping the familiar Sears, Roebuck or F. W. Woolworth stores in Europe, South America, and the Far East.

BRANCH-STORE EXPANSION. One of the most significant changes in department store retailing involves the growth and development of **branch stores**. Originally branches were, for the most part, small replicas of the parent (main) store. Most had limited stocks and contributed only a nominal percentage of the firm's total sales volume. Also, these branches were located close enough to the parent store so that the departmental buyers could visit each store frequently.

Today, however, many branch stores are as large as or, in some cases, even larger than the parent store, contributing in most cases more than 50 percent of the firm's total annual sales volume. In addition, branches are being established farther and farther away from the parent store, making meaningful buyer responsibility for sales and training supervision and management impossible. In such cases each branch, as well as the parent store, is treated as a separate entity, each with its own sales supervision and management.

Until recent years, department store branches were located principally in suburbs of the cities in which the parent stores were located, or in more distant cities, but always within the same or close neighboring states. Today, however, stores are opening branches far from the traditional trading areas of the parent store. Lord & Taylor, for instance, now has branches in Pennsylvania, Massachusetts, Maryland, Connecticut, Illinois, Texas, Georgia, Virginia, and New Jersey. Additional branches in other states are in the planning stage. Bloomingdale's, New York, has established branches in Connecticut, New Jersey, and suburban New York City areas. It also opened a branch in Washington, D.C., and has plans for opening branches in cities far removed from the main store, in states such as Florida and Texas.

Another current trend among branch-owning stores is to literally saturate the market in a new trading area by opening multiple branches. In this way not only sales volume is maximized but also the store's fashion impact in the community. For example, Lord & Taylor has six stores in the Greater Chicago trading area. It is interesting to note that as branch stores proliferate, the parent store organization takes on many of the merchandising, operational, and management characteristics of a chain organization.

TABLE 16-2 Selected Major Department Store Groups

ALLIED STORES CORP. (ALL), New York, N.Y.

THE WM. H. BLOCK CO., Indianapolis, Ind.	JOSKE'S, San Antonio, Tex.
THE BON, Seattle, Wash.	LEVY'S OF SAVANNAH, INC., Savannah, Ga.
CAIN-SLOAN, Nashville, Tenn.	MAAS BROS., INC., Tampa, Fla.
DEYS BROS. & CO., Syracuse, N.Y.	MILLER & RHOADS, Richmond, Va.
DONALDSON'S, Minneapolis, Minn.	MILLERS INC., Knoxville, Tenn.
GARFINCKEL'S, Washington, D.C.	MULLER CO. LTD., Lake Charles, La.
HEER'S INC., Springfield, Mo.	POMEROY'S INC., Harrisburg, Pa.
HERP'S CO., Grand Rapids, Mich.	POMEROY'S INC., Levittown, Pa.
JORDAN MARSH CO., Miami, Fla.	D. M. READ INC., Bridgeport, Conn.
JORDAN MARSH CO., Boston, Mass.	STERN'S, Paramus, N.J.
JOSKE'S OF DALLAS & PHOENIX, Dallas, Tex.	A. E. TROUTMAN & CO., Greensburg, Pa.
JOSKE'S HOUSTON, Houston, Tex.	EDWARD WREN STORE, Springfield, Ohio

ASSOCIATED DRY GOODS CORP. (ADG), New York, N.Y.

L. S. AYRES & CO., Indianapolis, Ind.
THE DENVER DRY GOODS CO., Denver, Colo.
GOLDWATER'S, Phoenix, Ariz.
HAHNE & CO., Newark, N.J.
JOSEPH HORNE CO., Pittsburgh, Pa.
LORD & TAYLOR, New York, N.Y.
THE H. S. POGUE CO., Cincinnati, Ohio
POWERS DRY GOODS CO., Minneapolis, Minn.

J. W. ROBINSON CO., Los Angeles, Calif.
ROBINSON'S OF FLORIDA, St. Petersburg, Fla.
SIBLEY, LINDSAY & CURR CO., Rochester, N.Y.
THE STEWART DRY GOODS CO., Louisville, Ky.
STIX, BAER & FULLER, St. Louis, Mo.

BATUS INC. (BAT), New York, N.Y.

THE CRESCENT, Spokane, Wash.
FREDERICK & NELSON, Seattle, Wash.
GIMBELS-EAST, New York, N.Y.
GIMBELS-PITTSBURGH, Pittsburgh, Pa.
GIMBELS-MIDWEST, Milwaukee, Wis.

IVEY'S CAROLINAS, Charlotte, N.C.
IVEY'S FLORIDA, Winter Park, Fla.
KOHL'S DEPT. STORES, Brookfield, Wis.
MARSHALL FIELD & CO., Chicago, Ill.
SAKS FIFTH AVE., New York, N.Y.

CARTER HAWLEY HALE STORES, INC. (CHH), Los Angeles, Calif.

THE BROADWAY-SOUTHERN CALIF., Los Angeles, Calif.
THE BROADWAY-SOUTHWEST, Mesa, Ariz.
EMPORIUM-CAPWELL, San Francisco, Calif.

NEIMAN-MARCUS, Dallas, Tex.
THALHIMIER BROS., INC., Richmond, Va.
JOHN WANAMAKER, Philadelphia, Pa.
WEINSTOCK'S, Sacramento, Calif.

DAYTON-HUDSON CORP. (D-H), Minneapolis, Minn.

JOHN A. BROWN CO., Oklahoma City, Okla.
DAYTON'S, Minneapolis, Minn.
DIAMOND'S, Tempe, Ariz.

THE J. L. HUDSON CO., Detroit, Mich.
MERVYN'S, Hayward, Calif.

FEDERATED DEPT. STORES, INC. (FED), Cincinnati, Ohio

ABRAHAM & STRAUS, Brooklyn, N.Y.
BLOOMINGDALE'S, New York, N.Y.
BULLOCK'S, Los Angeles, Calif.
BURDINE'S, Miami, Fla.
WM. FILENE'S SONS CO., Boston, Mass.
FOLEY'S, Houston, Tex.
GOLDSMITH'S, Memphis, Tenn.

F. & R. LAZARUS CO., Columbus, Ohio
I. MAGNIN & CO., San Francisco, Calif.
MILWAUKEE BOSTON STORE CO., Milwaukee, Wis.
RICH'S, Atlanta, Ga.
SANGER HARRIS, Dallas, Tex.
SHILLITO RIKES, Cincinnati, Ohio

R. H. MACY & CO., INC. (RHM), New York, N.Y.

BAMBERGER'S, Newark, N.J.
DAVISON'S, Atlanta, Ga.
MACY'S CALIFORNIA, San Francisco, Calif.

MACY'S HOUSTON, Houston, Tex.
MACY'S MIDWEST, Kansas City, Mo.
MACY'S NEW YORK, New York, N.Y.

THE MAY DEPARTMENT STORES CO. (MAY), St. Louis, Mo.

FAMOUS-BARR CO., St. Louis, Mo.
G. FOX & CO., Hartford, Conn.
THE HECHT CO., Washington, D.C.
KAUFMANN'S DEPT. STORES, Pittsburgh, Pa.
THE MAY CO., Los Angeles, Calif.
THE MAY CO., Cleveland, Ohio

MAY-COHENS, Jacksonville, Fla.
MAY D. & F., Denver, Colo.
MEIER & FRANK, Portland, Oreg.
THE M. O'NEIL CO., Akron, Ohio
STROUSS, Youngstown, Ohio

Source: Chain Store Guide—1984 Directory of Department Stores, pp. v–vi

Note: This listing does not include discount, variety, or specialty stores affiliated with these department store groups.

An alternative to branch expansion has been the revitalization of downtown shopping areas, stimulated in many parts of the country by the interest of merchants in urban renewal, and with the infusion of county, state, and government financial aid. Again, the changing lifestyles of customers, in this case the choice of living as well as working downtown, has been the impetus for this renewal.

EMERGING FORMS OF FASHION RETAILING

Seven forms of fashion retailing are emerging or have recently emerged as vital "new" businesses. Among them are off-price retailing, factory outlet stores, catalog showrooms, video-shopping, private labels, direct mail and its subcategory, mail-order catalogs.

Off-Price Retailing

It has been predicted that before long, off-price retailing will account for 25 to 30 percent of all name-brand soft goods in the United States. As it is right now, " 'off-pricers' [as they are called in the retail trade] sold an estimated 6 percent of the $85 billion of clothing sold in America last year."[1]

Off-price retailing is the selling of brand-name and designer-label merchandise at lower-than-normal retail prices, but still at the late rise or early peak of the fashion cycle. Discounters sell merchandise at the late peak and decline stages of the fashion cycle. Off-price retailers keep their selling expenses down to the discounter level by limiting services and maintaining austere surroundings in low-rent areas.

The first major off-price fashion retailer in the United States was Loehmann's, which set up a cut-rate outlet in 1920 in Brooklyn to sell "better" women's wear. Up to that point, such garments had been sold only through quality department stores. These stores demanded that if Loehmann's was to be allowed to sell the same fashions, Loehmann's must remove the labels so that customers could not know what was being sold off-price. To this day, Loehmann's stores throughout America, as well as reputable off-pricers everywhere, scissor some brand-name and designer labels out of garments before they put them on the racks. However, if a garment has the designer name on the lining or on the sleeve. . . .

Some stores and retail chain operations are entering the off-price apparel business. In the spring of 1983, K-Mart launched its off-price "Designers' Depot." F. W. Woolworth has its J. Brannam off-price soft-goods chain. Melville Corporation does off-price retailing of men's, women's, and children's fashions through its Marshalls Stores. And the Zayre Corporation features two off-price chains, T. J. Maxx and Hit or Miss. In addition, such fast-growing smaller companies as Syms and Suzanne S. continue to proliferate in the ever-increasing off-price fashion retail business.

Off-price retailers have provided an invaluable service to manufacturers and price-conscious customers alike. Because manufacturers must commit to fabric houses so early (up to 18 months before the garments are actually in the stores) they are at considerable risk of not having enough orders from their regular retail clients to use all the fabric. If this is the case, manufacturers can turn to off-pricers, who will often pay full price for the piece goods if the manufacturers will make them into garments at a lower cost. Selling to off-pricers helps manufacturers to avert financial difficulties and to keep their plants operating. Off-pricers benefit by getting garments for less than what regular retailers pay, and because of low overhead, are able to operate on a smaller markup. Customers benefit by being able to buy garments for far less than they would sell for in department stores or specialty shops.

Certainly, off-price retailers have taken a big portion of the brand-name clothing market. As designers such as Pierre Cardin, Bill Blass, Calvin Klein, and Halston grew stronger, they were able to deny exclusivity to any single store. Since these designers and many others license their names and designs to manufacturers, it is possible to purchase their brand-name garments in many department stores and specialty shops, and for much less at an off-price retailer.

While a department store puts designer spring and summer clothing on the floor in the winter of the previous year, an off-price retailer will not get the line until months later, with a resultant short selling period. However, the off-pricer will be able to make a nice profit while selling the garments for a great deal less than the price asked by prestige stores during the peak selling period.

The future of off-price brand- and designer-name retailers looks very favorable. Manufacturers will continue to periodically "miscalculate" the demand for fashion styles, the market will continue to present surprises, and educated consumers will continue to thrill to being able to purchase brand-name or designer gar-

ments at a fraction of their usual price. Off-price retailing seems to have found the right formula to satisfy growing ranks of customers.

Factory Outlet Stores

Another fast-rising source of discount fashion buying in the mid-1980s is the **factory outlet store**. This form of retailing began decades ago when a manufacturer would open a little store in one corner of the plant to sell company products at reduced rates to the company's employees. Kayser-Roth and William Carter Co. were two such factory outlet pioneers. Gradually, manufacturers opened their outlet stores to the public and these stores became popular with a diverse range of customers.

The severe recession in the United States in the early 1980s led to a proliferation of authentic (as well as ersatz) factory outlets. Major manufacturers with large outlet chains, such as Warnaco, Inc., Jonathan Logan, Kayser-

Here a 26th Street manufacturer opened a factory outlet store for customers.

FASHION FOCUS

THE *HORCHOW COLLECTION*: OF CATALOGS AND CONVENIENCE

Roger Horchow of Dallas, Texas, is a man who just hates to shop in a store. He detests standing in line to pay for merchandise! Roger Horchow is only one of an increasing number of Americans whose aversion to shopping has led them to purchase more and different items from mail-order catalogs. But Roger Horchow is a little different from his fellow catalog shoppers. He has his name on the catalog cover, not just on the address label. He is the Horchow of the *Horchow Collection*; he is the catalog king.

Because of people like Horchow, the mail-order business is growing by 15 percent a year, five times as fast as in-store business. Though mail orders accounted for only 4 percent of total sales in the United States in 1982, they are expected to account for a whopping 20 percent by 1990.[1] The increase in the number of women who work outside the home is probably the most obvious reason for the growth of the mail-order industry. But even people with plenty of time to wander around stores are choosing to spend their leisure hours doing other things, and are finding the effectiveness and ease of ordering from a catalog irresistible. It is these people who are the target of the fun, interesting, and impractical merchandise displayed on the glossy pages of the *Horchow Collection*.

Roger Horchow considers himself a full-fledged Texan, but was born in Cincinnati and graduated from Yale. Formerly vice president of Neiman-Marcus' catalog division and the head of the *Kenton Collection* (a prestige catalog that sold status items from other Kenton companies—Cartier's, Mark Cross, Valentino, and Georg Jensen), Horchow was well prepared for the task of producing a colorful catalog and expediting the ensuing orders. When the Kenton companies were sold in-

Roth, Blue Bell, and William Carter Co., continue to operate. In addition, a new phenomenon appeared: the shopping mall composed in large part of factory outlet stores.

Such a mall is the Charlestown Factory Out-

let Center in upstate New York. Its more than 39 factory outlets include Adidas, Bass Shoes, Carter Children's Wear, Ship 'n Shore blouses, Bates Bedspreads, Jack Winter sportswear, Van Heusen menswear, Wrangler jeans, and many

dividually in 1973, Horchow bought the financially unsteady Kenton catalog division and issued the first *Horchow Collection*. Other catalogs—*Trifles, Grand Finale, S.G.F., Another Perspective*— followed in the wake of the successful *Collection*.

The *Horchow Collection* is a deluxe catalog, issued 12 times a year. It appears in 1.5 million mailboxes each month—always in the most affluent neighborhoods. Roger Horchow himself chooses each item he sells and selection is based on his personal taste: either he personally wants the item, or he knows someone who does. Unlike some mail-order firms that concentrate only on wearing apparel or gear and provisions for special wants and needs, the *Collection* runs the gamut from white cotton pajamas to Lucite bathroom accessories to a one-of-a-kind antique Regency desk. Horchow travels all over the world foraging for interesting and unusual objects and ferreting out the exclusive, can't-be-found-anywhere-else items that he believes must comprise at least 25 percent of the *Horchow Collection*'s offerings to make it successful. Though this catalog features luxurious products, they are not necessarily expensive. There are usually several tasteful gifts under $50.

Preparing the Horchow catalogs is as important as selecting the merchandise, because these pictorial and written ads are the only thing the customers see until their parcels are delivered. The pictures must be visually attractive but never presented in such a way as to obscure any major feature, and the accompanying copy must clearly and accurately describe the merchandise. Horchow's gives a money-back-if-not-satisfied guarantee, so if there is an exaggeration in the written copy or if the photographs are not distinct and the goods are returned Horchow's does not stand to profit.

When Roger Horchow's book on the mail-order business, *Elephants in Your Mailbox* (published by Time Books), was offered in the *Horchow Collection*, he autographed every copy he sold. He is happy to give a personal touch to his catalogs as well, often posing in the glossy four-color photographs himself, showing off his family and mentioning friends in ads, and plugging pet causes such as the World Wildlife Preservation Fund. When he launched the spinoff catalog *Trifles*, which offers somewhat less expensive goods, he created an imaginary family to inhabit the pages: Mr. and Mrs. Michael Bradford Westfall II (Mrs. is G.G. and she loves monograms), their children Elizabeth and Brad, and their pets Muffy (dog) and Charlie (cat).

The new *Trifles* began to make a profit almost instantly, mainly because the new catalog was sent to the same people who bought from the *Horchow Collection*, and Roger Horchow had the list of buyers on his computer. Having a list, that is, knowing to whom to send catalogs, is probably the most important factor in building a successful mail-order business.

Roger Horchow's success has not gone to his head, but it may have gone to his feet. He's so enamored of the whole mail-order idea of comfort and convenience that he wears loafers—loafers he orders from the L. L. Bean catalog!

[1] "Catalog Cornucopia," *Time*, November 8, 1982, pp. 73–74.

This Fashion Focus is based on information from the article cited above and from these sources:

William G. Flanagan, "Roger Horchow: His Check Is in the Mail," *Metropolitan Home*, February 1982, p. 63.
Diane Justice, "Cut Rates on Luxury Items at Horchow," *Women's Wear Daily*, July 10, 1980, p. 1.
Elsa Kaplan, "Horchow: King of the Catalogs," *Advertising Age*, January 21, 1980, p. S-22.

more. This giant outlet operation is open to the public 7 days a week and advertises savings of 25 to 60 percent off regular store prices.

Like discount and off-price retailers, the factory outlets operate in austere surroundings with minimum service, and thus have low overhead. An outlet buys merchandise from the parent company at over 30 percent off regular wholesale prices. Most of the major manufacturers, such as Kayser-Roth, are careful to use their outlet stores only for closeouts and seconds. It is vital that these manufacturers continue to protect their status with the department stores and specialty stores that are their major regular-priced customers.

The future route that will be taken by factory outlet stores is unpredictable. The majority of factory outlets want to be located in areas with other off-price discounters since they realize that they would attract more customers if located near other retailers. In many cases manufacturers lack the retailing expertise of their competition—although they are quickly learning. The factory outlet store, depending as it does on manufacturers' closeouts and a price-conscious public, seems set for continued growth. For there will always be overproduction, and the educated customers of the 1980s and 1990s will continue to demand value for the price they pay.

Catalog Showrooms

The **catalog showroom** is set up like a trading stamp redemption center, with merchandise catalogs for customers to study and samples of the merchandise on display in the showroom. Orders are filled from a stockroom on the premises, and customers take their purchases with them. One of the largest catalog showroom chains is Best Products. Although only a minimal number of fashion goods besides jewelry and watches is offered in such catalog showrooms, it is likely that in the future more fashion-oriented merchandise, including apparel, will be available. Investment Clothiers of Columbus, Ohio, is an example of a fashion-oriented catalog showroom. It has been so successful that it plans to franchise its catalog showrooms.[2]

Videoshopping

With the growth of cable TV and home computers, the field opened in the early 1980s to **videoshopping**, the ultimate in shop-at-home. Since over a third of all homes in the country are wired for cable TV, and more are being wired all the time, the potential audience for in-home television shopping appears to be vast.

Of course, television has long been used as a direct-mail selling tool. One need only think of the gadget demonstrations of the 1960s, the perpetual storm window commercials, and the "golden oldies" record commercials of the 1980s. But the new videoshopping brings a whole store into the home screen, not just isolated items.

Some 3.5 million households receive "Home Shopping Show," a cable-TV program from the Modern Satellite Network. Manufacturers are charge $6,000 for a 10-minute product demonstration that is repeated five times in 35 days. The program airs Monday through Friday.[3] Market experts from Proctor and Gamble, Maytag, and Encyclopedia Britannica are among those highly pleased with results of airing their products via this method. Viewtron, a joint venture of Sears, Roebuck, Knight-Ridder Newspapers, and American Telephone and Telegraph, enables viewers to summon up a catalog's text and pictures on a specially adapted TV screen. Viewers make purchases using an order form that appears on the screen.[4]

Sears is also putting portions of its famed catalog on videodiscs to be viewed at leisure by the customer in the home. The success of sending videotaped catalogs to customers was proved in late 1982 by an enterprising boutique in New York, Votano, which now has a twice-a-year videotape catalog.

As two-way cable spreads, videoshopping continues to grow. With two-way cable, the viewer does not need to telephone the order into the store. Through a hand-held, calculator-like device linked to a central data base, the viewer just punches in the item's code.

The high cost per sale is still a problem of videoshopping. However, as new technologies

Television product demonstrations attract customers and help to sell fashion merchandise.

emerge, videoshopping will, undoubtedly, be the wave of the future for direct marketing.

Private Labels

While most well-established retail stores have long had their own name-branded merchandise, the apparel areas had, since the 1960s, put far more emphasis on designer names than on the store's own name. Designer shops had sprung up in all major stores, spurred by the excitement and image of the designer. But with the rise of off-price brand-name retailers and designers' refusal to grant exclusivity in the early 1980s, the department and specialty stores found it increasingly hard to compete or to improve their profit margins. More and more brand-name and designer-label apparel was being sold by discounters and off-price

retailers. At that point, the department and specialty stores realized they needed a new way of attracting customers. The stores decided to take advantage of the value associated with their names in the minds of their customers by actively promoting products under their own **private label**. New York's irrepressible Bloomingdale's had already proved the worth of the private-label concept. Its customers associated value and prestige with the Bloomingdale's name, so when the store began selling a myriad of merchandise, even toilet paper, under the "Bloomies" name, it proved very successful.

Today the private label has moved from its earlier use on shirts and underwear to include whole lifestyle concepts. Retailers, who previously would bring together apparel by various designers in one department, now contract for their own private label on all goods in a department. Sometimes the store name is used; sometimes a store chooses a special name of its own. Neiman-Marcus, in addition to its own name label, has developed the N-M Supplies name for use on all merchandise in the Down East way of dressing—a takeoff on L. L. Bean. All merchandise is made exclusively for Neiman-Marcus. Another Neiman-Marcus brand name, Red River, is used on its rugged-wear apparel for men, women, and children, as well as on various items for the epicure. Further emphasis on just how valuable Neiman-Marcus considers its private labels is shown through its national magazine advertising campaign, "What Makes Neiman-Marcus Neiman-Marcus?" At Lord & Taylor, always proud of its private label, as much as 30 percent of the total stock is under the store's own exclusive labels in men's, women's, and children's apparel and in home furnishings.

The resurgence of private labels offers stores more than just differentiation from other stores, or a way to fight inroads by off-price brand-name retailers into the designer business. Private labels, belonging exclusively to a store, allow the store an extra measure of quality control, complete design control, and a degree of profit control. And as many would say, they put the identity back where it belongs—with the store!

Direct Mail

By late 1982 the direct-mail explosion in the United States had reached such proportions that *Time* magazine featured "Catalogs" as one issue's cover news story. Inside, the national news publication devoted page after page to telling the story of this form of merchandise promotion so vital to the world of fashion.

Few readers were surprised by this acknowledgment of the importance of direct mail. For years, despite ever-increasing postal rates, direct mail has continued to grow by leaps and bounds.

The reasons are not hard to find. Direct mail is the one avenue of sales promotion that can be aimed at an individual customer. Equally, a piece of **direct mail**, whether a catalog or a statement insert, can provide the impact of full-color illustration and specific copy, along with an easy-to-use ordering coupon to persuade the customer to respond immediately. And because of the selective abilities of computer lists, merchandisers can select their target audience by sex, age, economic status, education—even lifestyle and hobbies. With such a personalized means of presenting fashion merchandise to selected customers, it is no wonder that both retailers and manufacturers have come to think of direct mail as a major medium for the merchandising of fashion.

MAIL-ORDER CATALOGS. Today, the convenience of shopping at home from a wealth of offerings has produced almost unbelievable sales figures. The average American home today receives over 40 catalogs a year. From these catalogs people can purchase everything from the latest fashions to foods and wines, from sporting goods to furniture, from robots to vacations in far-off lands. Department stores, specialty shops, and mail-order companies have been joined by catalog specialists who select goods from all over the world to be sold only by catalog. The Horchow Collection, American Express Company, Lillian Vernon, Spiegel, and many others produce a cornucopia of full-color gift catalogs to appeal to customers with a myriad of tastes.

Meanwhile, American mailboxes continue to be filled with a fabulous array of bill enclosures pinpointing specific fashion merchandise through the cooperative efforts of retailers and manufacturers. Stores send postcards and personalized letters to inform customers of special sales and events. Flyers and booklets extol products and service.

By the end of 1982, mail orders generated close to $40 billion in consumer sales, much of it from catalogs.[5] As the eighties continue,

A growing trend in fashion merchandising is for stores to feature their own labels as opposed to only designer labels.

the outlook for direct-mail impact on the shopping habits of the American populace is one of ongoing growth.

It was over a century ago, at the latter part of the 1800s, that Montgomery Ward and Sears, Roebuck sent out their first mail-order "lists" or "catalogs." Today, the catalog contents of the major mail-order houses bear little resemblance to those early offerings to rural America. Famous designers now create exclusive fashions for these catalogs. Mail-order companies employ the most up-to-date testing laboratories to assure that the fit, fabric, color, workmanship, and wearing qualities of the merchandise they offer are of the quality customers want. Because these mail-order houses print and distribute millions of copies of each catalog, they have tremendous purchasing power and prestige in the fashion market.

Mail order has, in the 1980s, achieved a highly enviable reputation as a means of selling even the most expensive and exotic merchandise. The prevalence of credit cards has now made it possible for customers to order everything from pearls to piano lessons to Paris weekends. Goods and services are presented in glowing four-color mailing pieces from an ever-growing group of sellers—department and specialty stores, credit card organizations, oil companies, museums, magazines, and music companies.

Catalogs have become highly creative works of art. And in today's households, where more often than not both husband and wife work, catalogs also represent valuable shopping hours saved to be used for leisure pursuits. Small wonder then that the business of mail order is today a very big business indeed!

REFERENCES

[1] Walter McQuade, "The Man Who Makes Millions on Mistakes," *Fortune*, September 16, 1982, pp. 106–116.
[2] "Catalog Cornucopia," *Time*, November 8, 1982, pp. 73–79.

[3] John Cooney, "Video Shopping Services, Goods You See on the Screen Can Be Delivered to Your Door," *The Wall Street Journal*, July 14, 1981, p. 52.
[4] Ibid.
[5] "Catalog Cornucopia," pp. 73–79.

MERCHANDISING VOCABULARY

Define or briefly explain the following terms:

Branch stores	Off-price retailing
Catalog showroom	Private label
Consumerism	Videoshopping
Direct mail	Voluntary associations
Factory outlet store	

1. Explain the meaning of the slogan, "An educated consumer is our best customer," and its significance to retailers.
2. What changes in organization and management will be needed to meet the challenges retailers face in the future?
3. Briefly discuss the trend toward large-scale retailing, as evidenced by (a) mergers and acquisitions, (b) voluntary associations, (c) chain expansion, (d) branch-store expansion.
4. Explain how the trend toward large-scale retailing has affected stores' fashion image.
5. How has off-price retailing affected the manufacturer? The consumer? The fashion cycle?
6. What factors enable off-price retailers and factory outlet stores to make a profit with such a low markup?
7. Explain the concept of videoshopping. What is currently the main problem in videoshopping?
8. What factors made it difficult for department and specialty stores to improve their profit margins on designer and brand name apparel in the early 1980s? Name one way in which they chose to deal with the problem.
9. What are the advantages of private-label merchandising to the retailer?
10. What are the advantages of direct-mail retailing to the merchant? To the consumer?

1. Explain and discuss the following statement, citing current examples to illustrate how it applies to fashion retailing: "Today, the catalog contents of the major mail-order houses bear little resemblance to those early offerings to rural America."
2. Compare and contrast off-price retailing and discounting. What effects have the growth of these emerging forms of retailing had on traditional department stores?

17.
RESIDENT BUYING OFFICES AND AUXILIARY SERVICES

When buying offices originated many years ago, their sole function was to place orders for out-of-town retailers. Back in the days of the outpost store, before travel became fast and relatively easy, the role of the resident buyer, then called a "buying agent," was simple. The agent would receive a request from a store, locate the required merchandise, and arrange for purchase and shipment.

A **resident buying office** is an organization, located in a major market center, that serves a group of noncompeting stores, usually in a different city. Its primary specialization and responsibility is coverage of the market. "Resident office" and "buying office" are used interchangeably in the trade; however, the term "buying office" is inadequate today. As the retail business changes, expands, and ventures into new concepts, the role of the resident buying office has changed also. Resident buying offices now offer an extensive array of product and merchandising services that can help all types of stores to run more effectively and profitably, from small mom-and-pop stores to giant department stores and chains. Most offer important additional services such as legal advice, market surveys, store planning, and computerizing.

HISTORY AND DEVELOPMENT

In their original form as active purchasing arms for groups of noncompetitive retail stores, buying offices were given the authority to make purchases from the major market, New York (and later, Los Angeles), and operated as retailers' representatives at a time when slow forms of transportation and communication limited stores' access to resources and market events. Buying offices wrote a large amount of business and were important contacts for stores in fashion markets.

But buying offices also originated as service organizations for their stores, clearinghouses of collective information used to help each store compete effectively in its trading area.

The telephone, the airplane, and the computer: these three forms of twentieth-century technology have successively altered the character of retailing and, consequently, the character of the resident buying office. Even with these tools, the demands on retailers' time are enormous. The challenge of running a profitable, growing business is equally demanding. In order to stay abreast of all they need to know and to analyze and act on an abundance of information, retailers rely more than ever on resident buying offices.

The buying function of resident buying offices remains, to varying degrees. But the most successful offices have enlarged their role in trend gathering, market evaluation, and strategic planning for all areas of the store.

So while buying offices began as only buying extensions of stores, present-day resident buying offices function in areas of fashion direction, merchandising techniques, assortment planning, vendor recommendation, and import coordination, along with a new concentration on sales promotion and advertising, personnel operations, and electronic data processing (EDP) systems, especially as the pace of change quickens. Today's retailers must keep abreast of many trends—technological, social, and economic, as well as fashion.

TYPES OF RESIDENT BUYING OFFICES

There are two major types of resident buying offices: independent offices and store-owned offices. An independent resident buying office actively seeks out noncompeting stores as paying clients, while a store-owned office is entirely owned by the store or stores it represents and works exclusively for them.

Independent Offices

The "salaried," "fee," or "paid" office is the most numerous of independent offices. A **salaried**, **fee**, or **paid office** is independently owned and operated and charges the stores it represents for the work it does for them. Another type of independent office is the commission or merchandise-broker office. In the case of the **commission** or **merchandise-broker office**, the store does not pay the office any fee. The merchandise-broker office collects a remuneration from manufacturers in the form of a commission based on a percentage of orders placed for their stores.

SALARIED, FEE, OR PAID OFFICES. Salaried, fee, or paid offices usually enter into annual contracts with noncompeting stores to provide market services in exchange for an annual, stipulated fee, or "salary," based upon each individual store's sales volume. The typical pay, on inverse scaling, is between 0.6 percent and 0.2 percent of a store's annual volume for a year's services.[1]

Salaried, fee, or paid offices strive to familiarize themselves with each client store's individual operation and needs and to meet those needs with a broad range of services. These offices primarily represent the moderate-priced independent department and specialty stores in mid-sized and secondary markets.

The fee-based offices secure their clients primarily through word of mouth. Stores hear about an office in the market from visiting manufacturer reps or from a satisfied customer. Mailings, regional market visits to meet the stores, or exposure in office-oriented national ads, which feature name merchandise and list the participating member stores of a particular office, are other methods the offices use to attract clients. To avoid conflicts, most offices restrict themselves to one client in a given trading area.

To better serve the clients and to strengthen their own market positions, offices concentrate on similar types of stores. The criteria vary from level of store volume to type of store and the merchandise carried.

Among the oldest and best-known offices of this type is Felix Lilienthal Company, founded in 1903. Almost half of the 150 stores served by Felix Lilienthal Company have been with the office more than 50 years, and some are charter clients![2] Also in this category are a number of specialized offices, such as the Youth Fashion Guild, which serves only children's stores and youth sections of department stores.

COMMISSION OR MERCHANDISE-BROKER OFFICES.
A commission or merchandise-broker office receives its fee directly from manufacturers in the form of a commission based upon a percentage of orders placed for their clients. While it might appear that the merchandise broker is more involved with the interests of the manufacturer than with those of the client store, this apparently has not been too great a handicap for a good commission office to overcome. There are many small commission offices operating, and they are the perfect answer for small fashion stores whose annual sales volume would not permit them to pay for the services of any of the other types of resident buying offices. One of the largest of the merchandise-broker offices is Apparel Alliance, which receives 5 percent of invoiced cost from manufacturers, while collecting an annual $800 postage and handling payment from each client store.[3]

Store-Owned Offices

Resident buying offices that are owned and operated by the stores they represent divide into three groups: associated or cooperative offices, syndicate or corporate offices, and private offices. An **associated or cooperative office** is jointly owned and operated by a group of privately owned stores for their mutual use. A **syndicate or corporate office** is maintained by a parent organization that owns a group of stores. A **private office** is owned and operated by a single, out-of-town store organization and performs market work exclusively for that store.

ASSOCIATED OR COOPERATIVE OFFICES.
Membership to an associated or cooperative office is by invitation only and is considerably more expensive than if the store were a client of a salaried office. In this type of shareholder arrangement, an accepted store buys stock in the associated office in an amount scaled to its volume. Today, for a store doing $20 million annually, the requirement might be $1,250 in stock shares for every million dollars in volume (or $25,000); for one doing $100 million it might be $750 in stock shares per million dollars in volume (or $75,000).[4]

Stores that belong to an associated office are usually highly homogeneous as to sales volume, store policies, and target groups of customers. As a result, their relationship is generally an intimate one that includes an exchange of operating figures and the sharing of merchandising experiences.

Typical of this type of buying office are the Associated Merchandising Corporation, (AMC), Frederick Atkins, and the Specialty Stores Association. However, there are rela-

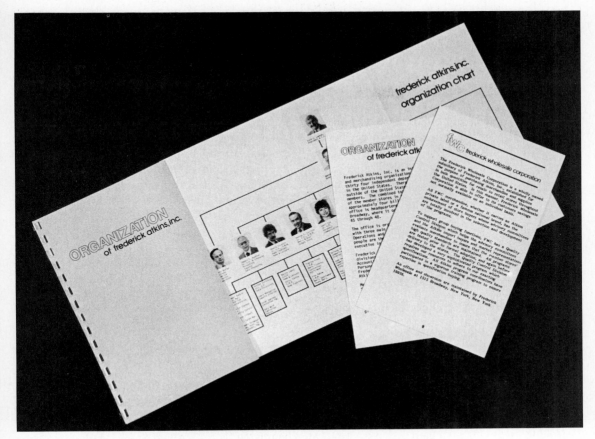

An associated buying office like Frederick Atkins is jointly owned and operated by a group of privately owned stores.

tively few associated resident buying offices, and their number is steadily decreasing as more and more privately owned store organizations are being absorbed by syndicates and holding corporations.

SYNDICATE OR CORPORATE OFFICES. A syndicate or corporate office is exclusively for those stores that are owned by the syndicate or holding corporation. Some offices of this type have more authority than do salaried or associated offices for the placing of merchandise orders to be delivered to member stores. In others, author-

ization from store buyers is required, despite the close corporate relationship. An example of a syndicate office is that maintained by Allied Stores Corporation, which owns Jordan Marsh in Boston, Stern's in New Jersey, The Bon in Seattle, and Joske's in Texas.

PRIVATE OFFICES. A private office is actually a staff bureau of a store, located in the market rather than in the store itself. Because of the investment involved and the high cost of operation, this type of office has virtually disappeared from the market. However, some stores maintain a private office within the facilities of an independent, associated, or syndicate buying office to which they belong. In this way, a store has access to all the services of the larger office, while the private office provides personnel to fulfill needs that are particular to that store. Such an office is usually under the direction of a manager who is on the store's payroll and is directly responsible to the store's management. Examples of this type of office are those maintained by Neiman-Marcus, a member store of the Carter Hawley Hale group; and Marshall Field's, now a member store of the Batus group.

Table 17-1 is a selected list of independent and store-owned resident buying offices.

ORGANIZATION AND SERVICES OF THE RESIDENT BUYING OFFICE

The typical resident buying office is organized along lines similar to those of a department or specialty store. Most have four divisions: merchandising, sales promotion, operations and research, and personnel; and many are adding a fifth division for foreign or overseas buying.

In the merchandising division, there are merchandise managers who supervise groups of market representatives. These market representatives' duties parallel, to a degree, those of retail store buyers. Just as store merchandise managers supervise a limited number of store buyers, the merchandise managers in resident buying offices also supervise a limited number of market representatives. Within this division there is also a fashion director, who is responsible for information on overall fashion trends. The fashion division collaborates with other parts of the merchandising division to offer to member stores interpretations of fashion direction. These interpretations are put into a fashion brochure that is sent to all member stores early in the season to serve as a guide to store

TABLE 17-1 A Selected List of Resident Buying Offices		
INDEPENDENT		STORE-OWNED
Salaried and/or Commissioned	Associated/Cooperative	Syndicate/Corporate
Anstendig, Blitstein & Gellenson, Inc.	Associated Merchandising Corp.	Allied Stores Marketing Corp.
Apparel Alliance	Frederick Atkins Co.	Associated Dry Goods Corp.
Atlas Buying Corp.	Mercantile Stores	Batus Retail Division
Jerry Bernstein	Specialty Stores Assoc.	Federated Department Stores
Jack Braunstein		Independent Retailers Syndicate
Carr Buying Office		R. H. Macy Corporate Buying Office
Certified Buying Service		May Merchandising Corp.
Clothiers Corp.		
Betty Cohn, Inc.		
Competitive Purchasing Service		
Henry Doneger Assoc.		
Fashion Guild		
Felix Lilienthal Company		
Loweth-National Buying Service		
Magerfield-Chernoff		
Retailers Representatives Inc.		
Van Buren-Newman Inc.		
Young Innovators		
Youth Fashion Guild		

presentation of the fashion message of the current season.

The sales promotion division of the resident buying office provides sales promotion ideas and aids to member stores. In this division, staff artists sketch some of the bulletins that are sent to stores. They also gather together for seasonal or special events color brochures for the member stores to send as mailers to their customers.

The operations and research division of the resident buying office provides advice, research, and in-depth studies relating to various specific issues. Included are exchange of sales, merchandising, expense, and profit information among member stores.

The personnel division generally keeps member stores up-to-date on current government regulations regarding personnel, and provides help and guidelines for placing the right person in the right position, not only in the resident buying office itself, but also for client stores.

In most of the larger resident buying offices (as well as some of the smaller ones whose clients buy a great deal of foreign merchandise) there is an overseas division or commissionaire located in key cities throughout the world. You will recall that a "commissionaire" is an agent representing stores in foreign market centers and is the equivalent of an American buying office. Because of the tremendous growth of foreign-produced merchandise being sold in this country, overseas divisions have gained added impact and importance in resident buying offices. The overseas division works very closely with the merchandising division, with many market representatives, and with client store buyers visiting and working in the foreign country in which the overseas division or commissionaire is located.

No matter how the organization of resident buying offices may differ, all resident buying offices are organized with one goal in mind. This goal is to provide their member stores a competitive edge, and to keep the stores well-informed on the most up-to-the-minute information and trends that affect their success.

The Market Representative

A **market representative** is a specialist who covers a narrow segment of the total market and makes information about it available to buyers of stores served by the resident office. Market representatives "live" in their markets and make themselves authorities on supply, demand, styles, prices, deliveries, and any conditions affecting supply and service to retailers. They visit resources, see lines, check into general conditions of supply and demand, verify trends, seek new, hot items, hunt up specific items requested by client stores, and follow up on delivery or other problems referred to them by client store buyers.

Although the market representative's responsibility is similar in many respects to that of a retail store buyer, it differs in one important aspect: market representatives cannot place orders for client stores except at the explicit request of the appropriate store buyer.

The market representative spends the early hours of each working day at a desk, reviewing mail from stores and seeing items and lines brought to the office's sample rooms by vendors' sales representatives. The market representative is also available to store buyers who may be in the market.

Afternoons are usually spent in the market, tracking down items, reviewing lines in producers' showrooms, and keeping in touch with what is happening in the industries assigned for coverage. In the late afternoon, the market representative returns to desk work, often to prepare a special bulletin to the stores on something they should know about immediately. It might be an opportunity for a special buy from a manufacturer who is closing out remainders, for instance, or the discovery of a new and exciting item that buyers should have a chance to consider without waiting for a market trip.

TO: BUYERS - BOYS' 8-20

FORM: ENID LeWINTER

NEW RESOURCE

CODE 18 BY GITANO

GITANO has introduced a new boyswear line called CODE 18. CODE 18 has successfully translated the Young Men's fashion influence for the boyswear customer. It is updated, yet not overdone or overpriced!

CODE 18'S first entry in the boyswear market emphasizes novelty bottoms. Fabrications featured are twill, sheeting, stone washed denim and off-the-wall canvas. Multi-pocket details and seaming interest are key treatments.

Screen printed T-shirts, french terry tops and novelty knit shirts complete the group.

Prices range from $10.00-$13.00 ea. for bottoms, $4.00 ea. for T-shirts and $5.50-$7.00 ea. for novelty tops. We strongly recommend that you shop this line.

RESOURCE: GITANO CODE 18
              112 West 34th Street
              New York, New York 10001

CONTACT: JOEL EISENBERG
              (212) 563-5360

#6105/sph
October 18, 1984

Market representatives sometimes issue special bulletins to keep client stores informed of developments and trends in the markets they cover.

Merchandising Services

Among merchandising services they provide to their client stores, resident buying offices report on current market information, conduct buyer clinics, in some cases provide central merchandising facilities, arrange for group purchases, sponsor a private-label or private-brand program, and place and follow up on orders.

CURRENT MARKET INFORMATION.

The market representatives are responsible for keeping appropriate buyers and merchandise managers of client stores continually informed of developments and trends in the market or markets that they are assigned to cover. They usually do this by sending out descriptive bulletins about new items, best sellers, and special price offerings, as well as market surveys.

When buyers arrive in the market, they check in first with their store's resident buying office and review their buying plans with the appropriate market representative. In the light of current supply and demand situations, fashion developments, and other pertinent factors, the buyer and market representative determine what changes, if any, should be made in the buying plan.

A great deal of market time is saved for buyers through such early conferences, since the market representative can direct them to those resources best able to fill their needs. If the buyers come to market hoping to locate some item they have not yet seen but have heard about and hope to find, the market representative will either suggest appropriate resources or advise against hunting for it, depending upon the availability and marketability of the particular item.

BUYER CLINICS.

Just prior to the start of major market weeks, the resident offices usually arrange a series of meetings or clinics for client store buyers of certain types of merchandise. These sessions are designed to give the buyers an idea of current fashion and market situations before they visit the showrooms of individual producers.

At such meetings the market representatives and other speakers discuss fashion trends, supply, retail prices, and market conditions. Often samples of the new season's merchandise are put on display. Occasionally a manufacturer comes before such a meeting to present a line, a new sales promotion program, or an idea for more effective product merchandising. In the course of such discussions, buyers may develop a new perspective in relation to their buying plans that enables them to make adjustments to improve the plans. Or they may emerge from the meeting with increased confidence in their plans.

CENTRAL MERCHANDISING.

With the information that unit controls provide, even a knowledgeable outsider, remote from a store, can gain sufficient insight into the preferences of a store's customers to be able to plan assortments and select merchandise for them. If a resident buying office is given this information about such fast-moving fashion categories as inexpensive dresses and budget sportswear, the buying office can perform this merchandising service for subscriber stores anywhere in the country. The advantage of a central merchandising operation of this type is that the buying office's representatives are in the wholesale markets daily and can make fresh selections or follow up on deliveries of orders constantly. This service, while not as extensively used today as it once was, is extremely valuable for smaller stores. They usually cannot afford to send their buyers into the market more than twice a year, which is not often enough to keep a stream of fresh, newsworthy fashions coming into stock.

In a central merchandising operation, each store provides the buying office with a dollar merchandise budget and an assortment plan, to which it adds general observations about its customers' preferences, such as ''no sleeveless dresses'' or ''our people like wide necklines.'' Using these guides, the resident buying office orders the garments it considers appropriate for each store. The store regularly reports to the buying office all receipts of merchandise, sales, markdowns, and customer returns, just as if it were reporting to a unit control department under its own roof. The records are kept in the buying office, however, so that the merchandiser in charge of the central merchandising operation has a finger on the pulse of demand in each store.

GROUP PURCHASES. Sometimes the market representative or the store buyer may suggest group action in a buying situation. Through **group purchase,** identical merchandise is bought by several stores at one time from a given resource, so that all participants may share in the advantages of a large-volume purchase. Such a group purchase might involve developing special merchandise for the exclusive use of member stores, pooling purchases in order to obtain financial benefits, or encouraging production of a new fashion item not yet widely available in the market but in which the stores have confidence. Group purchases may also include import items. Today in many offices import items form a majority of the group purchases.

A buying office may organize a group purchase when a manufacturer offers closeout merchandise in a quantity that is too large for one store to handle but that might be adequately apportioned among several stores. Group purchasing may also be used when the office prepares a group catalog for such occasions as Christmas or back-to-school promotions. When the catalog is one that can be used by a number of stores, a substantial reduction in printing costs can be realized by all the participating stores. Items selected for such a catalog, however, must be agreed upon by all the buyers, and each must plan to set aside sufficient money for the styles chosen by the group. Thus participation in group purchases may, on

occasion, involve adjustments in the planned assortments.

ORDER PLACEMENT AND FOLLOW-UP. Market representatives for resident buying offices, other than those maintained by syndicate or corporate holding companies, are not empowered to place orders for client stores. They may do so, however, at the request of store buyers. Frequently, a market representative will send out an illustrated bulletin on a new or hot item, suggesting that the appropriate buyer authorize a sample order for that store. Sometimes, store buyers may allocate a portion of their available money to market representatives to be used at the discretion of the latter.

Store buyers often send special orders to market representatives for placement with vendors. This is done to ensure faster service. Vendors might be inclined to overlook an order for one or two pieces of merchandise placed by a store buyer, but they are less apt to do so when that order is personally placed by the representative of a resident buying office that may have numerous potential store customers.

Some stores send copies of orders to resident buying offices for follow-up regarding delivery. Market representatives maintain tickler files on such orders and check with vendors to ensure that deliveries are made as specified.

PRIVATE-LABEL PROGRAMS. A continual search for items from good resources that can enable member stores to be exclusive with an item in their trading area has become a very important merchandising service. Private-label merchandise can be used for obtaining higher markups, better quality, lower retail prices, and the opportunity to build a store image. In addition to giving the store exclusivity and the opportunity for a higher markup, private-label merchandise helps protect the store from the promotional whims of its competitors. In many cases, the private label promotes customer loy-

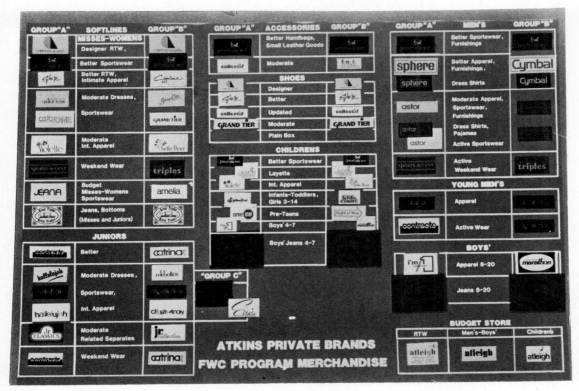

Private label programs are increasingly important services offered by resident buying offices.

alty and aids in securing the target audience the retailer is striving to attract.

Because of the larger amount of goods that an office can purchase, most stores work with their offices and participate in the private-label program to secure merchandise that is made specifically to their request. Because of this larger buying power, the merchandise can be produced at a lower cost, have a high degree of quality and performance traits, and be an exclusive in design, fabric, and color.

Sales Promotion Services

The sales promotion division of a resident buying office provides ideas and aids to member stores so that the stores can be more visible to customers. Color brochures or mailers, Christmas catalogs, and back-to-school inserts are some of the items provided to assist client stores in selling the goods they have selected and bought through the buying office.

COLOR
BROCHURES AND MAILERS.

Since most fashion stores encourage charge accounts, charge brochures and mailers are obtained by the office for the use of member stores. These are usually prepared by a manufacturer, but it is the office that negotiates for them and arranges to have its member stores' names imprinted on them.

FASHION FOCUS

FREDERICK ATKINS: A RESIDENT BUYING OFFICE AND MUCH MORE

"Stores have a need for exclusive merchandise that cannot be footballed by other companies,"[1] explains Ferd Lawson, president and chief executive officer of Frederick Atkins, Inc. And Frederick Atkins provides this type of merchandise for its members (and joint owners)—34 independent department store groups throughout the United States. Such brands as Triples in weekend wear, Jonathan Stewart in better sportswear, Grand Tier in shoes, and River Trader in women's and children's jeans are well-known to customers at Frederick Atkins' member retail corporations. They include such stores as Dillards in Texas and Arkansas, D. H. Holmes in New Orleans, Younkers in Des Moines, and B. Altman in New York. Each of the 34 stores has a "home" with Frederick Atkins in the form of an office on the 48th floor of a Times Square office building. Whenever a member buyer visits the New York markets, he or she has a private office to work from and a complete staff of Frederick Atkins advisers to work with.

The office is organized like a department store, with three main divisions: merchandising, operations, and finance. On the staff of 400 people are counterparts of every major executive in a store. And its merchandising departments include ready-to-wear, accessories, shoes, intimate apparel, children's, menswear and boys' wear, imports, home fashions/home and leisure, budget stores, and fashion. If a member store needs information on major fashion trends in weekend wear, or promotion and display ideas for better junior dresses, it can turn to Frederick Atkins for assistance. In fact, each store is regularly provided with complete merchandising and research reports on all markets and activities covered by full-line department stores. The office's Trend Intensification Program (TIP) is designed to help the

CATALOGS. The sales promotion division is expected to design and produce merchandise catalogs geared to important seasonal events and merchandise categories such as Christmas, back-to-school, and January white sales. The merchandise featured in these catalogs reflects the coordinated buying efforts for member stores. The sales promotion division will ar-

stores zero in on products that offer large volume and profit potential.

Frederick Atkins obtains its trend information by working with designers and manufacturers several months before each season in both the New York and California markets. Atkins is represented overseas by commissionaires in 28 European, Asian, and South American cities. Its American merchandise managers and market representatives also attend the spring and fall prêt-à-porter collections in Milan, Florence, Paris, and London. With this information in hand, the office sponsors two fashion directions meetings, one in March for fall trends and the other in September for spring. These meetings are attended by as many as 800 Atkins store personnel, including merchandise managers, sales promotion directors, buyers, and fashion directors.

In addition to the exclusive merchandise offered by the company, it has signed a licensing pact with the firm of Christian Aujard to market a designer women's sportswear line. The line will include dresses, coats, sportswear, shoes, lingerie, and a fragrance. Merchandising and marketing will be handled by Frederick Atkins. "We're recommending that the stores give [the line] a special identity with a special boutique and signing because we want to create awareness," explains Lawson.[2]

Frederick Atkins is an international research and merchandising organization. The research capability of the company enables member stores to gain valuable market information worldwide and comparative analyses that would otherwise be unavailable to relatively small department store organizations. The research division of the company coordinates the Performance Measurement Program, a series of reports showing departmental sales, expenses, and profit data from all member stores. It makes use of such data in analyzing departmental trends and provides members with in-depth studies, trend intensification reports, and prototype department reports.

Two other research-related services of Frederick Atkins that are valuable to member stores are in the sales promotion and personnel areas. Frederick Atkins assists the member stores in all areas of advertising, publicity, public relations, special events, visual merchandising, and marketing techniques. It also acts as a clearinghouse for the personnel divisions of member stores for the exchange of personnel-related surveys and information. Member stores are supplied with reports to update personnel executives on the latest issues and trends in employee benefit policies, turnover, and salaries. In addition to developing and conducting training programs for member stores, meetings are conducted with personnel executives from member stores throughout the year.

Atkins' newest service is provided by an off-price merchandise division that focuses on misses' sportswear and is planning to expand into men's sportswear and then into other apparel categories. This new off-price division also has some 30 nonmember customers.

Both the traditional and new services mentioned above give us a glimpse into the many and varied activities of a modern resident buying office—Frederick Atkins, Inc.

[1] Personal interview with Ferd Lawson, president and chief executive officer of Frederick Atkins, Inc., March 27, 1984.
[2] "Atkins Signs License Pact With Aujard," *Women's Wear Daily*, August 3, 1983, p. 8.

This Fashion Focus is based on information from the sources cited above and on these sources:

Samuel Feinberg, "From Where I Sit," *Women's Wear Daily*, January 27, 1984, p. 13.
"Organization of Frederick Atkins, Inc.," a 14-page booklet prepared and distributed by the company.

range to imprint the individual store's name, logo, special message, and prices so that the catalog appears to the customer to be the store's own promotion and production.

Operations and Research Services

The services provided to member stores from the operations and research division are the types of information and aid that support the

Resident buying offices plan catalogs so that they appear to be the store's own.

merchandising function. These services include market research and information exchange.

MARKET RESEARCH. In market research "the market" means not the market of producers, but the market of consumers. Market researchers conduct studies to determine customer preferences, lifestyle trends, and changing consumer purchasing patterns. Without this service, many stores would have little other than in-store aids and information to help them do any strategic or long-range planning. Market research and reporting provided by the resident buying office is especially helpful because it is correlated to the needs and wants of the target customer of the member stores.

INFORMATION EXCHANGE. The comparing and contrasting of pertinent information is helpful to member stores. Not only is the exchange of ideas and promotions that have been successful important, equally important is the exchange of information about

unsuccessful promotions. Learning through others' mistakes is sometimes quicker and easier than "doing it yourself."

Personnel Services

Because there are so many new government regulations concerning personnel practices, it is important for stores to be kept informed of these laws. Many smaller stores do not have official personnel departments, so it is important for them to be updated periodically on hiring and labor/management regulations.

RECRUITMENT SERVICE. This important service is performed differently in each of the different types of resident buying offices. In the large cooperative corporate offices, it is usual for them to have an actual executive recruitment office, both for the office and for the member stores. In the smaller offices, this function or service may be performed on a much less formal level. In some instances, the smaller buying office employs the service of an executive search or employment office on behalf of its store clients; in other cases, it may pass the word around informally in the market, using key manufacturing resources to attract the attention of executives from other stores or offices who might be interested in making a change.

Overseas Services

Because imports represent an extremely important and profitable segment of the fashion business, great attention is now paid to the markets of the world. Whether it is a store-owned office or an independent commissionaire office hired by the resident buying office in the foreign market, almost all offices are keenly aware that they must have representation in the fashion centers of the world.

These offices and commissionaires develop and maintain foreign resource relationships, assist office and store personnel on overseas trips, set up meetings, and follow through on orders after the buyers have left the foreign country. Many foreign offices also have product development and testing facilities that help to ensure that import items are sized and constructed to American specifications, and that, where necessary, American safety and labeling regulations are met. (See Chapter 14.)

CHANGING PATTERNS IN RESIDENT BUYING OFFICES

A resident buying office that satisfactorily serves its member stores across the nation easily becomes capable of also serving foreign stores, and of rounding up merchandise that can be sold to nonmember stores. Thus overseas divisions, wholesale divisions, and import-export activities have developed. All of these produce revenue for the resident buying office and extend its scope and range of services.

Off-Price Offices

The institution of off-price retailing, already mentioned in Chapters 15 and 16, is creating varied developments in resident buying office and store policies. A large number of off-price resident buying offices have recently been established.

Arthur B. Britten has been acknowledged as the pioneer in the off-price women's fashion field. In 1983 he had already built up a $100 million client volume, and offered a contract that called for a client to buy a minimum of $300,000 in yearly cost purchases. Typically, his remuneration is about 5 percent (at cost) of the quantities purchased.[5] Several stores of both minor and major volume are availing themselves of off-price office services with no thought of discontinuing the services of their traditional offices.

A few long-established offices have set up or are setting up in-house off-price divisions. It is still not clear to either retailers or resident buying office management just how important this type of buying will continue to be.

Product Development

In many resident buying offices, merchandise representative positions are being recast and divided into product managers, responsible for worldwide product development, and merchandise analysts, responsible for domestic market analysis. This move has been undertaken to intensify the role and effort in merchandising that the offices offer their member stores. Product managers and market analysts are better equipped to build and merchandise private-label programs, wholesale divisions, and overseas fashion importing, and to obtain the product and production know-how necessary for getting the best goods at the best price.

The Carter Hawley Hale group opened a New York product development office in the fall of 1981. This product development office develops exclusive merchandise, both domestic and imported, for private-label marketing throughout Carter Hawley Hale's various department and specialty store divisions.

This new office did not affect the relationship CHH divisions had with its resident buying offices. The new office was not a "buying office," but strictly a product development office. By 1986, CHH plans to have private-label merchandise represent from 8 to 10 percent of the volume in CHH's stores.[6]

TRENDS

In many buying offices the traditional role will change from reactor to anticipator in the coming decade. In order to succeed, buying offices must be prepared to monitor socioeconomic and psychological forces and be able to translate for member stores the implications for marketing and merchandising direction.

There is also evidence of strengthened status for the marketing function of resident buying offices and the people who will head this function. The marketing division will take the demographics and psychographics and integrate them into the merchandising, sales promotion, and selling efforts of their member stores.

Specialized resident buying offices are a major trend that is growing every year. There are specific offices for children's wear, boutique merchandise, women's wear, menswear, and offices catering and geared only to off-price merchandise. Many buying offices have begun to refer to their services as research and consultant services, rather than buying services.

The more market research, the more help made available to the retailer, the better the retailer's chance for survival in the highly competitive fashion business. Resident buying offices and the vast array of specialized services they offer appear to be flourishing.

REFERENCES

[1] Lewis Spalding, "Buying Offices: A Changing Business," *Stores*, April 1983, p. 18.
[2] Ibid., p. 20.
[3] Ibid., p. 19.
[4] Ibid., p. 18.
[5] Ibid.
[6] "Carter Hawley Hale Plans New York Product Development Office," *Women's Wear Daily*, August 12, 1981, p. 43.

MERCHANDISING VOCABULARY

Define or briefly explain the following terms:

Associated or cooperative office
Commission or merchandise broker office
Group purchase
Market representative

Private office
Resident buying office
Salaried, fee, or paid office
Syndicate or corporate office

1. What is the major function of the resident buying office? What additional services do they perform? Why are resident buying offices particularly advantageous to a small store?
2. List and briefly describe the differences between the five major types of resident buying offices.
3. Describe the organization of a typical resident buying office today.
4. What would a typical day's activities be for a market representative?
5. Name and briefly describe the six major merchandising services provided to clients by resident buying offices.
6. Describe the sales promotion services of a resident buying office.
7. What types of personnel services are provided by the buying office?
8. How does the resident buying office work with its clients in purchasing foreign goods?
9. How has off-price retailing affected the resident buying offices?
10. What is the relationship between product development responsibilities assumed by many resident buying offices and the growing popularity of private-label merchandise?

1. Discuss the differences between the responsibilities of the market representative and those of a store buyer.
2. Discuss the changing patterns of resident buying offices and the factors that have brought about these changes.

18. OTHER FASHION AUXILIARY SERVICES

The merchandising of fashion is a business aided by many enterprises that neither produce fashion nor physically distribute it. These are the many auxiliary services whose business it is to keep fashion in front of the public either through advertising or publicity. Chief among these are the independent agencies, offices, and companies that analyze various aspects of the fashion business and pass on their information and advice to producers and retailers. Through their constant efforts it is possible for the public—the ultimate consumers—to keep up-to-date with respect to the ever-changing fashion industry.

In their broadest context these auxiliary services fall into three major categories: advertising, publicity, and public relations. **Advertising** is the paid use of space or time in any medium. Advertising may appear in newspapers, magazines, catalogs, direct mail, and other printed media. It may appear also on radio and television. **Publicity** is the free and voluntary mention of a firm, brand, product, or person in some form of the media. The purpose of publicity is to inform or to enhance interest. **Public relations** is a broader term than publicity. Public relations works to improve the client's public image and may develop long-range plans and directions for this purpose.

You and this little bear can make a dream come true for a terminally ill child

Remember the wishes and dreams of your childhood? Since you've grown up, you've probably had the opportunity to make those dreams come true. Until the Teddi Project, children with terminal illnesses had little hope of realizing their dreams.

The Teddi Project, founded by Gary Mervis in memory of his daughter Teddi, is a very special fund that makes it possible for these boys and girls to have what the finest medical treatment and loving care can't provide: the joy of a trip to Disneyland, the excitement of meeting an idol, the honor of sitting on a favorite team's bench. Whatever their hearts desire, the Teddi Project is there to make it happen.

You can help grant a fervent wish for a terminally ill child this Christmas season, by purchasing one or more of these adorable little Teddi bears. At just $2 each, these bears will stuff a stocking, trim a tree, decorate a package and bring a smile to a small face on Christmas Day. All proceeds go to the Teddi Project; the $2 cost includes tax. The bears are available at all McCurdy's stores.

McCurdy's is proud to support the Teddi Project, an outgrowth of Camp Good Days and Special Times. Won't you join us in our efforts to make dreams come true?

McCurdy's

This ad represents good public relations—and a good cause.

FASHION MAGAZINES

Over 150 years ago, women suddenly had a new source to consult about fashion. Instead of just discussing new shapes and designs with friends, they could "read all about it" in *Godey's Lady's Book*. This periodical became the authoritative source for fashion news. Its editor, Sara Joseph Hale, is remembered as one of the first exponents of women's rights because of her influential editorials on the acceptance of women in the professions. With advertising, illustrations, and well-written text, *Godey's Lady's Book* provided women with information on latest styles and fabrics as well as a wealth of helpful hints and pertinent facts of interest. It was, therefore, the first fashion magazine.

Reporting and Interpreting

The business of reporting and interpreting the latest fashion news to their readers is still the primary aim of fashion magazines. In pursuit of this aim, fashion magazines send their editors to wholesale markets in America and overseas to report on important fashion trends and styles. *Vogue, Harper's Bazaar, Mademoiselle, Glamour, Seventeen* for younger devotees, *Working Woman* and *Savvy* for working women, and *Modern Bride* and *Bride's,* all are fashion authorities on women's apparel and accessories. These magazines also delve increasingly into health and fitness as well as fiction. Among publications for men, the monthly issues of *Playboy, M,* and *Esquire* focus on men's fashions and devote a good deal of space to a wide range of advertisements and editorials, while *Gentlemen's Quarterly* is devoted exclusively to fashions for men.

Fashion editors attend the various collections, taking notes on what they like best among the styles shown. They also sift through all the news releases that come into their offices, as well as do their own investigating by viewing the lines of designers and manufacturers throughout the year.

Editorial and Advertising Credits

The link between the manufacturers and the retailers of fashion is forged in magazine publicity through editorial credits. Fashion magazine editors visit manufacturers' showrooms and choose from the various lines the new apparel and accessories fashions that they feel are the most newsworthy. These they have photographed and shown in their magazine pages with the manufacturer's name given a credit. In addition, the magazine may list a few of the retail stores where each of the styles can be found, together with the approximate retail price of each. This listing or mention of retail stores that carry a photographed style is known as an **editorial credit.** Fashion magazines notify the selected stores of the editorial credit, and the stores are supposed to back it up by having the apparel and accessories in stock when the fashion magazine appears on the newsstands.

For stores that do not receive either advertising or editorial credit for an item, it is still possible to benefit from the magazine publicity by stocking and possibly advertising the item, and displaying it with signs identifying it "As featured in ———magazine." If the manufacturer uses hang-tags featuring an editorialized item and photo blowups of it, retailers can utilize these aids to inform customers of the fashion importance of these items.

Fashion magazines prepare editorial features on special designers, manufacturers, or retailers who are making important news in the merchandising of fashion. Though such reporting is supposed to depend solely on the merits of the fashion products themselves, the amount of free editorial publicity sometimes seems to be in a direct ratio to the amount of paid advertising placed in the magazine by the featured designer, manufacturer, or retailer.

Trend Information

Fashion magazines do provide invaluable services to the fashion industry. Their fashion

On a fast-moving day—Gianfranco Ferre's pants suit, op-
posite, with its perfect
man-tailored jacket, matching
wool trousers, silk shirt. And a
bigger coat—in leather, lined
with quilted covert cloth. Suit,
about $1475; blouse and
scarf, about $400; coat, about
$2125. Turnout, Gianfranco
Ferre Boutique at Torie Steele,
Beverly Hills. Coat and suit at
Bergdorf Goodman. Blouse to
order.... When you want
something that has a little
"more," *right* Perry Ellis' wonderful bordeaux velvet jacket
over his new draped skirt in
soft black satin wool, a cognac
silk blouse. Jacket, about
$320; skirt, about $190;
blouse, about $140. Bergdorf
Goodman; Lois Geans, Mag-
nolia **AR**, Balliet's; Mary V's,
Tyler **TX**; Neiman-Marcus...
Beauty Note: "Less is more" in
makeup, opposite--Merle
Norman's Fragile Beige Foundation. Hair, Louis Alonzo for
Nubest & Co.; makeup, Mar-
garet Avery. Details, additional stores, next to last pages.

Fashion magazines give editorial credits to retailers and producers. Note the mention of the Perry Ellis outfit pictured here at Bergdorf Goodman, Lois Geans in Magnolia, AR, etc.

forecasts of upcoming important colors and styles are vital to manufacturers and retailers. The information supplied by fashion magazines to retailers in the form of kits gives helpful tips on advertising, display, and fashion shows along with resources from which the featured fashions may be obtained. In addition, retailers can also look to fashion magazines to send editors to commentate fashion shows that are of value to both sides. The leading fashion magazines also provide research about their readers, in the form of published tables of facts and figures, which is important to retailers and manufacturers alike. Through their advertising and editorial presentations, fashion magazines are the medium in which fashion's newest and best are put forward. From the pioneering stage of fashion merchandising their pages take the readers along to the stage of full acceptance and ultimate purchase.

TRADE PUBLICATIONS

One of the most important aids to the merchandising of fashion is the **trade publication.** Unlike the fashion magazines just discussed, trade newspapers and magazines are published specifically for the professional people whose job it is to manufacture and sell fashion merchandise.

As general publications like city newspapers and national magazines keep the public informed about what is going on in the world, trade publications keep their special readers informed about what is going on at every level of the fashion business—raw materials, manufacturing, and retail selling. They announce new technical developments, analyze fashion trends, report on current business conditions, and generally help those involved in all parts of the fashion industry to keep up-to-date on a staggering number of new products, techniques, markets—even governmental regulations that have an effect on the fashion world.

Women's Wear Daily

Probably the best-known of the fashion trade publications is **Women's Wear Daily,** often referred to as the "bible" of the fashion industry. Certainly, *Women's Wear Daily* is one of the oldest trade publications, having been founded in 1890. Since that time, this trade newspaper, published by Fairchild Communications, has played a prominent role in the fashion business. *Women's Wear Daily,* also referred to as *WWD* in the trade, is a daily paper, published five times a week, and covers every aspect of the fashion industry. It plays an important role in the fashion communications system, reporting facts and events of common interest to fiber and fabric producers as well as to apparel producers. *WWD* also keeps retailers abreast of day-to-day developments and new directions within the various segments of the fashion industry. Additionally, in the last 20 years the paper has devoted a good amount of space to the social scene, covering fashions worn by the trend setters at social events and parties.

Women's Wear Daily, like other trade publications, serves as an advertising vehicle for both large and small firms comprising the fashion industries. Business notices, employment opportunities, industry-related want ads, and arrivals of buyers in the New York market are also included in each issue. The Monday, Thursday, and Friday issues highlight infants' and children's wear, lingerie and loungewear, and fashion accessories, respectively.

Other Trade Publications

Numerous trade publications are directed at and serve the needs of smaller and highly specialized segments of the fashion industry. *Fashion Accessories* and *Footwear News* are examples of publications that intensely cover one specific area of fashion. Department and specialty store management and merchandising executives read *Stores* and *Chain Store Age* to learn what other stores are doing, and to keep abreast of new developments in the retail world. The fiber and fabric companies have their trade publications, too—*Bobbin Magazine* and *Textile World.* Like *Women's Wear Daily,* the *Daily News Record* is an important trade newspaper published 5 days a week. It specializes in textiles and menswear news.

Certainly, the rapidly accelerating pace of the fashion industry has created a need for these specialized publications. There are just so many things going on and so many new discoveries, products, processes, systems, and markets evolving that no one publication could report on them fully and effectively. Since the editors and writers on these trade publications are experts in their areas of the fashion world, they are able to analyze and select the important concepts and pass them on. In addition, they provide vital market research to their readers, as well as serving as sources of information.

CONSUMER AND GENERAL PUBLICATIONS

In addition to the important roles played by fashion and trade publications in the merchandising of fashion, a great deal of help is also supplied by consumer and general publications. Practically every newspaper in the country has a "fashion/home section" that keeps the reading public up-to-date on new apparel, accessories, and home-furnishings fashion trends, important new designers, and innovations in textiles and manufacturing methods. *Women's Wear Daily*'s consumer weekly, *W,* is very successfully making inroads here.

Many retailers depend upon local newspapers to report trendy and current fashion news to the reading public. To do this, the large city newspapers, such as *The New York Times, The Los Angeles Times, The Chicago Tribune, Atlanta Journal, The Washington Post,* and others, regularly send their fashion editors and writers to cover fashion openings and showings wherever in the world they are happening. Semiannual press week showings of fashion in New York and Los Angeles are examples of industry efforts to provide fashion news and information to every community in the nation via large and small newspapers as well as various general publications, ranging from weekly newsmagazines, such as *Time* and *Newsweek,* to monthly consumer publications, such as *Family Circle, Good Housekeeping,* and *Ladies' Home Journal.* As a result, consumers living even in tiny towns in the United States have ready and immediate access to the changing world of fashion.

On the local scene, retailers depend on the "fashion pages" or "women's pages" of the local newspapers to get their specific fashion news stories told. Since these pages represent a great deal of space to be filled daily, the various fashion editors and women's page editors depend on local stores and shops to provide information about newsworthy merchandise (fashion or otherwise) or store events that have importance in the local community. The publicity department of a large retail store or the publicity-minded owner or manager of a small store recognizes the value of free publicity in local newspapers or magazines. As a result, these people keep in close touch with the various fashion and women's page editors and reporters and maintain friendly relationships with them. When the retailer sends a publicity story or item to the newspaper, the editor or reporter makes a special effort to see that it is presented, if it proves newsworthy.

The same sort of publicity effort with the press may well be directed by fashion merchandisers to consumer publications with special appeal to women, such as *Good Housekeeping* and *Ladies' Home Journal.* Even such news weeklies as *Time* and *Newsweek* frequently report on current fashion news and trends they believe will be of interest to their readers.

THE BROADCAST MEDIA

Today advertisers have a choice of the two standard broadcast media, radio and television, and the new offshoot of television—cable. Unlike print media, the broadcast media are time oriented rather than space oriented. Both radio and television offer three general kinds of commercials: network, spot, and local, in descending order of cost.

Television

One can seldom turn on a television set today without seeing fashion being promoted. From news programs to talk shows to the entertainment shows and the commercials themselves, what the people are wearing is presented in full, glowing color. And what they are wearing is right in tune with the fashions of the time. To verify this, just watch an old rerun of a

Television fashions are in tune with the times—thanks to designers like Nolan Miller who creates the clothes worn on *Dynasty*.

favorite show and see how strange some of the skirt lengths look!

In addition to this general across-the-board exposure to current fashions on regularly scheduled TV programs, occasionally short, specially planned fashion shows are televised as part of certain talk shows or news programs. These presentations of fashion "news" may publicize the work of a specific designer or be staged by a retailer. Either way they provide viewers with fashion news.

Because of its prohibitive costs, television has not been used by the manufacturers and retailers of fashion as widely as have other media. Only retail giants such as Sears, Roebuck and JC Penney, and giant fiber firms such as DuPont and Monsanto, have found it economically viable to use television for advertising. However, in the late 1970s and early 1980s the situation began to change. Shortening the length of commercials to 20 seconds or even 10 seconds allowed an advertiser to get across a specific message. The whole phenomenon of the "jeans revolution" was largely due to the extensive television advertising used by designers and manufacturers such as Gloria Vanderbilt, Calvin Klein, and Jordache.

Manufacturers and retailers of fashion know that in order to reach "the television generation" they must use television as an advertising medium. Many companies depend on outside specialists, or consultants, to aid them in preparing their advertising programs for television. These production firms prepare the TV storyboards, photograph the fashions, select (or create) the music, and provide tapes of the finished commercial for television airing. Because the viewing public demands a high quality of professionalism, very few manufacturers or retailers attempt to produce their own commercials.

Certainly cable TV is an important newcomer to the world of television. It can have tremendous impact on the medium as a valuable tool for fashion advertising. With the proliferation of cable TV stations, with their lower costs and unfilled air time, there is every reason to expect that by the late 1980s fashion advertising will be seen on television everywhere in America, from the largest metropolises to rural villages. All signs point to the fact that the time of television as a valuable medium in the merchandising of fashion has come.

Radio

While television is unsurpassed in the visual merchandising of fashion, radio remains the broadcast medium that can take a message, fashion or otherwise, everywhere. The emergence of the transistor freed radios from dependence on electricity so that now, in times of power outages, all of us depend on our transistor radios to keep informed. Equally, the radio can go along wherever we go, whether in the car, on a trip, or out in the yard.

The 1950s rise of rock 'n' roll began the love affair between America's young people and the radio. And while other styles of music have joined rock in popularity, the importance of the radio to the young has remained strong. Designers and retailers of fashion were quick to realize this. By the late 1960s they considered radio the most important medium they could use to reach the youth market.

Today radio commercials for fashion are directed at the whole family. Men and women hear these messages over the car radio during morning and evening "drive time." People at home during the day hear fashion commercials during various talk shows and variety shows. And teenagers (and their younger brothers and sisters) are reached by commercials during continuous "Top 40" disc jockey shows—commercials most often read by the disc jockeys themselves.

As with television, some retailers and manufacturers depend on outside agencies to write their radio commercials, provide music if desired, and record them for use by radio stations. Others provide the written commercial to a time-buying group, which supplies it to radio stations to be read by the station disc jockeys or announcers.

ADVERTISING, PUBLICITY, AND PUBLIC RELATIONS AGENCIES

Other help for the merchandising of fashion is provided by the agencies that specialize in advertising, publicity, and public relations. As previously stated, advertising is the paid use of space or time in any medium. Advertising may appear in newspapers, magazines, and other printed media. It may also appear on radio and television. Publicity, on the other hand, is the free use of space or time in any form of media. Another important difference between advertising and publicity is the amount of control the advertiser can expect. Since advertising is paid for, the advertiser controls when, where, and how much, while the publicist says "please, when, and where you can."

Advertising Agencies

An advertising agency provides a myriad of services for its clients, in addition to the preparation and placement of ads and commercials in the media. In fact, the very name "advertising agency" might well be changed to "marketing communicator," so broad is the scope of the services offered. From study of the product and its potential market to choice of ad-

Many retailers have their own in-store advertising departments since they advertise on a daily basis.

vertising media and execution of all creative areas, the full-service agency can provide a client with vital aid.

Advertising agencies come in all sizes, from one-person operations to giant agencies employing hundreds of people. A small agency typically concentrates on a few small clients and serves them with a highly personalized touch. Large agencies with many accounts divide their staffs into smaller groups, each handling specific clients and products.

In the fashion industry, only the very large fiber companies and wholesale apparel houses generally make use of advertising agencies. Retailers, by the very fact that their advertising is on a daily basis and their customers are not always nationwide, usually have their own in-store advertising departments that handle most of their promotional work.

Publicity and Public Relations Agencies

The Fashion Focus on page 372 shows how a public relations firm played a big part in setting up "The Great Lycra Try-Out." There are many other services public relations agencies offer to the fashion industry. Many direct their efforts to getting publicity for clients and products. This requires the agency to keep informed of what the client has that is "news," and involves sending press releases, photographs, and stories to the desired medium.

However, public relations for a client may well involve far more than this. Public relations firms help their client companies present a good image to the public. They may do this through such avenues as having the client provide a needed service or gift to the community. This might be a playground for children, an endowment of the arts, or scholarships and awards to deserving people. An example in the fashion industry is the Coty Fashion Award, which goes to designers. In addition, public relations firms often make it possible for their clients to receive awards or honors, which enhances their image and gleans favorable publicity in the print and broadcast media.

Sometimes retailers have within their stores a public relations, publicity, or special events department. This department works closely with top management in presenting the store's best face to the public. Giant fiber and fabric companies and important fashion producers more frequently depend on outside public relations agencies to achieve this aim. Eleanor Lambert, Inc. and Ruth Hammer Associates are two of the respected names in this field. Some new names include Jody Donahue, Madeline De Vries, and Christina Gottfreid.

CONSULTANTS AND MARKET RESEARCH AGENCIES

The fashion business is so huge and complex that it is almost impossible for any one individual or company to keep up with it. Instead they depend upon the expertise of various fashion consultants and research agencies to alert them to the new and ever-changing aspects of the world of fashion.

Fashion Consultants

Fashion consultants are independent operating experts who provide information and services to both producers and retailers of fashion, usually on a retainer basis. Probably the most famous of these, and certainly one of the pioneers, was Tobé. It was in 1927 that Mrs. Tobé Coller Davis founded Tobé Associates, which is to this day, under the ownership of Marjorie S. Deane, an important fashion consulting service for retailers. This service publishes weekly "The Tobé Report" and produces videotapes called "Tobé on Tape" for the five major market seasons. There are other inter-preters of the fashion scene whose services are important to all levels of the fashion industry. In the last two decades, specialized fashion consultants, dealing with specific areas of the fashion industry, have also become popular. Children's wear, accessories, fibers, and fabrics consultants are examples.

The Fashion Group, Inc.

Serving as a vital clearinghouse for fashion information is **The Fashion Group, Inc.** This association is made up of thousands of professional women from the fashion world. They represent manufacturing, retailing, advertising, education—every area of pursuit concerning fashion. The Fashion Group has its headquarters in New York, but maintains regional chapters in major cities of the United States and foreign countries. To be accepted for membership in The Fashion Group, an applicant must have at least 5 years of executive-level experience in the fashion industry, plus the sponsorship and recommendation of five Fashion Group members.

The original purpose of The Fashion Group was to increase the opportunities for women at executive levels within the fashion industry. But since this early goal has begun to be realized, it now offers a wide range of services, some of which are available to those outside the organization.

The Fashion Group is world-famous for its exciting and prophetic fashion presentations. Through lavish fashion shows and fabric displays, the group offers to all in the fashion industry—members and nonmembers alike—expert analysis and evaluation of upcoming seasonal fashion trends from the American fashion scene, as well as coverage of the European shows and, more recently, the growing fashion areas of the Far East.

To keep its members up-to-date on what is happening in fashion, The Fashion Group offers career-counseling workshops, fashion-career literature, and monthly bulletins. Re-

AUXILIARY FASHION SERVICES: THE GREAT LYCRA TRY-OUT CAMPAIGN

Sometimes a project comes along that brings together an advertising agency, primary and secondary producers of fashion, and retailers in one big effort. Such was the case in "The Great Lycra Try-Out" a few years ago. Here's what happened.

Du Pont, the giant fiber company, had a product called Lycra spandex, an elastic filament that provided great elasticity and shape retention when used with other fibers. The success of Lycra in hosiery, bras and girdles, sportswear, and playwear was phenomenal. Consumers found that the garments had a superior give-and-take, returning to their original shape no matter how often they were worn and laundered. In only one area was the addition of Lycra not successful as shown by sales figures: jeans. For some reason, though jeans made with some Lycra were superior, the customers were not buying them.

At this point, Du Pont turned to a retail-oriented advertising agency to research the problem, make suggestions, and create an exciting advertising promotion to bring "jeans with Lycra" be-

cently, the group's range of interest has expanded to include local community projects in cities where it has a regional chapter. The Fashion Group now also offers fashion and grooming clinics in hospitals and other helping institutions.

Market Research Agencies

In addition, producers, manufacturers, and retailers of fashion can look to market research agencies for all types of surveys and studies of buying patterns. Such well-known research firms as Yankelovich, Skelly and White are also of vital importance for their extensive work in demographics and psychographics.

Trade Associations and Trade Shows

Associations of manufacturers and of retailers assist fashion buyers in many ways. The nature and frequency of the assistance available, however, are not uniform throughout the fashion industries. Some associations offer more help to buyers than others, and buyers learn to familiarize themselves with the degree of assistance they may expect in the industries from which they buy.

RETAIL BUYERS' GROUPS. Associations or clubs for buyers of a single classification of merchandise provide an opportunity for the exchange of opinion with others. At the very least, such an opportunity aids buyers in clarifying their own ideas about fashion and market conditions. In some instances, groups of this kind provide a medium through which buyers can transmit to an entire industry their preferences in matters ranging from the dates when lines should be opened to the sizes of

fore the public's eye and into its buying habits. It soon became apparent that the buying public simply did not know of the important wear and comfort quality of Lycra in jeans, that the jeans made with Lycra were not separated in the stores from the jeans made without it, and that in many stores the salespeople were not informed enough to discuss Lycra benefits with customers. Also, jeans with Lycra were more expensive and it was only by trying them on that customers could experience the difference in feel and fit. Because of these factors Du Pont and the advertising agency set out to educate, stimulate, and sell.

A show business–oriented public relations company was called on to create an exciting nationwide promotion involving stores, jeans manufacturers, and Du Pont. Thus, "The Great Lycra Try-Out" was born.

Tied in to the very popular NBC-TV weekly show *FAME*, the promotion invited young people to go into the participating stores in their cities to try on a pair of Lycra jeans and register to win a one-time role in *FAME*. No purchase was necessary. An airline and a Los Angeles hotel were promoted to fly the winners to Hollywood and to house them while there.

For this promotion, the advertising agency produced a dramatic ad format that was personalized for every participating store. It also created display units for "The Great Lycra Try-Out" and signs, counter cards, ballot boxes, and registration forms. Radio commercials were also produced.

The result of this combined effort paid off handsomely. Sales of jeans with Lycra soared once people tried them on. Retailers saw fantastic traffic in their stores and benefited from the continuing excitement. Manufacturers were pleased with the lift that the promotion gave the slowly declining jeans business. And Du Pont had accomplished its primary task—to convince potential consumers of the value of Lycra in jeans.

This is an example of just one way an advertising agency can aid the merchandising of fashion. There are others. But the Du Pont Lycra jeans campaign demonstrates how auxiliary fashion services aid the fashion industry on every level. This Fashion Focus is based on a personal interview with Mary Collins of Mary Collins, Inc., a public relations firm.

---

stock boxes to be used. Many such associations are subsidized by the industries concerned, or by trade publications, or both.

TRADE SHOWS. Retail or manufacturer groups, and sometimes independent organizations, establish trade shows at which a great many manufacturers in a given industry exhibit their lines under one roof and at the same time. "Under one roof" usually means in a hotel, or two or three hotels, in which several floors are set aside for exhibit space. With a minimum of time and travel, buyers can see almost every line they want to see. They can make comparisons and can exchange opinions in "corridor talk" with other buyers from all over the country. The impact of seeing so many lines in so short a time is great, and a clear impression of what the market offers can be readily gained. This is especially helpful in industries in which small firms predominate. The buyer can look in on dozens of manufacturers in one day at such a show, instead of trekking from building to building, up and down elevators, and possibly covering only four or five showrooms in as many hours. Among the industries in which such shows are regularly staged for retail buyers are shoes, notions, piece goods, and men's sportswear.

FASHION BULLETINS. Many trade associations publish fashion bulletins for buyers, to alert them to fashion trends and to explain their significance in terms of retail opportunities. Since whatever helps the retailer to sell an industry's products also helps the industry itself, some of these associations retain experts in retail merchandising and promotion. These

Retailers' trade associations hold conventions regularly, providing merchants and buyers with the opportunity to keep abreast of subjects of interest.

experts contribute suggestions to buyers about advertising, selling, and display related to current fashions. Especially noteworthy are the bulletins of some of the associations in the raw materials fields, which discuss colors and textures to be featured in coming seasons.

RETAIL CONVENTIONS.   Retailers' associations regularly hold conventions or meetings for their members. Some of the sessions are devoted to subjects of interest to fashion merchants and buyers, especially in areas that present unusual problems or opportunities. The **National Retail Merchants Association** (NRMA), at its annual convention (always held in New York City in early January), devotes sessions to various selected categories of merchandise whenever fashion developments (or the lack thereof) in the merchandise concerned make these worthwhile. For many years, also, a regular feature of NRMA conventions has been a discussion of outstanding retail fashion promotions during the previous year and the elements that made each successful.

MERCHANDISING VOCABULARY

Define or briefly explain the following terms:

Advertising
Editorial credit
National Retail Merchants
  Association
Publicity

Public relations
The Fashion Group, Inc.
Trade publication
Women's Wear Daily (WWD)

MERCHANDISING REVIEW

1. How do fashion magazines help to presell consumers on the latest trends in fashion?
2. How do stores that do not receive editorial credits benefit from magazine publicity?
3. What other services do fashion magazines provide for retail stores?
4. What information is contained in trade publications such as *Women's Wear Daily*? What role do other consumer and general publications play in telling the fashion story?
5. How does the publicity department of a large retail store work with the local news media to disseminate fashion information?
6. Why was advertising via television considered impractical by most retailers for many years?

7. What types of services are offered to retail stores by advertising agencies?
8. What methods are used by a publicity or public relations firm in promoting a retail store or manufacturing firm?
9. What activities of The Fashion Group aid the fashion world?
10. What kind of information might be gathered by a market research agency that would aid a fashion retailer? A fashion manufacturer?

MERCHANDISING DIGEST

1. Discuss the following statement from the text: "Through their advertising and editorial presentations, fashion magazines are the medium in which fashion's newest and best are put forward."
2. Discuss the methods used by fashion auxiliary services in analyzing the Lycra spandex problem, discussed in the Fashion Focus on page 372. Consider the findings of the market research, and the resulting advertising campaign. Can you think of another fashion product that has had limited acceptance and try to analyze why it has not been successful? What alternative advertising methods would you suggest?

EXPLORING FASHION RETAILING POLICIES

The objective of this project is to allow the student to synthesize the information learned in this unit and to assess its impact on different types of retailers and how they function.

A. Choose three different types of retail distributors of fashion:
- One should be the local department store in town
- One should be a specialty store in town
- One should be a choice of your own from any of the following types of retail distributors—discount store, off-price store, mass merchandiser, mail order catalog firm

Compare and contrast each of the three different types of retail distributors on the following points:
- Target customer
- Type of merchandise assortment
- Place on the fashion cycle
- Quality standards
- Foreign vs. domestic merchandise
- Selling and other customer services

B. Choose one major department or classification of goods (i.e., sportswear, dresses, shoes, etc.) in each store that you used in question A above. (It should be the same for all stores!) Compare these departments on the following points:
- Manufacturers carried (brand names, designer names, store name labels, etc.)
- Type of advertising used (Clip ads over a three-week period, comparing and contrasting the ads on your chosen classification.)
- Publicity or promotional events used by each retailer

C. Set up a chart (model it after Table 15-2 in Chapter 15) that shows information for each of the retail distributors you chose.

D. Cut and mount one ad from each retailer showing the retailer's merchandising and advertising policies. Explain the differences between them.

Fashion has a future—a future for you!

The fashion business offers tremendous challenges and opportunities to those people who seek to make their careers in it. The scope of the fashion business is international, and fashion activity is evident in almost all consumer-oriented products. Because the fashion field is such an enormous one, beginners often need a guide to the various paths that may lead them to their goals. Unit 4 offers such a guide. Brief descriptions of the areas involved at all four levels of the fashion business may save you uncertainty and help direct you to that part of the fashion field for which you will be most suited. Choosing any career in fashion cannot be done without thought, study, and planning.

Choosing a career in fashion is an individual choice; realistic evaluations should be made before you start your career. Chapter 19 gives insight and information on career paths in a variety of fields that are all part of the fashion business. Manufacturing at the primary and production levels, retailing, resi-

dent buying offices, and fashion service organizations are all detailed and investigated for growth and movement.

However, working for someone else does not always satisfy the career goal of some people. Being "your own boss" is very important to these people and for them we present Chapter 20 on entrepreneurship. Not everyone is suited to being an entrepreneur because it requires a tremendous commitment of time, energy, and money. In Chapter 20 there is information on the "how to" of starting your own business and information on support services available to the new entrepreneur. The qualities of an entrepreneur as well as career opportunities are also discussed in this chapter.

The Fashion Project at the end of Unit 4 provides a structure for research in order for you to gain insight into the possible job opportunities available to you. Whichever way you choose to enter the fascinating field of fashion, the methods described in this unit will be of aid.

19. JOB OPPORTUNITIES AND CAREER PATHS

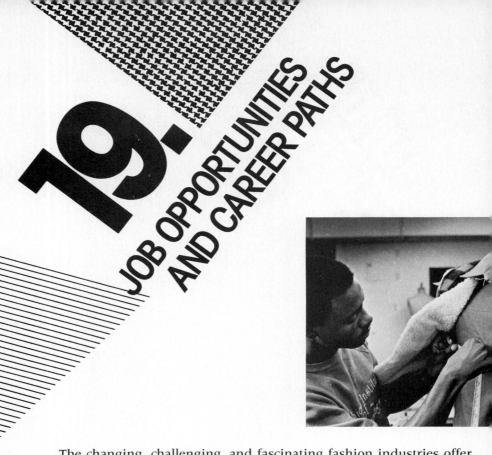

The changing, challenging, and fascinating fashion industries offer an endless variety of opportunities for people who are career-oriented and are willing to spend time preparing for their careers. Because the fashion field is enormous, beginners often need a guide to the various paths that may lead them to their goals.

This chapter offers such a guide. Brief descriptions of the areas open to people interested in fashion may save beginners some uncertainty and may help direct them to that part of the fashion field to which they will be most suited. A brief discussion of the steps to be taken when planning a career is also included.

There are opportunities in the fashion field for people of many different capabilities. Dedication, imagination, willingness to persevere, and sound business judgment are the important ingredients for success in this field.

SCOPE OF THE FASHION BUSINESS

The size and influence of the field of fashion cannot be measured in dollars alone. But out of every $100 in personal expenditures, $7.40 is used for apparel and accessories in the United States today.[1]

The fashion field, in terms of all that it includes, cannot be readily defined. Fashion in the broadest sense is a reflection of the consumer's way of life. It manifests itself in cars as well as clothing, in houses as well as hats—in any commodity or service in which the consumer exercises personal choice.

In the earlier part of this century, some fashion industries went along for years with little regard for consumer preferences and saw little consumer demand for style change. But as preferences and demands became more diverse, as a result of fast-changing lifestyles, most fashion industries came to accept the fact that consumers alone make fashions by their acceptance or rejection of proffered styles.

To the career seeker, the growing influence of fashion on industries unrelated to apparel and accessories means that experience is transferable: experience gained in the primary fashion industries can be applied to other industries serving consumers. The person who embarks on a fashion career today enters a field that is far-flung and many-faceted. In this field there is freedom to grow, freedom to change jobs or direction, and freedom to move to different cities or even to different countries without having to begin in an unrelated type of work.

International Character of American Fashion

The American fashion business today is international. Raw materials and manufactured goods, including both apparel and accessories items, are imported from all over the world. Also imported are ideas and inspiration, not only from the couture houses of Europe but from any part of the world where general news or fashion news is being made. Even outer space is within fashion's territory, as evidenced by jumpsuits and other apparel that have been inspired by astronaut gear.

American goods and ideas are exported.

Many American manufacturers contract to have their lines produced abroad under franchise and specification buying agreements. Producers in other countries send their young people to Seventh Avenue and to the fashion industries' technical schools in the United States to prepare them for fashion production careers. Sometimes the producers themselves seek United States know-how to help them establish or improve their fashion business in their home countries. In addition, the United States exports its know-how in fashion retailing. Stores from all over the world are members of the National Retail Merchants Association.

Within the borders of the United States, fashion activity is everywhere. Seventh Avenue in New York City remains the heart of the apparel-producing industries, but there are also creative centers in Los Angeles, Dallas, and Miami. Even in some seemingly unlikely small towns, there are mills and factories that need people to guide their output along current fashion lines. And there are retailers of fashion in every major city, in every suburb, and in every small town.

Thus, geography is not a limiting factor in a fashion career. Almost any location in this country and throughout the world is one in which fashion work of some sort can be found or created.

Facets of Fashion Activity

The fashion field is many-faceted, and the positions open to people starting a career are numerous and diverse. Some fields, such as designing, advertising, and display, usually demand a high degree of creativity and originality. Others, such as fiber and fabric research and development, require an interest and education in scientific subjects. Still others, such as plant management and retailing management, call for business know-how and administrative skills.

A pleasing personality, a genuine interest in people, and a willingness to work and learn are indispensable in the fashion field. A strong constitution and healthy feet are also helpful in the market work of retail buyers, buying office representatives, magazine editors, fashion coordinators, and their assistants. Skills in writing, sketching, typing, and photography are much in demand in the fashion field. Sewing and draping skills, even without a designer's creativity, can lead to such interesting work as sample making. In personnel, supervisory, and training work, an ability to teach is very helpful. This ability can also lead to a position as a teacher in one of the many schools devoted to fashion training.

Jobs may be classified by function, such as clerical, personnel, or sales positions; or by industry, such as the textile industry or the retail industry. There are sales and marketing and clerical positions in all phases of the fashion industry. Good work habits, basic typing and clerical skills, a willingness to please, and an interest in fashion can be all that are needed to start as a receptionist or secretary in one of the many branches of the fashion industry. Retail sales positions are available to the beginner, often with outstanding in-house training programs. Such jobs often offer the opportunity to discover and develop interest and talents useful to a career in fashion.

Another way to enter the fashion field is to begin as a model. Models are employed full- or part-time by many retail and manufacturing firms, the full-time jobs often being a combination of sales and modeling or clerical and modeling. A person's natural qualities, such as a certain type of face and figure, can be used to gain entry to a fashion career.

Entry-level jobs in some phases of the fashion industry, particularly in the apparel production trades, entail becoming an apprentice to an experienced worker. In other areas, such as the textile industry, college graduates become assistants to experienced workers such as stylists and colorists.

Education and experience requirements vary even between one business and another within the same industry. Many large retail organizations, for example, will not even interview a person for a position in the store's executive training program unless he or she has a baccalaureate degree. Others will accept associate degrees and certificates from specialized fashion schools. Still others hire for management training primarily those individuals on their sales staff who show the most promise. The wide variation in requirements, therefore, makes advance planning and research doubly important to the individual planning a fashion career.

CHOOSING A CAREER IN FASHION

Most successful people make things happen, rather than having things happen to them. Certainly, no one has yet discovered a guaranteed formula for success, but there are several things that can be done to smooth the path.

Evaluating Career Goals

An individual's career is usually the single most important factor in determining his or her lifestyle. Consideration should therefore be given to the effect career choice will have on such things as geographic location, family life, amount of time away from home, monetary compensation, degree of pressure and responsibility the job requires, and number of hours per week devoted to the job.

A realistic evaluation of personal talents and aptitudes should also be made. Does the individual aspiring to be a designer really have what it takes to reach the top? If not, at what point along the ladder of achievement will job satisfaction and monetary compensation bring sufficient rewards to make the effort worthwhile? What lateral moves within the fashion field could be made at various points in a career?

Too often dissatisfaction with a job is not the fault of either the job or the worker, but rather the result of a mismatch between the two. The scope and variety of job opportunities within the fashion field means that there is a fashion-related position for almost anyone who is interested, and a realistic evaluation of career goals will help eliminate many future disappointments.

In-Depth Job Study

Obviously, a wise decision cannot be made until the options are known. The importance of making an in-depth study of the career being considered cannot be overemphasized. As is true with many glamour jobs, there are a great many unrealistic perceptions of what a fashion career is really like. The average person, for example, sees a fashion buyer's job as one of exciting trips to the New York market, and does not realize either the extensive prep-

aration involved in planning for a buying trip or the exhausting demands of a week in the market. Fashion design and manufacturing are viewed from the perspective of the glitter and excitement of a fashion show, without consideration of the often unglamorous surroundings of the factory workroom where the garments are produced or the financial limits imposed upon the designer. A great many young people aspire to become fashion models without a realistic view of the extreme selectivity, grueling hours, short career span, or lack of even part-time positions. College graduates often expect to become buyers within a year, and are very surprised when they are asked to sell and do stock work, literally starting from the bottom in what might seem to be painfully slow progress toward their ultimate goal.

The project at the end of this unit provides an outline for an in-depth fashion career study. One of the most valuable aspects of the project

College graduates often start out with entry-level jobs selling and doing stock work.

is the student's interview with an individual working in his or her area of interest. In talking to a professional, the student can gain invaluable insight into the daily demands and rewards of the job.

Importance of First Jobs

First jobs in any industry can be critical, and the fashion business is no exception. Obviously, experience and training can be gained in any job, but will the job be a real plus on a résumé? What is the reputation of the firm or individual? What type of training program or apprenticeship is offered? Will in-depth exposure be offered in areas that will add to the trainee's credentials? The value of a good reference from an individual who is well respected in the industry cannot be overemphasized! And, it is often better to accept a lower-paying job that offers outstanding training, rather than a higher-paying position with narrower opportunity in the long run.

As the individual continues in the fashion world, he or she needs to be continually aware of new opportunities to grow professionally, by building a reputation for having worked with the best firms in the field. Keeping abreast of current trends and methods through reading trade publications, actively participating in professional organizations, and attending periodic workshops and seminars is also of the utmost importance.

A final note for those who aspire to own their own business: Experience is the best insurance against failure. Dun and Bradstreet cites lack of experience as the single most important factor in business failure.[2] Those who learn from experienced professionals and build a sound reputation in the fashion industry before trying to make it on their own have a much greater chance to succeed.

Career Paths

A **career** is a lifelong activity, involving all of the jobs an individual may have, both paid and unpaid. An aspiring designer may, for example, begin his or her career designing clothes for family and friends. As opportunities for education and experience occur, choices are made, and so an occupational **career path** or **career ladder** is formed: the order of occupations or periods of work in a person's life.[3] The culmination of a designer's career may be owning his or her own design and manufacturing firm.

A **job** is a specific position within an industry. In fashion retailing, typical **entry-level jobs,** requiring little or no specific training and experience, include salesperson, cashier, and stock person. **Mid-management positions,** requiring some experience and training and involving a higher degree of responsibility, include department manager or manager of a small store. **Management positions** include buyer, merchandise manager, and manager for a large store.

Those individuals who do some advance planning, who determine the goals they wish to pursue in the fashion industry, and what education, training, and experience are necessary to achieve those goals, are more likely to recognize a good opportunity when they see it. They are the ones who make things happen!

CAREERS IN MANUFACTURING

The principal manufacturing industries in the fashion field require fashion-oriented and fashion-trained people to guide their production, market their products to the industries they serve, and keep both their customers and fashion consumers informed about their products. Additionally, these industries employ technical experts of all kinds, skilled and unskilled factory labor, and clerical workers of various types.

Fashion-related careers to be found in manufacturing include those in the raw materials fields, in production of both apparel and accessories, in the cosmetics industry, in the home sewing industry, and with suppliers to these industries.

Raw Materials Industries

The greatest number and variety of fashion careers in the raw materials field are found among the producers of fiber and fabrics. This field not only is big but also is always in close contact with all phases of the fashion business. Similar positions, but in smaller number, are also to be found with other raw materials producers, such as leather and furs, and their respective industry associations.

FASHION EXPERT. Fiber producers and fabric firms have fashion departments headed by individuals with a variety of titles who attend worldwide fashion openings, keep in close touch with all sources of fashion information, and disseminate the fashion story throughout their respective organizations. Candidates for such positions either may have already acquired fashion expertise in other areas of the fashion business or are employees of the firm who have demonstrated an ability to handle such responsibilities.

The fashion department's activities usually require personnel with the ability to coordinate apparel and accessories, to stage fashion shows, to work with the press, to assist individual producers and retailers with fashion-related problems or projects, and to set up fashion exhibits for the trade or for the public. These extremely varied demands made upon all who work in such departments constitute an excellent training school. Even at the clerical level, the beginners in producers' fashion departments learn much about fashion and, if sufficiently motivated, are in the position to train themselves for promotion.

FABRIC DESIGNER. While it takes technical skills to produce a fiber, it takes both technical and artistic skills to produce a fabric. Fabric companies employ designers who have not only technical knowledge of the processes involved in producing a fabric but also artistic ability and the ability to successfully anticipate fashion trends. The fabric designer, who works

months ahead of the apparel trades, needs fashion radar of superlative quality. Some designers are allowed to concentrate on their own ideas, while others are expected to work out special fabric designs for certain customers. In either case, the chief designer for a fabric mill makes fashion decisions that can involve vast capital investments every time a new season's line is prepared.

HAND WEAVER AND SILKSCREEN ARTIST. These individuals execute the designer's ideas on hand looms and through the silkscreen process. The silkscreen artist makes screens as well as doing the printing. After a time, hand weavers and silkscreen artists may be given the opportunity to develop their own designs.

FABRIC STYLIST AND COLORIST. Many fabric companies employ a fabric stylist and/or colorist to revise existing fabric designs for a new seasonal line, try out various color combinations for an existing design, or adapt designs for specific markets. Some people find these jobs to be a career; others use them as stepping-stones to more creative jobs in fabric design.

FABRIC LIBRARIAN. Most major synthetic fiber sources maintain libraries of fabrics that are made from their fibers. These libraries consist of fabric swatches clipped to cards on which detailed descriptions and sources of supply are recorded. The librarian in charge is expected to be thoroughly capable of discussing fashion trends and fabric matters with interested designers and manufacturers. The librarian must also be knowledgeable not only about the firm's products but also about the market in general.

EDUCATIONAL CONSULTANT. Most of the fiber producers and some of the fabric houses maintain departments to convey technical information about their products to apparel producers, retailers, and consumers. Educational departments answer inquiries, prepare exhibits, address groups of retail salespeople or consumers, and stage demonstrations. In addition to a knowledge of both the technology and the fashion influence involved, graciousness along with an ability to talk to people at all educational and social levels are musts in this work.

INDUSTRY CONSULTANT. Most of the fiber companies and some of the fabric houses assign executives to study the needs of the individual industries in which their products are used. These executives act as a liaison between their firms and the industries in which they specialize. If a company is about to introduce a new fiber, fabric, finish, or treatment, its industry consultants work closely with consumer goods producers, encouraging them to try the new product and helping them to solve any problems related to its use. The help these consultants give may also extend to the retail level, where retailers may be assisted in launching fashions that employ the new product.

PUBLICITY EXECUTIVE. In both fiber and fabric companies, the publicity staff keeps in close touch with technical as well as fashion matters and makes information about company products readily available to the trade and consumer press. Usually product stories can be tied to fashion information, enhancing their appeal to editors and readers alike.

The publicity executive in charge of the department generally has a thorough understanding of fashion and journalism, along with a pleasing personality and a good memory for names and faces. These attributes are essential in preparing press releases, working with photographers who provide illustrative material for those releases, and working with members of the press who seek help on feature stories or who want background information. Skill in subtle selling is useful in placing unsolicited publicity, when an editor has to be convinced of the value and interest of the story to the publication's audience.

In the major fiber-producing companies, there may be a corps of publicity executives, each specializing in one or two closely related industries. One may concentrate on the use of specific fibers in apparel fabrics, for instance, while another may specialize in the use of the company's fibers in rugs and carpeting. In smaller organizations, there may be only one such executive. In any case, there are usually typists, secretaries, and assistants, and a beginner who starts in any such capacity is in an excellent position to learn fashion publicity.

JOBS IN TEXTILE TECHNOLOGY. Positions within the industry are also available for individuals with technical training in the production of textile products. Converters oversee the various processes in the transition of greige goods to finished fabric. Lab technicians perform tests on fabrics, yarns, fibers, and garments to determine durability, colorfastness, and shrinkage. Other positions involve responsibility for quality control, design of graphs for knits, fabric analysis, and color research.

MARKETING FIBERS AND FABRICS. Both fiber and fabric industries offer career opportunities in sales, market research, and promotion. These are not always fashion jobs, however, and they are rarely open to beginners. Some experience within the company and some specialized skill in the field are likely to be more important in getting such jobs than a knowledge of fashion alone. Advertising, including its more exciting aspects such as the production of TV shows, is often handled by advertising agencies rather than by the company's own advertising department.

Cosmetics Industry

The cosmetics industry offers many positions similar to the textiles industry, yet has jobs

Cosmetics demonstrators are in increasing demand as this industry booms.

unique to the field in the area of marketing. Individuals with technical knowledge, such as a background in chemistry or medical technology, are employed in research and development to create new colors and products and to produce those products. Market research plays a vital role in determining customer needs and preferences, pricing competitively, and packaging the lines. Heavy emphasis is placed on developing marketing strategies and effective sales promotion campaigns in this highly competitive fashion field.

Working closely with distributors and retailers, the sales representatives, who are responsible for large territories, help to develop merchandise plans, to maintain inventory records, and to offer sales clinics and incentive plans to retail sales personnel. Specialists in presenting consumer beauty clinics often travel throughout the country, presenting popular "how to" clinics to promote their lines.

The growing popularity of in-home sales by such firms as Avon and Mary Kay attest to the wide range of opportunity in the field of cosmetics. These firms offer basic sales training courses to their personnel, many of whom work on a part-time basis. Periodic sales meetings include extensive motivational work with groups of representatives, and the results are often outstanding, especially considering the limited background of the majority of the salespeople in the field.

Apparel Trades

For creative people, the plum of the fashion apparel trades is the designer's job. But the climb to this top job is often laborious and uncertain, and the footing at the top may be slippery. New talent is always elbowing its way in, and even the most successful couture designers are haunted by the prospect of a season when their ideas do not have customer appeal.

DESIGNING. Because so much of an apparel firm's success depends upon the styling of its line, the designing responsibility is rarely entrusted to a beginner, even a highly talented one. There are matters of cost and mass-production techniques involved, for example, and there is also the business of judging accurately the point in the fashion cycle at which the firm's customers will buy.

For moderate-priced and mass-market producers, the designer's job may be one of adapting rather than creating. Immense skill may be required, nevertheless, to take a daringly original couture idea and modify it so that it appears bright and new but not terrifyingly unfamiliar to a mass-market or middle-income customer.

The beginner, aside from offering designs on a freelance basis, can seek a number of jobs below the designer level in hopes of working up to that top level. Entry-level design jobs include Assistant Designer, Sketcher-Stylist, Junior Designer, Pattern Maker, Sketcher, and Sample Maker.

Assistant Designer. As a member of a large designing team, the assistant works under a head designer. Designing talent, indicated by submitted samples and good technical knowledge, is expected so that the assistant can help the designer in every aspect of the latter's job. Also highly desirable are a good disposition and the ability to accept and learn from criticism. Amid the tensions and frustrations that surround a head designer's job, corrections and suggestions may not always be made with utmost tact. In companies with several assistant designers, a cutting assistant may also be employed. This job involves cutting samples, altering patterns, and generally assisting in the design room.

Sketcher-Stylist. The sketcher-stylist works directly with principals of the firm. This job involves shopping stores for current trends, sketching ideas, and working with the pattern maker in developing these ideas. Additional duties often include assisting in fabric selection, coordinating the line, and working with buyers in the merchandising of the line. Designing talent and a good eye for trends in silhouettes, color, and fabric are musts.

Junior Designer. The junior designer sketches original designs and adaptations, executes the first pattern, and may frequently sew the sample. This individual must be able to provide the company with new design ideas and make accurate projections of what will sell in the next season within the firm's price range. Strong creative ability and excellent technical skills in draping, pattern making, and sewing are musts, as well as an ability to spot trends and develop a coordinated line of apparel.

Pattern Maker. From the designer's sketch or sample, a pattern is made from which a sample garment is cut. The sample is tested for fit and appearance, and adjustments or even a new pattern may be required. Once acceptable results have been achieved and production of the new style has been decided upon, the pattern maker grades the pattern, that is, makes up a separate pattern for each of the sizes in which the style will be produced. The need for patience and technical skill is obvious, and these should be coupled with an understanding of sketching, draping, construction, and good workmanship.

Sketcher. From the designer's rough drawings, working sketches may be made for the information of the sample maker and also for illustrations to be used in the showroom book. The showroom book includes fashion sketches of each style in a line, together with swatches of the materials used for each style illustrated.

Sample Maker. An all-around sewer is expected to construct a garment from a sketch or pattern. If it is to be modeled, the sample maker adjusts it to fit the designated model perfectly. The job of a sample maker is a particularly instructive one for future designers, since it provides training in the fundamentals of design, sketching, pattern making, and construction.[4]

APPAREL PRODUCTION. Positions in this field are with apparel manufacturing plants or offices. Skilled jobs for fashion graduates are available in both apparel production management and in pattern making.

Apparel Production Management. Entry-level positions in this field include junior engineers, costing engineers, assistant plant managers, production assistants, and quality control engineers. The responsibilities of each position are given below.

- *Junior Engineer*—Sets piece rates; does plant layout and time and motion studies; and is involved in methods engineering problems.
- *Costing Engineer*—Determines cost of manufacturing apparel, taking into account piece rates, material costs, and all other production considerations.
- *Assistant Plant Manager*—Assists in staffing the plant; assigns work loads; and assists in supervising plant operations including cutting, sewing, pressing, warehousing, and shipping.
- *Production Assistant*—Assists the production manager in keeping records that relate to production of merchandise; keeps clients informed on progress of orders; and expedites work flow and deliveries.
- *Quality Control Engineer*—Develops specifications for garments and fabrics and follows through to determine if such specifications are followed.

Production assistants may qualify for the job with training in either apparel production or fashion merchandising or buying. All other positions require strong apparel production skills.

Pattern Making. Entry-level positions in this field include assistant pattern maker, cutting assistant, grader trainee, and marker trainee.

The responsibilities of each position are given below.

- *Assistant Pattern Maker*—Works under the supervision of the production pattern maker in making perfect patterns, often assisting in cutting, grading, and marking.
- *Cutting Assistant*—Cuts and duplicates samples by hand or machine, altering and balancing patterns.
- *Grader Trainee*—Prepares production patterns in various size ranges.
- *Marker Trainee*—Lays out production patterns onto fabric for maximum usage of goods under supervision of the production pattern maker.

All of these positions require an extensive background of course work in pattern-making technology, as well as the ability to work under pressure in a fast-paced environment.

ADVERTISING AND PUBLICITY. An advertising manager, with possibly an assistant or two, may handle the advertising and publicity for an apparel manufacturer. Whether or not the firm is large enough to hire the services of an advertising agency (and most are not), there may be occasions on which ads are placed in cooperation with retailers or in cooperation with fiber and fabric sources. Publicity, usually a part of the advertising job, involves sending out press releases to interest consumer publications in some of the firm's new styles. Promotion kits for retailers are prepared under the direction of the advertising manager, as are statement enclosures and other direct-mail pieces offered for retail use. Aspiring assistants in this job have a distinct advantage if they have had enough retail advertising experience to be able to draw up rough layouts and suggest copy for store use.

SALES OPPORTUNITIES. Sales representatives who call upon retail stores should know the fashion points as well as the value points of their merchandise. Today, sales representatives are expected to be able to address retail salespeople, if invited to do so, or even to take part in consumer forums and clinics.

Showroom sales are sometimes handled by a junior sales representative who is awaiting the opportunity to cover a territory alone. At other times, a showroom assistant, with a good disposition, good feet, and a good memory, is hired. The assistant is expected to greet customers, understand their requirements, show the line, and help them place orders.

Sales representatives may work, at straight salary, exclusively for one large-volume manufacturer who assigns large territories to the company salespeople. More often, sales representatives handle one or more lines as independent representatives, receiving commissions on all orders taken in their assigned territory. Many spend the majority of their time in permanent showrooms in the larger merchandise marts, although some still rent temporary space in the marts or in trade shows in smaller towns outside of major market areas. Some time is always spent with major accounts in their territory, visiting the stores and buyers on-site.

An independent representative works under a loose contractual agreement with the manufacturer for a set commission on orders taken. After receiving the order, the rep forwards it to the manufacturer, who ships directly to the retail store. Commissions are received only after the retailer has paid the manufacturer.[5]

An understanding of retail merchandising, promotion, and fashion coordination is extremely helpful in all sales jobs in the apparel field. When selling to retailers, it is important to understand their needs, problems, and methods of operation, as well as what stage of the fashion cycle is of major interest to their customers. With such a background, sales representatives can present a line more effectively and can also gather and develop sound retail merchandising and promotion ideas for their accounts.

Suppliers to the Apparel Trades

Belts, buttons, zippers, and other minor but necessary components of garments are produced and sold by companies that range in size from one-person operations to large national firms. A great deal of business with apparel producers is done by tiny firms that offer little opportunity to the outsider. Some of the larger producers, however, offer job opportunities in selling to the apparel trades or to retailers, working either for one firm or as a commission representative for several firms.

Fashion trends cause ups and downs for producers in this field, with consequent changes in selling opportunities. When fashion favors the industrial zipper, for example, no amount of sales ability is likely to create a market for delicate buttons or ruffling. When shifts are in, the most persuasive salespeople fail in their efforts to sell belts. In this field, a knowledge of fashion is important if producers are to know what products to offer and when to resign themselves to temporarily diminished sales prospects.

Sales representatives calling on the apparel trades should know, in addition to the fashion significance of what they offer, something about garment production, for the mechanics of production play an equally important part in a line's profitability as fashion does. Representatives calling on the retail trade usually find themselves selling to the notions department, whose buyer may not be strongly fashion-oriented. They must be especially skilled in presenting the fashion story of their wares, not only to the buyer but also to the salespeople. A notions department carries such a miscellaneous assortment of goods, from shoe polish to swim caps, that the fashion aspects of some of its assortment are often overlooked in sales training programs. The representative who can help the department on this point becomes doubly welcome.

Some of the larger producers of such items as buttons and zippers keep close track of fashion's impact on their business. It is not unusual for these firms to employ fashion experts who analyze trends to guide production toward the most salable types, sizes, and colors. These people also may have responsibilities in other areas such as publicity and promotion. In a large button firm, for example, the fashion expert may work out new and acceptable ways to use buttons to highlight the current fashion features of garments, and may then publicize these uses to apparel producers, notions departments, and the press; or they may work out displays that help retailers sell the company's buttons to the home-dressmaking customer. Such fashion specialist jobs are few in number, but they are fascinating for those who like widely varied activities. Entry is through the position of understudy or through acquiring sufficient fashion experience in other fields to be hired from the outside as a full-fledged expert or consultant.

Designing accessories can mean an exciting and creative opportunity for the talented beginner.

Accessories Trades

For the artistic person, the designing of accessories is a huge field in which a talented beginner or an experienced freelancer can find exciting creative opportunities. Many of the firms in the field are small; they depend upon freelance designers to style their lines and upon their industry trade associations to promote and publicize their products.

A background in apparel fashions is necessary to design accessories that coordinate with the related garments. A knowledge of production procedures and problems is also essential, as designing for commercial purposes has to result in a practical as well as a fashionable style.

The larger firms and the large industries in the accessories field offer some positions that combine fashion coordination and publicity functions. Similar jobs also exist in some of the trade associations serving these industries. Those firms that do national advertising, such as the better-known makers of shoes, handbags, and hosiery, have advertising departments that work with agencies, and suggest or develop tie-ins for retailers.

Selling jobs require fashion knowledge. Sales representatives or showroom assistants who can give retail buyers the fashion background of the merchandise have a natural advantage over those who know only quality and workmanship points.

A particularly interesting field of work is that associated with millinery syndicates, which are so close to their industry that they are almost a part of production. In these syndicates, the fashion staff works closely with both producers and retail stores, not only on millinery trends but on overall fashion trends and fashion coordination as well. Entry to these fashion staffs is usually gained as an assistant or as an already established expert from an allied field.

Jobs in the accessories field can lead to other fashion fields, too. One of the country's most successful fashion coordinators, who headed the coordination work at a major buying office for years, got her start as a stylist for a millinery syndicate. She won the syndicate job because she looked better in hats than other aspirants, but she succeeded because she brought to the job an excellent mind and sound training in fashion fundamentals.

Home Sewing Industry

According to research conducted by Butterick, 59 percent of American women know how to sew and the median number of garments sewn each year is 3.62; *Vogue Pattern Magazine* readers average 18 garments each year! The 40 million individuals who make their own clothes are as fashion-conscious as those who buy ready-to-wear—and often more so.[6] Some sew for the pleasure of it. Others sew in order to have garments of better quality than they could otherwise afford. Still others make their own clothes because their fashion ideas are a jump ahead of what they can find in the stores.

The industries that serve these home sewers include sewing machine companies, notions producers, pattern companies, and the over-the-counter divisions of fabric companies. All of these industries have learned—some of them the hard way—that fashion provides a stronger motivation for home dressmaking than either the economy or figure problems. All of these industries use stylists who can interpret fashion trends in terms of what the home sewer wants and can accomplish. Designers for the pattern companies are as much in step with fashion as those for apparel producers, but the former emphasize ways to achieve currently important effects without taxing the skills of the average sewer or demanding too much time in the production of the garment. Skills in design, production, journalism, illustration, marketing, merchandising, and teaching are all needed in carrying total fashion information to home sewers.

The fashion staffs of industries serving those who make their own and their family's clothes have learned the art of making instructions simple and clear. They work with photographers and sketchers to achieve illustrations that will show both how to make the garment and how the finished garment will look. Particularly in the fabric and pattern fields, members of fashion staffs have to be able to stage fashion shows for stores and give talks to consumers describing and illustrating how easily fashion can be created at home.

Working with schools and with schoolchildren is also vitally important, for if this effort is allowed to lapse, the industry may lose a generation of home sewers. Sewing was once learned at home, but many families have relinquished the training to the schools.

For those with designing ability, pattern companies offer jobs as assistants with the opportunity to work up. For those with a flair for fashion coordination, publicity, sales, or a combination of these, excellent career opportunities are offered by pattern companies, sewing machine companies, and some of the larger firms in the sewing notions field. Entry can be gained as an assistant or as an established expert in a related field.

Custom Clothing

An interesting field that has recently experienced a revival is that of custom clothing production. Clothing (not necessarily original designs) is made to order for individual customers, who select the fabric and pattern for each garment. This service is often combined with a wardrobe consulting service. Individuals interested in this field should have an eye for fashion, knowledge of clothing construction and available resources, and the ability to work on an intimate basis with their clientele in developing and maintaining a suitable wardrobe.

One of the most successful custom clothing firms in the South is owned by a former menswear buyer who became a highly successful commissioned salesperson, then opened his own business in Houston. Ray Opio employs a staff of tailors and has offices in the United States and Europe.

CAREERS IN RETAILING

One of the best ways to begin a career in fashion is as a salesperson in a retail organization. Experience in selling to customers is a must for all people interested in any career in the fashion field. For it is the salesperson who has direct contact with the customer, and in the fashion field it is the customer who is always right.

Every phase of retailing demands the ability to deal pleasantly with people—with customers, suppliers, and fellow workers alike. One of the earmarks of the successful buyer, merchandiser, or fashion coordinator is the ability to win the cooperation of subordinates as well as superiors. A much-admired and successful department store buyer was fond of saying that she was so fortunate in the cooperation she received from the salespeople, the publicity director, her fellow buyers, and others who worked with her, that she would do nothing to complicate their jobs. Her subordinates and colleagues told the story differently: she was so thoughtful and considerate that there was nothing they would not do to help her.

Merchandising Careers

The starting place for most merchandising careers is in selling. Here one experiences face-to-face encounters with customers and the problem of anticipating what they will want.

Traditionally, the merchandising career ladder has moved from a sales position up through the ranks to the buyer's position. However, in recent years many large firms with many branches have provided a choice: an aspiring fashion merchant may choose either the traditional sales-to-buyer route or a strictly management route.

THE BUYING ROUTE. A person who chooses the buying route can go from head of stock to assistant buyer to buyer to divisional merchandise manager and finally to general merchandise manager. The responsibilities of each position are given below.

Head of Stock. This is a position in which one may do some selling, but it mainly involves replenishing stock in the selling area from the stockroom, reporting "outs," noticing and reporting slow sellers, and advising the buyer on unfilled customer wants. In branch stores, the head of stock is usually a department manager who acts as a liaison between the salespeople and the buyer, and who may be responsible for more than one related department. Both the head of stock in a large store and the department manager at a branch may do some of the more routine reordering, subject to the buyer's approval.

Assistant Buyer. The assistant buyer's job is the next step upward. As an understudy to the buyer, the assistant buyer may be called in to view the line of a visiting sales representative and may be taken occasionally to the market on a buying trip. Usually, however, the assistant buyer relieves the buyer of floor supervision, helps to train and supervise salespeople, processes branch questions and requests, and writes up reorders for basic stocks subject to the buyer's approval. The assistant buyer may verify prices on incoming merchandise, telephone resources in another city to expedite merchandise on order, verify advertising proofs, and post advertising tear sheets in the

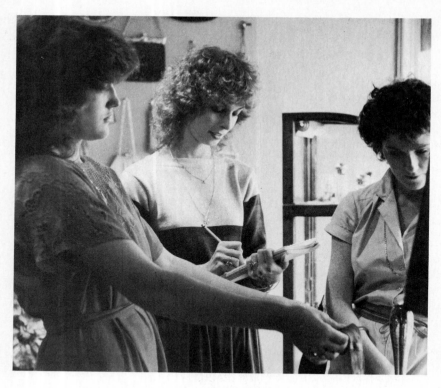

Assistant buyers perform a wide variety of tasks including helping out with inventory.

parent store department and dispatch other copies to the branches. The assistant buyer may also run meetings with salespeople on new merchandise or fashion or sales ability and schedule hours for sales and stock help.

Buyer. Buyers are virtually in business for themselves, in the sense that they have to budget and plan their expenditures, select the actual merchandise for resale, and decide what is to be advertised or displayed and why. The job usually involves from two to a dozen or more market trips a year. The buyer must have the ability to teach and train subordinates and the ability to work well with advertising, display, personnel, and other divisions of the store.

Divisional Merchandise Manager. In large stores, buyers of departments handling related merchandise are supervised by a divisional merchandise manager. Examples of related de-

partments are infants and children's wear, women's ready-to-wear, menswear, boys' wear, and home furnishings. In smaller stores, the supervisor of all the store's buyers is usually called the general merchandise manager. In either case, this person is often either a former buyer or a graduate of a school of retailing or business administration, or both. He or she has sufficient knowledge of budgetary controls and principles of management to supervise buyers. The merchandise manager coordinates the efforts of a group of departments, with or without the aid of a fashion director, so that the fashion picture each department presents to the public is related in theme, timing, and emphasis to those presented by the others.

General Merchandise Manager. The final rung on the merchandising career ladder is general merchandise manager, a top management position that demands, in addition to fashion and merchandising know-how, an understanding of every phase of store operation, from housekeeping to finances. To work from a selling position to a position responsible for policymaking is not impossible, but neither is it easy. A store may have hundreds or thousands of employees, but it has only a few people on its top management team.

THE MANAGEMENT ROUTE. A person who chooses the management route can go from assistant group sales manager to group sales manager to divisional sales manager and finally to store manager. The responsibilities of each position are given below.

Assistant Group Sales Manager. The assistant group sales manager works closely with the group sales manager in directing the activities of several related departments in a branch store. In this position, skills are built in sales and staff supervision, floor merchandising, inventory control, and business communications.

Group Sales Manager. The group sales manager (GSM) coordinates the personnel, merchandising, and operations aspects of several departments in a branch store. The person employed in this position must be both a merchant and a manager of people, learning to delegate responsibility in increasingly larger areas with a growing staff. A very large chain of stores might have several levels of group sales manager positions, with top-level GSMs managing the activities of two or three other executives. In such positions, success is measured by the ability to direct and train those executives in achieving their overall goals; their success becomes the senior GSM's success.

Divisional Sales Manager. The divisional sales manager is responsible for a large segment of a store. It is the responsibility of the divisional sales manager to develop the skills

of the group sales managers so that they can better manage, control, and direct the efforts of their areas to maximize profitable retail sales volume.

Store Manager. Store manager positions are near the top of the career ladder in management, second only to the chief executive officer and board of directors of the organization. The store manager is responsible for the total store operation in a single location.

BEGINNING IN RETAILING. For those interested in retailing as a career, well-qualified beginners may be recruited on college campuses or selected from among store employees who have demonstrated executive potential. For such people, large stores conduct formalized junior executive training programs. Total store orientation is provided through rotating job assignments in all phases of store operation and through regularly scheduled classes, usually conducted by heads of the various activities of the store. Those who successfully complete the training program qualify for junior executive positions, and they are assigned according to the talents and abilities they have shown during the training period.

The other way into large department and specialty stores is through their personnel departments, which interview, screen, and train desirable applicants 52 weeks of the year. A personal visit, with a preliminary mail contact if the store is in a distant city, is advisable. First, however, anyone interested in retail merchandising career should examine a store's advertising, display, and merchandise before making an application; unless one feels at ease in a particular store, he or she would be wise to look to other retail establishments for employment opportunities.

Smaller stores are necessarily less formal in their interviewing, hiring, training, and promotion procedures. Openings are fewer, and advancement may come more slowly than in a larger store. In a small organization, however, there is little chance of being overlooked for promotion, and there is ample opportunity to learn every phase of store operation as part of each day's work.

As a general rule, those who enjoy administrative work and prefer to function within the framework of clearly defined responsibilities are well advised to investigate the larger retail organizations for the start of their careers. Those who enjoy a shirt-sleeves atmosphere, who are versatile, and who enjoy dealing with all kinds of challenges (from digging out after a snowstorm to working up a spectacular fashion display) will probably enjoy the variety of work in a smaller store.

Sales Promotion Careers

Career opportunities in sales promotion include jobs on the advertising staff, the publicity and public relations staff, and the display staff.

COPYWRITERS AND ARTISTS.

Copywriters and artists who begin in retailing usually enjoy a tremendous advantage ever afterward. If they leave the field and go into advertising agencies or go to work for producers, they carry with them an understanding of consumer reaction that can be learned in no better school than the retail store. There is something exciting about a lineup of customers waiting for the store to open, telling a copywriter by their presence that the ad in last night's paper was good. Even if the merchandise offered was a real "doorbuster" special, the size and temper of the waiting crowd tell the copywriter just how effective the words were.

PUBLIC RELATIONS.

Publicity assignments usually grow out of copywriting jobs, although outsiders are sometimes hired for this work. Involved are such diverse activities as alerting the local press to newsworthy happenings, arranging for television interviews of visiting celebrities, and working up elaborate events—whether in the name of fashion, community,

or charity—that will brighten the store image. Writing ability and the ability to handle contacts are important, but in a large store the ability to keep track of details is even more important. If a department store undertakes to stage a fashion show, the publicity person assigned to the event may be responsible for checking on invitations, press and broadcast coverage, notices posted outside the store, notification of all store personnel, and so on.

DISPLAY EXECUTIVES.

Display executives usually start as assistants with a willingness to work hard. They advance in position if they demonstrate artistic sense, a knowledge of fashion, the ability to speak in visual terms to the store's customers, and the ability to pick up important selling points about merchandise.

Fashion Coordination and Fashion Direction

Partly merchandising and partly promotion, the jobs of fashion coordinator and fashion director are ideal for people who are extremely interested in fashion, know how to work with others, and have an unlimited supply of energy! These jobs involve working with a great many people, from merchandise or fashion information resources to store staff to customers, and their goals are accomplished largely through recommendations and advice rather than direct orders.

The job description and the degree of authority and responsibility vary widely from store to store, and unfortunately, the titles "coordinator" and "director" are often used interchangeably, even though the positions may be quite different. A fashion coordinator at one store may be primarily responsible for fashion shows and for coordinating efforts with the publicity director, and have very little if any work to do with buyers and merchandise managers. At another store, the fashion coordinator may be truly an experienced merchant who works closely with all phases of the fashion and buying-related aspects of the business. In the former instance, the fashion coordinator needs little more background than a flare for clothing coordination and the ability to organize a fashion show. In the latter, however, a strong fashion merchandising background, coupled with the ability to work with buyers and top management in making recommendations, is an essential requirement for success. Such an individual may have worked up through the merchandising or promotion staff, or may have come into the store with sufficient outside experience in fashion to qualify as a store's top fashion authority. The title "fashion director" is usually given to an individual with such experience and authority.

The fashion director's evaluation of a fashion trend or any aspect of it must be right, for he or she is making recommendations to experienced merchandisers who know their particular markets best. Each buyer is staking part of the budget on the director's judgment when the recommendations are followed. Every ad that is written in line with these suggestions and every sales training session that is staged with the director's help is done on the assumption that he or she knows how to read fashion's future. A beginner who has a chance to work as an assistant to such a fashion director soon learns that intuition is no match for systematic checking and rechecking. A considered opinion arrived at by one fashion expert alone is not always as safe a base for merchandising and promotion operations as the combined thinking of a store and a market full of expert watchers.

The fashion director is often one of the key store executives in a large chain who travel with buyers and merchandise managers to overseas markets as well as domestic markets. He or she may also be a member of a buying committee that travels to the Orient to contract for large orders to be produced exclusively for the chain according to store specifications.

As exciting as these jobs are, there are ac-tually very few full-time fashion directors or coordinators employed, even in large cities. In Houston, Texas, in 1985, there were only three fashion directors with the full responsibilities of the job. In most cases, the function of fashion director is handled by one of the store's top buyers or merchandise managers, along with his or her other duties.

Sales-Supporting Careers

Retail stores have openings in fields not directly related to the buying, selling, and promoting of merchandise. These activities, which may involve more than half the employees of a store, include personnel, employment and training, accounting, customer services, and adjustments, among many others. Even in the rapidly growing area of data processing jobs, fashion knowledge can be a valuable asset. For instance, add a knowledge of fashion merchandising to an understanding of computer programming, and the result is the kind of background that can lead to a career in computer program design for fashion-oriented companies.

Of the many sales-supporting job opportunities, training is the field in which a fashion background is most likely to be of direct use. Large stores with well-staffed training departments sometimes assign one training executive to each merchandise division to assist buyers in training salespeople. A training executive assigned to a group of fashion departments, for instance, might compile a reference library of basic information on fashion merchandise and also collect and route current information on fashions. Another assignment might be setting up courses to teach salespeople and prospective buyers the basic elements of fashion, or devising contests and quizzes to keep salespeople alert or to encourage them to sell related items. A background in fashion is extremely useful in this work, not only in the apparel and accessories departments but in any others that are part of the fashion business.

Owning a Retail Fashion Business

No discussion of careers in fashion retailing would be complete without mentioning the possibility of owning and operating an individual business. Having their own boutique or specialty shop is the dream of many individuals in the fashion business. (See Chapter 20 for a thorough discussion of owning your own business.)

Professional Fashion Sales Careers

Surprisingly enough, many commissioned salespersons in top fashion stores earn more than the buyers or store managers! Individuals who truly enjoy working one-on-one with a customer, who take a personal interest in the customer's lifestyle and clothing needs, and who derive a great deal of pleasure from completing a sale and seeing a satisfied customer walk out of the store should consider professional sales as a career. The excitement and pleasure of working with beautiful clothing and interesting people in an attractive atmosphere are key attractions—with few of the pressures and responsibilities that confront buyers and management!

Chain and Mail-Order Careers

Chain and catalog firms offer careers that are similar to those offered by independent stores, with this important exception: Buying, merchandising, publicity, and fashion coordination are handled by the headquarters staff rather than by the individual stores.

Career advancement up the retail management ladder, if one starts in a unit of a chain or in a catalog organization, begins with selling and moves to department manager, merchandise manager, store manager, and finally to district, regional, or central management. Those interested in such fields as buying, fashion coordination, promotion, catalog prepara-

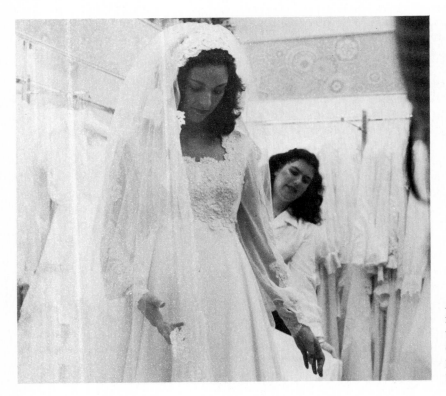

A bridal consultant is a fashion advisor who works one-on-one with customers, taking a personal interest in their wants and needs.

tion, merchandising, and quality control start as assistants in regional or central headquarters, where central buyers and merchandise managers are located.

Many highly specialized jobs in the chain and catalog companies call for intimate knowledge of the fashion business. For instance, the quality control department of one chain was called upon by the merchandising division to devise a size range for girls who fell between two size ranges currently offered by the children's market. The chain then made its new size range measurements available to any producers who wished to adopt them, whether or not they were resources of that chain.

Whatever special assets the beginner presents—apparel production techniques, laboratory know-how, or experience in copywriting, art, selling, buying, or coordination—the chain and the catalog companies can use them, but not always in the city or region where the applicant lives.

RESIDENT BUYING OFFICE CAREERS

Fashion careers in resident buying offices center around market work. Market representatives "live" in their markets, see every line that is important (and many that are not), and know supply and delivery conditions in those markets as well as they know the fashion aspects of the merchandise. Market representatives also learn to work with any number of bosses: their own supervisors, the heads of the client stores, and the buyers in the stores they serve.

Entry into the market representative's job is through the position of apprentice. Beginners work as assistants, literally running errands in the market all day. If the smile, the ability to remember, or the arches are weak, the career may never develop. The major job of an assistant is to follow up on details, to check with resources on deliveries and other questions that may arise, and to save the time of the

market representative. In the process, the beginner gets to know the markets, the buying office routines, and the needs of the client stores. If the work is done against a background of fashion training, it is more easily mastered and promotion is apt to be more rapid.

Buying-office people demonstrate tremendous physical and mental stamina in attending showings, handling mail and telephone calls, and working with visiting buyers. But they have no selling departments to oversee, no branch stores to visit, no weekend or holiday work, and no sales goals to meet. Their responsibilities are limited to specific markets.

Fashion directors in buying offices must function with an especially sure touch. Any errors of judgment on their part can mean wrong advice given to a number of client stores. They tour the major market sources to collect information, check their findings with appropriate market representatives, and consider what fashion publications have to suggest.

A fashion director for a resident buying office usually has a secretary and an assistant, at least one of whom is trained in fashion or sketching. In either job, a beginner with fashion training can quickly learn a great deal about fashion forecasting, markets, and coordination, knowledge of which is necessary in order to advance in the field.

Promotion staffs in resident buying offices are fairly small. In offices serving large stores, their function may be little more than reporting on what other stores are doing or what the New York stores are promoting. In offices serving small stores, they may draw up ads for the stores to use and send them out in the form of either rough layouts and copy suggestions or mats. The smaller the stores served by an office, the less likely the stores are to have full-fledged advertising departments and the more important it is for the buying office to supply them with such special assistance.

To find a place on the promotion staff of

such a resident buying office, it is necessary for an applicant to have retail advertising experience or to show examples of how to prepare a retail ad. Sketching and a flair for layout are helpful; writing ability is essential.

It is possible eventually to establish one's own buying office, provided one starts small, with a few client specialty shops and a versatile staff. Specialty shops have fewer departments, and they need fewer—but very capable—market representatives than department stores need. The outlay in capital, office space, and staff is relatively small if one starts with only the fashion departments.

CAREERS IN FASHION SERVICE ORGANIZATIONS

A wide variety of job opportunities is available in the service organizations that aid and assist the wholesale and retail fashion industries. These service organizations, such as advertising and publicity agencies, consumer and trade publications, trade associations, and consulting firms, perform functions that have a show-business quality about them. Work in these fields is hectic and, for those suited to it, fun. Each area has its own requirements, but in all of them there are important jobs in which an understanding of fashion is vital.

Advertising Agencies

Beginners, even those with special skills, often have a hard time entering the agency field. College graduates complain that they go to dozens of agencies and are offered nothing more exciting than a mail room or receptionist job. A solution to the beginner's problem may be to avoid the biggest and best-known agencies and seek a starting job in an agency of modest or small size. There the pay is likely to be small, the office tiny, and the future problematic, but the opportunities to work and learn are good and provide the experience necessary to qualify later for a good job in a major agency.

The careers in advertising agencies in which a fashion background can be useful include account executive, copywriter, illustrator, layout artist, and fashion consultant. The responsibilities of each position are given below.

ACCOUNT EXECUTIVE. The account executive solicits accounts and acts as liaison between client and agency staff. He or she also plans campaigns and calls upon the technical skills of the agency staff to develop them.

COPYWRITER. This creative person is expected to be an idea person, capable of originating campaign copy. The starting spot is copy cub; the top spot is copy chief.

ILLUSTRATOR AND LAYOUT ARTIST. These individuals must not only have creative talent and artistic ability, but also must understand the graphic arts, be able to specify typefaces and sizes, and know the problems of reproducing material in various media. An illustrator or layout artist starts with artistic skill and learns on the job how to adapt it to the needs of the ad agency.

FASHION CONSULTANT. In agencies that handle fashion accounts the fashion consultant guides campaigns, assists in client contacts, and provides the fashion background that other specialized agency executives may lack. Even an agency that does not handle fashion accounts may have a fashion consultant on the staff to make sure that the figures in illustrations and television commercials are wearing currently acceptable apparel, accessories, and hairstyles.

OTHER POSSIBILITIES. Clerical, secretarial, and various technical jobs abound in large agencies and can offer the beginner a foothold. For example, the media department is a haven

Sometimes large fashion staffs hire inexperienced assistants who learn on the job how to work with photographers, models, and an art department.

Consumer Publications

Nearly all consumer publications carry some sort of fashion material, and some are devoted exclusively to fashion. Career opportunities with such publications are immensely varied, ranging from editorial work to those numerous, behind-the-scenes activities that go into the publishing of a magazine or newspaper.

FASHION EDITOR. When fashion is presented in a publication, that publication's fashion judgment must be authoritative. Whether the publication is devoted entirely to fashion or simply runs a fashion section, the editor's job is to discover what the reader responds to, locate those fashions in the market, and illustrate examples of them at the right time. The editorial job can be all the more complicated because of pressures from publicity-hungry producers. An editor may cover the entire fashion market or just one segment of it, depending on the type of publication and the size of the publication's staff.

Large fashion staffs generally can absorb a few inexperienced assistants. For small pay, these people perform the necessary legwork in the market, and do a thousand other chores. They learn how to select and how to work with models, photographers, and an art department. They learn how to cut down a lengthy description of a new style to a dozen words, if that is all the space allowed for a caption. Fashion know-how, the ability to meet deadlines, and the ability to work with people are vitally important—at times even more important than writing or sketching skills.

Small fashion staffs, such as those on newspapers in small cities, do no market work but depend on press releases that come from the wire services and from producers and local retailers of fashion merchandise. Spending time as a general assistant in such a fashion department, which may also cover society news and

for those who understand statistics, since this department is responsible for measuring the worth of a publication's readership or a broadcast station's audience in terms of cost and increased exposure of the client's product. The research department investigates available information to guide the client's marketing and advertising efforts and often does some related studies on its own. The traffic department follows up on production schedules and makes sure that deadlines for advertising insertions are met.

Essential for any agency job is the ability to work well under pressure. Agency people do not acknowledge the word ''impossible'' in meeting deadlines.

garden-club activities, is useful preparation for big-city, big-publication jobs.

MERCHANDISING EDITOR. Behind the scenes, the merchandising editors of national publications and their staffs work to make sure that readers anywhere in the country can buy the merchandise that is featured editorially. They do this by reporting to retailers in advance of publication the details of what is to run, why it is important, and from what resources it is available. With their formidable knowledge of markets, merchandise, and retailing, these editors are also well equipped to offer retailers practical suggestions about how to successfully merchandise, promote, and display the items featured in their publications.

Developing a following among retailers is good sales strategy for a magazine that sells advertising to producers. Therefore, the merchandising staffs must be extremely knowledgeable and often quite creative about retail promotion. Some work up storewide or divisional promotional ideas that stores—even large stores with their own capable promotional staffs—can use. A typical ''package'' for a store may begin with a theme that ties in with a forthcoming issue of the magazine. To promote the theme, the publication's staff suggests merchandise and resources for it, as well as advertising copy for various types of media. If the merchandise lends itself well to fashion shows or displays, the retailer may receive scripts, posters, display diagrams, and even the offer of an editor's services as a commentator. Many of the awards given by the National Retail Merchants Association for outstanding retail fashion promotions are captured each year by just such packages developed by publications.

Merchandising staffs of consumer publications are usually large enough to absorb a beginner. Tirelessness and willingness to learn are essential; so is versatility. The beginner may be combing markets for weeks; then acting as host in a temporary showroom where future styles to be featured editorially are being shown to store buyers; then drafting copy for a suggested retail ad; then acting as liaison with outside experts hired to work up displays or the design of boutiques that have been suggested as part of a special promotion.

ADVERTISING SALES REP. Selling advertising space is the major source of revenue for a publication. The many aspects of selling accommodate various talents. Those who like selling deal with producers and their advertising agencies. People with a flair for research help the sales representatives to sell advertising space in the publication by supplying facts that indicate the publication's ability to enlist retail cooperation or that measure the buying power of the publication's readers. Those with a flair for persuasive writing may find a place on the advertising promotion staff, where presentations are developed to help the sales representatives conduct meetings with prospective advertisers.

Fashion background, sketching ability, and writing ability are aids to the beginner. Personality and contacts are vital in selling jobs, after one has become familiar enough with the publication to be entrusted with such assignments.

Trade Publications

Some trade publications are very narrowly specialized, such as *Accessories* and *Body Fashions and Intimate Apparel,* and are likely to be published monthly. Some are less specialized, such as *Retail Week,* and tend to be published weekly or semimonthly. A few, such as *Women's Wear Daily* (covering the women's apparel field) and *Daily News Record* (covering the menswear and textiles fields), provide in-depth coverage of a specific field and are published 5 days a week, Monday through Friday, except holidays. All may offer opportunities for beginners with an interest in fashion.

Editors of trade publications spend part of

their time in the market or investigating other sources of information and part of their time preparing material for publication. Assistants and secretaries to editors may be beginners learning how to make market calls, to select new products for illustration, and to write up what they have learned.

Trade publications hire beginners who are trained in publication procedures or journalism. Typing is indispensable, as are a durable smile for contacts with the trade and a good memory for names, places, and people. Knowing a particular industry is helpful, and knowing retailing even more so, because there is a regular need for articles for and about retailers. A good deal of rewriting is done from correspondents' reports and publicity releases.

Consulting Services to the Fashion Industry

The most glamorous of the consulting services involved in the fashion field is, of course, the fashion consultant. Of these, the oldest and best-known is the Tobé service, founded in 1927 by the late Tobé Coller Davis. As a young woman, she was hired to advise a retail store on its fashion merchandise by bringing the customers' point of view to bear on merchandise selections and promotions. From this start, she developed a syndicated service to which stores all over the country subscribed. With what is now a large staff, the firm continues to cover and interpret fashion news in such a way that buying, merchandising, and coordination executives can be guided by the views of skilled observers in every important fashion center. Reports, bulletins, clinics, videotapes, and individual advice are the subscribers' diet.

Some of the other services, like Amos Parrish & Company, combine general advice on store operation with some fashion advice. Others exist primarily to make the skill of an expert in fashion promotion, such as Estelle Hamburger or Mildred Custin, available to interested stores. Still others, such as the Retail News Bureau, offer a wide range of consultant services that may involve any subject from merchandise resources to advertising results.

In approaching any enterprise of this kind, the beginner is wise to offer other qualifications in addition to a background in fashion: typing, writing or sketching ability, or some retail experience. Some of the ''graduates'' of these services have gone on to become fashion coordinators for major retailers, buying offices, or producers. The opportunities to learn are great if one has the stamina, ambition, and the ability to work under pressure.

Some public relations and publicity consultants perform freelance services in manufacturing and retailing. Writing skills, resourcefulness, and a knowledge of how to handle contacts of many kinds are basic requirements for job applicants to such firms. The beginner can enter as a secretary or copywriter to learn the techniques of getting product publicity and favorable mentions for client firms.

Consulting Services to the Consumer

In recent years, fashion consumer consulting services have grown in popularity. Consulting services may be offered by fashion-trained individuals who wish to begin their own business on a part-time basis, and can often grow to a full-time, profitable business. Such businesses can be started with relatively little capital, but need a considerable amount of promotion from self-starting individuals with previous experience in the field of fashion to succeed.

WARDROBE CONSULTANT. Wardrobe, or image, consultants such as Emily Cho, who has also written several books on the subject, act as wardrobe counselors to individuals who wish to look fashionable and project an individual image. Such consumers may lack confidence in their own ability to plan a wardrobe, or may simply lack the time and knowledge necessary to choose the fashions that are most flattering and suitable for their lifestyle.

The wardrobe consultant begins with a complete analysis of the client's wardrobe, including inventory of all apparel and accessories, organizing closets, and discarding unsuitable items. New purchases are then recommended, which the client may either select or have selected by the consultant. An ongoing inventory of additional purchases may then be maintained by the consultant, who might be called upon in the future to purchase additional ensembles and accessories as they are needed. The consultant often accompanies the client on shopping trips. Charge may be by the hour or by the job, and the consultant often works out of his or her home.

COLOR CONSULTANT. Another type of consumer consultant that has become popular is the color consultant or specialist. The extent of services offered varies widely, as do the background and training of these individuals. Many color specialists offer only one service, that of developing a color chart for the individual client illustrating the client's best colors. This color chart is then used for all clothing purchases so that the individual can closely coordinate his or her wardrobe, thus avoiding costly mistakes in purchasing items that do not match other garments in the wardrobe. Other color specialists also offer services such as recommending the client's best fashion "type" or look, whether it be sophisticated, ingenue, or country. Many color specialists develop workshops each season to present fashion looks to their clients, drawing from the selections offered in many stores in their shopping area. Workshops are also presented to corporate groups who want to improve the personal image of their employees.

In recent years, consumer consultants, such as this color consulting service, have grown in popularity. Such businesses can be started with relatively little capital.

Television and Audiovisual Productions

Fashion-oriented specialists are beginning to find exciting careers in television. Many advertising agencies today engage outside companies to create fashion commercials for client producers or retailers.[7] The high cost of television time and production limits its appeal to retailers, but some make good use of television to present fashion. National advertising by major manufacturers and retailers—for example, Calvin Klein and Sears, Roebuck—is most commonly used.

Also, there has been a rise in the popularity of slide-tape, videocassette, and filmstrip presentations on fashion topics for retail stores and schools. A fashion background alone is not sufficient to provide a beginner with an entry into this field. Some understanding of the technical aspects of audiovisual production is essential.

Trade Associations

One of the more interesting areas of employment in the fashion field is trade association work. Industries, retailers, and professionals of all types form associations and hire executive staffs to do research, publicity, and public relations work. These associations also handle legislative contacts, run conventions, publish periodicals, run trade shows, or perform any other services members may require. Small or large, a trade association provides a great variety of work to its staff. Versatility is thus a paramount requirement. An assistant entering trade association work will find a background in the specific field served helpful, but the ability to communicate well is just as important.

The Bureau of Wholesale Sales Representatives, the National Handbag Authority, and the National Retail Merchants Association are only some of the many trade asociations active in fashion or retailing fields. Other trade associations include local chambers of commerce, and local and regional industry and merchants'

groups. Shopping centers have merchants' associations that employ promotion executives to keep the centers in the public eye. Producers in regional markets, like those in the New York and Los Angeles fashion markets, as well as traveling salespeople sometimes form associations to establish and publicize seasonal market dates.

Teaching

Opportunities to teach fashion-related courses are varied. Individuals with extensive experience in the industry can often teach in private schools offering 1- or 2-year training programs, without the necessity of a college degree. Teachers in secondary schools with specialized fashion merchandising and design programs generally are required to have a 4-year degree, often with additional college hours in teaching methods. To teach on the junior college or baccalaureate level, a master's degree is usually required. In any case, credibility is greatly enhanced by a solid background of direct experience in the fashion business. Other opportunities for teaching include working in the training department of a large store or chain, and providing freelance seminars on fashion-related topics.

FREELANCING

Opportunities for **freelancing,** working independently on an individual job or contract basis for a variety of clients, are available in almost all facets of the fashion business. Those experienced in fashion may, according to their background in the field, contract for individual jobs such as fashion designing for a manufacturer, coordinating fashion shows for various retailers, sewing samples for retail fabric stores, teaching wardrobing classes to teens in a local department store, or preparing displays for small boutiques.

For the creative individual who is not afraid to knock on doors, the opportunities are endless! A few words of caution, however. A strong background in fashion is essential, or the persuasive individual may win the first contract, but not be asked back! Freelancers must also be prepared for a slow start, for it takes time to establish contacts and build a regular clientele. Earnings at first will most likely be far short of what it takes to be self-supporting. Since freelancers are in business for themselves, these careers are discussed in more detail in Chapter 20.

Each year, tens of thousands of people seek fashion-related jobs. Those who win their jobs and turn them into satisfying careers are those who have that very important asset: fashion know-how.

FINDING A JOB IN FASHION

One of the first steps in career selection should be a self-evaluation to determine what the individual truly wants from a career. Listed below are some of the questions that should be answered to narrow down some of the many choices available to the fashion graduate:

- Do you want a career that will let you live in the same area that you live in now? If not, in what size community would you prefer to work? How will this affect your chances for job placement?

- Would you be willing to move to another area in the future if it meant a better job?

- Would you like to travel for your job? If so, how often?

- Would you like to be paid on straight salary so that you know exactly how much you will earn each month, or would you be willing to work strictly on commission?

- Is a short workweek important to you?

- Would you be willing to work on the weekends and have your days off during the middle of the week?

- Would you work overtime for pay? Without pay?

- Which of the following things do you want from your career? Which is most important? Which is least important?

Money	Self-satisfaction
Prestige	Challenges
Independence	Chance to be
Security	creative
Interesting experiences	Other things (list)

- Do you work well under pressure or would you prefer a job where you can work at a steady pace?

- Would you be willing to get more education to win a promotion?

- Which would you prefer: to have someone tell you how to do your job, to be fully responsible for your own work, or to plan and supervise the work of others?

- How much time and effort are you willing to give to be successful?[8]

Each response should be considered in light of various careers considered by the student.

When career choices have been narrowed, a thorough investigation of each should be made to determine how well a career area meets the needs of the individual. The project at the end of this unit can be most helpful in such an evaluation. Students will find that talking to professionals working in a specific field can be an invaluable experience. If no such individual is available in local businesses, other options might include attending a fashion career day sponsored at a regional mart or making a special trip to another city individually or with a group of students for the specific purpose of meeting a fashion professional in a pre-arranged interview.

As mentioned previously, part-time experience is an excellent way to explore job possibilities. Field experience and internship programs in colleges provide such opportunities, and students have the advantage of being able to share experiences with other students. Students should keep in mind that they must be flexible, as a specific position is not always available to part-time employees. However, because of the transferable nature of skills in the fashion field, experience gained in one area will almost always complement and enrich experience in other areas, and can often open doors of opportunity not available to inexperienced individuals.

Looking for Opportunities

Where can the student look for full-time jobs in fashion? One possible source—and often the best—is the campus interview. Each spring, retailers from all over the United States send recruiters to various campuses in an effort to select personnel for executive training programs in their stores. Former part-time employers can also be an excellent source of information for employment; often if they have no position available, they can give leads to other sources.

Fashion ads in newspapers can be scanned for information about retail stores to which the graduate may possibly apply. Another method is the "sidewalk survey," especially in smaller towns. On a walking tour of the community, leads are often brought to light. The telephone directory can be consulted for specific firms, as well as trade and consumer publications in the employment section.

Many personnel agencies specialize in specific types of job placement. A telephone survey of possible agencies can save time and make job hunting much more effective.

Finally, networking among friends in the fashion field can be one of the best ways to pick up leads. The job seeker should let everyone know that he or she is actively looking for employment. This multiplies the effort and can therefore often shorten the search.

After You Are Hired

The true professional never stops growing, whether through participation in professional organizations, taking advanced courses and seminars, or reading journals and other publications. It is also important to stay aware of opportunities for growth through promotion or moves to other firms. Such information is often acquired through a network of professional friends—valuable assets to any career. Such a network must be cultivated and nurtured, however, which means at least in part that "Don't burn your bridges behind you" is the policy to follow when moving from one organization to another!

REFERENCES

[1] Bureau of Economic Analysis, as reported in "The Work Revolution," *Newsweek*, January 17, 1983, p. 29.
[2] *Business Failure Record*, Dun & Bradstreet, 1981.
[3] Donald Super, *The Psychology of Careers*, Harper & Row, New York, 1957.
[4] Helen L. Brockman, *The Theory of Fashion Design*, John Wiley & Sons, New York, 1965, p. 7.
[5] Karen E. Wantuck, "In Business: Making It in Merchandising," *Working Woman*, November 1982, p. 88.
[6] Cecelia Reed, "Sew, You're in Fashion," *Advertising Age*, December 20, 1982, p. M18.
[7] Barbara Brenner, *Careers and Opportunities in Fashion*, E. P. Dutton, New York, 1964, p. 125.
[8] John Beaumont, Kay Lanagan, and Louise Taylor, *Your Career in Marketing*, McGraw-Hill, New York, 1976, p. 130.

MERCHANDISING VOCABULARY

Define or briefly explain the following terms:

Career   Freelancing
Career path   Job
Career ladder   Management positions
Entry-level job   Mid-management positions

MERCHANDISING REVIEW

1. How are transferable skills used within the fashion industry? Give examples within the production and the marketing areas of the fashion field.
2. In what parts of the country will most of the fashion manufacturing jobs be found?
3. Where will jobs in fashion retailing be found?
4. What types of fashion jobs are most likely to be found in a small town?
5. What considerations should be made in evaluating a career goal?
6. What are several misconceptions about jobs in the fashion industry that might be eliminated with an in-depth study?
7. Why is experience an asset in starting your own retail operation?
8. List and explain briefly three marketing jobs that may be found in fashion manufacturing.
9. Why is experience in sales important to a fashion buyer?
10. Where will jobs in resident buying offices be found? In fashion service organizations?

MERCHANDISING DIGEST

1. Identify a position in the fashion industry to which you would like to advance in the future. Without doing any further research, develop a career ladder that you might follow in achieving your goal, including the probable time frame. Then discuss your plans with other members of the class, comparing notes. Use this information as the basis for an in-depth research paper on your fashion career; then compare your findings with your original projections.
2. Discuss the options that are available in your town and within your state for an individual interested in a fashion career.

20. ENTREPRENEURSHIP

There are so many facets to the fashion business world that the possibilities for finding, entering, and pursuing a career path are almost endless. As discussed in the previous chapter, entry-level career opportunities exist in virtually every market and level of fashion merchandising, and many of these positions can lead, with experience, as far up the career ladder as an individual wants to go.

At the same time, there are many people who find greater satisfaction in "doing their own thing" than in filling a slot in someone else's company. These people generally thrive on challenge, exude creativity, and prefer the risks and rewards of running their own show to the security of collecting a regular paycheck. The willingness to assume risk is the prime characteristic of the people who go out and start new businesses. They are called **entrepreneurs.**

Not everyone is suited to being an entrepreneur. But for those with the right combination of creative spirit and initiative, the fashion business offers numerous opportunities and potential for entrepreneurial ventures. Depending on an individual's interests, background, and resources, those ventures could fall in the area of design, manufacturing, services, retailing, wholesaling—or could even combine two or more of these areas. But since starting one's own business requires a tremendous commitment of time, energy, and money, the field chosen should decidedly be one the person loves.

Running one's own business is an American dream. Yet it takes much more than just a dream to do it successfully. Aside from technical knowledge or skill in the area of concentration, an entrepreneur needs to have excellent business sense, perseverance, ambition, and the willingness to take chances. Successful entrepreneurs generally share a number of common traits, among them the abilities to organize, to take responsibility, and to lead others. The **Small Business Administration (SBA)** expressed the key qualities an entrepreneuer should possess in the rating scale on page 411. You can use it to test yourself as to whether or not entrepreneurship is for you.

CAREER OPPORTUNITIES

While it is doubtful that a new entrepreneur will attempt to form a new fiber company in the hope of someday rivaling a giant like Du Pont, or start a retail business destined to be as successful as Wanamaker's, there are certainly hundreds of ventures and opportunities to be considered. The direction taken depends heavily on the individual's own skills, background, interests, and ambitions, not to mention the availability of money to set up the business. Generally manufacturing, wholesaling, or retailing will demand more start-up funds than designing or a service business, but all these areas offer great potential for both personal and financial rewards.

There is even the possibility of combining two or more fashion businesses into one entrepreneurial venture. Jonal & Co., which manufactures and retails women's apparel of its own design, is such a business. Founded in 1980 by Susan McCone, a former lawyer who had designed many of her own clothes since college, the company has its own New York City shop selling both better ready-to-wear and custom-made clothing. An exclusive perfume and a line of made-to-specification luggage are also sold in the store, and McCone and her partner since 1981, Joanna Green, have pre-

pared a wholesale line of daywear to be distributed nationally. The success of the venture shows in more than just the merchandise expansion: By the fourth year in business, Jonal was projecting a sales volume of close to $1 million.[1]

Manufacturing

For those with the available resources and creations, a manufacturing concern might be the ideal entrepreneurial venture, and if successful, it can be extremely profitable. The start-up need not be overwhelming if you start small enough to test your concept and begin to establish a market. After all, there is always room to expand if a product catches on. When that happens, it is possible for a new manufacturing venture to become a huge business that branches into the other areas of entrepreneurship in a very short time.

An outstanding example is Jordache, which was featured in the Fashion Focus in Chapter 5. The enterprise of three brothers—Joe, Ralph, and Avi Nakash—Jordache was founded in 1978 to manufacture tight-fitting fashion jeans.

With each brother handling a different aspect of the business (one in marketing, one in styling and production, and one in operations and distribution), they further developed their business by expanding into sportswear, leisurewear, dresses, outerwear, and children's clothing. By 1982, the company's sales had grown to more than $300 million and its products were sold in some 25 countries.[2]

Certainly Jordache's almost immediate success is not typical of all new ventures. But recognizing a trend and marketing it well can play a big part in building a profitable business. For instance, Philip H. Knight wrote a research paper on track shoes for his master's in business administration theorizing that the Japanese could do for track shoes what they had done for cameras; that is, capture a large part of the market quickly. Not long after, he formed a partnership with his former track coach to

Instructions: *The following are personal traits that are important for a business proprietor. To rate yourself, place a check mark on the line at the point closest to your answer to each question. The check mark may fall between two suggested answers if your own answer lies somewhere between the two. Be honest in your answers.*

Are you a self-starter?

| I do things my own way. Nobody needs to tell me to get going. | If someone gets me started, I keep going all right. | Easy does it. I don't exert myself unless I have to. |

How do you feel about other people?

| I like people. I can get along with just about anybody. | I have plenty of friends. I don't need anyone else. | Most people annoy me. |

Can you lead others?

| I can get most people to go along without much difficulty. | I can get people to do things if I drive them. | I let someone else get things moving. |

Can you take responsibility?

| I like to take charge and see things through. | I'll take over if I have to, but I'd rather let someone else be responsible. | There's always some eager beaver around wanting to show off. I say let him. |

How good an organizer are you?

| I like to have a plan before I start. I'm usually the one to get things lined up. | I do all right unless things get too mixed up. Then I stop. | I just take things as they come. |

How good a worker are you?

| I can keep going as long as necessary. I don't mind working hard. | I'll work hard for a while, but when I've had enough, that's it! | I can't see that hard work gets you anywhere. |

How good is your health?

| I never tire. | I have enough energy for most things I want to do. | I run out of energy sooner than most of my friends seem to. |

Take this short test to see if you have the personal traits that are important for an entrepreneur in fashion. Do you have what it takes?

improve and market Japanese-made running shoes. The shoes he imported are Nike, and his company, Nike, Inc., soon captured about 30 percent of the quality athletic shoe market in the United States. In this case, the entrepreneur had literally done his homework regarding the market potential for his product.

Another way to enter your own business is by recognizing a need in the fashion marketplace that no other company has filled. Developing a product to meet that need can lead to a very successful venture. Naomi Sims, Inc. is a good example. A striking, 5-foot-10-inch model, Naomi Sims discovered that there were no well-styled, fashionable wigs for black women on the market. The only available choices were wigs for white women or Afro-styled wigs for black women. And although wigs are not as popular with the general public as they once were, they are frequently used by fashion models to create desired images. Sims tried wetting the fiber on the available Afro-styled wigs and baked them in the oven to make them come out looking like black hair that had been straightened. The result led to a successful new business for the already successful model.

Designing

An entrepreneur in the field of apparel (or accessories) design will probably need to rely more on his or her ability to sell designs to prospective customers than on amassing great amounts of capital to start up the business. A large number of designers actually work freelance, sometimes in their homes, turning out designs on their own, or sometimes based on a specific assignment from a client company. Other designers take their work a step further by establishing their own design firm to produce, coordinate, and market their creations.

The direction begun by an entrepreneurial designer may not be the course finally taken by the firm, but that freedom to move and shift emphasis is another lure of being an entrepreneur. Inger McCabe Elliott, president and founder of the textiles firm China Seas, began her career as a photographer. When a series of events led her to look for a new path, she began designing one-of-a-kind skirts, although she then knew nothing of the clothing business. Soon, however, she was selling her skirts in Henri Bendel and Bonwit Teller in New York, and working with a staff of pattern makers and seamstresses. Not happy with the methods used on Seventh Avenue, Elliott began a new business using batiks to make skirts and dresses. From that base, she proceeded to expand her products and designs. Today China Seas' line encompasses a full home fashions collection of Elliott's design, from yard goods to stationery and soap.

Mary Quant, best known for her miniskirt creations of the sixties, has also broadened her design enterprise into areas other than apparel. Employing her sense of design and her fashion awareness, she began marketing items from sunglasses to cosmetics in Europe in the late 1970s. By 1982, she was ready to reestablish a name for her designs in the United States, involving Max Factor for cosmetics and fragrances, Schoenfeld for ready-to-wear, and Nigel French Enterprises Ltd. for home furnishings.

Retailing

Retailing is the third fashion area offering tremendous opportunity for an entrepreneur. Most of the major department stores and chains in business today were started as small, one-store ventures by enterprising individuals. Wanamaker was discussed earlier; other examples are J. C. Penney, R. H. Macy, Frank W. Woolworth, and Marshall Field. Most boutiques and many small specialty stores and service businesses one sees in any town or city are run by entrepreneurs. But retailing also offers options for entrepreneurship other than starting a business from scratch.

BUYING A BUSINESS. Some people may be sufficiently interested and knowledgeable to run their own business, but simply don't have the time or money to risk in building it from the ground up. As the business failure rate of start-ups (brand new businesses) is greater than that of established businesses, by purchasing an existing business, an entrepreneur has a greater chance of staying in business. The reason for this is that the buyer of an existing enterprise has the opportunity to research what he or she is getting for his or her investment, what has made the business a success, and what can be done to make it more successful. Doing extensive research and retaining the services of a qualified attorney and accountant are critical because buying an existing business is not without dangers and problems.

In either manufacturing or retailing, another advantage to buying a business is that the new owner does not have to wait to build a steady clientele. In some cases, the entrepreneur may have been working for the business and at some point may have an opportunity to buy it. That is what happened to Geraldine Stutz, president of the chic New York specialty store Henri Bendel. When the ailing store was bought in 1957 by Genesco, a Nashville-based conglomerate, Stutz was made president, and within 5 years she managed to turn the store around by creating a new image with exciting merchandise and knowledgeable management. In 1980, Genesco decided to sell the operation, and Stutz asked for the right to match any offer. With the help of three European investors, she pulled together the necessary $8 million purchase price and took over as managing partner and owner of the store she had helped to build.

FRANCHISING A BUSINESS. Another alternative for entrepreneurs in retailing is the franchise route. As discussed in Chapter 5, franchising is a joint venture agreement whereby the entrepreneur, known as the franchisee, contracts to use a product or service and its name in his or her own business.

Beauty businesses are probably the most common example of fashion franchising, with companies such as Merle Norman and Georgette Klinger expanding their market shares through franchise operations. Other fashion franchises are Yves St. Laurent's Rive Gauche, and Comme des Garçons, from Japan.

Services

The service sector of the economy is growing very rapidly and provides many exciting career opportunities for fashion-oriented entrepreneurs. An increasingly popular area is beauty care services, especially those offered by makeup, wardrobe, and color consultants. Other opportunities include interior design and decorating, fashion illustration and photography, store display (interior and window), educational services (teaching sewing, modeling, fabric design, and so on), agency services for models, and even personal health and fitness services (for example, exercise salons).

For an aspiring entrepreneur, the service area is an excellent choice because a service business can be started with little or no capital. One man who owns a highly successful hairstyling salon started his business part-time by having customers come to his apartment for haircuts. To avoid the high cost of a sterilizer, he had customers bring their own hairbrushes and combs. His only investment was a pair of scissors and a hair dryer.

Another good example of a service company that was started on a shoestring is Ford Models, Inc., the well-known agency for fashion models. In 1946, Eileen Ford started the agency with two models. The company grew into a major force in the fashion industry, and has represented many of the country's top models.

Because service stresses personal contact, an individual service business will remain successful as long as the person conducting the service can offer the ability to do something better or more imaginatively than someone else. The key, as with any business, is to satisfy specific needs at sensible prices.

In addition, success in a service business involves two important marketing strategies: using tangible symbols and stressing benefits. Like packaging for a product, a tangible symbol is vital because it can help customers recognize and understand an intangible service. A brand name, ad logo, and uniform can all contribute to customers' positive perception of your service. Since a service is purchased without knowing the outcome, it is also important to stress the benefit that results from the service. An exciting new wardrobe for very little money may be the benefit of sewing lessons. And a new, radiant look may be the benefit of a color consultation.

As with retailing, franchising is popular in the service industry. One example is Color Me Beautiful, the color consultation company. Other examples include hairstyling salons such as Fantastic Sam's, The Barber's Hairstyling for Men and Women, and John Amico's Hair Performance Salons.

Wholesaling

The fifth fashion area that offers opportunities for entrepreneurs is wholesaling. However, there are not many examples of pure wholesaling businesses that have been started by entrepreneurs. For many people, the capital needed to invest in inventory is a deterrent. There is considerable risk involved in investing in a quantity of stock for resale unless the products can be tested at the retail level. In addition, it is often necessary for a wholesaler to be able to extend credit to a manufacturer or a retailer in order to make sales. This credit can involve a substantial dollar amount.

Despite these difficulties, the wholesaling function is frequently assumed by entrepre-

A large number of designers work freelance, turning out designs on their own.

neurs who are primarily either retailers or manufacturers. In most cases, they are able to eliminate the added cost of middlemen by assuming the wholesaling function.

One example of the retailing-wholesaling entrepreneur is a boutique owner who sells hand-knit sweaters and handmade baby clothes. When she found that she could not keep up with the demand for these items, she turned the retail aspect of the business over to an employee and spent the majority of her time locating and buying merchandise for resale. In doing this she became a wholesaler for her own shop.

An example of the manufacturing-wholesaling entrepreneur is Dotty Smith, a New York–based belt manufacturer who wholesales her products to retail chains throughout the country. She sells to retailers from samples and then assembles the belts in the quantity and colors required. "My strongest advice to anyone starting a business," she says, "is to start small; don't let a big overhead stare you in the face every month."[3]

Since retail stores are carrying a wide variety of merchandise, another wholesaling opportunity for entrepreneurs known as rack jobbers is increasing. Rack jobbers are wholesalers who furnish retailers with merchandise in an attractive display rack, usually on consignment. Display racks are common in hair care salons and supermarkets. These racks may offer a single item such as panty hose or a complete line of beauty products.

SUPPORT SYSTEMS FOR ENTREPRENEURS

Since the beginning of entrepreneurship, new businesses have been plagued by lack of capital, poor organization, or not presenting the right idea at the right time in the right way. All these pitfalls can be avoided by doing adequate research and preparation before jumping into a new venture. Luckily, there are a number of places an individual can turn to for help and guidance with a new business plan.

The **business plan** is the single most important instrument or tool for an entrepreneur to use prior to starting a business. It serves as a road map for the future paths the entrepreneur will take to ensure the success of his or her business. It is essential for the entrepreneur to have a business plan.

Governmental Support

Since 1953, governmental support has been available in varying forms through the Small Business Administration. As an agency fact sheet states, the SBA was created "to assist, counsel and champion America's small businesses. The agency's mission is to help people

There are a number of sources of help and guidance for those who are embarking on a new business plan.

get into business and prosper." The way the agency helps is through a program of low-interest business loans, as well as by management assistance and counseling. In recent years, the agency has placed higher priority on management aid, based on the estimate that 90 percent of all business failures are due to poor management.

The SBA has a central office in Washington, D.C., as well as 110 branch offices scattered throughout the country. All branches of the agency make a special effort to help those who face unusual difficulties in raising capital and finding sales markets, including women, minorities, the handicapped, and veterans. Approximately 6,000 of the agency loans in 1980 went to minority-run firms.

In addition, the Minority Business Development Agency of the Commerce Department was created specifically to help minority entrepreneurs. The agency coordinates all the government's minority business programs, and also offers management training and technical assistance to minority firms, especially in fields that have few minority-owned businesses, such as manufacturing.

LEGISLATION. Other methods employed by the SBA for aiding small businesses include helping to funnel federal government contracts to small businesses. In 1981, those contracts totaled $41 billion. The agency also has an Office of Advocacy, established in 1976 to monitor effects of legislation on small businesses. That office is currently keeping close tabs on the Regulatory Flexibility Act, passed in 1981, which requires federal agencies to consider the regulatory burden on small businesses in their rulemaking. Through Regflex, as the act is called, government agencies are required to give public notice of impending major rules so that small businesses may comment, and to fully weigh the effect of proposed rules on small businesses. Many believe the legislation to be a landmark ruling in aid to entrepreneurs.

STATE AID. The federal government is not alone in its cooperative efforts to support the small business sector. Many states have established advisory councils or committees on small business. In addition, a number of state legislatures have introduced bills that give small businesses a greater chance for success in areas such as capital formation and retention, regulation, and taxation. Because of geographic proximity, the cooperation of state governments is expected to be of equal if not greater importance to small business than that of the federal government.

Business Community Support

In addition to the federal and state government resources described above, there is a growing pool of both public and private organizations that offer assistance to entrepreneurs in the form of advice on investing, management counseling, seminars, and training.

INVESTING. The financial aspect is often the most difficult obstacle for an entrepreneur to overcome, since traditional banking facilities have tightened their reins on lending. However, a growing number of individual and business investors are pouring money into the ventures they feel will succceed. **Venture capital,** funds available for investment in the ownership element of a new enterprise, comes from a variety of sources, including pension funds, major corporations, individuals and families, endowments and foundations, insurance companies, and foreign investors. Small business investment companies (SBICs) handle some of the funds, routing them from the investor to an appropriate new enterprise.

COUNSELING. On the management side, aspiring entrepreneurs can turn to any one of dozens of groups that supply information and counseling on everything from how to raise capital to where to set up shop. Courses on starting and operating small businesses are now offered at hundreds of universities and

Small Business Studies Program

BT 261 – Starting a Small Business
Investigates the inherent problems and challenges in opening and managing a small business. Emphasis is placed upon analysis of financial statements and on developing an organizational plan for individual entrepreneurship.
3 credits

BT 4 — Interdisciplinary Senior Seminar
Explores and analyzes major areas of professional fashion marketing activities, from product development to distribution to ultimate consumption. Each student is assigned a phase of a team research project and papers are submitted as joint efforts. Guest speakers lead some seminar sessions.
3 credits

Fashion in Contemporary Living

CL 111 – Fashion in Contemporary Living
For one-year Fashion Design and Fashion Buying and Merchandising students. Involves the student with the world of fashion through visits to leading social, professional, civic, and cultural events. The ability to judge significant factors of fashion and to analyze potential trends is developed. Students are invited to fashion events, designer showings, and to similar functions. Special invitations to musical performances and to art galleries and museums are included. The preparation of reports develops critical judgment. Prominent members of the fashion world lecture and give presentations as a regular part of the course.
2 credits

CL 121 – Fashion in Menswear
For Menswear Design and Marketing majors. A series of lectures by experts in the world of fashion with emphasis on menswear and its relationship to the rest of the industry. Topics to be covered will include design, merchandising, marketing, advertising, publicity, and display. Guest speakers are invited by the instructor.
1 credit

Courses on starting one's own business are now being offered by a number of colleges.

colleges. Also, local small business organizations have cropped up around the country, many of them associated with a city's chamber of commerce. Through these groups, new or prospective business owners can get advice from other business owners, most of whom probably faced the same problems when they started out.

Other voluntary or nonprofit organizations have been established to provide aid and support to entrepreneurs. One such voluntary agency, Service Corps of Retired Executives (SCORE), provides experienced businesspeople to listen to ideas and give advice when needed. Professional groups, such as the National Society of Public Accountants, have also established programs of free counseling to small businesses.

TRAINING. Structured training programs for new entrepreneurs are also available from a number of organizations. The Entrepreneurship Institute (TEI), based in Worthington, Ohio, offers seminars and workshops nationwide on various aspects of small business ownership. In New York City, the American Women's Economic Development Corporation (AWED) offers a free 18-month comprehensive business training program. In biweekly sessions, women learn how to write business plans, apply for loans, and handle the financial, personnel, and planning problems unique to the woman entrepreneur. Besides this program, AWED provides a national telephone counseling service to match experienced business counselors with entrepreneurs in the same kind of business, and publishes a quarterly magazine, *WE,* for women entrepreneurs.

Publications
In addition to personal counseling from any of the above sources, an aspiring entrepreneur

can obtain information from a vast array of material available in books, pamphlets, and magazines. In the past several years, well over 50 books on entrepreneurship have been published, covering various aspects of starting and managing a small business. Magazines such as *INC.* and *Venture* are devoted specifically to the concerns of the entrepreneur, and provide practical news and tips as well as case studies of successful ventures. Additionally, a wealth of printed materials from the Small Business Administration can give a solid background to the would-be entrepreneur, including brochures on *Business Basics, Management Aids for Small Manufacturers,* and *Small Marketers Aids.* The Bank of America also offers a *Small Business Reporter* series, covering a range of business operations topics and business profiles for specific fields.

TRENDS IN ENTREPRENEURSHIP

More than a few entrepreneurs not only have succeeded in their initial enterprise, but have witnessed their businesses grow into giant companies. So many large corporations came into being and proved profitable in this century that through the 1960s, the concept of ''bigger is better'' overshadowed the lure of the independent small business. The 1970s, however, brought a reversal to that picture, as the number of nonagricultural and nonincorporated self-employed workers in the United States rose 29 percent. The number of people who classified themselves as self-employed but who had incorporated their businesses increased by 41 percent between 1976 and 1979. In 1982, the number of new businesses started in the United States hit an all-time high of 550,000 despite the fact that that year the country experienced one of the greatest business failure rates in its history. Even so, the number of new businesses established in 1982 was nearly twice the number that failed. An interesting sidelight is the fact that the SBA's most recent estimate is that there are over 3 million women business owners in America today.[4] Of the five main categories of entrepreneurship (retailing, wholesaling, designing, manufacturing, and service), service businesses are growing the most rapidly. By 1990 expenditures for services may reach 50 percent of all consumer expenditures.[5]

In the view of experts, the growth trend of entrepreneurship is not about to slow. In fact, they view the coming decade as ripe for independent small businesses, partly because of the increasing specialization taking place in all areas of business. The shift of the country from a mass industrial society to an information society is also seen as conducive to that entrepreneur who truly knows his or her business and how to manage it. Without a doubt, the rewards can be great, not only in profit and independence, but also in the satisfaction of succeeding in one's own personal venture.

REFERENCES

[1] Samuel Feinberg, ''From Where I Sit,'' *Women's Wear Daily,* May 4, 1983, p. 12.
[2] ''Jordache's New Executive Look,'' *Business Week,* November 2, 1981, p. 121.
[3] Claudia Jessup and Genie Chipps, *The Woman's Guide to Starting a Business,* Holt, Rinehart, and Winston, New York, 1980, p. 232.
[4] Alma Moore, ''Editor's Desk,'' *WE* (Women Entrepreneur), Winter 1984, p. 8.
[5] Statistics provided by Alvin Wormser, Small Business Center at Fashion Institute of Technology, December 30, 1983.

MERCHANDISING VOCABULARY

Define or briefly explain the following terms:

Business plan   Small Business Administration (SBA)
Entrepreneurs   Venture capital

MERCHANDISING REVIEW

1. What are some of the reasons why an individual would become an entrepreneur?
2. What are the key personal qualities necessary for success as an entrepreneur?
3. Which type of fashion business requires the most start-up funds: manufacturing, retailing, or designing? Why?
4. What are the advantages of buying an established business from someone else? What might be some of the disadvantages?
5. List the various organizations cited in the text that supply support for entrepreneurs, and briefly describe the functions of each.

MERCHANDISING DIGEST

1. Why do federal, state, and local government agencies encourage new entrepreneurial ventures rather than leaving the market entirely to the larger, established, and more experienced firms?
2. What aids to entrepreneurs are available in your local community? (Consult your local chamber of commerce, retail merchants' association, etc.)

EXPLORING CAREER OPPORTUNITIES

As a future graduate of a fashion merchandising or design curriculum, you should become aware of the many starting points in the field. You should be able to recognize and follow career development opportunities and know their movement either horizontally or vertically within one industry, or within the fashion business, since most merchandising and design activities are interrelated.

Research the following information and prepare a paper on career opportunities in fashion. Support your findings with references, including both printed material and a personal interview with an individual working in the position you would like to attain.

A. List the possible job opportunities that you will have upon graduation in the fiber or fabric industry. Then state what experience can be gained and applied to another type and level of job in fashion merchandising or production. Finally, list the career opportunities in this industry.

B. Find out the same information on possible job opportunities, experience to be gained and applied to another type and level of job in fashion, and available career opportunities for each of the following areas:
   1. Fashion apparel and accessory marketing.
   2. Manufacturing and design.
   3. Retail stores (all types).
   4. Buying offices (all types).
   5. Advertising, display, and promotion industry.
   6. Consulting and other support services.

C. Prepare a flowchart showing the possible jobs that would or could prepare you to advance from the beginning or entry-level job to a position as either a fashion buyer of a large prestigious department or specialty store or as a senior designer or owner of your own design business, or similar position.

D. Choose one specific position (*not* entry-level) that you now feel you would like to attain. Briefly describe the duties and responsibilities of this position.

E. What personal traits are suitable for this particular position? Personality? Likes and dislikes? Skills and aptitudes? Explain why you feel you are suited for this position.

F. Discuss the details of what this position involves: training offered by the firm, responsibilities, problems, rewards (other than monetary), hours worked, obligations.

G. What would the average day of a person in this position be like?

H. Discuss opportunities for growth and development and promotion in this position.

I. Discuss monetary compensation: average starting salary ranges, possible maximum salaries for tops in the field.

J. What firms in your city or state might hire you for this position?

K. What did the person you interviewed say he or she liked best and least about the job? What would he or she do differently if it were possible to plan his or her career knowing what he or she knows now?

Active sportswear The sector of sportswear that includes casual attire worn for sports like running, jogging, tennis, and racketball.

Adaptations Designs that have all the dominant features of the style that inspired them but do not claim to be exact copies.

Advertising The paid use of space or time in any medium. This includes newspapers, magazines, direct-mail pieces, shopping news bulletins, theater programs, catalogs, bus cards, billboards, radio, and television.

Apparel contractor A firm whose sole function is to supply sewing services to the apparel industry.

Apparel jobber (manufacturing) A firm that handles the designing, planning, and purchasing of materials, and usually the cutting, selling, and shipping of apparel, but does not handle the actual garment sewing.

Apparel manufacturer A firm that performs all the operations required to produce a garment.

Auxiliary level Composed of all the support services that are working with primary producers, secondary manufacturers, and retailers to keep consumers aware of the fashion merchandise produced for ultimate consumption.

Board of directors Chief governing body of the corporation.

Boarding (hosiery) A heat-setting process through which hosiery acquires permanent shape.

Bodywear Coordinated leotards, tights, and wrap skirts.

Boutique A shop associated with few-of-a-kind merchandise, generally of very new or extreme styling, with an imaginative presentation of goods. French word for "shop."

Branch store division A separate function or division within a large retail firm's organizational structure that is responsible for seeing that the firm's policies are carried out in the branches.

Brand A name, trademark, or logo that is used to identify the products of a specific maker or seller and to differentiate the products from those of the competition.

Brand-line representative (cosmetics) A trained cosmetician who advises customers in the selection and use of a specific brand of cosmetics, and handles the sales of that brand in a retail store.

Bridge jewelry Merchandise ranging from costume to fine jewelry in price, materials, and newness of styling.

Bridge (menswear) The area that spans young men's and men's collections; serves customers between ages 25 and 40.

Broad and shallow assortment An assortment of goods with many styles but only limited sizes and colors carried in each style.

Business plan Road map for the paths the entrepreneur will take in the future to ensure the success of the business.

Buyer's directory Lists manufacturers and sales reps and merchandise by category and by location within a mart.

Buying motivation The reasons people buy what they buy.

Buying on consignment Placement of an order with the privilege of returning unsold goods by a specific date.

Career A lifelong activity, involving all of the jobs an individual may have, both paid and unpaid.

Career path or ladder The order of occupations in a person's life.

Catalog showroom A place where customers study merchandise catalogs and sample merchandise on display. Orders are filled from a stockroom on the premises and customers take their purchases with them.

Category or classification buying A practice whereby a chain store buyer located in a central buying office is usually assigned to purchase only a specific category or classification of merchandise instead of buying all categories carried in a single department. See *Departmental buying.*

Caution A fee charged for viewing a couture collection.

Caveat emptor (pronounced "ka-ve-at EMP-tor") Latin phrase meaning "Let the buyer beware."

Caveat venditor (pronounced "ka-ve-at VEN-dee-tor") Latin phrase meaning "Let the seller beware."

Chain organization A group of 12 or more centrally owned stores, each handling somewhat similar goods, which are merchandised and controlled from a central headquarters office (as defined by the Bureau of the Census).

Chambre syndicale (pronounced "shahmbrah seen-dee-kahl") A French elite couture trade association providing many services for the entire French fashion industry.

Classic A style or design that satisfies a basic need and remains in general fashion acceptance for an extended period of time.

Classification An assortment of units or items of merchandise which can be reasonably substituted for each other, regardless of who made the item, the material of which it is made, or the part of the store in which it is offered for sale.

Commissionaire (pronounced "ko-me-see-ohn-air")

422

An independent retailers' service organization usually located in the major city of a foreign market area. It is roughly the foreign equivalent of an American resident buying office.

Confined style(s) Styles that a vendor agrees to sell to only one store in a given trading area. See *Exclusivity.*

Conglomerate A group of companies that may or may not be related in terms of product or marketing level but which are owned by a single parent organization.

Consignment selling A manufacturer places merchandise in a retail store for resale but permits any unsold portion to be returned to the wholesale source by a specific date.

Consumer The ultimate user of goods or services.

Consumerism The efforts of consumers to protect their own interests.

Contemporary menswear A type of styling that is often also referred to as "updated," "better," or "young men's." Applies to all categories of male apparel and furnishings.

Contract or specification buying A "development sample" of an item is made up so that it can be copied or adapted for sale at a price more advantageous to producers or customers. This type of buying is commonly used by chain organizations and mail order firms and often in foreign buying, as well.

Contract tanneries Business firms that process hides and skins to the specifications of converters but are not involved in the sale of the finished product.

Contractors See *Apparel contractor.*

Converter, leather Firms that buy hides and skins, farm out their processing to contract tanneries, and sell the finished product.

Converter, textiles A producer who buys fabrics in the greige, contracts to have them finished (dyed, bleached, printed, or subjected to other treatments) in plants specializing in each operation, and sells the finished goods.

Cooperative advertising Retail advertising, the costs of which are shared by a store and one or more producers on terms mutually agreed to.

Corporation An artificial being, invisible, intangible, and existing only in contemplation of law.

Cosmetics Articles other than soap that are intended to be rubbed, poured, sprinkled, or sprayed on the person for purposes of cleansing, beautifying, promoting attractiveness, or altering the appearance (as defined by the Federal Trade Commission).

Costume jewelry Mass-produced jewelry made of plastic, wood, glass, brass, or other base metals, and set with simulated or nonprecious stones. Also called fashion jewelry.

Couture house (pronounced "ko-tour") An apparel firm for which the designer creates original styles.

Couturier (male) or **couturiere** (female) (pronounced "ko-tour-ee-ay" and "ko-tour-ee-air") The proprietor or designer of a French couture house.

Culmination (stage) See *Fashion cycle.*

Customer A patron or potential purchaser of goods or services.

Customer demand Customer needs and wants for consumer goods.

Decline (stage) See *Fashion cycle.*

Demographics Studies that divide broad groups of consumers into smaller, more homogeneous target segments; the variables include population distribution, age, sex, family life cycle, race, religion, nationality, education, occupation, and income.

Departmental buying A practice whereby a department buyer is responsible for buying all the various categories of merchandise carried in that department. See also *category buying.*

Department store A store, as defined by the Bureau of the Census, that employs 25 or more people and sells general lines of merchandise in each of three categories: (1) home furnishings, (2) household linens and dry goods (an old trade term meaning piece goods and sewing notions), and (3) apparel and accessories for the entire family.

Design A specific version or variation of a style. In everyday usage, however, fashion producers and retailers refer to a design as a "style," a "style number," or simply a "number."

Details The individual elements that give a silhouette its form or shape. These include trimmings, skirt and pant length and width, and shoulder, waist, and sleeve treatment.

Direct mail A form of sales promotion aimed at an individual customer and sent through the mail. Includes letters, catalogs, statement inserts.

Direct selling Merchandise sold by its producer door-to-door or via in-home parties.

Discount store A departmentalized retail store using many self-service techniques to sell its goods. It operates usually at low profit margins, has a minimum annual volume of $500,000, and is at least 10,000 sq. ft. in size.

Discretionary income The money that an individual or family has to spend or save after buying such necessities as food, clothing, shelter, and basic transportation.

Disposable personal income The amount of money a person has left to spend or save after paying taxes. It is roughly equivalent to what an employee calls "take-home pay" and provides an approximation of the purchasing power of each consumer during any given year.

Diversification The addition of various lines, products, or services to serve different markets.

Domestic market A fashion market center located in the United States.

Downward-flow theory The theory of fashion adoption which maintains that to be identified as a true fashion, a style must first be adopted by people at the top of the social pyramid. The style then gradually wins acceptance at progressively lower social levels. Also called the "trickle-down" theory.

Drop (menswear) Refers to the difference between the waist and chest measurements of a man's jacket. Designer suits are sized on a 7-inch drop; traditional suits are styled with a 6-inch drop.

Dual distribution A manufacturer's policy of selling goods at both wholesale and retail.

Editorial credit The mention, in a magazine or newspaper, of a store name as a retail source for merchandise that is being editorially featured by the publication.

Entrepreneurs People who start new business ventures.

Entry-level job One requiring little or no specific training and experience.

Environment The conditions under which we live that affect our lives and influence our actions.

Erogenous Sexually stimulating or newly exposed.

European styling (menswear) Features more fitted jackets that hug the body and have extremely square shoulders.

Exclusivity Allowing a store sole use within a given trading area of a style or styles. An important competitive retail weapon.

Factory outlet store Manufacturer-owned store that sells company products at reduced prices in austere surroundings with minimum services.

Fad A short-lived fashion that affects relatively few people within the total population.

Fashion A style that is accepted and used by the majority of a group at any one time.

Fashion business Includes all industries and services connected with fashion: manufacturing, distribution, advertising, publishing, and consulting—any business concerned with goods or services in which fashion is a factor.

Fashion coordination The function of analyzing fashion trends in order to insure that the fashion merchandise offered is appropriate in terms of style, quality, and appeal to the target customer.

Fashion director A store's ranking fashion authority. Sometimes referred to as a fashion coordinator.

Fashion cycle The rise, widespread popularity, and then decline in acceptance of a style. *Rise:* The acceptance of either a newly introduced design or its adaptations by an increasing number of consumers. *Culmination:* That period when a fashion is at the height of its popularity and use. The fashion then is in such demand that it can be mass-produced, mass-distributed, and sold at prices within the reach of most consumers. *Decline:* The decrease in consumer demand because of boredom resulting from widespread use of a fashion. *Obsolescence:* When disinterest occurs and a style can no longer be sold at any price.

Fashion forecasting A prediction of the trend of fashion as determined by the prevailing elements in all the fashion industries.

Fashion image That aspect of a store's image that reflects the degree of fashion leadership the store strives to exercise and the stage of the fashion cycle that its assortments represent.

Fashion industries Those engaged in producing the materials used in the production of apparel and accessories for men, women, and children.

Fashion influential A person whose advice is sought by associates. An influential's adoption of a new style gives it prestige among a group.

Fashion innovator A person first to try out a new style.

Fashion jewelry See *Costume jewelry.*

Fashion marketing The marketing of fashion related apparel and accessories to the ultimate consumer.

Fashion merchandising Refers to the planning required to have the right fashion-oriented merchandise at the right time, in the right quantities, and at the right prices for the target group(s) of customers.

Fashion retailing The business of buying fashion-oriented merchandise from a variety of resources and assembling it in convenient locations for resale to ultimate consumers.

Fashion trend The direction in which fashion is moving.

Fiber A hairlike unit of raw material from which yarn and, eventually, textile fabric is made.

Fine jewelry Jewelry made of such precious metals as gold and all members of the platinum family (palladium, rhodium, and iridium), which may be set with precious or semiprecious stones.

First cost The whole price of merchandise in the country of origin.

Filaments Fibers of continuous, indefinite lengths produced by forcing liquid through a spinnerette.

Fords Styles that are widely copied at a variety of price lines.

Foundations The trade term for such women's undergarments as brassieres, girdles, panty-girdles, garter belts, and corselettes.

Fragrance Includes cologne, toilet water, perfume, spray perfume, aftershave lotion, and environmental fragrances.

Franchise A contractual agreement in which a firm or individual buys the exclusive right to conduct a retail business within a specified trading area under a franchisor's registered or trademarked name.

Franchise distribution (cosmetics) The manufacturer or exclusive distributor sells directly to the ultimate retailer.

Franchisee The individual who contracts a business from a franchisor.

Franchisor The parent company.

Free trade zone Secure areas, usually located in or near customs ports of entry, that are regarded as legally outside a nation's customs territory.

Freelancing Working independently on an individual job or on a contractual basis for a variety of clients.

Fur farming The breeding and raising of fur-bearing animals under controlled conditions.

Fusing A process in which various parts of a garment can be melded together under heat and pressure rather than stitched.

Garment District The center of the women's apparel market in New York City.

Gemstones Natural stones used in making jewelry. Precious stones include the diamond, emerald, ruby, sapphire, and real pearl. Semiprecious stones include the amethyst, garnet, opal, jade, cultured pearl.

General merchandise stores Retail stores which sell a number of lines of merchandise—apparel and accessories, furniture and home furnishings, household lines and drygoods, hardware, appliances, and smallwares, for example—under one roof. Stores included in this group are commonly known as mass-merchandisers, department stores, variety stores, general merchandise stores, or general stores.

General partner An individual who has unlimited liability and who may be called upon to furnish additional money from his or her own personal assets to pay the debts of the partnership.

General store An early form of retail store which carried a wide variety of mainly utilitarian consumer goods.

Going public Turning a privately-owned company into a public corporation and issuing stock for sale.

Graded Developed from a style's sample pattern; adjusted to meet the dimensional requirements of each size in which the style is to be made. Also referred to as "sloped."

Grade 6+ suit Man's suit that requires between 120 and 150 separate hand-tailoring operations and up to 15 hours of an experienced tailor's time for its production. Considered the finest quality available.

Grade X suit Man's suit that can be produced in 90 minutes with only 90 stitching and pressing operations. An acceptable but lower-quality, high-volume suit made possible by recent technological advances.

Greige goods (pronounced "gray goods") Unfinished fabrics.

Group purchase The purchasing from a given resource of identical merchandise by several stores at one time so that all participants may share in the advantages of a large-volume purchase.

Haute couture (pronounced "oat-koo-tour") The French term literally meaning "fine sewing" but actually having much the same sense as our own term "high fashion."

Hides Animal skins that weigh over 25 pounds when shipped to a tannery.

High fashion Those styles or designs accepted by a limited group of fashion leaders—the elite among consumers—who are first to accept fashion change.

Horizontal-flow theory The theory of fashion adoption that holds that fashions move horizontally between groups on similar social levels rather than vertically from one level to another. Also called the "mass-market theory."

Horizontal integration Merging with or acquiring other firms that function at the same marketing level, such as the merger of two fabric producers or one retail store with another store or store group.

Hot items Items, new or otherwise, that have demonstrated greater customer acceptance than was anticipated.

Impulse items Items a customer buys on an impulse rather than as a result of planning.

Inflation A substantial and continuing rise in the general price level.

Inside shops Garment factories owned and operated by menswear manufacturers who perform all the operations required to produce finished garments.

Intimate apparel The trade term for women's foundations, lingerie, and loungewear. Also called inner fashions, body fashions, and innerwear.

Irregulars Goods having defects that may affect appearance but not wear.

Job A specific position within an industry.

Jobber A middleman who buys from manufacturers and sells to retailers. See also *Apparel jobber.*

Kips Animal skins weighing from 15 to 25 pounds when shipped to a tannery.

Knocked-off A trade term referring to the copying, at a lower price, of an item that has had good acceptance at higher prices.

Laissez-faire economy A government policy of noninterference with business.

Last (shoe) A wooden form in the shape of a foot over which shoes are built.

Leased department A department ostensibly operated by the store in which it is found but actually run by an outsider who pays a percentage of sales to the store as rent.

Let-out (furs) A cutting and re-sewing operation to make short skins into longer-length skins adequate for garment purposes.

Licensed trademark (fibers) A fiber's registered trademark used under a licensing agreement whereby use of the trademark is permitted only to those manufacturers whose end products pass established tests for their specific end use or application.

Licensing An arrangement whereby firms are given permission to produce and market merchandise in the name of a licensor, who is paid a percentage of sales for permitting his or her name to be used.

Licensing agreement A contract whereby the licensor usually agrees to pay the licensee a royalty for use of the licensee's name.

Limited partner An individual whose liability extends up to the amount of his or her investment and who is not permitted to take an active part in the management of the business.

Line An assortment of new designs offered by manufacturers to their customers, usually on a seasonal basis.

Line-for-line copies These are exactly like the original designs except that they have been mass-produced in less expensive fabrics to standard size measurements.

Lingerie A general undergarment category that includes slips, petticoats, camisoles, panties of all types, nightgowns, and pajamas. Slips, petticoats, and panties are considered "daywear," while nightgowns and pajamas are classified as "sleepwear."

Long-run fashion A fashion that takes more seasons to complete its cycle than what might be considered its average life expectancy.

Loungewear The trade term for the intimate apparel category that includes robes, bed jackets, and housecoats.

Mail-order company A firm that does the bulk of its sales and delivery by mail.

Management positions Includes buyer, merchandise manager, and manager for a large store.

Manufacturer See *Apparel manufacturer.*

Market (apparel manufacturing) A long piece of paper upon which the pieces of the pattern of a garment in all its sizes are outlined and which is placed on top of many layers of material for cutting purposes.

Market (1) A group of potential customers. (2) The place or area in which buyers and sellers meet for the purpose of trading ownership of goods at wholesale prices.

Market center A geographic center for the creation and production of fashion merchandise, as well as for exchanging ownership.

Market representative A specialist who covers a narrow segment of the total market and makes information about it available to client stores.

Market segmentation The separating of the total consumer market into smaller groups known as "market segments."

Market weeks Scheduled periods throughout the year during which producers and their sales representatives introduce new lines for the upcoming season to retail buyers.

Marketing A total system of business activities designed to plan, price, promote, and place (distribute) products and services to present and potential customers.

Marketing process The series of activities involved in converting raw materials into a form that can be used by ultimate consumers without further commercial processing.

Markup The difference between the wholesale cost and the retail price of merchandise (sometimes called "mark-on" by large retail stores).

Mart A building or building complex housing both permanent and transient showrooms of producers and their sales representatives.

Mass distribution (cosmetics) Third-party vendors, such as wholesalers, divertors, and jobbers, often interposed between the manufacturer and the retailer.

Mass or volume fashion Refers to those styles or designs that are widely accepted. Also called "volume fashion."

Merchandise assortment A collection of varied types of related merchandise, essentially intended for the same general end-use and usually grouped together in one selling area of a retail store. *Broad:* A merchandise assortment that includes many styles. *Deep:* A merchandise assortment that includes a comprehensive range of colors and sizes in each style. *Narrow:* A merchandise assortment that includes relatively few styles. *Shallow:* A merchandise assortment that contains only a few sizes and colors in each style.

Merchandising The planning required on the part of retailers to have the right merchandise at the right time, in the right place, in the right quantities, at the right price (for the specific target group(s) of consumers), and with the right promotion.

Merchandising policies Guidelines established by store management for merchandising executives to follow in order that the store organization may win the patronage of the specific target group(s) of customers it has chosen to serve.

Merger A sale of one company to another with the result that only one company exists.

Mid-management position One requiring some experience and training and involving a higher degree of responsibility.

Mom-and-Pop store A small store run by the proprietor with few or no hired assistants.

Narrow and deep assortment One in which there are relatively few styles, but these styles are stocked in all available sizes and colors.

National brand A nationally advertised and distributed brand owned by a manufacturer or processor. Offers consistent guarantee of quality and fashion correctness.

Number, style number See *Design*.

Obsolescence (stage) See *Fashion cycle*.

Officers (corporation) Those responsible for carrying out the business objectives of the firm.

Off-price apparel stores Sell home-brands and designer merchandise at prices well below traditional department store levels.

Off-price retailing The selling of brand name and designer label merchandise at lower-than-normal retail prices, but still at the late rise or early peak of the fashion cycle.

Off-shore production Domestic apparel producers who import goods either from their own plants operating in cheap, labor-rich foreign areas or through their long-term supply arrangements with foreign producers.

Organization chart A visual presentation of the manner in which a firm delegates responsibility and authority within its organization.

Outside shops See *Apparel contractor*.

Partnership An association of two or more persons to carry on as co-owners of a business for a profit.

Patronage motives (consumer) The reasons that induce consumers to patronize one store rather than another; why people buy where they do.

Pelt The skin of a fur-bearing animal.

Personal income The total or gross amount of income received from all sources by the population as a whole. It consists of wages, salaries, interest, dividends, and all other income for everyone in the country. See also *Disposable personal income* and *Discretionary income*.

Personnel division A separate function or division within a retail firm's organizational structure that is responsible for employment, training, employee records, executive recruitment and development, and related activities.

Plateau See *Fashion cycle*.

Policy A settled, clearly defined course of action or methods of doing business deemed necessary, expedient, or advantageous.

Precious stones Include the diamond, emerald, ruby, sapphire, and real, or oriental, pearl.

Press release A written statement of news that has occurred or is about to occur, specifying the source of the information and the date after which its use is permissible.

Prêt-à-porter (pronounced "pret-ah-por-tay") French term meaning ready-to-wear.

Price line A specific price point at which an assortment of merchandise is regularly offered for sale.

Price lining The practice of determining the various but limited number of retail prices at which a department's or store's assortments will be offered.

Price range The spread between the lowest and the highest price line at which merchandise is offered for sale.

Price zone A series of somewhat continuous price lines that are likely to have major appeal to one particular segment of a store's or department's customers.

Primary level Composed of the growers and producers of the raw materials of fashion—the fiber, fabric, leather, and fur producers who function in the raw materials market.

Primary suppliers Producers of fibers, textile fabrics, finished leathers, and furs.

Prime resources Those producers from whom a department has consistently bought a substantial portion of its merchandise in past seasons.

Private corporation Ownership is usually held by a few owners and no shares of stock are sold on the open market.

Private label or store brand Merchandise that meets standards specified by a retail organization and which belongs exclusively to it. Primarily used to insure consistent quality of product as well as to meet price competition.

Private label manufacturers Produce merchandise to specification under the brand name of stores.

Profit The amount of money a business earns in excess of its income. See also *Net income*.

Prophetic styles Particularly interesting new styles that are still in the introductory phase of their fashion cycles.

Psychographics Studies that develop fuller, more personal portraits of potential customers, including personality, attitude, interests, personal opinions, and actual product benefits desired.

Psychological satisfactions (consumer) Those derived from the consumer's social and psychological interpretation of the product and its performance.

Public corporation Sells shares of its stock on the open market to the public.

Public relations Works to improve a client's public image and may develop long-range plans and directions for this purpose.

Publicity The free and voluntary mention of a firm, brand, product, or person in some form of media.

Purchasing power The value of the dollar as it relates to the amount of goods or services it will buy. A decline in purchasing power is caused by inflation.

Ready-to-wear (RTW) Apparel made in factories to standard size measurements.

Recession A low point in a business cycle, when money and credit become scarce and unemployment is high.

Regular tanneries Those companies that purchase and process hides and skins to the specifications of converters but are not involved in the sales of the finished products.

Release date The earliest date on which a publicity announcement can be made.

Resident buying office A service organization located in a major market area that provides market information and representation to its noncompeting client stores. *Associated/Cooperative:* One that is jointly owned and operated by a group of independently-owned stores. *Private:* One that is owned and operated by a single, out-of-town store organization and which performs market work exclusively for that store organization. *Salaried, Fee or Paid:* One that is independently owned and operated and charges the stores it represents for the work it does. *Syndicate/Corporate:* One that is maintained by a parent organization which owns a group of stores and performs market work exclusively for those stores. *Commission/Merchandise Broker:* One that is independent, whose fees are paid not by the store but by manufacturers.

Resource Vendor, source of supply.

Retail level The ultimate distribution level—outlets for fashion goods directly to the consumer.

Retailing The business of buying goods from a variety of resources and assembling these goods in convenient locations for resale to ultimate consumers.

Rise (stage) See *Fashion cycle*.

Rubber-banding Cosmetic products that can be returned to the manufacturer and replaced with other products, if not sold within a specified period of time.

Sales promotion The coordination of advertising, display, publicity, and personal salesmanship in order to promote profitable sales.

Salon selling The most exacting type of personal selling: Little or no stock is exposed to the customer's view except that which is brought out for the customer's inspection by the salesperson.

Sample hand A designer's assistant who is an all-around sewer.

Secondary level Composed of industries—manufacturers and contractors—that produce the semifinished or finished fashion goods from the materials produced on the primary level.

Seconds These are factory rejects having defects that may affect wear.

Section work The division of labor in apparel manufacturing whereby each sewing-machine operator sews only a certain section of the garment, such as a sleeve or hem.

Selection factors The various characteristics or components of an item of merchandise that influence a customer's decision to purchase.

Self-selection selling The method of selling in which merchandise is displayed and arranged so that customers can make at least a preliminary selection without the aid of a salesperson.

Self-service The method of selling in which customers make their selections from the goods on display and bring their purchases to a check-out counter where they make payment and their purchases are prepared for take-out.

Semi-precious stones Include the amethyst, garnet, opal, jade and other natural stones that are less rare and costly than precious stones.

Shop A small store or area within a large store that is stocked with merchandise for special end-use purposes; intended for customers with specialized interests.

Short run (apparel production) The production of a limited number of units of a particular item, fewer than would normally be considered an average number to produce.

Short-run fashion A fashion that takes fewer seasons to complete its cycle than what might be considered its average life expectancy.

Silhouette The overall outline or contour of a custume. Also frequently referred to as "shape" or "form."

Skins Animal skins that weigh 15 pounds or less when shipped to a tannery.

Sloped See *Graded*.

Slop shops A name associated with the first shops offering men's ready-to-wear in this country. Garments lacked careful fit and detail work found in custom-tailored clothing of the period.

Small Business Administration (SBA) An agency of the federal government created to assist, counsel, and champion America's small businesses; helps people get into business and to prosper.

Sole proprietorship An individual owns the business, assumes all risks, and operates the business for his or her own personal interest.

Specialty store A store that carries limited lines of apparel, accessories, or home furnishings (as defined by the Bureau of the Census). In the trade, retailers use the term to describe any apparel and/or accessories store that exhibits a degree of fashion awareness and carries goods for men, women, and/or children.

Specification buying See *Contract buying*.

Spinnerette A mechanical device through which a thick

liquid base is forced to produce fibers of varying lengths.

Stockholders Owners of the corporation.

Stockkeeping unit (SKU) A single or group of items of merchandise within a classification to which an identifying number is assigned and for which separate sales and stock records are kept.

Store image The character or personality that a store presents to the public.

Store policies Guidelines that affect areas other than merchandising, such as customer services, selling services, promotional activities, and fashion coordination.

Structured apparel Menswear garments whose construction involves many different hand-tailoring operations that give them a shape of their own when not being worn.

Style A characteristic or distinctive mode of presentation or conceptualization in a particular field. In apparel, style is the characteristic or distinctive appearance of a garment, the combination of features that makes it different from other garments.

Stylist Title given to persons employed to study consumer demand, who help buyers select and coordinate their assortment in line with this demand. Early title of fashion coordinator or director.

Subchapter S corporation One with 10 or fewer stockholders initially and 25 or fewer after 5 years that elects to be taxed in the same manner as a partnership.

Sumptuary laws Laws regulating extravagance in dress, etc., on religious or moral grounds.

Sweatshop A garment manufacturing plant employing workers under unfair, unsanitary, and sometimes dangerous conditions.

Tailored clothing firms Those menswear firms that produce structured or semistructured suits, overcoats, topcoats, sport coats, and/or separate trousers in which a specific number of hand-tailoring operations are required.

Tanning The process of transforming animal skins into leather.

Taste The recognition of what is and is not attractive and appropriate. Good taste in fashion means sensitivity not only to what is artistic but to these considerations as well.

Textile fabric Cloth or material made from fibers by weaving, knitting, braiding, felting, crocheting, knotting, laminating, or bonding.

Textile converter See *Converter, textiles*.

Texture The look and feel of material, woven or unwoven.

Trade association Professional organizations for manufacturers or sales representatives.

Trade publications Newspapers or magazines published specifically for professionals in a special field, such as fashion.

Trade shows Periodic merchandise exhibits staged in various regional trading areas around the country by groups of producers and their sales representatives for the specific purpose of making sales of their products to retailers in that area.

Trunk show A form of pre-testing that involves a producer's sending a representative to a store with samples of the current line, and exhibiting those samples to customers at scheduled, announced showings.

Unstructured apparel Menswear garments whose construction involves few if any hand-tailoring operations. A sports jacket, for example, often lacks padding, binding, and lining; it takes its shape in part from the person who wears it.

Upward-flow theory The theory of fashion adoption that holds that the young—particularly those of low-income families as well as those of higher income who adopt low-income lifestyles—are quicker than any other social group to create or adopt new and different fashions.

Variety store A store carrying a wide range of merchandise in a limited number of low or relatively low price lines.

Vendor One who sells goods to others; source of supply, resource.

Venture or start-up capital Funds available for investment in the ownership element of a new enterprise; comes from a variety of sources.

Vertical integration The acquisition or merger of firms at different marketing levels, for example, a fiber mill with a fabric mill or a garment producer with a fabric producer.

Video shopping In-home shopping using cable television and/or home computers.

Visual merchandising Everything visual that is done to, with, or for a product and its surroundings to encourage its sale. This includes display; print, broadcast, or film advertising; publicity; store layout; and store decor.

Volume fashion See *Mass fashion*.

Voluntary associations (retailers) Stores affiliated loosely with one another on a voluntary basis. Each store retains its own identity and owners retain complete control of their stores.

Yarn A continuous thread formed by spinning or twisting fibers together.

Textiles (Ch. 6)

American Printed Fabrics Council, Inc.
1040 Avenue of the Americas
New York, NY 10036

American Textile Manufacturers Institute, Inc.
(ATMI)
Wachovia Center
400 South Tryon Street
Charlotte, NC 28285

American Wool Council
200 Clayton Street
Denver, CO 80206

American Yarn Spinners Association, Inc.
P.O. Box 99
Gastonia, NC 28052

Belgian Linen Association
280 Madison Avenue
New York, NY 10016

The Color Association of the U.S.
24 East 38th Street
New York, NY 10016

Cotton, Inc.
1370 Avenue of the Americas
New York, NY 10019

International Silk Association, U.S.A.
299 Madison Avenue
New York, NY 10017

Knitted Textile Association
386 Park Avenue South
New York, NY 10010

Man-Made Fiber Producers Association, Inc.
1150 17th Street, N.W.
Washington, DC 20036

Mohair Council of America
1412 Broadway
New York, NY 10036

National Cotton Council of America
P.O. Box 12285
Memphis, TN 38112

National Knitwear Manufacturers Association
350 Fifth Avenue Room 4920
New York, NY 10118

National Knitwear and Sportswear Association
51 Madison Avenue
New York, NY 10010

Textile Distributors Association, Inc.
1040 Avenue of the Americas
New York, NY 10018

Wool Bureau, Inc.
360 Lexington Avenue
New York, NY 10017

Fur and Leather (Ch. 7)

American Fur Industry
100 West 31st Street
New York, NY 10001

Associated Fur Manufacturers, Inc.
101 West 30th Street
New York, NY 10001

Emba Mink Breeders Association
151 West 30th Street
New York, NY 10001

Fur Information and Fashion Council, Inc.
101 East 30th Street
New York, NY 10016

Luggage and Leathergoods Manufacturers of America, Inc.
350 Fifth Avenue
New York, NY 10018

Master Furriers Guild of America
101 West 30th Street
New York, NY 10001

Tanners Council
2501 M Street N.W.
Washington, DC 20037

United Fur Manufacturers Association
352 Seventh Avenue
New York, NY 10001

Women's Wear (Ch. 8)

Affiliated Dress Manufacturers
1440 Broadway
New York, NY 10018

Amalgamated Clothing Workers of America
15 Union Square
New York, NY 10013

American Apparel Manufacturers Association
1611 N. Kent Street, Suite 800
Arlington, VA 22209

American Coat and Suit Manufacturers Association
450 Seventh Avenue
New York, NY 10123

Apparel Guild
Statler New York Hotel
Seventh Avenue and 33rd Street
New York, NY 10001

Bureau of Wholesale Sales Representatives
1819 Peachtree Road, NE, Suite 515
Atlanta, GA 30309

California Fashion Creators
110 East 9th Street
Los Angeles, CA 90015

Chamber of Commerce of Apparel Industry
570 Seventh Avenue
New York, NY 10018

Costume Society of America
c/o Costume Institute
Metropolitan Museum of Art
Fifth Avenue & 82nd Street
New York, NY 10028

Costume Designers Guild
11286 Westminster
Los Angeles, CA 90066

Council of Fashion Designers of America
1633 Broadway
New York, NY 10019

The Fashion Group, Inc.
9 Rockefeller Plaza
New York, NY 10020

Federation of Apparel Manufacturers
450 Seventh Avenue
New York, NY 10001

International Ladies' Garment Workers' Union
1710 Broadway
New York, NY 10019

Ladies Apparel Contractors Association
450 Seventh Avenue
New York, NY 10001

National Association of Blouse Manufacturers
450 Seventh Avenue
New York, NY 10001

National Association of Uniform Manufacturers
and Distributors
1156 Avenue of the Americas
New York, NY 10036

National Association of Women's and Children's
Apparel Salesmen, Inc.
401 Seventh Avenue
New York, NY 10001

National Dress Manufacturers Association
570 Seventh Avenue
New York, NY 10018

New York Couture Business Council, Inc.
141 West 41st Street
New York, NY 10036

New York Fashion Designers
1457 Broadway
New York, NY 10036

United Garment Workers of America
31 Union Square
New York, NY 10003

Children's Wear (Ch. 9)

Bureau of Wholesale Sales Representatives
1819 Peachtree Road, NE, Suite 515
Atlanta, GA 30309

Childrenswear Manufacturers Association
112 West 34th Street
New York, NY 10120

Infants' and Children's Wear Salesmen's Guild
45 West 34th Street, Room 1102
New York, NY 10001

Infant and Juvenile Manufacturers Association
100 East 42nd Street
New York, NY 10017

Infants', Children's, and Girls' Sportswear and Coat
Association
450 Seventh Avenue
New York, NY 10123

United Infants' and Children's Wear Association
520 Eighth Avenue
New York, NY 10018

Menswear (Ch. 10)

Big and Tall Associates
P.O. Box 76
Glencoe, IL 60022

Boys and Young Men's Apparel Manufacturers Association
350 5th Avenue
New York, NY 10118

Clothing Manufacturers Association
1290 Avenue of the Americas
New York, NY 10104

Fathers Day Council, Inc.
47 West 34th Street
New York, NY 10001

International Association of Clothing Designers
Seven East Lancaster Avenue
Ardmore, PA 19003

Men's Apparel Guild in California
124 West Olympia Boulevard
Los Angeles, CA 90015

Men's Fashion Association of America
240 Madison Avenue
New York, NY 10016

Men's Retailers Association
2011 Eye Street, NW
Washington, DC 20006

Menswear Retailers of America
390 National Press Building
Washington, DC 20045

National Association of Men's Sportswear Buyers
535 Fifth Avenue
New York, NY 10017

Young Menswear Association
1328 Broadway
New York, NY 10001

Accessories (Ch. 11)

American Footwear Industry Association
1611 North Kent Street
Arlington, VA 22209

Association of Umbrella Manufacturers and Suppliers
11 West 32nd Street
New York, NY 10001

Belt Association
225 West 34th Street
New York, NY 10122

Footwear Council
51 East 42nd Street
New York, NY 10017

Jewelry Industry Council
608 Fifth Avenue
New York, NY 10020

Manufacturing Jewelers and Silversmiths
of America, Inc.
The Biltmore Plaza
Providence, RI 02903

Millinery Institute of America
37 West 39th Street
New York, NY 10018

National Association of Fashion Accessory Designers
2721 Clayton Street
Denver, CO 80205

National Association of Glove Manufacturers
30 South Main Street
Gloversville, NY 12078

National Association of Hosiery Manufacturers
516 Charlottetown Mall
Charlotte, NC 28204

National Handbag Association
350 Fifth Avenue
New York, NY 10001

National Shoe Retailers Association
200 Madison Avenue
New York, NY 10016

Intimate Apparel and Cosmetics (Ch. 12)

Associated Corset and Brassiere Manufacturers
535 Fifth Avenue
New York, NY 10017

Cosmetic Toiletry and Fragrance Association
1133 15th Street, NW
Washington, DC 20005

Intimate Apparel Council for the American Apparel
Manufacturing Association
1611 N. Kent Street, Suite 800
Arlington, VA 22209

Lingerie Manufacturers Association
41 East 42nd Street
New York, NY 10017

Retailers (Ch. 15)

National Retail Merchants Association
100 West 31st Street
New York, NY 10001

National Mass Retailing Institute
570 Seventh Avenue
New York, NY 10018

Auxiliary Services (Ch. 17 & 18)

American Advertising Federation
1225 Connecticut Avenue NW
Washington, DC 20036

American Association of Advertising Agencies
666 Third Avenue, 13th Floor
New York, NY 10017

Association of Buying Offices
100 West 31st Street
New York, NY 10001

Entrepreneurship (Ch. 20)

American Women's Economic Development Corporation
60 East 42nd Street
New York, NY 10165

National Federation of Independent Businesses
Capital Gallery E.
SW 600 Maryland Avenue
Washington, DC 20024